Routledge Revivals

The Pilgrimage of Grace 1536-1537 and The Exeter Conspiracy 1538

The Pilgrimage of Grace
1536-1537
and
The Exeter Conspiracy
1538

by

Madeleine Hope Dodds

and

Ruth Dodds

Volume II

First published in 1915 by Cambridge University Press

This edition first published in 2018 by Routledge
2 Park Square, Milton Park, Abingdon, Oxon, OX14 4RN
and by Routledge
52 Vanderbilt Avenue, New York, NY 10017, USA

Routledge is an imprint of the Taylor & Francis Group, an informa business

© 1915 by Taylor and Francis

All rights reserved. No part of this book may be reprinted or reproduced or utilised in any form or by any electronic, mechanical, or other means, now known or hereafter invented, including photocopying and recording, or in any information storage or retrieval system, without permission in writing from the publishers.

Publisher's Note
The publisher has gone to great lengths to ensure the quality of this reprint but points out that some imperfections in the original copies may be apparent.

Disclaimer
The publisher has made every effort to trace copyright holders and welcomes correspondence from those they have been unable to contact.
A Library of Congress record exists under ISBN:

ISBN 13: 978-0-367-18361-5 (hbk)
ISBN 13: 978-0-367-18362-2 (pbk)
ISBN 13: 978-0-429-06108-0 (ebk)

THE PILGRIMAGE OF GRACE
1536–1537

AND

THE EXETER CONSPIRACY
1538

IN TWO VOLUMES
VOL. II

CAMBRIDGE UNIVERSITY PRESS
C. F. CLAY, Manager
London: FETTER LANE, E.C.
Edinburgh: 100 PRINCES STREET

New York: G. P. PUTNAM'S SONS
Bombay, Calcutta and Madras: MACMILLAN AND CO., Ltd.
Toronto: J. M. DENT AND SONS, Ltd.
Tokyo: THE MARUZEN-KABUSHIKI-KAISHA

All rights reserved

THE PILGRIMAGE OF GRACE
1536–1537

AND

THE EXETER CONSPIRACY
1538

BY

MADELEINE HOPE DODDS
(Historical Tripos, Cambridge)

AND

RUTH DODDS

VOLUME II

Cambridge:
at the University Press
1915

Cambridge:
PRINTED BY JOHN CLAY, M.A.
AT THE UNIVERSITY PRESS

PRINTED IN GREAT BRITAIN

CONTENTS

CHAPTER		PAGE
XV	THE SECOND APPOINTMENT AT DONCASTER	1
XVI	THE KING'S POLICY	24
XVII	HALLAM AND BIGOD	55
XVIII	THE DUKE OF NORFOLK'S MISSION	99
XIX	THE KING'S PEACE	141
XX	THE END OF THE PILGRIMAGE	182
XXI	THE COUNCIL OF THE NORTH	226
XXII	THE WHITE ROSE PARTY	277
XXIII	THE EXETER CONSPIRACY	297
XXIV	CONCLUSION	329
	BIBLIOGRAPHY	335
	INDEX	340

ADDITIONS AND CORRECTIONS

PAGE
- **80** The Richmondshire articles are printed in full in "Richmondshire Wills," preface, p. xvii (Surtees Society).
- **126** Hutton of Snaith. Perhaps he was the bailiff of Snaith mentioned in connection with Hallam's rising, see pp. 49 and 64; but in that case it is odd that anything could be found against him in Durham. Norfolk calls him "one of the chief captains of the first rebellion." (L. and P. xii (1), 416 (2).)
- **130** *For* William Bowyer *read* Richard Bowyer.
- **151** On 22 February 1536–7 it was reported in Norfolk that seven of the Lincolnshire rebels had been executed by the Duke of Suffolk's orders. (L. and P. xii (1), 424; printed in full, Furnivall, "Ballads from MSS," vol. i, pt 2, p. 311 [Ballad Society].)
- **176** For another political play which probably dealt with the Pilgrimage of Grace, see "The Date of Albion, Knight," by M. H. Dodds in "The Library," April 1913.
- **189** Cromwell's name is used rather loosely throughout the passages relating to the evidence. As he was the moving spirit in the prosecution he is described as making all the notes and drawing all the conclusions found among the documents relating to the trials.
- **217** Delete Lord Cobham's name, as no expression of his opinions is recorded in the preceding pages.
- **219** Sir Ingram Percy's will is printed in "North Country Wills" (Surtees Society), i, 156.

CHAPTER XV

THE SECOND APPOINTMENT AT DONCASTER

The position and objects of the rebels having been set forth, it is now time to consider the situation from the King's point of view.

The Pilgrims had stated their grievances definitely, and begged the King to tell them what redress he was prepared to give. In order to discover what answer he would make, it is necessary to go back to the mission of Bowes and Ellerker at the beginning of November. On their first arrival Henry had himself drawn up a reply to the five articles[1], very much on the lines of his reply to Lincolnshire[2], but on the whole milder in tone. The King condescended almost to argument, as for instance in the recital of the names of his Privy Council, now full of noblemen, whereas at the beginning of his reign there had been but two nobles of the old blood, "others, as the Lords Marney and Darcy, scant well-born gentlemen." Also he demanded the surrender of only ten ringleaders, instead of a hundred, as in Lincolnshire[3]. It is not necessary to go into the details of the reply, however, for in essence it was simply a refusal to listen to any of the rebels' remonstrances, and it had no external result because it was never sent.

When he wrote it Henry seems to have been under the impression that the Pilgrims were already scattered, and that the affair would be over almost as quickly as the Lincolnshire rising. By the time the reply was received the rebels might be expected to be in a properly submissive frame of mind. As he gradually became convinced that the truce was merely a truce, and not a capitulation, the dreadful suspicion may have dawned in his mind that these traitors might not accept his gracious answer, written with his own hand, in the proper spirit. They might hesitate, argue, even reject it. The very idea of such a humiliation was too terrible to be entertained. The King would not run such a risk. Instead of issuing

---

[1] L. and P. xi, 957; printed in full, Speed, op. cit. bk. ix, ch. 21.
[2] L. and P. xi, 780 (2).   [3] Ibid. 957.

his reply to the Yorkshiremen, he caused his reply to Lincolnshire to be printed, thus returning an indirect answer to the rebels, without exposing himself. But his labour was not wasted, for he let it be known among the Pilgrims that he had answered their petition, but that he would not as yet allow them to see his reply. His letter to Ellerker and Bowes supplied this omission to some extent, and once the Pilgrims had made a full list of their grievances, as a substitute for their first general petition, the King's answer became quite insufficient. The stages by which Henry was reluctantly forced to acknowledge that he was obliged to treat formally with the Pilgrims have already been traced. On 14 November he had resolved to send Norfolk and Fitzwilliam to negotiate with them[1], and the first set of instructions was drawn up for their direction. They were to be provided with a safe-conduct under the Great Seal, "a proclamation implying a pardon," and the King's original answer. On their arrival at Doncaster they were permitted to arrange an interview with Darcy and three hundred others. They were to induce this company to come to them merely on their own promise of safety if possible, but if they could not be persuaded that this was sufficient security they might be given the safe-conduct. On this point of the safe-conduct the King was extremely sensitive. He seems to have felt that to grant one was a kind of recognition of belligerency; also it hurt his pride to acknowledge that any of his subjects were not wholly at his mercy. Apart from this we perhaps may see here one of the extraordinary freaks of his conscience. He would have had no hesitation in ordering Suffolk to seize the Pilgrims who had come to negotiate with Norfolk on the security of Norfolk's word, but he would prefer not to violate his own safe-conduct. Except for this matter there is not much of importance in these first instructions to Norfolk. Henry was not going to give way on any point. Darcy and his company must be persuaded and exhorted by the Duke to submit themselves entirely to the King, to make no further question concerning their petitions, and to accept the pardon which the King was willing to extend to all but a few persons specially named. If the rebels would conform themselves absolutely and surrender the aforesaid ringleaders they might be permitted to receive the King's answer "in a much more certain sort than the articles were proponed so that all indifferent men must be content."[2] If they would submit, Norfolk was to administer to them the oath of the Lincolnshire men; if they refused he was to gain as much time

[1] L. and P. xi, 1065.   [2] Ibid. 1064.

as possible by discussion, and at the first favourable opportunity he must break off the negotiations and straightway attack the rebels[1].

With these instructions Norfolk and Fitzwilliam set out. On 27 November the King wrote to them at Leicester. The rebels' attitude was still very threatening, and he seems to have thought that there was little prospect of peace, but he was still determined not to yield a single point; he would not give hostages for Aske; he would not grant fourteen days' truce for the appointment, "our instructions treat of a time to be won by policy, and not of an abstinence by pact, which would give them time to fortify themselves."[2]

These letters and instructions must have been very painful reading for Norfolk and the Admiral. It was abundantly evident by this time that there was no chance of winning over Darcy, and as far as could be discovered the other leaders were equally unapproachable. For a short while the royalists entertained some hope of winning over Aske, owing to the report of a spy. This man was called Knight, and was a servant of Sir Francis Brian[3]. Knight went into the rebels' country about 14 November[4], to learn what he could about their strength. When he was in York, his appearance aroused suspicion, but he escaped by saying that he was a servant of Sir Peter Vavasour. On 15 November, however, he was recognised as Brian's servant and taken before Aske. With great presence of mind and some humour Knight told the captain that Sir Francis had sent him in pursuit of his chaplain who was a thief[5]. Aske sent Knight back to his master with a letter to request a description of the missing chaplain, as he was determined not to protect bad characters[6]. It was Knight who told Sir Francis that Aske had only one eye. He had returned to his master by 18 November[7]. Apparently Knight had had some communication with Sir Peter Vavasour, whose name he had used as a protection, although Sir Peter was with the Pilgrims[8]. Knight told Sir Francis Brian that, according to Sir Peter, Aske had been heard to say that some men who were not suspected were worse than he, and that he would gladly accept the King's pardon. Brian repeated this to Sir Anthony Browne, who sent the report on to Norfolk and Fitzwilliam. The King's deputies reached Nottingham on Wednesday 29 November,

[1] L. and P. xi, 1064.   [2] Ibid. 1174.   [3] Ibid. 1103.
[4] Ibid. 1079.   [5] Ibid. 1103.
[6] Ibid. 1079.   [7] Ibid. 1103.
[8] L. and P. xii (1), 6, printed in full, Eng. Hist. Rev. v, 340.

and there they wrote to Sir Peter Vavasour[1]. They stated that it had been represented to them that Aske was wavering. If he would, he could do more service than a greater man, and Sir Peter must urge him to throw himself on the King's mercy. In token of his goodwill, let him come to the meeting at Doncaster without hostages, bringing with him this letter, which should be his safeguard[2]. This application to the supposed originator of the roundabout story demolished it altogether. Vavasour wrote back to say that there was no truth in the report that Aske was wavering. He himself dared not sign his letter, lest it should be intercepted. Thus all hope from this quarter vanished[3]. The reports from the north showed no signs of giving way on the part of the rebels. On the contrary, it was doubtful whether they would consent to treat at all. If they were really so much excited and so confident it was quite evident that they would not humbly accept any answer which the King might choose to make.

It may be asked why the royalists should fear the prospect of battle, when they had at their backs London, the King's treasure and the King's fleet. Norfolk and the nobles with him were honestly on Henry's side, but the particular sting lay in the fact that they would be fighting for Cromwell. They would be actually the protectors and maintainers of the man whom they most detested. While they were risking their lives and spending their money in his hated cause, he would be at the King's side, enjoying the King's favour, and probably poisoning the King's mind against them. In the circumstances it is not surprising that Norfolk, in particular, was ready to do almost anything rather than fight. The state of his feelings may be judged by the fact that between 24 November and 2 December he found courage to write to the King laying before him the situation at its very worst[4]. The letter seems to have been carried by Sir John Russell. It is lost, but there was a passage in it very irritating to Henry, in which Norfolk declared that everything depended on the weather; the waters of the river were falling and he could trust neither to Trent nor to Don[5]; moreover he enclosed the evidence of sixty gentlemen that "other parties were not to be trusted unto."[6] These other parties were probably the leaders of the Pilgrimage, Darcy, Latimer and the rest, and the report was that they would not be persuaded to betray their cause and come over to the King, as he hoped.

[1] L. and P. xi, 1196.   [2] Ibid.   [3] Ibid. 1242.
[4] Ibid. 1237, printed in full, Hardwicke, Miscellaneous State Papers, i, 30.
[5] See note A at end of chapter.   [6] L. and P. xi, 1241.

Henry was furiously angry at the contents of this letter. His situation with regard to Norfolk was indeed peculiarly galling to a man of his pride and temper. Norfolk for the moment was indispensable; he might not be a very good general, but he was the only one Henry possessed. Until the rebellion was suppressed the King could not afford to quarrel with him. But, while conscious of his own helplessness, Henry did not trust Norfolk in the least. He did not believe that the desperate letter contained a true account of the rebels' position; in his eyes it was all a trick to frighten him into coming to terms. Yet Norfolk could not be superseded, because there was no one to take his place, and he could not be forced to insist that the rebels should either fight or accept Henry's terms, because if Henry threatened him too boldly it was very probable that he would join the rebels himself. In the replies which were drawn up on 2 December, the King put a great restraint upon himself. Nevertheless the private letter which he sent to Norfolk was sufficiently alarming. Henry complained that Norfolk's desperate reports agreed neither with the information of spies nor with each other. In the first campaign he had particularly declared that he could hold the line of the Trent, and had attributed all his ill success to Shrewsbury's advance to the Don. Now he said that he could hold neither Don nor Trent, and yet it was evident that Shrewsbury's advance had saved a large district for the King[1]. From Newark he had written that he would esteem no promise made to the rebels nor think his honour touched in the breach of it[2], but nevertheless he had come to terms with them, disbanded his army without any exploit, and favoured their petitions at court. "We have now declared to you our whole stomach, as to him that we love and trust, which if you take as it is meant we doubt not but you will thank us, and by your deeds cause us eftsoons to thank you."[3] This was on the whole a temperate letter, but there is an undercurrent of restrained fury running through it which must have been very alarming to Norfolk. Such a rebuke might have goaded a loyal man into fighting immediately, or might have frightened a cautious man into going straight over to the rebels; but Henry knew Norfolk's character. The only emotion which it aroused in him was an intense desire to dispose of this tiresome business and return to court, where his "back-friends" must be intriguing against him.

---

[1] L. and P. xi, 1226; printed in full, State Papers, i, 518.
[2] L. and P. xi, 804; see above.
[3] L. and P. xi, 1226; printed in full, State Papers, i, 518.

At the same time the Privy Council received news that, according to letters from Sir William Musgrave, Tynedale and Reedsdale were loyal, Cumberland and Westmorland not ill-disposed, Lord Clifford was holding Carlisle and the Earl of Cumberland Skipton[1]. They thought therefore that Norfolk had only to deal with Yorkshire. They wrote to him to engage the rebels in conference while Suffolk prepared to attack them from the east, and Shrewsbury and Derby on the west. If the rebels could not be persuaded to accept the limited pardon and give up their ringleaders, he was to attack at once, for the King would on no account grant a general pardon. They enclosed the King's letter, but assured Norfolk that whatever it might contain the King was as gracious to him as ever he was in his life, from which it appears that they were rather nervous about the effect that Henry's remonstrance might have[2]. Sir John Russell also carried back a secret letter from the King to Shrewsbury. It is a high tribute to the old Earl's character that all parties trusted him; even the King placed more reliance on him than on Norfolk, although he now showed his confidence by asking him to do a dirty piece of work. In his reports Shrewsbury, whenever possible, had spoken a good word for his old friend Darcy. Henry now commissioned him to enter into secret negotiations with Darcy and Aske. He was not to allow the rest of the Council to know anything about it, but if he could by any means persuade them to come over to the King, he might give them the pardons, made out, one for Darcy, and the other for Aske, which Russell had in his possession. "The dates which are left blank you have power to fill up, but you must do so in such sort that there appear no diversity of hands." Was forgery one of the ordinary accomplishments of a Tudor nobleman? Russell also took a set of articles which Shrewsbury was empowered to declare if no terms were made with the rebels, but no copy of these articles has survived[3].

On the very day that these letters were despatched, Saturday 2 December, Norfolk wrote again to the King from Welbeck, still more emphatically setting forth the impossibility of inducing the rebels to submit unconditionally[4]. Sir Francis Brian carried this letter, and Suffolk also sent his opinion, which agreed with Norfolk's, that if the King would not grant a free parliament and a general

[1] L. and P. xi, 1207, 1208.
[2] Ibid. 1228; printed in full, Hardwicke, op. cit. i, 27.
[3] L. and P. xi, 1225; printed in full, State Papers, i, 519.
[4] L. and P. xi, 1237; printed in full, Hardwicke, op. cit. i, 30.

pardon there was no hope of coming to terms[1]. Sir Francis reached the court, at Richmond, on the night of Sunday 3 December[2]. After he had made his report the King could no longer doubt the gravity of the position. It was possible to believe that Norfolk was exaggerating, but Suffolk and Sir Francis himself were entirely loyal and their information must be taken seriously. Although he had urged both Suffolk and Norfolk to fight, Henry did not want to provoke actual warfare unless he could be quite certain of winning. Since there was no alternative between concession and battle he reluctantly gave directions for a new set of instructions to be drawn up[3]. In the beginning of this document he again complained of the desperate contents of Norfolk's letters. He reproached all the council of his army for neglecting to seize and fortify the Don, and for allowing the rebels to muster in such force at Pontefract without making corresponding levies. They were on no account to treat unless the numbers were equal on both sides,—either the Pilgrims must disband, or the King's troops must be increased. If this matter could be adjusted Norfolk, Fitzwilliam and the others were empowered to hold the conference. As usual the King held forth at great length on the reproaches that they must heap on the rebels for their disloyalty, ingratitude, etc., but if all their eloquence did not avail to make the Pilgrims accept the limited pardon, Norfolk was to say that his commission extended no further, but that if they would state clearly what they wanted he would venture to prolong the truce and himself lay their petition before the King. He was to persuade them that they only wanted a general pardon and a free parliament; they must be made to sign these articles and to undertake not to molest the King on any other point. Then Norfolk might make a truce for six or seven days, *as if to send to the King*, and at the end of this time he might present to them the general pardon which Sir John Russell would carry with him when he delivered these instructions. At the same time Norfolk might give them the King's promise that a parliament should be held, beginning on the last day of September 1537 at any place the King might appoint. If they insisted on any other articles, besides the pardon and the parliament, Norfolk was to make a truce for twenty days, to let the King know all particulars, and to send secretly to Derby to summon all the forces of Cheshire and Lancashire, to Suffolk to

---

[1] L. and P. xi, 1236; printed in full, State Papers, i, 521.
[2] L. and P. xi, 1237; printed in full, Hardwicke, op. cit. i, 30.
[3] See note B at end of chapter.

prepare Lincolnshire, while he himself got ready to seize all the fords of the Don until the King could make his preparations for advancing against the rebels in person[1]. The idea of prolonging the truce while secretly levying forces seems to have been suggested in the first place by Norfolk in a letter from Newark that has not been preserved. In a postscript the King replied to Norfolk's suggestion and to another letter from Nottingham. Although he approved of the general scheme, he would give no definite orders for further levies, as it would be so expensive. He promised to send three more safe-conducts, in addition to the one drawn up on 30 November which Norfolk had already received[2]; the new ones were made out for sixteen, twenty and forty days respectively, as he did not know what length of time might be agreed upon, and if a blank safe-conduct were sent, it would be visible that the date had been filled in by another hand[3]. Commissions of lieutenancy were also sent, made out to Norfolk and Shrewsbury, and to Norfolk and the Council. The King concluded by complaining again of their desperate letters. If they must send him so much bad news, he said, they might send some good news to balance it, or at least suggest some "honest remedy" for the evil. There is one other small but significant point: in the original draft orders are given for the payment of the men now with Norfolk, namely the "bands" of Sir John Russell, Sir Francis Brian, Sir Anthony Browne and Richard Cromwell, but the names of Sir Francis Brian and Richard Cromwell are struck out. Sir Francis had just brought up letters from Norfolk, and the rebels had refused to treat while Richard Cromwell was in Norfolk's company. The King silently yielded this point without any argument or blustering[4].

With these instructions Henry sent a letter to Suffolk[5]. After briefly telling him that he was prepared, in case of extremity, to grant a free pardon and a parliament to the rebels, "although we thought the granting of such a pardon would only encourage others," he gave orders that Suffolk must make up his companies to eight thousand men, and prepare to attack at once on receiving the word from Norfolk. The first plan was that on the alarm he should seize Hull and advance on York, sending word to Lord Clifford to set out from Carlisle and meet him. But this scheme was completely

---

[1] L. and P. xi, 1227; printed in full, State Papers, i, 511.
[2] L. and P. xi, 1205, 1206.   [3] See note C at end of chapter.
[4] L. and P. xi, 1227; printed in full, State Papers, i, 511.
[5] L. and P. xi, 1236; printed in full, State Papers, i, 521.

cancelled and he was ordered not to attempt to take Hull, but to await further advice. Letters and proclamations were enclosed to be sent by sea to Berwick and thence distributed to Lord Clifford, Sir William Musgrave, Edward Aglionby (of Carlisle), Sir Thomas Clifford, Sir Reynold Carnaby and the towns of Berwick and Carlisle. Suffolk received a commission of lieutenancy joining him with Norfolk and Shrewsbury[1], and a pardon and oath to be proclaimed and administered in Marshland and Holderness[2].

The Privy Council wrote to Norfolk at the same time, but their letter only hints at the King's change of attitude[3]. These Privy Council letters seem to have been composed to sweeten the King's more outspoken despatches. This one begins with warm praises of Norfolk and his colleagues. The King was making plans in case of war, but the Privy Council contemplated peace. If, as they did not doubt, Norfolk brought the affair to a satisfactory conclusion, the King was pleased with the Duke's plan that he should immediately advance into Yorkshire, with a good train of noblemen and gentlemen, to administer the oath; but Norfolk must send further particulars, as the King's charges had been great, and expenses must be kept down. They sent the Ten Articles and copies of the circular to the bishops[4], to be declared to the people. "There remains one thing to be considered which the King has much to heart and we all no less desire—the preservation of his Grace's honour, which will be much touched if no man be reserved to punishment." There is a certain humour in the earnestness with which the Council beseech Norfolk to "reserve" some vile persons, even if only a very few, and among them, if possible, Sir Robert Constable[5]. Sir Robert had offended the King mortally by saying that the truce had been broken when Edward Waters was sent to Scarborough. Henry, in his usual daring fashion, had retorted the reproach on the rebels in his instructions; Norfolk was to complain of the taking of Edward Waters as an innovation during the truce[6].

The Council also mentioned that the King had written to the Earl of Northumberland to come up to London "if nothing chance to him in the mean season,"[7] rather a sinister reservation. The Earl had sent a ring as a token to the King at the beginning of the month, through Suffolk's hands[8]. They added that Norfolk would

[1] L. and P. xi, 1236. [2] Ibid. 1235; cf. 1197.
[3] Ibid. 1237; printed in full, Hardwicke, op. cit. i, 30.
[4] See above, chap. xiii. [5] L. and P. xi, 1237.
[6] Ibid. 1227. [7] Ibid. 1237.
[8] Ibid. 1221.

doubtless see that the Earl's brethren did no displeasure, a task somewhat beyond his power[1].

Such were the final instructions despatched to Norfolk before the conference. They did not arrive till Wednesday 6 December, and would have been too late if the meeting had not been deferred for a day.

On Saturday 2 December Norfolk was at Welbeck writing desperate letters to the King. On Sunday 3 December he was at Hatfield, and with him were his half-brother Lord William Howard, Sir William Fitzwilliam and Sir Anthony Browne[2]. He had summoned Shrewsbury to join them, but Shrewsbury that day sent word that he was so ill that it would be impossible for him to reach Doncaster before Wednesday[3]. Probably Lancaster Herald arranged to defer the meeting when he went to Pontefract that eventful Sunday. Shrewsbury's letter was written in the morning, and after dinner Norfolk mentioned in a letter to the King that the meeting would not be till Wednesday. The principal object of the letter was to give warning that William Steward of Scotland was on his way to France and had passed right through the rebel country. It would therefore be well to stop him, as he might be carrying messages from the rebels to the King of Scotland. Norfolk reported that the nobles at Pontefract were in half captivity to the commons, who were very numerous and wild, but he was not without hopes of winning over some of the gentlemen[4]. This no doubt is an allusion to the Archbishop's sermon and the tumult in the church. Norfolk must have written on the report of Lancaster Herald. It is rather difficult to discover exactly what arrangements the Herald made for the first meeting on Monday. Robert Aske said afterwards that he delivered the King's safe-conduct for ten knights and esquires, each accompanied by three servants[5]. On the other hand Fitzwilliam, writing on Monday 4 December, told the King that the gentlemen were coming with only two servants each and "upon our honours without your Grace's safe-conduct."[6] Fitzwilliam would be the better authority, as Aske may easily have forgotten the exact particulars, if it were not possible that Fitzwilliam was trying to soothe the King, whose angry letters of 2 December had just been received. They seem to have arrived early on Monday morning before the meeting, and Norfolk and Fitzwilliam answered them at 8 A.M. In

[1] L. and P. xi, 1237; printed in full, Hardwicke, op. cit. i, 80.
[2] L. and P. xi, 1234.   [3] Ibid. 1233.   [4] Ibid. 1234.
[5] L. and P. xii (1), 6; printed Eng. Hist. Rev. v, 340.   [6] L. and P. xi, 1243.

these replies therefore there is no record of what passed. Norfolk wrote to the King and to the Council. Both his letters are full of protestations of loyalty; he insisted that he had only spoken the plain truth all through, as it was his duty to warn the King of the danger in which he stood. Doubtless he had mismanaged affairs, but that was due to his old age and feebleness, unfit as he was for the great duties which the King had forced upon him. He hoped now that they would not send him north, as he had suggested, because he wanted to go home[1]. The letters are very picturesque but they contain no information about the negotiations with the rebels.

After despatching these letters from Hatfield, Norfolk must have gone to Doncaster to meet the Pilgrims' representatives. Sir Thomas Hilton and his companions had received full instructions from the Pilgrims' council. They were (1) "to declare to the Duke of Norfolk and other lords that our meeting of our part is meant of assured truth without any manner of deceit or 'male ingyne': (2) to receive the King's safe-conduct, and to deliver our safe-conduct for the assurance of the lords there: (3) to entreat of our general pardon, including all persons who in heart, word or deed aided the federation in this our quarrel, and that we be not mentioned in the pardon, nor in any records as rebels and traitors: (4) that Richard Cromwell nor none of his kind nor sort be at our meeting at Doncaster: (5) to receive the King's answer by the declaration of the lords, and to certify the very intent thereof to us here: (6) to know what authority the lords have to promise: (7) to demand what pledge they would deliver for the captain: (8) if the particulars are required, then to descend to divers particulars."[2]

To all this Norfolk had no very truthful reply, particularly if it is correct to suppose that he did not receive the King's final instructions until Wednesday. He could not honestly answer to (1) that he came to the meeting "without any manner of deceit or 'male ingyne,'" seeing that he knew his object was to gain time until the King's troops were ready to make an attack. On that very day Suffolk was writing to ask for guns, gunners, arrows, etc., saying that he was making musters and every day expected the King's two ships[3]. With regard to (2) Norfolk's orders were if possible to withhold the King's safe-conduct and to persuade the Pilgrims to

[1] L. and P. xi, 1241, 1242.
[2] Ibid. 1246; printed in full, Speed, op. cit. (3rd ed.), bk. ix, ch. 21.
[3] L. and P. xi, 1239, 1240.

come to the meeting on no security but his own word. He was not authorised to promise a general pardon, as the King in his last letters[1] had insisted that some of the rebels must be reserved for punishment[2]. He could indeed satisfy them with regard to (4) as Richard Cromwell had already withdrawn. But as to (5) he had particular instructions not to reveal the King's reply until the rebels had submitted; and though he was to assure them that it was quite satisfactory he must have known that this was far from being the case. As to (6) he had no authority to promise anything but the limited pardon, while he had been particularly forbidden to give a pledge for Aske. Though he was permitted to go into particulars, it was only that he might persuade the Pilgrims not to trouble the King with them, the one point on which his orders were most emphatic being that he should take every means to detach the gentlemen from the commons[3].

At this point there comes a complete break in the contemporary letters and reports. No account of these first negotiations at Doncaster survives. Aske alluded to the meeting once or twice, but always said that as he was not there he could not be certain of what passed. He knew, however, that Robert Bowes delivered a copy of the articles to the Duke. The principal business of the meeting was probably to arrange for the final conference. It was decided that the appointed three hundred should come to Doncaster next day, and there choose forty of their number, twenty gentlemen and twenty commons, to treat with the Duke[4]. The King's safe-conduct seems to have been sent, although there is no absolute statement to that effect, but it does not appear that any hostage was given for Aske[5]. Perhaps the matter of the safe-conduct was compromised on those terms. When this had been decided the ten gentlemen returned to Pontefract.

However Norfolk may have endeavoured to gloze the matter over, it could not be denied that the preliminaries had been very discouraging. The commons realised this, and on Tuesday they were uproarious. They threw the blame on Archbishop Lee, rightly thinking that his wavering had encouraged the royalists, and there was another tumult in the church, where the Archbishop was performing service[6]. In order to prevent a breach of the truce, it was

---

[1] L. and P. xi, 1241.
[2] Ibid. 1228; printed in full, Papers of the Earl of Hardwicke, i, 27.
[3] L. and P. xi, 1226, 1228.
[4] L. and P. xii (1), 6; printed Eng. Hist. Rev. v, 340, 341.
[5] See note D at end of chapter. [6] L. and P. xii (1), 786 (ii, 2).

agreed that Lord Neville, Lord Lumley and Lord Conyers should remain at Pontefract to control the commons, while Lord Scrope, Lord Latimer, Lord Darcy and Aske, with the three hundred knights, esquires, gentlemen and commons, rode to Doncaster[1]. During these two days the clergy had been drawing up their articles, which were not completed and accepted until Tuesday afternoon[2], and it must have been after the close of the short December day that the three hundred rode across the bridge to the Grey Friars' house in Doncaster. Next morning, Wednesday 6 December, they chose ten knights, ten esquires and twenty commons to go to the conference with Norfolk. Robert Aske was their leader, and was empowered to speak in the name of all. This being determined, the forty set out for the house of the White Friars, where Norfolk and his council were prepared to receive them. By this time the King's last instructions must have arrived, which gave Norfolk something to base the treaty upon.

When the Pilgrims came into the presence of the council, Aske made three low obeisances. Then he and all his companions fell on their knees and humbly begged for the King's free pardon and gracious favour, notwithstanding anything which they might have done contrary to the laws of the land. These respectful preliminaries might have satisfied Henry, but the subsequent proceedings did not follow the lines which he had laid down, for without any representation of the King's grievances they passed immediately to the discussion of the articles. Here again Norfolk seems to have disregarded the King's desire for repeated delays. He had obtained authority to grant a full and free pardon to all, and to promise that the King would hold a free parliament; he thought, very reasonably, that no good would result from disguising the fact, as the more the negotiations were prolonged the wilder and more suspicious the commons would become[3].

On this basis, therefore, the representatives of the King and of the Pilgrims argued the particulars of the petition. About the first article, for the suppression of heresy, no difficulty could be made[4]. The King was as anxious for this as his subjects, and the arrest of several heretics had already created a good impression[5]. Norfolk at this point could use with some effect a passage in the King's answer to the men of Yorkshire in which he promised to punish any

---

[1] L. and P. xii (1), 6; printed in full, Eng. Hist. Rev. v, 341.
[2] See above, chap. xiv.
[3] L. and P. xii (1) 6; printed in full, Eng. Hist. Rev. v, 340–2.
[4] L. and P. xi, 1246.   [5] Ibid. 1250.

members of his council or others, who could be proved to be subverters of the law, and he would be free to suppress the King's addition that nobody would be able to prove such a thing[1]. The King's circular to the bishops was well received. In it the bishops were ordered " to commend all the honest ceremonies of the Church in such wise that they be not contemned," and were forbidden to retain in their service any person who spoke of the ceremonies " contentiously or contemptuously."[2] They were to watch the preachers vigilantly, and silence any who were indiscreet, even if they had the King's licence, and they were to seek out and apprehend any priests ' who have presumed to marry.'" Darcy afterwards forwarded a copy of this letter to Lee, saying that in it "all true Catholics may joy."[3] The rest of the articles dealing with religion might all be referred to the coming parliament. The royal supremacy, the tenths and first-fruits, and the rest had all been granted by act of parliament. It would be highly unconstitutional for the King to annul them merely on his own authority, but what one parliament had done another could undo. It seems that the Pilgrims assented to this, in all but one point. They insisted, however, that the suppressed abbeys must be allowed to stand until their case had been brought before parliament again. Norfolk had no power to grant this, but the Pilgrims firmly refused to give it up.

Leaving that aside for the moment, the other articles may be considered. With regard to constitutional reforms, the repeal of the various statutes included under that head might be left to the coming parliament, and it will be observed that by this device Norfolk would be able to avoid the discussion of such dangerous topics as the treason laws and Mary's legitimacy. Even the punishment of Cromwell, Audley and Rich might possibly take the form of an impeachment, and here Norfolk's obvious sincerity must have helped him. It must have been evident that he wished for Cromwell's downfall as much as the Pilgrims did. He would be able to make the most of the withdrawal of Richard Cromwell, and he might represent that the King's eyes had been opened by this insurrection to Cromwell's enormities. It was, however, impossible to defer the consideration of when and where the parliament should meet and how it should be composed. With regard to the date, Henry had at first proposed

[1] L. and P. xi, 957; cf. 1410 (4).
[2] Ibid. 1110; printed in full, Burnet, History of the Reformation, iv, 396; Wilkins, Concilia, iii, 825.
[3] L. and P. xi, 1336.

next Michaelmas¹, which was too far distant to satisfy the Pilgrims, but in the end he left the matter open, which enabled Norfolk to pretend that a near date would be appointed, while it gratified Henry to feel that it really rested entirely with him. As to the place, he was determined to name that himself. The question of additional representation for Yorkshire and kindred subjects were fully argued at Doncaster; but no definite promise was made². Finally Norfolk was able to show them a full and free pardon without exceptions. All the other grievances, legal and economic, might safely be referred to the parliament.

In all this conference it is evident that the greatest importance attached to Norfolk's representation of the King's attitude. If he had spoken the strict truth, he would have said that Henry was very angry, that the few concessions which he had made had been forced from him by sheer necessity, that he was absolutely determined not to yield an inch more, that in particular he would not give up the monasteries or the supremacy, and that he was extremely anxious to punish the leaders of the rising. There is no reason to believe that Norfolk was so tactless as to reveal any of this. He probably encouraged the Pilgrims' idea that Henry had been so far misled by Cromwell and that witch Anne Boleyn that he did not realise what he had been doing. The Pilgrimage had opened his eyes, and for this he was grateful. But it would be undignified in him to grant petitions which were backed by force. Only let the Pilgrims submit and disperse, and the King, now restored to his right mind, would do all they desired, if they would proceed by entreaty and constitutional means. As the Pilgrims regarded Norfolk as almost one of themselves, his words would have all the more weight. But on the one point they were still unpersuadable; the monasteries must be allowed to stand. Norfolk knew perfectly well that the King would never agree to this, but he had received a significant hint from his master as to how he should act in these circumstances. In his letter of 2 December Henry had reminded him: "you said you would esteem no promise you should make to the rebels nor think your honour touched in the breach of it."³ The implication is clear:—
"Why do you trouble me about making concessions to the rebels? Promise anything they demand for yourself, but leave me free to repudiate it afterwards." Finding that there was no other way of

---

¹ L. and P. xi, 1227; see note E at end of chapter.
² L. and P. xii (1), 901 (37); printed in full, Eng. Hist. Rev. v, 553, 567.
³ L. and P. xi, 1226; printed in full, State Papers, i, 518.

dealing with the problem of the monasteries, Norfolk and the Pilgrims finally agreed upon a compromise. The abbots must surrender their houses to the King's commissioners, but they should then be restored by the King's authority until the next parliament, which was to settle their fate[1]. At the end of the day Aske and his companions returned to the rest of the three hundred at the Grey Friars with these terms: a free pardon, the promise of a free parliament, and the provisional restoration of the abbeys. After laying the proposed treaty before them, Aske, at Norfolk's request, rode back to Pontefract the same night to communicate the terms to the assembly there[2].

Meanwhile Norfolk and the rest of his council wrote to the King, stating the terms they had made, and honestly declaring that they did not believe there would be any possibility of peace unless the King would give up the abbeys, at any rate temporarily[3].

Early next morning, Thursday 7 December, Aske sent the bellman about Pontefract to summon the commons to hear the result of the negotiations[4]. There were about three thousand in all, who gathered at the market cross, where Aske announced the terms that had been made. When they heard of the King's most liberal and free pardon, all raised a shout of joy. Under the impression that the terms were ratified by acclamation, Aske set out for Doncaster again, accompanied by Lord Neville. As soon as they reached the town they went again to Norfolk, but while Aske was declaring the result of his mission a letter came from Lord Lumley, who was in command at Pontefract, to warn them that affairs there had changed for the worse. Now that they had had time to discuss the terms, the commons were not so well pleased with them, and the leaders of their own rank, such as Hallam and Pulleyn, who were always suspicious of the gentlemen, were encouraging them to give the alarm and raise all Yorkshire again, if they were not shown the King's pardon under seal, and if the lords would not agree to the continuance of religious houses and promise that the parliament should be held at York. This news plunged the negotiations into confusion again. After some debate, Aske suggested that he should return to Pontefract and lay the proceedings before the commons once more. His offer was accepted. When he arrived at Pontefract his eloquence was effective and by night he had persuaded everyone

---

[1] L. and P. xii (1), 787.
[2] Ibid. 6; printed in full, Eng. Hist. Rev. v, 841.　　　[3] L. and P. xi, 1271.
[4] L. and P. xii (1), 6.

that the terms were perfectly satisfactory[1]. To complete the work he sent back to Doncaster a request that Lancaster Herald would bring the King's pardon. Norfolk wrote gleefully to Suffolk that all was going well at Pontefract[2]. The herald arrived with the pardon the same night[3]. Possibly he was accompanied by the three hundred lords and gentlemen, for next day, Friday 8 December, they all assembled on St Thomas' Hill and heard the pardon read. Then the commons dispersed to their houses, and the gentlemen rode to Doncaster once more. When they again presented themselves before Norfolk, Aske gave an account of all that had happened, and Norfolk then proceeded to rehearse the King's grievances, which in Henry's opinion ought to have come first. Norfolk required to know how the King's rents were to be collected, to which it was replied that they were ready for him. He also demanded the restoration of Edward Waters and his ship. The Pilgrims were prepared to redeliver everything that had been taken except the money, which had been divided among the captors. Several other small points were similarly adjusted. After this Aske knelt down and humbly besought the whole assembly that he should no longer hold the office or be called by the name of captain. When they had assented to this he tore off the badge of the Five Wounds which he was wearing, and all the other Pilgrims did the same, crying "We will all wear no badge nor sign but the badge of our sovereign lord." Finally Norfolk gave orders for the restoration of the grantees of the monasteries, and the conference broke up[4].

It is an interesting point to consider whether the Pilgrims believed that the prisoners in Lincolnshire would be included in this pardon. They had so far prevented any executions from taking place there, but although they probably hoped that they might be able to obtain mercy for the Lincolnshire men the Pilgrims were not in a position to treat on their behalf. They had deserted Yorkshire and made terms for themselves; now they must abide by these. Darcy, however, made a daring effort for them. On 15 December he wrote to Suffolk that he would not allow Waters' ship to be delivered unless the appointment at Doncaster was observed in Lincolnshire, and his intervention had the effect of preventing any executions for the time[5].

The end of the second conference at Doncaster is the end of the Pilgrims' success. They had allowed the issue to be changed from a

---

[1] L. and P. xii (1), 6, printed in full, Eng. Hist. Rev. v, 341; cf. L. and P. xii (1), 29.
[2] L. and P. xi, 1271.   [3] L. and P. xii (1), 6; printed Eng. Hist. Rev. v, 341-2.
[4] Ibid.   [5] L. and P. xii (1), 848 (i, 4).

trial of strength to a trial of diplomacy, and though Henry might have been overcome by force, he had not his match as a diplomat. The leaders, who were on the whole rather old-fashioned and simple-minded, were baffled without the slightest difficulty and Henry's triumph was almost ridiculously easy and complete.

There is one peculiarity of the conference at Doncaster which strikes the modern reader instantly, namely, that the terms do not appear to have been written down. It was later a part of Henry's plan of action to slur over the second conference as much as possible. Not a single interrogation about it was addressed to any of the prisoners, and the only information on the subject is derived from a few chance remarks, and from the brief account which Aske drew up for the King while he still believed that the terms would be observed. In these references there is absolutely nothing to show that the Pilgrims either signed any document themselves, or demanded any written copy of the terms from Norfolk. Henry had suggested that the leaders of the Pilgrimage should be required to sign a document pledging themselves to demand nothing from the King except a free pardon and a free parliament, but it seems that this paper was never drawn up.

The omission was not quite so surprising at that date as it would be now, for Yorkshire gentlemen were still accustomed to transact most of their business by word of mouth, and writing was unfamiliar to their ideas. But Darcy and Aske must have known how important it was to have the King's terms in black and white. We can only conclude that the absence of a written agreement was due to Norfolk's skill and prudence. It seems to have been agreed on both sides that the terms were only provisional. Norfolk might explain that he would go and represent to the King what he had promised and what the Pilgrims had demanded, and that he would bring back the King's answer in full legal form under the Great Seal. That would be the real treaty. Until that was drawn up there was no need for writing. It will be shown in the next chapter that Norfolk's speedy return with the King's confirmation of the terms was fully expected by gentlemen and commons alike, and that his delay produced fresh agitation. At present the only one of the King's concessions which the Pilgrims actually saw in writing was the pardon. They did not see the promise of the parliament, which the King offered to concede in his instructions to Norfolk; neither did they see any written promise concerning the monasteries, for which Norfolk had no authority.

The only report of the proceedings at the time occurs in a letter to Lady Lisle, wife of the Governor of Calais, from her agent in England, John Husee. With the delightful inconsequence of a contemporary he writes " news has just come that the Northern men have obeyed the King's proclamation, and submitted to mercy. The wine and herrings are come, and will be delivered to Mr Sulyard."[1] This, it will be observed, was the report circulated in London by the King on Monday 11 December. Needless to say, it was not true. The northern men had not submitted to mercy, but had made terms. The difficulty lies in discovering what those terms were. In order that the narrative should not be interrupted, we have stated above as an actual fact the terms which we believe were made, but it is now necessary to give the grounds for this belief. There is no doubt about the pardon and the parliament. The problem lies in the agreement as to the monasteries. About this the evidence is conflicting. In the first place, on Wednesday night, when Aske returned to Pontefract to communicate the terms to the commons, Norfolk wrote to the King that it would not be possible "to appease the commons unless the King consented to the standing of the abbeys in those parts which are to be suppressed by act of parliament."[2] This looks as though he had made some provisional promise, which he was trying to persuade the King to ratify, but unfortunately his letter has not been preserved. The quotation is from the King's reply. Before Norfolk's return to the north, "the King examined him in the gallery of his opinion in causes of religion," and Norfolk promised that no default should be found in him, "in the suppression of the Abbeys and treatment of the traitors therein."[3] There would have been no reason for the King to examine Norfolk if he had not made some unwelcome concession on the subject, which he repudiated "in the gallery" before the King.

Secondly, there is Aske's narrative drawn up for the King. In this account he described only his individual acts; as the progress of the negotiations must have been reported to the King by Norfolk, Aske says hardly anything about them[4].

His statements are (a) that on Thursday morning he proclaimed at the market cross at Pontefract "the said order (taken at Doncaster) and...the knowledge of the King's most liberal and free pardon." The commons received the news joyfully.

(b) After he had set out for Doncaster again the commons

[1] L. and P. xi, 1282.
[2] Ibid. 1271.
[3] L. and P. xii (1), 416.
[4] Ibid. 6; printed Eng. Hist. Rev. v, 841.

became dissatisfied and demanded to see the King's pardon and also "that the abbots, new put in of houses suppressed, should not avoid their possession to (until) the parliament time," and that the parliament must be at York.

(c) When the news of this reached Doncaster, Aske, after consulting with Norfolk, went back to Pontefract and persuaded the commons "to abide the said order at Doncaster."[1] He seems to have had a good deal of difficulty, for Marmaduke Nevill reported that the commons were so much excited that the gentlemen thought "we should be fain to divide, calling all them that were disposed to take the King's most gracious pardon to come to a side."[2] This may mean that they thought of putting the treaty to the vote. In the end on Friday morning all formally accepted the terms[3].

(d) The last business transacted by Norfolk on Friday was to "take order for the putting in of the King's farmers."[4]

(e) After the conference Aske took part with Sir Ralph Ellerker and Sir Robert Constable in "the putting in of the King's farmers into the abbeys of Haltemprice and Feriby."[5]

In all this there is no definite statement of what was the order taken at Doncaster, but the general impression which the narrative gives is that the monks were to be turned out and the farmers restored. The third witness in the matter is John Dakyn, and he makes a definite statement, the only definite statement, be it observed, that exists. Dakyn, it will be remembered, was one of the ecclesiastics at Pontefract. He was an elderly, cautious man, very anxious to avoid committing himself. During the conference William Collins, the bailiff and one of the representatives of Kendal[6], came to him and asked his advice concerning the monastery of Cartmell. All the monks had been restored by the commons, but the prior would not go back[7]. Dakyn promised to write to him on the subject. On Saturday 9 December, after the conference was over, Dakyn left Pontefract for York. He did not write to Cartmell as yet, because he wished to have definite information as to what had been determined. As he had been at Pontefract all the time, he might have been expected to know, but probably he had had no opportunity of learning the details from any of the leaders and he wanted to be quite certain. Collins came to him at York for the letter, and Dakyn, having no real doubt on the subject, wrote on Sunday 10 December

---

[1] L. and P. xii (1), 6; printed in full, Eng. Hist. Rev. v, 341.
[2] L. and P. xii (1), 29,   [3] Ibid. 6; printed Eng. Hist. Rev. v, 342.
[4] Ibid.   [5] Ibid.   [6] L. and P. xii (1), 914.   [7] Ibid. 787.

to the priors of Cartmell and Conishead[1] that by the King's consent all religious persons should re-enter suppressed houses again till further direction was taken by parliament[2]. Collins sent these letters to the monasteries[3]. Dakyn went home to his own parish of Kirkby Ravensworth[4]. Within a week of his arrival Robert Bowes and Sir Henry Gascoigne requested him to go and explain to the canons of St Agatha's at Richmond that they must "be put forth by the King's authority and taken in again by the same authority until the next parliament." The prior agreed and it was done. "This manner of putting out and taking in again was commonly spoken of to be true, after our return from Pontefract, in all those parts as well with gentlemen as others."[5] Robert Bowes was one of the principal men at Doncaster, and must certainly have known all that passed, and Dakyn's evidence shows decisively that he believed that the monasteries were to make a formal surrender, but were to be allowed to stand.

In the fourth place there is the evidence of William Collins. Clarencieux King-of-Arms arrived at Kendal on 22 December, bringing the King's pardon. The farmers of the priory of Cartmell and the restored monks were quarrelling over the rents and corn, and when they heard of the herald's arrival two of the monks came to him and begged him to write an order for them. The herald would not write himself, but he directed Collins to write, which he did, in the herald's presence, to the following effect: "Neighbours of Cartmell, so it is that the King's herald hath made proclamation here that every man, pain of high treason, should suffer everything, as farms, tithes, and such other, to be in like stay and order concerning possessions as they were in time of the last meeting at Doncaster, except ye will of your charity help the brethren there somewhat towards their boards, till my lord of Norfolk come again and take further order therein."[6] All the monasteries of the north had been restored before the last conference at Doncaster, and putting together Dakyn's and Collins' statements it appears that the monks were to be left unmolested, but that the rents, etc., were to remain in the hands of the farmers and grantees of the monasteries, who should, however, make an allowance to the monks.

Finally it appears that as soon as he returned home Sir Thomas Hilton, who, like Bowes, had been prominent at Doncaster, insisted on restoring the Friars Observant of Newcastle[7].

[1] L. and P. xii (1), 787.   [2] L. and P. xi, 1279.   [3] L. and P. xii (1), 914.
[4] Ibid. 787.   [5] Ibid.
[6] Ibid. 914.   [7] L. and P. xi, 1372.

From the evidence of all these persons, the majority of them being men who had every opportunity of knowing the truth, it seems certain that Norfolk promised at Doncaster that the monasteries should be allowed to stand, subject to an agreement with the farmers of them, until the promised parliament met.

Norfolk had no authority for making any such promise, and in the absence of any proof of his actual words, it is not fair to accuse him of treachery. It is not likely that he pretended to have the power which he did not possess. In all probability he only promised to make suit to the King that the monasteries should stand, although he may have held out strong hopes that the King would grant his suit, while he knew very well that the King would do nothing of the sort.

The first news of the terms made Henry exceedingly angry[1]. A letter was at once drawn up addressed to Fitzwilliam and Russell, in which he scolded them roundly. He was amazed that they could not achieve the thing that the King most desired, namely, the reservation of certain persons for punishment. As for the monasteries, so long as he wore the crown of England he would never give them up. Various persons from the north had been interrogated by the King[2], in particular Steward, the Scot of whom Norfolk had given warning[3], and they all reported that the commons of the north were weary of the rebellion, penitent and ready to submit unconditionally. He would have been a brave man who dared to say otherwise, when face to face with Henry. The King desired Russell and Fitzwilliam to send a detailed account of all the negotiations. It is very much to be wished that they had done so, but in all probability the King's letter was never sent. It is undated and endorsed by Wriothesley "The minute that was devised to have been sent to my lord Admiral and Master Russell," which implies that it never was despatched[4]. When it was drawn up Henry must have expected that the negotiations would last at least a week, as he had suggested in his instructions. The minute cannot have been written before 8 December, as it alludes to a letter from Norfolk to Suffolk dated Thursday 7 December and forwarded to the King[5]. The despatch of the King's letter may have been prevented by further letters from Doncaster, announcing that the conference was over, or it may be simply that the King had changed his mind. As soon as his first outburst of rage was over, he must have become aware of the great

---

[1] L. and P. xi, 1271.   [2] Ibid.   [3] Ibid. 1234, 1238.
[4] Ibid. 1271.   [5] Cf. ibid. 1267.

advantage which he had gained. He had been thwarted for the moment, which his passionate self-will could hardly bear, but cunning was really more in accordance with his tastes than violence. A very little reflection would show him that it only required time, patience and diplomacy for him to recover everything that he had yielded for the moment, and to recover it, moreover, without the risk and expense of war. Therefore his angry letter was cancelled, and the King gave no sign as to his opinion of the terms made at Doncaster. He did not ratify them, but on the other hand he did not repudiate them. One of the heralds who was sent to the north with the pardons, as we have seen, encouraged the people to believe that the monks were to remain in their houses for the present. It is here that a charge of treachery will fairly lie. Henry had no intention of keeping the unauthorised promise which Norfolk as his representative had made, but he did not repudiate it. He permitted and encouraged those whom it most concerned to believe that he regarded the promise as binding, until he found a favourable opportunity for denying it altogether, and punishing those who had trusted him.

NOTES TO CHAPTER XV

Note A. In the Letters and Papers this passage runs "if we shall trust either to treat or do, we shall be deceived," but in the State Papers it is printed "either to Trent or to Don" and a reference to the original shows this to be correct.

Note B. These instructions are undated and are printed among the letters of 2 December[1]. They seem, however, to belong to 4 December. Possibly they were first drawn up on the 2nd but held back and modified after Norfolk's letter from Welbeck was received.

Note C. Henry attached great importance to the point that there should be no diversity of handwriting in the pardons and safe-conducts; the reason for this anxiety is not apparent.

Note D. The question of the hostages aroused a great deal of interest at the time. The Spanish Chronicler says[2] that the King sent as hostages for Aske the Earl of Surrey, Lord Darcy, the Earl of Rutland, Lord William Howard Norfolk's brother, the Marquis of Exeter and Lord Thomas Howard Norfolk's second son. This account of the insurrection is interesting as showing the rumours current in London, but it is quite without authority as evidence of what occurred.

Note E. This date is written and then cancelled. In his letter to Suffolk[3] the King mentions Michaelmas as the date of the parliament, but in the end the date was left open.

[1] L. and P. xi, 1227.
[2] Spanish Chron. ed. Hume, chap. xvii.
[3] L. and P. xi, 1236.

CHAPTER XVI

THE KING'S POLICY

After the conference at Doncaster had concluded on Saturday 9 December 1536 there was a general dispersal of the gentlemen and nobles who had been together for so long. The commons had already gone home, rather disappointed that there had been no fighting, and half-suspicious that they had been betrayed after all. Norfolk and his colleagues set off for London to make their report to the King[1]. Shrewsbury returned to Sheffield to keep an eye on the disaffected region[2]. Suffolk, who had been petitioning for some time to be recalled to court, dismissed all his men but five hundred to guard the ordnance and prisoners, and went up to London[3]. The northern gentlemen departed to their homes, where they endeavoured to keep order and to adjust the disputes between the monks and the farmers of the monasteries.

Some of the gentlemen, however, went south with Norfolk. Marmaduke Nevill[4] asked the Duke's leave before starting, and was told that no leave was required[5]. These gentlemen rode south in great spirits, telling everybody that they had obtained a pardon and a parliament, and that they had set up all the abbeys again in their country. In the parliament the pardon would be confirmed and the Act of Uses repealed, for younger brothers would not have it. Marmaduke Nevill visited the Abbot of St John's at Colchester on Saturday 16 December. The justices of the peace were dining there, and one of them asked, "How do the traitors of the north?" Nevill retorted with a catch phrase of the time, "No traitors, for if ye call us traitors, we will call you heretics." He said that the answer of the King's Council had been known at Pontefract before Norfolk declared it at Doncaster, and that all the south had been with the plain fellows of the north, but dared not speak their minds[6].

---

[1] L. and P. xii (1), 29.
[2] Ibid. 1283, 1288.
[3] L. and P. xii (1), 29.
[4] L. and P. xi, 1320.
[5] See note A at end of chapter.
[6] L. and P. xi, 1319.

His boasting was quickly put to silence. The justices reported his words to Cromwell and on Twelfth Day [6 January 1536-7] he was arrested by the Earl of Oxford and thrown into the Tower[1]. His name is still to be seen there, the first of many such sorrowful memorials which were to find place on its walls in the next few months, but his fate is unknown.

On receiving a full account of the conference at Doncaster, the King's first care was to conceal the fact that he had received a check. A report spread that the northern men had submitted unconditionally[2]. On Friday 22 December the King, accompanied by the Queen and the Imperial Ambassador, made a magnificent progress through London to Greenwich, where he intended to keep a particularly festive Christmas. "Such a sight has not been seen since the Emperor was here. The streets were hanged with arras and cloth of gold. Priests in their copes with crosses and censers stood on one side, and the citizens on the other. It rejoiced every man wondrously."[3] The weather was so severe that the Thames was frozen, and the procession went down to Greenwich on the ice[4]. The King's daughters had preceded him and were already established there[5].

Cromwell wrote to the English ambassadors in France on 24 December that it was false that the nobles had been forced to come to terms with the northern men because they distrusted their own levies. The King's soldiers were entirely loyal. The King had consented to treat with the rebels only because of his merciful disposition and kindly wish to avoid bloodshed. The rebellion was now completely at an end. It was true that the rebels had at first attempted to make conditions, but finally "they submitted entirely to the King's pleasure with the greatest repentance."[6] On Christmas Eve Latimer preached at Paul's Cross, "moving to unity without any special note of any man's folly."[7]

When he came to review the situation, Henry found that it was not very bad, but required caution. With regard to the monasteries, he did not consider himself as bound in any way, but he wished to create a good impression. Since March 1536, when the act for the suppression was passed, exemptions from its operation had been granted from time to time. From June to December 1536 eighteen

[1] L. and P. XII (1), 16, 27-29.   [2] L. and P. XI, 1282.
[3] Ibid. 1358, 1369; and all the Chronicles under 1536.
[4] Hall, Chronicle, ann. 1536.   [5] L. and P. XI, 1291.
[6] Ibid. 1363; printed in full, Merriman, op. cit. II, no. 174; extracts in Tierney, op. cit. I, 482.
[7] L. and P. XI, 1374; printed in full, Latimer's Remains (Parker Soc.), p. 375.

monasteries had been permitted to stand, the greatest number exempted in any one month being six in August. It must be due to something more than a coincidence that in January 1536–7 the number of exemptions was seventeen[1], only one less than the total previously exempted in the course of seven months. There is an undated list of 123 monasteries which were to be allowed to stand. Of these twenty-four are in Yorkshire, twenty-four in Lincolnshire, and not more than six in any other one county[2]. So great was the uncertainty as to the King's real intentions with regard to the monasteries that in Norfolk and Somerset the commissioners for the suppression suspended their work until they received further orders[3].

Although he was angry at being forced to make a definite promise, Henry had no objection to holding a parliament. It was characteristic of him that he was not in the least afraid of his parliaments, and never doubted that he could do anything he liked with them. In this case he was prepared to be even better than his word, for though he had not promised to do so, he intended to hold the parliament at York[4].

After Norfolk's report had been laid before the King, a minute was drawn up, containing suggestions for the settlement of the north. It is undated, but probably belongs to the last days of 1536. There was every intention of holding a parliament in the north, but as "there remain persons who desire, either by Parliament or else by another rebellion, to compass a change from their present state... means ought therefore to be devised for the maintenance of perfect quiet in the future." When the King went north, loyal noblemen must be put in authority to keep the southern counties in order, especially in certain counties where there was much disaffection[5]. A mass of treasure must be raised, "as money is necessary for the enterprises of princes and adds heart and courage in danger to all men." Garrisons must be planted in the disaffected regions, but "so ordered as not to offend the people." The King's ordnance must be reviewed and properly bestowed, and a supply of weapons of all sorts must be laid in[6]. These were not very encouraging preparations for holding a free parliament where every man should speak his mind openly, though of course the King was justified in taking precautions for his own safety and he can hardly be blamed for trusting the north less than he pretended.

---

[1] Gasquet, op. cit. II, append. 1.
[2] Stevens, Monasticon, II, append. 17–19.
[3] L. and P. XII (1), 32.
[4] L. and P. XI, 1410 (1); XII (1), 108.
[5] See coloured map.
[6] L. and P, XI, 1410 (1).

Henry soon hit upon a very ingenious scheme for introducing a sufficient force into the north without exciting suspicion. He had originally intended that Queen Jane should be crowned at Westminster on the Sunday before the feast of All Hallows 1536, but when the day came round the northern rebellion was at an acute stage, and the King had neither money nor men to waste over pageants. A convenient excuse for postponing the coronation was supplied by the prevalence of the plague in London during the autumn[1]. At Christmas, however, the King's policy was to make a lavish display of splendour and security, and he allowed it to be known that not only would he himself travel to York to hold his parliament, but the Queen would accompany him to be crowned in York minster[2]. No one could object to such an honour being conferred upon the city of York, while at the same time it gave a good excuse for extensive military preparations, and for filling the city with the King's own men.

The only one of the concessions made at Doncaster which Henry could not tolerate was the general pardon. The rising had been a stain upon his honour which blood must cleanse. He had brought himself to consent to certain limitations; he would be content with a specified number of victims, and that number should be a small one; if he could not have the leaders, he would be satisfied with vile persons; but executions there must be, and he would not feel he had done his duty as a king until someone had suffered.

His council advised that he should allure the northern gentlemen into obedience by affability, and thereby "by little and little find out the root of this matter"; also that those whose goods had been spoiled should be encouraged to prosecute the robbers, "whereby some offenders may yet be punished, and the beginners of the rebellion detected."[3] In the meanwhile there was no help for the general pardon, and the heralds were accordingly sent out to proclaim it.

An inclusive pardon for all the rebellious districts, provided that the inhabitants made submission to the Duke of Norfolk or the Earl of Shrewsbury, was issued on 9 December, and an order was given for separate pardons to be granted to applicants from the various counties[4]. Suffolk had already received the pardon for Hull, Marshland, Howden, Holderness, Beverley and the East Riding[5]. It was at first

---

[1] Wriothesley, op. cit. I, 55–6; L. and P. XII (1), 47 (4), (11).
[2] Ibid. 20. [3] L. and P. XI, 1410 (1).
[4] Ibid. 1276; printed in full, Speed, op. cit. bk. 9, ch. 21.
[5] L. and P. XI, 1235.

proposed that Thomas Hawley, Clarencieux King-of-Arms, should carry the pardon to the North Riding, Richmond, Durham and Northumberland, while Thomas Miller, Lancaster Herald, should take it to the West Riding, Lancashire, Westmorland and Cumberland. But as the former was considered the more dangerous mission, it was finally assigned to Lancaster Herald, who had acquitted himself so well before among the rebels. This was a slight which Clarencieux King-of-Arms never forgave[1], and the effect of his resentment will be apparent later[2].

Clarencieux King-of-Arms proclaimed the pardon at Wakefield on Tuesday[3] 12 December, at Halifax on Wednesday 13 December, at Bradford on Thursday 14th, at Leeds on Friday 15th, at Skipton on Saturday 16th, at Kendal on Tuesday 19th. His doings at Kendal have already been described. He was at Appleby on Wednesday 20 December, at Penrith on Thursday 21st, at Carlisle on Saturday 23rd, and Cockermouth on Tuesday 26th, and at Lancaster on Sunday 31st, whence he sent back his report[4].

Lancaster Herald wrote from Berwick on Tuesday 26 December that he had proclaimed the pardon at York, Ripon, Middleham, Barnard Castle, Richmond, Durham, Newcastle-upon-Tyne, Morpeth, Alnwick and Berwick. He found the commons everywhere very repentant and eager for the coming of the Duke of Norfolk, but the spiritualty were most corrupted and malicious, and the originators of all the mischief[5].

It was no wonder that the spiritualty were offended by the pardon, which ran as follows:

"Albeit that you the King's Highness' subjects and commons dwelling and inhabiting in the shires of York, Cumberland, Westmorland, Northumberland, the Bishopric of Durham, the city of York and the shire of the same, the town of Kingston-upon-Hull and the shire of the same, the town of Newcastle-upon-Tyne and the shire of the same, and in other shires, towns, dales, places privileged, the franchises and liberties within the limits of the said shires, cities, towns, or any of them or being reputed or taken for any part, parcel or number of any of them and such other the King's said subjects inhabited in the town of Lancaster or elsewhere by north in the shire of Lancaster have now of late attempted and committed a manifest and open rebellion against his most royal majesty, whereby was like to have ensued the utter ruin and destruction of these whole countries, to the great comfort and advancement of your ancient enemies the Scots, which as his Highness is credibly informed do with a great readiness watch upon the same, and to the high displeasure of God, Who straitly commandeth you to obey your sovereign lord and king in all things and not with violence to resist his will

---

[1] L. and P. xiii (1), 1818. [2] See below, chap. xxiii.
[3] See note B at end of chapter. [4] L. and P. xi, 1892. [5] Ibid. 1871.

or commandment for any cause whatsoever it be : Nevertheless the King's royal majesty perceiving as well by the articles of your pretences sent to his Highness as also duly informed by credible reports your said offences proceeded of ignorance and by occasion of sundry false tales never minded or intended by his Highness or any of his council but most craftily contrived and most spitefully set abroad amongst you by certain malicious and perverse persons, and thereupon his Highness inclined to extend his most gracious pity and mercy towards you, having the chief charge of you under God both of your souls and bodies, and desiring rather the preservation of the same and your reconciliation by his merciful means than by the order and rigour of justice to punish you according to your demerits, of his inestimable goodness, benignance, mercy, and pity, and at your most humble petitions and submissions made unto his Highness, he is contented and pleased to give and grant and by this present proclamation doth give and grant unto you all and to all and every your confederates wheresoever they dwell, of whatsoever estate, degree, or condition so ever you or they be, or by what name or names so ever they or you be or may be called, his general and free pardon for all manner treason, rebellions, insurrections, misprisions of treason, murders, robberies, felons, and of all accessories of the same and of every of them, unlawful assemblies, unlawful conventicles, unlawful speaking of words, confederacies, riots, routs, and all other trespasses, offences and contempts done and committed by you or any of you against the King's Majesty, his crown or dignity royal, within and from the time of the beginning of the said rebellion whensoever it was unto the present day of proclaiming of this proclamation, and of all pains, judgments, executions of death and all other penalties, forfeitures, fines and forfeitures of lands, tenements, hereditaments, goods or chattels, by any of your forfeitures incurred by reason of the premisses or any of them; which fines, forfeitures, lands, tenements, hereditaments, goods and chattels, the King's said Highness of his special grace and mere motion by these presents giveth to such of you as have or should have forfeited or lost the same by occasion of the premisses or any of them : And also his Highness is pleased and contented that you and every of you from time to time shall and may have upon your suits to be made hereafter in his Chancery his said most gracious and free pardon under his Great Seal concerning the premisses, without any further bill or warrant to be obtained for the same, and without paying any thing for the Great Seal thereof: And that you and every of you, from time to time, may freely and liberally sue for his said pardon when and as often as it shall like you, without any trouble, vexation or impeachment for the premisses or any of them by his heirs or by any his officiaries, ministers, or subjects, by any manner of means or in any manner of wise.   Provided always that you and every of you in token of a perfect declaration and knowledge that ye do heartily lament and be sorry for your said offences, shall make your humble submission unto his Highness in the presence of his right trusty and right entirely beloved cousins and councillors the Duke of Norfolk and the Earl of Shrewsbury, his Lieutenants General, or any of them, or to their deputy or deputies of them, or any of them, or such other person or persons as the King's Highness shall appoint for the same : Furthermore, the King's most royal Majesty straitly chargeth and commandeth that you and every of you shall from henceforth like true and faithful subjects use yourselves, in God's peace and his, according to the duties of allegiance, and that you shall in no wise hereafter attempt to make or procure any such rebellion, intent, unlawful assemblies, riots, routs and conspirations, nor at the commandment nor by the authority of any person of what estate or degree or for what cause so ever it be, shall arise in any forcible manner and array, unless it be at the special commandment of the King's Highness or his Lieutenant sufficiently authorised for the same.

In witness whereof the King's most royal Majesty hath caused this his proclamation to be made patent and sealed with his Great Seal at Richmond the IX day of December in the XXVIII year of his reign."[1]

Henry was so much accustomed to scolding his subjects and praising himself in his public documents that the pardon would appear, to those who were used to his ways, to be rather a moderate production, but it was very aggravating to the independent spirit of the northern men, and in addition to its irritating tone there were special points in it which must have been deliberately provocative. The King referred once more to the "false tales" as the causes of the insurrection, in spite of the Pilgrims' repeated endeavours to set him right on that point. He insisted that he had "the chief charge of you under God, both of your souls and bodies," although that was the main point at issue. Finally the proclamation was not an actual pardon, but merely the promise of a pardon when each individual Pilgrim had first made his submission to the King's lieutenants, who had not yet even set out for the north, and had secondly sued out his private pardon in Chancery. It is difficult to know how far this phraseology is to be taken literally. The King cannot have expected all the inhabitants of the north to make a journey up to London for their private pardons. For the greater number the proclamation would have to be sufficient; but its wording was so vague as to throw a disagreeable doubt upon its validity. Consequently while the King thought the pardon far too liberal, the commons were by no means satisfied with it. Lancaster Herald did not dare to read the proclamation as it stood at Durham. He was reported to have read the pardon one way in the city of Durham and another way in the loyal town of Newcastle-upon-Tyne. When this was known in Durham the citizens were so angry that they attacked the Herald on his return, and he had great difficulty in escaping from them[2].

On Sunday 31 December the parishioners of Kendal declared that the priest must bid the beads in the old way, praying for the Pope and the cardinals. Collins brought the King's pardon to show them, and Bricket, one of the King's servants, warned them that if

---

[1] L. and P. xi, 1276 (1); printed in full, Speed, op. cit. bk. 9, ch. 21, from which this is copied with corrections from the original.
[2] L. and P. xii (1), 50, 201 (p. 101).

they were to enjoy the pardon they must keep the peace, but they cried, "Down, carle, thou art false to the commons," and one of them, William Harrison, declared that he cared for no pardons. Collins was obliged to retreat, and left the pardons in the vestry. Parson Layborne persuaded the congregation to let the priest bid the beads as he would until the coming of the Duke of Norfolk. Collins summoned two justices of the peace to punish the ringleaders, but one magistrate was out of the country, and the other could only do his best with words[1].

In the East Riding the pardon was also received grudgingly. Hallam said that they had liever have had some of their petitions granted[2].

The division between the commons and the gentlemen became greater, because the gentlemen based their hopes on the coming parliament, but the commons, having no concern in the parliament, did not feel much interest in it. They did not care about the constitutional point, and wanted the King to reverse the statutes which they disliked on his own authority. All were united, however, in an eager expectation of the Duke of Norfolk's coming. In spite of their experience in the case of Ellerker and Bowes, they still hoped that he would come very soon, perhaps immediately after Christmas, to bring the King's reply to their petitions and to announce the date and place of the new parliament[3]. But now that Norfolk had returned to court, he was in no hurry to set out again, and Henry was in no hurry to despatch him. The King had begun a very difficult game. Nothing would suit him better than a slight rising among the commons, one which could easily be suppressed and yet would give him an excuse for repudiating the terms granted at Doncaster. Yet if he went too far, and allowed distrust to grow too rapidly, the next rising might be as formidable as the last had been, and in that case it would be much less easily suppressed. Henry quickly discovered the solution of the problem. The lower classes without leaders were not formidable. The insurrections which they raised by themselves collapsed at the first opposition. The King's plan, therefore, was to detach the gentlemen to win them over to his side, if possible, or at any rate to entertain them with hope and fair words until the commons were provoked into calling them traitors and rose without them.

The best opportunity for this policy was immediately after the

---

[1] L. and P. xii (1), 7, 914, 671 (iii).   [2] Ibid. 201 (p. 91).
[3] L. and P. xi, 1387; xii (1), 171.

conference at Doncaster, as from 9 December until the beginning of January, in spite of some grumbling and rioting, the north was fairly quiet in the expectation of the Duke's coming. But the departure of the gentlemen who travelled south to sue their pardons alarmed the commons and caused rumours and threats of a new rising[1].

On Friday 15 December Henry made his most skilful move. Peter Mewtas, a gentleman of the Privy Chamber, was despatched to Robert Aske, with a letter from the King. Henry wrote that, as he had granted a free pardon to Aske, he had conceived a great desire to speak with him, and therefore summoned him to come up to court, where he trusted that by frankness Aske would deserve reward. A safe-conduct was enclosed, from the date until Twelfth Day, 6 January 1536–7. Aske was instructed not to inform anyone of the summons[2]. The King's object in enjoining that the visit to court must be secret was to inspire the other leaders of rebellion with fear and suspicion of Aske. If he disappeared from the north and was next heard of in London, everyone would conclude that he had gone up to turn King's evidence. His credit would be destroyed, and the other gentlemen, trembling for their lives, might be induced to turn traitors in fact. Simple-minded as he was, Aske was not quite so foolish as to fall into this trap. He had been living in his old home at Aughton since the conference at Doncaster[3], and did not receive the King's messenger until after 18 December[4], for travelling must have been slow in that bitter winter. When the letter arrived Aske sent his brother-in-law William Monketon to Lord Darcy with a copy of it, and a message that he intended to go, and that he begged Darcy to keep the country in order while he was away. After despatching the messenger he set out for London, accompanied by six servants, without waiting for an answer from Darcy. When Aske returned to the North, Monketon told him that Darcy said "he did well to venture, seeing that he had the King's letter therefor."[5] Darcy was afterwards accused of having counselled Aske to take six servants and to leave one at Lincoln, another at Huntingdon, another at Ware, and to lodge the rest in different parts of London, so that if the King attempted any treachery they might bring back news to Darcy, who would come to his rescue[6]. Aske never received any

---

[1] L. and P. xi, 1294.
[2] Ibid. 1806; printed in full, State Papers, i, 523.
[3] L. and P. xii (1) 6; printed in full, Eng. Hist. Rev. v, 342.
[4] L. and P. xi, 1843.   [5] L. and P. xii (1), 1175.   [6] Ibid. 1119, 1206.

such message[1], and the story in its elaborated form must be untrue[2], but it sounds as if it might have had some foundation in Darcy's impetuous form of humour. If Monketon hinted that he feared Aske was really on his way to the Tower, Darcy may have exclaimed, "If he is in any doubt, let him lay posts along the road to bring me early news, and I will come and fetch him out myself,"—or words to that effect. He might easily make a hasty remark of that nature, without the smallest idea that anyone would take it seriously, but Henry, like all despots, was extremely suspicious of a joke. Without any such precautions, therefore, Aske rode up to London about Christmas time.

Henry summoned Sir Thomas Wharton to court, but he excused himself[3]. Bishop Tunstall, who was still at Norham, was also summoned. The letter, despatched on 24 December, did not reach him until 4 January, and he replied that he dared not attempt the journey through the disaffected region[4]. Sir George Darcy and Sir Nicholas Fairfax went up on their own account at Christmas, the former carrying messages from the Earl of Northumberland[5]. Archdeacon Magnus, who had been with Archbishop Lee since the beginning of the rising, went to the Earl of Shrewsbury and thence to London as early as 13 December[6]. Sir Oswald Wolsthrope and Sir Ralph Ellerker had gone up to London, as well as Sir Ralph Evers, who held Scarborough so long[7]; Lord Latimer set out, but was turned back by an order from the King[8].

The news that so many had gone up to court gave rise to rumours. The commons said that the only object of the conference at Doncaster and the "counselling above" was to betray them, and that they would trust the gentlemen no more[9]. This was the result which the King wished to obtain, and he took no trouble to conciliate the lower ranks of the Pilgrims.

His Council had determined that a mass of treasure must be accumulated. To achieve this, the King's rents and taxes must be collected[10]. The collection was not contrary to the agreement at Doncaster. The gentlemen had declared there, perhaps over hastily, that the King's money was ready for his Highness[11]. But considering the state of the country it would have been wiser to defer the

[1] L. and P. xii (1), 1175.   [2] See note C at end of chapter.
[3] L. and P. xi, 1389.   [4] L. and P. xii (1), 22.
[5] L. and P. xi, 1337, 1368.   [6] Ibid. 1293.
[7] L. and P. xii (1), 7, 66.   [8] Ibid. 131, 173.
[9] L. and P. xi, 1294.   [10] Ibid. 1410 (1).
[11] L. and P. xii (1), 6; printed in full, Eng. Hist. Rev. v, 342.

collection for a time, if the King's object had really been peace. The servants of John Gostwick, the treasurer of the tenths and first fruits, went north to collect the King's rents immediately after the conference at Doncaster[1]. They were accompanied by Sir George Lawson the treasurer of Berwick, who had himself been involved in the rebellion[2]. At Templehurst, Doncaster, Wakefield, and Sheriffhutton the rents were paid quietly, but as the King's servants went further north they began to encounter opposition[3]. On Christmas Eve Lawson reported to Gostwick from Barnard Castle that it was impossible to induce anyone to pay at present in those parts. They all said that they had been ruined by the late disturbances. At Barnard Castle the tenants had demanded respite until twenty days after Christmas, and at Bishop Middleham until a week before Candlemas (2 February), and he could make no better terms. He himself and some other friends were advancing the money to pay the garrison at Berwick, whither he was going, while Gostwick's servants were returning to Lawson's house at York to wait until the appointed time for the new collection[4]. One of the servants, Thomas Ley, wrote to Gostwick from York, confirming Lawson's report. He added that at Middleham Lord Conyers had rather hindered than helped them[5]. Lawson on the contrary said that Lord Conyers had done his best for them[6].

The tenth from the clergy fell due at Christmas. The thought of it had been weighing on Archbishop Lee's mind for some time; he requested that Norfolk should be consulted about it at Doncaster[7]. About 31 December he received orders from the King that the tenth must be collected. As Lee felt sure that this would create disturbances he wrote on 5 January 1536–7 to consult Darcy[8], who advised him to lay the matter before Shrewsbury. Darcy warned Shrewsbury on 7 January that it would be very dangerous to levy the tenth north of Doncaster and begged him to make the King understand this[9]. Shrewsbury forwarded the letters to Henry on 9 January, with his own advice that the collection should be foreborne for the time[10], but he wrote to Lee on the same day that he dared not counsel him to delay, as he had had express commands to begin it, and if the King changed his mind he would soon be informed[11].

[1] L. and P. xi, 1365.
[2] L. and P. xi, 1337, 1380.
[3] See above, chap. viii.
[4] Ibid. 1365.
[5] Ibid. 1380.
[6] Ibid. 1365.
[7] L. and P. xii (1), 1022.
[8] Ibid. 20.
[9] Ibid. 89.
[10] Ibid. 50, 51.
[11] Ibid. 52.

Henry's reply was to have been a peremptory order to carry on the collection; but though there is an undated draft of it, the order was probably never sent, as before it could be despatched the situation had changed[1].

Other measures were taken which increased the irritation of the lower classes. Preachers were sent to the north to expound the King's orthodoxy and to represent the enormity of rebellion to their congregations, and tracts on the same subjects were circulated[2]. The King's reply to the first five articles[3] was printed and sent to the north. This step may have been due partly to the King's natural partiality for his own writing, partly to a deliberate intention of exasperating the people. The reply was extremely provocative. Even at the present day the reader of it longs to argue with the King. The Council had seen how unsuitable it was for publication when it was first written, and with great difficulty had persuaded the King to withhold it. When it was at length issued, the effect was even more aggravating than it would originally have been, for the circumstances in which the reply had been drawn up had all changed, and the reply was no longer applicable to the situation. Both the beginning and the end of the reply referred to the earlier state of affairs. It was absurd to complain that the terms of the articles were "so general that hard they be to be answered," when a detailed list of grievances had been drawn up and sent to the King, and it was very alarming to find the King still insisting that the ringleaders must be given up before he would think of a pardon, when a general pardon had just been proclaimed[4].

The Pilgrims believed that they had won their object; the King's reply showed that they had lost it. In the very first clause the King spoke once again of the "light tales"; this always annoyed his opponents. They might ask, was it a light tale that the monasteries were being suppressed? Was it a light tale that the Pope's name was omitted from the service and the King's substituted? The King proceeded to outrage the feelings of the conservatives still further by asking, when they spoke of the maintenance of the Church, what Church they meant? The very idea that there could be more than one Church was a horrible innovation. The King went on to talk about his own Church, of which he was the Supreme Head, and to declare that this was an affair in which the commons had no right to interfere. He implies that as they had nothing to do with

---

[1] L. and P. xii (1), 21.
[2] L. and P. xi, 1410 (1), 1459, 1481-2; xii (1), 5.
[3] See above, chap. xii.
[4] L. and P. xii (1), 67.

the government of the Church in the Pope's days, so they had nothing to do with it now. Their part was to believe its doctrines and bow to its authority, whoever wielded it. But if a layman might be Supreme Head of the Church, it seemed only reasonable that other laymen might express their opinion on the subject, especially as many of them believed the choice between King and Pope so vital as to affect their eternal welfare.

The King's defence of his Council was mere quibbling. Norfolk, Exeter and Sandys might be nominal members of the Privy Council, but their advice was never followed, and the King's policy was determined by their chief enemy, Thomas Cromwell. Although the King boasted that the rest of his realm was loyal, the northern men had good reason to believe that a great part of the south sympathised with them. This was afterwards admitted by Henry's panegyrist William Thomas, who said that the King was forced to treat with the rebels because he had such difficulty in mustering troops[1].

While the King was goading the commons to further rebellion, he was drugging the gentlemen with gracious promises. Aske was most flatteringly received at court. The Spanish Chronicler gives an account of his reception which, though unreliable in details, represents the King's general attitude in a picturesque manner:—

"When he [Aske] arrived where the King was, as soon as the King saw him he rose up, and throwing his arms around him said aloud that all might hear: 'Be ye welcome, my good Aske; it is my wish that here, before my Council, you ask what you desire and I will grant it.' Aske answered, 'Sir, your Majesty allows yourself to be governed by a tyrant named Cromwell. Everyone knows if it had not been for him the seven thousand poor priests I have in my company would not be ruined wanderers as they are now. They must have enough to live upon, for they have no handicraft.' Then the King with a smiling face and words full of falseness, took from his neck a great chain of gold, which he had put on for the purpose, and threw it round Aske's neck, saying to him: 'I promise thee, thou art wiser than anyone thinks, and from this day forward I make thee one of my Council.' And then on the spot he ordered a thousand pounds sterling to be given to him, and promised him the same amount every year as long as he lived.

"The unhappy Aske, carried away with the chain and the thousand pounds and grant of annual income, was quite won over, and the King said to him, 'Now return to the north, and get your people to disperse and go to their houses, and I will grant a general pardon for all. In order that the priests may have enough to live upon I will divide them among the parish churches and give them an allowance. Let them come at once, that this may be done. I order that

[1] William Thomas, The Pilgrim, ed. J. A. Froude.

in York each of the parishes shall take two of these priests, and give them £10 a year to live upon, but the others I will divide amongst all the towns and villages.' When Aske saw the good tidings he had to take back he determined to return at once; and the King ordered that after all was pacified he should come to court, and he promised to make him one of his Council."[1]

It will be noticed that the Spaniard misses the point with respect to the monks, and greatly exaggerates the King's gifts. Yet he preserves correctly the spirit of the interview. The King gave Aske " a jacket of crimson satin,"[2] and requested him to write an account of his part in the Pilgrimage. Aske drew up a full narrative of all that he had done since the beginning of October. This narrative, to which we have so often referred, is the first and best history of the Pilgrimage. In it we see clearly mirrored Aske's character and views, and it also shows the King's flattering attitude towards him while he was at Court. Aske evidently believed that he could speak very plainly to the King without giving offence, and, with the standing explanation that he was "only declaring the hearts of the people," he spoke out with a bluntness which must have been an unusual experience to Henry. He did not hesitate to say that if Cromwell remained in favour there would be danger of more rebellions "which will be very dangerous to your Grace's person."[2] The King professed himself to be so much pleased by this frankness that he gave him " a token of pardon for confessing the truth."

There was no difficulty in persuading Aske that the King had not known the real state of affairs in the north, and that now his eyes were opened all would go well. Cromwell, indeed, either could not win Aske over, or did not consider him worth winning. He said that all northern men were traitors, which Aske resented, and his hostility to Norfolk was very evident[4]. Henry, however, convinced Aske of his good will. He declared that he fully pardoned all the north, that he intended to hold the parliament at York, where the Queen should be crowned, that there should be complete freedom of election, and that convocation should be held at the same time, at which the spiritualty should "have liberty to declare their learning."[5] The free parliament was the chief object for which Aske had been labouring, and it seemed as if that object was now within reach.

On one point, however, he was disillusioned. He discovered that

---

[1] Spanish Chron. ed. Hume, chap. xvii.
[2] L. and P. xii (1), 1224.
[3] Ibid. 6; printed in full, Eng. Hist. Rev. v, 331.
[4] L. and P. xii (2), 292 (iii); printed, State Papers, i, 558.
[5] L. and P. xii (1), 43.

the King did not mean to give his consent to the temporary restoration of the monasteries. The only evidence on this point is very slight. When Aske was arrested a letter was found in his possession written to him by his sister Dorothy Green. According to his accusers it appeared from this letter that Aske had written to Dorothy's husband Richard Green that the King would not be as good as he promised concerning the Church and the abbeys. Dorothy Green's letter has not been found, and Aske's alleged letter to Richard Green was never produced; consequently it is impossible to know how much Aske really learned about the King's intentions[1]. His first impulse, on learning some part of the truth, must have been to send north the news that the King would not confirm the order for the monks which had been made at Doncaster; but he was convinced by the King's professions of good-will, and believed that if only there were peace in the north until the parliament met, the Pilgrims might still be successful without bloodshed. Nothing was more likely to provoke a serious outbreak than the repudiation of the terms made for the monasteries, and it may be assumed that these considerations weighed with Aske so much that he was silent about the King's determination.

The situation of the monks was a very uneasy one, even without knowledge of the King's intentions. They were apt to be bullied by their own champions. William Aclom had carried off "two trussing bedsteads" at the sack of Leonard Beckwith's house, and had deposited them at the Priory of the Holy Trinity at York. He wrote to the Prior on 12 December: "Mr Prior, I marvel at your doubleness, which is a great vice in a religious man, touching a bed of Beckwith's you promised to send to me. I think you reckon our journey in vain. Send it or I will do you further displeasure."[2] The Abbot of Jervaux lost thirty wethers during the rebellion and appealed to one of the rebels named Edward Middleton, a hunter, to "find" them. It was probably a case of "no questions asked, upon my honour."[3]

The monastery of Tynemouth was harried; the mutilation of a letter leaves it doubtful by whom[4]; but perhaps the loyal burgesses of Newcastle had some hand in it, for they had long been at feud with the Priory[5]. The monks had no prior at the time. They appealed for protection to Darcy, who recommended them to Sir Thomas Hilton[6].

[1] L. and P. XII (1), 848 (ii), (4).   [2] Ibid. 586.
[3] Ibid. 1035.   [4] L. and P. XI, 1293.
[5] Leadam, Select Cases in the Court of Star Chamber (Selden Soc.), II, p. 68.
[6] L. and P. XI, 1293.

Some monks suspected that after Doncaster there was little hope for the success of the Pilgrimage. Dan Ralph Swensune, a monk of Lenton Abbey, Notts., said at Christmas time,

"In the misericorde while sitting by the fire on a form...'I hear say that the King has taken peace with the commonty till after Christmas, but if they have done so it is alms to hang them up, for they may well know that he that will not keep no promise with God Himself but pulls down His churches, he will not keep promise with them; but if they had gone forth onward up and stricken off his head then had they done well, for I warrant them if he can overcome them he will do so by them.' 'Peace,' said the sub-prior, 'you rail you wot not whereof.' 'Nay,' said he, 'I say as it will be.' 'Peace,' said the sub-prior, 'In the virtue of obedience I command you speak no more at this time.'"[1]

A certain Dan Robert Castelforth had begged Aske to help him to the priorship of Blyth in Nottingham. On 12 December he wrote to ask for his letters back again, which was a very prudent measure, unfortunately defeated by the fact that this letter was preserved[2]. The Abbot of St Mary's, York, on 18 January, did his best to make his peace with Cromwell by sending him a gift and abject apologies for the part that he had taken in the rising, which, as he said, had been forced upon him by the commons[3].

The less cautious religious were induced to go back to their houses. Reference has already been made to the cases of Conishead, Cartmell, and the Friars Observant of Newcastle-upon-Tyne[4]. The Abbot and monks of Sawley had been restored and were living on the alms of their neighbours. Nicholas Tempest sent them a fat ox, a mutton and two or three geese, and others also contributed[5]. A little before Christmas the Abbot sent a request to Sir Stephen Hamerton that he would write to Robert Aske to know what should become of the house. The first messenger returned without an answer, Aske being in London. A second man, George Shuttleworth, was sent, and returned with the required letter. The Abbot despatched him with it to Aughton, as Aske had now returned. Aske knew by this time that the King was not going to allow the monasteries to stand and therefore advised the Abbot to submit to any man who came to him in the King's name and to keep the commons quiet[6].

Several of the greater monasteries, though not yet dissolved, had been thrown into confusion by the fact that the abbot or prior had been deprived, and the house was left either without a head, or with

---

[1] L. and P. xiii (1), 892.   [2] L. and P. xi, 1287.
[3] L. and P. xii (1), 132, 133.   [4] See above, chap. xv.
[5] L. and P. xii (1), 1014; printed, Yorks. Arch. Journ. xi, 254.
[6] L. and P. xii (1), 491.

one who was a mere creature of Cromwell's. Tynemouth was without a prior. The Prior of Watton had fled to London, greatly to the indignation of the monks and the neighbouring commons[1]. In February 1535-6 the visitors of the monasteries had induced James Cockerell, the Prior of Guisborough, to resign[2]. They appointed in his place Robert Sylvester alias Pursglove, who was "meet and apt both for the King's honour and the discharge of your [Cromwell's] conscience, and also profitable." James Cockerell, however, had provision made for him on his retirement, including a mansion called "the Bishop's Place" in Guisborough[3]. With a new prior of this temper and with the old prior still living in the neighbourhood it was not surprising that the internal affairs of the monastery did not go smoothly, and twice in the course of the rebellion Sir John Bulmer, as steward of the Priory, was called in to mediate. The second time it was the new prior who appealed to him, from which it may be inferred that Sir John strove to keep the peace and did not favour the monks unduly[4].

Although the Pilgrimage had been undertaken on behalf of the monks, the secular clergy had been the moving spirits in it, and their ardour had not yet cooled. On 12 December 1536 Dakyn wrote to William Tristram, the chantry priest of Lartington, to rebuke him for being over-zealous in bearing arms, collecting money, and urging his parishioners to fight[5]. Lancaster Herald reported on 26 December that the spiritualty of the north were "most corrupted and malicious... inward and part outward,"[6] and on 22 January 1536-7 Sir William Fairfax wrote to Cromwell accusing all the clergy of the north, both regular and secular:—

"The houses of religion not suppressed make friends and wag the poor to stick hard in this opinion, and the monks who were suppressed inhabit the villages round their houses and daily wag the people to put them in again. These two sorts hath no small number in their favours, arguing and speaking. The head tenants of abbots, bishops and prebendaries have greater familiarity with their landlords than they used to have. None are more busy to stir the people than the chief tenants of commandry lands of Saint John of Jerusalem. Where the archbishop, bishops, abbots and spiritual persons have rule the people are most ready at a call. The insurrection in Lincolnshire began at Louth, the Bishop of Lincoln's town, next at Howden, Yorks, the Bishop of Durham's town, Sir Robert Constable, a virtuous pilgrim of grace, there being steward, and then at Beverley, the Archbishop of York's town, York being worst of all....The King

---

[1] L. and P. xii (1), 201 (p. 102), 870 (p. 169); see above, chap. xii.
[2] L. and P. x, 271.   [3] Ibid. 927.
[4] L. and P. xi, 1135 (2), 1295.   [5] Ibid. 1284.
[6] Ibid. 1371.

should command his lord deputy to put out the rulers made by spiritual men, for their bailiffs are brought up from childhood with priests, and are malicious in their quarrels."[1]

The dean and canons of York were supposed to be laying in a store of weapons[2]. At Kendal on 28 January there was a tumult in the church at the bidding of beads; Sir Walter Brown "second curate," said, "Commons, I will bid the beads as ye will have me," and prayed for the Pope and the cardinals[3].

It was very difficult for Darcy and the other gentlemen to control this ferment, and the difficulty was increased by the behaviour of some of the gentlemen.

Since Sir Thomas Percy had gone to Northumberland, the whole country had been plunged in disorder. "The Percys and their friends and the Grays and their friends take contrary parts and make contrary proclamations who shall be sheriff."[4] Thomas Gray, Darcy's nephew, who represented him at Bamborough, sent word to him that twenty-four score ploughs were laid down in Northumberland on account of the raids made by the mosstroopers of Tynedale and Reedsdale; "the most part of Northumberland is broken amongst themselves, and open forays made by Sir Ingram Percy and others against the Grays."[5] Darcy sent this news to Norfolk on 15 December 1536[6].

Before the appointment Sir Thomas Percy was living at his castle of Prudhoe on the Tyne, "where the most noted offenders of Tynedale and Hexhamshire resorted to him, especially John Heron of Chipchase, Edward Charleton, Cuddy Charleton, Geffray Robson, Anthony Errington and others." Sir Thomas, however, was not very often at Prudhoe, as he was continually riding about the country. He acted as lieutenant of the Middle Marches, although he had received no authority, and in this capacity summoned a great meeting at Rothbury for the redress of spoils and the establishment of Tynedale and Reedsdale. The aggrieved royalists complained that nothing was done except the proclamation of a peace for twenty days, which was not observed, and the administration of the Pilgrims' oath to all the gentlemen who had not taken it before at Alnwick. In addition to this Sir Thomas proclaimed that anyone who captured a Carnaby or a follower of the Carnabys should have the prisoner's goods. At Hexham market he demanded of the people "what help he might have in the quarrel of the commons." As lieutenant of the Middle Marches he attempted to hold the "warden's day" with the Scots, but

[1] L. and P. xii (1), 192.   [2] Ibid. 582–3.   [3] Ibid. 914.
[4] L. and P. xi, 1294.   [5] Ibid. 1293.   [6] Ibid. 1307.

they refused to meet him as he had no authority. On this occasion he spent the night with John Heron at Harbottle Castle, and then rode to join his brother Sir Ingram at Alnwick. Sir Ingram was very anxious as to the result of the conference at Doncaster, for it was only too clear that the private interests of the brothers were a matter of very little concern to the commons, while their removal was a great object with the King. "In the chapel at Alnwick" he confided his fears to Sir Thomas. If the King came to an agreement with the commons it could do the Percys no good. Sir Thomas reassured him as well as he could. The leaders had promised to grant nothing without sending him information, and they would never consent to any terms but a general pardon,—" wherefore let us do that we think to do whiles we may, and that betimes."[1]

In Cumberland the feud between the Dacres and the Cliffords broke out again, though affairs were not so bad as in Northumberland. Lord Clifford, Cumberland's eldest son, was still in Carlisle, but Lord Dacre had gone up to London some time before. On Saturday 9 December, the last day of the conference at Doncaster, Richard Dacre, coming to Carlisle with a company of Lord Dacre's tenants, met Lord Clifford at the church door "and looked upon him with a haut and proud countenance, not moving his bonnet." In the churchyard he encountered Sir William Musgrave. "Without speaking one word," Dacre attacked Musgrave with his dagger, and would have killed him but for "a son of the laird Featherstonhaugh," who snatched out his dagger and leapt between the two. Dacre and Featherstonhaugh drew their swords, but Musgrave's men separated them. Dacre cried through the town "A Dacre! A Dacre!" and a great company assembled in the market-place. Lord Clifford took refuge in the Castle. The mayor and Edward Aglionby, a prominent citizen, "commanded Richard Dacre to avoid the market-place," but he refused to stir until the mayor summoned the townsmen to arms and joined Clifford in the Castle. In spite of the preparations that were being made to attack him Dacre "went to his lodging and dined and departed at his leisure." Next Sunday, 17 December, Dacre appeared at Carlisle again, accompanied by twenty men of Gilsland "in harness for some unlawful purpose." By Clifford's orders the mayor and Aglionby went out to stop him from entering the town, but he would not be stayed and entered the market-place. However he found that Clifford was in possession this time; "he perceived the

[1] L. and P. xii (1), 1090; printed in full, De Fonblanque, op. cit. i, Append. lii, and Raine, Priory of Hexham (Surtees Soc.), i, Append. p. cxxx et seq.

lord Clifford, well accompanied, come to the market cross and make a proclamation..." He probably announced the terms made at Doncaster, but the account breaks off at this point[1].

The zeal of the loyalists was almost as embarrassing to those who were trying to keep the peace as the lawlessness of the Percys and Dacres. Shrewsbury demanded the restitution of cattle which had been driven away during the disturbances[2]. Derby kept a great Christmas at Lathom and strengthened the Castle, proceedings which the commons watched with a jealous eye[3]. The Earl of Cumberland was ill about Christmas time, but he summoned several of the gentlemen who had taken part in the Pilgrimage to come and see him. Sir Richard Tempest excused himself on the grounds that he was as "sore a crasyd" as the Earl[4]. Sir Stephen Hamerton did not dare to go[5]. On 14 December Cumberland reported that since the appointment at Doncaster, bills had been set on the church doors of Gargrave, Rylston, Lynton and Burnsall in Craven. These bills bade the priest order the constable of the parish to charge the parishioners to be at Rylston on Tuesday [12 December] to kill all the deer they could find[6]. Cumberland's retainers had been in the habit of hunting at Rylston, which belonged to John Norton, whenever they felt inclined[7], and the commons were following their example; but, as Cumberland observed, the insurrection had begun with bills set on the church doors, though the contents of the bills had been different. The Earl declared his intention of arresting the instigators of the bills; he suspected that they were "gentlemen, some of them the King's servants," but he had as yet no certain information[8]. He was evidently hinting at Sir Richard Tempest. Before Christmas the Earl imprisoned in Skipton Castle "one of Harry Amarton's sons, a man of law, and also one Thomas Porter." They must have been Ribblesdale men, as Lord Clifford was nearly captured in Christmas week when he went to mass at Giggleswick; the commons declared that they would take and hold him until his father released the prisoners[9]. Shortly after Christmas the travellers assembled in an alehouse at Kettlewell talked of "how gently my lord of Cumberland had treated such prisoners as had been a-hunting in his chaces, and Tenande, who had been with them in gaol for the said matter, affirmed the same."[10] It does not appear whether they were speaking

[1] L. and P. xi, 1331.
[2] Ibid. 1320.
[3] L. and P. xii (1), 7.
[4] L. and P. xi, 1401.
[5] L. and P. xii (1), 7.
[6] L. and P. xi, 1299 (ii).
[7] See above, chap. iii.
[8] L. and P. xi, 1299.
[9] L. and P. xii (1), 7.
[10] Ibid. 491.

sarcastically, or whether Cumberland was really a model gaoler, whose praises were sounded by his ex-prisoners. The arrests were injudicious, considering the unsettled state of Westmorland, and Darcy wrote on 17 January that the Earl of Cumberland was "likely to have business for two prisoners he keeps."[1]

About Christmas time it was reported that Robert Pulleyn, who had been a leader in the Pilgrimage, had paid the detested levy of the neat geld and had taken bribes and put men into possession of lands. His neighbours of Kirkby Stephen attacked him, and "would have spoiled his goods, but upon sureties and entreaty of certain men they delivered him again." "Shortly after the goods of one Mr Rose were taken away by night of thieves and the country was afraid of burning."[2] On Saturday 29 December the tenants of Broughton and Talentire turned the threshers out of the tithe barns and locked the barn-doors; the movement against the tithes threatened to spread to the neighbouring villages[3]. On 12 January the Earl of Cumberland wrote to the King that there had been musters about Cockermouth since the pardon and that the Westmorland men were turning against their captains in the late rising "for such money as they had gathered among them." Also bills were being set on the church doors in Yorkshire. The Earl urged emphatically that Carlisle must be strengthened, as the fortifications were in a state of decay and the commons would certainly attack the town if they rose again[4].

In Richmond a new insurrection was talked of soon after Christmas, and Dakyn, who preached against the Pope, was saved from being pulled out of the church only by the intervention of "Ralph Gowre and other honest men."[5] Lancaster Herald was attacked in Durham after Christmas, and on 2 January the Earl of Westmorland was warned that there were stirrings about Auckland[6]. When Lawson and Gostwick's servants returned to Barnard Castle to collect the King's rents at the time appointed they found that there was still no money and no prospect of it[7].

The burden of all the letters from Darcy, Cumberland, and Lawson, is the same; the Duke of Norfolk must be sent at once. If he came and brought a satisfactory answer from the King the commons would be pacified. It did not suit Henry, however, to do anything in a

---

[1] L. and P. xii (1), 115.
[2] Ibid. 687 (2); printed in full, Wilson, op. cit., no. xxii.
[3] L. and P. xii (1), 18.   [4] Ibid. 71-2.   [5] Ibid. 788.
[6] Ibid. 11.   [7] Ibid. 116.

hurry. The gentlemen could scarcely expect Norfolk to return before Christmas, but Christmas passed, and the new year came, and January was slipping away, and still there was no news of his approach. Meanwhile so far from soothing the commons and making the task of the gentlemen easier, all the reports that came from "above" were of an alarming nature. The King's answer to the first five articles put the commons in doubt of their pardon[1]. It became known that the King was demanding the tenth, and the commons were quite clever enough to see that any money sent out of the north weakened them and strengthened the King[2]. It was said that their harness was to be taken from them and stored at York[3]; that the appointment was not observed in Lincolnshire[4] but that the prisoners there were already being brought to execution[5]; that the monasteries were not to be allowed to stand; and that the King intended to fortify Hull and Scarborough[6]. These rumours described very accurately the King's real intentions. The gentlemen tried not to believe them and tried to persuade the commons that they were false, but there was all the more difficulty in doing this as the promise of a parliament did not pacify the commons at all. They murmured among themselves that "the Parliament men would not get them what they rose for."[7] As they never even thought of being represented in the new parliament, they were much more inclined to pin their faith on the arbitrary power of the King, and all their hopes centred in the coming of the Duke of Norfolk.

The hero of Flodden was very popular in the north—"no man... would withstand the Duke of Norfolk, but as for Suffolk they would hold him herehence the best they could."[8] The gentlemen therefore found it easiest to keep order by exhorting the commons to hold over their grievances until the Duke of Norfolk came. Yet still there was no news that he had set out. The commons grew more and more uneasy. Another matter troubled them, Aske had ridden up to London before Christmas, and since then nothing had been heard of him. The gentlemen suspected him of betraying them. The commons were more faithful to their leader. They did indeed suspect treachery, but it was on the King's part. The rumour ran that Aske had been beheaded in London[9] and that Norfolk was in the

---

[1] L. and P. xii (1), 67.
[2] Ibid. 192, 201 (p. 91).
[3] Ibid. 1036.
[4] Ibid. 201 (p. 88).
[5] Ibid. 64.
[6] Ibid. 64, 201 (p. 85).
[7] Ibid. 201 (p. 88).
[8] Ibid. 201 (p. 92); see above, chap. xi, note A.
[9] L. and P. xii (1), 56.

Tower. The story of Norfolk's arrest is a spirited narrative, which shows the pathetic confidence that the northern men had in the Duke, and also how entirely baseless a most circumstantial story may be:—

"My Lord Cromwell came to the King and said, 'Sir, and please your Grace, ye are minded to send the Duke of Norfolk northward shortly?' And the King said 'Yea.' And my lord said again, 'Sir, as far as I can perceive, my lord of Norfolk hath granted the commonty all their demands or else he would take their part, and as far as I perceive he will lose no part of his honour.' Then the King sent for my lord of Norfolk and asked him whether he would do so. And he answered the King that he would be loath but that the commons should have their demands, and would be loath to lose any part of his honour. Then the King commanded him to the Tower. And thereupon my lord William [Howard] went to the lieutenant of the Tower and desired that he might speak with my lord of Norfolk, and could not; and returned again toward the Rolls to speak with my Lord Privy Seal, and he was gone and had taken his barge to go to the Court. Then as my Lord William came along Chancery Lane he met with Richard Cromwell; and there (said) my lord : ' By God's blood I will be revenged of one of you,' and took out his dagger and did stick him therewith, and turned him with his hand and so killed him."

This story was told "in Johnson's house at Minstergate in York" on Saturday 13 January[1], but it had probably been travelling about the country before that date. When Sir Robert Constable heard it he said, "As in the chronicles of the Romans there was a gentleman who, having killed the Emperor's secretary in mistake for the Emperor, ran unto a pan of coals and burnt off the hand that missed the Emperor; so the said lord William may burn his hand for missing of killing my lord Cromwell."[2]

In the East Riding the agitation was strongest. The commons feared that Hull and Scarborough were to be fortified and held by the Duke of Suffolk, to become a refuge for the gentlemen and a menace to the commons if the King resolved to deny their petition. The leader of this agitation was John Hallam[3]. His position with regard to the gentlemen leaders of the Pilgrimage was rather similar to that of a Labour member towards members of a Liberal government at the present day. Having no responsibility himself, he was always ready to urge on the most sweeping measures and the most dangerous enterprises. He was quite shrewd enough to see through the King's moves, but not wise enough to realise that policy must be met by policy, and that to resort to violence was to play into his opponent's hand. It was not without reason that he distrusted the gentlemen, and he had not sufficient tact to conceal his suspicions and strive at all costs to preserve unity among the Pilgrims. The fatal cleavage

[1] L. and P. xii (1), 201 (p. 89). [2] Ibid. 891. [3] Ibid. 201.

between class and class was broadening rapidly; as always happens in the many causes which it has wrecked, each party had a certain amount of reason, the gentlemen to fear the commons, the commons to distrust the gentlemen; but to quarrel among themselves merely increased the danger. Their only chance of obtaining their purpose and securing their pardon lay in strict co-operation. Neither party could understand this. The commons could not be patient, and raised a cry of treachery at each delay. The gentlemen grew more and more alarmed by their turbulence, and were continually tempted to throw over the cause and make themselves safe individually.

Hallam made his headquarters at Watton parish church. As early as Christmas, before the appointment was a month old, he was whispering to its frequenters that Hull was false to the commons, and that the men of Holderness were ready to rise again. He saw as plainly as did the King that if Hull and Scarborough were fortified and garrisoned " they were able to destroy the whole country about."[1] Twelfth Day, the feast of Epiphany, 6 January, fell this year on a Saturday. The following Monday, 8 January, was called Plough Monday, and was a festival and holiday[2]. Hallam and his friends celebrated it by drinking at John Bell's tavern in Watton, and after the festivity was over, Hallam, Hugh Langdale, Philip Uty, Thomas Lunde, William Horskey and the vicar of Watton returned home together. When they came to the church they turned in to say a paternoster; the vicar left the laymen, who went to Our Lady's altar, a chantry in the church. Hallam remarked that Langdale had come into the country recently and had never taken the commons' oath. He brought out a copy of the oath and asked Langdale whether he thought there was anything unlawful in it. Langdale said no, and took the oath willingly[3]. Then Hallam said to the others, "Sirs, I fear me lest Hull do deceive us the commons, for there is ordnance daily carried in thither by ships, and they make prie yates [privy gates] and Scarborough shall be better fortified, and the gentlemen will deceive us the commons, and the King's Grace intends to perform nothing of our petitions. Wherefore I think best to take Hull and Scarborough ourselves betimes; and to the intent that we may do that the better, I think best that ye, Hugh Langdale, do go forth to William Levening and Robert Bulmer or William Constable whether [whichever] he would; you, Horskey,

---

[1] L. and P. XII (1), 201 (p. 85).
[2] Cox, Churchwardens' Accounts (the Antiquary's Books), chap. XVIII.
[3] L. and P. XII. (1), 201 (p. 87).

to Sir Robert Constable, and I will go to Hull to inquire what tidings goeth abroad in those parts and how they are minded there, and after that let us meet all in this place together again upon Wednesday next, then to take further counsel what is to be done in this matter." The other two promised to take their messages, but next morning, when they were already mounted and about to start, Hallam met them with a letter from Robert Aske, announcing that he had returned to the north and was about to hold a great meeting next day, Tuesday 9 January at Beverley. He asked Hallam to met him first at Arras and to ride with him to the meeting. On receiving this great news they all agreed that they must go to Beverley instead of performing their errands[1].

Aske left London on Friday 5 January, riding north secretly and "with most haste."[2] It was an amazingly clever stroke of policy on Henry's part to send back the leader of the Pilgrims to pacify the disturbance that the King himself had fomented, and to prevent it from passing beyond control. Aske rode swiftly and reached home on 8 January, the very day when Hallam was plotting in Watton church.

As soon as Aske arrived he wrote to Darcy, repeating the King's gracious promises, and saying that he intended to visit Templehurst next day. He was already busy quieting his own neighbourhood[3], and scarcely had he arrived when appeals for assistance came pouring in from all quarters. Hallam's agitation was known to Sir Marmaduke Constable, who wrote to welcome Aske home and to beg him to pacify Beverley, which was ready to rise in consequence of a rumour that the King was secretly sending ordnance to Hull. Sir Marmaduke said that Hallam would not listen to him, but Aske might have more influence[4].

In consequence of this message Aske appointed the meeting at Beverley next day. Two manifestos containing the King's reply were issued to pacify the country. They are undated, but must have been issued immediately after Aske's return. One was by Aske himself, and announced the King's promise of a general pardon, and that "your reasonable petitions shall be ordered by Parliament." The King himself was coming to hold the parliament at York, the Queen was to be crowned there, and the arrival of the Duke of Norfolk might soon be expected[5]. Sir Oswald Wolsthrope, who had perhaps ridden

---

[1] L. and P. xii (1), 201 (p. 86). [2] Ibid. 23.
[3] Ibid. 43. [4] Ibid. 46.
[5] Ibid. 44.

north with Aske, in another manifesto repeated and amplified these statements. Norfolk was to bring the particulars concerning the parliament. He would come "with a mean company and after a quiet manner." The parliament, the convocation and the coronation were all to be held in York at Whitsuntide; until then the commons had only to keep the peace and refuse to listen to any who bid them make new disturbances[1].

On Tuesday 9 January, instead of going to Templehurst, Aske rode to Beverley. The Twelve Men and the whole town had assembled, besides many people from the neighbourhood, among them Horskey, Langdale and Hallam. Aske addressed the assembly, beginning: "The King's Highness is good and gracious unto us the commons all, and he hath granted us all our desires and petitions, and he will keep a Parliament shortly at York, and there also for the more favour and goodwill that he beareth to this country he purposeth to have the Queen's Grace crowned..." "adding many other good words on the King's behalf." He went on to declare that the Duke of Norfolk was coming shortly, and would bring "a better report unto them from the King's Grace under the Great Seal."[2] After Aske's speech, questions were asked, as at a modern meeting. Hallam wanted to know why, if the King's intentions were so favourable, he had given orders for the collection of the tenth and of his rents before the parliament time. Aske had not heard of these orders, and the news must have been a disagreeable shock to him, but he put the best face he could on the matter, and said that the King had probably sent only for the money that had already been collected and was in Archbishop Lee's hands[3]; in any case the clergy had freely granted the tenth[4], and the Pilgrims had decided that "it might be borne well enough."[5]

After the meeting Aske and all the principal men who attended it were invited by Mr Crake and the Twelve Men to dinner at Christopher Sanderson's house. When Hallam and Horskey entered the room Crake drew them aside to a window and said, "Mr Hallam, I pray you stay the country about you. Ye see how good and gracious the King's highness is to us and will be undoubtedly. There be certain lewd fellows abroad in the country that would stir the people to naughtiness again, as Nicholson of Preston in Holderness and the bailiff of Snaith. I pray you stay them and be not counselled by them." The appeal was

---

[1] L. and P. xii (1), 45. [2] Ibid. 201 (p. 86); see note D at end of chapter.
[3] L. and P. xii (1), 201 (p. 88). [4] Ibid. 201 (p. 86).
[5] See above, chap. xiv.

judicious, and Hallam was reassured and pacified. He promised that he would not stir. For the moment this danger seemed to be averted[1].

Aske rode back to Aughton, but next day Wednesday 10 January Sir Marmaduke Constable appealed to him again. He congratulated him on quieting Beverley, but a rising was now threatened at Ripon and there was mustering on a moor near Fountains. The commons said that Aske had been beheaded in London, and his presence was urgently needed[2]. Next day, 11 January, Sir Marmaduke wrote to Cromwell to report that Aske had pacified Beverley and the East Riding, but that the North Riding was still dangerous, and Norfolk was very much wanted[3].

Aske received Sir Marmaduke's letter on Thursday 11 January, and at the same time he was summoned by Darcy to come and help to stay the parts round Templehurst[4]. He sent news of his return and of the King's goodwill to Ripon and rode to Templehurst[5]. Darcy had received on 10 January a summons from the King to go up to court "in order that the King may show he retains no displeasure against him."[6] Sir Robert Constable, who was also at Templehurst, had received a similar summons. Aske described to them his encouraging interviews with the King, and, as he had kept a copy of it, he showed them his narrative of his own doings during the rising. Darcy asked how the King had spoken of him. Aske replied that the King had referred to him and others as "offenders before the pardon," but he had not otherwise mentioned him. They consulted together over the King's summons, and decided that as the country was "in a floughter and a readiness to rise," it would be very unwise for Darcy and Constable to alarm the commons by going up to court. Aske advised Sir Robert to go back to Holme and Darcy to stay where he was, and promised to write to the King to explain their delay and to beg him to excuse them[7].

On Friday 12 January Aske had returned to Aughton once more, and sent the King a report of all that had happened and all that he had done since his return home. The frank and outspoken tone of his letter is a great contrast to that of Norfolk's reports. He described how he had pacified Beverley. The people were very joyous to hear that the King himself proposed to visit them, and that Norfolk was coming, and the gentlemen were anxious to keep

---

[1] L. and P. XII (1), 201 (p. 86).   [2] Ibid. 56.   [3] Ibid. 64.
[4] Ibid. 1175; see note E at end of chapter.
[5] L. and P. XII (1), 67; extracts in Froude, op. cit. II, chap. XIII.
[6] L. and P. XII (1), 26.   [7] Ibid. 1175.

order; but the commons were still very wild, bills were posted on the church doors, and unless Norfolk came soon, accompanied by the worshipful men now with the King, another rising was to be feared. The points which caused the most uneasiness were as follows:—

(1) The people suspected that the parliament would be delayed.

(2) The King had summoned the leading gentlemen to London.

(3) The answer to the first five articles made the people doubt whether the King would confirm the pardon.

(4) They were afraid of the cities being fortified, especially in the case of Hull.

(5) The tenths were being demanded.

(6) Cromwell (my lord Privy Seal) was in as great favour as ever.

Aske concluded:

"Finally, I could not perceive in all the shires, as I came from your Grace's homewards, but your Grace's subjects be wildly minded in their hearts towards commotions or assistance thereof, by whose abetment yet I know not; wherefore, Sir, I beseech your Grace to pardon me in this my rude letter and plainness of the same, for I do utter my poor heart to your Grace to the intent your Highness may perceive the danger that may ensue; for on my faith I do greatly fear the end to be only by battle."[1]

He proposed to ride to Ripon on Saturday 13 January to pacify the North Riding. Darcy seconded Aske's efforts by issuing a proclamation against rebellious assemblies[2]. On Saturday 13 January Dorothy Darcy, Sir George Darcy's wife, wrote to her husband from Gateforth, begging him to come home and protect his poor children and herself, as the wildness of the country filled her with terror. She had heard that the disturbance at Beverley was due to the arrival of some ships at Hull laden with wine, corn, and Lenten stores. Although Beverley was pacified, the country all round Lady Darcy's home was very much disturbed. In Kirkbyshire captains had been appointed and at Leeds bills had been set on the church doors[3]. One of these bills has been preserved and runs:

"Commons, keep well your harness. Trust you no gentlemen. Rise all at once. God shall be your governor and I shall be your captain."[4]

Darcy wrote to the King on Sunday 14 January to excuse himself for not obeying the summons to court. He did not speak of the

[1] L. and P. xii (1), 67; extracts printed by Froude, op. cit. chap. xiii.
[2] L. and P. xii (1), 68.
[3] Ibid. 81; printed in full, Everett-Green, Letters of Royal and Illustrious Ladies, ii, no. cxliv.
[4] L. and P. xii (1), 201 (p. 39).

unsettled state of the country, which made his presence in the north desirable, but described his illness. Since the meeting at Doncaster he had not thrice left his chamber. Nevertheless he was ready to come if his health would mend a little and if the King would give him leave to come by water[1]. This may have been merely an excuse, but the journey to London from Templehurst in mid-winter must really have been a dangerous undertaking for a man of Darcy's age in a bad state of health.

On the news of the disturbance in Beverley the northern gentlemen at court were sent home. Sir Ralph Evers wrote to Sir John Bulmer that the Duke was to be at Doncaster on the last day of January, and Sir John was appointed to attend him with ten men[2]. Sir Ralph Ellerker was despatched on Monday 15 January with instructions to be delivered to the corporation of Hull[3]. On 16 January the King sent to Sir Robert Constable a countermand of the summons to come up to London[4].

Henry was satisfied with the result of his manoeuvres. The disturbance at Beverley, although it had been checked before it came to anything, gave him an excuse for disregarding the general pardon. A competent number of victims could now be sacrificed to the cleansing of the King's honour. Norfolk was to be sent north at last. A device was made by the King and his Council "for the perfect establishment of the North parts." Not only was Norfolk to be sent into Yorkshire with a council of "personages of honour, worship and learning," but Suffolk was to return to Lincolnshire "and put the men of substance there ready at an hour's warning to enter Yorkshire in aid of my lord of Norfolk," while Sussex went to assist the Earl of Derby to "put the parts [of Lancashire] not corrupted with the late rebellion ready to serve the King at an hour's warning." Cheshire was also to be prepared to muster, and "certain discreet and learned personages" were to be sent into all these parts "to preach and teach the word of God that the people may the better know their duties." The Lord Admiral was to take over Pontefract from Lord Darcy, and to garrison the castle. Sandall Castle was to be delivered by Sir Richard Tempest to Sir Henry Saville, who would command a garrison there, and Ellerker and Evers would place garrisons in Hull and Scarborough. The other nobles, Shrewsbury, Rutland and the rest, and the gentlemen who had held command

---

[1] L. and P. xii (1), 84; printed in full, State Papers, i, 524.
[2] L. and P. xii (1), 66.   [3] Ibid. 90.
[4] Ibid. 96.

in the King's army, such as Sir Francis Brian and Sir William Parr, were to call out their men, ready to march to Norfolk's assistance. Provision was made for Norfolk's train and salary, for levying the tenth and so forth. This was the end, or almost the end, of the idea that Norfolk would bear a conciliatory reply from the King. The Council, which always favoured moderate measures, drew up a list of suggestions which were not quite so drastic; they proposed that the more favourable parts of the King's reply should be embodied in proclamations to be issued in the north, and that the people should "be given hope of pardon, for despair might cause them to reassemble," but the King would temporise no more[1]. A minute was drawn up of a letter which directed the gentlemen of the north to have their servants ready to assist Norfolk in the punishment of those who had offended since the proclamation of the pardon. The King trusted that this might be effected without difficulty, but although the most part of his subjects were sincerely repentant, "there may remain some desperate persons who might move further sedition."[2]

The King was determined to have his executions, even if they provoked a new rising; but he was to be more fortunate than he as yet dared to hope.

NOTES TO CHAPTER XVI

Note A. Froude adds to the complication of the huge Constable family by calling Marmaduke Nevill Sir Marmaduke Constable. The historians of the Tower have assigned the inscription of Marmaduke Nevill to some unknown relation of the last Earl of Westmorland who may have taken part in the Rising of the North[3], but it is more likely to have been cut by the Marmaduke Nevill who is known to have existed in 1537.

Note B. The herald says Monday 12 November, but this must be a mistake.

Note C. The evidence is that George Lassells said that Thomas Estoft said that Thomas Saltmarsh said that Darcy had said this[4]. Thomas Estoft was interrogated and deposed that Thomas Saltmarsh had told him that Darcy advised Aske to lay post horses and if he sent bad news Darcy would rescue him, but without the details, which seem to have sprung from Lassells' imagination[5]. "One Saltmarsh" had quarrelled with Aske at the beginning of the rebellion "disdaining that he should be above him"; possibly this was the Thomas Saltmarsh who spread the story[6].

[1] L. and P. xi, 1410 (1) and (3).
[2] L. and P. xii (1), 97.
[3] Gower, The Tower of London, i, chap. i.
[4] L. and P. xii (1), 1119.
[5] Ibid. 1206.
[6] Ibid. 392.

Note D. The Spanish Chronicle gives a confused account of this speech:

"When [Aske] arrived to where his people were he made them a speech after this fashion: 'Oh, my brothers and gentlemen, what a wise and virtuous prince we have! He recognised the justice of our cause, has given us a general pardon, and to you, the priests, he will give enough to live upon. Here is an order for York, providing for many of you in the parishes there, and you are to go thither at once to be apportioned to various places.' When the people heard this they all cried with one voice, 'Long live our good King!' and the hostages were sent back to the Duke's quarters, and, in short, in a few hours all the people were on their way home, for they were already tired of it, and had wasted a good deal of their cattle."[1] The Spaniard confuses Aske's return from London with his return to Pontefract after the second conference at Doncaster.

Note E. In his letter of 12 January Aske says that he has already gone to Lord Darcy[2]. Afterwards, in his examination, he said that he received Darcy's letter four or five days after he was at Beverley[3], but it was natural that his memory of such hurrying days should be rather confused.

[1] Spanish Chron. ed. Hume, chap. xvii. [2] L. and P. xii (1), 67.
[3] Ibid. 1175.

CHAPTER XVII

HALLAM AND BIGOD

The leaders of the Pilgrimage undertook an impossible task when they promised at Doncaster to keep the north quiet until Norfolk's return. When a large region has been in open insurrection for three months, it cannot be restored to order at a word. It is true that the gentlemen did not realise then what they were required to do. They expected Norfolk to return within a month, and they expected that the King would make allowance for the difficulties of their position. They were mistaken in both points. Norfolk's return was delayed, and Henry was prepared to exact from the north a state of immaculate order to which few counties in England ever attained, even in times of peace. As soon as the Pilgrims allowed themselves to be put off by vague promises their cause was lost. Even if they had exacted a definite agreement with proper guarantees at Doncaster, it would probably have made no difference in the end. Nothing but force could have induced Henry to observe such a treaty. Even if the parliament which they desired had met, it is unlikely that it would have achieved anything. Henry was no Charles I. With Cromwell's help he knew how to manage parliaments. The Pilgrims' one chance of success had lain in battle. The two parties were very evenly balanced. Henry had a better general and on the whole better supplies, but the Pilgrims had the advantage in numbers and enthusiasm, and were on their own ground. They did not choose to push the matter to fighting, and they failed.

It is impossible to regret their failure now. If England had been rent by a religious civil war at the very outset of modern history, as the Reformation has rightly been called, she must have been seriously, perhaps fatally, crippled, and prevented from taking her place among the greater European powers. No country which had undergone the strain of the Hundred Years War, followed by the Wars of the Roses, could have borne in succession a third war more terrible than either of these. The Pilgrims cannot be accused of weakness when their decision was so truly patriotic, but it was fatal to themselves and their cause. Once that decision was taken the result was inevitable. Henry would observe no treaty with rebels when he could safely repudiate it. The rising of Hallam and Bigod gave him a good excuse, but before that excuse was offered he had already found others. The disturbance at Beverley, the deer-stealing at Rylston, the tithe riots in Cumberland, the restoration of the monks at Sawley—anything was a sufficient pretext for declaring that the King was no longer bound by the terms, and for bringing the champions of the old faith to trial and execution; but the catastrophe was precipitated by an ally of the most fatal kind, a political theorist.

During the progress of the first rising a glimpse has been caught from time to time of Sir Francis Bigod. As might have been expected from his previous history, he was by no means in sympathy with the Pilgrims. His attempted flight and capture have already been described[1]. The band of commons who took him all unconsciously did their cause a great disservice. Once involved in the rising Sir Francis quickly grew interested. The movement gave him plenty of scope to indulge in his chief passion, which was to reform monasteries. He was far from acting in the spirit of Cromwell's commissioners. The welfare of the abbeys was his real object, and he made no profit for himself, but his views were in every way peculiar. His activities began about Martinmas (11 November 1536) at the monastery of Guisborough[2].

The resignation of James Cockerell, Prior of Guisborough, and the appointment of a new prior by the visitors have been mentioned above[3]. As usually happened in these cases, the new prior accused the old one of having embezzled some of the revenue of the monastery[4]. Sir Francis Bigod acted in this matter on behalf of Cockerell, who is always called the Quondam of Guisborough[5]. Having thus a footing in the affairs of the monastery, he made up his mind that the new prior had not been chosen formally according to the laws of God and the old custom, and that the house ought to be reformed. He wrote to consult the Earl of Westmorland on the subject, pointing out that the new prior had been put in only by Cromwell's authority and that the people did not consider him a true prior. His proposal was that to quiet the country the new prior's accounts should be made up and

---

[1] See above, chap. IX.
[3] See above, chap. XVI.
[5] L. and P. XII (1), 584.

[2] L. and P. XII (1), 1087 (p. 499).
[4] L. and P. XI, 1438.

the prior himself expelled. Then another prior might be chosen "by virtue of the holy comentie and by the assent of all the religious brethren belonging to their chapter."[1] In consequence of these disturbances Sir John Bulmer was ordered by the council of York to regulate the affairs of Guisborough, but the prior was not deposed[2].

Bigod himself was not at the council of York, but before it met his brother Ralph told him that the clergy were to assemble and decide "what they judged to be reformed concerning the faith and for heresy." After the council was over Aske sent Sir Francis as a captain to Scarborough, probably to look into the affair of Edward Waters. Hallam came from York to Scarborough and reported what the council had resolved upon[3]. Sir Francis attended the great meeting at Pontefract[4], and like several of the other gentlemen, he wrote down his opinion on the various questions which were under discussion, "the title of Supreme Head, the statute of suppression, and the taking away the liberties of the Church."[5] His "book" made no particular impression at Pontefract. It is never mentioned by the leaders, while the commons looked upon him as one of Cromwell's agents, and he was even in danger of his life[6]. Sir Francis, however, had naturally an author's pride in his own work. It seems to have been much longer and more elaborate than the books of the other gentlemen. The views which it expressed were entirely individual and did not conform to the standards either of Rome or of the government. The author attempted to define "what authority belonged to the Pope, what to a bishop, and what to a king, saying that the head of the Church of England might be a spiritual man, as the archbishop of Canterbury or such, but in no wise the King, for he should with the sword defend all spiritual men in their right."[7]

The Quondam of Guisborough read the book, and, by Sir Francis' account, praised it highly, "saying no man could mend it, and he durst die in the quarrel with Bigod," and when the author promised him a copy, he said that "he would make as much thereof as of a piece of St Augustine's works." The Quondam admitted that he had seen the book, but he denied that he had commended it. He took exception to one passage, at any rate, in which Bigod asserted that the King held his sword immediately from God. The Quondam pointed out that "we hold opinion that the King has his sword

---

[1] L. and P. xii (1), 1087 (p. 499).
[3] L. and P. xii (1), 533.
[5] Ibid. 1087 (p. 499).
[7] Ibid. 201 (p. 92).

[2] See above, chap. xiii.
[4] Ibid. 145.
[6] Ibid. 145.

by permission and delivery of the Church into his hands and not otherwise." Bigod seems to have accepted the correction[1].

The Quondam of Guisborough was not Bigod's only literary friend among the regular clergy. Sir Francis was also a frequent visitor at the monastery of Malton in Rydale, where he was told of a prophesy by the Prior, William Todde[2]. It was at the Prior's table that he first heard the rumour that Cromwell was plotting to marry Lady Margaret Douglas and to become the King's heir[3].

Sir Francis also lent a hand in the disordered affairs of the monastery of Watton, which was, like Malton, a Gilbertine priory[4], containing both monks and nuns to the number of between three and four score[5]. The flight of the Prior appointed by Cromwell and Aske's intervention to help the deserted religious have already been mentioned[6]. The absconding Prior had previously held the same office at St Katherine's, Lincoln[7]. During his brief term at Watton he had made himself universally disliked; "while he was there he was good to no man and took of Hallam 20 marks where he should have been paid in corn when God should send it; and he gives many unkind words to his tenants in his court, more like a judge than a religious man."[8] The monks afterwards declared that it was only the commons who were discontented with the Prior. He had put Hallam out of a farm, and Hallam in revenge during the insurrection brought a number of his soldiers to the monastery, just as the brothers were sitting down to dinner, and ordered them to elect a new prior[9]. The priors of Ellerton and St Andrew's, York, were both present, and Hallam advised the canons to nominate the former, Dan James Lawrence[10]; if they did not obey him, Hallam threatened to plunder their house and make a new prior himself. Thereupon the canons nominated the Prior of Ellerton, but only as a form to satisfy Hallam[11]. Lawrence never acted as prior, and the canons wrote to Aske to beg him to appoint a new one for them[12]. By his advice they accepted the sub-prior as the prior's deputy[13].

Hugh Langdale, Hallam's friend, attended his new master the Prior on his flight to London, leaving his wife behind him[14]. A little before

[1] L. and P. xii (1), 1087 (p. 499).
[2] Ibid. 584, 1087 (p. 499).
[3] Ibid. 533.
[4] Tonge, op. cit. 71.
[5] L. and P. xii (1), 6; printed in full, Eng. Hist. Rev. v, 339.
[6] See above, chap. xiii.
[7] L. and P. xii (1), 65.
[8] Ibid. 201 (p. 92); cf. Tawney, op. cit. pp. 197-8.
[9] L. and P. xii (1), 201 (p. 100).
[10] Ibid. 201 (p. 102).
[11] Ibid. 201 (p. 100).
[12] Ibid. 849 (p. 382).
[13] Ibid. 6; printed Eng. Hist. Rev. v, 339.
[14] L. and P. xii (1), 201 (p. 87).

Christmas she wrote to tell him how much she had suffered during the rising and to beg him to come back to her. Her letter was carried by Thomas Lownde of Watton Carre, who returned about 26 December. Lownde met Hallam in a house by the Priory gates at Watton and Hallam asked him for the London news. Lownde said that " my lord prior was merry," to which Hallam rejoined, " no more of that, for an ye call him lord any more thou shalt lose thy head." He wanted to know what was the opinion of the south about the insurrection. Lownde answered that some Nottingham men with whom he had ridden from London to Stamford, told him that they wished the northern men had come forward, " for then they should have had me to take their parts." Also when he was in London at a " corser's " [calcearius, shoemaker] house between Cow Cross and Smithfield, the good man said to him, " Because ye are a northern man ye shall pay but 6d. for your shoes, for ye have done very well there of late: and would to God ye had come to an end, for we were in the same mind that ye were."[1]

The sub-prior of Watton, the confessor of the nuns, the vicar of Watton, and Anthony one of the canons, were all heard to say that there would be no real restoration of religion so long as the King held the title of Supreme Head, and that the only way to force him to lay it down was by a new insurrection[2].

In this hot-bed Hallam's plans had been flourishing, but at the Beverley meeting on Tuesday 9 January 1536-7 he received a check, and he returned to Watton with the intention of waiting at least until he saw the King's next move.

While Hallam was being persuaded to trust the King, Bigod was becoming more and more convinced that it would be folly to do so. On the same Tuesday 9 January he set out from Mulgrave to ride to York " for a matter between the Treasury and the old prior of Guisborough." He had with him a copy of the King's pardon, which he had been considering very seriously. In discussing it with his friend the Prior of Malton, whom he visited on his journey, he remarked that the pardon would enrage the Scots, who were called " our old ancient enemies." The Prior, in return for the pardon, showed him a copy of the Pilgrims' articles, and Sir Francis gave the Prior's servant two groats to copy it and send the copy after him[3]. He left Malton for Settrington, where he expected to meet his brother Ralph. Next day, Wednesday 10 January, he arrived at

[1] L. and P. xii (1), 201 (p. 95).   [2] Ibid. 201 (p. 87).
[3] Ibid. 534.

Watton, still on his way to York, and went to Hallam's house. They visited the Priory together, and once more urged the canons to elect a new prior[1]. Bigod drew up a form for them, in which the present Prior was referred to as "the late prior of St Katherine's, Lincoln."[2] The canons thought that this was not respectful; they sent to Beverley for a notary and had another document drawn up, which appointed James Lawrence to be their prior[3]. The canons gave this paper to Wade a bachelor of divinity dwelling near by, in order that they might show the new nomination to the commons if there were a fresh insurrection; but they protested that they did this through fear of the commons, and not with any serious idea of deposing their prior[4].

Hallam and Bigod both supped at the Priory. Bigod produced the King's pardon and explained his doubts about it. He pointed out that it did not run in the King's name, but "began as another man's tale, 'Albeit the King's Highness,'" and that it was in the third person throughout, from which he judged that it was really the work of Cromwell[5] who was higher in favour than ever[6]. In Bigod's opinion a pardon in that form would not prevent a sheriff from imprisoning a man and seizing his lands and goods; besides it was dated two days after it had been read[7]. He also objected to the statement in the pardon that the King had charge of his subjects both body and soul. Sir Francis declared that the King should have no cure of his soul. Hallam, the sub-prior Harry Gill, and two of the canons sat together over the fire while Sir Francis expounded his views to them, but at this point he drew Hallam aside into a window and they talked privately together for a long time[8].

Sir Francis read to Hallam his book concerning the supreme head of the Church. From that they passed to the question of Hull and Scarborough. Everyone in the countryside, said Bigod, was convinced that the towns ought to be held by the commons until the meeting of the parliament. Moreover he did not believe that the Duke of Norfolk would do any good when he came. It would be better and safer either to drive out of the north any general sent by the King, or to capture Norfolk as he ascended from the plain of York into the hills about Newborough and Byland, and to make him take their oath. Hallam, by his own account, hesitated to attack

[1] L. and P. xii (1), 201 (p. 86).   [2] Ibid. 65.
[3] Ibid. 201 (pp. 100, 101).   [4] Ibid. 201 (pp. 99, 100).
[5] Ibid. 201 (p. 91).   [6] Ibid. 201 (p. 99).
[7] Ibid. 201 (p. 102).   [8] Ibid. 201 (p. 99).

Norfolk[1]. Others, however, said that they had heard him threaten, if the Duke were captured, to strike off his head[2]. Leaving Norfolk out of the question, Hallam was soon persuaded to revive his former scheme of capturing Hull and Scarborough. Bigod told him that all the Dales, Swaledale, Wensleydale and the rest, were rising, that Sir Thomas Percy was coming forward from Northumberland, and that the East Riding had no choice but to rise as well[3]. It is impossible to say how much of this Sir Francis believed himself, but there had been disturbances and bills posted on the church doors in the Dales, and Northumberland had never been quiet since the last insurrection.

Sir Francis Bigod stayed at the Priory of Watton that night, but Hallam went home. Next day, Thursday 11 January, Hallam took William Horskey into his confidence. After repeating to him all that Sir Francis had said, he laid before him their plan of campaign. Hallam was to surprise Hull, while Sir Francis seized Scarborough; they would then meet at Beverley and march to take Pontefract. The day for the attempt was not yet appointed[4].

Bigod left Watton on Friday 12 January and rode to Settrington. On Saturday 13 January he sent a servant to bid Hallam come to Settrington. Hallam arrived on Sunday 14 January, and found that Ralph Fenton of Ganton and "the friar of St Robert's" were also there. Bigod told them that he had news of a rising in Durham and another in the west country. Lord Latimer had fled, and the commons had spoiled the property of Archdeacon Franklin and Robert Bowes, whom they accused of betraying them[5]. Dr John Pickering had sent news of the attack on Lancaster Herald at Durham[6]. Fenton and Hallam both agreed that Yorkshire must rise too[7].

Hallam returned to Watton on Monday 15 January. That day he was visited by three Beverley men, Richard Wilson, Roger Kitchen, and John Francis a baker. Francis was a quiet man with dangerous friends. The day before, Wilson and Kitchen had asked him to go with them "as it were a-mumming," to break up an assembly of "the most ancient men" of Beverley, who were making merry at Catherell's house, "because they were of a contrary faction in a dispute concerning the privilege of the town." Francis refused to go with them, and when on Monday they invited him to accompany them to Calkhill he was suspicious, but they assured him that their

---

[1] L. and P. xii (1), 201 (p. 92).   [2] Ibid. 1087 (p. 495).   [3] Ibid. 201 (p. 86).
[4] Ibid. 201 (p. 86).   [5] Ibid. 201 (p. 92).
[6] Ibid. 1087 (p. 500).   [7] Ibid. 201 (p. 92).

only object was to make merry with Hallam, and Francis agreed to go with them. They met Hallam at Hutton Cranswick, and all drank together at Mr Wade's[1] house. Francis observed that Wilson and Hallam talked together privately for some time. When the Beverley men went out to get their horses, Hallam came with them. On the way to the stable he told them that Sir Francis Bigod had sent the friar of St Robert's to Durham to find out whether there was a new rising. Francis did not like this conversation, and to change the subject he asked Hallam to sell him "half a score of wheat." Hallam replied that he would pass through Beverley on his way to Hull next day, and they could talk over the bargain then. After Francis had mounted, the other three went into the stable together and talked for a long time, until Francis called to them to come. Wilson and Hallam in the stable revealed their plans to Kitchen. Wilson promised to bring "a great sort out of Beverley" as soon as he heard that Hallam had set out to take Hull. Hallam asked Kitchen to be ready on receiving his message to go to Holderness and desire Richard Wharton, John Thomson, the bailiff of Brandsburton, William Barker and William Nicholson to meet Hallam in Hull and drink a quart of wine with him. At last the Beverley men set out for home with the impatient Francis[2].

While Hallam was drinking and plotting in Mr Wade's house at Hutton Cranswick two messengers sent by Sir Francis Bigod had arrived at Hallam's home. Not finding him there, they went to the Priory, where they gave a man 2d. to bring Hallam to them. The messengers represented themselves as Bigod's servants, but one of them was Friar John Pickering in disguise[3]. Before long Hallam came to the Priory and they delivered to him a letter from Sir Francis. He sent news that Durham and Richmondshire were up, that he would attempt to seize Scarborough next day, and that Hallam must take Hull at the same time and meet him at Beverley on Wednesday[4].

All this was read aloud and supplemented by the messengers in the presence of the sub-prior, the Prior of Ellerton, Dr Swinburne and other canons of Watton assembled in a chamber called the "Hal sied" [Hall Side]. After the reading of the letter, Hallam picked out two of the convent servants, Anthony Wright or West and Lancelot Wilkinson, to accompany him to Hull next day, and directed the sub-prior to send them and a third, Clement Hudson, and

---

[1] See above, chap. xiv.
[3] Ibid. 1087 (p. 500).
[2] L. and P. xii (1), 201 (p. 97).
[4] Ibid. 201 (p. 99).

to provide them with money, but they were not to bring horses or harness. His men were to enter the town in small groups of two or three, like market folks; they were to go to the market, and begin bargaining for goods until they heard Hallam cry, "Come hither to me all good commons!" whereupon they must join him and take the town. After making these arrangements Hallam left the Priory. The canons were naturally somewhat fluttered, but either from fear or from sympathy they obeyed Hallam[1], and the cellarer, Thomas Lather, delivered to the chosen men 3s. 4d. to last them for two days[2].

There was no time to be lost if Hull was to be taken next day, for it was already nearly 7 o'clock at night[3]. Taking up his station at the Priory gates, Hallam began to despatch messengers. He sent Andrew Cante and John Lowrey, labourers of Watton, to Kitchen at Beverley to bid him deliver the message that he knew of in Holderness. John Prowde was despatched to bid William Horskey, Philip Uty and Thomas Lownde to be at Beverley next day by sunrise. All were directed to meet Hallam at Beverley next day as soon as they had done their errands[4].

Early next morning, Tuesday 16 January, the little band set out from Watton in the dark in order to be at Beverley by sunrise. Hallam wore "a privy coat of fence made with many folds of linen cloth rosined, and a privy skull on his head, a sword and a buckler."[5]

At William Cooper's house in Beverley Hallam met Uty, Horskey and Langdale; he read Bigod's letter to them and sent them on to Hull to open communications with some friends in the town[6]. Although these men were Hallam's chosen confederates, they were not very reliable. Langdale said that "what he did was for fear of his life, for Hallam was so cruel and fierce a man amongst his neighbours that no man durst disobey him."[7] Both Langdale and Horskey distrusted Sir Francis Bigod, while Uty knew Hallam but slightly. As they rode to Hull together their hearts failed them, and they resolved to betray Hallam to the magistrates. After some discussion they decided to warn William Crockey, Robert Grey and Stephen Clare of Hallam's plot[8]; they would ask them to inform the mayor without mentioning who had given the warning.

The first person whom they visited was Crockey, the deputy-

---

[1] L. and P. xii (1), 201 (pp. 99, 101, 102).
[2] Ibid. 201 (p. 96).
[3] Ibid. 201 (p. 95).
[4] Ibid. 201 (p. 96).
[5] Ibid. 201 (p. 94).
[6] Ibid. 201 (p. 87).
[7] Ibid. 201 (p. 88).
[8] Ibid. 201 (p. 87).

customer. Their pretext was that they wanted to buy a tun of wine, which had been ordered by the sub-prior of Watton[1]. It was now about 11 o'clock, and as Hallam had intended to be in Hull by 9[2], the informers knew that they must make haste. Langdale and Uty put Horskey forward, and he, "abashed and trembling," took Crockey apart. Their embarrassment alarmed the deputy-customer so much that he exclaimed, "What news? How do ye all in your parts?" Horskey answered, "Naught[3], for we were commanded yesternight about midnight, pain of death, to be here this day, and for to take the town, as I suppose."[4]

Crockey at once went and told Robert Grey, who said "he trowed all would be nought, wherefore let every man do his best." Not finding much support in this enigmatic remark, Crockey went next to Mr Johnson, an alderman, who took him to the mayor's house. There they found that they had been forestalled, as "one Fowbery" was already laying the matter before the mayor[5]. This man was John Fowbery of Newbold, a servant of the Earl of Surrey[6]. He had taken part in the first insurrection[7], and was in Hallam's confidence[8]. By the time Crockey arrived, Fowbery had disclosed everything to the mayor and aldermen[9]; and they all went to their houses to arm and prepare to take Hallam[10].

Meanwhile the plot was going badly. On entering Hull Hallam met William Nicholson of Preston, who had often promised, in the case of a fresh rising, to join him with 100 or 200 men from Holderness. It was Nicholson who had suggested the plan of smuggling men into Hull on market-day as if to attend the market, and Hallam had sent Kitchen to warn him of the attempt the night before[11]. By ill-luck Nicholson had set out for Hull before Kitchen arrived[12]. He had not received the message and therefore had brought no men. Hallam told him to see what friends he had in the town who could be trusted in the matter[13]. The bailiff of Snaith had sent to Hallam after Christmas to let him know that if he made any fresh attempt all the commons of that part would join him, and it would seem that Hallam had sent a message to Snaith which also miscarried, but this is not certain.

[1] L. and P. xii (1), 201 (p. 88).
[2] Ibid. 201 (p. 95).
[3] See note A at end of chapter.
[4] L. and P. xii (1), 201 (p. 88).
[5] Ibid. 201 (p. 89).
[6] Ibid. 141.
[7] Ibid. 466.
[8] Ibid. 201 (p. 93).
[9] Ibid. 141.
[10] Ibid. 201 (p. 89).
[11] Ibid. 201 (p. 93).
[12] Ibid. 201 (p. 97).
[13] Ibid. 201 (p. 95).

Thus Hallam found himself with no support but his own small band. The attitude of the commons in the town was hostile, and he resolved to abandon the enterprise. He told the men who were with him to go home, mounted his horse, and rode out of the Beverley Gate to a watering-place beside a windmill. Looking back, he saw the town gates were "a-sparring" [being fastened]. At the watering-place he met Marshall, clerk of Beswick, and John Fowbery the traitor. Marshall, who really sympathised with Hallam, exclaimed, "Fie! will ye go your ways and leave your men behind you[1]?" The situation was a very tempting one. Hallam was mounted and free to join Bigod, or, if all else failed, to make his way to Scotland. He had warned his men, and the town gates were on the point of being shut. To go back was certain death. This history contains many examples of weakness and betrayal, but from time to time they are redeemed by some act of high courage and faith, such as that which Hallam now achieved. He turned and rode back to Hull.

The traitor Fowbery played his part to the last; exclaiming, "And I will turn again to seek for some of my neighbours that be there too," he rode ahead of Hallam to the gates, where two of the aldermen, William Knolles and John Eland, were giving orders[2]. These were the aldermen who had surrendered Hull to the rebels[3]. Fowbery called out, "An you look not shortly of your man Hallam, he will subdue you all." Eland answered, "I know him not," and Fowbery said, "Yon is he that is on horseback in the yeatts [gates] and ye may see the people assemble hastily till him." Eland grasped Knolles by the arm, crying, "Go way, for we will have him," and they went up to Hallam together[4]. He, from outside, asked them to let his neighbours come out before they barred the gates[5]. The two aldermen came out and asked him his name; he answered, "My name is Hallam." Knolles said, "Then thou art the false traitor that I look for."[6] The aldermen were standing one on each side of his horse, and at the word they both attacked him with their daggers, but his coat of fence saved him. There was a general struggle. Hallam's neighbours and the city guard both ran out to help their respective champions. Knolles was knocked down, but rescued by his men, and seized Hallam's companions. Eland clung to Hallam, and, striking at him, cut his bridle rein. He was afraid that Hallam would escape, but the horse fell into the Busse ditch, and Hallam was

---

[1] L. and P. xii (1), 201 (p. 93). [2] Ibid. 141, 142.
[3] See above, chap. viii. [4] L. and P. xii (1), 142.
[5] Ibid. 201 (p. 93). [6] Ibid. 141.

forced to dismount. He drew his sword and "many stripes were taken among them." They "bickered together" until they were both badly wounded and Hallam was at length captured[1]. There were only two men with him, Thomas Water and John Prowde[2]. As the prisoners were being led through the streets, William Nicholson attempted to create a diversion in their favour. He cried to the guards, "Jesus! What mean ye? Will ye murder me now?" and there was another fray, in which Nicholson was wounded and captured[3]. So ended the disastrous attempt to recover Hull.

Bigod's letter declared that he had received positive news that the commons of Durham and Richmond intended to rise on 16 January, the day on which the simultaneous attempts on Hull and Scarborough were made. These messages have not been preserved, but Sir Francis acted on them at once, and on Monday 15 January his servants were despatched in every direction to call out men for the new rising. Besides the two who went to Watton, one was sent to Bigod's friend the Prior of Malton, to order a muster there next day[4]. Another was sent to Durham with letters for Auckland, Staindrop, Richmond and the city of Durham, enclosing a new oath[5]. This man arrived at Brancepeth on Wednesday 17 January[6]. On the same Monday Bigod summoned to him William Levening of Acklam, and caused him to take the new oath. He told him the news from Durham and Richmond, and ordered him to send a summons to a muster at Borough next day to all the neighbouring constables[7]. At night the beacon at Settrington was lighted[8].

The nearest gentleman was George Lumley of Thwing, who was just recovering from an illness. Richard Simpson, the constable of Thwing, came to him as he lay in bed on Tuesday morning, 16 January, with news of the summons and the beacon. Lumley, his wife, and the constable, were all thrown into great perplexity, as they did not know whether this was a muster on behalf of the King or against him. At first Lumley thought of sending a servant to make inquiries, but in the end he decided to go himself, "for an if the assembly were for the King,...it was his duty to be there. And if it were about any new business of commotion, then he thought it was best for him to go thither also for to stay them, or else it

[1] L. and P. xii (1), 142.   [2] Ibid. 201 (p. 93).
[3] Ibid. 201 (p. 95).   [4] Ibid. 1023, cf. 139, 532.
[5] See below.
[6] L. and P. xii (1), 148; printed in full, Longstaff, A Leaf from the Pilgrimage of Grace, p. 9 n.   [7] L. and P. xii (1), 730 (2).
[8] Ibid. 369; printed in full, Milner and Benham, op. cit. chap. v.

might be laid to his charge afterward that seeing there were few gentlemen else in that quarter that he did not endeavour himself to stay them....Thinking at the least way, if he could do no good among them, he would do no harm." He set out, therefore, taking with him two servants[1].

At Borough they met a body of men, who conducted them to an assembly of about thirty or forty persons on a little "howe" [hill]. These men had no idea why they were summoned, but had come in response to the beacon. Presently Sir Francis Bigod appeared at the head of about a hundred horsemen. George Lumley tried to draw him aside to question him, but Bigod said that "he would commune with no man of any thing but that the whole company should be privy unto." Thereupon he mounted the hillock and addressed those who had assembled. George Lumley afterwards gave the substance of his speech in a medley of oratio recta and oratio obliqua:—

"He declared to the people that there were many causes that they had need to look upon, or else they should be all shortly destroyed; for the gentlemen of the country (said he) had deceived the commons. And said that the Bishopric and Cleveland were up already and would go forward to have their articles fulfilled, trusting that you will not now leave them in the dust seeing they took your part afore, and it is in the defence of all your weals. For my Lord of Norfolk is coming down with twenty thousand men to take Hull and Scarborough and other haven towns, which shall be our destruction unless we prevent him therein and take them before. And so I and my fellow Hallam purpose to do, for we are both appointed to meet at Beverley this night and so to raise the country and go forward to Hull[2]. And I think it necessary that you command Mr Lumley here to go with you to Scarborough to take the Castle and town and keep the port and haven from any such as should come in there to be your destruction, as I have written a letter to the bailiffs of Scarborough that they should help thus to do with the aid of you the commons that I shall send unto them."[3]

Sir Francis then brought out two letters, which he gave to Lumley, charging him on pain of death to deliver them. One was to the bailiffs of Scarborough, and the other was to the dowager countess of Northumberland to request her to summon Sir Thomas Percy to come forward with all his men, with the promise that Bigod and the commons would restore his lands to him. Lumley opened and read the second letter, and then despatched one of his servants with it.

---

[1] L. and P. xii (1) 869; cf. Ibid. 780 (2).
[2] See note B at end of chapter.
[3] L. and P. xii (1), 869; printed in full, Milner and Benham, op. cit. chap. v. See note C at end of chapter.

After giving him the letters, Bigod continued his speech:

"Also ye are deceived by a colour of a pardon, for it is called a pardon that ye have and it is none but a proclamation."

At this point he read aloud a copy of the pardon, and then went on:

"It is no more but as if I would say unto you, the King's grace will give you a pardon, and bade you go to the Chancery and fetch it. And yet the same is no pardon. Also here ye are called rebells, by the which ye shall knowledge yourselves to have done against the King, which is contrary to your oath."

The commons, who had always been suspicious of the pardon, were very much moved by this. One cried out, "The King hath sent us the fawcet and keepeth the spigot himself!" while another said that "as for the pardon it makes no matter whether they had any or not, for they never offended the King nor his laws, wherefore they should need to have any pardon." After the clamour had died down, Bigod proceeded:

"A parliament is appointed as they say, but neither the place where nor the time when it should be kept is appointed. And also here is that the King should have cure both of your body and soul, which is plain false, for it is against the Gospel of Christ, and that will I justify even to my death. And therefore if ye will take my part in this and defend it, I will not fail you so long as I live to the uttermost of my power; and who will so do assure me by your hands and hold them up."

Thereupon all present held up their hands with a great shout and cried that they would strike off the head of any man who did not do as they did. A tall man dressed like a priest, who had come with Bigod, said that "if they went not forward, all was lost that they had done before, for all was but falsehood that was wrought against them." He was probably one of the ever-zealous friars of Knaresborough. Bigod promised the commons that "the fat priests' benefices of the south that were not resident upon the same and money of the suppressed abbeys should find the poor soldiers that were not able to bear their own charges." He told Lumley and the commons who were to remain with him that he had already summoned the wapentake of Dickering to join them[1].

Then Sir Francis rode away with his horsemen in the direction of Hull, and Lumley was left to occupy Scarborough with about forty men. His position was a very awkward one. Bigod's speech must have made a great impression even on Lumley, as he was able to

---

[1] L. and P. xii (1), 369; printed in full, Milner and Benham, op. cit. chap. v; L. and P. xii (1), 578.

repeat so much of it three weeks afterwards, and it had roused intense enthusiasm among the commons. As Sir Francis disappeared they exclaimed, " Blessed was the day that Sir Francis Bigod, Ralph Fenton, John Hallam and the friar of St Robert's met together, for an if they had not set their heads together this matter had never been bolted out." They were ready to be led on any enterprise, but unfortunately George Lumley was far from being ready to lead them. In character he bore a marked resemblance to one of Sir Walter Scott's weaker-minded heroes, such as Edward Waverley; he was a well-meaning but ordinary young man, quite unequal to the task of making up his mind, or assuming a grave responsibility. He had hesitated before setting out, and his vague hopes that it might prove to be a muster for the King, or that he might induce the commons to disperse, were now at an end. In all the previous course of the rebellion he had never done anything on his own initiative. At the present moment, although his intentions were loyal to the King, he found himself with a single servant surrounded by forty excited and resolute countrymen. The number was not great for taking a fortress, but it was too many for him to persuade or command to depart. Accordingly he submitted to circumstances and set out for Scarborough. On the way, at a place called Monyhouse, he found a muster of the Dickering men, as Sir Francis had expected. They were all ready to march to Scarborough, but Lumley would take with him only two men from each township, and dismissed the rest to their homes. Even with this limitation his force was raised to six or seven score, too many for Lumley's comfort, but too few to please his followers, who insisted on summoning Pickering Lythe to muster next day at Spittels to give them aid if they should need it[1].

At the same time they sent to the Priory of Bridlington for help. The prior asserted that he ordered his men not to obey the summons and armed them in order that they might resist the rebels if they came that way, but he was accused of arming them for and not against Lumley[2].

Lumley's company entered Scarborough without encountering the least opposition. Lumley issued a proclamation that no one should take anything without paying for it, and that no revenge should be attempted against the men who had defended the castle during the last rebellion. By this time it must have been evening, and he went to his lodging for the night, but the commons were not yet

---

[1] L. and P. xii (1), 369; printed in full, Milner and Benham, op. cit. chap. v.
[2] L. and P. xii (1), 1019, 1020 (ii).

satisfied. They were afraid that forces might make their way into the castle, which was unoccupied. In order to secure it, they wished to take up their quarters in it. Lumley would not permit this. He replied that "he would not be of their counsel to enter into the castle, for it was the King's house, and there had they nor he nothing to do. And their oath was to do no thing against the King." In the face of this argument the commons did not insist upon entering the castle, but they set a watch round it, in order that no one should surprise it. Lumley went back to his lodging, where he found some more of his servants. About midnight he sent one of them to old Sir Ralph Evers to warn him that the castle was guarded, and to assure him that Lumley would do his best to persuade the commons to go home quietly, and that he hoped in a short time young Sir Ralph would be able to occupy the castle without any opposition.

Next morning, Wednesday 17 January, Lumley and the commons met the bailiffs of the town at the Grey Friars. The town officers took the oath to be true to the commons according to a new form prescribed by Sir Francis Bigod, "the effect whereof was in all things like the former oath with this addition, that no man should give counsel to any man to sit still until such time as they had obtained their former wishes."[1] Bigod seems to have drawn up several forms of the oath; another draft enjoined the commons to keep their former oath, "and not urging any to join them, to prepare themselves to battle against the undoers of Christ's Church and the common wealth."[2]

After administering the oath the commons demanded that three of Sir Ralph Evers' servants should be surrendered to them. These were Guy Fishe, Lancelot Lacy and one Lockwood. The commons had resolved to put them to death on account of their part in the defence of the castle. Lockwood and probably the other two also were present at the Grey Friars. By "fervent request and long entreaty" George Lumley prevailed upon his men to spare them.

The commons next resolved to enter the castle, but here again the exhortations of Lumley and the bailiffs of the town induced them to give up their purpose for the present.

By this time Lumley and his followers must have been heartily tired of one another, and accordingly he met with no opposition when he said that he must go home and attend to his own business.

[1] L. and P. xii (1), 369; printed in full, Milner and Benham, op. cit. chap. v.
[2] L. and P. xii (1), 147.

John Wyvell was chosen captain in his place, and Lumley prepared to depart. He said that Wyvell had enough men to keep the town, and ordered his own company to return with him; he also took Lancelot Lacy, one of the threatened men. Wyvell complained that he would be "left very sklender," and that men from the neighbouring villages must be summoned to supply the place of Lumley's men. Lumley promised to send him aid next day and rode off.

Lumley went first to Spittels, the place appointed for the muster of Pickering Lythe. On the way he met small bands of commons going to or returning from the muster. He told them that their fellows had resolved to hold Scarborough, and ordered them to go to its defence that night and to return home next day, as he would then send more men. By the time he reached Spittels those who had attended the muster had all gone home, for he had purposely delayed his arrival. He felt himself now in a position to dismiss his own men, and. therefore ordered them all to depart to their houses and not to rise in response to any summons or beacon unless he sent for them in his own name. In the meanwhile he promised to lay their doubts before the Duke of Norfolk and "know his pleasure therein." They said that they would not rise at the summons of any man but Lumley himself or Sir Thomas Percy. Lumley urged them to make no exceptions—"if ye should rise at his calling or any other man's then were I in a sore case, for then should I be left alone." But they still persisted that if Sir Thomas summoned them they must rise; on this understanding they disbanded, and George Lumley went home[1].

Sir Francis Bigod was sufficiently clear-sighted to see that Hull was the point on which his energies must be concentrated. With Hull in his possession, the King could overawe all the East Riding, where disaffection was most active, but if the town were in the hands of the commons, it would be a substantial guarantee for the forthcoming parliament. Accordingly on the first day of the rising he set out to support Hallam's attack on Hull, which was of vital importance to his success, leaving only a small party to occupy Scarborough, which was a point of much less value, as the experience of the last insurrection had proved. In all his movements his characteristic qualities appear. He had very good ideas, but he was quite incapable of carrying them out. He could see what might be done, and what ought to be done, but he had no power of organisation. Having decided that Scarborough ought to be taken, he despatched

[1] L. and P. xii (1), 369; printed in full, Milner and Benham, op. cit. chap. v.

the first gentleman whom he encountered to take it, without stopping to consider whether his agent was capable of performing the task.

After Sir Francis left Borough on Tuesday morning, his movements cannot be definitely traced for the next two days, but he had given orders for a muster at Bainton, a place within a few miles of Beverley, on Wednesday 17 January[1]. During these two days there was great activity among the responsible leaders of the Pilgrimage. The news of the attempt on Hull spread quickly. On the very day, Tuesday 16 January, the mayor of Hull sent to the Ellerkers for help, and they passed on the news to Darcy. Bigod's letter had been found on Hallam, and thus they learnt of the attack on Scarborough[2]. Sir Robert Constable received warning of what had taken place the same day, and wrote about it to Aske from his house at Holme in Spalding Moor. He attributed the rising to the alarm caused by the printed answer to the first petition, and suggested that Aske should come to him and that they might ride to Hull together to declare the King's true answer[3]. At the same time he sent out several manifestoes to the disaffected parts of the country, assuring all men that the parliament, coronation and convocation were to be held at Whitsuntide in York; "wherefore, good and loving neighbours, let us stay ourselves and resist those who are disposed to spoil."[4] He explained that he was prevented by illness from coming in person to reassure them, as he was suffering from a severe attack of gout[5].

One of these manifestoes was sent to his son Sir Marmaduke Constable, who despatched it to Thwing. George Lumley sent it on to Scarborough on Thursday 18 January, with orders that the commons there must all depart to their homes, after receiving such a favourable answer[6].

Aske was at Osgodby on Wednesday 17 January, where he received Constable's letter. He was very much distressed by the news, as he saw that it threatened to destroy the hopes of success which he still entertained. He obeyed Sir Robert's summons and set out for Holme, after forwarding the letter to Darcy with a request for advice and an exhortation that Darcy would maintain order in his own quarter[7]. Darcy replied immediately that although

---

[1] L. and P. XII (1), 780 (2).   [2] Ibid. 104.   [3] Ibid. 102.
[4] Ibid. 103; printed in full, Longstaff, A Leaf from the Pilgrimage of Grace, and by Froude, op. cit. II, chap. XIV.
[5] L. and P. XII (1), 146.
[6] Ibid. 369; printed in full, Milner and Benham, op. cit. chap. v.
[7] L. and P. XII (1), 112.

he heard very dreadful rumours he was able to keep his own parts quiet, in spite of the fact that he was confined to his bed[1]. Darcy also sent congratulations to Hull on the capture of the rebels[2].

On the morning of Thursday 18 January Sir Francis Bigod reached Bainton, and held a muster there[3]. By this time he had of course received news of Hallam's failure, and his first object was to rescue the prisoners in Hull. From Bainton he wrote to Sir Robert Constable, enclosing the new oath. He stated the reasons for the new rebellion, and begged Constable to send him advice as there was no man whom the commons trusted so much[4]. He despatched three men to Hull to demand the release of Hallam and the other prisoners, and awaited the replies to both messages at Bainton[5].

Sir Robert Constable's answer was soon brought. Aske was with him at Holme and they both sent remonstrances. Their position was a very difficult one. If they disowned the new movement uncompromisingly, they would forfeit their influence over the commons, with the result that they would be regarded as traitors and their words would have no effect. As they were sincerely opposed to Bigod's rising, they wished to check it and prevent ill consequences, not merely to demonstrate their own loyalty. Accordingly the gist of their letters was an assurance that the King's pardon was genuine, that the parliament and the coronation were to be held in York, and that the Duke of Norfolk was coming with only a small train.

Aske's letter was addressed to the commons, and warned them that "Bigod intended to have destroyed the effects of our petitions"; and that they had done very foolishly in listening to him. However, Aske would represent to the King that they had acted through ignorance and fear, and if they dispersed quietly he did not doubt that the King would pardon them[6]. Sir Robert Constable wrote to Bigod. He repeated the assurances of the King's good intentions. He could not come himself because he had gout, but Aske was willing to come to them and tell them what he had heard from the King's own lips. The commons ought to be satisfied with this and remain quiet until Norfolk's coming. The present rising was contrary to the appointment at Doncaster, and it was a bad time of year for fighting. The best thing that Bigod could do would be to send the commons home again[7].

---

[1] L. and P. xii (1), 115.
[2] Ibid. 135; see note D at end of chapter.
[3] L. and P. xii (1), 730 (2).
[4] Ibid. 145.
[5] Ibid. 174.
[6] Ibid. 187; see note E at end of chapter.
[7] L. and P. xii (1), 146.

These letters were received by Sir Francis Bigod at Bainton and when they were read aloud it was agreed that a safe-conduct should be sent to Aske, in order that he might come and speak to them. Just then Woodmancey came to Bigod with a private message from Beverley, and orders were given that the host should enter the town[1]. Old Sir Ralph Ellerker had taken up his quarters there at the first alarm[2], but he was not able to offer any resistance, and Bigod entered Beverley at about four o'clock on Thursday afternoon with between three and four hundred men[3].

There he received a letter from Sir Oswald Wolsthrope commanding the commons to disperse[4]. Bigod replied that the commons would not trust Sir Oswald, because he and the other gentlemen had deceived them before[5]. With this reply he sent a letter to the Dean and Chapter of York[6], to whom he announced that the commons assembled at Beverley demanded their support[7]. This letter shows once more Bigod's extraordinary mixture of insight and stupidity. The commons are represented as saying that "all will be undone if they do not go forward whilst they yet have pledges for the performance of their petitions and are not in captivity like the men of Lincolnshire and even of Hull. It behoves the clergy to prevent the danger, for the King understands from the gentlemen that the Church began the last assembly." No warning could have been more true, yet no attempt to avert the danger could have been more futile than Bigod's. When he wrote these letters his plans were all in confusion, for the one to the Dean and Chapter indicates that he intended to advance on York, while in the other to Sir Oswald Wolsthrope he said that his forces would withdraw into Richmondshire, there to draw up a petition to the King[8]. His bewilderment was natural, for his prospects were becoming more and more gloomy.

Young Sir Ralph Ellerker, who was in Hull, made two of Bigod's messengers prisoners, on the ground that they were traitors and had no safe-conduct, and sent the third back with an answer which he thought was enough to terrify Sir Francis out of Beverley. Old Sir Ralph sent to his son for help; the latter promised to be with him next day at noon and gave orders for the mustering of Holderness[9]. Bigod had written to Rudston, who had been the captain of Holderness in the last rising, but Rudston replied that he was

[1] L. and P. xii (1), 730 (2). [2] Ibid. 174.
[3] Ibid. 161. [4] Ibid. 177.
[5] Ibid. 143. [6] Ibid. 177.
[7] Ibid. 144. [8] Ibid. 143.
[9] Ibid. 174.

pledged to the King and went to join Ellerker. Sir Robert Constable also wrote to Rudston, as soon as he heard that Rudston was going to Hull. He commissioned him to ask Ellerker to come to Holme with a copy of "the King's letter," in order to pacify the commons. Sir Robert was keeping a watch upon Bigod's movements and had his men in readiness, but he had just written to Bigod and would not stir until he had received an answer. His advice was that Ellerker should set free Bigod's messengers, as they had only done their master's bidding[1].

As nothing but messages of disapproval and news of hostile musters poured in upon Sir Francis at Beverley that night, he and his followers entirely lost heart, while old Sir Ralph Ellerker and the loyalists of the town were much encouraged. Young Sir Ralph was to arrive next morning, Friday 19 January, but long before he was expected his father decided that the forces in the town were strong enough to attack without further delay. No details of the fray have been preserved, but before the late winter dawn had broken, old Sir Ralph and his men had chased the rebels out of Beverley and made sixty-two prisoners[2].

Young Sir Ralph, who had sent to Lincolnshire for reinforcements and to the King for ammunition, mustered the men of Cottingham and Holderness within two miles of the town before 8 o'clock in the morning, and arrived at Beverley too late to do anything but congratulate the victors and carry off the prisoners to Hull. Gratifying as the victory was, young Sir Ralph, in his report to the King, criticised some of the proceedings. He was disappointed that no one had been killed; if he had been there no quarter should have been given. It was also a great blemish that Sir Francis Bigod had been able to make his escape; no one knew whither he had fled[3]. Nevertheless, in spite of these drawbacks, the danger in the East Riding was at an end, and it remained only to spread the news up and down the country[4].

After Sir Francis Bigod's flight the papers which he left in his room at Beverley were seized by Matthew Boynton[5], son-in-law of Sir John Bulmer[6]. Among them was the "book" containing his opinion on the supremacy and on other points of church government, which Sir Francis had read to Hallam[7], and some letters directed to

---

[1] L. and P. xii (1), 113.   [2] Ibid. 174.
[3] Ibid. 140, 174, 179.   [4] Ibid. 154–162.
[5] Ibid. 174, 369; see note F at end of chapter.   [6] Tonge, op. cit. 25.
[7] L. and P. xii (1), 369; printed in full, Milner and Benham, op. cit. chap. v.

the Lord Mayor of York, which were forwarded by the town officers of Beverley with the news that Bigod had "left early in the morning," and a warning that the city and neighbourhood of York must be kept in order[1].

Boynton wrote to his father-in-law to warn him that Bigod was thought to have fled to Cleveland with the intention of raising the commons there. It would be a most acceptable piece of service to the King if Sir John could capture him[2]. Boynton did not know the painful situation in which Sir John was placed. It is tolerably certain that Sir Francis Bigod had revealed his intentions to Bulmer, who was his uncle by marriage. Margaret, Sir John's second wife, William Staynhus his chaplain, and Ralph his eldest son by his first marriage, also knew of the scheme. His wife and the chaplain urged him to join his nephew, saying that the commons wanted but a head, that if one rose all would, and that if the other gentlemen rose he must do the like[3]. Sir John himself had no inclination for rising. He was the lessee of the suppressed nunnery of Rosedale[4], and had been taken by the commons with violence in the first insurrection[5], in which he had played no particular part. He was a nervous, excitable man, very unfit for any dangerous enterprise. Yet in consequence of his temperament Sir Francis' doubts about the validity of the pardon made a great impression upon him. He would not join his nephew's hopeless attempt, but he sent his son Ralph up to London in order to discover the King's real purpose. When he received Boynton's message he was anxiously expecting news from Ralph[6]. In the circumstances it is not surprising that he did not take Sir Francis.

The King was well informed as to the progress of events. On Thursday 18 January Aske sent news of Hallam's attempt, Bigod's musters, and the agitation in the north and west. He reported that the commons of the north and west "repaired to no worshipful men," but made their fellows captains. All the gentlemen were doing their best to quiet the people, and he begged the King to send Norfolk immediately[7]. On the same day the mayor of Hull sent the King a full report of Hallam's attempt and the arrival of Bigod's messengers, enclosing the first examinations of six of Hallam's men and John Eland's own account of Hallam's capture[8]. Since its

---

[1] L. and P. xii (1), 161.
[2] Ibid. 164.
[3] Ibid. 1087 (pp. 494–5).
[4] Ibid. 543, 1277 (iii).
[5] Ibid. 1011.
[6] Ibid. 1087 (pp. 494–5).
[7] Ibid. 186.
[8] Ibid. 141, 142.

capitulation to the Pilgrims, the town of Hull had been in disgrace with the King, and trade had been interrupted[1]. Consequently the burgesses were delighted to have this opportunity of re-establishing their credit with the government. Other letters spread the tidings of the rebels' defeat[2].

The news from Scarborough was equally favourable to the King. George Lumley, anxious to prove his ignorance of Bigod's plot, resolved to surrender to the Duke of Norfolk. He has been compared to a hero of Sir Walter Scott's, but unfortunately real life does not show the happy turns of a romance; there was no quick-witted outlaw or faithful gipsy to spirit him away to Scotland and safety in spite of himself, and in the innocence of his heart he went straight to his death[3].

The leaders of the commons at Scarborough were Ralph Fenton and John Wyvell. They must have heard of Bigod's flight after they were abandoned by Lumley, and finding themselves completely deserted by their leaders and without support, they offered no resistance when young Sir Ralph Evers occupied the town. The date of this is not certain, but he probably set out as soon as Lumley surrendered himself. Sir Ralph imprisoned Wyvell and Fenton, but used no further severity. He "gave the people comfortable words," and induced them to promise obedience and "to wear a cross of St George." The wearing of these crosses was a sign that they thankfully accepted the pardon and meant to be as loyal as before the insurrection[4]. Gregory Conyers, who seems to have been at court about Twelfth Night, on his return to the north spread the story that "the King himself of Sunday after Twelfthtide...openly in the presence of all noblemen and worshipful men of the country and many other...laid his hand of his breast and swore by the faith that he did bear to God and St George he had not only forgiven and pardoned all his subjects of the north by his writing under seal, but also freely in his heart."[5] The neighbourhood of Scarborough appeared to be quiet, but for fear of disturbances in other parts Evers garrisoned and prepared the castle[6].

Sir Ralph Evers had prudently taken only two prisoners, but at Hull there were over seventy, and the first question which confronted the gentlemen there was how to deal with them. All those who

---

[1] L. and P. xi, 1285.
[2] L. and P. xii (1), 159, 169, 170, 171, 177, 178.
[3] Ibid. 369; printed in full, Milner and Benham, op. cit. chap. v.
[4] L. and P. xii (1), 234.   [5] Ibid. 271.
[6] Ibid. 234–235.

had come to the defence of Hull met on Saturday 20 January to consider the matter. There were now in prison at Hull Hallam, Kitchen and six of their company, Bigod's two messengers, and the sixty-two prisoners who had been taken at Beverley; it must have been difficult to find room in the town to keep so many safely. It was impossible to release Hallam and his fellows, but while some of the gentlemen advised that all the prisoners should be kept in ward, others wished to keep only the leaders of the Beverley captives, while others again thought that all might be released on bail. Monketon, who was sent by Robert Aske, strongly urged the last-named course upon them, and it was finally adopted, partly because it was the most convenient, partly because there were no prisoners of importance and all declared that they had come against their wills, and partly because the responsibility for it could be laid upon Aske[1].

The result of the attempt on Hull was to bring about the very thing that the commons had feared, namely, the fortification of the town by the King. When the prisoners had been disposed of, young Sir Ralph Ellerker made a full report to Henry, with a request that gunners and gunpowder might be sent to him, and that he might be allowed a body of two hundred horsemen until the country was in better order[2]. The request was justified by the fact that Bigod's agitation had spread much further than the East Riding. Bigod believed that Durham, Richmondshire and the west were on the point of rising; when the immediate danger had been averted at Hull and Scarborough it still remained to be seen whether there might not be a more formidable host coming from the north.

On Wednesday 17 January two of Bigod's messengers to the north were taken. Sir William Mallory discovered one of them near Northallerton, and sent to the Duke of Norfolk a letter from Bigod, which was found in the man's possession, urging the commons of Swaledale to rise[3]. The other messenger took a letter and a copy of the new oath to Durham, and delivered them to the bailiff and Cuthbert Richardson. The officers of the town returned answer that the men of Durham had sworn to rise for no one but the Earl of Westmorland or the King, and that they would "stick to the King's pardon." As the Bishop of Durham was still at Norham, they sent the letter and the messenger to the Earl of Westmorland at Brancepeth[4]. The Earl was rather an incapable character, but at

[1] L. and P. xii (1), 174.   [2] Ibid.   [3] Ibid. 139, 217.
[4] Ibid. 148; printed in full, Longstaff, op. cit.

least he had the wisdom to know his own weakness. Having heard a rumour that he was to be made warden of one of the Marches, he had hurried south to his uncle Lord Sandys, in order, if possible, to prevent the dreaded appointment[1]. He left an efficient deputy in the person of his wife Katharine, daughter of the late Duke of Buckingham, who "rather playeth the part of a knight than of a lady."[2] When the bailiff of Durham brought Bigod's letter and messenger to the countess on Thursday 18 January, she gave orders for the apprehension of any others who might come, thanked the bailiff, and sent a copy of the letter to her husband, directing him to show it to the Lord Privy Seal. Her conclusion was, "I and all honest men long for your coming home." The letter was laid before the Privy Council[3], but in spite of the Countess' vigour, when the townsfolk of Durham heard what their bailiff had done, they seized him and threatened to strike off his head if the messenger was not released, and the bailiff was obliged to contrive that the prisoner should be set free[4].

It was not Bigod's letters, however, which were the real danger in the north, but a secret agitation going on among the commons. Its originators are unknown. Proclamations and manifestos appeared and passed from hand to hand, or were fastened on church doors, no one knowing whence they came. Several of these manifestos were seized and sent to the King. They were all of a popular character, and show no trace of Bigod's influence. One of them was headed, "These be articles that men may perceive that this entreaty is but feigned policy to subdue the commons withal," and proceeded to show that the terms made at Doncaster had not been kept. The abbeys had been restored only by the commons, and many of the farmers had sold the abbey lands and fled out of the country. A parliament had been promised in York "on the twentieth day," but it had never been held. Cromwell was as high in favour as ever. No man was pardoned unless he would acknowledge the King to be Supreme Head of the Church. Aske had received great rewards in London for betraying the commons. Hull was being fortified. Therefore if the commons would save themselves, they must rise at once and make their own leaders, trusting the gentlemen no more[5]. This may have been the bill sent up to Norfolk by Lord Scrope from Bolton on 27 January[6].

On Friday 19 January a bill appeared in Richmond ordering the

[1] L. and P. xii (1), 151. [2] Ibid. 345.
[3] Ibid. 148. [4] Ibid. 362.
[5] Ibid. 188. [6] Ibid. 253.

commons of every township to rise on pain of death, to seize the gentlemen and to make them swear upon the mass-book to maintain the profit of Holy Church, to take nothing of their tenants but the rent, to put down Cromwell and all heretics, and to prevent all lords and gentlemen from going up to London. If any gentlemen refused to take the oath he was to be put to death and his heir seized and sworn in his stead. This bill was taken by Sir Thomas Wharton on Sunday 21 January[1].

The fact that this agitation was going on further north was known at Hull, and it was feared that Sir Francis Bigod had fled only to raise Cleveland[2]. On Saturday 20 January Darcy informed Shrewsbury that the commons of the north were coming forward, and that they entered the houses of Lord Latimer, the Earl of Westmorland, and other gentlemen who had gone up to the King, and made inventories of their goods with the intention of seizing them if their owners did not return at once[3]. Lord Latimer heard on the same day that the commons of Richmondshire had seized his house at Snape. He was on his way to London, but had been ordered to turn back and wait on Norfolk in York[4]. The property of the detested Beckwith at Stillingfleet was plundered again on Friday 19 January[5].

In addition to the disturbances in Richmond and Durham, no one knew what might be happening in Northumberland. When the first news of Bigod's rising spread to Lincolnshire, it was said that Sir Thomas Percy had seized Scarborough[6]. The suspicion against him increased when George Lumley came to York on Saturday 20 January, and laid before Sir Oswald Wolsthrope his connection with the rising[7]. It is true that he was able to state definitely that Sir Thomas Percy had not been at Scarborough, but he represented that the commons of the neighbourhood were so deeply attached to Sir Thomas that he was the "lock, key and ward of this matter." When examined, Lumley denied that, to his knowledge, Sir Thomas had had any complicity in the rising; he used these words to indicate Sir Thomas' popularity[8].

The parson of Leckonfield, Sir Thomas' chaplain, was at Beverley during Hallam's attempt. Bigod asked him whether his master was prepared to take part in another insurrection, and he replied that

[1] L. and P. xii (1), 163.   [2] Ibid. 164.
[3] Ibid. 169.   [4] Ibid. 173.
[5] Ibid. 176; Star Chamber Proceedings, Hen. VIII, bdle. xix, no. 893.
[6] L. and P. xii (1), 140.   [7] Ibid. 176.
[8] Ibid. 369; printed in full, Milner and Benham, op. cit. chap. v.

Sir Thomas would rise for no man¹. As soon as Hallam's failure was known, the chaplain hurried off to Northumberland with the news². He travelled so fast that he arrived before Bigod's own letter to Sir Thomas, which was sent to the dowager countess of Northumberland and forwarded by her with a message that Sir Thomas "should take a substantial way in that matter upon her blessing." Sir Thomas declared that he understood this to mean that he should have nothing to do with Bigod, and that he was prevented from sending the letter and the messenger who brought it up to the King only by his respect for his mother³. Whatever the countess may really have meant, for her words scarcely seem to bear her son's interpretation, he was not likely to make any move after he had heard of Hallam's ill-success, but he was already compromised in more ways than one. On Wednesday 17 January he had proclaimed a county meeting at Morpeth. Sir John Widdrington and Lord Ogle prohibited it. The Percys, contrary to their wont, took this prohibition very well. The coincidence of the proposed meeting with Bigod's rising is suspicious, but as Sir Thomas acquiesced in its abandonment, it was probably no more than an unfortunate chance. On Monday 22 January the common people swore that they would burn all Tynedale and Reedsdale, but as the reivers were Percy's friends, this was a movement against, rather than for, him. Lord Ogle succeeded in quieting the people⁴.

The threat of a Northumberland rising was hanging over the heads of the gentlemen at Hull when on Tuesday 23 January they examined Hallam and his accomplices. In consequence of this Aske warned them not to proceed to execution as yet, for fear of provoking the north⁵, and his advice was so far followed that some of the prisoners were sent to York to await Norfolk's arrival⁶.

The special commissioners who examined them on 23 January were William Rogers the mayor, Sir Ralph Ellerker the younger, Sir John Constable of Holderness, Sir William Constable, Sir Christopher Hillyard, and Richard Smytheley. The chief informer, John Fowbery, was not examined, or at least his evidence has not been preserved. The justices heard Horskey and Langdale, who had turned King's evidence and had accused the sub-prior and several of

---

¹ L. and P. XII (1), 393; printed in full, De Fonblanque, op. cit. I, chap. IX.
² L. and P. XII (1), 467; printed in full, De Fonblanque, op. cit. I, Append. no. liv.
³ L. and P. XII (1), 393; printed in full, De Fonblanque, op. cit. I, chap. IX.
⁴ L. and P. XII (1), 220; printed in full, Raine, Mem. of Hexham Priory (Surtees Soc.) I, Append. p. cxlvi.
⁵ L. and P. XII (1), 1087 (p. 497).
⁶ Ibid. 410.

the canons of Watton[1]. Hallam was carefully examined on the 24th and 26th, but said nothing to implicate the monks of Watton[2]; in fact he did not accuse anyone but those who were already prisoners[3]. On 25 January William Nicholson of Holderness, who had tried to rescue Hallam, Roger Kitchen and John Francis of Beverley were examined. William Crockey the deputy-customer to whom Horskey and Langdale revealed the plot gave his evidence on Friday 26 January. The rest of the prisoners were servants and labourers who were examined on Friday and Saturday[4].

The case against all these men was perfectly clear. They had risen in open rebellion since the pardon. The extenuating circumstance that the King had deliberately provoked the rising could not be pleaded by them, and the only question was how far the King would be inclined to show mercy. On this point the gentlemen were still in some doubt, and accordingly only Hallam and two others, probably Nicholson and Kitchen, were condemned to death[5]. The rest were remanded to await the coming of the Duke of Norfolk[6]. The three were executed before 4 February 1536–7[7], but probably not until Norfolk had been consulted about their fate.

On the information of Horskey and Langdale three of the canons of Watton were arrested before Tuesday 30 January[8]. These were Dan Harry Gyll the sub-prior, Thomas Lather the cellarer and granator, and Richard Wilkinson the cellarer of the kitchen. When examined they all three confessed that they had taken part in the election of a new prior, but all declared that it had been done through fear of the commons. They also confessed that it was the general opinion of the monastery that the King could not be Supreme Head of the Church, that they had heard Sir Francis Bigod express doubts as to the validity of the pardon, and that they had sent three men with money to take part in Hallam's enterprise. The two cellarers professed to have opposed the sending of the men; they said that they were unpopular in the monastery because they were the servants of the prior appointed by Cromwell. Gyll did not attempt to defend himself. The canons were reserved for Norfolk's judgment[9].

Another instance of a monastery becoming implicated, justly or unjustly, in the rebellion occurred at this time. Thomas Hungate,

---

[1] L. and P. xii (1), 201 (pp. 87–88).
[2] L. and P. xii (1), 201 (pp. 88–94).
[3] Ibid. 338.
[7] Ibid. 338.
[9] Ibid. 201 (pp. 98–102).
[2] See note G at end of chapter.
[4] Ibid. 201.
[6] Ibid. 410.
[8] Ibid. 292.

a servant of Sir Arthur Darcy, informed Sir Oswald Wolsthrope that George Shuttleworth, a servant of Sawley Abbey, had been in Durham when the herald was attacked (on or before 9 January)[1] and had given out that he was going to Sir Thomas Percy for counsel[2]. Shuttleworth was arrested about Wednesday 24 January. As suspicion had been so strongly excited against Sir Thomas, this information was naturally believed to be very important. When it became known that Shuttleworth had been in company with William Leache, one of the Lincolnshire refugees, the case against Sir Thomas and the Abbot of Sawley seemed to be almost proved[3]. Yet when the matter is as far as possible unravelled, with the help of Shuttleworth's deposition, their guilt still remains dubious.

The Abbot of Sawley's letter to Aske has already been mentioned. Sir Thomas Percy was regarded as the founder of Sawley, that is, as the representative of William, Lord Percy, who founded and endowed the monastery[4]. The living founder of a monastery was the person to whom the monks usually appealed in any secular difficulty. After writing to Aske, the Abbot of Sawley decided to apply to his founder also, and wrote a supplication to Sir Thomas Percy[5]. He took counsel in this matter with no one but three monks of the house, his chaplain Estgate, Bradforde and Parishe.

Estgate took this letter to Sir Stephen Hamerton whom he found hunting at Settle Spring. Estgate offered him for nothing a wood which he had wished to buy from the Abbey two years ago, but Sir Stephen refused such a dangerous gift. The chaplain told him of the letter to Sir Thomas Percy, and repeated the most important part of its contents,—that the commons had restored the monks to their abbey, and that the monks begged for Sir Thomas' favour. Hamerton said that he did not see what Sir Thomas could do for them "but they might do as they list," and Estgate left him without any further conversation upon the subject[6].

When Shuttleworth returned with Robert Aske's letter, the Abbot straightway despatched him to Sir Thomas Percy with the supplication. At this point a serious difficulty in chronology arises. Shuttleworth said that he set out at once and reached Richmond on Innocents' Day, 28 December 1536[7]. Sir Thomas Percy supported this statement by saying that he received the Abbot's letter a month

---

[1] See above, chap. xvi.
[2] Ibid. 247.
[5] L. and P. xii (1), 491.
[7] Ibid. 491.
[3] L. and P. xii (1), 218.
[4] Harland, The Monastery of Sawley, p. 3.
[6] Ibid. 1034.

or six weeks before Bigod's rising[1]. Against this is to be set the fact that Shuttleworth was accused of having been in Durham on his way *to* Sir Thomas, on or before 9 January 1536–7[2], and that he himself said that he had been with Robert Aske at Aughton at a time when Aske must have been in London[3]. William Maunsell, who took part in arresting Shuttleworth on 24 January, implied that the latter had just returned from his errand[4]. The only deduction from all this conflicting evidence is that it is impossible to determine exactly when Shuttleworth's errand was performed; more is known about the way in which he performed it.

The Abbot delivered to him 10s. for his expenses, "a bent royal of gold for a token to Sir Thomas Percy," and the supplication, the contents of which Shuttleworth did not know. After receiving these articles, Shuttleworth went to Richard Broderton's inn near the Abbey gates, to have a drink before setting out on his new journey. A friend asked him to come next day to "an ale," and he was obliged to refuse the invitation because he had an errand to Sir Thomas Percy. Another man heard this, and offered to accompany Shuttleworth, saying that he also had an errand to Sir Thomas. They set out together, and Shuttleworth soon discovered that his companion was William Leache, a Lincolnshire rebel who had been excepted from the King's pardon.

Leache told Shuttleworth that he had received a letter signed by Lord Darcy, Robert Aske and Sir Thomas Percy summoning Lincolnshire to rise again. He had sent this letter into Lincolnshire with one of his own to the same effect, but before any answer came "they in Yorkshire took another way with them." The letter had fallen into the King's hands and consequently Leache had been excluded from the pardon. Now he was going to Sir Thomas Percy to ask for his intercession with the Duke of Norfolk. He showed Shuttleworth one of the letters, but it is not clear whether this was his own letter, or the one alleged to have been signed by Darcy, Aske and Percy[5]. This letter to Lincolnshire must have been written before the second appointment at Doncaster, when they "took another way," if it was ever written at all, but the whole story is improbable, for Darcy, Aske and Percy were never together, except for a few days before the first appointment at Doncaster, and Leache had been excepted

---

[1] L. and P. xii (1), 393; printed in full, De Fonblanque, op. cit. chap. ix.
[2] L. and P. xii (1), 247, 490.   [3] Ibid. 491.
[4] Ibid. 490.   [5] Ibid. 491.

out of the Lincolnshire pardons from the beginning, before the King was even aware that Yorkshire had risen[1].

Leache and Shuttleworth spent the first night of their journey at Kettlewell, and the next at Ralph Gower's house in Richmond, where they fell in with a party of five priests and two or three laymen. On hearing that Shuttleworth came from Sawley the laymen said, " Fye on them that dwell nigh about that house, that ever they would suffer the monks to be put out of it. And that was the first house that was put down in this country. But rather than our house of Saint Agatha should go down, we shall all die; and if any insurrection should happen here again, where there was but one in the same before, now there would be three."

Next night the travellers were in Durham, but Shuttleworth said nothing about their adventures there. On the following day they reached Prudhoe, but Sir Thomas Percy was out hunting, and Shuttleworth did not see him until 9 o'clock on the morning after he arrived. Shuttleworth presented the letter and the token, and Sir Thomas told him he should receive his answer in the afternoon. When Shuttleworth came again, Sir Thomas gave him a verbal message that the Abbot should "make no resistance if any commission came down from the King, but speak fair to such as should come withal, for the Abbot had as many friends as any man, and if any house should stand, his was like to do so." Sir Thomas also told him to desire Sir Stephen Hamerton's best counsel for the Abbot and the house, and as a token that the message came from Sir Thomas he was to say "that I [Sir Thomas] spake to him at our last being together that he should be good unto my lady my mother."[2]

Leache had not yet accomplished his ambiguous errand. After Shuttleworth left Sir Thomas, Leache had an interview with the latter, but what passed between them Shuttleworth did not know[3]. The two men went back to Sawley together, but when the Abbot was told who Leache was, he ordered him to "avoid that quarter," lest he should bring trouble upon the house[4].

The supplication which aroused so much curiosity in Sir Thomas Percy's enemies afterwards fell into Norfolk's hands[5]. It appears to be a very harmless document. The monks of Sawley begged Sir Thomas to consider their present need, and to let them know his

---

[1] See above, chap. vii.
[2] L. and P. xii (1), 491.
[3] Ibid. 490.
[4] Ibid. 491.
[5] See below, chap. xviii.

pleasure for the succour of their house. They feared their "most sinister back friend Sir Arthur Darcy," and wished to know whether Sir Thomas would advise them to follow the counsel of the neighbouring commons and remain in their house. Sir Stephen Hamerton and Nicholas Tempest had been true friends, and the monks begged Sir Thomas to give them some reward, as they themselves could requite them only by their prayers. The one passage to which any seditious meaning could be attached ran as follows:—"The whole noise and bruit in these parts is, the captain should have left and discharged himself of the captainship, but also is judged and supposed an order to be taken for religious houses suppressed, the farmers or other to enter and occupy, and the abbot or prior and brethren to have and taken at their delivery their necessaries, and so to be avoided of possession unto the Parliament, whereof not only the place but also the time is as yet not perceived to be; wherefore men's hearts hath no little suspect, vexation, and great disdain, in doubting the great enormities and danger that may ensue and come to them."[1] Even this, which is the most incriminating part of the letter, is too vague to bear any genuinely treasonable interpretation. The unfortunate monks, in fact, only begged to be told what they ought to do, as they were quite ready to submit to any orders which they might receive from a competent authority; but no one was in a position to relieve their perplexity. The Abbot was accused of being the author of the bills which were posted on the church doors in the neighbourhood, but no evidence of this was produced[2].

The most suspicious circumstance in the communications between Sir Thomas Percy and the Abbot was the presence of William Leache. He was a man of a savage, determined character. On this occasion he made his escape to Scotland, but in 1541 he and another fugitive murdered Somerset Herald near Dunbar, as he was returning from a mission to James V. For this barbarous deed they were both surrendered to the English government and executed[3]. It can have been with no very peaceful object that such a man appeared at Sawley, visited Sir Thomas Percy, and returned to Sawley again; but the nature of his errand was never discovered.

The gentlemen had accomplished a good deal in the week which followed Bigod's rising. They had arrested and examined most of his accomplices, they were accumulating evidence against Sir Thomas

[1] L. and P. xi, 785; printed in full, De Fonblanque, op. cit. i, Append. li; see note H at end of chapter.
[2] L. and P. xii (1), 490, 1034.   [3] Archaeological Journal, xiv, 381.

Percy, and George Lumley was a prisoner in York. The only remaining task was the capture of Bigod himself. This did not appear to be a very difficult affair, as everyone had turned against him. The gentlemen were trying to arrest him as a rebel against the King, and the commons were ready to put him to death as a traitor to the commons.

The particulars of Sir Francis' flight from Beverley on Friday 19 January are not known, but the commons declared that he had deserted them. His only idea was to go home again, and as he neared Settrington he sent forward his horsekeeper Harry Soulay to discover how he would be received. At Yeddingham Bridge Soulay heard the threats of the disappointed rebels, and came back to warn his master to go no further. Bigod took refuge at William Middlewood's house in Ebberston, and sent Soulay on again, with orders to go right to Settrington for news and to return to Ebberston the same night. Before Soulay's return Middlewood's brother-in-law came in and reported some of the angry sayings against Sir Francis which he had heard by the way. Sir Francis was so much alarmed that he set out again and rode all night for his castle at Mulgrave. On the morning of Saturday 20 January he reached Sandsend, a little village on the coast a couple of miles east of Mulgrave. Soulay, on returning to Ebberston to find his master, was seized by the commons and would have been beheaded if he had not been rescued by Sir George Conyers.

The feeling against Sir Francis was so strong that his inveterate enemy Gregory Conyers for the moment took up the popular cause. His one object was to be on the opposite side to Sir Francis, and consequently when the latter changed sides, and again when both sides turned against him, Gregory's position was a complicated one. On Saturday 20 January he proclaimed to the fishermen all along the coast that Sir Francis Bigod was a traitor to the King and to the commons, and ordered them to keep watch that he did not escape by sea[1]. This formula linking the King and the commons was the usual one, which occurs in the Lincolnshire oath and elsewhere. It does not imply that Gregory was commissioned to act for the King. William Neville, brother of Lord Latimer, and Serjeant Roger Middlewood went to Mulgrave to seize Bigod's goods[2]. Gregory Conyers arrived there shortly afterwards; hearing of the previous seizure, he said to Bigod's wife, "Madame, and here are twain come

---

[1] L. and P. XII (1), 533.
[2] Ibid. 234.

for the commons," and seized what remained in the commons' name, on the grounds that Sir Francis had betrayed them[1].

While this was going on Bigod was in hiding somewhere near his despoiled castle. On Sunday 21 January Gregory Conyers went to Hinderwell in search of him, warning all the country to give the fugitive no aid, but at this point Gregory seems to have abandoned his alliance with the commons, as he joined the King's representatives, Neville and Middlewood[2]. They were so close upon Bigod's track that they surprised him in his hiding-place, and Gregory seized him by his sleeveless coat, but Bigod slipped off the loose garment and fled into the woods on foot. His assailants had to be satisfied with the capture of his servants and horses[3]. Dismounted as he was, Bigod eluded pursuit for nearly three weeks[4].

On Thursday 25 January young Sir Ralph Evers reported to the King the retaking of Scarborough and Bigod's flight[5]. He petitioned Cromwell to further his suit for Sir Francis' lands[6]. Next day he wrote again enclosing the names of those who had been rulers of the commons in the last insurrection but had served the King well on this occasion. He hoped that the King would acknowledge their services, and particularly praised Sir John Bulmer's son-in-law Matthew Boynton[7].

The King must have been pleased to find that his policy had produced such excellent results. The breach between the gentlemen and the commons was now complete. The former had been busy quieting the latter, while Henry felt himself absolved by the rising from any obligation to keep his promises.

On receiving young Sir Ralph Ellerker's report dated 20 January, the King sent letters to both the writer and his father. He thanked them for their services, sent money and ammunition, and gave permission for 100 horsemen to be retained in Hull, but he was displeased that the prisoners had been admitted to bail. He ordered that they should be re-arrested and tried, and as many as possible executed; for this purpose he sent a commission to the Ellerkers. These letters are undated, but probably reached Hull before 24 January, the day of Hallam's trial[8]. John Eland was thanked and rewarded for his service in taking Hallam[9].

Sir Arthur Darcy wrote to his father from court on 23 January

---

[1] L. and P. xii (1), 533.
[2] Ibid. 234.
[3] Ibid. 810, 870.
[4] Ibid. 234, 810, 870.
[5] Ibid. 234.
[6] Ibid. 235.
[7] Ibid. 248.
[8] Ibid. 227, 228.
[9] Ibid. 279.

that the King had received Lord Darcy's letters very graciously[1], and next day Henry wrote himself to Darcy to thank him for his services and to order him to victual Pontefract Castle secretly, so that he and his sons might hold it if the people rose again[2]. On Thursday 25 January Henry thanked Shrewsbury for his "discreet proceedings" in the "new tragedy moved by that false traitor Bigod."[3] The old Earl had written to his master that he was very ill and feared he should "not long be here."[4] The King in reply sent him his own physician Dr Butts, and expressed the hope that he would see and thank Shrewsbury in person on "his repair into those parts, which, God willing, shall be shortly." The King repeated the contents of his letter to Darcy, and declared that so long as Darcy did his duty, he would regard him with as much favour as if the rebellion had never occurred[5]. Darcy's pardon was made out on 18 January[6].

The King wrote to Robert Aske on 24 January thanking him for his letter and goodwill. Henry concluded by saying that he "would be glad to hear of some special deed in answer to our expectations."[7] The meaning of this was clear. Aske was already regarded with suspicion in Yorkshire on account of his intercourse with the King. If he took a leading part in the capture and execution of the new rebels, his influence over the commons would be completely destroyed. Then Henry, if he pleased, might safely execute the discredited captain, or extend to him a contemptuous pardon if he seemed likely to become a useful tool. Aske did not take the hint. Throughout the rebellion he had been acting not for himself but for his cause. He was entirely opposed to Bigod's attempt, because he saw that it was foolish, useless, and dangerous. As he held this opinion he did his best to suppress the movement, but he was full of pity for the unfortunate men who had taken part in it. His voice was always on the side of mercy. He advised that Bigod's messengers should be released from Hull, that the prisoners should be bailed, and that Hallam's execution should be delayed in the hope of a pardon. Several of those who had been with Bigod threw themselves upon Aske's mercy, and he promised to try to procure their pardon[8].

Perhaps Aske still believed in the King's humane intentions, but it is scarcely possible that he should have kept this illusion after

[1] L. and P. xii (1), 169, 170, 188, 197.
[2] Ibid. 208.
[3] Ibid. 226.
[4] Ibid. 169.
[5] Ibid. 226.
[6] Ibid. 134.
[7] Ibid. 209; printed in full, State Papers, i, 529, and Longstaff, A Leaf from the Pilgrimage of Grace.
[8] L. and P. xii (1), 1087 (p. 497).

Henry's letter, particularly in face of the opposite conduct of the other gentlemen. They for the most part realised that they had made their choice between the King and the cause, and that it remained for them to make themselves secure with the King by denouncing others. Beneath the steady stream of gracious messages which still flowed down from the court, there is an eddy in the opposite direction of messages vaguely or definitely hostile to the former leaders of the Pilgrimage, sent up by their former comrades.

Eland and Knolles had taken an active part in the surrender of Hull to the insurgents, but they had now redeemed their characters by capturing Hallam. Sir Ralph Ellerker had been one of the messengers to the King, and Nicholas Rudston had been the chief captain of Holderness, but they were now anxious to retrieve themselves by implicating Sir Robert Constable in the new rising. They discovered a means by which this might be done in the letter which Aske and Constable had written to Rudston before Bigod's flight from Beverley; it contained the advice that Bigod's messengers should be released, as they had only done their master's errand[1]. The letter was delivered to Rudston on the morning of Friday 19 January, just before the advance on Beverley; after the gentlemen had entered the town Rudston showed the letter to young Sir Ralph Ellerker whom he met on Westwood Green. Rudston read it aloud in the presence of two of Sir Robert's servants, who perceived that it was considered treasonable[2].

On Saturday 20 January at Hull Sir Ralph Ellerker caused his chaplain to make a copy of the letter to be sent up to the King, while Rudston went to dine with Sir Robert Constable on Sunday 21 January. Constable's servants must have warned him that the letter was being used against him, for he asked Rudston to show it to him, and inquired what fault he found with it. Rudston seems to have implied that it was a very faulty performance in every respect, but he said, "The greatest fault that Sir Ralph Ellerker and I do find is against the messengers that ye write for." Sir Robert unwisely attempted a prevarication, saying that there was no harm in that, for he meant Langdale and Horskey, who went to Hull to buy their Lenten store. Rudston answered that Sir Ralph Ellerker thought that he had meant Bigod's messengers. Sir Robert retorted with an oath, "And if so, what harm?" and gave back the letter. Later in the day he asked Rudston to show the letter to Dr Waldby. Rudston handed it over, and Sir Robert stood talking about it beside

[1] L. and P. xii (1), 113.   [2] Ibid. 1130.

the Doctor. Presently he took it out of Waldby's hands "and conveyed it into his bosom or sleeve." Rudston saw this, but pretended to notice nothing. Happening to find Waldby by himself, Rudston asked him whom Sir Robert had really meant, and Waldby admitted that the allusion was to Bigod's messengers. The conclusion is rather humorous:

> "Within a while I [Rudston] put my hand into my bosom and said, as if speaking to myself, 'What have I done with the letter?' adding, 'Marry, Mr Constable hath it himself.' The Doctor said, 'Even so hath he.' And forasmuch as I did somewhat mistrust the said Sir Robert, and perceived indeed that he had conveyed the letter, I durst not ask the letter of the said Sir Robert, and specially because I was sure of a copy."[1]

Rudston might well be afraid of Sir Robert; it is a matter for wonder that he had sufficient impudence to go and dine at his house, when he was doing his best to ruin him. It was unfortunate for his case that Sir Robert tried to prevaricate about the persons mentioned in his letter, as he was afterwards accused of having asked Rudston to deliver Hallam[2]. Constable could never have imagined that he could procure Hallam's release by letter; such an attempt would have been both treasonable and useless, but the ambiguity of his phrase enabled his accusers to read that meaning into the words.

For some reason, both Aske and Constable were firmly convinced that Sir Ralph Ellerker had brought north a letter from the King. Constable asked to be allowed to read it in his letter about the messengers[3]. On Sunday 21 January Aske, who had returned from Holme to Aughton, wrote to ask Ellerker to send him a copy of the mythical letter from the King. Aske's request has not been preserved. Sir Ralph Ellerker replied that he had no such letter; his conclusion is curious: "I will be glad to confer with you at Ellerker if you will send me word, for I am not so good a clerk as to read your letter perfectly."[4] Aske's letter was probably the one in which he recommended Ellerker not to execute Hallam while the north was still so much disturbed, and this passage in Ellerker's reply must be an allusion to the same dangerous subject. Ellerker was collecting evidence against Constable; he may have wished to entrap Aske also, but it is possible to give him the benefit of the doubt. The Ellerkers had an old feud with Sir Robert Constable, which revived as soon as the enforced truce of the

---

[1] L. and P. xii (1), 1130.
[2] Ibid. 848 (ii) (10).
[3] Ibid. 113.
[4] Ibid. 191.

Pilgrimage ended, but the Ellerkers and the Askes were friends and related by marriage. Young Sir Ralph never produced Aske's letter as evidence against him, and his comment on the letter which he could not read perfectly may have been meant as a warning that there was something in the letter which ought not to have been written. In response to this invitation Aske set out for Ellerker. On the way he met William Levening and one Fulthorp, who appealed to him to help them, as they had been forced to take part in Bigod's rising against their will. Levening said that he had already been to Sir Robert Constable and to Lord Darcy, in order to enlist their sympathy. Both he and Fulthorp promised, if Aske would take their names, to be ready to appear before Norfolk whenever he summoned them. Aske undertook to do his best for them, and afterwards requested William Babthorpe to lay their case before the Duke[1].

The gentlemen who had been loyal throughout the insurrection were now busily accumulating evidence against the late leaders. Sir Henry Saville on 29 January sent to Cromwell a letter from the Vicar of Brayton which showed that the Vicar had acted by Aske's orders. Sir Henry mentioned a summons which Darcy had sent out to the gentlemen of the Honour of Pontefract, calling them to assemble at Pontefract Castle. Before they came he had surrendered the castle, and on their arrival they all took the Pilgrims' oath. Sir Henry Saville reported that there had been riots between the servants of the Abbot of Kirkstall and those of Sir Christopher Danby. His advice was that the abbot should be deposed, and he suggested that the real movers in the last insurrection had never appeared, but "had set light persons on to prove the country."[2]

The easiest way for anyone to prove his loyalty was by accusing someone else, and Sir George Darcy reported that there were "great exclamations against Aske." The King's orders to Darcy to hold Pontefract Castle with his two sons, though put in the form of a compliment, were really a source of strife, for Lord Darcy found it impossible to work with Sir George Darcy, who did his best to obtain evidence against his father. Through Shrewsbury's mediation, Sir George had a fairly amicable meeting with his father on Friday 26 January[3], but as soon as the King's orders concerning Pontefract arrived, about Monday 29 January, trouble followed. On receipt of the King's letter, Sir George wrote to his father

---

[1] L. and P. xii (1), 698 (3).   [2] Ibid. 281.
[3] Ibid. 247.

to ask him what he meant to do. Darcy replied that he did not wish to make preparations until Sir George came in person to see the letter which he had received, and that as Norfolk was expected on Saturday 3 February, and as the country was quiet, he thought that there would be no harm in waiting until Norfolk arrived before doing anything[1]. In fact this cunningly framed compliment placed Darcy in such a position that whatever he did could be used as evidence against him. If he set to work energetically to provision Pontefract Castle, he would be accused of preparing for a new insurrection, but when he chose the other course of doing nothing without express orders, he was represented as being slack and reluctant in the King's service.

As soon as Lord Darcy had declared his opinion, Sir George took the opposite side. He wrote back on Tuesday 30 January that the country was far from quiet and that he dared not wait the three days which must elapse before Norfolk arrived without beginning to prepare the castle; neither did he dare to leave the castle even for the few hours which were required for a visit to Templehurst, and he therefore refused to come to his father to see the King's letter. This was the point at which matters stood when Norfolk arrived at Doncaster.

Before the Duke reached the north, Cromwell sent an agent of his own, Sir Ralph Sadler, to see how the land lay. Sir Ralph's ostensible mission was to go to Scotland and to demand from the government the surrender of the Lincolnshire fugitives[2], but with this he combined the duty of writing careful reports on the state of the disaffected districts. On Tuesday 23 January he reached York. He heard many rumours on the road of fresh risings further north, and found that there were bills on all the church doors between Doncaster and York, urging the commons to stick together as the gentlemen had deceived them. All the country through which he had passed was quiet, but if there were a new insurrection, the people would take the part of the army which arrived first, to save their goods.

Sadler talked with many of the "honest householders," who declared that Aske had caused the first rising by spreading bills that the parish churches should be pulled down, and that taxes were to be levied on marriages, burials, and christenings. They were also positive that the gentlemen had been willing enough to take part in the rising. "Why," quoth Sadler, "the gentlemen were taken by the commons and compelled to be their captains." "Yea, yea," was the reply, "an the gentlemen had been as they should be they might

[1] L. and P. xii (1), 280.   [2] State Papers, i, 526 n.

have stayed them well enough at the first; but when the gentlemen took their parts, then such poor men as we be could do no less than do as they did or else have been spoiled of all that we have." Sadler was particularly intimate with the hosts of the various inns at which he stayed. The host of the village inn has always been an oracle of almost equal authority with the village priest. At Tadcaster Sadler's host, a merry fellow, said to him, "Why, how say ye to my lord Darcy? Did he not turn to the commons as soon as they came to Pontefract and took their part? And yet being within the castle he might have resisted them if they had been ten times as many as they were."[1] When the King was receiving such reports, it was not very likely that he would keep his promise to take the first insurrection "but for a dream."[2]

Sadler wrote again on 28 January from Newcastle. A day or two before he set out on his journey, there had been great danger of a new rising in Cleveland, owing to bills which were scattered abroad to warn the people that the Duke of Norfolk was coming with a great army "to hang and draw from Doncaster to Berwick," so that the north would be "brought in worse case than the Lincolnshire men." The rising had been prevented by Robert Bowes, who was travelling all over the district to quiet the people. Sadler remarked that as the gentlemen had been able to repress the present attempt, they could have dealt with the first rebellion just as easily if they had wished. In spite of the recent disturbance, all the country through which he had passed was quiet except Darlington, where he had spent a night and found the people very "tickle." He alighted at his inn at about 6 o'clock, and saw not more than three or four people in the street, but he had scarcely mounted the stairs to his room, when thirty or forty armed men had gathered round the inn door, "and stood together in a plompe whispering and rounding together." Sadler, as usual, had recourse to the host, "who seemed to be an honest man." He said that the townsfolk always assembled when any traveller came from the south, because they wanted to hear the news. Sadler admonished him that the town authorities ought not to permit such unlawful assemblies. The host replied that the heads of the town dared not for their lives interfere, but that no harm would come of it. "Quoth he, 'Ye shall see that I shall cause them to scatter abroad, and every man to go to his home by and by.' 'Mary,' quoth I, 'if ye do well, ye should set some of them by the

---

[1] L. and P. xii (1), 200; printed in full, State Papers, i, 526.
[2] L. and P. xii (1), 66.

heels.' 'No,' quoth he, 'God defend, for so might we bring a thousand in our tops within an hour; but ye shall see me order them well enough with fair words.'" Then he went down into the street with his cap in his hand, and assured them that the new-comer was one of the King's servants on an embassy to Scotland. The crowd replied that this could not be true, because the King of Scotland was in France, which indicates a very low state of political knowledge. The host, however, persuaded them that his story was true, and they all with one voice asked when the Duke of Norfolk was coming and with what company. The host came back to Sadler to ask his opinion on this subject. Sadler by this time was converted to the host's policy of fair words, and replied that Norfolk would be at Doncaster on Candlemas Eve, with none but his household servants. This contented the people and they dispersed, but the occurrence had impressed Sadler: "I assure your lordship the people be very tickle, and methinks in a marvellous strange case and perplexity; for they stare and look for things, and fain would have they cannot tell what." From Darlington Sadler went to Durham, where he met Bowes, and thence to Newcastle-upon-Tyne, where the mayor and aldermen maintained very good order; they showed him how strong the town was, and he remained there waiting for a safe-conduct from Scotland[1].

On his way through Cleveland, Sadler had stayed at Wilton Castle, where Sir William, brother of Sir John Bulmer, was constable. Soon after Sadler left, another traveller from London arrived. This was Thomas Fulthorp, a servant of young Ralph Bulmer, who was bringing a letter from his master to Sir John. Fulthorp told Sir William that the Duke of Norfolk "was not in so good favour with the King as the north country took him to be"; in other words, the Duke's influence was not sufficient to make the King observe the appointment at Doncaster. Sir William did not believe this, because Sadler had told him the contrary[2].

Fulthorp then went on to Lastingham, where Sir John Bulmer was living. Soon after he reached home, one of Sir John's servants brought a terrified letter to Wilton. Ralph, who had gone up to London to discover the King's real intentions, sent word that thirty ships were being prepared to sail against the north, that Aske and Sir George Darcy had accused several people, including Lord Darcy

---

[1] L. and P. xii (1), 259; printed in full, State Papers, i, 259, and in part by Surtees, Hist. of Dur. sub Darlington, and Longstaff, Hist. of Darlington (misdated 1538). [2] L. and P. xiii (1), 568.

and Sir Robert Constable, and that Norfolk was coming with the worst intentions. Sir John begged his brother to lay a watch along the coasts and to prepare beacons, and warned him not to leave his house "for no fair letters nor words."[1] Sir William may have been used to his brother's panics, for he paid so little attention to the letter that he did not even trouble to destroy it[2].

Although Sir John was afraid of fair letters and words, he was also alarmed because he had not been summoned to meet the Duke of Norfolk. He wrote to Sir Ralph Evers to inquire the meaning of this, and received a comforting reply. The Duke meant to send for him; the arrangement at London was that either Sir John should attend the Duke with ten servants or his brother Sir William with six[3]. Somewhat relieved, Sir John agreed that his brother should go[4].

Until he could make up his mind what to do, Sir John had been trying to keep the commons quiet, but his servants attended their musters, and he had made quite a collection of their treasonable bills, with the intention of using them in any way that would serve his own interest. One of these bills originated at Kendal. It was a semi-rhyming production, which urged the commons to insist upon having their old customs and tenant right, "to take your farms by a God's penny, all gressoms and heightenings to be laid down." It expressed the general idea that the lords and gentlemen had undertaken a pilgrimage to protect Holy Church, and that the commons would support them if they would grant the commons' demands concerning rent and ingressum[5]. It was shown to Sir John by Priestman, a fugitive from Lincolnshire, who asked him how he liked it. Sir John replied, "Marry, very well, for when two dogs fight for a bone the third will take it up; for this will make the gentlemen and the commons fall forth, and the King shall take up the matter." A second bill came from the south and began, "Good Northern men, stick to your matter, for the lord of Norfolk comes to beguile you"; it continued with a repetition of Norfolk's promises, which he had not performed. A third bill ordered the men of Cleveland to take Sir William Bulmer and Sir James Strangways, and the men of the Bishopric to take the Earl of Westmorland, Lord Lumley and Lord Neville, while the men of Pickering and Blackmoor would seize Sir John Bulmer, and all the bands would

---

[1] L. and P. xi, 1408.
[2] L. and P. xiii (1), 568.
[3] L. and P. xii (1), 66.
[4] Ibid. 1083.
[5] Ibid. 163 (2); see above, chap. xii, note F.

advance to capture the Duke and force him to keep the promises which he made at Doncaster[1].

This scheme had a particular fascination for Sir John. It had originally been devised by Sir Francis Bigod. The plan seems to have been that Richmondshire should rise as soon as Norfolk reached Doncaster. He would probably hurry forward with no troops but his escort, and might be attacked by the men of Cleveland as he went up from the plain of York into the Hambleton Hills about Byland[2]. Two men of Bilsdale came to Sir John to propose this plot. They brought a list of articles similar to those which were circulating in Richmond "for the swearing of all lords and gentlemen or their sons or else to strike off their heads." Sir John was to take up his abode at Wilton Castle, when the commons of Guisborough would capture him by arrangement, and he would then go with them to seize the Duke. His wife knew of this plot and did not advocate lenient measures. "She said divers times that if the Duke's head were off, Sir Ralph Evers' and Sir Ralph Ellerker's men might go where they would."[3] Before any steps were taken to put this plot into practice, Sir William Bulmer visited Lastingham on his way to Doncaster, and convinced his brother that so long as they remained quiet they had nothing to fear. Sir John handed over to him his collection of bills, in order that they might be laid before the Duke. He reversed his tactics, suppressed the musters of the commons, and for a short time lived in comparative security[4].

Sir John Bulmer's is an extreme case of the uneasiness which filled all the northern gentlemen, as they awaited the Duke of Norfolk. They felt that, like the knight of the legend, they had blown the horn without drawing the sword, and they were now unarmed at the mercy of an opponent whose next move was incalculable.

NOTES TO CHAPTER XVII

Note A. "Naught" in Henry VIII's reign usually meant "evil," as it does here; similarly "naughty" has a much stronger meaning than at the present day and is equivalent to "wicked," not to "mischievous."

Note B. This was not really inconsistent with the fact that Hallam was to attempt to take Hull before Bigod arrived, for after securing the town he intended to advance to meet Bigod at Beverley.

Note C. The original of Sir Francis Bigod's letter to the bailiffs of Scarborough has disappeared, but it is printed in Speed's "Great Britain," book IX, chapter 21, as follows:

[1] L. and P. XII (1), 1083. [2] Ibid. 201 (p. 92).
[3] Ibid. 1087 (pp. 494–5). [4] Ibid. 1083.

"To the Bailiffs and Commons of the Town of Scarborough.

Wellbeloved, we Francis Bigod, Knight, and John Hallam, Yeoman, in the name of all the commons, command and charge you that ye assemble yourselves together immediately upon receipt hereof, and so take this oath which we here send unto you, and then after in all haste possible to assist and aid these our brethren whom we send to you to keep and make sure the Castle, Town and Port of Scarborough, that no man enter into the same Castle that belongs unto Ralph Evers the younger, Knight, nor any other which did not take full part with the commons at our first and last assembling, in whose name, authority or attorney soever they come, unless they have licence of all the commons; in like manner ye shall truly keep all such ordnance and ship[s] to the use of the commons, with which we charged you at our last being here, and this not to fail, upon pain of your lives. Ye shall refer credence unto these messengers, thus in haste: Fare you well.

From Setterington this Monday Saint Maurus' day[1]. Francis Bigod Knight, in the name and by commandment of all the commons."

Note D. This letter is dated 18 January, but endorsed 17 January, and the latter appears to be the more probable date.

Note E. It was afterwards alleged that Aske had written to Bigod promising that Hallam should be released, but no trace of this letter remains[2]. The two letters upon which the prosecution based the charge are both fully discussed in the text; they were (1) Sir Robert Constable's letter for the release of Bigod's messengers, and (2) Aske's lost letter for the delay of Hallam's execution. The prosecution, which was not at all scrupulous in its methods, combined these two letters and asserted that Aske had written either to request or to promise that Hallam should be released, thus producing a charge of treason out of two harmless documents.

Note F. Sir Ralph Ellerker reported that Boynton arrived on the 20th[3], but he signed a letter at Beverley on the 19th[4].

Note G. In the summary of the evidence and in Norfolk's letter it is said that "Hallam" accused the monks of Watton[5], but this is a mistake; it was the prisoners who were examined at the same time as Hallam who accused them. It is perhaps scarcely necessary to say that the leader of a rebellion is often mentioned loosely as having done actions for which his followers were really responsible. A well-known name is attached by rumour to the deeds or words of obscure persons, and instances have already been given in which Robert Aske was supposed to have written letters or issued manifestoes with which, in fact, he had nothing to do. Hallam's is a similar case.

Note H. The supplication of the abbot and monks of Sawley is printed among the Letters and Papers of October 1536, but this is evidently too early, as its real date was either the end of December 1536 or the beginning of January 1536–7. The reference in it to the fact that the captain had laid down his office shows that it was written after the second appointment at Doncaster and that it is, in fact, the same document which was carried by Shuttleworth to Sir Thomas Percy. The summary in the Letters and Papers is a good deal more definite than the vague rambling clauses of the original.

[1] 15 January.
[2] L. and P. XII (1), 1087 (p. 497).
[3] Ibid. 174.
[4] Ibid. 161.
[5] Ibid. 202, 292.

CHAPTER XVIII

THE DUKE OF NORFOLK'S MISSION

While these things were happening in the north, the Duke of Norfolk, so urgently needed and so long expected, was living quietly at Kenninghall in his own county. His orders directed him to go northwards at Candlemas, and he had no intention of stirring before that time. On 6 January 1536–7 he wrote to Cromwell; as the quarter sessions were about to be held at Norwich, he suggested that the commissioners of the subsidy and of the suppression who attended them should be ordered to proceed with their work, which had been suspended during the rebellion. The religious living in the houses which ought to be suppressed were a great cost to the King, and if they were allowed to remain and the subsidy was not levied, it " might put folly into the light northern heads."[1]

On 16 January Norfolk was with the King at Greenwich, receiving instructions for his mission to the north. Considering that the news of Hallam's attempt had not yet reached the King, these instructions were severe, and showed little prospect that the King would fulfil the promises which he had made to Robert Aske a few days before. Norfolk was to go to the counties recently disturbed, accompanied by a council, and there to take such steps as the King thought necessary for their final settlement. His first stopping-place was at Doncaster, where the most trustworthy of the northern gentlemen would meet him. He was to administer to them the King's oath, and then to summon the gentlemen of the district, and, when they had taken the oath, the commons. Everyone must take the oath in turn, and this procedure must be followed at every place where the Duke halted.

After Doncaster the Duke would proceed to Pontefract, and, when the West Riding had taken the oath, to York, where he was to be met by the remaining leaders of the Pilgrimage and all other gentlemen of importance. Thence he would travel through all the

[1] L. and P. xii (1), 32.

country that had risen, administering the oath and enlarging upon the King's wonderful clemency and goodness to his disobedient subjects. He was to reproach the justices of the peace with their lack of vigilance, and to let them see that they were blamed for the disturbances. Any loyal subjects suing for restitution of goods taken during the period covered by the pardon were to be put off with fair answers, and asked to wait until the coming of the King; neither they nor the present holders of the goods must be driven to despair.

The Duke was to make every effort to search out the beginners of the insurrections, the devisers of the articles, and the real reasons of the outbreak. Any man who refused to take the oath must be executed if Norfolk dared to proceed to extremes. If the attitude of the people forbade severity, " he shall pretend to make light of such a fool and proceed to swearing the rest till a better opportunity."

When the whole country was sworn, the next step was to turn out the monks, nuns, and canons who still occupied suppressed houses, and to put the farmers in possession. As the Duke himself had promised to make suit to the King that they might remain till the next parliament, he was to explain to the people " how far they vary from true religious men, yea, from true subjects."

Norfolk must see that the King's rents were collected and order other men's tenants to pay their landlords; but he must also inquire into the matter of enclosures and fines, hear complaints about them, and mediate between gentlemen and tenants, in order that they " may live together as they be joined in one body politic." This clause in the instructions had a double object; " the King's instructions to Norfolk, under their fair show of conciliatory words, by enjoining the reception of complaints against enclosures, were deftly intended to widen the breach between the confederated classes of the north."[1]

As it was through ignorance that the north had been seduced into horrible treason, the King intended " to send thither certain grave, discreet and learned personages to teach and preach the truth " and the Duke must recommend them to the people.

Finally Norfolk was to sit on cases of common justice, and all offenders since the pardon were to be sought out and executed, " if it may be done without danger, especially if they have been ringleaders." If there was danger, he must simply " look through his fingers at their offences, and free them to continue till the King's Majesty's arrival in those parts," taking care that they did not fly the country[2].

---

[1] Royal Hist. Soc. Trans. (New Ser.) xviii, p. 197.　　[2] L. and P. xii (1), 98.

The government seems to have felt the difficulty of finding a form of words suitable for the oath which was to alter all the feelings, aims and ideals of the Pilgrims, to make them forget their vow to God and the Commonwealth, and to induce them to concentrate their allegiance upon the King. The form must be as sweeping as the King dared to make it, and yet must not go too far. The drafts of the oath remain[1], and the last, which is the simplest, was probably the one used. "You shall swear to be true liegeman to the King our sovereign lord, Henry VIII King of England and of France, etc,"[2] it began, sliding over the obnoxious title of Supreme Head of the Church, which is inserted in another draft. Those who took the oath swore to do no treason, murder or felony, but to discover the doers of such crimes; to renounce the oaths taken during the insurrection, and in future to resist such movements; to be obedient to the King, his lieutenant, and all his laws. Several irritating items in the other drafts are omitted in this, such as expressions of contrition and desire of forgiveness for the rising, and a declaration of willingness to assist the commissioners in the suppression of the abbeys. With these drafts for the oath is a set of instructions for its administration. Every man was required to "confess and knowledge" his traitorous demeanour and submit himself to the King's mercy: he was then to declare the names of the rebel leaders, and to give up his arms in token of complete submission; finally he was to take the King's oath and to hold all others vain[3]. It is, however, practically certain that these instructions were not carried out, as the Duke of Norfolk did not disarm the north, and could not have done so without the greatest danger.

On 16 January 1536-7 the King sent out letters to various gentlemen ordering them to be in readiness to attend the Duke on his northern progress[4]. One was addressed to Sir Robert Constable, who was to meet Norfolk in York; another to Lord Darcy, who was to await him at Pontefract[5]. Norfolk summoned Sir William Fairfax and Sir Oswald Wolsthrope, who were trusted by the government, to meet him at Doncaster on Candlemas Eve (1 February) with all their servants, unharnessed[6].

After his visit to court, Norfolk returned to Kenninghall to prepare for his journey at leisure. He was there when the news of Bigod's rebellion reached him. All accounts agreed in attributing the new

---

[1] L. and P. xii (1), 98 (4) (6) (7).
[2] Ibid. 98 (8).
[3] Ibid. 98 (3).
[4] Ibid. 97.
[5] Ibid. 96, 99, 100.
[6] Ibid. 101.

outbreak to his long delay[1], but the Duke was not disturbed on that account; he had his orders and he was obeying them. It is probable that he was expecting some such news.

On 28 January old Sir Marmaduke Constable's eldest son was with him, bringing from the north a full account of all that had taken place. He showed Norfolk a copy of the manifesto sent out by his uncle Sir Robert Constable and Aske to stay the parts about Beverley. "He has written more than I can perform," said Norfolk in a letter to Cromwell, "and his large sayings might be for a scant good purpose about the coronation and parliament, etc." Yet they were given on the authority of the King's own words. Norfolk congratulated Cromwell on the news. If the country were settled before he reached the north he would grudge no man the praise; if something were left to be done he would show his good-will. "This young man [Constable's nephew] cannot speak too much good of my lord Darcy and his uncle; sickness now hath kept them both at home, which could not do so at the first business at Doncaster."[2] Norfolk was in bad health, "but desire to serve my master and anger mine enemies will, I trust, make me shortly strong and lusty."[3] By way of precaution he sent to Cromwell his will and the details of a whole string of suits which he hoped Cromwell would forward in his absence. Fortunately we have no concern with the family affairs of the wicked old Duke. A proverb which he quoted, "God shall send a shrewd cow short horns," unhappily was not true in his own case[4].

On 30 January Norfolk was in Lincoln on his way to Doncaster. Here he met messengers with letters for the King from Hull, which he opened to see if they contained anything urgent; but all was going well. Several canons of Watton and others implicated in Hallam's rebellion had been captured. Norfolk wrote to ask the King if the prisoners should be executed in York, and how many the King desired him to "justify." He had also received letters from the Bishop of Durham, Lord Scrope, and the Earl of Cumberland. Norfolk thought that the timid bishop was over-anxious about the state of the country, but to satisfy him he promised to go to Newcastle-upon-Tyne after he had settled Yorkshire[5]. Cumberland and Scrope both enclosed seditious bills, and the latter reported from Bolton that the country was much stirred by such

---

[1] L. and P. xii (1), 200; printed in full, State Papers, i, 526.
[2] L. and P. xii (1), 198.   [3] Ibid. 252.
[4] Ibid. 216, 252.   [5] Ibid. 292.

writings, which "misdeedy" persons sent about, though the honest men were content to wait for the parliament[1].

Norfolk was puzzled by learning on the road that Sir Anthony Browne had just ridden northwards on a mission from the King. The Duke had been told nothing of this, and as he was the King's Lieutenant in the north, he marvelled that the matter had not been laid before him. The Privy Council were writing to him on the subject that same day, 30 January[2]. The office of Warden of the Marches was vacant, owing to the ill-health of the Earl of Northumberland. The King had proposed to bestow it on the Earl of Westmorland, but the Earl was exceedingly anxious to escape from such a difficult and dangerous post. Henry had no intention of increasing the Earl of Cumberland's power, for it was already too great for the peace of his neighbours. Therefore he determined to adopt some old advice of Norfolk's, and, keeping the office of warden in his own hands, to appoint meaner men as his deputies. He had chosen Sir William Evers and Sir John Widderington; Sir Anthony Browne had been sent down post to receive their oaths and give them their instructions. A later chapter will be devoted to the government of the Borders and relations with Scotland[3], but Sir Anthony Browne's mission is mentioned here in order to emphasise the double nature of Norfolk's task. The King had entrusted to him the subjection of the rebellious counties and the punishment of the men with whom he was supposed to sympathise. This is the part of his duty which concerns us at present. The King did not trust to Norfolk alone the establishment of order on the Marches. He had not even explained to him the new arrangements before the Duke set out, but none the less Henry expected Norfolk to help the matter forward. He could not do without his lieutenant, although he did not trust him. Norfolk knew how extremely dangerous this position was. The King asked his advice, and did not take it; the King needed his presence on the Borders for the furtherance of his plans, but he did not confide those plans to the Duke. In Yorkshire Norfolk knew what was expected of him and intended to do it; in Northumberland he was to do nothing without explicit orders.

Norfolk reached Doncaster punctually on Candlemas Eve, 1 February 1536-7. He was met there by the gentlemen whom he could best trust with their servants. Among those who welcomed him were Sir Marmaduke Constable the younger, Sir Robert's son,

[1] L. and P. XII (1), 253.   [2] Ibid. 291.
[3] See below, chap. XXI.

and William Babthorpe, Aske's kinsman. They brought a message to the Duke from Aske, who wished to know if Norfolk desired his presence. Babthorpe wrote that night to Aske that the Duke expected to meet him in York, but not sooner. He was not to be disheartened if the Duke showed him "no very friendly countenance." It would be for certain reasons which would be opened to him in secret. Old Sir Marmaduke Constable, who had lately been at court, was assured that Aske possessed Norfolk's favour and that the King and Council esteemed his services[1].

Aske was only too anxious to believe such assurances. He had spoken to the King, and had been convinced of his graciousness and good faith. He had returned to the north to find the whole country equally convinced that they had been beguiled. He was not unmoved by this; his letters to the King himself show that he was sometimes beset by doubts, but the belief of a man like Aske in one who has secured his loyalty and trust is very hard to shake. When Aske used every means to quiet the agitation, when he declared Bigod's attempt disloyal not only to the King but to the Pilgrims' cause, he was pledging his honour to his followers that the King was true. On that he staked everything, including his life. He clung to his belief and went on hoping against hope until the very end. Yet there was no lack of warning; the matter was plain to all who could look on unconcerned. For example, Ralph Sadler had carried special orders by word of mouth to Sir Thomas Clifford, the captain of Berwick, concerning the Percys. Clifford was first to send them letters from the King which summoned them to his presence; if they did not immediately obey he was to arrest them and send them by sea from Berwick to Grimsby, to avoid the danger of rescue if they passed through the northern shires as prisoners[2].

Sir Thomas Clifford met Sadler at Newcastle-upon-Tyne on 28 January, and was more worried than surprised by these secret instructions. The matter had leaked out, in spite of precautions, and Sir Thomas Hilton had told him a week before that he would be commanded to arrest the Percys. The rumour was bruited abroad in the country, and Clifford knew that if it came to the ears of those most nearly concerned he would be in danger of his life. As he heard that the Percys were preparing to go to meet Norfolk at Doncaster, he sent them the King's letters. They had already set out before the letters arrived, and Clifford was spared further

[1] L. and P. XII (1), 315.
[2] Ibid. 259, 294; the former printed in full, State Papers, I, 533.

embarrassment, and was able to declare that he would have risked everything to carry out the King's commands. The royal letters reached the Percys at Doncaster[1], and with the recklessness of their race Sir Thomas and Sir Ingram obeyed the summons to London. They scarcely needed the Duke's wily encouragement, though he provided them with a letter recommending them to the Council, which, as he was careful to explain in another despatch, was not to be taken seriously[2]. Before the week was out the two brothers were in the Tower. The other leaders of the Pilgrimage did not take alarm. The Percys had behaved with utter lawlessness, and many of their actions could not be connected with forwarding the Pilgrims' demands; moreover the King had special private reasons for wishing them out of the way. Thus, no doubt, Aske and Darcy explained the omen.

Norfolk found the north in no very settled condition when he reached Doncaster. Even in the country round him there was much sedition. He sent Cromwell the rhyming prophecy about "a crumb well set in a man's throat."[3] Bills were posted on the church doors, but they were all of the type described above which called upon the commons to stick together and choose their own leaders, as the gentlemen had betrayed them. The King's policy was a complete success; he had broken up the alliance of rich and poor which had brought him into danger. Norfolk found that he could trust almost all the gentlemen and rich yeomen "which without doubt is most principally for their own safeguards, being in the greatest fear of the people that ever I saw."[4] They forgot all grievances in anxiety for their property, and welcomed Norfolk as a saviour from general anarchy. The Duke was satisfied that all would go well. News of abortive risings came from Cleveland, Sheriffhutton, and Middleham, but in each case the gentlemen had dispersed the rebels without difficulty[5]. The only serious news was from the north and west. Northumberland was a prey to the Border thieves, but they were a separate problem. Cumberland and Westmorland were in commotion; the tithe barns were seized and enclosures were pulled down. A great muster had been ordered at Richmond by the secret leaders of the commons.

Every sort of rumour agitated the country. At Cockermouth the people said that the Duke of Norfolk would never be sent to them,

---

[1] L. and P. xii (1), 319. [2] Ibid. 319, 821. [3] Ibid. 318; see above, chap. iv.
[4] L. and P. xii (1), 337; printed in full, State Papers, 1, 534.
[5] L. and P. xii (1), 319.

for he was in disgrace with the King[1]. In Cleveland it was rumoured that he "came down with a great army and power to do execution, to hang and draw from Doncaster to Berwick...notwithstanding the King's pardon."[2] Norfolk tried to inspire confidence by issuing a proclamation, as Lieutenant-General from Trent northwards, prohibiting all assemblies, ringing of alarm bells, lighting of beacons and setting up of bills on posts and church doors without the King's authority; he set forth that Bigod and other traitors had falsely declared the King's pardon void, assured all men, by the King's express command, that the pardon held good, and offered £40 for the capture of Bigod and £20 each for that of Leache, of Horncastle, Morland of Louth Park, and the friar of St Robert's of Knaresborough[3]. He thought that this proclamation would prevent the threatened disturbances in Richmondshire[4].

Very little can be discovered about the musters at Richmond. The depositions which remain are not so illuminating as they might be, since the government persisted, for its own reasons, in regarding Jervaux Abbey as the headquarters of the agitation. The monks played their part, but the real plotters were shadowy characters who haunted the boundaries of Yorkshire, moving from Richmond to Kirkby Stephen. Nicholas Musgrave and Thomas Tibbey were two of these leaders on the Westmorland side. Lobley, Servant and Hutton sent out the bills from Richmond[5].

On Saturday 3 February the bills and letters which were constantly passing about the country took a more definite tone. These letters came from Richmond and were passed from bailiff to bailiff; they bade every parish send two representatives to meet at the Grey Friars' at Richmond on Monday 5 February, to consult "for the common wealth," and particularly to decide how they should treat with the Duke of Norfolk in the matter of tithes. Collins, the bailiff of Kendal, was very earnest in setting forward the matter in his part of the country, and sent on the summons to Beetham, Windermere, and other parts. The meeting was held, but Norfolk's proclamation had reached Richmond, and the townsfolk refused to have anything to do with the men from other districts. The gentlemen had all gone to meet the Duke, and in consequence there was no one in authority. The leaders of the commons proved

---

[1] L. and P. XII (1), 185; printed in full, Wilson, op. cit. no. XIX.
[2] L. and P. XII (1), 259; printed in full, State Papers, I, 530.
[3] L. and P. XII (1), 322.
[4] Ibid. 337; printed in full, State Papers, I, 534.
[5] L. and P. XII (1), 1012.

incompetent at the last. No conclusion was reached, and the assembly soon dispersed[1].

There are more details about the rising at Jervaux. The Abbot had lost some sheep during the insurrection, and asked Edward Middleton, who had been one of the rebel leaders, to seek for them, "because he was a hunter." About the middle of January he met Middleton in the abbey church and asked for news of the sheep. Middleton said that he had done his best, but he could not find them. "Ye have taken pains, although ye could do no good," said the Abbot, and told his "storer" to give the man some drink money. The storer had no money, and the Abbot sent Middleton to the cellarer, or the quondam Abbot of Fountains who was staying in the house, to ask one of them to pay him[2]. A servant led Middleton and Ninian Staveley, who was with him, to the quondam Abbot's room, and delivered the Abbot's message that the quondam was to give the men forty pence. William Thirsk the quondam abbot took out an angel noble and asked Middleton to change it. Staveley snatched it and said it was cracked. The quondam gave him another and bade him change that; but Staveley calmly put the two nobles in his purse, saying, "Ye churls monks, ye have too much and we have nothing, and neither of these thou gettest again." "Ye shall not have my money so," cried the quondam, "If ye be true men ye will not take my money away, and ye should have but forty pence of me." Middleton interfered, whispering that Staveley was mad and that he would see the quondam's money restored, and so they left him[3]. According to Staveley the quondam Abbot offered them twenty nobles to restore him to Fountains if there was a new insurrection. This may be true or it may not. Staveley's excuse for his violence was that two of the monks of Jervaux, Roger Hartlepool and John Stainton, had been urging both himself and Middleton to raise a company, fall upon the Duke of Norfolk, and slay him, for they said that if Norfolk were allowed to come peaceably "their abbey would be put down and they would go a-begging." The stories about the two nobles and the thirty sheep point to the conclusion that Staveley and his friend were the men to entrust with such a desperate scheme, and that they probably knew all the bad characters in the Dales.

In January the Abbot of Jervaux had sent a servant to gather the Abbey's rents in Lincolnshire; the man was also to tarry about Newark until the Duke came and bring back word as to how large a force he brought with him. The servant did not wait long enough to

[1] L. and P. XII (1), 914, 959, 965.   [2] Ibid. 1035.   [3] Ibid. 1023 (ii).

see the Duke's train, but he returned with the news "that the Lincolnshire men were busily hanged, and their charter stood them in no stead," and that Norfolk was coming to do the same in the north. This spread dismay in the country[1]. Lord Latimer left his house at Snape and with Sir Christopher Danby set out for the court, which alarmed the commons, who were always ready to listen to the cry that the gentlemen were betraying them, and at the same time removed the men best able to keep order. The people were so angry that they were ready to plunder the houses of the absentees[2].

When the news came that Norfolk had reached Doncaster, Staveley and his accomplices determined to take action. On Sunday 4 February they set up bills, provided by the two monks, on every church door in Richmondshire, commanding every man between the ages of 16 and 20 to be at Middleham Moor in harness on Tuesday next (6 February). On Monday the leaders quarrelled among themselves, and the whole matter would have fallen through, if the two monks had not come to Staveley's bed at midnight, in harness with battle-axes in their hands, and called upon him to rise and go forward or else they would all be destroyed[3]. Staveley sent to Middleton and they called together their friends and went to Jervaux Abbey about midday. They bade the Abbot come forth with all his brethren and go with them to the muster; but "the Abbot said and desired them to be contented to leave his brethren at home and to take his servants with them, and said further that he and all his brethren would come unto them next day. And then he gave the company such meat and drink as he had." The muster at Middleham Moor was poorly attended. Staveley and his band, the Abbot's servants, and a few of the Abbot's tenants of Witton were the only companies mentioned as being present. The leaders stayed there two or three hours, but when news came of the failure of the meeting at Richmond on the day before they all went home[4]. The Abbot of Jervaux fled next day to Lord Scrope at Bolton Castle; there is no proof that he knew of the plans of his monks. Middleton and Roger Hartlepool the monk fled to Scotland, thereby showing more prudence than the majority of the captains[5].

On Sunday 4 February Norfolk was at Pontefract. In spite of the unruly state of the north-west he was in good spirits, and trusted soon to have it in more quietness. As long as the gentlemen were so thoroughly afraid of their own tenants there was no chance of serious

[1] L. and P. xii (1), 1012.   [2] Ibid. 173.   [3] Ibid. 1012.
[4] Ibid. 1035; see not A at end of chapter.   [5] L. and P. xii (1), 1012.

rebellion¹. Lord Latimer had been appointed to meet Norfolk in York, "but he liked so ill his being at home" that he came to meet the Duke at Doncaster. Lord Conyers was in doubt as to whether his people would let him leave home at all. None of the gentlemen dared attempt to turn the religious out of the restored abbeys; Norfolk could hardly persuade them to pursue the leaders of the late commotions, not because they sympathised with them, but because they were afraid the people would attack them².

All the country about Pontefract was in good order when Norfolk arrived³. Darcy took some pride in this, but really it told against him. If he could keep his country quiet when he liked, why had he failed on the first rising? When Norfolk reached the castle, he found himself in the middle of a family quarrel. Lord Darcy had come up from Templehurst to meet him, and had joined issue with Sir George Darcy, whom he found in possession. Lord Darcy refused to share his authority with his son; he would be the sole keeper of the castle or not at all. Sir George had the King's orders and would not give way unless the Duke commanded him to do so. In the end Norfolk decided in favour of Darcy, who undertook to lie in the castle himself and put the King to no expense; but Sir George was to be ready to come in with all his power at an hour's warning. Norfolk trusted Sir George, who would serve the King against his father and all the world. "I pray God the father be as good in heart as the son, which by the proof only I shall believe."⁴

Norfolk went on to York, probably on Monday 5 February. Here he was met by almost all the gentlemen of Yorkshire, the very men who had held the council there as leaders of the Pilgrimage two months before. The oath was administered in the Duke's presence to the head men of the city and of all the three Ridings; it was taken without the least dissent or opposition. The gentlemen were to carry back the oath to the districts which Norfolk did not intend to visit, but it was by no means certain that the business would be accomplished so quietly in those parts. He wrote to the King on 7 February from York, where he was to sit on the indictments of eighteen persons, spiritual and temporal, on Saturday 10 February; he thought that many would be found guilty and trusted shortly to have more⁵. On Friday the 9th, in the midst of his session work, he found time to answer a letter from Cromwell. He was glad to receive Cromwell's assurances of friendship, and begged that he might soon

---
¹ L. and P. XII (1), 336. ² Ibid. 337; printed in full, State Papers, I, 534.
³ L. and P. XII (1), 349. ⁴ Ibid. 362. ⁵ Ibid.

hear good news of his various suits and causes. In order to show that the friendship was not all on one side, he narrated how he had "caused one of the sheriff's officers to be set in the pillory and for ever put out of office for speaking ill of Cromwell. If the matter would have served by law he should, on Tuesday next, have stretched a halter with others."[1]

On Saturday 10 February Sir Francis Bigod was taken by Sir John Lamplough and a party which Norfolk had sent out to capture him on information received from Sir Thomas Curwen[2]. Bigod was seized in "a chapel in Cumberland" with two servants[3], and was taken to Carlisle Castle to await Norfolk's orders, as his captors did not dare to bring him through Westmorland. The circumstances of his pursuit and arrest are unknown, as they were reported to the King by word of mouth[4].

On Monday 12 February nine prisoners were arraigned before Norfolk in York for treason. There was not yet enough evidence to convict the rest, who remained in prison. Of the nine who were condemned, one named Graystoke was "reprieved by desire of all the gentlemen." Norfolk sent Cromwell a list of the others, with the places where they were to be executed. There were three religious, two canons of Warter who were hanged in chains in York, and the sub-prior of Watton, who suffered at Watton. Wyvell was hanged at Scarborough, and Fenton and Cante in York. A yeoman called Otterburn had been the leader of an obscure rising at Sheriffhutton some days before, and was hanged on Yersley Moor five miles from Sheriffhutton[5]. Another man, not named on Norfolk's list, seems to have been executed at the same time. He was one Stokton who had brought treasonable bills to Guisborough, "but would not say how he came by them when he was hanged."[6] Finally, as Staveley, Middleton and the other Richmond leaders were not yet caught, Anthony Peacock was hanged in chains on Richmond Moor as a warning to the district. He had been stirring the people about Barnard Castle[7].

On Thursday 15 February Peacock was in Richmond waiting for his death. That night half-a-dozen boon companions met at John of Blade's alehouse in the little village of Grinton in Swaledale. Among them was Harry Wycliff, Sir Ralph Bulmer's servant and brother-in-law. While they were drinking he turned to the others and exclaimed,

---

[1] L. and P. xii (1), 381. [2] Ibid. 401.
[3] Wilfred Holme, The Downfall of Rebellion. [4] L. and P. xii (1), 401.
[5] Ibid. 416 (2).   [6] Ibid. 1088.   [7] Ibid. 416 (2).

"Sirs, what mean ye? Is your hearts done? Let me have 200 men and I shall give the Duke of Norfolk an onset, and I shall either save Peacock's life or have the Duke's chain (meaning to have slain him) ...with many other such seditious words, meaning to make a new commotion." No one was ready to aid him in such a desperate attempt, though the men of Swaledale were Sir Francis Bigod's tenants and no doubt sympathised with the rebels. Peacock was hanged next morning and no hand was raised to save him[1].

Norfolk intended to turn his attention next to the restored abbeys. He mentioned, in a letter to the Earl of Sussex, that the gentlemen did not dare to meddle with them. When Sussex showed the letter to the King, Henry was especially interested in this point. He said that the gentlemen had undertaken at Doncaster to restore his farmers to the abbeys; "he saw not but if the gentlemen had broken promise with him, he might much better break promise with them." He left the matter vague, however, saying that if all went forward satisfactorily he would not "take any advantage thereof."[2]

Cromwell spurred Norfolk on by hinting that he was thought to be too warm a supporter of the old faith to deal sternly with the abbeys and "the traitors therein." Norfolk indignantly repudiated the accusation; he was no "papist nor favourer of naughty religious persons." In the north his feelings were now so well known that he had been warned not to eat or drink in monasteries[3]. He was going to Leeds on Tuesday 20 February, thence to Sawley Abbey, and then to Ripon[4]. As he would be very busy, he suggested that the ordinary justices of assize, whose arrival was almost due, should be joined in a commission with the Earls of Cumberland and Westmorland. He thought it very necessary to have someone to help him with the law work, for his health was bad, and it would be a pity if the "dreadful execution" begun at York were not carried out in other places. Norfolk was constantly expecting news of the arrest of more ringleaders. "As concerning the monks of Sawley and other abbeys I cannot yet speak of their offences but ere Sunday I doubt not to do so." The leaders in Westmorland were Nicholas Musgrave and Thomas Tibbey, "whom I trust be taken by this time."[5]

These two men upset Norfolk's plans. Ever since Christmas there had been trouble in Westmorland[6]. On Twelfth Day, 6 January 1536-7, the deputy captain of Carlisle, Thomas Clifford the bastard,

---

[1] L. and P. XII (1), 775.
[2] Ibid. 416.
[3] Ibid. 416.
[4] Ibid. 378.
[5] Ibid. 408.
[6] See above, chap. XVII.

came to Kirkby Stephen to arrest Nicholas Musgrave. Musgrave was warned and with Thomas Tibbey he took refuge in the church steeple, so defensible a position that Clifford was obliged to withdraw without his prisoners, " which thing stirred the country greatly. And they sent abroad word to keep watches in every town." The men of Kirkby Stephen plucked down all the enclosures in their parish, and sent orders to the surrounding parishes to follow their example[1].

In Cumberland things were no better. The west parts " from Plumland to Muncaster is all on floughter," wrote Sir Thomas Curwen[2]. The chief reason for the agitation was the departure of so many gentlemen to court. The commons distrusted the King, who might have the gentlemen beheaded, and they distrusted the gentlemen, who might betray them to the King. When the gentlemen were away, the bailiffs and other officers found it impossible to keep order[3]. As soon as he knew the state of affairs, Norfolk urged Cromwell to send home the Cumberland gentlemen. Sir Thomas Curwen told a story which showed the feelings of the commons. On Saturday 13 January a servant of Dr Legh came to Muncaster. The whole country rose and made him prisoner. He was carried to Egremont and thence to Cockermouth. A great crowd filled the market-place, crying, " Strike off his head!" and "Stick him!" He was searched for letters from the King, but all that were found on him were from his master about private matters. Nevertheless he would have been put to death; but young John Swinburn saved him, by advising the people to spare him for a week, during which inquiries should be made about his conduct. At the end of the week twenty-four men might try him in open market, and if it could be proved that he had carried letters from the King to the gentlemen, he might be put to death. The people agreed and sent through all the countryside to inquire if he had delivered letters. Whether he was brought to trial or not he must have escaped death, as nothing more is heard of him. On 18 January all the tithe barns on the south bank of the Derwent were plundered. Private feuds were pursued as vigorously as public grievances. Sir Thomas Curwen fled to Yorkshire because the commons had determined to take him and force him to take the oath or die. He went first to Sheriffhutton, then to Richmond and finally to York, meeting with many seditious bills on the way[4].

---

[1] L. and P. xii (1), 687 (2); printed in full, Wilson, op. cit. no. xxii.
[2] L. and P. xii (1), 185; printed in full, Wilson, op. cit. no. xix.
[3] L. and P. xii (1), 386.
[4] L. and P. xii (1), 185; printed in full, Wilson, op. cit. no. xix.

Norfolk sent orders to Carlisle for the apprehension of Musgrave and Tibbey[1], and accordingly Thomas Clifford set out again for Kirkby Stephen in search of them with a troop of horse. His followers were mosstroopers from the waters of Esk and Line, "strong thieves of the westlands." Musgrave and Tibbey fled to their old fastness in the steeple, and there defied their pursuers. The townsfolk took no part either for or against the rebels, but while Clifford and some of his men were debating how to take their quarry, the rest of the riders, following their inbred vocation, fell to plundering. This was more than flesh and blood could bear. The burgesses caught up their weapons and fell upon the spoilers, causing a timely diversion in favour of the men in the steeple. Scattered about the narrow streets of the town, the horsemen were at a disadvantage and soon showed that their prowess was not equal to their thievishness. Two of the townsmen were killed in the skirmish, but their enraged fellows drove the borderers from the town and followed up their retreat until they were forced to take refuge in Brougham Castle[2].

The commons saw that they were committed to a new rebellion, although they had risen in defence of their property; indeed, a panic seems to have spread through the countryside that they would all be treated like the people of Kirkby Stephen. The two captains raised all the surrounding country and sent the following summons to the bailiff of Kendal, whom they knew to be on their side:

To the Constable of Mellynge

Be yt knowen unto you Welbelovyd bretheren in god this same xii day of februarii at morn was unbelapped on every syde with our enimys the Captayne of Carlylle and gentylmen of our Cuntrie of Westmerlonde and haithe destrowed and slayn many our bretheren and neghtbers. Wherfore we desyre you for ayde and helpe accordyng to your othes and as ye wyll have helpe of us if your cause requyre, as god forbede. this tuysday, We comande you every one to be at Kendall afore Eight of the clok or els we ar lykly to be destrowed.

Ever more gentyll brether unto your helpyng honds.

Captayn of Povertie.

[*Note at the top of the sheet.*] the like letter was sent to bethom by colyns which we sent in our letters to the kinges highnes from preston xxi march[3].

William Collins, the bailiff of Kendal, had just returned from York, where he and other men from the town had met Norfolk[4]. The whole country was stirring. Atkinson, Musgrave, Leache and Staveley were issuing such bills as the one given above, urging the

---

[1] L. and P. xii (1), 416 (2).
[2] Ibid. 411, from original at P. R. O.
[3] Ibid. 419, 439, 687 (2).
[4] Ibid. 914.

people "that they should come and take their neighbours of Westmorland's part." Collins forwarded such letters to the surrounding townships.

Nothing is known of the musters and counsels of the Westmorland rebels. No gentlemen joined their ranks and very few priests. Their plans were simple. They had long before decided that the first step in case of a new rebellion was to seize Carlisle[1]. A new motive for this was added by the fact that Bigod was a prisoner in the castle[2]. The idea of a rescue always appeals to the human heart, and though a week before everyone had been cursing Bigod, now that he was captured and his fate assured there was a reaction in his favour. After all, everything that he had prophesied had come to pass. Here was the Duke "busily hanging" at York; here were loyal subjects robbed and slain in spite of the pardon.

The town of Carlisle was little prepared to stand a siege. The walls were out of repair and the garrison, though loyal, was not strong[3]. The gentlemen coming in with their own servants, however, soon formed a force of five hundred or so within the city, and these troops were much superior in arms and equipment to the six thousand commons who presently assembled outside the walls. The rebels carried a cross as "their banner principal."[4] There was not a single gentleman amongst them, but though their leaders were poor yeomen, they did not lack determination, and were for the most part men already outlawed for their share in earlier risings. They were in hopes of capturing men of position, and it was said that one of the Percys would join them with a strong company. The rumours of taxes on christenings and burials were repeated among them and had perhaps only now reached these shires, the most remote in the kingdom[5].

Norfolk was at Fountains when the news of the outbreak reached him on Wednesday 14 February. He wrote to the King, and set to work to raise a sufficient force to march against the rebels[6]. He thought that he would be ready to set out on Saturday. On Thursday and Friday he was at Richmond, calling in to him all the nobles and gentlemen, but not daring to muster the commons. He was determined not to risk defeat, and laid several plans. He sent Sir Thomas Wharton, Sir Thomas Curwen and other Westmorland gentlemen

---

[1] L. and P. xii (1), 185; printed in full, Wilson, op. cit. no. xix.
[2] Wilfred Holme, The Downfall of Rebellion.   [3] L. and P. xii (1), 71, 72.
[4] Wilfred Holme, op. cit.   [5] L. and P. xii (1), 520.
[6] Ibid. 419.

back to their own estates to persuade their tenants, if possible, to take the King's part. They were to be joined by two or three hundred light horse when Norfolk could spare the men, and were to burn and plunder the rebels' houses, in the hope of making them abandon Carlisle and return to defend their own goods. Norfolk was not a little pleased at the prospect of fighting, even under the difficulties which burdened him. It was true that " this journey will pluck the bottom out of my purse," but he trusted to bring the realm to better quiet. "Now shall appear whether for favour of these countrymen I forbare to fight with them at Doncaster."[1]

The success or failure of the new insurrection depended upon the part taken by Lord Dacre's tenants. They had not yet risen for the commons; the Dacres, if they chose, could raise them for the King. Lord Dacre was in the south, but his uncle Sir Christopher Dacre was at Gilsland and wielded authority in his nephew's absence. During the first insurrection the Dacres had remained loyal, but had not taken an active part. Their conduct had been most circumspect, for they lay under suspicion of treason. Their one offence had been an outbreak of the feud with the Cliffords and Musgraves. Was Sir Christopher's loyalty strong enough to urge him to rescue his blood-foes now pent by the commons within Carlisle? The Earl of Cumberland had been ordered by the King to reconcile himself with Dacre, but these official hand-shakings went for nothing.

Norfolk showed his fears in a letter to Sir Christopher dated 15 February. The commons were about to assault Carlisle, and Norfolk conjured him by their old friendship, by his hopes of the King's favour, by his care for his nephew's safety to come to the relief of the city. "I will not instruct you what ye shall do, for ye know better than I. Spare for no reasonable wages, for I will pay all." Let him but prove the Duke's saying that "Sir Christopher Dacre is a true knight to his sovereign lord, an hardy knight, and a man of war. Pinch now no courtesy to shed blood of false traitors; and be ye busy on the one side, and ye may be sure the Duke of Norfolk will come on the other. Finally now, Sir Christopher, or never." He signed it "your loving cousin if ye do well now, or else enemy for ever."[2] Two copies of this letter were sent by different hands to insure its safe delivery[3].

On the same day, 15 February, the captains of Carlisle were also

---

[1] L. and P. xii (1), 439.
[2] Ibid. 426; printed in full, Raine, Mem. of Hexham Priory (Surtees Soc.), i, Append. p. cxlix.   [3] L. and P. xii (1), 439.

writing to Sir Christopher, but their letter was much calmer than Norfolk's. Men in a desperate strait do not let their enemy know that he alone can save them. They commanded Dacre, in the King's name, to join them at Carlisle Castle with all the men he could trust "in goodly haste." If he could trust "the prickers of Gilsland," he was to leave "the landserjeant" with them to attack the rebels, but if the prickers would not fight for the King, he must bring the landserjeant with him, and in any case he must come to Carlisle himself. This was signed by Sir John Lowther, Thomas Clifford, and John Barnfield[1].

Unfortunately there is no account of the rising written from the commons' point of view, nor, indeed, any full contemporary account at all. It is extremely difficult to form a coherent idea of the fighting round Carlisle from the scattered references which remain. The first move of the commons is clear. On Friday 16 February they mustered on Broadfield Moor to the number of about 6000 men, more or less effectively armed and mounted; thence they marched to Carlisle.

A wanderer came to the Abbey of Holm Cultram, and the Abbot asked him "What news?" "There was never such a gathering to the Broadfield as there was that day afore," said the other. "Almighty God prosper them, for if they speed not, this abbey is lost," said the Abbot. He sent his servants out in haste to summon his tenants to the Abbey church, and called the subprior to him, "and commanded him to cause the brethren to go daily with procession to speed the commons' journey." All the men of the lordship of Holm assembled in the church. The Abbot came to them and in the commons' name bade Cuthbert Musgrave, his deputy officer, ride to Broadfield at the head of the tenants and join the host there. Musgrave refused to go, and argued the point with the Abbot. The tenants declared that they would not go unless the Abbot went with them. "And so they departed and none went." The Abbot had enemies among his own brethren; he had compromised himself past hope before them, and he had not even helped the cause[2].

On Saturday 17 February the commons prepared for the assault on Carlisle. It does not seem to have been such a vigorous attack as the word now implies. They approached within bow-shot, and showered arrows on the defenders who appeared on the city walls. This went on until they exhausted their supply of arrows, when they retired

---

[1] L. and P. xii (1), 427.
[2] Ibid. 1259; printed in full, Wilson, op. cit. nos. xxiv–xxvii.

a little way to consider what to do next. Perhaps they had actually advanced to the attack when Sir Christopher Dacre unexpectedly appeared with five hundred border-spearmen. The commons broke and turned to fly; whereupon Thomas Clifford issued from the castle and fell upon them, pressing on the pursuit for twelve miles or more. His mosstroopers were in no mood to spare the countryfolk who had beaten them so ignominiously on Monday[1].

Several heroes on the King's side distinguished themselves. One Roger Middlewood, who had been in the Kirkby Stephen skirmish and there was taken prisoner and stripped, "was the first man out of the town and slew one with his own hand."[2] But his honour was challenged by Robin Grame, a noted spy in Scotland, who, with only two other men, had been skirmishing with the commons before the assault, and "continued crying and shouting at them more than one hour before any man came to help him." He was one of the last to turn back from the pursuit[3]. Others of his name won no less praise. The Grahams of Esk, four brothers, "proper men," had come in with half their grayne to serve in the castle without wages. "Whosoever take the thank, these were the first that break spear on the rebels after the assault."[4] They were foremost in the chase, captured seven score rebels and one of the captains, who seems to have been Thomas Tibbey himself. On the strength of these services they afterwards petitioned the King that they might hold their lands on the Esk rent-free, as their father did before them[5].

On Saturday 17 February Norfolk was at Barnard Castle, where the gentlemen of his train had mustered their servants and head tenants—everyone, in short, whom they could trust. The Duke was overjoyed with the army which had assembled; there were about 4000 men, all well tried, harnessed, and mounted on "the best geldings he ever saw." Their only anxiety was to atone for their former fault; such a band would be fearful for the King's enemies to look upon. Hardly was this splendid little army in array, when news came from Carlisle which showed that it would not be needed. Before 9 o'clock in the morning messengers rode in who had seen the assault upon Carlisle and the rout of the commons. The chase was not ended when the messengers set out. Norfolk wrote to Henry: "Your Highness hath as much cause to thank God as ever had prince. Sir

---

[1] Wilfred Holme, op. cit.; L. and P. xii (1), 448, 478–9, 520; see note B at end of chapter.   [2] L. and P. xii (1), 992.
[3] Ibid. 1216.   [4] Ibid. 1215.
[5] Ibid. 1217 (1) and (2); (2) printed in full, Raine, op. cit. i, Append. p. clx.

Christopher Dacre has shown himself a noble knight." Seven or eight hundred prisoners were taken and the Duke was about to travel in all haste to Carlisle to see execution done[1]. The rejoicings in London were great. Sir Christopher Dacre was the hero of the hour. It was said that he had slain 700 rebels or more and taken the rest prisoners, hanging them up on every bush. Cromwell declared at court that "if it lay in him he would make him an earl."[2]

This magnificent victory was won over the wretched, desperate commons of the poorest shire in the realm, fighting in defence of their property and lives. There is no means of knowing how many were killed, as the number reported in London, 700, seems to be too large. Wilfred Holme estimated that 300 prisoners were taken, and this seems a more likely figure than the 800 reported to Norfolk. The victory was certainly decisive; in defeat more than at any other time strong captains are needed; the leaderless commons of Westmorland and Cumberland were utterly broken.

Norfolk was in Carlisle on Monday 19 February. There were so many prisoners in the town that he found great difficulty in providing for their safe-keeping. He wrote that night to the Council to promise that if he might go his own way for a month he would order things to the King's satisfaction. It would take some time, because he must himself be present at all the convictions and proceed by martial law, and there were many places to punish. Not a lord or gentleman in Cumberland and Westmorland could claim that his servants and tenants had not joined in the insurrection. "And, good Mr Comptroller[3], provide you of a new bailiff at Embleton, for John Jackson your bailiff will be hanged Thursday or Friday at the furthest."[4]

Norfolk wrote to Cromwell with assurances that if he did not at once proceed to "sore justice" it was for no love he bore the traitors, but for reasons evident to anyone on the spot, but too long to be explained. Nevertheless more should suffer "than should do if I would believe so many were compelled to rebellion as is showed me....I was never so well-beloved here as I shall be feared if I live another month." No doubt Norfolk trusted by the last suggestion to please the King, who was always jealous of popular noblemen[5].

Amidst all his business Norfolk found time to examine Sir Francis Bigod and "communed with him at great leisure." Bigod said very little, and Norfolk sent up his first confession to Cromwell, promising

[1] L. and P. xii (1), 448.
[2] Ibid. 492.
[3] Sir Wm. Paulet.
[4] L. and P. xii (1), 468.
[5] Ibid. 469.

that the prisoner should be strictly interrogated from time to time[1]. Sir Francis' examinations are not now extant, but there is a summary of his evidence[2]. He said nothing against Darcy, Constable, and Aske, which must have vexed the authorities.

Norfolk issued proclamations which commanded all who had been in rebellion to come to Carlisle and submit themselves humbly to the King's mercy. Accordingly on Tuesday 20 February the country-people began to straggle into the city in scattered, dejected bands. They had lost their horses, harness, and weapons in the chase; they were in instant fear of a traitor's death for themselves, and of fire, plunder, and outrage for their homes and families. Norfolk imprisoned seventy of the "chief misdoers," that is of the braver and more determined of them, and turned the rest away without even a promise of pardon; but he dared not proceed to execution until all the country had submitted. He sent orders to the Earl of Derby and Lord Mounteagle in Lancashire to apprehend all who might flee in that direction; in Durham the Earl of Westmorland had made thirteen prisoners, not fugitives, but men who favoured the rebels; thus there was no encouragement to try to escape eastward[3].

Norfolk's strategy was successful. Every day more and more of the "poor caitiffs" came in from all districts of Westmorland and Cumberland, even Cockermouth, the wildest part of all. They were contrite enough to satisfy any tyrant, "and if sufficient number of ropes might have been found would have come with the same about their necks." Seventy-four out of six thousand who submitted were selected for trial. A Cumberland jury had not then attained the bad name which it earned long afterwards, and Norfolk, though a master of the art of choosing juries, dared not trust one with the work in hand, lest "many a great offender" were acquitted. He appointed Sir Ralph Ellerker as marshal and Robert Bowes King's attorney to prosecute. This must have been a sufficient humiliation for the Pilgrims' ambassadors to the King.

All the prisoners were condemned to die by law martial, the King's banner being displayed. Not the fifth part would have been convicted by a jury. Some protested that they had been dragged into rebellion against their will. The most part had only one plea, saying, "I came out for fear of my life, and I came forth for fear of loss of all my goods, and I came forth for fear of burning of my house and destroying of my wife and children."[4] They had not,

---
[1] L. and P. XII (1), 473.   [2] Ibid. 532.   [3] Ibid. 478.
[4] Ibid. 498; printed in full, Wilson, op. cit. no. xx.

in fact, turned against the law, they had risen to defend all that the law should have defended for them from Clifford's police, the thieves of the Black Lands[1]. "A small excuse will be well believed here, where much affection and pity of neighbours doth reign. And, sir, though the number be nothing so great as their deserts did require to have suffered, yet I think the like number hath not been heard of put to execution at one time." Thus Norfolk wrote to the King; his chief anxiety was lest it should be thought that he had not put a sufficient number to death. He assured his master that every man who had taken a forward part in the rising was to suffer. He had done his best, helped by Sir Christopher Dacre, Sir Thomas Wharton, Sir Thomas Curwen, Sir John Lamplough and the other gentlemen, to try out sufficient matter against more of the prisoners; little as was needed, he had failed, though he still hoped to swell his numbers with some who had fled or were in hiding[2].

No time was lost over the executions, as Norfolk was in haste to be in Northumberland, where Tynedale and Reedsdale were giving trouble. The rebels were hanged in their own villages, " in trees in their gardens to record for memorial " the end of the rebellion[3]. Twelve were hanged in chains in Carlisle for the assault on the city, eleven at Appleby, eight at Penrith, five at Cockermouth and Kirkby Stephen, and so on; scarcely a moorland parish but could show one or two such memorials. Some were hanged in ropes, for iron was "marvellous scarce," and the chain-makers of Carlisle were unable to meet the demand. The victims were all poor men, farm hands from the fields and artisans of the little towns; probably the bailiff of Embleton was the highest man among them. Only one priest suffered with them, a chaplain of Penrith. The government's conviction that the clergy were at the bottom of the new rising was mistaken; Norfolk, with the best will in the world, could only implicate one priest, but he made the vicar of Brough-under-Stainmore prisoner, although he had done nothing unlawful since the pardon, except that he had prayed for the Pope. Norfolk wished to know the King's pleasure as to whether he must suffer or not[4].

Later times have seen assizes more bloody than Norfolk's in Carlisle—Sussex' in York after the Rising of the North—Jeffreys' in the west country after Monmouth's rebellion. The horror of the Carlisle assizes lies less in their cruelty than in their injustice. Those

---

[1] L. and P. xii (1), 489.   [2] Ibid. 498.
[3] Wilfred Holme, op. cit.
[4] L. and P. xii (1), 498; printed in full, Wilson, op. cit. no. xx.

who take up arms for a political cause must look to be punished for political reasons, but what principle can condemn men miserably poor for defending the little they have ? The judges knew well that they were doing an indefensible act, and they spared the people as far as they dared. This is the final indictment of Henry's government, that his greatest nobleman hanged men whom he knew to be guilty only of having turned against intolerable oppression. Norfolk wrote to Cromwell : " What with the spoiling of them now and the gressing of them so marvellously sore in time past and with increasing of lords' rents by enclosing, and for lack of the persons of such as shall suffer, this border is sore weaked and especially Westmorland; the more pity they should so deserve, and also that they have been so sore handled in times past, which, as I and all other here think, was the only cause of the rebellion."[1] Perhaps Norfolk told his conscience (if it ever troubled him) that another man would have made more sure of the King's favour by greater severity.

When the news of the rebels' defeat reached the King, he sent orders for the harshest measures to be enforced. His instructions have been quoted so often that a summary of them is sufficient here. First the King thanked all who had served him, especially Norfolk and Sir Christopher Dacre ; " you shall have good cause to rejoice of your doing in that behalf." He heartily approved of Norfolk's declaration of martial law, and his banner was not to be closed until the country was in such fear as would insure better behaviour.

Bigod, the Friar of Knaresborough, Leache, " the vicar of Penrith," Chancellor Towneley and Pickering of Bridlington or as many of them as were in Norfolk's hands, were to be sent to the King. The lands and goods of these and any other traitors who owned such were to be seized, and the King would consider the question of rewarding faithful subjects with them.

Finally Norfolk was to proceed to Sawley, Hexham, Newminster, Lanercost, St Agatha's at Richmond, and such other monasteries as had " made any manner of resistance," and to cause the monks or canons found faulty " to be tied up, without further delay or ceremony, to the terrible example of others ; wherein we think you shall do us high service."[2] This is one of the most famous commands King Henry ever gave, and nobody knows whether it was obeyed. This ignorance is due to the fact that from 24 February to 5 March there is a blank in Norfolk's correspondence with the King. The

---

[1] L. and P. XII (1), 478.
[2] Ibid. 479; printed in full, State Papers, I, 537, and Raine, op. cit. I, Append. p. cl.

Duke intended to ride from Carlisle to Hexham, there to suppress the Abbey, take order for Tynedale and Reedsdale, hear any cases of sedition in Northumberland, and take the oaths of the gentlemen. From Hexham he meant to go to Durham and thence to York, "sitting in execution" at both cities[1].

His own account of this expedition is lost. He did not go to Newminster in Northumberland, for it was not suppressed until August 1537, when all the monks received pensions[2]. It is not known why the King named it as a centre of sedition. Nothing is known about the fate of Lanercost Priory and its inmates, nor about that of St Agatha's at Richmond. Sawley was suppressed by Norfolk's orders, though not by the Duke in person, and the Abbot and some of the monks were executed[3]. Norfolk went to Hexham, but in his next letters, from Newcastle-upon-Tyne, there is no account of what he did there. A letter to Cromwell about the suppression of Hexham Priory exists, however, and as there is no mention in it of the "tying up" of any monks, it is probable that Henry's orders arrived too late, that Norfolk had already closed the King's banner in token that martial law was ended, and that he therefore had a sufficient excuse for sparing the canons.

A fragment of Norfolk's reply to the King's famous letter has been preserved by a Cumberland historian, although the original is lost. No doubt if it still existed the problem of the monks' fate would be solved, for if martial law was no longer in force Norfolk would have no power of summary execution. The remains of the letter are as follows:

"Aglionby, I doubt not, or now hath shewed you highness what was done at Carlisle. And though none were quartered because I knew not your pleasure therein before: yet all the threescore and fourteen be hanged in chains or ropes upon gallows or trees, in all such towns as they did dwell in. And whereas your Majesty would have sent the vicar of Penrith to you; it is not of Penrith, but of Brough that your grace doth mean, for there is none such; for whom I have sent to my lord of Cumberland, for I left him in his keeping. And also I have for Doctor Towneley, and doubt not within three days to have them both with me, and so shall send them up."[4]

In order to conclude the matter of the rebellion in Cumberland, it is necessary to look forward for some weeks. Sir Thomas Curwen, the sheriff of Cumberland, received anonymous letters accusing the Abbot

---

[1] L. and P. xii (1), 498; printed in full, Wilson, op. cit. no. xx.
[2] Gasquet, op. cit. ii, chap. iv.   [3] See below.
[4] Nicolson and Burn, op. cit. i, p. 569; see Wilson, op. cit. p. 14 n.

of Holm Cultram of treason. With Sir Thomas Wharton and others he paid a secret visit to the Abbey on 22 May 1537, collected enough evidence to hang the Abbot, and forwarded it to Norfolk. As usual the Abbot's fate is uncertain[1].

The Cumberland magistrates were no doubt trying to regain Norfolk's favour by their zeal in the case of the Abbot, because they had incurred his displeasure in another matter. Two months after the Duke's session in Carlisle, he heard that the bodies of all the rebels who were executed had been cut down and buried. He rebuked the magistrates with "quick messages," and ordered them to search out the ill-doers. They sent him nine or ten confessions in reply, but he did not consider these nearly enough. "It is a small number concerning seventy-four that hath been taken down, wherein I think your Majesty hath not been well served." Norfolk asked the King on 8 May how these offenders were to be punished; they were all women—the widows, mothers and daughters of the dead men. Of all the records these brief confessions are the most heart-breaking and can least bear description. The widows and their neighbours helped each other. Seven or eight women together would wind the corpse and bury it in the nearest churchyard, secretly, at nightfall or daybreak. Sometimes they were turned from their purpose by the frightened priest, and then the husband's body must be buried by a dyke-side out of sanctified ground, or else brought again more secretly than ever and laid in the churchyard under cover of night. All was done by women, save in two cases when the brother and cousin of two of the dead men were said to have died from the "corruption" of the bodies they had cut down[2]. The Earl of Cumberland was blamed by Norfolk for the loss of the bodies, and it must be counted to the Earl's credit that he was ashamed to look too closely into so pitiful a story. Norfolk wrote to Cromwell:

"I do perceive by your letter that ye would know whether such persons as were put to execution in Westmorland and Cumberland were taken down and buried by my commandment or not: undoubtedly, my good lord, if I had consented thereunto, I would I had hanged by them; but on my troth, it is 8 or 9 days past sith I heard first thereof, and then was here with me a servant of my lord of Cumberland's called Swalowfield dwelling about Penrith, by whom I sent such a quick message to my said lord, because he hath the rule in Cumberland as warden, and is sheriff of Westmorland and hath neither advertised me thereof, nor hath not made search who hath so highly offended his Majesty,

---

[1] L. and P. xii (1), 1259; printed in full, Wilson, op. cit. nos. xxiv–xxvii, and Raine, op. cit. i, Append. p. cliv; see note C at end of chapter.
  L. and P. xii (1), 1214 (2), 1246.

and also commanding him to search for the same with all diligence, that I doubt not it shall evidently appear it was done against my will."[1]

The Duke was anxious to shift the blame on to someone else's shoulders, as the King was very angry at this defiance of his authority. He remarked characteristically that he did not believe it "had come of women's heads only," although the depositions do not mention the names of any living men concerned in it. On 22 May Cromwell insinuated that Norfolk must have countenanced the offenders, and sent most positive orders that somebody must be punished, but the fate of the women is unknown[2].

To return to the main course of our narrative, Norfolk was at Hexham on Monday 26 February. There he met Sir Reynold Carnaby, the farmer of the Priory, and put him in possession. The canons were turned out "with very good exhortation to the inhabitants" of Hexham uttered by Norfolk. With the Duke and his train in their midst they were "very tractable and sorry for what they had done amiss." They professed themselves ready to obey Carnaby "as their officer," when they saw Cromwell's orders to that effect, though without these he was likely to have been "discouraged." Norfolk asked him if the canons had done anything contrary to their allegiance since the pardon. Carnaby answered, "No, otherwise I would have been an untrue man to conceal it."[3] Sir Reynold was already held in evil report among his neighbours, and if he had informed against the canons his life would not have been safe. The people of the neighbourhood loved their Priory, and to this day Carnaby is spoken of with hatred in the countryside.

From Hexham Norfolk went to Newcastle-upon-Tyne, where he stayed for some time, chiefly engaged in his second task of bringing the Borders into comparative peace[4]. He visited Prudhoe Castle, Sir Thomas Percy's home, and gave it into the keeping of the Percys' deadly foe Sir Reynold Carnaby; but he first had an inventory made of the goods in the castle, and redelivered them to Lady Percy by bill indented. He seems to have been touched by the desolation of Lady Percy, "a good woman" who obeyed him in all things. She gave him the Abbot of Sawley's supplication, which seemed to the casual reader so innocent but proved in the end evidence sufficient to take five men's lives. Lady Percy sent it to Norfolk, no doubt in obedience to a demand for papers; if she had read it she could

---

[1] L. and P. xii (1), 1156; printed in full, Raine, op. cit. i, Append. p. clxi.
[2] L. and P. xii (1), 1257.   [3] Ibid. 546.
[4] See below, chap. xxi.

scarcely have guessed that it was worth her husband's head. Norfolk thought it would "touch the Abbot very sore" but does not seem to have considered it compromising to Percy. Lady Percy was setting out for London, to be near Sir Thomas, who was in the Tower. She herself carried Norfolk's letters[1].

The Earl of Northumberland was preparing to surrender his estates into the King's hands. He was stricken by his last illness. To Norfolk's great indignation he had sent down servants to sell the woods on his lands in Yorkshire, probably in a last attempt to raise money to satisfy some of his creditors. "As good to pull down the houses as destroy the woods,"[2] wrote the Duke, and sent peremptory orders to Topcliff that nothing of the sort was to be attempted[3].

On 3 March the Privy Council sent Norfolk special orders concerning Sir Robert Constable. The King had despatched letters which bade him repair to court; the messenger found him at Flamborough and "he made no satisfactory answer to the letters." Norfolk was ordered to send word to Sir Ralph Ellerker at Hull and Sir Ralph Evers at Scarborough to watch the ports so that Sir Robert might not escape by sea; at the same time the Duke was to advise him to obey the King, and if he did not at once address himself to the journey, he must be sent up by a serjeant-at-arms[4]. Norfolk did not think that Sir Robert was likely to fly, though if he intended to do so, he could take ship from Flamborough, which was his own town, without anyone being the wiser. Constable seems to have gone up on receiving Norfolk's letters, as nothing is ever said about his arrest, and it was not likely to pass off quietly in the midst of his own country. The King also desired that Dr Pickering should be sent up, and Norfolk promised to arrest him at once[5].

After suppressing the lesser monasteries within his commission Norfolk had about three hundred religious persons on his hands wanting capacities, which he had no power to give; neither had he a commission for levying the subsidy. These were mere hitches, however, and he was soon to find himself face to face with a serious difficulty[6]. On Thursday 8 March he rode to the city of Durham, and next day sat on the indictments of about twenty offenders; but before the beginning of the session he discovered that the Bishopric of Durham was not included in his commission. All the country had come in, everything was ready for the trial, and Norfolk had no legal

[1] L. and P. xii (1), 577. [2] Ibid. 609. [3] Ibid. 617.
[4] Ibid. 558; printed in full, Miscellaneous State Papers (ed. the Earl of Hardwicke), i, p. 38.
[5] L. and P. xii (1), 609. [6] Ibid. 594.

power to proceed with it. He decided, with the advice of his council, to keep secret his lack of authority, and accordingly the jury was charged and the indictments were found[1]. Thirteen offenders, including the Priory porter and two of the Priory cooks[2], would have been condemned next day in the ordinary course of justice, but Norfolk graciously respited them until after Low Sunday [7 April 1537], as he was too busy to wait in Durham for an answer to the letters which he despatched to the King and Cromwell.

In these letters Norfolk humbly asked pardon for not having perused his commission more carefully; in future he would have such documents read by counsel. He was about to return to Newcastle-upon-Tyne for a brief visit devoted to Border affairs, and after that he proposed to ride to York by way of Beverley and Hull, taking with him from those towns the offenders whom Ellerker had admitted to bail after Bigod's rising[3]. Norfolk was very anxious to know how many the King wished him to arraign; his own inclination was to be sparing of executions. "Folks think the last justice at Carlisle great, and if more than twenty suffer at Durham and York it will be talked about."[4]

The King received these letters on 17 March; in his reply he thanked Norfolk for his proceedings, sent him a complete commission, and assured him that he did not consider him to blame for the omission in the last one. The King particularly desired the conviction of Hutton of Snaith, against whom, as he understood, new matter had been found; "we and our Council thought his assembly on pretence of making a supplication no less than high treason, even if this matter had not turned up." Nothing is known of Hutton's "assembly." The man is something of a mystery, as no account remains of the rising round Snaith, which was part of Darcy's country. Hutton, along with Aske and Constable, was excepted by name out of the intended Yorkshire pardons in November[5]. A theory that seems to meet the circumstances is that Snaith rose at the beginning of the rebellion, perhaps earlier than the East Riding, and sent a private supplication to the King, as the people of Louth did. This petition, the first to come from Yorkshire, might have especially angered Henry. If this were the case, Hutton's assembly must have occurred during the period covered by the pardon, yet the King thought it enough to hang him without further evidence, a clear sign of the way things were going. It is of course possible that

---

[1] L. and P. xii (1), 615. [2] Ibid. 478 (2). [3] Ibid. 615-6.
[4] Ibid. 609. [5] See above, chap. xii.

his offence was committed after the pardon, but in that case Norfolk need not have waited for fresh evidence before acting against him.

The King's further orders were that Norfolk must bring to trial the Abbot of Jervaux[1] and the quondam Abbot of Fountains, for whose apprehension he was heartily thanked. If enough matter could be found against the Abbot of Sawley, as the King did not doubt, remembering his supplication to Sir Thomas Percy, he was to be disposed of with the others. The men let out on bail by Sir Ralph Ellerker were left to Norfolk's discretion. The King perceived from the evidence before him that the Friars Observant were "disciples of the Bishop of Rome and sowers of sedition"; therefore the Duke must arrest the friars of that order and imprison them in the houses of other friars, strictly forbidding any man to converse with them until the King's pleasure towards them was known. Finally the King was about to send for Lord Darcy, as Norfolk himself had advised in a lost letter[2].

Lord Darcy lay quietly at Pontefract Castle, victualling and garrisoning it at his own cost. He sent Sir Arthur Darcy to Norfolk with instructions to show him that all was quiet round Pontefract, the castle prepared, and Darcy ready at his command. Sir Arthur was to ask for a copy of the King's oath, which Darcy and his friends and retainers had taken in Pontefract Priory, and he must consult the Duke about Thomas Strangways, Darcy's steward[3], who had carried to Aske in York Darcy's messages—and some of his own, too[4]. Strangways' cousin, Sir Oswald Wolsthrope, had warned him that Cromwell bore him no goodwill, and he had gone to Whitby Abbey and the parts about Guisborough in order that Darcy and his friends might not be troubled on his account, although he still trusted to the King's pardon. He had offered to leave Darcy's service, but his master was loth to part with him unless Norfolk advised him to do so.

Sir Arthur Darcy was with the Duke in York on 9 February. Norfolk intended to go to Sawley in person to expel the monks, and as Sir Arthur was the farmer, he was expected to attend the Duke with a company of friends and kinsmen suitable to the occasion. He wrote to his father, requesting him to send such a company to join him on Wednesday at Leeds[5]. Darcy asked for further particulars. Were the men to be harnessed, and were they to be paid, and how

---

[1] See note E at end of chapter.
[2] L. and P. xii (1), 666.
[3] Ibid. 850, 871.
[4] See above, chap. viii.
[5] L. and P. xii (1), 388.

many must there be[1]? On 10 February, the day after he received Sir Arthur's letter, Lord Darcy wrote to Robert Aske, desiring him to deliver secretly to the bearer, Darcy's constable, all the arrows, bows and spears which had been taken from the castle during the insurrection[2]. It must have occurred to Darcy that this action might be misinterpreted, when he asked for secrecy; or perhaps he was afraid of provoking the commons, who were still on the alert when they saw a royal castle being put into a state of defence; for this took place while Richmond was still in a state of turmoil and before the rising in Cumberland. These considerations might make secrecy desirable, although otherwise it was unnecessary. It was perfectly natural that Aske should take arms from a captured fortress, and equally natural that Darcy should want them back again after the insurrection when he was suddenly called upon to equip an armed force. The King had laid great stress on the refortification of Pontefract, and Darcy was carrying out these orders as well as he could, knowing that any delay or inefficiency would be turned against him and reported as proof of a traitorous disposition.

Sir Arthur Darcy answered his father's questions on 12 February. He wanted thirty or forty "clean fellows" besides his own servants; the well-horsed men must be provided with spears and the worse with bows, and he was willing to pay their costs. Norfolk sent Darcy thanks for his good offers; he advised him to put away Strangways, but if the man had not offended since the pardon he might live where he chose without fear[3].

Darcy sent the men, but the Duke's plans were altered by the rising in Cumberland, and Sir Arthur rode with him to the musters at Barnard Castle. "I beg you to be no less nigh to his person than ye would be to me," wrote his father to him[4]. When news was received at Barnard Castle of the rebels' defeat, Norfolk gave Sir Arthur his choice of riding with him to Cumberland or departing with his own men to Sawley. Sir Richard Tempest had been sent to Sawley, where he turned out the monks and put three of his servants into possession. Sir Arthur prudently decided to look after his goods. He came to Sawley none too soon, for he found Tempest's servants wasting the Abbey stuff and collecting his rents. The abbot had been allowed to depart, and at first Sir Arthur could not learn where he was. Before he left, however, secret information was brought and twelve of his servants hunted down the

[1] L. and P. xii (1), 391.
[2] Ibid. 390.
[3] Ibid. 408.
[4] Ibid. 470.

abbot and made him prisoner; the poor man protested that he was fit neither to ride nor walk, and had done no wrong, for the commons had forced him to re-enter the Abbey against his will. Sir Arthur took depositions from some of the abbot's tenants which, he said, showed that the religious were the stirrers of all this pestilent sedition "and not only that but would have eftsoons quickened and revived the same." When Sir Arthur was leaving the Abbey, he heard that Leache of Lincolnshire "and others of his like" were hiding in Lonsdale. He sent out his men in search of them, and rode himself to Kettlewell, where they were said to be hidden, but did not find them.

On 25 February he returned to Pontefract and sent a report to Cromwell. The country was quiet, thanks to Norfolk's severities. His father was in the castle, ready at the King's command, "but his disease grows upon him and he desires licence to withdraw and live with a small company till he be out of debt." He had dismissed Strangways[1]. On 22 March Darcy wrote to the King, suggesting that as the country was in such quiet it was no longer necessary to keep a full garrison at Pontefract. He wished to come up to the King at Easter, even though he were able to travel "but six miles a day."[2] Shortly afterwards he was commanded to repair to the King's presence. It may have been on this occasion, or perhaps earlier, that Darcy wrote down a number of memoranda, in which mention is made of his journey up to court. The notes are disjointed, not always intelligible, and chiefly connected with his public life. Among them this passage occurs:

"Item, to counsel with Sir Arthur for bestowing of my servants or helping [them] with fees, annuities or [other] ways: and himself. For I peremptor feel my broken heart, and great diseases, without remedy, to the death of [my] body, which God not offended I most desire, after His high pleasure and my soul's health: and He be my judge never lost King a truer servant and subject without any cause but lack of furniture and by false reports and pick-thanks. God save the King: though I be without recovery."[3]

Towards the end of March 1537, Lord Darcy set out for London.

On the 22nd Norfolk was in York, resting a little after all his riding, but otherwise as busy as ever. As he was staying for two or three days in the same place "about execution," he thought it a good opportunity to hunt out the devisers of the articles of the spirituality, which the divines at Pontefract had drawn up and submitted to him at Doncaster. About this matter he thought that

[1] L. and P. XII (1), 506. [2] Ibid. 699. [3] Ibid. 303.

Dr Dakyn, William Bowyer the alderman of York, and Friar Pickering could disclose most, and he sent them up to London. Dakyn had written out the articles for the council of divines, and he could tell " what sort the Archbishop was of," but Robert Bowes and other gentlemen bore witness that Dakyn had stood firmly to the King's part in the first insurrection, and had endangered his life in consequence of his loyalty. Bowyer could tell much if he chose, for he had been in Lord Darcy's favour and was " as naughty a knave as any." Norfolk advised Cromwell that Pickering should be gently handled and given fair words. He would be able to give information about the prior of Bridlington and Sir Robert Constable, who was a close friend of the prior. By this means Cromwell ought to be able to discover any offences of Darcy or Constable since the pardon[1].

Norfolk had taken Aske with him when he rode north, though he regarded him with less suspicion than scorn. It must have been a terrible journey for Aske. Did he at last abandon all belief in Henry's faith ? Or did he still hope that a northern parliament would be called and that it might carry the King and the nobles along with it in a violent reaction ? Whatever the thoughts of his heart, with Norfolk he assumed confidence. " The man is marvellous glorious, often time boasting to me that he hath such sure espial that nothing can be done nor imagined against the King's Highness, but he will shortly give me warning thereof," wrote the Duke scoffingly. He did not believe a word of this; fear in his mind was the instrument of power, never love. Aske might boast of his influence over the commons, but the gentlemen were never tired of telling Norfolk how much they hated him and that he was the only cause and head of the insurrection, the most guilty of all :—

"I have by policy brought him to desire me to give him licence to ride to London, and have promised to write a letter to your Lordship for him ; which letter I pray you take of like sort as ye did the other I wrote for Sir Thomas Percy. If neither of them both come never in this country again I think neither true nor honest men would be sorry thereof, nor in likewise for my lord Darcy nor Sir Robert Constable. Hemlock is no worse in a good salad than I think the remaining of any of them in these parts should be ill to the common wealth."

Norfolk believed that the articles were Aske's work and that Sir Robert Constable and Lord Darcy were the most earnest maintainers of them. For both these men Aske had a great love, and the King would do well to give him secret interviews, " and wade with him with fair words, as though he had great trust in him. This would make

[1] L. and P. XII (1), 698.

him cough out as much as he knows concerning" them. Nevertheless the Duke could not find the slightest sign that they had stirred sedition since the pardon; on the contrary they did their best to prevent and put down Bigod's rising[1]. Norfolk caused Aske to draw up several written statements concerning the rising. One was a list of the spoils in which he had shared, though he had never plundered anyone himself[2]. Another concerned his correspondence with his brother Christopher, the articles of the clergy, his intercourse with the Earl of Northumberland, and his promise to Levening[3]. The third was about the taking of Pontefract[4]. On 24 March Aske left York for London, with Norfolk's letter of recommendation to Cromwell and another to the King, which Cromwell was to see "weighed accordingly."[5]

On the same day the Duke was at York sitting in justice on those who had been concerned in Bigod's rising. It may be presumed that some were condemned, but this is not certain, and two at least were acquitted on the ground that they had been dragged into the business against their wills. One of these was called Lutton; the other was William Levening of Acklam, the gentleman who had appealed to Aske, Darcy and Constable to help him[6]. Norfolk saw at once that there would be trouble about this acquittal. It was difficult to find anything incriminating against the leaders of the Pilgrimage since the pardon; it could be proved, not only by Levening's confession but by Aske's own statement that they had promised to help Levening. If he was a traitor, the three leaders were guilty of misprision of treason and there was a sufficient case for the crown. It is true that they had not in fact concealed the matter, for Aske had reported it to the Duke, but such a fine point could easily be overlooked in the sweeping measures of Tudor justice[7]. Levening's acquittal was therefore very inconvenient, and the King demanded the names of the offending jurors. Norfolk replied that he would find them out; he advised the King not to summon them to London or it would be said "that men should be compelled to pass otherwise than their conscience should lead them."[8] No doubt he was thinking of the scandal and indignation which Wycliff's case had caused[9]. If the King would let Norfolk come himself, he would bring with him "the greatest stickers in the King's part to

[1] L. and P. xii (1), 698 (1).
[2] Ibid. 698 (2).
[3] Ibid. 698 (3).
[4] Ibid. 852; see note D at end of chapter.
[5] L. and P. xii (1), 698, 710, 712.
[6] Ibid. 730-1.
[7] Ibid. 847 (12); 698 (3).
[8] Ibid. 777.
[9] See above, chap. iii.

have the indictments pass," who would explain the matter. "Some that were acquit was not without good grounds," and if Lutton had been condemned the Duke would have reprieved him. Sir Ralph Ellerker, who was the only witness against him, said that if he had been on the jury " he would not for all his lands have cast him."[1]

The Council sent in reply strict orders that the Levening affair should be "boulted out." The King thought Levening's treason manifest; therefore the jurors must be examined[2]. As to this intimidating others, as long as the King gained by that, he seems to have cared little what justice lost. Norfolk, who was very busy, delayed to send the names[3], and probably contrived never to show a full list, for he saw clearly that the north was not yet ready for a full revelation of the King's methods; but Thomas Delariver, one of the gentlemen on the jury, went up to the King. He had not been named by the sheriff, but Norfolk trusted him and Sir Henry Gascoigne so much that he put them on the jury in spite of this, and they were the principal "stickers" on the King's behalf[4]. In a deposition which he made concerning Levening's trial he displayed the secret deliberations of the jurors and the inside of the case. Sir Ralph Ellerker was the chief witness against Levening; Delariver, Sir Henry Gascoigne, Thwaites of Maston and two other jurors thought that his evidence was enough, and were ready to find the prisoner guilty of death. John Donnyngton, Henry Rasshall, Wentworth and four more held the contrary. Some of them were Levening's neighbours, and they believed that the evidence was given maliciously, because the King had granted Ellerker some of Levening's lands. Delariver urged that it was impossible the King should have disposed of a man's lands before he was attainted, and pressed them to give a verdict of guilty. They debated the point from 9 o'clock on Friday morning until Saturday night. The majority said that if Levening was guilty, so were all Bigod's company, and yet Lutton had been acquitted. The others replied that Lutton was less guilty than Levening, for he had gone with Bigod against his will, and had substantiated his plea by flying to the Ellerkers. Finally Delariver declared that an acquittal would be " the destruction of us all." Between 12 and 1 o'clock on Saturday an usher came from the Duke to ask if they had yet agreed on their verdict. The majority

[1] L. and P. xii (1), 777, 1172.
[2] Ibid. 864; printed in full, Miscellaneous State Papers (ed. Hardwicke), i, p. 46.
[3] L. and P. xii (1), 916. [4] Ibid. 942.

answered that they had, and the rest, for very weariness, let silence assent. The Duke of Norfolk came to the Castle, and just as they were going before him Delariver heard Rasshall say to Thwaites that old Sir Marmaduke Constable would rather lose a hundred pounds than that Levening should be condemned. On hearing this Delariver exclaimed that he would die rather than find Levening not guilty:—

"The Duke then rose up and went to his lodging, appointing his men Scarlit and Brigham to keep the jury more straitly; who took away from them all that might keep them warm. At night the Duke sent Leonard Beckwith and Mansfield to them and they fell all to prayer and rose up and agreed to acquit Levening; for some of them would not have agreed to the contrary to have died in the cause."[1]

The jury may have escaped the King's anger; at least no record of their punishment remains.

Norfolk had further trouble in the matter of sending prisoners up to London. Cromwell had sent for sixteen, and later the King added five more. The Duke explained that he would have to send a guard of at least thirty horsemen with them, and he could not spare so many before his second visit to Durham and Newcastle[2]. By way of economising escorts, he suggested that letters under the privy seal might be sent to summon some of the intended prisoners to court; this would be quite safe in the cases of Sir Stephen Hamerton, Nicholas Tempest and the Prior of Bridlington, who were in no fear of arrest[3]. Norfolk was surprised that Gregory Conyers was named among the proposed arrests; no man had done better service than he at the taking of Bigod, and it would be a mistake to send him up in custody "unless there be pregnant matter against him."[4] Conyers was probably sent for on the accusation of Sir Francis Bigod. The King was quite willing that as many as could be trusted should come up to London as free men[5]. Sir Thomas Tempest was to have charge of the prisoners, among whom was Sir John Bulmer[6].

Norfolk was at Newborough during the first days of April[7]. He rode thence to Newcastle-upon-Tyne about Border affairs, and was at Durham on the 11th[8]. There he received letters from the King, dated the 8th, which contained the news that Lord Darcy, Sir Robert Constable and Robert Aske had been arrested, and ordered Norfolk to take inventories of their goods, and seize all their rents and evidences, "so that they may be forthcoming to our use if" the

[1] L. and P. xii (1), 731. [2] Ibid. 809.
[3] Ibid. 777. [4] Ibid. 810.
[5] Ibid. 864; printed in full, Miscellaneous State Papers (ed. Hardwicke), i, 40.
[6] L. and P. xii (1), 917–8. [7] Ibid. 810. [8] Ibid. 902, 916.

prisoners "shall not be purged of the treasons whereof they be now accused." In a postscript the King added that this was an additional reason for prolonging Norfolk's stay in the north, as, in his own elliptical phrase, "Lord Darcy, Sir Robert Constable and Robert Aske...we doubt not will by their confessions detect such matter touching those parts as we would trust no man there so well with the execution of as yourself."[1]

On 12 April Norfolk was busy with the trials of the prisoners whom he had been obliged to leave alive at Durham on his first visit. The Earl of Westmorland had arrested thirteen men for some unidentified disturbance, perhaps for "ungoodly handling" Lancaster Herald, or for threatening to hang Westmorland's bailiff. One of these prisoners had escaped or had been acquitted. Norfolk had picked up two prisoners in Cumberland, John Follansby, gentleman, and Henry Brasse; their offences are never mentioned. Another prisoner, Michael Swayne, appeared in the interval between the first and the second assize[2]. The Sheriff of Yorkshire sent Hutton of Snaith to Durham by Norfolk's command, as no sufficient matter could be found against him in his own county; "nor would have been here," wrote Norfolk, "unless great diligence and circumspection had been used." Of these sixteen prisoners there was "not one acquit," as the Duke triumphantly noted, and they were hanged in chains near their homes. Norfolk boasted to the King that people were in such fear that no one now alive was likely to see another insurrection. The King's visit to the north would establish its loyalty for ever. He need not stay for more than six or eight days, and there would be no lack of food "after the fashion of the country" nor of forage, if he did not come until late in July. Many full-grown people had never seen the King, and the King of Scots, "your scant kind nephew," was shortly to return "into his proud populous realm." Those who thought that the King could not come in safety without a very large company had only to see the state of the country to be undeceived[3]. After finishing the assizes at Durham by attending to the restitution of spoils, Norfolk went to Sheriffhutton and took up his abode in the King's castle there[4]. He was very much occupied with Border affairs, which will be dealt with later, but he did not forget the King's order to seize the goods of the Pilgrimage leaders[5].

On 24 April William Blytheman wrote to Dr Legh from York. He confirmed Norfolk's account of the peaceful state of the country.

[1] L. and P. xii (1), 863. [2] Ibid. 478 (ii), 918. [3] Ibid. 918.
[4] Ibid. 942. [5] Ibid. 991.

Every malefactor was afraid; the spirit of the people had changed much since the insurrection. Complaints were no longer heard against the visitation of the monasteries: "I dare well say there is no religious man that will avouch any grief for that matter." By midsummer another visitation might be instituted without any danger of opposition. The gentlemen whom Norfolk was sending as prisoners to London in the charge of Sir Thomas Tempest and Robert Bowes had just passed through York[1].

On Monday 7 May Norfolk received letters from the King and Cromwell[2] accompanied by the indictments charging Lord Darcy, Robert Aske, Sir Robert Constable, Sir Thomas Percy, Sir Francis Bigod, Sir John Bulmer and Margaret his wife, Sir Stephen Hamerton, George Lumley, Ralph Bulmer, Nicholas Tempest, James Cockerell, quondam prior of Guisborough, William Wood, Prior of Bridlington, Adam Sedbar, Abbot of Jervaux, and William Thirsk, quondam abbot of Fountains, with treason and conspiracy against the King[3]. According to the usual procedure, these indictments must be found a true bill by a Yorkshire jury before the offenders could be tried in London. At first Norfolk was puzzled by the fact that there were two indictments exactly the same, but after consulting his council, he concluded that he was intended "to have two divers inquests; which, if ye do so I think ye do well, for they being so kept that one of them shall not know what an other doth, shall make them the more quick to find the matter." This was a method of guiding the hands of justice which entirely recommended itself to the Duke's ingenious mind. So many gentlemen from all parts of the shire were with him on their own business that he was able to hold the assize at once, and he expected "to have the greatest appearance that was seen at York of many years, on Tuesday at night and Wednesday in the morning." He was careful to provide for as many juries as might be needed— "we shall lack no number, if I should have four inquests....My good lord, I will not spare to put the best friends these men have upon one of the inquests, to prove their affections whether they will rather serve his majesty truly and frankly in this matter, or else to favour their friends. And if they will not find then they may have thanks according to their cankered hearts. And, as for the other inquest, I will appoint such that I shall no more doubt than of myself." Everything was being done in the greatest haste; Cromwell need not doubt that the

[1] L. and P. xii (1), 1025.   [2] Ibid. 1156.
[3] Ibid. 1207; printed in full, Deputy Keeper's Report, iii, Append. ii, p. 247. The Yorkshire indictment is printed by De Fonblanque, op. cit. i, Append. lv.

matter would be found "according to the King's pleasure," and the result would be in his hands by Friday night[1].

Accordingly on Wednesday 9 May the Duke was at York amidst the fullest assembly of gentlemen that had been seen there for forty years; no one who was still able to sit his horse was missing. Norfolk selected his two juries, one of twenty-one and the other of twenty men. The first was composed chiefly of kinsmen of the Pilgrimage leaders. Sir Christopher Danby, "cousin german removed to the lord Darcy" was the foreman; Sir Edward Gower and Sir Roger Chambley, Constable's sons-in-law, five more gentlemen related or allied to Darcy, and John Aske, Robert's brother, were all on the "quest," and their kinship to the accused was carefully noted by Norfolk himself.

As to the other jury, the foreman was Sir James Strangways, and it included Darcy's enemy Sir Henry Saville, Thomas Delariver who distinguished himself at Levening's trial, Nicholas Rudston who had been as deep as any man in the first rising and later turned King's evidence, and Gregory Conyers, who ran Bigod down. It will be observed that Rudston was one of the principal witnesses for the prosecution in Constable's case, yet he sat on the grand jury. All the others were men whom Norfolk could trust, though two or three were related to Bigod or the Bulmers[2].

The position must have been clear to everyone present. If the first jury dared to differ from the second, who were certain to find the prisoners guilty, their decision would be declared a traitorous favouring of their kinsmen and another jury would be called from among the gentlemen whom Norfolk had in readiness. The jurors might compromise themselves, while they could not save their friends. It seems almost incredible that such a thing should have been done in England. It is true that juries were easily bribed or intimidated, and Levening's case shows how much family politics had to do with a gentleman's sense of justice, but Wycliff's case and Sir Thomas More's charming story of the juror who would not agree with the rest for the sake of good company indicate that men were not devoid of conscience then any more than they are now, and that there was a standard of true justice, however much below it the actual practice might fall. It must have attracted notice that so many kinsmen of the accused were on one jury; but Darcy and Constable between them were related to most of the gentry of the north, and the selection might almost have happened by chance, if Norfolk's letter did not

---

[1] L. and P. xii (1), 1156; printed in full, Raine, Mem. of Hexham Priory (Surtees Soc.) I, Append. p. clxi.   [2] L. and P. xii (1), 1172.

prove that it was purposely done. John Aske's appointment was a different matter. In the days when even distant relationship was a binding tie, it must have appeared still more monstrous than it does now that one brother should be forced to pass sentence on another. John was probably too weak and too much frightened to protest, but why did Norfolk venture upon such an outrage? He had warned the King against the scandal that would follow any public punishment of the jury which had acquitted Levening. Yet little more than a month later he did not hesitate to commit this far greater abuse of power. It is hard for us to-day to imagine an adequate motive for such an action. No doubt Norfolk wished to be able to say "The prisoners must have been guilty: their own friends convicted them"; and he seems to have been moved partly by vanity, wishing to show the King and Cromwell that he could do anything with the northern gentlemen. He boasted that if he had known them before as he did now Levening would not still be alive[1].

The juries were sworn, the Duke addressed them, and they retired separately. Shortly they returned and found the indictments "billa vera." The fate of the Pilgrims was soon decided, for if the chance of acquittal by their own friends was small, with a London jury it would be smaller still.

The business of the court was not yet done. After the indictments of the Pilgrims the case was taken of two Carthusian monks who denied the King's supremacy. These were John Rochester and James Whalworth of the London Charterhouse, who had been sent to the Charterhouse at Hull. Rochester had written to Norfolk in March, offering to explain before the Duke and his council how much the King was deceived by those who persuaded him to assume the title of Supreme Head of the Church of England; he begged Norfolk to help him to the King's presence, for he would rather die than hide the truth[2]. Norfolk forwarded the letter to Cromwell, remarking rather peevishly that the monk should never have been sent north, as he had always expressed his opinions openly, and that he certainly ought to be "justified" in the south[3]. Norfolk, however, was obliged to see to both of them himself. They might have recanted at their trial, but they both stood firm. "Two more wilful religious men in manner unlearned I think never suffered," wrote Norfolk. They were condemned to be executed on Friday 11 May[4].

[1] L. and P. xii (1), 1172; see note F at end of chapter.
[2] L. and P. xii (1), 778.   [3] Ibid. 777.
[4] Ibid. 1172.

The indictments were despatched to London, where they were received in plenty of time for the trials, which began on Tuesday 15 May 1537.

NOTES TO CHAPTER XVIII

Note A. Staveley's dates are entirely incomprehensible. We have done our best to construct a reasonable chronology from the facts.

Note B. It is not clear from the accounts whether Sir Christopher Dacre came up and attacked the commons in the rear, or whether he was already in the town. Wilfred Holme says that five hundred horse "came forth" from the city; as he does not give the names of the leaders, he may have been thinking of Thomas Clifford's troop, which certainly came out of the castle. On the whole it seems most probable that Dacre was not in Carlisle but came upon the rebels while riding to the relief of the town.

Note C. The problem of the fate of Holm Cultram Abbey is rather curious. Abbot Carter had undoubtedly taken part in the second insurrection. Yet he was never attainted, for on the attainder of an abbot the King seized the abbey, as in the cases of Whalley and Barlings, but Holm Cultram was surrendered by the Abbot and monks on 6 March 1537-8[1]. The Abbot who conducted this surrender was Gawen Borrodale, a monk of the house who had been accused of poisoning a former abbot, Abbot Ireby[2]. Borrodale had been appointed before 23 January 1537-8[3]. It is possible that Abbot Carter escaped attainder by a natural death. Gasquet suggests this, but confuses Carter with his predecessor, Ireby[4].

Note D. The third of Aske's papers is entered separately in the Letters and Papers, but it was obviously written before his imprisonment, and should probably be placed with the other two.

Note E. On 13 May 1537 the King desired the Duke of Norfolk to go in person to suppress the Priory of Bridlington and the Abbey of Jervaux[5], as the Duke had offered to perform the work, if it was the King's pleasure, in a letter of 10 May:—"I think I should be at the suppressing because the neighbouring country is populous and the houses greatly beloved by the people, and also well stored with cattle and other things that will not come all to light so well if I be absent." He suggested that he should take with him Mr Magnus, Sir George Lawson, Leonard Beckwith, Blytheman and his own two servants Uvedale and Rous, to survey the lands. He remarked frankly, "these men look for none of the farms, and therefore will see to your profit."

Jervaux was "well covered with lead," and as to Bridlington, Norfolk went into raptures over the roofs there. "It has a barn all covered with lead, the

---

[1] V. C. H. Cumberland, II, p. 171. [2] Ibid. p. 170.
[3] Ibid. p. 171.
[4] Gasquet, op. cit. II, chap. v; cf. V. C. H. Cumberland, II, p. 170.
[5] L. and P. XII (1), 1192.

largest, widest, and deepest roofed that ever I saw." Altogether there must be at least three or four thousand pounds' worth of lead, and that so near the sea that it could be easily taken away[1]. Norfolk was at Bridlington from 16 to 18 May. Inventories were made of all the goods and the best part were sent to Sheriffhutton. The priory church of Bridlington was also the parish church for 1500 "houseling people" [communicants]; Norfolk suggested that part of the land might be granted to the parishioners, to keep up the church and the shrine of St John, and to repair the harbour, which was a dangerous place[2].

Even in the matter of the monasteries, Norfolk was not entirely trusted. Cromwell wrote that commissioners would be sent down from court to survey the lands, estimate the value of the lead, and so forth. If £20 would repair the haven, it might be done. The King did not intend to make grants of the land till Michaelmas, when he would put in substantial men to comfort the tenants and stay the country. As to the shrine, it was to be taken down, in order that the people might not be seduced into offering money there; all the jewels and plate were to be sent direct to London, except such as Norfolk chose to buy. The cattle and corn might be sold at once[3]. These orders were executed before 5 June, when Tristram Teshe carried to London the tenths and two chests full of the gold and jewels taken from the Bridlington shrine. Among them were three "wrought tablets" of which Norfolk wrote to the King "if I durst...be a thief I would have stolen them to have sent them to the Queen's Grace, but now your Highness having them may give them unto her without offence." There was also "a proper thing of *radix Jesse* to be set upon an altar." There remained the silver plate; Norfolk said contemptuously that it was very old and had better be broken up[4], and no doubt it was destroyed according to his advice. The church itself is said to have been demolished[5].

Jervaux was disposed of in as short a time; the monks had been dispossessed by Norfolk before 31 May, and Sir George Lawson, Robert Bowes, Blytheman and others were left in charge. The abbey church was covered with lead, half of which belonged to the parishioners. Norfolk made a choice selection from the spoils, including a ring, a silver cross and censers. Beckwith, who carried letters to London, was charged to give the King "this stone called the best stone." "Item, after this manner all men will be desirous to see dissolution."[6] It is a matter for conjecture whether the defrauded parishioners were so well satisfied, or whether they received their own part of the lead and preferred that to their parish church. Sir Arthur Darcy, in a letter to Cromwell of 8 June, commended Jervaux as "one of the fairest churches I have seen, fair meadows and the river running by it and a great demesne." He thought that Jervaux would be a better place for the King's stud of mares than Thornbury[7]. If this arrangement would have saved the abbey it is a pity it was not carried out.

When Richard Pollard surveyed Bridlington in June, it is satisfactory to learn that he found most of the movables had been stolen by the poor folk of the neighbourhood[8].

[1] L. and P. xii (1), 1172.
[2] Ibid. 1307.
[3] Ibid. 1257.
[4] L. and P. xii (2), 84.
[5] Gasquet, op. cit. ii, chap. v.
[6] L. and P. xii (1), 1807 (2).
[7] L. and P. xii (2), 59; printed in full, Wright, Three Chapters of Letters relating to the Suppression of the Monasteries (Camden Soc.), p. 158.
[8] L. and P. xii (2), 92.

Note F. It has been suggested to us that if we are neither satisfied with the jury of enemies nor with the jury of friends, it is because whatever the government did is wrong in our eyes. The third possibility, a jury of indifferent men, does not seem to have occurred to our critic. Norfolk had all the gentlemen of the north to choose from; and if it be urged that indifferent men would be difficult to find at such a time of political excitement, still he could easily have avoided the Pilgrims' near relatives, and enemies who had actually given evidence against them on the charge that was being tried. (For Rudston's evidence against Constable see L. and P. xii (1), 1130; for Saville's evidence against Darcy see L. and P. xii (1), 1087 (p. 497).) It is true that to appoint an indifferent jury is a counsel of perfection which in similar circumstances would very likely not be followed in our own age. If Norfolk had merely named two juries of loyalists, we should not have called it justice, but it would have been so natural and indeed inevitable as to merit no special comment. It appears to us that Norfolk's actual proceedings, as set forth in his own letters, were very far from natural, and were deliberately calculated to give the greatest possible pain both to the accused and to those jurors who were forced either to condemn their relatives or to show "their cankered hearts" to a jealous government. And we believe that "outrage" would not be considered too strong a word for his conduct by most honest men either in that age or our own.

CHAPTER XIX

THE KING'S PEACE

The Act for the Suppression of the Monasteries may be compared to a stone flung into a pool, where its fall causes first a wave, then circle beyond circle of ripples, each one fainter than the last. After the wave of revolt had passed, there followed a succession of conspiracies, none showing any promise of success, and each giving the King an excuse for further bloodshed.

Lancashire was not included in Norfolk's commission, but disturbances had taken place there which the King was not inclined to overlook. Towards the end of February 1536-7 he sent down Robert Ratcliff, Earl of Sussex, as his lieutenant in those parts, jointly with the Earl of Derby[1]. In January Sussex had married for a second time; the lady was Mary daughter of Sir John Arundel. "Some are glad of it, and some sorry, for the gentlewoman's sake," wrote John Husee[2].

On 18 February Sussex was preparing to set out for Lancashire[3]. The instructions provided for himself and his fellow lieutenant were similar to Norfolk's. They must administer the oath, first to the gentlemen, then to the commons. They must seek out the beginners of the insurrection, and punish all offenders since the pardon. The monks were to be expelled, their evil lives exposed, and the article in their favour which had been promised at Doncaster must be explained away. The Lieutenants were also to reform any pressing grievances as to enclosures and fines, and to discover the full strength of Lancashire and Cheshire when mustered[4].

Sussex, with Sir Anthony Fitzherbert, reached Warrington on Monday 26 February. Next day the Earl of Derby and the gentlemen appointed to form the Lieutenants' council joined them, together with most of those who were on the commission of oyer and terminer.

---

[1] L. and P. xii (1), 302. [2] Ibid. 86.
[3] Ibid. 457. [4] Ibid. 302.

The meeting was held at the Friary, where the new oath was taken, and proclamation was made that all complaints would be heard. Next day the commons took the oath with great good will, and on Thursday the Lieutenants went on the same business to Manchester, whence they would proceed to Preston and Lancaster. A refugee from Carlisle, who was spreading the rumour about a tax on ploughs, christenings, and burials, was brought before them. They were anxious to execute him, but were obliged to postpone the matter, as the offence had been committed in another county[1].

Sussex was at Lancaster during the first weeks of March, very busy with the assizes. His expedition was particularly aimed against the religious; he boasted to Cromwell that he was keeping his promise " for the punishment of such traitorous monks."[2] Whalley was the first house to be attacked. No documents concerning its fall remain, except some examinations of monks about the sale of the abbey plate[3], but the accusations against the abbot were bound up with the affairs of Sawley. It has been shown that Sir Arthur Darcy occupied Sawley and arrested the abbot. He took some depositions against the house, but these are lost. There was evidence against the abbot without them; his supplication had been found among Sir Thomas Percy's papers, and his servant Shuttleworth had made his confession[4].

Shuttleworth was sent up to London and examined there on 23 February, when he told all the details of his mission to Percy[5]. At the same time Sir Arthur Darcy arrested the abbot. No doubt this alarmed the scattered brethren, and Richard Estgate, the abbot's chaplain[6] who had been in his confidence, fled to Whalley Abbey, where his brother John Estgate was a monk. According to Sanders the fugitive reached Whalley while the brethren were at supper, and was sheltered by the monks unknown to the abbot, yet for this offence alone the abbot of Whalley was hanged[7]. This story receives some confirmation from the fact that Richard Estgate, a monk of Sawley, was hanged at Whalley the day after the abbot's execution, in company with William Heydock, a monk of Whalley, ten laymen and some of the canons of Cartmell[8].

The indictment of the abbot has not been discovered among the records of riots, thefts and so forth which were tried at the spring

[1] L. and P. xii (1), 520.
[2] Ibid. 630; printed in full, Beck, Annales Furnesienses, p. 348.
[3] L. and P. xii (1), 621.   [4] Ibid. 218, 490.
[5] Ibid. 491.   [6] Ibid. 1034.
[7] Sanders, De Origine ac Progressu Schism. Angl., lib. i, p. 129 (ed. 1588).
[8] L. and P. xii (1), 632.

assizes in Lancaster that year, but it is known that John Paslew, twenty-fifth and last abbot of Whalley, was convicted of high treason before the Earls of Sussex and Derby and was executed at Whalley on 10 March 1536–7, "in a field opposite his birth-place."[1] Stow says that John Estgate was executed with the abbot[2], but this is a mistake, as John Estgate went to the monastery of his order at Nethe on the dispersal of the brethren[3]. Stow must have confused John with his brother Richard Estgate, the monk of Sawley. Sussex believed that the abbot of Whalley's conviction was brought about by a special providence, because he had so many friends that it might have proved difficult; "it will be a terror to corrupt minds hereafter."[4]

It is not known when the abbot of Sawley suffered or whether any of his brethren were with him. He was within Norfolk's not Sussex' jurisdiction, and the King sent special orders that matter must be found against him[5]. There is only one reference to his death. Sir Stephen Hamerton, examined in the Tower on 25 April 1537, related that "the abbot [of Sawley] when condemned to die, sent to ask his forgiveness for having named him in the said letter [the supplication]... this Sir Arthur Darcy can himself show."[6] The abbot's "most sinister back-friend" was with him at the last. In the end of the Coucher Book of Sawley Abbey are written some latin verses which have been regarded as a lament for the death of the last abbot. Examination shows, however, that they cannot be interpreted as referring to him, for the writing is of too early a character, and is probably not later than the beginning of the sixteenth century. The verses are, in fact, a short poem on the Crucifixion, but Whitaker, who printed an incorrect copy of them, thought they contained an allusion to the death of the last abbot, and Harland, the historian of the abbey, accepted Whitaker's conjecture. The version printed by both these antiquaries is unintelligible; a new transcript is given below[7].

According to some accounts the abbot of Sawley was executed at Lancaster but this must be a mistake arising from a confusion between the two abbots of Whalley and Sawley. It is said that the prior of Sawley was executed with the abbot[8]. There is no proof of this, but it is not improbable.

[1] Whitaker, Whalley and the Honour of Clitheroe, I, 108–9 (ed. Nichols and Lyons).
[2] Stow, Chronicle, ann. 1537.
[3] L. and P. XII (1), 706, 896; 706 printed in full, State Papers, I, p. 541.
[4] L. and P. XII (1), 630; printed in full, Beck, op. cit., p. 848.
[5] L. and P. XII (1), 666.   [6] Ibid. 1034.
[7] Harleian MS. no. 112, B.M.; see note A at end of chapter.
[8] Harland, The Monastery of Salley, p. 48.

However many Sussex executed, there were still some who escaped him. These included the sub-prior and two brethren of Cartmell, Captain Atkinson, the bailiffs of Dent, Milnthorpe and Kendal, and four or five more[1]. Atkinson and the bailiff of Kendal, however, were afterwards captured by Norfolk. Atkinson was betrayed by "his own sister's son."[2]

Sussex wrote to Norfolk that Sir Richard Tempest "was neither good first nor last"; his brother Nicholas and his servants were the first men who stirred Lancashire. As for the present state of the country, "as long as the world standeth this will be a dreadful example"; the commons were sorrowful for their offences and meekly made submission[3].

In a letter to the King written on 11 March 1536–7, but now lost, Sussex told the story of an old man, who, on being condemned as a traitor, made lamentation at the bar, crying out that he had thrice served the King against the Scots. The Lieutenants, whether from pity or policy, respited him and referred the matter to their master. Henry replied that he took their action in good part, but none was more worthy to suffer than a man who had so often taken the King's wages. In this letter, dated 17 March, the King heartily thanked the Earls for their diligence in redressing the grievances of true subjects and in punishing corrupt ones. He was especially pleased with their seizure of the goods of Whalley Abbey, and the execution of the abbot. As the house had been so evil, he thought it would be better in his own hands; the crown was entitled to it, as he explained, by the attainder of the abbot. The Earls were to persuade the monks to enter other houses, as they would be safer there than wandering about the country. If some would not consent to this, they might be given capacities. Above all the Earls must take care that the abbey goods were not embezzled[4].

On 21 March 1536–7 Sussex wrote to Cromwell from Preston. He had been very busy with the assize work, but expected to have finished it in five or six days. He needed the King's letters for bestowing the monks of Whalley; after that was arranged, there would be no longer any need of his presence in Lancashire. He did not believe horse meat and man's meat could be so hard to get in any other shire in England. He would leave the people in very good obedience, but he thought the monks of Furness had been concerned in the insurrection. Cromwell had asked for Richard Estgate's confession,

---

[1] L. and P. XII (1), 632. [2] Ibid. 825, 863 (3).
[3] Ibid. 632. [4] Ibid. 668; printed in full, State Papers, I, p. 540.

but neither before nor after his condemnation could the Earl bring him to accuse anyone, save that he once said Nicholas Tempest was a great favourer of the house of Sawley[1]. Henry's nobles always hated being sent to the north, which they naturally regarded as "the last place God made," in a phrase of the time. Sussex did his best to earn a speedy recall and a sunny welcome to court, and the monks suffered in consequence.

Furness was the next house to which the Earl turned his attention. On 14 March 1536–7 Alexander Richardson, the bailiff of Dalton, deposed what he knew against the monks. His evidence as to the first rebellion was all hearsay; he was told that their tenants had been summoned to come out with horse and harness, that the abbot had "taken a way to be sure both of King and commons," and that money had been sent to the rebel host. About a fortnight before he made his deposition a friar told him that one of the monks named Henry Sawley had said, "there should be no lay knave head of the Church." Meeting the same friar on 13 March, just after the execution of the abbot and monks of Whalley, the bailiff asked what was likely to happen to Dan Henry Sawley "now at my lords' being here?" The friar answered, "Nothing, I will say nothing."[2] This friar was Robert Legate, who had been "put into that monastery of Furness to read and preach to the brethren," and also, probably, to act as one of Cromwell's spies[3]. Sussex received orders from the King to "search out the whole truth" about the disloyalty of the Furness monks and to imprison them till further orders were sent. The King enclosed letters for the brethren of Whalley to go to other houses, but those who wished to go to Jervaux must choose another place, as that abbey was likely to be suppressed for the same offence as their own. Those who had chosen capacities might be given "bedding, chamber stuff and some money." Richard Estgate must be sent to London, for Sir Arthur Darcy knew such matter against him as might lead him to confess[4]; but the monk was already hanged. The affairs of Whalley were soon despatched, and an inventory of the plate and goods was taken on 24 March[5]. The prior, a man of eighty, who had been fifty years a monk, begged that he might be appointed to the parish church; Sussex thought this would be charitable, and the prior was not likely to live long[6].

[1] L. and P. xii (1), 695; printed in full, Beck, op. cit. p. 344.
[2] L. and P. xii (1), 652.   [3] Ibid. 841–2.
[4] Ibid. 706; printed in full, State Papers, i, p. 541.
[5] L. and P. xii (1), 716.
[6] Ibid. 840; printed in full, Beck, op. cit. p. 347.

Sussex attended to this suppression, while Derby was still at Preston sitting in justice. The Abbot of Furness was ordered to attend at Whalley, and beheld the ruin that was soon to overtake his own house. The commissioners made every effort, but they could find only two out of his thirty-three brethren who had offended since the pardon. A good deal of evidence was produced by Robert Legate, the vicar of Dalton, and the abbot himself. The monks had repeated prophecies which were supposed to foretell the King's death[1]. They had favoured the Pilgrims and one of them had spoken against the supremacy since the pardon. Dan Henry Sawley, who used to speak slanderously against the King when overcome with ale, was committed to Lancaster Castle, with another of the monks. Robert Legate did not say "nothing," but accused him of traitorous words, and related that when he, Legate, preached a sermon commending the King's just laws, Sawley said "it was a marvel that God did not take vengeance of us both, of him for his preaching and of us for hearing him." Legate accused the abbot of ordering the monks to make no complaints to the King's commissioners; another charge was that he concealed Sawley's traitorous words about the "lay knave" who was head of the Church[2].

The abbot had boasted that he had made himself safe both with King and commons; but now he was in the gravest peril, while a brother abbot was not a fortnight dead. He must have gone to Whalley full of the darkest fears and eager to clutch at any chance of escape. Those who had anything to give and were weak enough to give it could often buy a pardon from the King. The abbot was again examined before Sussex, more straitly than ever. Still nothing could be found that would "serve the purpose," and the Earl wrote to the King quite frankly that, one way failing, he sought out another to dispose of the monks, that the abbey "might be at your gracious pleasure." Sussex suggested to the abbot that he might surrender the house of his own free will. The abbot was "very facile," and wrote out a form of surrender immediately in the presence of Sussex and his council[3]. He said that with their aid the brethren might be brought to ratify it under the convent seal. Three knights were sent off to take charge of the house, and to see that nothing was embezzled. Sussex proposed to follow them shortly[4]. Henry was entirely satisfied with this prudent conduct of the affairs of Furness;

---

[1] See above, chap. iv.
[2] L. and P. xii (1), 841–2; 841 (4) printed in full, Beck, op. cit. p. 342.
[3] L. and P. xii (1), 832; facsimile in Beck, op. cit. pp. 346–7.
[4] L. and P. xii (1), 840; printed in full, Beck, op. cit. p. 347.

he ordered inventories to be taken of the goods and jewels of the house, and arrangements to be made for the confiscation of the lands. The monks were to be dealt with as in the case of Whalley; the Earl might allow them apparel and "other things as be of no great value," considering the King's profit, "and yet rid the said monks in such honest sort as all parties shall be therewith contented."[1] So anxious were Sussex and his council to make no blunders about the King's claim that no less than three forms of surrender were drawn up[2]. The final suppression of Furness Abbey did not take place until July[3].

Besides the trial of offenders and the suppression of monasteries, Sussex had a third duty to perform, the collection of evidence against the leaders of the Pilgrimage. A clue was provided when a copy of Norfolk's letter to Darcy about the second meeting at Doncaster[4] was discovered in the chamber of Randolph Lynney, the vicar of Blackburn[5]. Lynney was imprisoned in Lancaster Castle. While Sussex was at Whalley he sent for the vicar and examined him as to how he obtained the letter. This examination is lost, but there is one still extant which was taken at the same time. This second prisoner was William Talbot, one of Darcy's servants[6]. Before the second appointment at Doncaster Talbot had been sent from Templehurst into Lancashire with letters to the Abbot of Whalley. Among them he brought the copy of Norfolk's letter, which had been given to him by one of Aske's servants. It must have been sent as definite proof that Norfolk had consented to a meeting, and the vicar of Blackburn must have received it from the abbot.

Talbot was a Lancashire man, and had Darcy's orders to raise the country, but not, probably, unless the negotiations fell through. The vicar of Blackburn was ready to help him, and said that if the commons rose again "he would bear the cross afore them and said God speed them well in their journey," but, receiving no further orders, Talbot remained quietly in Lancashire until Sussex sought him out. He recalled a number of anecdotes and sayings of Darcy's, but they all related to the period covered by the pardon, as Talbot had never seen his master since the second appointment. Nevertheless they are endorsed "Talbot's Confession against Lord Darcy, traitor."[7] On 8 April 1537 Sussex sent to Cromwell this document and the

---

[1] L. and P. xii (1), 896.
[2] Ibid. 832, 880, 908; the two first in full, Beck, op. cit. pp. 846, 850.
[3] L. and P. xii (2), 205–6; printed in full, Beck, op. cit. p. 856.
[4] L. and P. xi, 1014, 1065.
[5] L. and P. xii (1), 706; printed in full, State Papers, i, 541.
[6] L. and P. xii (1), 878. [7] Ibid. 853.

vicar of Blackburn's lost confession[1], together with the depositions of the monks of Whalley about the sale of plate[2], some evidence against William Colyns bailiff of Kendal[3], and Dr Dakyn's letter to the Prior of Cartmell[4]. Information was also required against the Tempests[5], whom Sussex believed to be very blameworthy.

The King was delighted with all this evidence, and particularly with Dakyn's letter, by which another monastery might be brought into his hands. Sussex received gracious permission to return to court when the affairs of Furness were settled, and the King promised that the abbey lands should not be bestowed without the Earl's advice[6]. Sussex set out for London about 18 April. Sir Anthony Fitzherbert, his companion, sent Cromwell a eulogistic account of the wisdom and diligence by which he had brought Lancashire into perfect obedience[7].

At the same time as the Lancashire assizes the prisoners at Lincoln were being tried and put to death. The insurgents there may have shown weakness at the crisis of their attempt, but the expiation of their failure was very terrible. The swift execution that the King had designed for them would have been more merciful than the long winter of captivity during which their fortune swung between life and death. In order to understand the circumstances it is necessary to go back to 12 October 1536, when Suffolk sent up to the King the names of the gentlemen who had surrendered themselves at his camp. They were all the principal commissioners who had been taken by the commons, Tyrwhit, Skipwith, the Dymmokes and the rest[8].

The King's lieutenants, the Duke of Suffolk and the Earl of Shrewsbury, were anxious to treat the matter as an ordinary riot. A certain number of the commons might be executed, and the whole affair forgotten. They both assured the King of the gentlemen's loyalty[9]. Henry was not so easily satisfied. The inclination of the gentlemen to join the rebels was the most dangerous feature of the situation, and on 15 October he sent orders that they were all to be examined. Those whose conduct had been suspicious must be sent up to London; the rest might be "dismissed with good words," but they were to remain in Suffolk's custody until the commons had surrendered their weapons. Hudswell and Cutler must be sent up to

[1] L. and P. xii (1), 878.
[2] Ibid. 621.
[3] Ibid. 411.
[4] Ibid. 878; see above, chap. xv.
[5] L. and P. xii (1), 785.
[6] Ibid. 896.
[7] Ibid. 970.
[8] L. and P. xi, 672.
[9] Ibid. 673, 728.

London, and the Lieutenant might keep for execution four captains of Louth, three of Horncastle and two of Caistor as a beginning[1].

Suffolk reported that the sheriff, Edward Dymmoke, had already presented to him "an arrant traitor," who was in ward at Stamford and would be executed in two or three days[2], but this did not satisfy Henry. He suspected that the gentlemen would persuade Suffolk to execute out of hand the commons who could bear evidence against them. He therefore instructed his Lieutenant to be cautious as to whom he hanged. Also he was not to execute one alone, but to proceed as instructed at Louth, Horncastle and elsewhere with "as many of the common traitors as shall seem requisite." No gentlemen need be executed there. Any who had notably offended must be sent up to London[3]. Henry despatched his answer to the Lincolnshire petition on 19 October. In it the number of victims necessary to satisfy the royal vengeance was appointed at a hundred[4].

Hitherto the King had felt no serious doubt that he could do as he liked in Lincolnshire, and he seems to have reproached Suffolk with slackness, in that not a single execution had yet taken place. But at this point the effect of the rising in Yorkshire began to be experienced. Suffolk dared not hang men; he dared not even "take them cruelly," or Lincolnshire would join Yorkshire[5]. Nevertheless he proceeded slowly with the examinations. Cutler, Hudswell, and Lord Hussey were sent up to London on 18 October[6]. The confession of Abbot Mackerell of Barlings was taken on 20 October[7], and numbers of others followed[8].

On 22 October it was known at court that two hundred men of Louth had taken the oath to the King and surrendered fifteen of their ringleaders, including Nicholas Melton, otherwise Captain Cobbler[9]. On the same day Horncastle submitted. Suffolk prepared books of the examinations to be sent to the King and apologised for the delay in the executions. "We have so much to do that we cannot possibly provide for all things," but he promised that the traitors should receive their full deserts in time[10], and sent lists of the gentlemen who had taken the King's oath and of the rebels whom he held prisoner[11]. The King sent back a list of the points on which the prisoners must be interrogated in order to reveal the complicity

---

[1] L. and P. XII (1), 717. [2] Ibid. 728. [3] Ibid. 764.
[4] Ibid. 780 (2); printed in full, State Papers, I, p. 463.
[5] L. and P. XI, 789. [6] Ibid. 772.
[7] Ibid. 805. [8] Ibid. 828.
[9] Ibid. 834; printed in full, State Papers, I, p. 471.
[10] L. and P. XI, 838. [11] Ibid. 842 (3), (4).

of the gentlemen[1]. Wriothesley was disgusted that they were not to be sent up to London for examination[2], but the King did not wish to alarm the gentlemen, who might still escape to Yorkshire. George Hudswell, however, who had already been sent up, was examined[3], and, probably on his accusation, Thomas Moigne was arrested and sent to London on 26 October. Richard Cromwell informed his uncle of Moigne's arrest. His letter contains one of those minor mysteries which cannot be explained. "This night, by my Lord's command I have, with much business, taken George Wyndessor."[4] Perhaps the business involved the wounding of the captive so severely that he did not survive; at any rate his name is never mentioned again, although Richard Cromwell attached so much importance to his arrest.

The council at Lincoln still used the gentlemen very gently. Cromwell's servants looked forward to more rigorous measures[5], when the first appointment at Doncaster stopped the proceedings altogether. Norfolk's letter, which announced the truce to the Privy Council, concluded "for God's sake help that his Highness cause not my lord of Suffolk put any man to death unto my coming."[6] The prisoners were kept in the castle at Lincoln[7]. Only one man is known to have been executed[8], but it is probable that some others suffered at this time, just before the first appointment. There were rumours to that effect[9], and it is significant that the names of Nicholas Melton (Captain Cobbler) and Thomas Foster the singing-man of Louth never occur after their examination on 21 October. It is not likely that they were spared. The probability is that they and perhaps others were executed without any record of their death. The Abbot of Barlings was saved from execution by the truce[10]. After the truce the examination of the prisoners continued[11].

On 14 November 1536 the King sent a pardon to be proclaimed in Lincolnshire for all except the prisoners[12], of whom there were at this time about 140 in Lincoln Castle and more in the town[13]. After this nothing more is heard of them, except that they were safely guarded[14], until 12 January 1536–7. By that time twelve, including

[1] L. and P. xii (1), 843.
[2] Ibid. 842; printed in full, State Papers, i, 490.
[3] L. and P. xii (1), 853.
[4] Ibid. 880.
[5] Ibid. 888.
[6] Ibid. 909.
[7] Ibid. 938 (2).
[8] Ibid. 1086.
[9] See above, chap. xiii.
[10] L. and P. xi, 1155 (5) (ii).
[11] Ibid. 967–75.
[12] Ibid. 1061, 1224 (2).
[13] Ibid. 1155 (5) (ii).
[14] Ibid. 1267, 1283.

the Abbot of Barlings, had been removed from Lincoln to the Tower, where they were examined again[1].

There was still a party in Lincolnshire eager for a new rising. Aske was told "that if any power had come [from Yorkshire] into Lincolnshire before the agreement at Doncaster, the commons of Lincolnshire would have taken their part."[2] There are traces of a plot for a new rebellion in January 1536-7[3]. The leader of the project was William Leache, who, though he had been excepted from the pardon, had never been captured. A man who carried messages from him was taken and sent to the Duke of Norfolk before 14 February[4]. Leache's two brothers, Nicholas vicar of Belchford, and Robert, were among the prisoners, and the long delay, during which it seemed sometimes that the prisoners would be freed, sometimes that they must die, could not but produce an attempt in their favour, but it came to nothing.

On Monday 5 March Sir William Parre arrived at Lincoln to try the rebels. After him came Sir Walter Luke, Serjeant Hinde, William Horwood the King's Solicitor, and the gentlemen of the county who were royal commissioners; they were all royalists. The trials were not disgraced by the unnatural proceedings which had characterised Norfolk's assizes at York[5].

There were now a hundred prisoners in the charge of the sheriff[6], exactly the number which the King had named[7]. Yet in November 1536 there had been over 140. It is unknown what became of the rest. Perhaps they were discharged; perhaps they died in the overcrowded and insanitary prisons; perhaps some of them were executed, for it was reported in Yorkshire in February that "they were busily hanged" in Lincolnshire[8].

Thirty-four prisoners were brought to trial on the morning of Tuesday 6 March 1536-7. In spite of the King's efforts to discover the guilt of the gentlemen, only one of them appeared among the prisoners, Thomas Moigne the lawyer, who served as a scape-goat for the rest. His execution was desirable, from Henry's point of view, as he was a very able man, but in one way it would have been safer to select a less capable victim, as he "for three hours held plea with such subtle allegations, that if Sergeant Hinde and the Solicitor had not acquitted themselves like true servants to the King and profound

---

[1] L. and P. xii (1), 70.
[2] Ibid. 946 (8).
[3] Ibid. 420, 490, 491.
[4] Ibid. 420.
[5] Ibid. 590.
[6] Ibid. 591.
[7] L. and P. xi, 780 (2); printed in full, State Papers, i, p. 463.
[8] L. and P. xii (1), 1036 (iv).

learned men, he had troubled and in a manner evict all the rest."[1] Moigne's labour, however, was thrown away, as all the prisoners were condemned[2].

The sentence cannot be described as unjust. Not only according to Tudor laws, but by any law, it is treason to bear arms against the government, or to give aid to rebels. The prisoner may plead that he acted from fear, or in the hope that he might acquire sufficient influence over the rebels to make them alter their intentions, but if the judge does not choose to listen to the plea, he may be blamed for harshness but not for injustice. The lives of the Lincolnshire men were forfeit, for they had made no terms. When they had weapons in their hands they had not tried to save themselves, and now they paid the penalty.

Among the condemned were fourteen laymen, including Moigne and Guy Kyme[3], who acted as an intermediary between Yorkshire and Lincolnshire, six parish priests, including Thomas Yoell a native of Louth but priest of Sotby, who was aged and blind[4], four monks of Barlings, six monks of Bardney, three monks of Kirkstead and Richard Harrison the Abbot of Kirkstead. All the monks of Kirkstead had been with the host, and the abbot sent money and food, though he excused himself as he was ill. The monks said in their defence that the commons had threatened to burn the house if they did not come, and that the abbot rejoiced when they came back and thanked God that there had been no business[5].

Moigne, Kyme and the abbot were executed at Lincoln on Wednesday 7 March 1536–7. Moigne suffered the full penalty, but the other two were only hanged[6].

Meanwhile on Tuesday afternoon and Wednesday morning the other sixty-four prisoners were tried. They were found guilty and condemned, but apparently it was understood that they were not to be executed, and the court presented a formal petition that the King would show them mercy[7]. They were all laymen[8], and among them may be noticed Robert Horncliff and Anthony Curtis, whose adventures have already been related[9]. Curtis was indicted but not arraigned, "because it is thought he is within the compass of the pardon and would plead it."[10] The other two prisoners who made up

---

[1] L. and P. xii (1), 590.
[2] Ibid. 581 (ii).
[3] See note B at end of chapter.
[4] L. and P. xi, 973.
[5] Ibid. 828 (viii) (ix) (x).
[6] L. and P. xii (1), 590, 591; Wriothesley, op. cit. i, 61.
[7] L. and P. xii (1), 590, 591.
[8] Ibid. 581 (i).
[9] See above, chaps. iv and xiii.
[10] L. and P. xii (1), 591.

the hundred were Roger New of Horncastle, who was in the Tower[1], and Robert Carre of Sleaford, who had been discharged by Cromwell's orders[2]. The goods of all the prisoners were forfeited to the King by their attainder. Sir William Tyrwhit, the new sheriff, petitioned for the property of Guy Kyme in recompense for his expenses over the prisoners[3].

Those who had been pardoned were set at liberty upon sureties. The rest of the condemned were executed on Friday 9 March at Horncastle and on Saturday 10 March at Louth, before all the people assembled for the market[4]. The country was then reported to be in perfect quiet, and Parre proceeded to take inventories of the lands and goods of Kirkstead and Barlings. A monk had been discovered at Bardney who had not been tried at the last assize, and Parre wished to know what was to be done with him[5].

The first business of the court at Lincoln of 5 March had been to find a true bill for high treason against the twelve prisoners in the Tower, Matthew Mackerell Abbot of Barlings, Thomas Kendall vicar of Louth[6], Thomas Ratford vicar of Snelland[7], Robert Southbye[8], George Hudswell[9], Roger New[10], Bernard Fletcher[11], Brian Staines[12], Philip Trotter[13], Nicholas Leache[14], Robert Leache[15], and William Burreby alias Morland the monk of Louth Park[16]. The prisoners were brought up for trial at the Guildhall on Monday 26 March 1537. The charge was that they

"did on Monday 2 October [1536] 28 Henry VIII at Louth riotously assemble with others in great numbers, compassing and imagining the death of the King; and for that intent held a discourse amongst themselves that they with a great multitude and power would rule and govern the King against his will and deprive him of his royal liberty and power, and subvert and annul divers statutes ordained in the reign of the said King for the common weal and government of England; and for such purpose did levy war against the King. And that they with arms, etc., levied war against the King, and slew divers of the lieges who

---

[1] L. and P. XII (1), 70 (vii).
[2] Ibid. 591.
[3] Ibid. 608.
[4] Ibid. 639.
[5] Ibid. 676, 677, 700.
[6] L. and P. XI, 843, 970; XII (1), 19, 69, 70 (1).
[7] L. and P. XI, 827 (2), 828 (xi), 971, 975 (fo. 3); XII (1), 70 (ii).
[8] L. and P. XI, 842 (4), 967 (i); XII (1), 70 (iii).
[9] L. and P. XI, 747, 772, 853; XII (1), 70 (vi).
[10] L. and P. XI, 827 (ii), 967 (viii); XII (1), 70 (vii).
[11] L. and P. XI, 842 (4); XII (1), 70 (viii).
[12] L. and P. XI, 568, 975 (fo. 2); XII (1), 70 (ix).
[13] L. and P. XI, 828 (2), 842 (4); XII (1), 70 (x), A, B.
[14] L. and P. XI, 828 (i, 2), 975 (fo. 1); XII (1), 70 (xi), C.
[15] L. and P. XI, 843, 967 (ii), 975 (fo. 1), 1224 (2); XII (1), 70 (xii).
[16] L. and P. XI, 975 (fo. 8); XII (1), 380, 481.

refused to fulfil their traitorous intent; and made proclamations, and rang the common bells and so assembled 4000 persons until Wednesday 4 October, when, having chosen captains and assembled 6000 persons, they proceeded to Caistor and compelled Sir Robert Tyrwhit and his fellow justices, then holding sessions there, to fly, and took certain of the said justices. Further, that the said Leache, etc., continued in arms, etc., at Louth, Caistor, Legbourne and elsewhere from that Wednesday until the Thursday following, when they assembled at Towys to the number of 10,000 persons, and thence on the following Friday, to the number of 12,000 with banners displayed, went towards Lincoln and continued the same day in a field at Netlam, called Netlam Field, at war against the King. And thus the said Leache, etc., compassed and imagined the King's death, etc."[1]

The prisoners pleaded "not guilty" but were all found guilty and condemned to death. The sentence was carried out with the usual barbarities at Tyburn on 29 March 1537, and the bodies were buried at Pardon Churchyard by the Charterhouse[2].

These were all the prisoners from Lincolnshire who are known to have been executed. There were a few others whose fate is unknown. William Longbottom was examined in the Tower on 12 January 1536–7, but he was not among those tried at the Guildhall[3]. A canon of Barlings was in the Tower on 18 March 1536–7[4], but he has no further history, and no directions concerning the monk of Bardney, about whom Parre wrote, have been preserved.

The most interesting of the sufferers is Matthew Mackerell Bishop of Chalcedon and Abbot of Barlings. He is described as a man of remarkable eloquence. In 1524 he preached the funeral sermon of the old Duke of Norfolk, and so moving was his discourse on death and the Resurrection that the whole congregation was seized with a dread that the dead duke was about to rise from his coffin, and all rushed tumultuously from the church[5]. It is singular that priestly eloquence played so small a part in the rebellion. Several of the laymen could sway multitudes by their speech, but the only two instances of priests using this their chosen weapon were the "collation" of Thomas Kendall the vicar of Louth and Archbishop Lee's unfortunate sermon at Pontefract. Abbot Mackerell might have been a powerful ally and his gift must have made him a special object of dread to the King. According to all the historians before and including Froude, the Abbot played a distinguished part in the

---

[1] L. and P. XII (1), 734 (3); printed in full, Deputy-Keeper's Report, III, Append. II, p. 245.
[2] Grey Friars' Chron. (Camden Soc.), p. 89.
[3] L. and P. XII (1), 70 (iv).   [4] Ibid. 677.
[5] Brenan and Statham, op. cit. I, chap. III; Henry Howard, Earl of Northampton, A Defensative against the Poison of Supposed Prophecies (1583).

rising, although he was not, as some chroniclers imagined, Captain Cobbler. Recently, however, it has been pointed out that his activity was much less than had been supposed. As his is in a sense a test case, it may be as well to go into it in detail.

The Abbot of Barlings was accused of having had foreknowledge of the rebellion, because about a month before it broke out he had sent away much of the plate and ornaments of the monastery to be hidden in the houses of laymen[1]. To this charge he replied that when the King's surveyors were seizing the goods of the lesser monasteries, it was reported that after Michaelmas they would return and take those of the greater houses, beginning at Barlings. When he heard this he called the brethren together and advised them to make provision for themselves by selling their plate and vestments, as the government pension was only 40s. a-piece. The monks agreed and he proceeded to sell the plate[2]. This was not very honest dealing, as the possessions of the monastery did not, of course, belong to the individual monks. On the other hand, neither did they belong to the King, who had received the lesser monasteries, but not the greater, by Act of Parliament. It was easy for the monks to persuade themselves that they had a better right to the valuables than the King. Nevertheless the abbot can be acquitted of treason only by acknowledging embezzlement.

Second, he was charged with inciting the commons to plunder the house of John Freeman, one of the surveyors, and to murder Freeman himself[3]. This charge rested only on Freeman's own assertion, and therefore is not worthy of consideration.

Third, he was accused of having aided and encouraged the rebels. He confessed that he had aided them by the gift of provisions and money, but he protested that he acted through fear, weeping and trembling in a far from encouraging manner. The main charge was that when he brought the provisions to the rebel host, he urged the captains to proclaim what he had brought. He defended this by saying that he hoped the proclamation would appease the commons and prevent them from demanding more[4]. His words were, " Masters, I have according to your commandment brought you victual, beseeching you to be good unto me and preserve my house from spoil, and if ye will let me have a passport I will go to a lordship of mine called Sweton, where, against your coming to Ancaster Heath, I will prepare

---

[1] L. and P. xii (1), 677. [2] Ibid. 702.
[3] L. and P. xi, 725. [4] Ibid. 805.

for you as much more victual"[1]; but it was reported that he said, "Go forward and stick to this matter," and the messengers to Beverley told the Yorkshire men of the abbot's great present and his comfortable words[2].

The case of Abbot Mackerell is typical of those of the other abbots and religious men who were involved in the rebellion. It is curious that their most ardent apologists dwell particularly on the small share that the monks took in it, as this does not at first sight appear to be to their credit. The Pilgrims were putting themselves, "lives, wives, children, lands, goods and chattels...to the utter adventure of total destruction," on behalf of the monks. In return they were received with terror, helped grudgingly, and dismissed as soon as possible. Their champions might risk their all, but the monks would risk nothing in return if they could help it. They were ready to share the fruits of victory, but they had no mind to suffer for a possible defeat. The attitude of the Abbot of Furness was only too common—they wanted to be safe with both sides.

In extenuation it may be urged that the arrival of a band of rebels at a monastery was often indistinguishable from the arrival of a gang of marauders. At the beginning of the rebellion, moreover, the commons often compelled the monks to serve in their ranks, which was contrary to the monastic vow; it is not suggested that the religious should have borne arms, but that they might have been more liberal of money, encouragement and prayers.

Then too the monks were landowners, sharing all the interests and terrors of the propertied class. They might on the whole be better landlords than laymen were, but in individual cases they had aroused hatred, and they feared the consequences. The Abbot of Jervaux's tenants were ready to murder him. Mackerell said that many of the commons were his mortal enemies[3]. The poor were groping towards a policy of their own, that they would defend the monasteries if the landlords would remedy their grievances. The religious were not farsighted enough to understand and adopt this policy. They would not take part with the commons; they were merely afraid of them and thought that somebody ought to keep them in order. They did not see that by their own faith they might convert a disorderly rabble into a body of crusaders. It was not impossible; the miracle had been wrought before and would be again, but the English religious of that age were not the men to perform it. They were in the main

---

[1] L. and P. xi, 805; xii (1), 70 (v), (viii).
[2] Ibid. 392; printed in full, Cox, op. cit.   [3] L. and P. xii (1), 70 (viii).

worthy creatures enough, but incapable of either a martyr's complete self-abnegation or a rebel's courage and decision:

" The life of the monastery was cut off from the life of the nation. Narrowness of sympathy was the most serious fault of the monk. He had little interest in what went on outside the abbey close. He had nothing to care for or to work for, except the maintenance of the wealth and position of his house. His whole life was spent in its corridors and gardens, except when he was sent out in company with another brother to gather the rents of its distant estates, or to accompany the abbot on his occasional visit to London. He spent all his waking hours in company with several score of other men, as singly devoted as he was himself to the interests of the place....It is not wonderful that he developed a narrowness of mind which made him, in questions of local or national interest, a dead weight on society."[1]

When the order came for the monks to go, they lamented—and accepted the King's pension. There were among them some martyrs and some rebels, but even out of those who were executed many would have submitted to the King on any terms if he would have accepted their submission.

Henry was not inclined to be lenient, and he had no difficulty in satisfying his anger against the clergy, regular and secular, but that was not enough; he wanted also to punish the gentlemen, whom he suspected of great negligence and probable disloyalty, because they had not prevented the rebellion at the first signs of disturbance. In this he was partially baffled by the strong class spirit of the gentlemen. His lieutenants were reluctant to gather evidence against men of their own order. They were quite willing to sacrifice the commons, and they could not save the monks, but as far as possible they protected the gentlemen and even the higher of the secular clergy[2].

This reluctance could not be more than a temporary check to the King. If he could not trust his agents, he would act himself. There is reason to suppose that he did not intend to permit some of the northern gentlemen who rode up to court at Christmas 1536 to return to the north again, but if this were so the outcry of the commons in the north temporarily saved their lords, and convinced the King that the time for the blow had not come. The commons were inspired more by fear than by love. They were not so much anxious lest their masters should be put to death as suspicious that they were plotting with the King against the commons. As it turned out the effect of the gentlemen's return was greatly in the King's favour, as it encouraged those whom he summoned later to come up to him

---

[1] Trevelyan, England in the Age of Wycliff, chap. v.
[2] L. and P. xi, 728, 764, 1043, 1084; cf. xii (1), 697.

without fear. In this way the Percys, Sir Robert Constable, and Lord Darcy went unsuspiciously up to London.

The proceedings of Norfolk and Sussex and the executions in Lincolnshire shook the confidence of the gentlemen who remained in the north. They could not help seeing that the King's oblivion of the past extended only to the appointment of Doncaster. He had forgotten his own promises, but he was not inclined to forget the behaviour of the gentlemen, and he was prepared to strain the law to the utmost in order to evade the observation of the pardon. As this came to be realised in Yorkshire the uneasiness which it produced was the cause of the last Yorkshire plot, devised by that particularly unsuitable conspirator, Sir John Bulmer.

About the middle of March the Bulmers' peace was suddenly disturbed by the delivery of a royal citation summoning both Sir John and Margaret his wife to go up to London[1]. This part of the affair is difficult to follow, but it is probable that information had been laid against them by Gregory Conyers, who played so mysterious a part in Bigod's rising[2]. Norfolk must have sent his accusations to London, but the letter containing them is lost.

On receiving the summons the unfortunate couple realised that it was probably their death warrant, but Sir John resolved to make sure. He obtained licence from Norfolk to delay his journey until Easter, and wrote privately to his son Ralph, who was still in London, to ask whether he might safely obey the summons[3]. Ralph sent back a servant named Lasingham with the message that Sir John "should look well to himself, for, as far as he could perceive, all was falsehood that they were dealt withal,"[4] a true but dangerous message. The gentlemen who were summoned to London at that time were all wanted for trial, and the Bulmers, conscious of their secret, were driven desperate by fear.

Lady Bulmer was terrified lest she should be parted from her husband. Their connection had been irregular, and she knew that there was no hope of mercy if her conduct were called in question. Sir John Watts, the parish priest of Easington, Yorks, said, "She is feared that she will be departed from him for ever...she peradventure will say, 'Mr Bulmer for my sake break a spear,' and then he like a dow will [say], 'Pretty Peg, I will never forsake thee.'" His servants heard him say that "he had liever be racked than part from his wife,"[5] and she for her part declared that "she would liever be

---

[1] L. and P. xii (1), 1084.   [2] Ibid. 870.   [3] Ibid. 1084.
[4] Ibid. 1087 (p. 495).   [5] Ibid. 1084.

torn in pieces than go to London." Apart from other considerations, her baby son was not three months old, and it would be equally hard to take or to leave him. In spite of the priest's assertion that Margaret encouraged her husband to plan a new insurrection sooner than obey the royal summons, it seems that she really used her influence to persuade him to escape by sea either to Ireland or to Scotland[1]; but it was very difficult to induce a man to leave his father's home and his native land in those days. In almost every case a suspected man preferred the probability of death to the certainty of exile. Sir John would not fly, but neither would he go to London. He preferred the desperate expedient of an attempt to raise a new insurrection, saying, "As good be slain and die in the field as be martyred as many other were above."[2] The exact date when Ralph Bulmer's warning was received is not known, but it was about Palm Sunday 25 March 1537. In "Palm Sunday week" Margaret begged Sir John to fly, but he resolved to stay and make a last effort to revive the Pilgrimage.

On Thursday 29 March Sir John Bulmer's chaplain, William Staynhus, set out from Lastingham, where Sir John was living, on a tour among the neighbouring parish priests " to inquire if the commons would rise again, which they should know by men's confessions." Margaret suggested that he should go to Bartholomew Cottam and Parson Franke, rector of Lofthouse, who had been a captain in the first insurrection[3]. The chaplain was also to visit John Watts the parson of Easington, the parson of Hinderwell and, perhaps, Gregory Conyers. His message seems to have been that an attempt should be made to seize Scarborough on Easter Day[4], though if this is correct Bulmer was allowing very little time for preparation as it was already Thursday and Easter was the following Sunday.

Other messengers were sent out besides the chaplain. Robert Hugill went to the vicar of Kirkby in Cleveland, and Sir John Bulmer wrote to Lord Lumley " to come and live with him till they might provide some way for themselves."[5] With the letter he sent a copy of a treasonable bill which had been brought to him by his servant Blenkinsop[6]. Lord Lumley's son was in the Tower, with very little hope of obtaining mercy from the King. Staynhus told Sir John that Lumley had said, "If he were commanded to come up [to London], he would bring 10,000 at his tail." Sir John replied that it was impossible for both himself and Lord Lumley together to raise

---

[1] L. and P. xii (1), 1087 (p. 494).
[2] Ibid.
[3] Ibid. 1087 (p. 495).
[4] Ibid. 1084.
[5] Ibid. 1087 (p. 494).
[6] See note C at end of chapter.

enough men to save them from the King. Staynhus did not press the point and merely said, "Nay, that is truth, but thus speak they there."¹ Shortly before Good Friday Sir John visited Lord Lumley, who was living at Kilton near Guisborough; although Lumley had intended to spend Whitsuntide at Kilton, after Sir John's visit he left the place hurriedly, "which things causeth a great murmur to be here in the country."²

Bulmer was counting on the help of Lord Latimer, who had also been summoned to London, and of Sir James Strangways, an old friend of his, but it does not appear that he sent them any messages³. When he received his son's warning, however, he sent it on to Lord Darcy and perhaps to Sir Robert Constable⁴, but they probably had set out for London before the message arrived; at any rate they paid no attention to it.

After despatching his messengers Sir John went to Rosedale, where he was the lessee of a suppressed monastery⁵. The parish priest, Sir James Otterburn, said to him on Good Friday, "Here is great destruction of people since my Lord Norfolk came," and hinted that the country was ready to rise again⁶. Sir John received further encouragement from a very unexpected quarter. Young Sir Ralph Evers had occasion to write to him about the presentation to the living of Settrington, and in his letter he sharply criticised both Norfolk and Cromwell. It is true that Evers afterwards denied that he had written this part of the letter, and asserted that it had been forged by his enemies, but Norfolk, who investigated the affair, came to the conclusion that Evers was really responsible for the words⁷. As he, next to the Earl of Cumberland, had been the chief supporter of the King's cause in the north, the fact that even he was turning against the King's measures is highly significant, and must have been very encouraging to the Bulmers. This, however, was the end of their success, for William Staynhus' mission was a failure.

Staynhus went first to see John Watts, parson of Easington, and revealed his master's purpose to him in the presence of Bartholomew Cottam. Watts, a garrulous but harmless old man, entered into a long discourse about "the chronicles." Probably, like Wilfrid Holme, he proved from history to his own satisfaction that "treason can never

---

¹ L. and P. xii (1), 1088.   ² L. and P. xii (2), 12 (1).
³ L. and P. xii (1), 1084.
⁴ Ibid. 1087 (p. 497); the passage is partly obliterated.
⁵ L. and P. xii (1), 543.   ⁶ Ibid. 1088.
⁷ L. and P. xii (2), 248, 741, 828, 850; 828 printed in full, State Papers, v, p. 109.

prosper." By his account his arguments completely baffled Staynhus, who could not of course complete the rhyme. " He gave no answer, but I answered that," " he answered no word"—are Watts' report of Staynhus' share in the conversation. He managed to say that he was on his way to Parson Franke at Lofthouse, and Watts determined to forestall him; " my purpose was that he [Franke] being a marvellous witted man as we have in all our country might have his answer surely."

Although Watts said service before he set out, he arrived at Lofthouse before Staynhus, whose horse was weary. Watts repeated the chaplain's message to Franke, " he hearing me patiently," and then suggested that he had better go home again before Staynhus arrived, so that his errand should not be suspected. The two priests set out together, but they met Staynhus on the road. Staynhus said, " I have a message to show you from my master and my lady." Franke answered, " If ye have any message to say to me, my brother parson shall hear and the bailiff and the constable both, because your master was with my Lord Lumley within these two days, saying he had both brewed and baked and slain his beefs, and suddenly my Lord Lumley is gone." As Franke was angry, Staynhus gave him a harmless message: " My master and my lady commended them to you, desiring you to show them whether they may make a proctor to excuse them. They are sent for to London."[1] Franke exclaimed, " Twisshe, straws! I can neither thee neither thy master thanks for sending to me for any such counsel...If thy master be sent for to London let him go as he is commanded. I can give him none other counsel."[2]

Watts, " hearing that cloaked matter contrary to his [Staynhus'] saying before Bartholomew Cottam," cried out, " ' Parson, these be not the matters he said he would show to you, but if ye will hear I will rehearse them before you.' " Franke had no desire to assist at so dangerous a rehearsal, and replied hastily that he would hear nothing, and that Watts was " frantic." Watts, angry in his turn, said " he should hear them whether he would or no," but Franke went away and summoned the bailiff to hear Staynhus' message, and in the interval Watts cooled. When the bailiff came Franke repeated the " cloaked " message, and asked if there were any harm in it. The bailiff said none that he could perceive, and went home. Watts and Staynhus followed him[3]. The chaplain had a letter for Franke from Sir John Bulmer, but " finding the parson did not favour his master,"

[1] L. and P. xii (1), 1084. [2] L. and P. xii (2), 12 (1). [3] L. and P. xii (1), 1084.

he tore up the letter and threw the pieces "into a water between the bailiff's house and the church."[1]

The two priests talked together as they went along. Staynhus asked Watts what he thought would happen to the gentlemen whom the King had sent for; Watts replied vigorously but discouragingly, "All false harlots should be hanged by the neck." He asked how Sir John hoped to resist the summons, and Staynhus said that Lord Lumley had promised to succour him to his power. Watts had no confidence in Lumley, and said he would forsake Sir John. He also declared that he was sure the whole plot was devised by that wicked woman Margaret, Sir John's pretended wife. He gave as his reason for this the story of one of Bulmer's tenants at Rosedale, who had heard a servant of Sir John's say that his master had said that he would rather be racked than parted from his wife. This was merely a fourth-hand report, and Watts' conviction was based on his disapproval of Margaret's past life rather than anything in her present conduct.

Staynhus said nothing to confirm Watts' opinion that Margaret was at the bottom of the plot. When Watts went so far as to say, "Sir William, take heed of yourself, an ye are a wanton priest, beware ye fall not in love with her, for if ye do ye will be made as wise as your master and both will be hanged then," he was moved to protest, "Of a truth I never wist she loved me but of late," i.e. I was never on friendly terms with her until lately.

Watts reported the conclusion of the conversation as follows:

"Then at last of all I said, 'Sir, ye are a priest, counsel your master to take heed of himself, and also take ye heed, for surely ye must be first hanged; for surely, Sir William, there is not one man in all England will take your master's part.' Then said Sir William, 'Parson, I dare show my mind to you.'

'What else?' said I, 'I am sure enough, and that know ye well enough.'

'Thus it is, if my master mistrusted that the commons would not be up at a wipe, surely he will flee to Ireland, and he trusts to get his lands again within a year.'

Last word that ever I said to the said Sir William, I said: 'Fare well Sir William, for of a truth thou wilt be hanged by the neck.'"

With this encouragement Staynhus departed. Watts passed the night at the bailiff's house at Lofthouse, and next day went home to serve mass on Easter Even. He confessed himself to be "marvellously 'commeryd' in the mind how I should do in this matter which passed greatly my wit...I knowing all this, some men would think I had no

[1] L. and P. xii (2), 12 (1).

cause to be very merry at my heart...I could not compass in my mind how I should disclose this hideous and parlous case which passeth my rude understanding."[1]

If the worthy parson was troubled and frightened, the situation of Sir John and his fellow conspirators was still more "hideous and parlous." The chaplain's visit to Lofthouse was on Good Friday, 30 March, and by 8 April they were all under arrest. The matter came to light through Gregory Conyers, who must have laid information very soon after Staynhus parted from Sir John Watts, as Norfolk had time to collect some confessions, which probably included that of Watts, before he sent up to London on 8 April Nicholas Rudston, Gregory Conyers, William Staynhus and Margaret Bulmer[2]. Already the husband and wife were parted, for Sir John was to be sent up later, and did not reach London until 21 April[3]. Sir William Bulmer, on hearing of his brother's arrest, went to Norfolk to find out whether anything was laid to his charge, but after examination Norfolk acquitted him and sent him up to London, not as a prisoner but as a messenger[4].

As Staynhus, Rudston and Conyers were making their weary journey up to London, Rudston asked the chaplain who were his accusers[5]. Staynhus replied that they were the vicar of Easington and the rector of Lofthouse. Rudston, sympathising with him, remarked that Franke had done much worse than the acts with which he charged Staynhus, as he was a head captain in Howdenshire, and caused Sir Thomas Percy to rise; "he [Rudston] could say more if he list,...he [Franke] was the unknownest fellow in Yorkshire."[6] Rudston's accusation was correct; Franke is mentioned as a captain in one of the earliest of Aske's manifestos[7].

It is not certain where Lady Bulmer was imprisoned at first, but when Sir John was sent up they were reunited in the Tower[8]. Staynhus was confined in the Marshalsea, and found there another prisoner, John Pickering the priest—not the friar—who was an old friend of his. They were not harshly treated, and after they had heard each other's confession and dined, Staynhus told his friend why he was committed. His story was that Sir John Bulmer had sent him to Parson Franke with the letter of citation to London, because Bulmer wanted Franke's advice about it. Staynhus had called upon

[1] L. and P. XII (1), 1084.　　　　　[2] Ibid. 870.
[3] Ibid. 918.　　　　　　　　　　　 [4] Ibid. 902.
[5] L. and P. XII (2) 12 (1).　　　　　 [6] L. and P. XII (1), 1085.
[7] L. and P. XI, 622.
[8] L. and P. XII (2), 181; printed in full, Archaeologia, XVII, 294.

the priest of Easington on the way about his private affairs, and the priest, when he heard that Sir John was cited to London, said that he would lose his head. Franke had been angry at Sir John's message, and consequently Staynhus had never delivered his master's letter. He repeated to Pickering Rudston's accusation of Franke, and said that Gregory Conyers was a witness to the words. Pickering thought the matter so important that he repeated it to another prisoner and also to the keeper of the Marshalsea. Staynhus was a vindictive man. He declared that if he were hanged he would cause Parson Franke to hang Rudston or Rudston Parson Franke[1].

Thus by the beginning of May 1536 all the principal leaders of the Pilgrimage were in the Tower, and the last hope that the appointment of Doncaster would be observed had vanished. The humiliation of the north was completed by the mock trial of the prisoners before a jury of their own relations; no further resistance was possible when men had been reduced to this infamy. In the south, however, the failure of the insurrection caused keen disappointment in some quarters, while the people had not the evidence of the King's severity before their eyes to restrain the expression of their grievances. It is true that the south could not be induced to rise simultaneously and complete the work of the Pilgrims. The southern sympathisers were less warlike and less enthusiastic than the northerners. They hoped that the northern rebels could do all that was required, and that they would enjoy the result without sharing in the risk.

After the second appointment of Doncaster, there was an outburst of activity among the conservative priests which the government suppressed as far as possible. On 23 December 1536, Richard Southwell announced that he had arrested two priests who were circulating copies of the rebels' oath[2]. His brother Robert Southwell reported about Easter 1537 the execution of two priests who were taken in Sussex and were perhaps the same men[3].

On 31 December 1536 another priest was charged with sowing abroad slanderous bills against Cromwell in Cambridgeshire, where many such bills passed about[4]. Richard Jackson, the parson of Witnesham, Suffolk, was reported on the same day to have brought into the pulpit the King's Book of Articles, and said, "shaking the book in his hand, 'Beware, my friends, of the English books...he

---

[1] L. and P. xii (2), 12 (1). [2] L. and P. xi, 1356.
[3] L. and P. xii (1), 725; printed in full, Ellis, Original Letters, 3rd Ser. iii. 95.
[4] L. and P. xi, 1875.

that was the first and chief setter forward of them shall be the first that shall repent him '"; besides other speeches in favour of the Pope's supremacy¹. Hugh Payne, the curate of Hadley in Suffolk, taught that one paternoster said by a priest's commandment was worth 1000 said voluntarily. Archbishop Cranmer enjoined penance upon him, but he continued to preach at Stoke Nayland in Suffolk, and Cranmer reported to Cromwell on 28 January that he was a " wolfish Pharisee."² Payne was imprisoned in the Marshalsea, where he "was like to die of sickness and the weight of his irons."³ Robert Canell was accused of preaching a seditious sermon at Windsor on Advent Sunday 1 December 1536⁴, and John Woodward was committed to Stafford gaol for the same offence at Christmas⁵.

Early in January 1536–7 the rumours began to spread again. It was said in London that the King had levied a tax on christenings in the north⁶; another story told at Rochester was that the Earl of Cumberland had refused to obey the King's summons to court and was holding a castle against him⁷, while in Buckingham it was said that the churches would be pulled down and their jewels sold. A barber's boy of Aylesbury was examined about this tale; he said he heard it from his dame, and she in her turn had heard it "at the common bakehouse, where they were to set their bread."⁸ The same rumour was discussed in the ale-houses of Shrewsbury early in March⁹. It had probably spread from Wales, where there had never been more rioting than there was that spring¹⁰. The Bishop of St Asaph banished one priest from his diocese "for not rasing the Bishop of Rome's name and for other crimes."¹¹ Another priest was accused of repeating a rumour that the King would pull down parish churches. He had also said "that if the men of Holy Church would rise with one assent that they would not give a point for the King's Grace," and other words against the King. Although he denied the words the Council of Wales were satisfied of his guilt by the evidence¹². The Abbot of Wigmore was accused of having in his service a suspected northern rebel¹³.

There was very little heresy in Wales, "for their language does not agree to the advancement thereof," but on 15 January 1536–7

---

¹ L. and P. xi, 1393.
² L. and P. xii (1), 256; printed in full, Cranmer's Works (Parker Soc.), p. 333.
³ L. and P. xii (1), 257.   ⁴ L. and P. xi, 1404.
⁵ L. and P. xii (1), 193.   ⁶ Ibid. 62.
⁷ Ibid. 63.   ⁸ Ibid. 456.
⁹ Ibid. 808.   ¹⁰ Ibid. 1148, 1271, 1272.
¹¹ L. and P. xi, 1446.   ¹² L. and P. xii (1), 1202.
¹³ Ibid. 742 (3).

the Bishop of Coventry sent up to London articles against a heretic who had been preaching in the diocese of St David during November 1536. One effect of his doctrine was that the Prior of Woodhouse in Cleobury Mortimer (Cleeland) "without authority despatched the goods of his monastery and changed his vesture in this ruffling time."[1]

The only article of the second appointment of Doncaster which the King was inclined to observe was the promise that he would summon a council of divines to show their learning on religious questions. They were not, of course, permitted to discuss the royal supremacy or the other most important points which the rebels wished to lay before them, but they were entrusted with the revision of the Ten Articles. By 18 February 1536–7 "most part of the bishops have come [to London], but no one knows what is to be done."[2] The tendency of the assembly was on the whole reactionary. The four sacraments which had been omitted from the Ten Articles were "found again,"[3] and it was rumoured, incorrectly, that "Our Lady is now found again, thanked be God, that was lost before."[4]

Another sign of conservatism was the renewed prosecution of heretics which occurred in the early part of 1537[5]. The northern rebels had a saying, "If you call us traitors we will call you heretics." The reverse of this was literally true in the heresy cases, for the accused always retorted that his accuser had used treasonable words during the rebellion; all the preacher's friends swore to the treason, and all the accuser's friends to the heresy, and the whole countryside was filled with quarrelling and counter-accusations.

An instance of this occurred in the neighbourhood of Ipswich. John Bale, formerly Prior of the White Friars there, gave up his office on account of his changed opinions, and became vicar of Thorndon. He was constantly in trouble for his preaching, and in return accused his parishioners of sympathy with the Lincolnshire rebels[6]. While he was accused of heresy, the Prior of Butley, who was also Suffragan of Ipswich, was accused of treason, as he was inconveniently reluctant to surrender his house[7].

Bishop Latimer's diocese of Worcester was torn by dissensions, some of the clergy supporting their bishop, others calling him a false

---

[1] L. and P. xii (1), 98; printed in full, Strype, op. cit. i (2), 271.
[2] L. and P. xii (1), 457.
[3] Ibid. 708, 789 (ii), 790; xi, 60, which is misdated, see note in xii (2), p. vi.
[4] L. and P. xii (1), 1147 (iii, 6).
[5] L. and P. xi, 1424; xii (1) 98; printed in full, Strype, op. cit. i (2), 271.
[6] L. and P. xi, 1111; xii (1), 40, 807.
[7] L. and P. xi, 1357, 1377.

harlot and a "horesone" heretic¹. John Kene parson of Christchurch, Bristol, despised the new preachers and condemned their doctrines. Most of his parishioners were offended because he "prayed not for the King four Sundays together in his chief wars against the rebellious and traitors," but a few were on his side, and William Glaskeryon said at the time of the rising, "We may bless the time that we were born; they rise to strengthen our Faith." Another man, when he heard the rebels had fallen, hoped that they would rise again, and said that he would join them himself. About Candlemas seditious bills appeared on the steps of Christchurch, Bristol, and during Lent the warden of the Grey Friars, who was of the old way of thinking, and the Prior of the Friars Preachers, who was of the new, preached one against the other².

The hopes of the reactionaries were dashed by a proclamation issued by the King about the middle of Lent which permitted the eating of white meats, milk, eggs, etc., during the fast³. This was a new source of strife. A mariner of Brighton was accused of saying that "he could not judge how the King should be Pope and have power to license people to eat butter, cheese and milk in Lent"; but the justices decided that the accusation was malicious and false⁴.

The diocese of Salisbury was in much the same condition as that of Worcester. Bishop Shaxton was a reformer, but his people were conservative, and when the King's dispensation was posted up in the city of Salisbury it was immediately torn down. The Bishop's chaplain, John Madowell, urged the mayor to investigate the matter, and was promptly thrown into prison⁵. He complained to Cromwell both on his own behalf and on that of another man, who had posted a bill against the seditious preaching of a certain friar and had been imprisoned for it⁶. On Cromwell's remonstrance the prisoners were reluctantly set at liberty under surety, but the mayor defended his conduct on the grounds that Madowell was a Scot and had used himself uncharitably and slanderously against the corporation⁷.

There was a similar breach in Kent between the Archbishop and the lower clergy⁸. At the time of the insurrection "one Sir Davy, a priest" quarrelled with a man called John Drewry in a tavern. The priest said that the King was "a tyrant more cruel than Nero; for Nero destroyed but a part of Rome but this tyrant

---

[1] L. and P. xii (1), 308, 1147.
[2] Ibid. 508, 1147.
[3] Ibid. 679.
[4] Ibid. 927, 941.
[5] Ibid. 824, 868.
[6] Ibid. 746, 755–6.
[7] Ibid. 888.
[8] Ibid. 256.

destroyeth his whole realm." Drewry called him a traitor, whereupon the priest drew his dagger and chased Drewry into the kitchen, " where my host and hostess were, he grinding of malt and she dressing her child by the fire." Davy wounded Drewry and fled, thinking he had killed him. The fugitive was protected by the commissary of Maidstone and by the curate of Headcorn[1]. In April certain of the curate's parishioners brought charges against him, but the rest of the parish were so much enraged that they said " there would be no peace till five or six of these new fellows were killed," and kept the accusers in terror of their lives[2].

The complete failure of the insurrection was generally known in the south by Easter. The executions in the north and in Lincolnshire, the King's Lenten proclamation, and the absence of any preparations for a parliament, showed that there was no further hope. The result of this was two-fold, for while the timid ceased to murmur against the government, the bolder spirits dreamed of a last effort which might snatch a victory when all seemed lost. There were certain districts where the disaffection was so strong that definite ideas of resistance were entertained. It often happened that these were the places where there was also a good deal of heresy. Sedition and heresy in fact went hand in hand, for where one party was strong, the other was provoked into violence.

Particular efforts were made to force the acceptance of the King's reforms upon the two universities. Not much is known about the attitude of Cambridge during this period, except that the vicar of All Hallows, who was a chaplain of the Bishop of Ely, caused much offence by the manner in which he ministered the Sacrament, and the vicar of Caxton was accused of giving his parishioners ale instead of wine at the mass on Easter day[3].

There is more information about Oxford, where several royal preachers spoke against the primacy of Rome and in favour of justification, without obtaining much acceptance[4]. A certain John Parkyns laid information against the Abbots of Oseney and Eynsham and against Serls, vicar of St Peter's in the East, Oxford, but the man seems to have been a lunatic, as even Cromwell admitted, for he endorsed one of Parkyns' letters " a fool of Oxford or thereabouts."[5] Although Parkyns' tales cannot be credited, there are other signs that there was disaffection both in the country and in the university.

---

[1] L. and P. xii (2), 908.   [2] L. and P. xii (1), 957.
[3] Ibid. 876, 877, 1182; printed in full, Cooper, Annals of Cambridge, i, 887.
[4] L. and P. xii (1), 212, 757-8, 1325.   [5] Ibid. 79, 127, 182, 211, 264.

The people of Thame insisted upon celebrating the day of St Thomas a Becket [29 December 1536]. Thomas Strebilhill said to the vicar, "Master Doctor, ye have kept a solemn feast this day, where had ye such authority?" The vicar replied that the people would have it so. Strebilhill persisted that within a mile and a half there were men at work, whereupon another man said, that "he wished their horses' necks had been to-braste and their carts fired." Strebilhill remonstrated, "I think thou art one of the northern sect; thou wouldst rule the King's Highness and not be ruled." In May there was a rumour at Thame that the King would take away the church jewels[1]. An Oxford scholar was heard to say on 19 January 1536-7 that "if the northern men should continue rebellious his Grace would be in great danger of his life or avoid his realm before the end of March."[2]

About the beginning of February the Abbot of Whalley sent a letter to "his scholar at Oxford" and to the Abbot of Hailes, of whom he said in his message: "I would be glad to see him once more ere I departed out of this world, seeing I brought him up here of a child." The proctor of Blackburn sent a letter to the scholar by the same messenger, William Rede, a baker of Oxford. On his journey Rede spent the night at his usual halting-place, the house of Richard Oldfelden, a schoolmaster at Knutsford[3]. In order to be a successful schoolmaster it was necessary to be a conservative in religion; all parents like to think that their children are being taught what they themselves learnt when they were young. The failure of Gervase Tyndale, the reformer, in the profession has already been recorded[4]. Robert Richardin, another reformer and would-be schoolmaster, was driven out of Lincolnshire by the insurrection[5]. Oldfelden, however, was a conservative and must have prospered, as he had a son Philip at Oriel College, Oxford, and was thinking of sending another son there, if he could get him a place as a butler[6]. Oldfelden asked Rede to carry a letter to Philip, and especially charged him not to show it to any man, and to deliver it into Philip's own hands[7]. In this letter, among various items of family interest, Oldfelden told his son that he would send him "a hundred verses and more made by Roger Vernon in your brother John's name, concerning the insurrection in the north. Cave dicas resurrection [beware lest thou say resurrection]." Philip might show these verses and others which his father was sending to

---

[1] L. and P. xii (2), 357 (2) and (3).
[2] L. and P. xii (1), 298.
[3] Ibid. 389.
[4] See above, chap. iv.
[5] L. and P. xii (1), 5.
[6] L. and P. xi, 1403.
[7] L. and P. xii (1), 889.

his master. At the end of the letter Oldfelden was seized with caution and added that he would not send the verses, lest the poor man who carried the letter should show them to anyone or be searched[1]. This omission is a pity; it would have been interesting to see the verses, which might have been preserved with the letter, and Oldfelden's danger could not have been increased, as they had been mentioned. The schoolmaster's fears were justified; Rede spent the next night in the constable's house at Wotton. He told the constable that he was ill and would be glad to go back to Lancashire if he could find anyone to deliver his Oxford letters. The constable took the letters, opened and read them, and laid them before a magistrate at Kenilworth Castle. He promptly imprisoned Rede who was examined on 10 February 1536–7[2]. As he had been solemnly warned not to part with the letters, he deserved his misfortune.

Thomas Reynton, another north country man at Oxford, corresponded with his friends at Durham in no loyal terms. He told them that the most part of the King's levies were but boys, and that the people of Oxfordshire were so weary of being summoned to musters and then countermanded " that they say ere they rise again the King shall as soon hang them up at their own doors."[3] The King's levies, and particularly the pressing of horses, caused complaints in several places[4].

At Oxford there was opposition to the new opinions, but in the more remote parts of England there was an obstinate adherence to the old customs. In September 1536 John Tregonwell reported to Cromwell that the people of Cornwall were as quiet and true to the King as any in the realm, and rejoiced greatly " that the King has allowed the festum loci of every church to be kept holy, at Cromwell's intercession."[5] Either a special indulgence had been granted to Cornwall for a limited time, or Tregonwell had misunderstood Cromwell's injunctions, as not all the church holy days were permitted. One of those which were prohibited was the day of St Keverne [St Kevin's day, 3 June], who was the patron saint of a large and unruly parish in Cornwall, the first to rise in the insurrection of 1497[6].

It is probable that the discontent which the suppression of the local feast caused was encouraged by a copy of the Pilgrims' oath and articles which some Cornish soldiers had obtained at King's Lynn,

[1] L. and P. xi, 1408.
[2] L. and P. xii (1), 389.
[3] Ibid. 798.
[4] Ibid. 126, 152.
[5] L. and P. xi, 405.
[6] L. and P. xii (1), 1001.

when Norfolk disbanded his troops[1]. Early in April 1537 two fishermen of St Keverne's, named Carpyssacke and Treglosacke, when selling their fish at Hamell beside Southampton, met two men who were evidently agents of the rebellious party. They asked the Cornish men why they had not risen with the north, and the fishermen were so much moved by their words that they " swore upon a book to help them," and began their preparations by buying 200 jerkins.

When the fishermen went home they directed a local painter to make a banner for the parish of St Keverne, " in the which banner they would have first the picture of Christ with his wounds abroad and a banner in his hand, Our Lady on the one side holding her breast in her hand, St John à Baptist on the other side, the King's Grace and the Queen kneeling, and all the commonalty kneeling, with scripture above their heads, making their petition to the picture of Christ that it would please the King's Grace that they might have their holidays." Carpyssacke intended to display this banner on Pardon Monday, and he expected that the people would follow it[2]. In consequence prophecies of the King's death and rumours of musters arose in the neighbouring county of Devonshire[3]. The plot, however, was a very ingenuous one, and was quickly discovered. The painter was alarmed at so dangerous a commission, and reported the matter to a local magistrate, who wrote on 22 April to Cromwell for orders, with assurances that the whole county was quiet and well-disposed, and that Carpyssacke was the only traitor; nevertheless he begged that the King would permit the people to "hold the day of the head saint of their church."[4] He was commanded to arrest the two fishermen and send them to London, but they had gone back to Southampton and Treglosacke seems to have escaped altogether[5]. Carpyssacke was eventually taken and imprisoned in Cornwall. He was not sent up to London, and there must have been some powerful influence at work in his favour, for the justices of assize said that they had no authority to inquire for high treason and refused to try him[6]; he is last heard of on 28 August 1537, still uncondemned[7]. In July it was reported that the people of Exeter were "half afraid of a privy insurrection of Cornishmen."[8]

These mutterings and plots are all connected with the religious discontent, but the failure of the rebellion was also a severe

---

[1] See above, chap. XIII. [2] L. and P. XII (1), 1001; see note D at end of chapter.
[3] L. and P. XII (1), 685, 1000. [4] Ibid. 1001.
[5] Ibid. 1126. [6] Ibid. 1127.
[7] L. and P. XII (2), 595. [8] Ibid. 182 and n.

disappointment to the commons who had hoped for social reforms, and the methods in which they vented their baffled feelings were more dangerous than the feeble efforts of the religious.

In Somerset, although the suppression of the monastery of Clyffe[1] caused much lamentation[2], social grievances were uppermost. The levying of the subsidy had been stopped in several counties during the insurrection. In April 1537 it began again, and the commissioners inquired "whether we shall stand to the old taxation or attempt higher sums."[3] As the King was badly in need of money after the expenses of the insurrection, they were probably ordered to get as much as they could, but the exaction which provoked the rising was not the subsidy. The outbreak was caused by a "certain commission... to take up corn," apparently an exercise of the hated royal right of purveyance, due to the King's poverty. The commons tried to rise against the commissioners, but were repressed by "young Mr Paulet and other great men." Sixty rebels were imprisoned, of whom fourteen were executed for treason, one being a woman. The rest were pardoned[4].

It is curious that there is no reference to this attempt among the "Letters and Papers of Henry VIII" until 13 May, after the prisoners had been executed at Taunton. There was a rumour in the county that the King was displeased with Thomas Horner for "his taking the men imprisoned at Nonye"[5] and causing them to be executed at Taunton. It was said that Horner's life had been saved only by the intercession of Sir John St Low and that the King said that "he had liever have given Sir John 1000 marks a year."[6] Sir John St Low wrote to Cromwell to request that the rumour might be contradicted and its authors punished, as it was greatly to Horner's detriment[7]. It is unlikely that Henry took any active measures to suppress the story, as he encouraged the popular view of his character, upon which it was based, that he was a good-natured but careless man, who left too much to his agents, but was shocked and grieved when his attention was called to their severity.

It is interesting to notice the previous history of Somerset. The peasants of the shire had risen in the great revolt of 1381. In the fifteenth century lollardy was widely diffused there. Without entering into the vexed question as to how long lollardy survived as a creed[8],

---

[1] Cleeve. [3] L. and P. xii (1), 4.
[2] Ibid. 152, 1070; see note F, chap. iv.
[4] Wriothesley, op. cit. i, 61. [5] Nunney.
[6] L. and P. xii (1), 1194. [7] Ibid. 1195.
[8] Trevelyan, op. cit. chap. ix; Gairdner, Lollardy and the Reformation, i, chap. i.

it may be remarked that the lollards of 1447 were nearer in point of time to the men of 1537 than John Wesley is to our own time, and it is possible that their influence may have lasted as his has done.

It is still more interesting to trace the history of revolt in Norfolk and Suffolk. In 1381, under the vigorous rule of Bishop Spencer, these counties were considered the most orthodox in England[1]. Nevertheless the peasants' revolt there in that year was exceedingly violent and unusually well organised. Its objects were purely social, and many parish priests and chaplains were with the insurgents, still the monasteries were savagely attacked, not on religious grounds, but because their tenants felt themselves oppressed[2]. The hatred of the monks was so strong that it is surprising that their fall 150 years later should have excited any regret, but the changed feeling of the people is accounted for by the changed social conditions. The monasteries were above everything conservative. In 1381, after the great catastrophe of the Black Death, they insisted on exacting the old dues, which had become oppressive, and in paying the old wages, which were inadequate. The peasants in consequence wanted to force their lords to move with the times. In Henry VIII's reign, on the contrary, it was the lords who were moving faster than the peasants liked. The monasteries became popular because they still practised the old hospitality, and to some extent cultivated the land in the old way.

After the death of fighting Bishop Spencer, lollardy spread rapidly through East Anglia; the large lollard communities there underwent vigorous persecution in 1428[3]. Social discontent, more than religious conservatism, caused the commons of this region to meditate a rising in 1537, and the rebels of 1549 definitely professed themselves to be protestants[4]. Yet the first suggestion of a revolt was connected with the suppression of Buckenham Priory. As three men were riding home from Stone Fair on 1 August 1536 [Lammas Day], one of them, Hugh Wilkinson, said to the other two: "Let us go home, for now are the visitors in putting down of our house. And if ye will do after me, I have here an angel noble in my purse that never did me good, and that shall ye have between you, if ye will come in the evening and kill them in their beds, for I know the gates of every door, so that I shall let you into every chamber. And when ye have done ye may soon be out of the way for the wood is at hand. And when

---

[1] Trevelyan, loc. cit.
[2] Powell, The Rising in East Anglia.
[3] Trevelyan, loc. cit.
[4] Russell, op. cit. Introduction.

they be in their beds ye shall be sure that they have no weapon at hand to defend themselves withal. And if I had no more to lose than one of you hath, it should be the first deed I should do." But the two others refused the rather inadequate bribe[1].

Later in the year 1536 there were disturbances in Norfolk which were suppressed by the Duke of Norfolk[2]. When the Lincolnshire rebellion broke out there was much anxiety lest it should spread to Norfolk, and this was prevented only by prompt and severe measures[3].

In November copies of the Yorkshire oath and manifesto appeared at King's Lynn and Walsingham[4] and murmurs were heard of an intended rising[5]. The great shrine of Our Lady of Walsingham was naturally a centre for all the rumours of the country. One of the priests, Henry Manser, was accused of having discussed the rebellion with some Lincolnshire pilgrims to the shrine on 7 December 1536; in the course of the conversation they had regretted that Norfolk and Suffolk had not risen at the same time as Lincolnshire, for then the rebels " would have gone through the kingdom." The way in which the conversation was revealed is rather suspicious. In June 1537 the priest caused " a sore and a diseased " beggar to be turned out of Our Lady's Chapel and set in the stocks. The beggar in revenge accused the priest of the treasonable conversation which he asserted that he had overheard[6].

Information was laid on 15 February against John Hogon, a fiddler, who went about Norfolk and the neighbouring counties singing seditious songs[7]. During Lent Harry Jervyse of Fincham said that he wished the Yorkshire men had prospered, for then " the holydays that were put down should be restored again," and after Easter he rebuked some of his friends, saying that if they had been ruled by him he would have cried " Fire ! " at mass time at the house of John Fincham, the principal gentleman; when he ran out they might have taken him, and if he would not be ruled by them " they would make a cart way betwixt his head and his shoulder." Jervyse also urged his friends to ring the bells in every town to raise the commons[8].

The suppression of the monasteries and the levying of the subsidy were suspended in Norfolk during the rebellion, but on 6 January 1536–7 the Duke of Norfolk recommended that the commissioners

---

[1] L. and P. XII (1), 1268; printed in part, Russell, op. cit. Introduction.
[2] See above, chap. IV.
[3] See above, chap. VI.
[4] See above, chap. XIII.
[5] L. and P. XII (2), 56.
[6] Ibid. 21.
[7] L. and P. XII (1), 424.
[8] L. and P. XII (2), 150; printed in part, Russell, op. cit. Introduction.

should begin their work again[1]. One of the collectors went to John Cokke, a worsted weaver of Norwich, for his payment during Lent. Cokke was accused of saying, in reply to the collector's demand: "I cannot pay for I can sell no worsted, wherefore I see no remedy without poor men do rise." Cokke denied having said the words, unless he was drunk at the time[2].

After Easter a plot for a rising began to be discussed at Walsingham Priory. The chief mover was Ralph Rogerson, a singing man of the Priory. Nicholas Myleham the sub-prior was also accused of taking part in the conspiracy, but there was little evidence against him[3]. About the middle of April Rogerson discussed the state of the nation with his friend George Guisborough. Guisborough said that "he thought it very evil done for the suppressing of so many religious houses, where God was well served and many other good deeds of charity done." Rogerson agreed and said that the living of poor men went away with the abbeys, for now the gentlemen had all the farms and cattle of the country in their hands. They decided that "some men must step to and resist them," and they resolved that they would raise a company by firing some beacon and go to the King to complain. They appointed St Helen's Day, 21 May, as the date on which to proclaim their intentions; the mustering place was to be Shepcotes Heath, and meanwhile they sounded their friends on the subject[4].

It is difficult to judge of their success, as Guisborough was honourably reluctant to accuse others, and Rogerson's confession has not been preserved, but the conspirators held several meetings. On one occasion they made use of the opportunity offered "at a game of shooting of the flyte and standard" at Benham, where they held a consultation[5]. Their fully developed plan was to assemble the people in the night, fire the beacons on the coast, and cause the head constables and under constables of the hundreds to summon the musters. Then the rebels would kill and plunder all who resisted them, seize Brandon Ferry and Brandon Bridge in order to cut off communications with London, and march to help the northern men.

Unfortunately for themselves, they admitted into their secret John Galant, a servant of Sir John Heydon. In spite of their threats that they would kill anyone who betrayed them, this man informed his master of the plot on 26 April. Sir John immediately

---

[1] L. and P. XII (1), 32.
[2] L. and P. XII (2), 18 (3).
[3] L. and P. XII (1), 1125, 1300.
[4] Ibid. 1056; printed in part, Russell, op. cit. Introduction.
[5] L. and P. XII (1), 1125.

sent the news to London and arrested George Guisborough and his son William, who was in the plot[1]. The rest of the conspirators were taken on 30 April[2], and orders were sent down on 8 May that the offenders were to be executed without sparing[3].

The social discontent was strong in Suffolk, although it did not culminate in an organised conspiracy. On May day there was a May game at some place in Suffolk, "which play was of a king how he should rule his realm, in which one played Husbandry and said many things against gentlemen more than was in the book of the play."[4] After the games Husbandry prudently disappeared and could not be found[5].

On 11 May Richard Bushop of Bungay had a long conversation with Robert Seyman in Tyndale Wood, Suffolk. Bushop asked, "What tidings hear you? Have you any musters about you?" Seyman replied no, and asked if there were any at Bungay. Bushop complained that it was a hard world for poor men, and when Seyman agreed, he went on: "Methinketh ye seem to be an honest man, such a one as a man may trust to open his mind unto. We are used under such fashion now a days as it hath not been seen, for if three or four of us be communing together the constables will examine what communication [we have] and stock us if we will not tell them: good fellows would not be so used long if one would be true to another. And as I have heard, now lately at Walsingham the people had risen if one person had not been; and as I hear some of them now be in Norwich Castle, and other be sent to London....If two men have communication together, a man may go back on his word as long as no third man is there; three may keep counsel if two be away."[6] Bushop offered to show Seyman a prophecy "which one man had watched in the night to copy." In it the King was called a mole who should be put down this year or never[7]; also "There should land at Walborne Hope the proudest prince in all Christendom, and so shall come to Mousehold Heath, and there should meet with two other kings and shall fight and shall be put down, and the white lion should obtain." Bushop had been told that the Earl of Derby had rebelled, and that the Duke of Norfolk was so beset in the north that he could not escape[8]. The man must have been drunk to run on like this to a stranger. He paid a heavy price for his folly. Seyman

---

[1] L. and P. xii (1), 1045, 1046. [2] Ibid. 1068, 1125. [3] Ibid. 1171.
[4] Ibid. 1212. [5] Ibid. 1284.
[6] See note E at end of chapter. [7] See above, chap. iv.
[8] L. and P. xii (1), 1212; printed in part by Russell, op. cit. Introduction.

informed against him, and Bushop was forced, probably by torture, to confess his words, and was then executed. It seems that Seyman shared his fate[1]. It is rather surprising that Cromwell was able to find such a number of informers, considering that they were occasionally imprisoned and hanged with the guilty person.

The disaffection in East Anglia was due to the subsidy, the bad state of the cloth trade, the government espionage, and particularly to the aggressions of the gentlemen. In spite of its connection with Walsingham Priory the religious motive was not strong. The conspirators objected to the suppression of the monasteries partly because their almsgiving ceased, but chiefly because the confiscated lands went to increase the wealth and influence of their chief enemies, the country gentlemen. The prisoners at Norwich were heard to say that " if any great man had two dishes on his table, they would have had the one if they had gone forward with their business."[2]

The evidence from Aylesham is still more clear. This town was quite a centre of heresy, but it was also a centre of sedition. About the beginning of May seven persons were accused of heretical speeches. One case was very singular. Thomas Rooper " set up in the town of Aylesham a cross of wood whereon was made the image of the Pope with his three crowns, gilded, and a cardinal, which was gilded by John Swan of Aylesham and Simon Cressy the carver and setter up thereof." It is difficult to deduce the religious belief of the designer of this curious symbol. Two persons said that they knew a hundred traitors in Aylesham, which is perhaps partly explained by the conduct of four other men who " reported that there was an Act of Parliament made that if their church lands were not sold before May Day the King would have it; whereupon they sold it to defeat the King thereof, and have converted the money coming of the sale thereof to their own use." They tried to get hold of the church jewels also, but the churchwardens refused to give them up, saying " if the King wished to have it he was most worthy." Again the thieves' religious convictions cannot be deduced from their action; the devout stole church property to prevent the sacrilege of its falling into the King's hands, the reformers did the same to prevent idolatry[3].

There can be no doubt about the opinions of Elizabeth Wood of Aylesham, who on 12 May said to John Dix, tailor, as she was leaning upon his shop window, " It is pity that these Walsingham men were

---

[1] L. and P. xii (1), 1284.   [2] L. and P. xii (2), 56.
[3] L. and P. xii (1), 1316.

discovered, for we shall have never good world till we fall together by the ears:

> And with clubs and clouted shoon
> Shall the deed be done,
> For we had never good world
> Since this King reigned.
> It is pity that he 'filed
> Any clouts more than one."[1]

She was singing or saying an old rhyme which played its part in the later Norfolk rising[2].

Twenty-five men were imprisoned at Norwich for the Walsingham plot[3]. According to the report of some prisoners, Rogerson and George Guisborough thought of accusing several others who had known their plans, especially "a rich gentleman" who had promised them six or seven score sheep, and had said they should not lack sheep as long as he had any. They had even written out their accusation, when William Guisborough, George's son, remonstrated with them, saying, "Father, there is no remedy but death with us, and for us to put any more in danger, it were pity." His gentleness touched the others and they tore up the paper. Several of the prisoners gave evidence that they had seen pieces of paper "as small as pence or two pence" flying about; one had seen a fragment "about the breadth of a groat...stamped in the water by James Biggis, his fellow that he was coupled unto."[4] Five prisoners were prepared to give the names of those whom they had heard Rogerson mention as his fellow-conspirators, but others whom they named as witnesses declared that they had never heard Rogerson speak in the prison. They were in a different house from him, and saw the other prisoners only occasionally from a distance in the chapel. All the accused denied absolutely that they knew anything about the plot[5].

The conspirators were tried on Friday 25 May 1537. Twelve were condemned to execution, three to perpetual imprisonment, two were remanded to prison without judgment, and the other eight were pardoned. Rogerson and four others were executed at Norwich next day. On the scaffold a most unusual incident occurred; Rogerson attempted to address to the crowd a justification of his conduct. He was cut short by the executioner[6]. This gives one reason why the

---

[1] L. and P. XII (1), 1301.
[2] L. and P. XII (1), 1300.
[3] Ibid. 68.
[4] Russell, op. cit. Introduction.
[5] L. and P. XII (2), 56.
[6] L. and P. XII (1), 1300.

last words of the condemned at this period are nearly always said to have been a confession of the crime, an acknowledgment of the impartiality of their trial, and a humble apology. If the criminal attempted to say anything inconvenient he was promptly silenced for ever. Two more of the prisoners were executed at Yarmouth on Monday 28 May, George Guisborough and Nicholas Mileham suffered at Walsingham on 30 May, and William Guisborough and another at Lynn on Friday 1 June. The twelfth man seems to have been spared[1].

After the executions at Norwich two men of Houghton juxta Harpley were discussing the news. One of them, Thomas Westwood, had been sent to ask the other, Thomas Wright a carpenter, to come and work for his master. Westwood remarked that the wife of one of the traitors fell down in a swoon when her husband was executed, and lay so for an hour, but her husband had as he deserved. Wright was accused of answering, "They that did for the commonwealth were hanged up."[2]

The state of England cannot be considered healthy or happy when such an unscrupulous watch was exercised over every careless word and every expression of ordinary humanity, but it is a good sign that this spying was deeply resented by the people themselves. The monks of Lenton Abbey, Notts, talking together at Easter, said: "It is a marvellous world, for the King will hang a man for a word speaking nowadays," to which another replied, "Yea, but the King of Heaven will not do so, and He is King of all kings; but he that hangs a man in this world for a word speaking, he shall be hanged in another world his self."[3] These sentiments were very natural, but they provoke the reflection that it was the Church which had taught the King that a man otherwise blameless might be put to death "for a word speaking" or for holding heretical opinions. For centuries Church and State had played into one another's hands. So long as the clergy felt certain that the heretics whom they condemned and "relaxed to the secular arm" would be burnt, they were ready to teach that obedience to the King was a duty second only to obedience to the Church, and they blessed with their approval and imitation the barbarous penalties for treason. Now that the age-long alliance was broken, they were shocked and indignant to find themselves suffering the fate that they had complacently inflicted on others.

[1] L. and P. xii (1), 1300 (3).
[2] L. and P. xii (2), 13 (2).
[3] L. and P. xii (1), 892 (ii).

NOTES TO CHAPTER XIX

Note A.
Pacem emit armorum precio
O quam letus dolor in tristi gaudio
Grex respirat pastore mortuo
Plangens plaudit mater in filio
Quia vivit victor sub gladio.

Then follow rubrics with the beginnings of versicles:—

Versus—justus igitur...
Collecta—Deus per cujus...
Capitulum (?)—gloriosus pontifex...

Note B. It is interesting to observe that Anne Askew, the protestant martyr of 1545, was the daughter of Sir William Askew, one of the commissioners who helped to check the Lincolnshire rebellion. She became the wife of Thomas Kyme of Kelsey, whom she was forced to marry although he was devoted to the old religion[1]. He must have belonged to the same family as Guy Kyme, which would make his relations with his wife still more difficult.

Note C. One of Sir John Bulmer's papers, seized after his arrest, was a letter from his sister-in-law Anne, the wife of Sir Ralph Bulmer[2]. The writer referred to a message which she had sent to Sir John by his servant Blenkinsop. She mentioned her "brothers" Richard Bowes and Harry Wycliff, but as she was one of the two daughters and co-heirs of Roger Aske of Aske, she had no brothers by blood[3]. Richard Bowes was her brother-in-law, the husband of her sister Elizabeth. Harry Wycliff may have been her step-brother or even her foster-brother. He was accused on 30 March 1537 of inciting the commons to rescue Anthony Peacock, the Richmondshire rebel[4]. The letter from Anne Bulmer is dated Easter day, but without the year. She says that she has received letters from Sir John on Good Friday, and that she and her two "brothers" have arranged that her husband Sir Ralph shall meet Sir John at Northallerton on Easter Tuesday in order to arrange some business over which, apparently, Sir John and Sir Ralph had quarrelled. The nature of the business is not stated.

This may be the treasonable letter that Blenkinsop brought, but it does not bear any outward trace of treason. In fact, if its date was Easter 1537, it is rather evidence for than against Sir John, as it indicates that, so far from plotting a rising, he was busy with private affairs. But the government lawyers were quite unscrupulous in their use of documents, as for instance in the case of the Abbot of Sawley's supplication. They may have forced a treasonable interpretation upon the innocent letter, or it is possible that the business alluded to may not have been as harmless as it appears. In the absence of a date it is impossible to discover the true importance of the letter. It may have been written at some other Easter years before.

Note D. Froude made up his mind that the Marquis of Exeter must have encouraged the Cornish rising, and in consequence of this preconceived opinion he jumbled together several documents without any regard for their dates. First

---

[1] Dict. Nat. Biog. art. Askew, Anne.
[2] L. and P. xii (2), 189.
[3] See above, chap. iii.
[4] See above, chap. xviii.

he described the ordering of the banner by the Cornish fishermen, but assigned the intended display of it to the year 1538. In a note he admitted that this date was inconsistent with the fact that "the queen" was to be painted on the banner, as Henry in 1538 was a widower, but Froude explained this by saying that the banner was ordered in the summer of 1537, but the painter delayed his information until 1538; in order to fit in with his theory the insurgents must have ordered their banner a year before they meant to use it.

The passage continues, "At length particular information was given in, which connected itself with the affair at St Kevern. It was stated distinctly that two Cornish gentlemen named Kendall and Quyntrell had for some time past been secretly employed in engaging men who were to be ready to rise at an hour's warning." The implication is that the machinations of the two gentlemen were discovered in 1538, in consequence of the exposure of the Cornish plot; yet the evidence quoted in a foot-note sufficiently contradicts this, for it was a report addressed to Cromwell that Kendall and Quyntrell had told many people that "Henry Marquis of Exeter...would be king, if the King's Highness proceeded to marry the Lady Anne Boleyn, or else it should cost a thousand men's lives." This discrepancy passed unnoticed by Froude[1].

The conspiracy of Kendall and Quyntrell, in fact, took place and was discovered in 1531, when Exeter was banished from court for some time on account of its discovery[2]. It had nothing to do with the present agitation in Cornwall, and there is not the smallest reason to connect the Marquis of Exeter with this later movement.

Note E. This was a favourite proverb of the King's: "'Well then,' quoth the King, 'Let me alone, and keep this gear secret between yourself and me, and let no man be privy thereof: for if I hear any more of it, then I know by whom it came to knowledge. Three may,' quoth he, 'keep counsel, if two be away; and if I thought that my cap knew my counsel I would cast it into the fire and burn it.'"[3]

---

[1] Froude, op. cit. II, chap. xv.   [2] See below, chap. XXIII.
[3] Cavendish, Life of Wolsey (ed. Singer, 2nd ed.), p. 899.

CHAPTER XX

THE END OF THE PILGRIMAGE

It is not likely that any tidings of the new attempts at insurrection reached the prisoners in the Tower. They were cut off from the world and forgotten; the conspirators who still maintained their cause did not even plan a rescue.

The champions of the old faith lay at the mercy of the reformers, but even this was not perhaps the most deadly feature of the prisoners' position. Their plight was rendered still worse by the fact that they were the upholders of the common law, but they had fallen into the hands of the civilians. There was a new influence at work in the law courts, inimical to the ancient free customs of England:—

"In 1535, the year in which More was done to death, the Year Books come to an end: in other words, the great stream of law reports that has been flowing for near two centuries and a half, ever since the days of Edward I, becomes discontinuous and then runs dry. The exact significance of this ominous event has never yet been duly explored, but ominous it surely is. Some words that once fell from Edmund Burke occur to us: 'To put an end to reports is to put an end to the law of England.'"[1]

One sign of this new influence was very significant, namely, the interrogation of the prisoner before trial. This practice, which was closely connected with the use of torture, was contrary to the usages of English common law, but it was so freely employed in Henry VIII's reign that "in criminal causes that were of any political importance an examination by two or three doctors of the civil law threatened to become a normal part of our procedure."[2] Every one of the prisoners after the Pilgrimage of Grace was repeatedly interrogated and their answers were used as the chief evidence against themselves and each other.

Norfolk expected the last batch of prisoners from the north to arrive in London on 21 April 1537. Sir John Bulmer and Margaret

---

[1] Maitland, English Law and the Renaissance.

[2] Ibid.; for the form of criminal trial at this period see Holdsworth, Hist. of Eng. Law, II, 160, 164.

were reunited in the Tower, never to be "departed" again, except for a few hours[1].

The King was not satisfied with such a small number of prospective executions, and several of the gentlemen had narrow escapes. It was characteristic of the royal gratitude that two of the three noblemen who had served him most faithfully in the north were among those in danger. The Earl of Cumberland paid no penalty for his loyalty, but the Earl of Northumberland, who had refused the rebels' oath at the risk of his life, was threatened with a prosecution for treason. He had made the King his heir, but he was "an unconscionable time a-dying." Henry wanted to settle the north, and entertained the idea of sweeping away all the three Percy brothers at once. The Earl was charged with the surrender of Wressell Castle to Aske, although this event was undoubtedly covered by the pardon[2]. The accusation was made about the end of April, and on 29 April the unfortunate man wrote to declare his unswerving loyalty[3]. It was probably not so much his innocence as the state of his health which saved him from a traitor's death. On 3 June he sent word that although he had made the King his heir on condition that certain articles of his devising were performed, he now withdrew all conditions and submitted everything wholly to the King[4]. Perhaps the threat of a prosecution had been made in order to secure this submission. On 29 June 1537 the Earl died and the King at last entered upon the inheritance that he had coveted so long[5].

Young Sir Ralph Evers, who had defended Scarborough Castle against the rebels, must have appeared to be perfectly secure of the King's favour, yet he also fell under suspicion. He had been ordered to seize the goods of the quondam prior of Guisborough and of Dr John Pickering, and he was charged with embezzling some of the money[6]. The charge was very likely true, but his gains cannot have been great, and at a time when pickings were so plentiful his conduct was hardly worthy of remark.

A more serious matter against him was his alleged letter to Sir John Bulmer, which contained disrespectful comments on Norfolk and Cromwell[7]. Norfolk examined him about it on 11 July and was

---

[1] L. and P. xii (2), 181; printed in full, Archaeologia, xviii 294.
[2] L. and P. xii (1), 849 (53); printed in full, De Fonblanque, op. cit. i, append. liii.
[3] L. and P. xii (1), 1062.
[4] L. and P. xii (2), 19; printed in full, de Fonblanque, op. cit. i, chap. ix.
[5] L. and P. xii (2), 165; printed in full, de Fonblanque, op. cit. i, chap. ix.
[6] L. and P. xii (1), 535, 979, 1293; xii (2), 12 (2).
[7] See above, chap. xix.

favourably impressed by his answers. The Duke advised that Evers should be summoned to London, although he was in very bad health, suffering apparently from a serious abscess in his ear. Norfolk did not think he could live long, and suggested that the letter had been forged against him by his enemy Sir Roger Cholmeley[1]. Evers insisted that he had not written the treasonable passages, on the very good grounds that he could neither read nor write more than his own name[2]. Sir Ralph was at Windsor in July[3], but returned safely to the north in August[4]. His summons to London at such a time naturally caused his family the greatest anxiety. His wife was reported to have said, "There is twenty of the best in Yorkshire hath sent me word that if my husband were in any danger, that they would rise and fetch him out or else die therefore," and also that if her husband were in any danger above, it would turn to a worse business than the death of any man that died in Yorkshire. Two servants who tried to lay information against her were imprisoned by John Evers, Sir Ralph's brother, in the parsonage of Lythe, near Whitby. They contrived to escape to Sir Ralph's enemy Sir Roger Cholmeley, and laid their accusations against Lady Evers[5] and her brother-in-law, but Norfolk treated the matter lightly, perhaps because her words were true and he dared not meddle with her[6]. Norfolk came to the conclusion that the incriminating letter had been written by one of Evers' servants, but he was satisfied with the punishment of the servant, and overlooked the offence of the master[7].

The King's auditors on 28 December 1536 accused Lord Conyers of hindering them in their collection of the royal rents, "for some said if he commanded [the tenants] they would pay, insomuch that Mr Fulthorpe, constable of the Castle [of Middleham] urged him to further the audit."[8] This was duly noted, and as soon as the King could act with safety Lord Conyers was sent for and put in ward. By Norfolk's advice, however, he was released instead of being brought to trial. Lord Conyers returned home and incurred the King's further displeasure by breaking "his promise at his departure from Windsor," whatever that may have been[9]. Nevertheless he escaped further trouble.

Lord Latimer's danger was even greater. He was vaguely implicated in the Bulmer conspiracy, and it was known that he had

---

[1] L. and P. xii (2), 248, 583, Append. 1.   [2] Ibid. 291.   [3] Ibid. 356.
[4] Ibid. 519.   [5] Ibid. 733.
[6] Ibid. 828; printed in full, State Papers, v. p. 109.
[7] L. and P. xii (2), 828, 850.   [8] L. and P. xi, 1380.
[9] L. and P xii (2), 14.

suggested at Pontefract that the clergy should be asked whether it was ever lawful for subjects to rebel. He was also connected with Sir Francis Bigod, whose baby son Ralph was pledged to Lord Latimer's daughter Margaret[1]. Latimer was summoned to London at the same time as Sir John Bulmer, but he never obeyed the summons[2]. At length, about the middle of June, Norfolk induced him to go up to London as a suitor on his own affairs; the Duke was not scrupulous in such matters, but perhaps it was as a salve to his conscience that he wrote to Cromwell that he could find no evidence against Latimer[3].

Lord Latimer had been proposed as a member of the Council of the North, but his name was struck off the list[4]. He arrived in London about 29 June[5], and his friends gave him up for lost. His brother Thomas Nevill, hearing of his journey, exclaimed to his wife, "Alas, Mary, my brother is cast away. By God's Blood, if I had the King here I would make him that he should never take man into the Tower." Hearing a poor woman lamenting that the parson of Aldham, Essex, who had been arrested for treason, "should be put to death upon a false wretch's saying," Nevill replied, "No, Margaret, he shall not be put to death, for he hath no lands nor goods to lose; but if he were either a knight or a lord that had lands or goods to lose, then he should lose his life."[6] Yet lands and goods might save a life as well as destroy it. Lord Latimer escaped for the time by means of a bribe to Cromwell in the form of his house within the Charterhouse churchyard, the lease of which had cost Latimer 100 marks, besides his expenses on many improvements[7].

Lord Lumley came up to London with Lord Latimer, and saved himself in the same way. The evidence which connected him with the Bulmer conspiracy was fairly clear, but he sent a substantial bribe to Cromwell, with the hint that, in consequence of his son's attainder, he could make whomsoever he pleased his heir[8]. By these means he was enabled to die in his bed.

It is not likely that Latimer and Lumley would have been able to buy themselves off if the King had really determined upon their death, but in the case of Lumley the royal vengeance was satisfied by the execution of his son George Lumley, and after the trials of Darcy and Hussey Henry must have realised that it would not be easy to secure a conviction on the very slender evidence which was all that

---

[1] L. and P. XII (2), append. 28.   [2] Ibid. 14.   [3] Ibid. 101.
[4] Ibid. 102 (3).   [5] Ibid. 166.   [6] Ibid. 665.
[7] Ibid. 784.   [8] Ibid. 8.

could be produced against Latimer. Barons and lesser nobles were the only men whose trials gave Henry any difficulty. The great nobles, Buckingham, Exeter, Norfolk, made so many enemies, that it was easy to accomplish their fall. Knights, country gentlemen, and common people were at the King's mercy. But barons must be tried by their peers, who were collectively too powerful to be intimidated; and these judges were led by a strong class spirit to sympathise with their unfortunate fellow-peer who stood before them. Before this Lord Dacre had been acquitted[1]; later the King found it impossible to bring Lord Delaware to trial[2], and even at the present crisis the peers made an effort to save Lord Darcy. Lord Hussey excited less sympathy, being comparatively an upstart.

Darcy was committed to the Tower on 7 April 1537[3], and on the 8th the King sent orders to Norfolk to seize his lands, papers, etc.[4] There was some apprehension at court that his arrest might provoke a fresh rising, but Norfolk had taken his precautions, and assured Cromwell that there was no danger[5], while he seized the goods in accordance with his orders[6].

Darcy was examined at the Lord Chancellor's house about 16 April[7]. He did not make a patient subject for cross-examination; he knew that his doom was fixed and, like Macbeth, he turned upon his enemies:

"They have tied me to a stake; I cannot fly,
But bear-like I must fight the course——."

He greeted his examiners with the words: "I am here now at your pleasure; ye may do your pleasure with me. I have read that men that have been in cases like with their prince as ye be now have come at the last to the same end that ye would now bring me unto. And so may ye come to the same."[8] He accused Surrey; he most probably accused Norfolk[9]; he defied Cromwell with the famous challenge: "Cromwell, it is thou that art the very original and chief causer of all this rebellion and mischief, and art likewise causer of the apprehension of us that be noble men and dost daily earnestly travail to bring us to our end and to strike off our heads, and I trust that or thou die, though thou wouldst procure all the noblemen's heads within

---

[1] See above, chap. II.   [2] See below, chap. XXIII.
[3] L. and P. XII (1), 885, 846; printed in full, Miscellaneous State Papers (ed. the Earl of Hardwicke), I. 48.
[4] L. and P. XII (1), 863.   [5] Ibid. 967.
[6] Ibid. 991.   [7] Ibid. 981.
[8] Ibid. 1120.   [9] See above, chap. XI.

the realm to be stricken off, yet shall there one head remain that shall strike off thy head."¹

Darcy was examined again in the Tower before his trial², but the fragments of his answers on the first occasion show plainly the reason why the full record of them has not been preserved. It must have been a very spirited document, but too many people were interested in its destruction for it to survive, while there was no motive for keeping it, as it incriminated none of the other Pilgrims. This is proved by the summaries of the evidence against the different prisoners, and the memoranda for the prosecution. In these the names of the witnesses against each prisoner are given, with references to the examinations and depositions containing the evidence. Not a single person was accused by Darcy; not a single charge was strengthened by his evidence. He made good his vaunt that "Old Tom has not one traitor's tooth in his head."

All Darcy's papers were seized and sent to London; they were very numerous, for he kept copies of almost every letter that he ever received or wrote³. His method of writing was to make a rough copy of the letter himself in his large, bold, uncouth hand-writing with individualistic spelling; this was given to one of his secretaries who made one fair copy, or perhaps several if the matter was important. Out of this correspondence the Crown lawyers proceeded to pick treason, and their notes show the kind of evidence which must have been given at the trial as proof of the charges in the indictment⁴.

This evidence falls into three classes, (1) the treasonable acts which he was accused of committing since the King's pardon; (2) those which he committed during the rebellion; (3) those which he had committed before the period covered by the pardon which extended from 10 October to 10 December 1536⁵.

(1) The principal evidence in the first category was that Darcy in his letters about Bigod's rising had repeatedly stated that Norfolk was coming down to confirm the general pardon and to appoint the time for the new parliament and convocation, that he came with but a small company, and that the commons must remain quiet until he arrived⁶. This was twisted into treason on the grounds that it implied, if the terms were not confirmed, according to the rebels' unreasonable requests, "they will revive their traitors' hearts; meanwhile they are

---

[1] L. and P. xii (1), 976. [2] Ibid. 1079.
[3] L. and P. xi, 929; L. and P. xii (1), 1088.
[4] L. and P. xii (2), 186. [5] L. and P. xii (1), 1207 (8).
[6] *Darcy's Letters*: L. and P. xii (1), 115, 135, 155, 162, 184. *Evidence*: ibid. 847 (5), 848 (2) (5) (15) (16), 1087 (pp. 497–8).

to stay but upon the Duke's coming." This charge is obviously nonsense. Darcy believed the King's solemn and repeated assurances that he pardoned everybody, and that he would hold a free parliament. Now that the King did not mean to keep his promises, it was suggested that Darcy's faith in the royal word was treason. Darcy believed that Norfolk brought from the King conciliatory messages which would satisfy the commons, and take away their wish to rebel again. In this mistaken belief he pacified the country, and this was also considered a proof of treason.

Another piece of evidence on which stress was laid was that Levening, "one of the principal traitors with Bigod," had asked Darcy to speak to Norfolk on his behalf, and that Darcy had never reported his application[1]. This shows the King's superb command over circumstances. Levening was not a traitor. He had been tried and acquitted; legally he was an innocent man, and it could not possibly be treason to help him to clear his character. But in spite of the verdict of the jury the King had made up his mind that Levening was a traitor, and as a traitor he was to appear in all other trials.

More evidence against Darcy was gleaned from Parker's letter which described the state of Lancashire at Christmas time[2]. It was a report of muttered discontent and threatening preparations. Cromwell commented on it that Parker would not have written this if it had not been Lord Darcy's pleasure[3], which shows the kind of report that he expected from his own spies; but it appears from the letter itself that Parker was far from sure that Darcy would be pleased, for he said, "My lord, I beseech your lord[ship] be not miscontent with me if [I show your] lordship what their communing is in all this country." Cromwell's other objection, that Darcy never reported Parker's warning to the royal lieutenants, was absolutely false. Darcy wrote to Shrewsbury about it on 7 January[4].

Further evidence related to Darcy's alleged message to Aske before the latter went up to London at Christmas. This has already been discussed and disproved[5].

Sir John Bulmer's statement that he sent Darcy warning not to go to London was mentioned, but this point was not dwelt upon, as even Cromwell must have realised that there was no proof that

[1] *Levening*: L. and P. xii (1), 730, 731. *Evidence*: ibid. 848 (10), 1087 (p. 497).
[2] Ibid. 7. *Evidence*: ibid. 848 (ii) (13), 849 (6) (37), 1087 (p. 498).
[3] Ibid. 847 (13). [4] Ibid. 39.
[5] Ibid. 849 (33), 974, 1087 (p. 498), 1175. See above, chap. xvii.

Darcy had received the message, and he certainly had not acted upon it[1].

Darcy's recent stewardship of Pontefract Castle was called in question, and it was considered equally treasonable that he had suggested the delay of its re-equipment for a few days[2], and that, when Sir George Darcy insisted on speed, he had applied to Aske for the weapons which had been carried off by the rebels[3].

One of the notes deals with an interesting point in the second negotiations at Doncaster. It was alleged that Darcy wrote to Suffolk and Shrewsbury to require that the appointment should be observed in Lincolnshire, and that no prisoners should be executed. As none is known to have been put to death until March this probably was in fact part of the appointment[4].

The last accusation of this class was that Darcy, in a letter which has not been preserved, invited Aske to meet Chaloner, Grice and Sir Robert Constable at Templehurst, ending "I trust in our being together shall stay many things, and all good men I find well-minded thereunto, your faithful, Thomas Darcy." Against this it was objected that the meeting was suspicious, and that "by the words 'your faithful' it appears there is great fidelity betwixt the Lord Darcy and Robert Aske, being but a mean person."[5]

A puzzling note in the evidence states that Darcy, in Lent, sent a copy of one of Norfolk's letters to "the prior of Whalley now attainted"; this showed that he favoured a traitor[6]. There is some mistake here, for the prior of Whalley was not a traitor; it was the abbot who was condemned for treason[7]. Talbot deposed that one of Aske's servants gave him a copy of a letter from Norfolk to Darcy, which he delivered to the abbot of Whalley, but the witness did not state when this happened[8]. It is by no means improbable that Cromwell simply invented the date, "in Lent," and that the letter referred to was really the one found in the vicar of Blackburn's house, which had been sent out in November with the summons to the council at Pontefract[9]. Aske's letter about the same council is also mis-endorsed "since the appointment."[10]

---

[1] L. and P. xii (1), 1087 (p. 497).
[2] *Delay*: ibid. 280, 295. *Evidence*: ibid. 849 (82), 1087 (p. 498).
[3] *Application*: ibid. 390. *Evidence*: ibid. 848 (1), 1087 (p. 497).
[4] *Evidence*: ibid. 848 (4), 1087 (p. 497). *Letter*: L. and P. xi, 1293, illegible in the essential passage.   [5] L. and P. xii (1), 848 (8).
[6] Ibid. 847 (10), 848 (ii) (12), 1087 (p. 498).
[7] Ibid. 840; printed in full, Beck, op. cit. 347.
[8] L. and P. xii (1), 853.   [9] Ibid. 878.
[10] L. and P. xi, 1128; xii (1), 849 (7).

(2) The second class of evidence against Darcy ought not to have been brought into the case, as the events were covered by his pardon. It was no longer a matter of importance whether the surrender of Pontefract Castle was collusive[1], whether Darcy took the rebels' oath[2], what he said to Somerset Herald[3], or whether he proposed to send a message to Flanders[4]. All this should have been obliterated by his pardon of 18 January 1536-7[5]. Nevertheless minute inquiries were made on all these points in order to blacken the case against him.

Owing to his high office and influential position there were naturally a great many papers relating to different periods of the rising in Darcy's possession. Some had been sent to him before the siege of Pontefract by the King's lieutenants, while he was still acting for the King[6]; others had been intercepted during the rebellion or had been sent to him by the rebels[7]; while others again were later than the pardon, when he was once more acting for the King[8]. The possession of these letters was the necessary consequence of the position which Darcy had filled for many years, yet it was considered highly suspicious, and was magnified into treason.

Other accusations which fall under this head had more point. By investigating the problem of the Pilgrims' badges it might have been possible to prove that Darcy had foreknowledge of the insurrection, although as a matter of fact nothing incriminating was discovered[9]. The government was naturally anxious to learn who were the Pilgrims' southern friends, as although Darcy's share of the correspondence was covered by the pardon, the other parties' share was not; but Darcy accused no one[10]. On this subject a story was sent to Cromwell that a certain beggar "said he had a letter from Lord Darcy to my lord of Exeter in his cape." The cape was cut to pieces, and the remains of a letter, also cut up, were discovered. The finder, Sir Walter Stonor, sent the fragments to Cromwell, but he did not put much faith in the tale, as both the beggar and his accuser were "very simple men."[11] In an age of such universal suspicion there was an immense temptation to half-witted people to acquire

[1] L. and P. xii (1), 852 (iii), 853, 900 (56) (60–64), 1022.
[2] Ibid. 900 (65–72). [3] Ibid. 944; cf. L. and P. xi, 1086.
[4] L. and P. xii (1), 1079, 1080. [5] Ibid. 134.
[6] Ibid. 848 (3), 849 (11) (12) (19) (20), 1087 (p. 498).
[7] Ibid. 849 (15) (45) (47); 849 (2) (p. 382); 849 (18), and L. and P. xi, 1080; L. and P. xii (1), 848 (7), 849 (46), 1087 (p. 498), 849 (5), and L. and P. xi, 1051.
[8] L. and P. xii (1), 849 (44) and 850; 849 (48) and 144.
[9] Ibid. 900 (78–87); printed in full, Eng. Hist. Rev. v. 554–5.
[10] L. and P. xii (1), 849 (8) and xi, 1128; xii (1), 852 and 852 (iv).
[11] Ibid. 797.

a dangerous importance by making accusations and professing to know secrets. Instances of this tendency have been given already, and this must have been another case, for although Cromwell was eager to implicate southern noblemen in the rebellion, nothing more is heard of the story.

(3) Finally comes evidence that Darcy had committed treason before the beginning of the insurrection. Here the prosecution was really on firmer ground. They suspected as much, but they had even less real proof than in other parts of the case. At this point a curious problem arises. There was no substantial evidence that Darcy had committed treason since the pardon; but from Chapuys' correspondence we know now that he had been guilty of treason two years before. The government suspected the earlier plot, but had never been able to prove it. Can it be said that justice was done when Darcy was executed?

So many innocent persons were put to death in Henry's reign that historians are apt to dwell with relief on any defects in the character of the condemned, no matter how irrelevant they may be to the charge on which he suffered. Darcy was tried and executed for a crime which he had not committed, but he had committed a crime for which, if his guilt could have been proved, he would have been executed. Unless the principle is adopted that the wickedness of some people is such that it is right to shoot them at sight, this is not a satisfactory way of administering justice. Even a criminal is entitled to a fair trial, and to acquittal when he is not guilty of the particular crime with which he is charged.

To return to the evidence against Darcy,—nothing could be proved, but a few rash speeches were brought up against him, which did not amount to treason. He had said that he would be no heretic[1], and that it was better to rule than to be ruled, but the utmost severity was needed to construe this into a plot against the King's title or life[2]. A witness was found in the person of a chantry priest, who deposed that he had been told that Darcy said, on hearing of the rebellion in Lincolnshire, "Ah, are they up in Lincolnshire? If they had done this three years ago it had been a much better world than it is now." The same deponent had also been told of another speech of Darcy's, apparently after the pardon, "By God's blessed mother, if the commons should happen to rise again, where there were then two shaven crowns that did take their parts, there will

---

[1] L. and P. xii (1), 900 (45-49), 945 (48); printed in full, Eng. Hist. Rev. v, 553, 572.
[2] L. and P. xii (1), 848 (11), 974.

now be four."[1] These speeches are reported on no authority but that of hearsay, and were repeated eight and four months after they were alleged to have been uttered. They would not be admitted as evidence in any law-court now, but no such nice scruples were entertained in Henry VIII's reign.

There may have been an attempt to accuse Darcy of plotting to murder Wolsey. The following notes are in the "articles against Lord Darcy":—"First, the destruction of the Cardinal in the Chancery"; "For the gunpowder to burn my Lord Cardinal."[2] Apparently the charge broke down. Norfolk tried to support it by sending Darcy's "book" against Wolsey. Darcy had taken the chief part in the Cardinal's prosecution and this "book" probably contained the charges brought against the latter with the consent of the King. Norfolk, however, said it showed that "the said lord has been long dissatisfied with the King's affairs, and the King may by his great wisdom pick out some matters long since imagined."[3] "The book that the Lord Darcy made against the Cardinal" was entered among the evidence against Darcy[4].

Other pieces of evidence were picked out of Darcy's old papers,—an indenture with a servant of quite an ordinary type[5], an order dated June 1536 for a statute book, which Cromwell thought "might be conspiracy before the insurrection."[6] But these points, and perhaps some of the others, must probably have appeared even to the King's lawyers too slight to be brought up at the trial.

It is difficult to know what to say about such pieces of evidence as these, so trivial, so disingenuous, and yet treated as of sufficient weight to cost a man his life. When the morality of another age is strikingly unlike our own, we are apt to excuse it on the grounds that it was the custom of the time, and that people knew no better. But this will not serve to excuse the treason trials of Henry VIII. People did know better. All intelligent and honourable men knew that the King was not doing justice. There is abundant proof in the preceding pages of this book that no class of society believed it to be just or right or necessary for the common safety to put men to death "for a word speaking," particularly when the evidence that the word had been spoken was only hearsay or was supplied by those who had an interest in the death of the accused. The treason laws, and trials such as those of More, Fisher and the

---

[1] L. and P. xii (1), 1087 (p. 497), 1200.
[2] Ibid. 848, 850 (2); see note A at end of chapter.
[3] L. and P. xii (1), 1064; see L. and P. iv (1), Introduction, p. dlv; (3), 5749-50.
[4] L. and P. xii (1), 848.   [5] Ibid. 849 (49).   [6] Ibid. 849 (50).

Carthusian monks, in the previous year, excited so much horror as to provoke the rebellion. The rising was at first successful; it was overcome not by force, nor by the rally of any considerable party round the throne, but by treachery. The King in the moment of victory was able to do as he pleased, for the defeated opposition was bewildered, terrified and helpless. But laws and legal proceedings of the kind which in part caused the revolt cannot reasonably be called a bulwark of national safety, nor is it altogether just to say that they were willingly accepted and supported by the nation.

On 15 May 1537 Lord Darcy was brought to trial in Westminster Hall on the indictment which had been found at York. The Marquis of Exeter was appointed Lord High Steward for the trial, and the panel of peers was composed of the Marquis of Dorset, the Earls of Oxford, Shrewsbury, Essex, Cumberland, Wiltshire and Sussex, Viscount Beauchamp, and Lords Delaware, Cobham, Maltravers, Powes, Morley, Clinton, Dacre of the South, Mountjoy, Windsor, Bray, Mordaunt, Borough and Cromwell[1]. It will be observed that Cromwell, who took the chief part in drawing up the indictment, was also one of the judges.

Darcy pleaded not guilty, and his peers were by no means willing to convict him according to a friend of Delaware, who said that Delaware, on coming from the trial, had told him he trusted Darcy would lose neither life nor goods, as Cromwell had promised to do his best for him[2]. Darcy could have told them the folly of listening to such a promise,—"he that will lay his head on the block may have it soon stricken off,"[3] but the tale served its purpose. The lords found him guilty, and if Cromwell intervened his petition was useless. The trial was on Tuesday, and it was at first intended that the execution should take place on Saturday. Darcy faced the prospect with great firmness; "Lord Darcy is a very bold man," wrote Husee[4]. On Friday Darcy sent for his confessor to be with him early next morning; he asked for either Doctor Aglabe of the Black Friars nigh Ludgate, or "the Doctor of Our Lady Friars in Fleet Street, a big, gross, old man."[5] His death, however, was postponed. The King could not make up his mind whether it would have a better effect to execute Darcy in London or in his own country, and until this point was settled he remained in the Tower.

On 3 June Norfolk sent up to London Thomas Strangways, Darcy's

---

[1] L. and P. xii (1), 1207 (16–21); printed in full, Deputy-Keeper's Report iii, append. ii. p. 247.   [2] L. and P. xiii (2), 808.
[3] L. and P. xi, 1086.   [4] L. and P. xii (1), 1239.   [5] Ibid. 1234.

steward, who had just been arrested at Beverley[1]. He had in his possession letters to Darcy from Norfolk, Bowes and Ellerker, and the King's letter to Bowes and Ellerker[2]. Norfolk said that the discovery of these letters showed that the Pilgrims had had spies in the royal camp, but it is not clear why he thought this, for all these were public documents which would naturally be circulated in the north. Strangways was "sore crazed" and could travel only very slowly[3]. When he reached London it was supposed that he would "open many matters,"[4] but "like master, like man." Strangways showed all Darcy's resolution, and made the King very angry by "labouring to excuse wholly Lord Darcy and Constable and that with such advancement of the fame of the country towards them as though our subjects there do much repine at their punishments, saying also plainly that they be more meet to rule there than you [Norfolk] be and much better beloved than you be, amongst the people of those parties." These words give an impressive picture of the faithful old servant, sick and helpless, yet daring to speak out before the terrible King.

The effect of Strangways' words was to make Henry almost determined to send down all the prisoners for execution in the north. He wrote to Norfolk:

"Considering that this matter of the insurrection hath been attempted there, and thinking that as well for the example as to see who would groan at their execution, it should be meet to have them executed at Doncaster and thereabouts; minding, upon their sufferance, to knit up this tragedy, we think it should not be amiss that we should send the said Darcy, Constable and Aske down for that purpose; requiring you, with diligence, to advertise us of your opinion in that behalf."[5]

Norfolk's reply has not been preserved, but he dared not risk the effect of Darcy's execution in the north; the idea was given up, and the old lord's life was prolonged again.

Darcy never entertained any hope of mercy. In June he sent a petition to the King, asking, not for pardon, but "that the straitness of the judgment may be mitigated at the King's pleasure." He had been condemned to the usual death for treason, but he was allowed the privilege of his rank and was beheaded. He also requested "to have confession and, at mass, to receive my Maker"; and begged that his whole body might be buried by that of his second wife Lady Nevill in the Friary at Greenwich. He sent in

---

[1] L. and P. xII (2), 22, 23. [2] Ibid. 43; xI, 1009, 1064 (2), 1065.
[3] L. and P. xII (2), 30. [4] Ibid. 105.
[5] Ibid. 77; printed in full, State Papers, I, 551.

a list of his debts, which were small, begging that they might be paid; "the premises served is great merit in, and to me a singular comfort, and to his Grace a small matter." He added that he forgave the King a debt of £4400 which the Treasury owed him, and therefore trusted that his Grace "will the rather command the within-written debts to be paid."[1] On June 30 1537 Lord Darcy was beheaded on Tower Hill[2]. His last wishes were not observed, for his head was exposed on London Bridge, and his body was buried "at the Crossed Friars beside the Tower of London."[3] On 22 July Darcy was posthumously degraded from his rank as Knight of the Garter, and his vacant stall was bestowed upon Cromwell[4]. The overthrow of the old by the new could not be more emphatically marked.

During Darcy's imprisonment his sons were in the north, scrambling for a share in the monastic lands. But there is perhaps a touch of natural feeling in a letter dated 3 May to the King from Sir Arthur, Darcy's younger and favourite son, in which he requested that if his father was condemned, he might be allowed to change his lands for others in the south, because he would never again "rejoice to abide here."[5]

Lord Hussey's wavering fortunes since the insurrection have already been traced. He had been accused, but never brought to trial; the accusation had been allowed to fall into abeyance, but he had never been pardoned. His trial was in one sense fairer than Darcy's, but in another even less fair. Darcy had openly committed treason, and borne arms against the King, but he had been pardoned. Hussey had never received a pardon, and consequently he was liable at any time to be brought to judgment for his behaviour during the rising in Lincolnshire, but on the other hand he had never committed any definitely treasonable act.

Hussey was arrested at about the same time as Darcy, and was imprisoned in the Tower[6]. He was present at Darcy's first examination[7]. His wife, who was living at Limehouse, was allowed to visit him, and he repeated to her such of Darcy's answers as are given above. All her misfortunes had not taught Lady Hussey discretion. She repeated the words to her servant Katharine Cresswell, the wife of Percival Cresswell, and the story soon spread abroad[8].

---

[1] L. and P. xii (2), 1. [2] Ibid. 166.
[3] Wriothesley, op. cit. i, 65.
[4] L. and P. xii (1), 1078; xii (2), 313, 445; the last printed in full, Anstis, The Order of the Garter, ii, 407. [5] L. and P. xii (1), 1129.
[6] Ibid. 905; L. and P. xii (2), 181; printed in full, Archaeologia, xviii, 294.
[7] L. and P. xii (1), 981. [8] Ibid. 976, 981.

The evidence against Hussey was much less bulky than that against Darcy, and it falls into two classes. The first was that relating to his conduct during the Lincolnshire insurrection. This has been fully discussed above[1]. His acts all showed him to be loyal; he sent out warnings, he tried to raise men, he kept his district quiet, and when resistance was hopeless he fled to the royal camp. Against the evidence of such conduct there was nothing to oppose but spiteful gossip, conjectures and perversions of evidence. It was said that though he received warning of the revolt on Monday, he did nothing until Wednesday[2], a statement which was contradicted by the Mayor of Lincoln's evidence that Hussey ordered him to prepare to resist the rebels on Tuesday[3]. It was brought up against Hussey that his servant Cutler, when in the power of the rebels, had told them that his master was at their commandment[4], but as the rebels had two days before killed Lord Borough's servant because his master opposed them, Cutler's words were clearly an attempt to save his own life, and no weight could attach to them. Finally Hussey was said to have ordered his servants to hide his weapons, but the witness admitted that this was probably to keep them out of the rebels' hands[5].

In Hussey's case, as in Darcy's, there was a second set of accusations which really had more foundation in fact. He had been in communication with the Imperial ambassador in 1534, although he had only sent him a single message of no importance[6]. His prosecutors laboured hard to prove his earlier offence. On his arrest he had uttered some imprudent words about the supper party with Darcy and Constable which had happened so long ago[7], but he gave a perfectly clear and simple account of what had passed there[8]. One witness was found who deposed that Hussey had said two years before that heresy would never be mended "without we fight,"[9] but even the crown lawyers could not consider this sufficient to condemn him, and in the end he was indicted only for his share in the Lincolnshire rising.

Lord Hussey was tried with Darcy, pleaded not guilty, and was condemned[10]. No one seems to have made any effort to obtain the

---

[1] See above, chap. vi.
[2] L. and P. xii (1), 1012 (4); 1087 (p. 500).
[3] Ibid. 964.
[4] Ibid. 1087 (p. 501).   [5] Ibid. 1213.
[6] See above, chap. ii.
[7] L. and P. xii (1), 973.
[8] Ibid. 899; printed by Froude, op. cit. ii, chap. xiv.
[9] L. and P. xii (1), 576.
[10] Ibid. 1207 (5), (7), (11–21); printed in full, Deputy-Keeper's Report, iii, Append. ii, p. 247.

King's mercy on his behalf. If Norfolk had been in London he might have done something. His connection with Hussey was not very creditable to either, being based on the relationship which Norfolk's mistress bore to Hussey, but it was useful, as he had interceded for Hussey before[1]. Norfolk went so far as to say that he was sorry for the sentence, though no doubt it was deserved[2]; the Duke suggested that Hussey might have sent the rebels information during the insurrection[3].

Hussey sent a petition to the King praying that his debts might be paid, and earnestly asserting his innocence, but he made no useless appeal for mercy[4]. He remained in the Tower until late in June, when the King resolved that he should be executed at Lincoln[5]. On 28 June he left the Tower on his last journey, in the custody of Sir Thomas Wentworth[6]. The King sent orders that he was to be beheaded and that the Duke of Suffolk must supervise his death, "which we desire may be done notably, with a declaration that of our clemency we have pardoned all the rest of the judgment."[7] The exact date of his death is not known, but it did not have altogether the required effect of striking awe into the hearts of the people, as it was followed by a riot in the city, about which unfortunately no details are preserved[8].

Hussey's fate was more sordidly tragic than Darcy's. Darcy died a martyr to the faith which he loved; he desired nothing better than "so high perfection," and to pity him would be an impertinence. But Hussey was killed merely to satisfy the causeless suspicion of the King and the malice of his enemies. There is even reason to suppose that his religious views had undergone some modification since he said he would be no heretic. No religious rites are mentioned in his last petition to the King[9], and a friend had shortly before promised to send him "a fair Bible."[10] The evidence is slender, and the point is not of much importance; if we are right it serves to emphasise the needless cruelty of his death.

The trial of the other Pilgrims followed immediately after that of the two lords. On Wednesday 16 May 1537 at eight o'clock in the morning[11] Sir Francis Bigod, George Lumley, Sir John Bulmer,

[1] L. and P. xii (2), 143; printed in full, Nott, Lives of the Earl of Surrey and Sir T. Wyatt, Append. xxviii; L. and P. xii (2), 1049; printed in full, Everett-Green, op. cit. ii, no. cxlix.
[2] L. and P. xii (1), 1252.
[3] L. and P. xii (2), 43.
[4] Ibid. 2.
[5] Ibid. 156 (2).
[6] Ibid. 926.
[7] Ibid. 156 (2).
[8] Ibid. Append. 31.
[9] L. and P. xii (2), 2.
[10] Ibid. 187 (2).
[11] L. and P. xii (1), 1199 (4).

Margaret Cheyne alias Lady Bulmer, Ralph Bulmer, Sir Thomas Percy, Sir Stephen Hamerton, Sir Robert Constable and Robert Aske were tried in Westminster Hall[1] upon the indictment which had been returned as a true bill at York and ran as follows:—

"That [the prisoners] did, 10 October 28 Henry VIII [1536] as false traitors, with other traitors, at Sherburn, Yorks., conspire to deprive the King of his title of Supreme Head of the English Church, and to compel him to hold a certain Parliament and convocation of the clergy of the realm, and did commit divers insurrections etc. at Pontefract, divers days and times before the said 10 October. And at Doncaster, 20 October 28 Henry VIII, traitorously assembled to levy war, and so continued a long time. And although the King in his great mercy pardoned the said [prisoners] their offences committed before 10 December 28 Henry VIII; nevertheless they, persevering in their treasons, on 17 January 28 Henry VIII [1536-7] at Settrington, Templehurst, Flamborough, Beverley and elsewhere, after the same pardon, again falsely conspired for the above said purposes and to annul divers wholesome laws made for the common weal, and to depose the King; and to that end sent divers letters and messengers to each other, 18 January 28 Henry VIII, and at other days and times after the said pardon. And that Sir Francis Bigod and George Lumley, 21 January 28 Henry VIII, and divers days and times after the said pardon, at Settrington, Beverley, and Scarborough, and elsewhere, with a great multitude in arms, did make divers traitorous proclamations to call men to them to make war against the King, and having thereby assembled 500 persons, did, 22 January 28 Henry VIII, levy war against the King.

And thus the said jury say that Bigod and Lumley conspired to levy cruel war against the King. And moreover the said jury say that the others above named, 22 January 28 Henry VIII etc. falsely and traitorously abetted the said Bigod and Lumley in their said treasons."[2]

The clumsy practice of including so many people accused of different offences under one vague indictment makes it necessary to disentangle each case in detail and in the order named above.

The Grey Friars' Chronicler records that "On 13 March 1536-7 Sir Francis Bigod was brought out of the North to the Tower through Smithfield and in at Newgate, riding so through Cheapside and so to the Tower, and Sir Ralph Ellerker leading him by the hand with that he was bound withal."[3] Bigod was in the Tower for a little less than three months, but the government was scandalously overcharged for his maintenance, as the Lieutenant put his charges down for six months at 10s. a week[4].

Before Sir Francis was sent up to London, he had been examined

[1] L. and P. xii (1), 1227 (13).
[2] Ibid. 1207 (8); printed in full, Deputy-Keeper's Report, iii, Append. ii, p. 247; de Fonblanque, op. cit. i, app. p. lv.
[3] Grey Friars' Chron. (Camden Soc.), p. 40.
[4] L. and P. xii (2), 181; printed in full, Archaeologia, xviii, 294.

repeatedly by Norfolk, who was rather annoyed that, though Bigod did not disguise his own offence, he would not accuse anyone else except Gregory Conyers[1]. In his confession he was obliged to mention the names of his brother Ralph and a friend Thomas Wentworth, but he was careful to add, "and whereas I take testimony at [*call to witness*] my brother and Mr Wentworth, I trust you will bear them no displeasure, and if you send for them, do not say why, else the country and they will fear I have accused them as councillors in this naughty matter of Hallam's and mine, of which [so] help me the blessed Body of God which yesterday I received, an they are any [*sic*] more guilty than the child unborn; so far as I know; and my mother, having no more children but us twain, would be too full of sorrow." Bigod's confession ended with a petition that, whatever his own fate might be, Norfolk would help two preachers, Mr Jherom, who had not his fellow for preaching, and one Cervington, "who in my country dare not come because he is a true favourer of God's word; he is a proper gentleman and honest, and can do good service at a table among other qualities."[2] So Sir Francis concluded, enigmatical to the last. He was about to die for the old religion, and his last written words are a commendation of the new. His former friend Latimer overlooked his backsliding and protected his widow and children[3].

Bigod's accomplice George Lumley had been in the Tower since the beginning of February. He was examined there on 8 Feb. by Cromwell and Drs Tregonwell, Layton and Legh[4]. Nothing is known about the details of his imprisonment.

Sir Christopher Hailes, the Master of the Rolls, appeared against Bigod and Lumley at their trial[5]. They both pleaded not guilty, and were both condemned[6]. There can be no doubt as to the justice of their sentence; their offences were apparent and openly confessed by themselves. The simplicity of George Lumley's conduct might have pleaded for him in more favourable circumstances, but where there was little hope of justice there was none at all of mercy. The King had a particular reason for his death. It had seemingly been decided that the government dared not attempt to arrest Lord Lumley, but he could be made to suffer for his offences through his son.

---

[1] L. and P. XII (1), 473, 533.
[2] Ibid. 533.   [3] L. and P. XII (2), 194.
[4] L. and P. XII (1), 369; printed in full, Milner and Benham, op. cit. chap. v.
[5] L. and P. XII (1), 1199 (3) (ii).
[6] Ibid. 1227 (13).

After his trial George Lumley wrote to his wife to beg her to pay his debts, of which he enclosed a list. His letter continued:

"Be good mother and natural to my three children to whom I give God's blessing and mine, desiring you further always to instruct my son to honour God and be obedient to His laws, and next God to give his diligent attendance to do his duty in loving, dreading and fearing his presence (?prince), observing his laws and to be obedient to them, and so doing I trust I shall pray in Heaven for you."[1]

The Bulmers were not long in the Tower, as Sir John and his wife had been placed there on or after 21 April. Ralph Bulmer had been committed to the Fleet, whence he wrote to Sir Oswald Wolsthrope on 6 May that he doubted not but that the truth would justify the declaration of his allegiance to his sovereign[2]. Before the trial he was sent to join his father in the Tower[3]. Humphrey Browne serjeant-at-law conducted the prosecution against Sir John and Lady Bulmer, and John Baker the attorney-general against Ralph Bulmer[4].

The case against Sir John was fairly clear, although the most incriminating piece of evidence, his letter to his brother Sir William Bulmer, was not discovered until nine months after his death, when it came to light in consequence of a family quarrel. On 23 February 1537–8 Sir William visited his wife and had a violent dispute with her over some of her title deeds. After he had left her, she imagined that he might have taken possession of some valuable documents, and proceeded with the help of a servant and a friar to go through her husband's papers. Among them she discovered Sir John's letter, and seeing that it was treasonable, she laid it before the Council of the North, "as in duty bound," said Bishop Tunstall[5]. Sir William was arrested and imprisoned in Pontefract Castle in consequence of her information, and from his examination some particulars of Sir John's conduct appear, which were not known at his trial in 1537[6]. Nevertheless enough was proved by the evidence of his chaplain William Staynhus, who seems to have saved his life by turning King's evidence against his master and mistress. He was corroborated to some extent by Lord Lumley, John Watts, and Ralph Bulmer's confession[7].

Just before the trial Norfolk sent up to London some papers which he had seized at Sir John Bulmer's house. He admitted that these letters had been written before the pardon, but said that they showed that "no man had a more cankered heart" than Sir John, for

[1] L. and P. xii (1), 1324; printed in full, Milner and Benham, op. cit. chap. v.
[2] L. and P. xii (1), 1142.
[3] Ibid. 1227 (13).
[4] Ibid. 1199 (3) (ii).
[5] L. and P. xiii (1), 865.
[6] Ibid. 568, 706–7.
[7] L. and P. xii (1), 1087 (p. 494).

"I think ye never read more lewd nor more malicious letters which I, Babthorpe, Thirleby and Uvedale every of us have perused his part for haste."[1] No letters which correspond with this description have been preserved. They must have been written to Sir John, unless he, like Darcy, kept copies of his own letters, of which there is no proof. Most of the letters to Sir John which are still extant were written after the pardon and are very loyal in tone[2]. There is also a collection of deeds relating to the Bulmer estates[3], and one family letter[4]. The only papers which could be turned against Sir John Bulmer relate to the monastery of Guisborough; one was the order sent by the Pilgrims' council of York, which directed Sir John to maintain the Prior of Guisborough in the enjoyment of his office, and the other was an appeal sent by the Prior to Sir John for help in the management of his unruly monks[5]. As the Prior had been put in by Cromwell, this appeal is evidence rather in favour of Sir John, but it was very dangerous for any gentleman to meddle in the affairs of a monastery, and an equally innocent document was sufficient to cost the lives of Percy, Hamerton and Tempest. It may be, therefore, that these were the lewd letters to which Norfolk referred.

Sir John Bulmer had not borne arms against the King since the pardon, but he had become involved in a succession of plots, none of them sufficiently well-contrived for success, but each enough to cost him his life. His case shows the danger which the over-severity of the law brought upon the government. Sir John had been drawn into treason by accident. There is no proof that he desired Sir Francis Bigod's confidence, or that he wished to help him. His original crime was a natural reluctance to hand his nephew over to the executioner. Knowing that the government would refuse to take this into consideration, he was driven by terror and despair from plot to plot, whereas if he could have expected mercy, he would probably have committed himself no further.

The charges against Margaret and Ralph Bulmer rested only on the evidence of William Staynhus and Sir John himself, the two men whom above all others they must have believed to be most trustworthy[6]. It is not just to blame Sir John too much for this. In his written confession he neither admitted his own guilt nor accused anyone else. He offered to find a hidden treasure for the King, which was perhaps as good a defence as any[7]. But a weak-willed, impetuous

---

[1] L. and P. xii (1), 1184.
[2] Ibid. 66, 164, 236, 271.
[3] L. and P. xiv (1), 976.
[4] L. and P. xii (2), 189.
[5] L. and P. xi, 1135 (2), 1295.
[6] L. and P. xii (1), 1087 (p. 493).
[7] Ibid. 1083.

man of his type must have been helpless under cross-examination. He was brought to confess his own offences, and those of his family, although against the will of his judges he persisted in calling Margaret his wife to the last[1]. Their union may have been irregular, but it was founded on sincere affection. Margaret knew all his plans; she hoped for success while success was possible, and when all had failed she counselled him to fly and save both their lives. Sir William Bulmer's lawful wife dutifully betrayed him. Margaret was faithful to the last. She seems to have given no evidence and made no confession.

Ralph Bulmer was accused both of foreknowledge of Bigod's rising and of sending treasonable messages from London. The only witness against him who is named is his father[2].

At the trial Sir John and Margaret pleaded not guilty, but Ralph's plea is not recorded. After the jury had retired, however, they withdrew their plea and substituted guilty. In consequence of this the jury was exonerated from giving a verdict and they were both condemned, Sir John to the usual penalty for treason, Margaret to be burnt. The jury was also exonerated from giving a verdict in Ralph's case, and he was re-committed to the Tower[3]. His name remains carved on the wall in the Beauchamp Tower. He was still imprisoned there in the following year and it is not certain when, if ever, he was released[4].

Sir Thomas Percy and his brother Sir Ingram had come up to London immediately after Norfolk's arrival in the north. As they were perfectly well aware that the King was anxious to get rid of them, the very fact of their coming shows a strong conviction of innocence. There are two points in Sir Thomas' behaviour since the pardon which are suspicious, but it is a remarkable circumstance that neither of these is mentioned in the notes for the proceedings against him. The first was his interview with William Leache, the Lincolnshire fugitive, as deposed by George Shuttleworth. The second was the meeting at Rothbury in January, at which he was alleged to have forced some gentlemen to take the Pilgrims' oath. As neither of these charges was brought forward, it must be concluded that the evidence was insufficient to support them. There was in fact nothing to show what passed between Sir Thomas and Leache; it is not even certain that he knew who Leache was, as the fugitive may have concealed his name. The evidence with regard to the Rothbury meeting rests on an unsigned paper which was

---

[1] L. and P. XII (1), 1087 (p. 494). [2] Ibid. 1087 (p. 495).
[3] Ibid. 1227 (13). [4] L. and P. XIII (1), 568.

probably drawn up by Sir Reynold Carnaby, the Percys' mortal enemy.

The charges which were brought against Sir Thomas might be substantiated by evidence, but they were of a very trivial character in themselves, as they rested merely upon letters which had been sent to him, for which he could not justly be considered responsible. The prosecution laid great stress on the Abbot of Sawley's supplication, yet it was not only harmless in itself, but Sir Thomas could not possibly have prevented the Abbot from writing and sending it. Sir Thomas' reply was non-committal, and the only accusation which could be founded upon it was that he had not arrested the messenger, a step for which there was no apparent reason[1].

The second incriminating document was Bigod's letter, which was forwarded to Sir Thomas by his mother. To this he had returned no answer, and he declared that it was respect for his mother which had prevented him from arresting the messenger, her servant[2].

The third alleged letter was a very mysterious one, connected with the rising in Richmondshire. Ninian Staveley deposed that the Abbot of Jervaux and the quondam Abbot of Fountains ordered himself, Middleton, Lobley and Servant to send a message to Sir Thomas Percy, bidding him come forward. They sent a servant to Northumberland, after Twelfth Day [6 January 1536-7], and the man told them on his return that Sir Thomas had written down their names and had said that he would send for them when he came to the country. Both the abbots denied that they had sent any such message[3]. Sir Thomas never referred to the matter in his deposition, and the supposed messenger was never named or produced. Staveley was quite untrustworthy, and it is probable that the story was a mere invention.

Sir Thomas was further charged with his disorderly behaviour in Northumberland[4], and with George Lumley's statement that he was the "lock, key and ward of this matter."[5] There were some grounds for the first of these two charges, although it rested on the testimony of his enemy. As for the second, Lumley had been careful to explain that he was describing Sir Thomas' influence in Yorkshire, and did not mean that he had any particular knowledge of the new insurrection.

---

[1] L. and P. xii (1), 1087 (p. 496), 1088.
[2] Ibid. 893; printed in full, de Fonblanque, op. cit. i, chap. ix.
[3] L. and P. xii (1), 1012 (1), 1023 (ii), 1035 (1), (iv).
[4] Ibid. 1086.   [5] Ibid. 1087 (p. 496).

Sir Stephen Hamerton came up to London as unsuspiciously as Sir Thomas Percy. He was examined in the Tower on 25 April by Tregonwell, Layton and Legh[1]. The only points alleged against him were the occurrence of his name in the Abbot of Sawley's supplication and his meeting with the Abbot's messenger[2]. Even the prosecution admitted that in this there was no matter against him except before the pardon[3], but as usual it was laid to his charge that he had not arrested the messenger[4]. A modern lawyer might as well accuse a man of failing to arrest the postman who delivered a letter containing a forged cheque. There was a general feeling in the north that messengers ought to have something of the privilege of heralds; their exemption from responsibility was both convenient and just, as they were servants who were obliged to obey their masters' orders, and did not necessarily know the contents of the letters that they carried. The government was doing its best to destroy this privileged position.

John Hynde, King's serjeant-at-law, who had been so successful in Lincolnshire, conducted the prosecution of Sir Thomas Percy and Sir Stephen Hamerton[5]. Like the Bulmers they first pleaded not guilty, and then withdrew the plea and substituted guilty[6]. There is something suspicious in this change. The King was always anxious to obtain a confession of guilt from those whom he intended to execute, and he did not care what means were employed to attain his object. It is possible that the prisoners were induced to plead guilty by the promise of a mitigated sentence.

Sir Stephen Hamerton was probably a victim to his feud with the Stanleys[7]. No other reason can be found for his condemnation, as the extant evidence against him is trifling and he had not distinguished himself during the insurrection. The Earl of Derby had done Henry good service; he probably interested himself in his cousin's quarrel, and if he asked for any favour from the King, such as the life of a man, he was not likely to be refused. Sir Stephen's son Henry Hamerton died about two months after his father; it was said that his death was caused by grief at his father's execution[8].

Sir Robert Constable was arrested about the same time as Lord Darcy[9]. He was examined, but his answers have not been preserved[10].

---

[1] L. and P. xii (1), 1034. [2] Ibid. 1087 (p. 496). [3] Ibid. 1088.
[4] Ibid. 1086. [5] Ibid. 1199 (3) (ii).
[6] Ibid. 1227 (13). [7] Ibid. 1321; see above, chap. iii.
[8] Yorks. Arch. and Top. Journ. viii, 404.
[9] L. and P. xii (2), 181; printed in full, Archaeologia, xviii, 294.
[10] L. and P. xii (1), 900 (47); printed in full, Eng. Hist. Rev. v, 553.

The evidence against him was of the slightest description. He had been present at the famous dinner party when Darcy, Hussey, and he declared themselves no heretics[1], but there was and is nothing to show that he knew of Darcy's communications with Chapuys.

At the beginning of the Lincolnshire rising he "took Philips, a captain of the commons of Lincolnshire, servant to Lord Hussey, and brought him to the lords at Nottingham." They sent Sir Robert to pacify the East Riding, with orders to join Darcy at Pontefract "if the commons were in great number." He was in the Castle when it was surrendered, but he could not be considered responsible for the act of the commander[2].

The principal evidence against him was based on the letters which he had received from and sent to Bigod[3]. In particular Bigod had said that there was no man whom the commons trusted so much as Constable[4]. In his reply Sir Robert urged Bigod to give up his purpose. The concluding words of his letter, in the original draft which is in Aske's handwriting, were "Thus in all your worshipful affairs our Lord be your governor."[5] It is very much to be wished that the history of this draft could be traced. Perhaps after writing it Aske handed it over to a servant to be copied. This was Lord Darcy's method of letter-writing. The copy would be sent to Bigod, and the original would remain in the possession of Sir Robert Constable, at whose house it was written. The copy might fall into the hands of the government when Bigod's, and the draft when Constable's, papers were seized[6]. But the copy, if it ever existed, has not been preserved.

There is a reason for this theorising. At Constable's trial a certified copy of the letter was produced, but it does not tally with the draft. The most important difference is in the conclusion, which, in the certified copy, runs "Thus in your worshipful affair, our Lord be your governor."[7] The prosecution, of course, insisted that Bigod's "worshipful affair" was the insurrection, and that Constable was praying for its success. The phrase "all your worshipful affairs" has much less significance. Unless the theory outlined above is accepted as the history of the letter, the certified copy must have been deliberately altered from the original draft to strengthen the case against Sir Robert. On the other hand, if a copy of the original draft was sent to Bigod, it may have contained whether by accident or

[1] L. and P. xii (1), 899, 978.
[2] Ibid. 1225.
[3] Ibid. 847 (1) (2) (11), 848 (ii), (7) (17) (18).
[4] Ibid. 145.
[5] Ibid. 146 (3).
[6] See above, chap. xviii.
[7] L. and P. xii (1), 146 (1) (2).

intention, the slight but important variation in the conclusion. Yet if such a version were in the possession of the government there seems no necessity for a certified copy.

Constable was accused, like Darcy, of saying that the King had promised a general pardon and a free parliament. He had also told the commons to stay only until the Duke of Norfolk came[1]. To this he replied that such were the King's orders: "The King's letters to me were to stay the country till the Duke of Norfolk's coming, and so I did."[2] But it was useless to plead his own orders to Henry when he did not choose to acknowledge them.

Constable's letter which requested Rudston to liberate Bigod's messengers was brought forward, and also the mythical letter to the mayor of Hull for the deliverance of Hallam[3]. These letters have been discussed above[4].

Finally Constable was one of the leaders to whom Levening had appealed, and in his case, as in the others, Levening's acquittal was overlooked[5].

When the prisoners were brought out of the Tower for trial, a mistake was made in the destination of Sir Robert Constable and Lady Bulmer, who were sent first to the Guild Hall. The trial took place in Westminster Hall, and the two mis-sent prisoners were despatched thither[6]. At the trial Sir Thomas Willoughby, serjeant-at-law, appeared against both Constable and Aske[7]. Sir Robert pleaded not guilty and maintained the plea, whatever inducements may have been used to make him withdraw it. The jury returned a verdict of guilty[8].

Sir Marmaduke Constable the younger was honourably free from the fear or coldness which kept the relations of the other prisoners from exertions on their behalf. He was now in London doing what he could for his father, who wrote to tell him how to use in his favour all the influence at court which the Constable family possessed. Sir Robert had hopes of obtaining the intercession of Lord Beauchamp, the Earl of Rutland, and the Queen, to whom he was distantly related. If all were in vain he charged his son to see that his debts were paid[9]. Sir Robert petitioned Cromwell, not for his life, but for the payment of these debts. He had no money himself; it had all been

[1] L. and P. xii (1), 847 (5) (6) (9), 848 (ii) (8) (9).
[2] Ibid. 1225. [3] Ibid. 847 (8), 848 (ii) (10), 1088, 1130.
[4] See above, chap. xvii, note E. [5] L. and P. xii (1), 730, 1087 (p. 497).
[6] Grey Friars' Chron. (Camden Soc.), 40.
[7] L. and P. xii (1), 1199 (8) (ii). [8] Ibid. 1227 (13).
[9] Ibid. 1225.

spent during his imprisonment, for prisoners had to maintain themselves in the Tower, as the government allowance went into the Lieutenant's pocket. Four gentlemen had lately been Sir Robert's sureties for a payment to the King, and he particularly desired that they should not be allowed to lose by their bond; "Alas, that these poor gentlemen that were so lately bound for me and never had profit by me should be undone!"[1] The matter weighed upon his mind, and before his death he sent in another list of his debts[2].

Robert Aske went up to London on 24 March[3]. He knew that he was going into danger, and left a horse at Buntingford in order that he might send back a message as to how he fared[4]. It need hardly be explained that this cannot have been with any idea of a fresh rising, as all the other leaders came up to London at the same time; it was simply a private means of communication with his friends. On 7 April 1537 he was arrested and committed to the Tower[5] He was repeatedly examined and both the interrogatories and the replies have fortunately been preserved[6]. It is easy to see why this happened. Darcy's and Constable's examinations can have been only of personal interest, but Aske's were of real value to the government. They describe the state of the north and the whole course of the rebellion as seen by a very thoughtful and able man. In writing his long, careful answers to the interrogatories Aske perhaps cherished to the last a desperate hope that he might do some good to his country. His cause had failed, his life was forfeit, but his words might still be carried to the King's ear and might have some effect. His most elaborate replies were begun on 11 April, almost immediately after his arrest and imprisonment, and were continued on the 15th. His next set, undated, but written later, concluded with a partly illegible petition to his examiners:

"I most humbly beseech you all to be so good unto me...measures or by your favor to my lord privey....yt mr....tenant myght discherg my comyns to myn hostes as...might know....whether I might send for my rentes or fees or not without any....disples....to any man for onles the kinges highnes and my lord privey seall be mercifull and gracius unto me....I am not able to lyf for non of my frendes will not do nothing for me, and I have ned to have a payre of hous a

---

[1] L. and P. xii (1), 1226.
[2] L. and P. xii (2), 160.   [3] L. and P. xii (1), 712.
[4] Ibid. 1082; printed in part, Froude, op. cit. ii, chap. xiv.
[5] L. and P. xii (1), 846; printed in full, Miscellaneous State Papers (ed. the Earl of Hardwicke), i, 43.
[6] L. and P. xii (1), 852, 900, 901, 945, 946, 1175; 900, 901 and 945 are printed in full, Eng. Hist. Rev. v, 550–573.

dublet of fusthean a shirt for I have but one shirt her and a pare of showes I beseech you hertely that I may know your mynd herin and how I shalbe ordered yt I may trust to the same for the luf of god."[1]

No attention was paid to this pitiful appeal. On 11 May Aske was examined for the last time by Dr Legh and John ap Rice. At the end of his replies is another petition:

"Good mr doctor I beseech you to send me mony and my stuf as a shirt a paire of hous a dublite and a paire of shown for nether I have mony nor ger to were as ye sawe yourself for the reverence of god send me the same or els I know not how to do nor lyf and that mr pollerd be remembred for the same."[2]

Aske had now been more than a month in the Tower without the common necessities of life. He remained there about two months longer, and some sort of allowance must have been made to him, as the King wanted him to be kept alive for the royal purposes.

There was one charge against Aske which, if it could have been proved, would have warranted his condemnation, but it was not discovered until after his execution and was never properly investigated. On 2 August 1537 the Bishop of Rochester informed Cromwell that he had arrested at Bromley a priest called Matthew Fisher, who confessed that he had fled from the north at Whitsuntide. This priest stated that on Midlent Sunday, 11 March 1536–7, the captains of "his country" had received letters from Aske which ordered them to rise again, and 400 men had mustered, he himself being among them. The Bishop added that he believed there were other fugitives in his diocese who had fled from the north when Aske was arrested[3]. There seems to be no foundation for this vague story. The Bishop never mentioned the name of Fisher's "country," but it is certain that in Midlent Aske was riding in Norfolk's train under close surveillance[4]. The reports from the north on and after 11 March are full, and not a word is said of any stirring[5], while the royal lieutenants were so anxiously watchful that it was impossible for 400 men to muster without some report reaching one of them. The Bishop, who may not have been very well informed about northern affairs, probably misunderstood Fisher, who was perhaps concerned in the Cumberland or the Richmond rising; or possibly Fisher was one of the half-insane informers who appear from time to time.

Apart from this, the evidence against Aske is the same which has been repeated with wearisome regularity in the cases of Darcy

[1] L. and P. xii (1), 946.　　[2] Ibid. 1175 (3).　　[3] L. and P. xii (2), 420.
[4] L. and P. xii (1), 698.　　[5] Ibid. 629, 630–1, 641, 651.

and Constable. There is a certain probability that Aske knew about the intended rebellion before it broke out, but there was no proof of this foreknowledge then and there is none now. Aske had taken a small part in the Lincolnshire rebellion, but for that the King had expressly pardoned him[1]. It was objected against him that during the insurrection he made himself the chief rebel and that at the same time he had "a proud and traitorous heart,"[2] but for this also the King had pardoned him.

By Norfolk's advice Aske was questioned as to what had become of his money, "for he received no small sums in these countries of abbots, priors and others during the insurrection."[3] It was highly characteristic that Norfolk should imagine Aske to have been quietly feathering his own nest by extortions from the religious houses which he was nominally defending, but an insurrection is a costly affair and Aske had spent all the money he could obtain as fast as he received it on necessary expenses. He had made a declaration of the spoils that he had shared in when he was at Court, and the King was then "gracious to him therein."[4]

As Aske's replies are preserved, some of the evidence which was brought against both himself and Darcy is discredited. He had received no message from Darcy on going up to London for the first time[5], and he had informed Norfolk of Levening's petition[6]. Like Constable he was charged with an attempt to secure the liberation of Hallam and of Bigod's messengers[7], and with bidding the commons stay only till the Duke of Norfolk's coming[8].

The chief point against him, as against the others, was that in the middle of January he still expected that there would be a parliament, convocation and a general pardon; thereby showing that if his "unreasonable requests" were not granted, he would "revive his traitor's heart."[9] He had written to Darcy on 8 January 1536-7 that the King had granted free election of knights and burgesses, and free speech in convocation. He concluded, "Trusting your Lordship shall perceive I have done my duty as well to the King's grace, under his favour, as also to my country, and have played my part, and thereby I trust all England shall rejoice." This was held to prove that "he continues in his traitor's heart and rejoices in his treasons, and it is to be noted that he, by writing of the same letter,

---

[1] L. and P. xii (2), 292 (iii).
[2] L. and P. xii (1), 849 (51) (52).
[3] Ibid. 847 (8), 848 (ii, 11), 849 (3), 991.
[4] Ibid. 698 (2).
[5] Ibid. 849 (33), 974, 1119, 1175, 1206.
[6] Ibid. 847 (12), 848 (ii, 14), 698 (3).
[7] Ibid. 847 (3), 848 (ii, 10), 1087 (p. 497).
[8] Ibid. 847 (4) (5) (9).
[9] Ibid. 848 (ii, 15), 1087 (p. 497).

committeth a new treason."[1]. He also committed a new treason by saying to the commons "your reasonable petitions shall be ordered in parliament."[2]

Although it was plainly treason that Aske should believe the King's promise, it was also treason to write that "it was reported the King would not be as good as he promised concerning the church lands."[3] This lost letter of Aske's has already been discussed[4].

These accusations were based chiefly on the papers which had been seized at Aske's lodgings in London when he was arrested[5]. He does not seem to have kept copies of the letters which he wrote, except in the case of one manifesto[6]. There are only thirteen letters preserved which were written to him and of these seven are copies which were in the possession of other people[7]. The remaining six must have been found in his rooms[8]. The leader of a prolonged insurrection must have had many more documents than this meagre number. When he was interrogated about them his reply was, "To his remembrance they [the papers] be in his chamber in his brother's house and in the chamber in Wressell Castle where he lay; albeit he thinks there be few at Wressell, but they be all in his said chamber or else in some other place in his brother's house, where his servants left them. Also he thinks there be some in a little coffer which his niece keeps, which is plated with silver [?]...there unlocked in his brother's house at Aughton....Also there be bills of complaint betwixt party and party during that time in a little trussing coffer in his said niece's chamber, albeit to his remembrance they be but of small effect touching any article of the petitions or requirements, and if he can remember there be any writings in any other place, he shall always declare the same as it cometh to his remembrance."[9]

With these ample directions Norfolk caused the papers at Aughton to be seized, but a certain mystery envelopes their fate. On the day of the trial, 17 May, Cromwell wrote to Norfolk for the papers, which he had expected to receive long before. Norfolk's reply was curiously shuffling. He expressed deep regret that they had not been sent earlier. He had devoted all one night to reading them, with two helpers, and he had believed that they were sent up to London long ago. The bearer of the letter would explain how

---

[1] L. and P. xii (1), 43, 848 (i, 13).
[2] Ibid. 848 (ii, 3).
[3] Ibid. 848 (ii, 4).
[4] See above, chap. xvii.
[5] L. and P. xii (1), 848 (ii).
[6] Ibid. 44.
[7] L. and P. xi, 945, 1107, 1306; xii (1), 46, 102, 115, 390.
[8] L. and P. xi, 1211, 1287; xii (1), 56, 191, 209, 315.
[9] Ibid. xii (1), 901 (2) (58); printed in full, Eng. Hist. Rev. v, 565-6.

XX] *The End of the Pilgrimage* 211

they had been forgotten. Amid all these apologies Norfolk never said that he was now sending or that he would send the papers[1]. They have never been discovered, and it is probable that they never left the north. A great many people there must have been interested in their suppression, and Norfolk may have been bribed to destroy them, or they may even have been stolen. In any case they certainly were not produced at the trial.

Aske, like Constable, pleaded not guilty; both were found guilty and condemned to death[2].

The other prisoners, James Cockerell, quondam Prior of Guisborough, Nicholas Tempest of Bashall, William Wood, Prior of Bridlington, John Pickering of Lythe, clerk, John Pickering of Bridlington, friar, Adam Sedbar, Abbot of Jervaux, and William Thirsk, quondam Abbot of Fountains, were brought up for trial on the same indictment, but were remanded until the next day, Thursday 17 May[3].

James Cockerell, the quondam Prior of Guisborough, was arrested shortly after Easter by Sir Ralph Evers[4], and was on his way up to London as a prisoner on 19 April[5].

The case against him was, first, that about Martinmas Sir Francis Bigod had attempted to restore him to his house[6]; this was covered by the pardon.

Second, he had read and praised Sir Francis' book about the royal supremacy since the pardon. He confessed that he had read the book, but denied that he had praised it[7].

Third, he had heard Sir Francis throw doubts upon the King's pardon[8].

The only witness against him who is mentioned was Sir Francis Bigod; the prosecution was conducted by John Baker, the attorney-general[9]. Cockerell pleaded not guilty, but was found guilty by the jury[10]. Under the new law of treason the fact that he listened to Sir Francis' book without arresting the author was sufficient to constitute his guilt.

Orders were sent to Norfolk for the arrest of Nicholas Tempest, to which he replied on 31 March that if Tempest were summoned to London he would go without hesitation, as he was in no fear[11]. Accordingly he was summoned, together with Sir Stephen Hamerton

---

[1] L. and P. XII (1), 1252.
[2] Ibid. 1227 (13).
[3] Ibid.
[4] Ibid. 582, 585, 1296.
[5] Ibid. 979.
[6] Ibid. 1087 (p. 499).
[7] Ibid. 1012 (4, v); 1087 (p. 499).
[8] Ibid. 1087 (p. 499).
[9] Ibid. 1199 (3) (ii).
[10] Ibid. 1227 (13).
[11] Ibid. 777.

and the Prior of Bridlington, on 7 April[1]. It was no wonder that he went without fear, as the sole charge against him was that he had been mentioned in the Abbot of Sawley's supplication to Sir Thomas Percy, which even the prosecution admitted was "no apparent matter against" him[2]. It was stated in general terms that he was a "principal doer in the second insurrection," but of this there was absolutely no evidence[3]. He was accused of maintaining the Abbot of Sawley, and in particular it was said that he had sent provisions to the monastery, but this was during the first insurrection and ought to have been covered by the pardon[4]. William Whorwood, the solicitor-general, appeared against him at the trial[5]. Tempest pleaded not guilty, but was condemned[6]. It is probable that he owed his death to the feud between his family and the Savilles. Sir Henry Saville had been loyal during the insurrection, and he was now reaping his reward. He had the ear of the Government, and was able to dispose of his enemies who had joined the rebels[7]. There does not appear to have been any other reason for Nicholas Tempest's death, as he was both innocent and inconspicuous.

William Wood, the Prior of Bridlington, came unsuspiciously up to London with Nicholas Tempest. There was, however, a little more evidence against him than against his companion. He was accused of giving aid to Lumley during his occupation of Scarborough in the second insurrection. The Prior's defence was that on hearing the first news of the rising he had warned Matthew Boynton; that he agreed with the neighbouring gentlemen to defend Bridlington against the rebels, that he had called out his own men for this purpose, and that he had endeavoured to prevent them from joining the rebels[8]. Matthew Boynton did not altogether bear out this story. He said that he had sent to the Prior for help to take Bigod and that the Prior had refused it to him. The Prior replied that he had needed all his men for his own protection[9].

The Prior's chief offence had been committed during the Pilgrimage. He had read and praised Friar Pickering's rhyme beginning "O faithful people," and had given money to the insurgents[10]. The King was exceedingly sensitive to ballad criticism, and the Prior's conduct during Bigod's rising was sufficiently suspicious to

---

[1] L. and P. xii (1), 846; printed in full, Miscellaneous State Papers (ed. the Earl of Hardwicke), i, 43.
[2] L. and P. xii (1), 1088.
[3] Ibid. 1020.
[4] Ibid. 1020, 1087 (p. 501).
[5] Ibid. 1199 (3, ii).
[6] Ibid. 1227 (13).
[7] Ibid. 632, cf. 783-4.
[8] Ibid. 1019.
[9] Ibid. 1020 (ii).
[10] Ibid. 1021 (3), 1087 (p. 499).

give an excuse for bringing him to the scaffold. The solicitor-general conducted the case against the Prior[1], who pleaded not guilty, but was condemned[2].

John Pickering of Pickering Lythe, clerk, seems to have been arrested solely because he was Sir Francis Bigod's chaplain[3]. He was imprisoned in the Marshalsea, where on 2 June he made a deposition against the Bulmers, although they had been executed the week before[4]. No evidence against him has been preserved. He pleaded not guilty, and was condemned[5], but eventually he was pardoned[6].

Friar John Pickering, his namesake, was a prominent Pilgrim, and the author of the popular rhyme just referred to. He had attended the council of divines at Pontefract, and had argued against the royal supremacy[7]. From the first it was known that he had taken part in Bigod's insurrection, and the King ordered his arrest on 22 February[8]. For a short while he evaded pursuit[9], but he was captured and despatched to London before 22 March[10]. He confessed to carrying messages from Bigod to Hallam, and to informing Bigod about the state of Durham[11]. In his case, at any rate, there was no miscarriage of justice. He had worked for his cause until the last, and had failed.

Adam Sedbar, the Abbot of Jervaux, was arrested early in March[12] and sent up to the Tower, where his name may still be seen inscribed on the wall. He was not a popular landlord, and had taken part in the Pilgrimage to some extent against his will. He was examined twice, first on 25 April and again on 24 May, just before his execution. He maintained his innocence to the last, and declared that the insurrection had little to do with religion, but was the work of the discontented commons[13].

The case against him was as follows:—

(1) About Christmas he had sent a servant into Lincolnshire to report on the state of the country. The servant brought back word that the Lincolnshire men were "busily hanged," and on this news the Abbot began to plot a new insurrection.

---

[1] L. and P. xii (1), 1199.
[2] Ibid. 1227 (13).
[3] Ibid. 1239.
[4] L. and P. xii (2), 12.
[5] Ibid. 1227 (13).
[6] Ibid. 192.
[7] L. and P. xii (1), 1021.
[8] Ibid. 479; printed in full, State Papers, i, 537.
[9] L. and P. xii (1), 609.
[10] Ibid. 698.
[11] Ibid. 1087 (p. 500).
[12] Ibid. 666.
[13] Ibid. 1035, 1269.

(2) He gave money to Ninian Staveley and others for the purpose of inducing them to rebel.

(3) He ordered Staveley to send a message to Sir Thomas Percy that he must come forward to help the Abbot in the new rising.

(4) When the men of Richmondshire rose, the Abbot sent his servants to join them, and promised them further help[1].

The Abbot's defence was:—

(1) He had sent the servant to Lincolnshire only to collect the rents belonging to the Abbey and for no other purpose.

(2) He had ordered money to be given to Staveley and his companion by way of a tip, because they had been trying to find some lost sheep belonging to the Abbey.

(3) He had never sent or ordered a message to Sir Thomas Percy.

(4) He knew nothing about the Richmondshire insurrection until the commons surrounded the Abbey and insisted upon carrying off his servants. As soon as they had gone, the Abbot fled to Bolton Castle, where he remained with Lord Scrope until the tumult was over[2].

Staveley and Middleton, the witnesses against the Abbot, were men of bad character, and on the whole it is probable that the Abbot's defence was true and that his only crime was his office.

William Thirsk, the quondam Abbot of Fountains, lived at Jervaux, and was involved in the same charges as Sedbar[3]. His defence was the same and was equally sound. Both were found guilty and condemned to death[4].

On Friday 25 May 1537 Sir John Bulmer, Sir Stephen Hamerton, Nicholas Tempest, James Cockerell, the quondam Prior of Guisborough, William Thirsk, the quondam Abbot of Fountains, and Pickering were executed at Tyburn. Bulmer and Hamerton enjoyed the privilege of their knighthood and "were but hanged and headed." The others suffered the full penalty of the law. Their heads were set on London Bridge and the gates of London[5].

These executions had, on the whole, a settling effect on the country. The reformers were delighted. The large and powerful class who desired peace above everything were reassured. Most of the

---

[1] L. and P. xii (1), 1012, 1028 (ii), 1087 (p. 500). [2] Ibid. 1035.
[3] Ibid. 1012, 1028 (ii), 1035, 1036, 1087 (p. 500).
[4] Ibid. 1227 (18). [5] Wriothesley, op. cit. i, 63.

conservatives were frightened into silence. But one Yorkshire man called William Moke, who was present at the executions, felt such indignation that when he heard Sir Richard Tempest and Thomas Grice were summoned to London he set out at once to warn them not to come. He foolishly mentioned his object at an inn in Lincolnshire, and as innkeepers were among the best of Cromwell's sources of information, Moke was at once arrested and brought back to London[1].

On the day when Sir John Bulmer died, 25 May, another execution took place. Lady Bulmer, or Margaret Cheyne as she was called, was drawn after the other prisoners from the Tower to Smithfield and there burnt. Burning was the ancient penalty for treason in the case of a woman, but it was seldom exacted. The poor women in Somersetshire, for instance, suffered the same fate as the men. The death of Margaret caused some sensation at the time. There is a touch of pathos even in the dry record of Wriothesley's Chronicle; she was burnt, he says, "according to her judgment, God pardon her soul, being the Friday in Whitsun week: she was a very fair creature and a beautiful."[2] At Thame in Oxfordshire her fate was discussed on the Sunday before she died. Robert Jons said that it was a pity she should suffer. John Strebilhill, the informer, answered, "It is no pity, if she be a traitor to her prince, but that she should have after her deserving." This warned Jons to be careful, and he merely replied, "Let us speak no more of this matter, for men may be blamed for speaking the truth."[3]

Froude says, "Lady Bulmer seems from the depositions to have deserved as serious punishment as any woman for the crime of high treason can be said to have deserved." The depositions show only that she believed the commons were ready to rebel again, and that the Duke of Norfolk alone could prevent the new rebellion. In addition to this she kept her husband's secrets and tried to save his life. She committed no overt act of treason; her offences were merely words and silence. The reason for her execution does not lie in the heinous nature of her offence, but Henry was not gratuitously cruel, and her punishment had an object. It was intended as an example to others. There can be no doubt that many women were ardent supporters of the Pilgrimage. Lady Hussey and the dowager Countess of Northumberland were both more guilty than Lady Bulmer. Other names have occurred from time to time, Mistress

---

[1] L. and P. xii (1), 1819. [2] Wriothesley, op. cit. i, 64.
[3] L. and P. xii (2), 357; printed in part, Froude, op. cit. ii, chap. xiv.

Stapleton, old Sir Marmaduke Constable's wife, who sheltered Levening[1], and young Lady Evers. But these were all ladies of blameless character and of respectable, sometimes powerful, families. Henry knew that in the excited state of public opinion it would be dangerous to meddle with them. His reign was not by any means an age of chivalry, but there still remained a good deal of the old tribal feeling about women, that they were the most valuable possessions of the clan, and that if any stranger, even the King, touched them all the men of the clan were disgraced. An illustration of this occurred in Scotland during the same year (1537). James V brought to trial, condemned, and burnt Lady Glamis on a charge of high treason[2]. She was a lady of great family and James brought upon himself and his descendants a feud which lasted for more than sixty years[3].

James' uncle Henry VIII was more politic. He selected as the demonstration of his object-lesson to husbands, which should teach them to distrust their wives, and to wives, which should teach them to dread their husbands' confidence, a woman of no family and irregular life, dependent on the head of a falling house. This insignificance, which might have saved a man, was in her case an additional danger. She had no avenger but her baby son, and we only hear of one friendly voice raised to pity her death. The King's object-lesson was most satisfactorily accomplished.

On Saturday 2 June 1537 Sir Thomas Percy, Sir Francis Bigod, George Lumley, Adam Sedbar the Abbot of Jervaux, and William Wood the Prior of Bridlington were executed at Tyburn. Sir Thomas Percy was beheaded, and was buried at the church of the Crutched Friars on Tower Hill[4]; the others suffered the full penalty and their heads were exposed on London Bridge and elsewhere[5].

Darcy, Hussey, Aske and Constable were still in the Tower, but with these exceptions the end of the treason trials and executions had been reached.

It is customary at this point to comment on the stolid indifference of the general public to such events, but a study of contemporary depositions shows that this placidity has been rather over-rated. Short of another insurrection, there was no way in which sympathy could be expressed with the sufferers; the lightest words laid a man at the mercy of any chance informer. Yet a perceptible murmur followed the death of the northern men. Thomas Strangways,

---

[1] L. and P. xii (1), 780.
[2] L. and P. xii (2), 346; printed in full, State Papers v, 94.
[3] Lang, James VI and the Gowrie Mystery.
[4] Grey Friars' Chron. (Camden Soc.), 41.   [5] Wriothesley, op. cit. i, 65.

Thomas Neville, William Moke, Robert Jons, Lord Delaware, Lord Cobham and Lord Montague each in his way uttered a protest which must have voiced the feelings of many others who dared not speak or who escaped detection. The feeling of Scotland was probably expressed by the Bishop of Aberdeen. "Ye have put down many good Christian men," he said to an English pursuivant, and when the latter protested, added, "ye that are poor men are good, but the heads are the worst."[1] The Spanish Chronicler, who seems to have come to England a few years later and depended for his information entirely on hearsay, never even mentions the second insurrection. His story is that the people were pacified by the King's promises, that as soon as there was no danger of any further rising Aske was persuaded by fair words to reveal the names of those who had helped him, and that the King then threw off the mask and caused all the leaders to be executed[2].

The attitude of the King's apologists is also very significant. Knowing that Henry's conduct was always severely criticised in France, Cromwell wrote to Sir Thomas Wyatt, the English ambassador there, that he must affirm that, although it was true Darcy and the others had been pardoned, yet they had all most ungratefully offended again and were justly sentenced to death. If it had not been for their second treason, the King would never have remembered their former crime[3]. In 1546 William Thomas wrote a panegyric of Henry VIII in the form of a dialogue between an Englishman and an Italian. The Italian objects against Henry, "After the Insurrection in the North, when he had pardoned the first rebellers against him, contrary unto his promise did he not cause a number of the most noble of them, by divers torments to be put to death?" Thomas of course makes the usual answer, that they had offended a second time[4]; but the objection shows that the executions were not accepted as just, and were not forgotten, or Thomas would have had no occasion to allude to them. Finally the Yorkshire Chronicler, Wilfred Holme, begins by stating that the pardon was not universal:—

> "And to the Duke of Norfolk's intercession
> There was granted a pardon and that general,
> From Don to Tweed for their whole transgression
> Of all contempts and trespasses as well as things vital
> *Nine* only reserved."

[1] Hamilton Papers, Vol. I, p. 44; see below, chap. XXI.
[2] Spanish Chron. (ed. Hume), chap. XVII.
[3] L. and P. XII (2), 41; printed in full, Nott, Lives of Surrey and Wyatt, p. 321, and Merriman, op. cit. II, no. 199.   [4] Thomas, The Pilgrim, p. 11 (ed. Froude).

But he presently adds that later these nine were also pardoned at Norfolk's intercession[1].

Considering the conditions of the period it may be said that this was quite a powerful body of criticism to be directed against Henry. He was exceedingly sensitive to public opinion, and although he had still a number of prisoners on his hands the executions ceased. There was a simpler way of disposing of the prisoners which attracted less attention. The plague was raging in London, and a few months in one of the prisons were enough to prevent anyone obnoxious to the King from troubling his Majesty again.

Sir Richard Tempest's case illustrates this point. On 11 March 1536-7 the Earl of Sussex reported to Norfolk that Sir Richard "was neither good first nor last."[2] He was accused of having called out the men of Halifax before 10 October 1536[3], which was the date of the beginning of the insurrection for the purposes of the pardon. A letter of his to Sir George Darcy was discovered in which he declared that he would take Lord Darcy's part against any lord in England[4]. Sir Richard Tempest was summoned to appear in London during Trinity term to answer these charges, or others[5]. William Moke's warning never reached him[6], and on 2 June 1537 Norfolk thanked Cromwell for telling him that the King "did not much favour" Sir Richard[7]. Tempest came up to London and was thrown into the Fleet. He petitioned Cromwell to be released on bail, because he was in jeopardy of his life, "the weather is so hot and contagious and the plague so sore in the city."[8] His petition was disregarded and on 25 August he died. "He willed his heart to be taken out of his body and carried to his own country, to be buried in the place he had prepared for his corpse and his wife's to lie in."[9]

Some prisoners fared better than this. William Aclom's name is mentioned among those who were accused of treason[10], but he was not included in the indictment. Leonard Beckwith summoned him before the Court of Star Chamber for robberies committed during the insurrection[11] and Aclom was imprisoned in the Fleet until his case should be tried. He made himself comfortable there by marrying

---

[1] Holme: The Downfall of Rebellion.
[2] L. and P. xii (1), 632.
[3] Ibid. 784.
[4] Ibid. 849 (9).
[5] Ibid. 1178.
[6] Ibid. 1319.
[7] L. and P. xii (2), 14.
[8] Ibid. 179.
[9] Ibid. 576.
[10] L. and P. xii (1), 1087 (p. 501).
[11] Star Chamber Proc. Bdle. xix, 393; Yorks. Star Chamber Proc. (Yorks. Arch. Soc. Rec. Ser.) ii, no. xlix, misdated 1535.

the sister of the keeper, with the result that Beckwith complained Aclom had "a very small imprisonment."[1]

Aclom's case was exceptional and several of the other prisoners must have died. Thomas Strangways was sick at the time of his arrest, and did not long survive[2]. Robert Thompson the vicar of Brough-under-Stainmoor was arrested before 24 February. Norfolk proposed that he should be tried and executed at Carlisle, although there was no proof that he had taken any part in the second insurrection, except that he had once prayed for the Pope[3]. Thompson was sent up to London on 8 March[4], and was examined in the Tower on 20 March[5]. He was never brought to trial, but from the Tower he was transferred to the King's Bench Prison where he found "his body...what with years, what with corrupt and stinking smells, what with cold and hunger, so sore pricked" that he earnestly petitioned Cromwell for mercy. The petition is endorsed "no" and the vicar was left to die in his miserable prison[6]. Sir Ingram Percy was imprisoned in the Tower at the same time as his brother Sir Thomas. There was no evidence of any kind that he had offended since the pardon, but he was kept a prisoner in the Tower for about a year. There he carved his name and motto

"Ingram Percy. Sara fidele." [*I will be faithful.*]

He was probably released in November 1538[7], when there was a rumour that he had fled to Scotland, but this was unfounded. His health must have been completely broken, for he never returned to the north and died in a few months. His will, dated 7 June 1538, was proved at Canterbury on 21 March 1538–9[8].

The fate of the other prisoners is unknown. Some must have saved themselves by turning King's evidence, as for instance Staynhus and Staveley. Richard Bowier did so well in this respect that although in March Norfolk had called him "as naughty a knave as any,"[9] in the summer he was petitioning Cromwell for a grant of monastic lands[10]. There were others who probably shared the fate of Robert Thompson in prison. A case was carefully made out against William

---

[1] L. and P. xii (1), 1163; xii (2), Append. 16, 17.
[2] L. and P. xiii (1), 706.
[3] L. and P. xii (1), 498; printed in full, Wilson, op. cit. no. xi.
[4] L. and P. xii (1), 609.
[5] Ibid. 687 (2); printed in full, Wilson, op. cit. no. xxii.
[6] L. and P. xii (2), 1339; printed in full, Wilson, op. cit. no. xxxi.
[7] L. and P. xiii (2), 996.
[8] Information supplied by Mr J. Crawford Hodgson.
[9] L. and P. xii (1), 698.   [10] L. and P. xii (2), 400.

Collins, the bailiff of Kendal, who was certainly guilty[1]. He was examined in the Tower on 12 April 1537[2], but after that nothing more is heard of him, saving that in a list of Cromwell's memoranda, probably drawn up in July 1537, there occurs the item, "for Collins, bailiff of Kendal."[3]

It remains, in Henry's words, "to knit up this tragedy," and to conclude with the fate of the two principals, Sir Robert Constable and Robert Aske. They remained in the Tower after the trial on 16 May for more than a month. The King made up his mind on 12 June that they should be executed in the north[4]; Constable, who had held Hull, was to be hanged there in chains, and Aske was to be executed at York "where he was in his greatest and most frantic glory." It was decided that they should be sent with Lord Hussey to Lincolnshire, in order that their appearance might be a warning to the rebellious people there[5]. On 28 June the three prisoners left the Tower under the escort of Sir Thomas Wentworth[6]. At Huntingdon they were delivered to Sir William Parr, who conveyed them to Lincoln, where Hussey was handed over to the Duke of Suffolk. Parr conveyed Constable and Aske to Hull, where they were transferred to the custody of the Duke of Norfolk[7].

Sir Robert Constable was kept in Hull until the next market day, in order that his end should have all possible publicity. He was asked whether his written confession contained all that he knew about the insurrection. He answered that he had omitted some "naughty words and high cracks which my lord Darcy had blown out," because he did not wish to repeat them while Darcy was alive. "He was in doubt whether he had offended God in receiving the Sacrament concealing this"; but now he was able to free his mind, "saying that they could hurt no man now my lord Darcy was dead."[8]

On Friday 6 July 1537 Sir Robert Constable was brought out to the Beverley Gate for execution. The government chaplain could not bring him to confess that he had committed treason since the pardon, "howbeit his open confession was right good." The passivity with which prisoners submitted to death in Tudor times is somewhat repugnant to modern ideas. When a man knows that his cause has been overthrown by treachery and his life forfeited by the most cruel

---

[1] L. and P. xii (1), 671, 849 (27) (29) (30), 878, 959, 965.
[2] Ibid. 914.   [3] L. and P. xii (2), 192.
[4] L. and P. xii (2), 77; printed in full, State Papers, i, p. 551.
[5] L. and P. xii (2), 156.   [6] Ibid. 166.
[7] Ibid. Append. 31.   [8] Ibid. 178.

injustice, we feel that he ought to make some protest at his death, that his warfare on behalf of right and justice, as he conceives it, ought to be carried on up to the very last breath. Any submission appears like a compromise with evil. In Henry VIII's reign public opinion was very different. In the first place, as we have seen, the officials who conducted the execution took summary measures to prevent the prisoner from saying anything in his own justification. In the second place an execution was a public amusement, and the people did not want to be made uncomfortable by it. They guarded against mental uneasiness in a very simple manner. If the prisoner submitted to his sentence and acknowledged that he had received a fair trial, they applauded him. There was no need to trouble about a man who was quite satisfied with his own fate. If, on the other hand, he did by any chance protest, they said that he must be a bad man because he died "uncharitably"; therefore he must have deserved his fate, and again there was no need to pity him. The prisoner had usually no power to resist the weight of public opinion, broken as he was in body by most rigorous imprisonment, and in spirit by his long conflict with the most paralysing human vices, injustice, cruelty and selfishness. He was worn out—

"Let the long contention cease,
 Geese are swans and swans are geese.
Let them have it as they will,
 Thou art tired, best be still."

There is something noble in this quiet resignation,—something which makes the protests of the modern martyr sound petty and shrill.

In the strength of this resignation died Sir Robert Constable. Norfolk reported that his body "doth hang above the highest gate of the town, so trimmed in chains...that I think his bones will hang there this hundred year."[1] The Beverley Gate was the scene of Hallam's sacrifice, when he turned his back on safety and chose to share the fate of his comrades. It was fitting that Sir Robert should die there, he who worthily fulfilled his motto:

"As to the ship is anchor and cable,
 So to thy friend be thou, Constable."[2]

A very different scene of friendship was enacted at his execution. Norfolk entered into conversation with Sir William Parr, saying that he was as much bound to Cromwell as ever nobleman could be to

---

[1] L. and P. xii (2), 229; printed in full, State Papers, v, 91.
[2] Tong, op. cit. Append. p. i.

another. Parr replied that he had heard and partly knew how willing Cromwell was to further Norfolk's interests. The Duke exclaimed, "Sir William, no man can report more than I know already, for I have found such assured goodness in him to me, that I never proved the like in any friend before; and therefore myself and all mine shall be, as long as I live, as ready to do him pleasure as any kinsman he hath." Parr, as was expected of him, repeated all this to Cromwell[1]. Such were the professions of the man who afterwards arrested Cromwell in the Council Chamber and "snatched off the order of St George which he wore in his neck."[2]

As the plague was raging in Hull, Norfolk left the town immediately after the execution, and conveyed Aske to York, where he was to suffer on the next market day[3].

Ever since he had assumed his perilous office as grand captain of the Pilgrimage, Aske had been haunted by the nightmare of an execution for treason, from which he had not even the protection of knighthood. His was not that unhealthy type of mind which despises life and seeks for death in any form. He had none of the hysterical enthusiasm which carries some martyrs through their sufferings in a state of happy insensibility. He saw that the death which threatened him was horrible and shameful, but he had the supreme courage to face it, not because he drugged himself with the thought of future bliss, but because it was necessary for the sake of his cause.

Aske was prepared to suffer martyrdom if it must be so, but he did not pretend to desire it. During the rebellion he was heard to say that "he had rather die in the field than be judged like a traitor."[4] On his last journey up to London he was accompanied by Robert Wall his foster brother and constant companion. When Wall heard of Aske's arrest, he cast himself upon his bed, and cried, "Oh my master! Oh my master! They will draw him and hang him and quarter him." A few days afterwards the faithful servant died of sorrow[5].

After his trial Aske sent a petition to the King, and another to an unnamed lord, probably Cromwell. He begged that his debts might be paid, and that his lands in Hampshire might revert to the right heirs, as he held them only for life. He solemnly declared that none of his kinsmen took any part in the insurrection, and begged that the King would be gracious to them, and not visit his offences

---

[1] L. and P. xii (2), Append. 31.
[2] L. and P. xv, 804.
[3] L. and P. xii (2), 203.
[4] L. and P. xii (1), 853.
[5] Ibid. 1082; printed in part by Froude, op. cit. ii, chap. xiv.

upon them. He requested that "other men's evidences," which had been in his charge at Gray's Inn and were seized with his papers, might be restored to the rightful owners. Finally he begged that his sentence might be commuted to perpetual imprisonment " or else let me be full dead ere I be dismembered."[1] On this point the King showed mercy. Aske was allowed to hang "until he died."[2]

The day appointed for Aske's execution was Thursday 12 July, which was market day in York[3]. Richard Coren, the government chaplain, was with him on the last morning, and received from him a list of the spoils which he had taken and not restored; he begged they might be discharged by the King. As with Constable, the chaplain tried hard to draw fresh details of the rising out of him, and noted, with some annoyance, that both men "thought a religion to keep secret between God and them certain things rather than open their whole stomach; from the which opinion I could not abduce them." The secret which the chaplain was so anxious to discover must have been the identity of the Pilgrims' friends in the south. The evidence that they had such friends has already been discussed[4]. When interrogated on the subject in the Tower Aske replied, "the common report of all that travelled in the south parts was then that if the north parts would come forwards that the countries as they came would take their part and join with them,...he never received letter nor special message with any promise of help from the South. The gentlemen of Yorkshire adjoining Lincolnshire told him that if any power had come into Lincolnshire before the agreement at Doncaster the commons of Lincolnshire would have taken their part. By such reports the said Aske knew the minds of the countries and none otherwise."[5] When this statement is compared with Aske's letter to Darcy in November 1536[6], it is evident that he was lying to his examiners. He probably confessed the falsehood to the chaplain, but still refused to betray the names of his allies. He stated, out of confession, that Darcy had told him during the Pilgrimage of his communications with the Imperial ambassador in 1535, which though suspected had not been known to the government before, and he also mentioned Darcy's intention of sending to Flanders, which had been discovered during the trial.

Two things troubled Aske because they had "somewhat aggrieved"

---

[1] L. and P. xii (1), 1223, 1224.   [2] Wriothesley, op. cit. 1, 65.
[3] L. and P. xii (2), 229; printed in full, State Papers, v, 91.
[4] See above, chap. xiii.
[5] L. and P. xii (1), 946 (8).   [6] L. and P. xi, 1128.

him. One was a speech of Cromwell's, who "spake a sore word and affirmed it with a stomach," that all the northern men were but traitors. The other was the fact that Cromwell had several times promised him a pardon, and the King had given him a token of pardon for confessing the truth, yet he was now to die. He said that he had kept these matters secret, and of course the chaplain, in his report to Cromwell, promised never to repeat them. Another secret which Aske had learnt was that Cromwell "did not bear so great a favour to my lord of Norfolk as he thought he did."[1] These blunt statements of facts that no one in diplomatic circles ever mentioned caused a slight flutter among those concerned. Norfolk and Cromwell were obliged to exchange more assurances of perpetual amity[2] and the English ambassador in Brussels wrote on 22 January 1539–40 that Chapuys "professeth with great oaths the King's good service and true intent in the place he was in, wherein he showed me of the accusation that Aske had made against him, and of his innocence therein."[3]

After his confession Aske was brought out of the prison and openly confessed he had offended God, the King, and the world. "God he had offended in breaking of his commandments, many ways; the King's Majesty, he said, he had greatly offended in breaking his laws whereunto every true subject is bounden by the commandment of God, as he did openly affirm, and the world he had offended, for so much as he was the occasion that many one had lost their lives, lands and goods. After this he declared openly that the King's Highness was so gracious lord unto all his subjects in these parts that no man should be troubled for any offence comprised within the compass of his gracious pardon." He was then laid upon a hurdle and drawn through the main streets of York, "desiring the people ever, as he passed by, to pray for him."

On reaching the Clifford Tower, Aske was made to repeat his confession, and then taken into the Tower to await the coming of the Duke[4]. All the principal gentlemen of the West Marches had been summoned to attend the execution, and others of Yorkshire including Aske's brother John, who afterwards had a severe illness[5].

When Norfolk arrived he pronounced an exhortation[6]. Aske was brought out upon the scaffold on the top of the tower, and there

---

[1] L. and P. xii (2), 292; printed in full, State Papers, i, 557.
[2] L. and P. xii (2), 291.   [3] L. and P. xv, 97.
[4] L. and P. xii (2), 292; printed in full, State Papers, i, 557.
[5] L. and P. xii (2), 203, 261.   [6] Ibid. 203.

repeated his confession, "asking divers times the King's Highness' forgiveness, my Lord Chancellor, my Lord of Norfolk, my Lord Privy Seal, my Lord of Sussex and all the world, and thus, after certain orisons, commended his soul to God."[1] So died Robert Aske, begging the forgiveness of the men who had done him to death. "And all the trumpets sounded for him on the other side."

NOTE TO CHAPTER XX

Note A. There are three long papers (L. and P. XII (1), 847, 848, 849) filled with notes on the evidence against Darcy and Aske. We have taken these to be notes for the prosecution, showing the material for the various charges brought against the prisoners. It has been suggested that our view is mistaken, and that these are really notes for the interrogation of the prisoners, but this seems improbable for the following reasons:—

(1) Against some of the items a note is made that a question is to be asked about that particular point, but if they were all intended for questions, there would be no reason to mark a few in this way. So far as the notes were used as interrogatories, it was chiefly in the matter of the dates of various letters mentioned in them, such dates being added in the margin.

(2) Against some of the items are written such comments as "this shows him a traitor," "thereby he committed a new treason." There could be no reason for such notes on a mere list of questions.

For these reasons therefore we take the notes to be the general outline of the case for the crown against Darcy and Aske.

---

[1] L. and P. XII (2), 292; printed in full, State Papers, I, 557.

CHAPTER XXI

THE COUNCIL OF THE NORTH

There is documentary evidence that 185 persons were executed in the north for their share in the risings between October 1536 and March 1537, and that 31 were executed in the south, making a total of 216. In addition to this there is reason to believe that some executions took place of which no record remains, and there were a certain number of prisoners who died in prison without trial. The slaughter at the assault on Carlisle was considerable, but there is no means of discovering how many fell there, as the only number mentioned, 700, seems to be much too great. Making allowance for these omissions, however, the death-roll, although much longer than historians have acknowledged, is short considering the standard of the period. It is said that 100,000 peasants were slaughtered in Germany after the revolt of 1525. In comparison with this Henry's modest total of little over 200 looks like humanity itself. If he won the victory by treachery, he is entitled to the praise of having used it with moderation, although this mercy was forced upon him by circumstances and was not much to his taste.

It may be doubted whether this punishment would have been sufficient to overpower the opposition to Henry's policy, if the King had not found an effective ally in the plague. The fatal disease which had raged in the south during 1536 spread northward in the summer of 1537, and continued its ravages in the northern counties during the next four or five years. Men had no time to trouble about the wrongs of the Church with that terrible spectre at the door. According to the King's servants it was the direct work of God on behalf of the King. At any rate it had a great deal to do with the peaceful close of Henry's reign.

The north of England at the beginning of the sixteenth century was the poorest and most backward part of the kingdom, the part, therefore, which required most attention and care at the hands of a competent ruler. So far Henry had not done well by it. He found the north poor, and he robbed it of the only treasure it possessed in the wealth of the abbeys. He found it backward, and he nearly destroyed the only civilising influence at work there, the Church. He found that the people cherished, among many faults, a few rude virtues, truthfulness, personal honour, fidelity to family and friends. He made no serious effort to reform their faults, but he did his best to eradicate their virtues. By his system of justice oaths were made so common that it was impossible they should be respected. Treacherous and false witnesses were encouraged. The brother was forced to condemn the brother, and the wife was tempted to betray her husband. It was impossible that the gentlemen should preserve the same standard and feel the same self-respect after they had been half bribed, half frightened into taking part in the arrest and condemnation of their kinsmen and friends. In short, the north was impoverished and degraded by Norfolk and the King.

Nevertheless Henry VIII was a statesman, and he had long intended to reform the north. His experimental councils are one sign of this. His intrigues against the Percys are another. The Pilgrimage of Grace afforded a very suitable opportunity to put his ideas into practice. By its means he at last laid hands on the whole of the Percy inheritance, and destroyed a power which had menaced the throne for two hundred years. This dangerous power had been delegated to the Earls of Northumberland in the hope that it would enable them to control the Borders, but time had proved the folly of the measure. The Percys could plunge the kingdom in turmoil whenever they chose, but they could not maintain any appreciable amount of good government on the Borders. At length Henry VIII destroyed the family by violence and treachery. The means were bad, but the end was worth attaining, and the King was firmly determined that no act of his should confer similar power on another great family, which his son or grandson would in turn be obliged to destroy.

Henry had determined to try a new plan of government on the Borders. No satisfactory way to hold the moss-troopers in check had ever been devised. The councils were in a perpetual state of reorganisation. The wardens of the Marches were often in trouble for treason and at other times pursued spirited blood-feuds among themselves or with the Scots wardens. It was no wonder that the King took the wardenships into his own hands and secretly resolved that no nobleman should hold them again.

The East Marches were offered to the Earl of Westmorland, but he was allowed to refuse the office[1], which would not have been the case if the King had really wanted him. Henry intended that the work should be done by knights and gentlemen appointed as his deputies and dependent on his own orders. They were to be assisted by the Council of the Marches. This body, which had been in existence for a long time, was composed of all the principal Border gentlemen, and the King decided to grant them pensions in consideration of the services which he hoped they would perform. The powers of the council were confined to the Borders; its members were officials such as Sir Thomas Clifford the captain of Berwick, Lionel Grey porter of Berwick, and Northumbrian gentlemen such as the Forsters, the Ogles, the Carrs and the Fenwicks. It was now proposed to include the headmen of the principal surnames of Tynedale and Reedsdale, the Charltons, Robsons, Dods, Halls and others. The presidents of the council were the deputy wardens, and its business was confined to Scots and English raids, outrages in Tynedale and Reedsdale, the safe-keeping of Border castles, and dealings with the English spies who infested the Lowlands of Scotland.

This council must not be confused with the Council of the North, as it was a totally distinct body. It was a makeshift means of dealing with the problem of the Borders. While England and Scotland were hostile, it was impossible to rule these districts justly and firmly. The reivers were not to blame for their situation. There is no real moral distinction between deliberately laying waste a fair country in time of war, and carrying off a neighbour's cattle under cover of night, except that the first is wanton destruction and the second is sometimes a work of necessity. The mosstrooper naturally lost all respect for the law which praised and rewarded the first and hanged him for the second. The King did his best to deal fairly by the Borders. It was not his fault that all plans failed; or at least it was his fault only in so far as he stirred up tumult and encouraged the terrible Warden raids which so often set the Scots fields ablaze just before harvest time. He had let a lawless genie out of the pot, which he could by no means conjure back again.

In January 1536–7 the Earl of Northumberland was dying. He made no difficulty about the surrender of the wardenships of the East and Middle Marches into the King's hands. The younger Percys were soon to be disposed of in the most definite way possible. There remained the West Marches, of which the Earl of Cumberland was the warden. On 24 January the King commanded the Earl

---

[1] L. and P. xii (1), 291.

to reconcile himself with Lord Dacre. Shortly afterwards the Privy Council desired the Earl to resign his office as warden, and announced at the same time that it was the King's pleasure to advance him to the Order of the Garter[1].

The King decided to appoint Sir William Evers to the East and Sir John Widdrington to the Middle Marches as his deputies, with Roger Fenwick as Keeper of Tynedale and George Fenwick Keeper of Reedsdale[2].

It might have been expected that the King would consult the Duke of Norfolk before making these appointments, as he was just about to start for the north. But perhaps he wished to show Norfolk that he was not entirely trusted. At any rate Sir Anthony Browne set out secretly with the commissions for the new deputy wardens several days before Norfolk, and the Duke was much surprised to find himself following in the steps of a royal messenger about whom he knew nothing[3]. Norfolk's authority was limited also in another way. From the first it had been determined that he should be accompanied by a council of "personages of honour, worship and learning," appointed by the Privy Council[4]. Their commission set forth the powers of the council "whose advice the Duke shall in all things use, and for whose entertainment he shall have allowance, as in a book, wherein the Duke and every councillor is rated at a certain ordinary, is contained." Some of these councillors accompanied the Duke to the north, the rest were gentlemen already resident there[5]. On 14 January "the Earl of Westmorland and Bowes were sworn of the King's Council in the North."[6] Sir Marmaduke Constable was vice-president, and William Babthorpe was a councillor[7].

The Council of the North was thus constituted in 1537, but as yet it had no independent authority. The members did not even sign Norfolk's despatches, and the Duke quoted their advice only when he was suggesting measures which would be disagreeable to the King[8].

When Norfolk was at Doncaster on 2 February he received from the Privy Council an explanation of Browne's errand. Besides the appointment of the new deputies[9], he carried letters patent to all the headmen of Tynedale and Reedsdale granting them fees as the King's

---

[1] L. and P. xii (1), 372-3; 372 printed in full, State Papers, v, 64.
[2] L. and P. xii (1), 222-5. [3] Ibid. 293.
[4] L. and P. xi, 1410 (3). [5] L. and P. xii (1), 98.
[6] Ibid. 86. [7] Drake, Eboracum, Bk i, chap. viii.
[8] L. and P. xii (1), 594; xii (2), 291, 369.
[9] L. and P. xii (1), 319.

servants[1]. At first Norfolk was not opposed to the general outlines of the plan, but he strongly objected to some of the King's pensioners. Edward and Cuthbert Charleton, Henry and Geoffrey Robson, Christopher and David Milburn, John Hall of Otterburn, and Sandy and Anthony Hall were all either thieves themselves or maintainers of thieves[2]. They had been involved in the murder of two gentlemen. "Light persons will say that the King is obliged to hire the worst malefactors and overlook their offences." Norfolk ventured to send after Sir Anthony Browne the advice that he should not deliver the patents to these men without further orders[3].

The Duke was snubbed by the Privy Council for his pains. "The King marvelled he should be more earnest against retaining such as have been murderers and thieves than such as have been traitors. These men rather did good in the late trouble, though they did it for their own lucre, and if they can be now made good men the King's money will be well spent." To grant them fees was not the same thing as to grant them pardons; if they were murderers they could still be punished for that. Norfolk must write at once to Sir Anthony and tell him to carry out his original orders without modification[4]. Henry always believed that the mosstroopers might be turned to good use if he could but manage them. On the approach of war with Scotland they became a valuable asset.

Sir Anthony Browne arrived at Berwick on Saturday 3 February. Besides the delivery of their commissions to the deputy-wardens, he was instructed to arrange a general pacification, to demand restitution from Tynedale and Reedsdale for the raids they had made in Northumberland during the rising, to appoint certain persons to advise the deputies, and to put Ford Castle into safe-keeping. In addition to these tasks, some of them not easy, he had still more delicate work to do. He must warn the Borderers against all breaches of the peace with Scotland; he must inform Sir Thomas Clifford that the Earl of Cumberland had been reconciled to Lord Dacre, and he must order Sir Thomas to "cast away his ancient grudges"; he must persuade the Northumbrian gentlemen "to live more in the heart of the Marches than they do now"; finally he was not to leave the north until the two younger Percys were safely in London by dint of force or strategy, and with them their henchman little John Heron of Chipchase[5].

---

[1] L. and P. xii (1), 291.   [2] Ibid. Append. 2.   [3] Ibid. 319.
[4] Ibid. 332; printed in full, Miscellaneous State Papers (ed. the Earl of Hardwicke), i, 33.   [5] L. and P. xii (1), 225.

Sir Anthony Browne sent for the gentlemen of Northumberland to meet him at Berwick on Tuesday 6 February. There were some who failed to answer his summons—Cuthbert and Edward Charleton, Henry Robson, Christopher and David Milburn, and Sandy Hall— all names on Norfolk's black list. The Bishop of Durham, who was making himself very useful, explained that they were noted freebooters who would not come in "for fear of their evil deeds;"[1] the deputy wardens confirmed this opinion[2]. The absentees would have received a pleasant surprise if they had plucked up heart to come; against all likelihood it was gold, not halters, that the King had sent them.

All the gentlemen who assembled at Berwick took the new oath to the King and received their patents. They took "not a little comfort" in being the King's servants, and would "think long" until they had earned their pensions by some deed. The Greys were at feud with the Carrs, the Forsters and Ogles with the Halls; indeed it is safe to say that there was not a family in Northumberland without a blood enemy and a sworn ally. Sir Anthony Browne commanded them in the King's name to forget their hatreds, and in the fullness of their new-found loyalty they all replied that the King should be obeyed in everything, "and each agreed to set his hand to an instrument."

They were heartily agreed on one point. Tynedale and Reedsdale had spoiled the plains "so sore that many are weary of their lives"; the reivers must be forced to make restitution, or if that was impossible at least some revenge must be taken. Sir Anthony Browne promised redress and sent to the hill graynes to demand pledges for their good behaviour[3]. Reedsdale made no difficulty, but sent in seven or eight of these hostages at once. There was likely to be more trouble over the Tynedale pledges, and the dalesmen had an excuse for their lawlessness ready. They said that they would never have "broken" if Sir Reynold Carnaby had not called upon them in the King's name to rise against the rebels of Northumberland. Of course everyone in Northumberland swore that he had no thoughts against the King and took up arms only to protect his goods from the reivers[4]. It is difficult to discover who was responsible for the raising of the two dales, the Percy or the Carnaby faction. The

---

[1] L. and P. xii (1), 351.
[2] Ibid. 421; printed in full, Raine, Mem. of Hexham Priory (Surtees Soc.), I, Append. p. cxlvii.
[3] See note A at end of chapter.   [4] L. and P. xii (1), 351.

Carnabys laid the mustering of Tynedale to the charge of little John Heron, Sir Thomas Percy's man, and supported their story by many circumstantial details[1]. This still leaves Reedsdale unaccounted for, and the mosstroopers themselves said that they rose for Sir Reynold. In the King's opinion, though they acted for their own gain, they did more good than harm. He must have meant by spoiling their neighbours, for they did nothing else. It may have been that when John Heron raised Tynedale, the Carnabys raised Reedsdale against him, and that both dales thought it more profitable to spoil the lowlands than to fight each other. It was in nobody's interest to defend the falling house of Percy, and it may be suspected that a list of spoils nearly as long as those attributed to the Percys might have been made against the Carnaby faction.

The members of the Council of the Marches assembled at Berwick. They were Sir Thomas Clifford, Sir William Evers, Sir John Widdrington, Robert Collingwood, Lionel Grey, Cuthbert Radcliff and John Horsley. On 14 February they wrote to the King to inform him that it had been necessary to modify some of the orders brought by Sir Anthony Browne. First they had requested him not to deliver the King's letters patent which granted the keeping of Reedsdale to George Fenwick, because a change at such an unsettled time would be sure to cause disorder, and the deputy warden of the Middle Marches, Sir John Widdrington, felt himself hampered in his duties if Reedsdale were not under his direct control.

Further, after much debate, they had determined to advise the King humbly against enlisting as pensioners in his service Cuthbert and Edward Charleton. These two men were leaders of the Tynedale thieves. They had resorted to Sir Thomas Percy during the insurrection. They had busily devoted themselves to stirring up the disorder so favourable to the practice of their calling. The feeling was general that in asking these reivers to assist their natural enemies the wardens, the King was obeying too implicitly the old saw about catching thieves. Moreover, the Charletons had not been loyal since the end of the rising. The greater number of the dalesmen had been ready to take the King's oath, but the Charletons had refused to swear to be true to the King, unless they might make a special reservation in favour of Hexham Priory, which they had sworn to maintain against all the world, receiving 20 nobles a year from the canons in guerdon of their allegiance. This is some proof

---

[1] See above, chap. ix.

that the marchman's respect for his oath was more than a chivalrous fiction of the Border minstrels.

The Charletons would not agree to send in pledges for restitution of the cattle and gear they had plundered. They had plenty of friends on the Marches, and being in league with the reivers of Liddesdale, Jedworth Forest, Harlaw Woods and Esk Water, they could defy the King's officers with impunity. The Council of the Marches suggested that it would be better to catch and hang them than to enrich them with the nation's gold. They were so formidable that it would take a force of 300 men to penetrate Tynedale and run them to earth.

Finally the King had commanded that John Heron of Chipchase should be arrested and sent up to London by water; but the Council of the Marches thought that his arrest would alarm the Reedsdale men, who were so far fairly quiet, and found it expedient merely to bind him over for 200 marks to appear before the King when summoned[1].

Some of these arrangements did not please Henry. From a fragment of a despatch to the Council of the Marches, it appears that he marvelled at the demand for 300 soldiers, considering that Northumberland was quiet; he expected the Council to arrest and send up the Charletons without any such aid. He saw no reason against employing the Charletons in Norfolk's objection that they were murderers, but it was a very different matter if they had refused to take his oath. The draft breaks off, and it is impossible to say what further orders were in the completed letter[2].

On Monday 26 February the Duke of Norfolk dissolved Hexham Priory. All passed quietly. Edward and Cuthbert Charleton were safe in the fastnesses of North Tynedale, and did not consider that their oath bound them to attack the King's Lieutenant when he had superior forces[3].

On Tuesday 27 February Sir Anthony Browne received the last of the Reedsdale pledges, and the Tynedale men agreed to send in theirs on Monday 5 March. Well pleased at seeing the end of this difficult task, Sir Anthony left Berwick for Newcastle-upon-Tyne[4]. At Morpeth he was met by 300 of the King's subjects who had been "sore harried and spoiled" and begged for redress against the mosstroopers. Browne replied to their petition that he had taken order

---

[1] L. and P. XII (1), 421; printed in full, Raine, op. cit. I, Append. p. cxlvii.
[2] L. and P. XII (1), 422.   [3] See above, chap. XIX.
[4] L. and P. XII (1), 552.

for the restitution of their lost goods, "whereat they are right joyous and glad." Browne wrote that all went well, and that he expected to be at court again in a fortnight[1]. If he had had more experience of the Borders, this very look of peace would have made him uneasy.

On Saturday 3 March Sir Anthony Browne was complacently sure that no part of the realm was in better stay than the Middle Marches. That very day Roger Fenwick, the Keeper of Tynedale, went to Bellingham to receive the pledges of his dale. At midnight he was set upon and murdered "for old grudges, by three naughty persons"; the murderers were John of Charleton, Rynny Charleton and John Dod[2].

Norfolk was at Newcastle-upon-Tyne at the time. Feeling his position strengthened by the early failure of the King's new policy, he drew up, with the assistance of his council, an alternative scheme for the government of the north. Henry was determined to be served no more on the Marches by noblemen, who were as lawless as the reivers and might use their isolation to become too powerful. Norfolk, on the other hand, was convinced that only a nobleman, wielding such powers as any king might fear to entrust to a subject, could keep order on the Marches[3]. According to Norfolk's scheme, this nobleman ought to be a member of the King's Privy Council. He should be the King's Lieutenant, president of the proposed Council of the North, and the ultimate authority in Cumberland, Westmorland, Northumberland, Durham and Yorkshire. He was to have power to levy forces whenever he saw need. He must be chief warden of all the Marches, with deputies under him. He was to spend most of the year in the north and to sit two or three times at Newcastle-upon-Tyne to administer justice in Northumberland, in such cases as murders, felonies and debts, as the wardens had no authority to judge between Englishman and Englishman except in cases of March treason[4], but only between Englishman and Scot.

In this proposal Norfolk showed his hand. During the following months there was a continuous subterranean struggle between the opposite schemes of Henry and Norfolk for the government of the north. Although little is to be found as yet about the Council of the North, there can be no doubt that that was the form of government which Henry had in his mind from the first. Against it Norfolk set up his scheme of a northern dictator, with himself holding the dictatorship. It was a tempting but a dangerous dream,

[1] L. and P. xii (1), 553.
[2] Ibid. 594, 596, 859.
[3] Ibid. 594–5.
[4] See note B at end of chapter.

and Norfolk dared not allow it to appear except by hints and glimpses such as this.

To strengthen the hands of the dictator of the north the Duke and his council made a number of suggestions less open to criticism than the main proposal:

(1) Reedsdale belonged to Lord Tailboys, but it "is wholly inhabited by thieves and has always been used as a lord marcher's liberty and is not geldable." Harbottle Castle, where the Keeper of Reedsdale ought to dwell, was so ruinous that it was fit neither for a dwelling-place nor a prison. The King ought either to compel Tailboys to repair Harbottle, or take the whole valley into his own hands, giving Tailboys compensation.

(2) Some fortress ought to be built in Tynedale, or else Simonburn Castle, belonging to Heron of Ford, must be put into repair and made over to the Keeper of Tynedale.

(3) "Some true and hardy gentleman" was needed as Keeper of Tynedale, which was to include Hexhamshire, Corbridge and the Barony of Langley. All the gentlemen of the South Tyne valley should be ordered to rise at his word in case of raiding or Scots invasions.

(4) The Earl of Northumberland's castles and lands should be taken into the King's hands, and the tenants instead of paying ingressum and such charges should be commanded to be ready with horse and harness at short notice.

(5) Lord Dacre must be ordered to keep his tenants, the prickers of Gillsland, in good rule, and they must be ready to attend the King's officers at the Border meetings.

(6) The pensions granted to the gentlemen and headmen of Northumberland, designed to encourage them in the King's service, were not likely to have that effect. The money would be better spent in rewarding good service already done, or in making the castles defensible.

(7) Finally the laws of the Marches ought to be fixed and written down, as at present they worked with all the uncertainty of traditional custom.

These suggestions, headed "A remembrance for order and good rule to be had and kept in the north parts," were sent up to London[1]. In his letter to the Privy Council dated 7 March Norfolk again urged that a nobleman should be appointed warden, at least of

[1] L. and P. xii (1), 595.

the West Marches. "Every man of wit" about him was agreed that no "mean person" could curb the Marches. This was the moral he drew from the murder of Roger Fenwick[1].

The Privy Council answered this letter on 12 March. They pointed out that the King had offered the wardenship of the East and Middle Marches to two noblemen, who had both been reluctant to accept the office; instead of reluctant servants he had taken the best men who would serve him willingly. Norfolk had expressed approval of the scheme at first, only objecting to a few of the pensioners, whose unfitness the Privy Council now acknowledged. The King had been badly served on the West Marches because of the Clifford feud; it would become still more bitter if he appointed Lord Dacre to an office which the Earl of Cumberland had just given up. Was not the King's authority enough to make the meanest man respected? "The King retaining all the gentlemen and headmen as he doth shall not be ill served; at least it shall not be ill to assay it." They asked for the names of the "wise men" who had advised with Norfolk[2].

The Privy Council remained blandly unconscious of Norfolk's very broad hint that there was one nobleman who would not refuse to be warden of all the Marches. Their reply also shows why Norfolk resented so much the pensions which the King had granted. The recipients received the money direct from the King; a special messenger had brought them their patents, and it was made very plain that the Duke had nothing to do with the gift. This struck a blow at Norfolk's power of buying adherents by a promise of court patronage, and when all the gentlemen and headmen were the King's servants, it became much more difficult for anyone else to gather a strong band of retainers and allies.

When Norfolk's proposal was laid before the King, he replied in no uncertain terms. On 17 March the Privy Council report to Norfolk the following speech which the King himself had deigned to make. Henry marvelled that Norfolk seemed so resolved that only noblemen should serve him on the Marches:

"When I would," quoth his Highness, "have preferred to the wardenry of the East and Middle Marches my lord of Westmorland, like as he did utterly refuse it, so my lord of Norfolk noted him a man of such heat and hastiness of nature that he could not think

[1] L. and P. xii (1), 594.
[2] Ibid. 636; printed in full, Miscellaneous State Papers (ed. the Earl of Hardwicke), i, p. 39.

him meet for it. When we would," quoth his Grace, "have conferred it to my lord of Rutland, he refused it also; and my lord of Norfolk noted him a man of too much pusillanimity to have done us good service in it, if he would have embraced an overture in it. And we think," quoth his Highness, "he would not advise us to continue in it my lord of Northumberland. Now if we shall prefer none of these three to that room, we would be glad," quoth his Grace, "that my lord of Norfolk shall name a nobleman that he thinketh meet for that office. For gladly we would have such a one in store to appoint it unto, if we should hereafter alter our device, which we be not yet determined to do, nor shall apply to that sentence, till we have better experiment what should enforce us unto."[1]

Norfolk could not, of course, name the "nobleman that he thinketh meet for that office." He had indicated the identity of that desirable personage as plainly as possible. The King's snub revealed to him his mistake, and he remained silent for a considerable time, deep in his multifarious duties in the north[2].

On 11 March Norfolk was at Newcastle-upon-Tyne, making the final arrangements, as he thought, for bringing in the Border pledges[3]. Sir Anthony Browne, who was about to ride south, thought that there would be little more trouble with Tynedale as certain men "of good estimation" had undertaken to send pledges for all the inhabitants except the murderers[4]. Norfolk intended to return in Easter week to see that his orders had been executed and to "hear many poor men's causes."[5]

All that is known of the terms of Norfolk's treaty with the men of Tynedale may be gathered from the following letter, apparently addressed to the Council of the Marches by the heads of the four graynes[6]:

"Worshipful master, this is our answers being the heads men of Tynedale, it is so that we were called before the Duke of Norfolk's grace for such misorder as we have done in the late rebellion within our sovereign lord's realm, and there was commanded to make restitution of the third part of all such goods as we had by our oaths, and to find our felons given forth by the commissioners, and that [what] we have not done we shall do. Also the said commissioners hath given forth another decree, the which we may not bide marvelling what is the cause thereof. This bill made the xvii day of March. Also all conditions made before the Duke of Norfolk we will fulfil and do to the uttermost. Also if they be any

---

[1] L. and P. xii (1), 667; printed in full, Miscellaneous State Papers (ed. the Earl of Hardwicke), i, p. 41.
[2] L. and P. xii (1), 651.   [3] Ibid. 594.
[4] Ibid. 596.   [5] Ibid. 594.
[6] See note C at end of chapter.

that be obstacle to do the same, we bind us by this our writing to had [*hold*] him and forcify him. By us—

Thomas Charlton	John Robson of the Pawston
Gylbert Charlton	Jaffray Robson
Gerret Charlton of Wark	Arche Robson.
Gerre Charlton of the Boure.	
Umfray Mylborn	Henry Dode
Rynyone Charlton	Arche Dode
Henry Yarro	
John Wilkinson"[1]	

There was no trouble, at present, between England and Scotland. The deputy wardens, who had nothing to do with internal justice, could send in satisfactory reports. The East Marches were quiet. On the Middle Marches Sir John Widdrington and the Scots officers arranged for redress between Liddesdale, Tynedale and Reedsdale according to the agreement made at the last Border meeting. The King of Scots had sent special orders that this should be observed on his side. Nevertheless there was a general feeling that war would follow on James' return from France[2].

At Easter Norfolk returned to Northumberland, as he had intended. He made a tour of inspection round the Border castles and held a meeting with the Scots warden of the Middle Marches. Norfolk was convinced by his demeanour that there was no immediate intention of war[3].

The Duke was at Newcastle-upon-Tyne on 5 April, where he was met by Sir John Widdrington, Sir William Evers, the Council of the Marches and most of the gentlemen. He was much displeased with the state of affairs. Tynedale and Reedsdale had made no restitution, and were not likely to do so unless they could be constrained by more effectual means than keeping their kinsmen in prison[4]. Neither dale would begin to make restitution before the other. In spite of their thievings the borderers were miserably poor, and in some cases they were in fact unable to restore even a part of what they had stolen, for the cattle often went to supply a pressing lack of meat.

Some of the Reedsdale men had just raided Tynedale and harried one of the Milburns. This was no doubt a surprise expedition, for Tynedale could muster more spears than Reedsdale. The inhabitants of the two valleys might fairly be said to eke out a precarious existence by driving away each other's cattle. A servant of the Carnabys had been attacked. The mosstroopers scorned the garrison left

---

[1] Raine, op. cit. I, Append. p. clvii. [2] L. and P. XII (1), 889.
[3] Ibid. 804. [4] Ibid. 857.

to protect him and burned his house to the ground. Sir John Widdrington had nowhere to bestow the nine Reedsdale pledges except in the decayed tower of Harbottle where "they cannot be kept strong, ne yet hath any victual for them."

Sir William Evers had held two meetings with the Scots on the East Marches, but no meeting had been held by the deputies of either the Middle or the West Marches. If nothing more than this were done, Norfolk thought the disorders would increase. He reported the unsatisfactory state of affairs to the King on 7 April[1]. He did not mention his earlier scheme in the letter, but he sent a verbal message that only a nobleman, armed with sufficient powers, could hope to keep order; as for the name of anyone fit for the post, "the King knows his nobles."[2]

Perhaps Norfolk was a little afraid of the effect which his sullen message might produce, for on 12 April he wrote a hedging letter to Cromwell. He thought that the Earl of Rutland would be the best warden of the East and Middle Marches. Rutland was allied to all the gentlemen of Northumberland, and also to the Earl of Westmorland. He was a man who would listen to counsel, and as war was threatened "it is perilous for a hasty, heady man to have the rule of such people, for the Scots can train men to ambushments as well as any man living." This remark was aimed at Westmorland; but nevertheless the Duke considered him the best man for the wardenship, failing Rutland.

Norfolk had inquired of both my lord and my lady of Westmorland why the Earl had refused the office, and found that it was for the following reasons,—that the Earl's servants had refused to serve the King during the Pilgrimage, and he was busy dismissing them by degrees; the Earl was not assured of the friendship of Robert Bowes, whose influence was so great among Westmorland's kinsmen and allies that he feared it would outweigh his own; during the rebellion the Earl had defended Sir Reynold Carnaby, and thereby attracted to himself some of the hatred felt on all hands for Northumberland's favourite. Norfolk thought that these reasons were good. As to Bowes he "is not only very much esteemed but is a wise, hardy man and dare well enterprise a great matter." The King could not do better than attach him to his service by a valuable grant. "Though I dare not speak assuredly of a man so lately reconciled, yet if he may be assured he may be very useful."

On the West Marches Norfolk put no faith in Sir Thomas

[1] L. and P. xii (1), 857-8. [2] Ibid. 858, 978.

Wharton, who was suggested for the post of deputy warden. No one could do such good service as Lord Dacre, but as he had been heavily fined so lately it would not look well to restore his office; people would say that the King was simply making everything he could out of him. The Earl of Cumberland was the only suitable person left; "but he must be brought to change his conditions and not be so greedy to get money of his tenants." Norfolk declared that this was his final opinion, and begged the King to keep it secret[1]. Needless to say, the King did not change his plans, nor was he deceived as to Norfolk's real ambition.

About this time, the middle of April 1537, the rumours of an approaching war with Scotland became alarming. In order to understand their origin, it is necessary to trace the relations of England, France and Scotland during the last five months.

James V, King of Scotland, was at Tournelles near Paris in December 1536, preparing for his wedding with Francis I's daughter Madeleine[2]. The French were pleased with his gentleness and Faenza, the Papal Nuncio, with his devotion to the Holy See[3]. To the English ambassadors he was cold and distant, and Wallop described him, not without malice, as a countrified youth. "His manner of using himself by that we do perceive is after the northern fashion, as the lords of those parts doth use themselves when they come first to court, now looking over one shoulder, now over the other, with a beck to one and a beck to another, and unto us nothing. He is a right proper man after the northern fashion. His being here shall do him much good, and to us little profit; for here he shall learn many things."[4] It seems to have been the fashion at the English court to talk of the Scots as if they were barbarians, but James probably had his own reasons for seeming shy to the English ambassadors.

He spent much of his time practising for the jousts which were to be held at his wedding[5]. Francis showed him every courtesy and when he entered Paris in state on 31 December 1536 the Court of Parliament went before him clad in red cloaks, an honour not usually accorded to any but the King of France[6]. The marriage took place on New Year's Day, with great magnificence, and a proper display of sumptuous apparel, cloth of gold, and precious stones. After the wedding was a banquet, and after the banquet a mask and dancing. Next day there was jousting at Tournelles. The King of Scots was a true sportsman, and appeared

[1] L. and P. xii (1), 919.   [2] L. and P. xi, 1305.   [3] L. and P. xii (1), 88.
[4] L. and P. xi, 1305.   [5] Ibid. 1315.   [6] Ibid. 1852, 1895.

at his wedding with a wound caused by "a great stroke with a spear upon the left side of his head...being a sore blemish in his face all this triumphing time."[1]

On 19 January 1536-7 Faenza wrote that there was good hope of English affairs going well. The people stood firmly to their demands. The King had received ambassadors from them graciously, which showed that he must be aware of his own weakness. No doubt some report of Aske's reception at court had reached France. The Nuncio suggested that Pole should be sent to England and that the Censures should be published at once[2], but as soon as he received definite orders to publish them he hung back[3]. This made little difference, however, as the time when they would have been useful had passed.

James V desired to return home through England, but he felt some difficulty about requesting Henry's hospitality. The King of England had always opposed the French marriage, and James, to avoid his remonstrances, had not consulted him on the subject. Henry professed himself grieved and offended by this neglect[4]. Nevertheless James did not wish to take the long voyage home with his young bride in the stormy season of the year, and as he was anxious to return to Scotland, he ventured to make his request through the French ambassador in England.

Henry was by no means inclined to do his nephew a favour. He considered it very strange that the King of Scots should not make the request in his own name. On 4 February the Privy Council asked Norfolk's advice on the subject[5]. The Duke's position was a delicate one. James was possibly the future King of England. His friendship would in any case be very valuable to the dictator of the north. In spite of Henry's obvious wishes Norfolk ventured to consult his own future interests, and replied that it would do no harm for James to pass through England, except on the score of expense. It was probably Scots pride which prevented him from writing to the King himself, and the peace and riches of England could cause nothing but wholesome humiliation to one with "a very enemy's heart in his body."[6] But Henry determined to show his nephew no courtesy. "The King's honour is not to receive the King of Scots into his realm unless he will come as his Grace's vassal. For there came never King of Scots into England in peaceable

---

[1] L. and P. XII (1), 12, 58.   [2] Ibid. 165.
[3] Ibid. 326.   [4] Ibid. 397.
[5] Ibid. 333; printed in full, Miscellaneous State Papers (ed. the Earl of Hardwicke), I, p. 35.   [6] L. and P. XII (1), 398; printed in full, State Papers, v, p. 68.

manner but after that sort." Henry enumerated all his grievances against James, and concluded with the argument that the country must appear peaceful and loyal to an enemy who was passing through it, and to secure this appearance it might be necessary to make concessions to the disaffected which would afterwards cause trouble. James' overtures met with no response, and he was obliged to face the sea voyage[1].

This affair did not improve the relations between the two countries. James became more gracious than ever to the Papal Nuncio at Paris. He was ready to further the Pope's plan of reconciling Francis and Charles, and he cherished the splendid dream of all young kings, that he would go in person to fight against the infidels. The Scots disliked Henry's policy and his person. They saw that his growing despotism was a menace to Scotland. David Beaton, the Abbot of Arbroath and Keeper of the Privy Seal, was willing, if the Pope desired it, to send the Censures secretly into England and cause them to be published suddenly when Henry VIII was in the north[2]. It is impossible to say what the effect of this bold scheme would have been, but the Papal court had not sufficient energy to take it up, and Henry did not travel north after all at this time.

The Pope sent James V a consecrated cap and sword, as a special token of his favour, together with an exhortation against heresy[3]. The King of Scots was pleased and stirred by the symbol. "With as many words as he can say in French, [he] again thanks his Holiness for the sword. I know it has touched his heart and tomorrow morning the ceremony [of presentation] shall be," wrote the Papal Nuncio on 18 February[4].

On 8 March the King and Queen of Scots took leave of Francis at Compiègne and went to Rouen, whence they were to sail[5]. They waited there for nearly two months before they embarked. The young Queen was consumptive and could not well bear the voyage, which was therefore delayed until a more favourable time of year. James distrusted Henry's intentions. The English ships held command of the sea and before now a King of Scotland had been captured on his voyage and carried prisoner to London. Rumour said that there were ten armed English ships on the coast and ten more in Flanders, and though James had fourteen ships of his own and eight

---

[1] L. and P. xii (1), 899; printed in full, State Papers, i, 535.
[2] L. and P. xii (1), 463.   [3] Ibid. 166.
[4] Ibid. 463.   [5] Ibid. 600.

lent for the voyage by Francis, he feared that Henry might begin hostilities by an attack on his fleet.

Henry, however, was not on such good terms with the Emperor as Francis imagined, and was not disposed for war. Though relations were strained between France and England, neither was prepared to fight[1]. The war with the Emperor kept Francis busy, and Henry needed time to recover after the late crisis in England. James had no intention of attacking England without his father-in-law's support. Nevertheless the news that he was bringing home his French bride raised a general expectation of war with Scotland.

At a friend's house in West Malling, Kent, James Fredewell a priest, was playing at tables with Adam Lewes, the schoolmaster, one day in April 1537. The priest asked a man who was going to London to buy him a book. Lewes asked if he would buy the New Testament, but Fredewell replied he wished all the Testaments in English were burnt.

"What! will ye burn the Gospel of Christ and the word of God?" said the schoolmaster.

"Tush!" quoth the priest, "I will buy me a portresse to say my service on, as I was wont to do."

They finished their game and went to John Doomright's shop, where a pile of Acts of Parliament lay, concerning artillery, dress and unlawful games. Lewes remarked that he hoped they would be better enforced when the King had finished with the work in hand.

"Yea," said Fredewell, "the King is like to have more to do yet."

"Why so?" said the shop-keeper, "his Grace hath overcome his enemies of the north, for they hang at their own doors."

"What then?" returned the priest, "there is another bird abreeding that came not forth yet which will come forth before midsummer, that the King had never such since he was King of England."

Being asked what he meant, he told them that the Emperor had given the King Flanders, but if Henry took the Emperor's part, both the King of France and the King of Scots would be on his neck, and Francis had made James Admiral of the sea. The schoolmaster declared that they could do little hurt; but if the King made war beyond the sea he would do well to cut off the priests' heads first or they would betray him. Fredewell retorted that that was easier said than done. Lewes went away and another priest called Cuthbert came into the shop. He picked up an English Testament and said he was an evil man who translated it, or the Emperor would not have

[1] L. and P. xii (1), 760-2; 760 printed in full, State Papers, v, 72.

burnt him. The shop-keeper asked if no good men were ever put to death by the Bishop of Rome. "Yes," said Fredewell, "there were some put to death within this two year that was as good livers and as faithful as be now alive." Cuthbert said that the Bishop of Rome never put good men to death, and the two priests left the shop discussing whether it were lawful for priests to marry[1]. Fredewell probably meant the Pilgrims when he spoke of the faithful who were put to death.

At Whitsuntide a citizen of Leicester, who had been making a circuit of pilgrimages in the north of England and Scotland, reported the rumours which he had heard by the way. In Edinburgh it was said that King James would make war on England for "the Seven Sheriffdoms" unless the King of England would give them to him freely, and that James had proclaimed himself Duke of York and Prince of Wales. There were said to be 15,000 Englishmen in Scotland, fugitives who had fled from Norfolk. Two of them were pointed out to the pilgrim in Edinburgh; one was a gentleman wearing a black velvet coat, and yet it was said that he had been but a poor man in England. The other, a priest, was now a canon in a house of religion near Holyrood. These Englishmen had promised to be in the van of an invasion of England, and to raise all Northumberland[2].

Scots rhymes, prophecies and ballads aimed against Henry spread into England from time to time. An instance of this came to light at Royston, Hertford. The story is painful and rather perplexing. Robert Dalyvell of Royston went to Scotland "to learn the cunning in the craft of a saddler" about April 1535. He lived in Edinburgh with a saddler for about eight weeks and heard many Scots, both light persons and men of reputation, say that their king should be crowned King of England in London before midsummer three years later, i.e. 1538. They had read this in books of prophecy. Dalyvell returned to England and wandered about the north, working for a few weeks at York, Gateshead and Chester-le-Street; at the last place he heard several Scots say that their king was worthy to be king of England, and next in blood. He told them they were false traitors and their master rebuked them. Dalyvell went back to Edinburgh and "the Scots that railed before read the prophecies of Merlin in his hearing." He returned home to Royston in 1537 and "on Tuesday night after Palm Sunday at midnight, his wife being asleep" an angel appeared to him, saying, "Arise, and show your

---

[1] L. and P. XII (1), 990.
[2] L. and P. XII (2), 6.

prince that the Scots would never be true to him." The next night he had the same vision, but he did not obey it.

On 11 June 1537 Dalyvell told a serving-man in the stable of the Greyhound, Royston, some of the prophecies which he had heard from the Scots, that if the King did not amend he should not live a month after the feast of the Nativity of St John the Baptist 1538, and that before that day a horse worth 10s. "shall be able to bear all the noble blood of England."[1] Whether the serving-man reported the matter, or whether Dalyvell himself confessed in a panic does not appear, but he was examined by seven magistrates and admitted the words[2]. He was sent to London and made a fuller statement next day. It is difficult to see why so much importance was attached to the story of a poor man who seems to have been half-witted. Perhaps Cromwell hoped to get hold of some Scots spies by his means; and he endeavoured to make Dalyvell accuse priests. Though he was racked and cross-examined the prisoner had only one story to tell, and declared that of all the religious men he had known not one had spoken of prophecies even in confession[3].

That Henry himself was anxious about James' intentions is shown by the matters treated in the Privy Council on 3 April 1537. It was decided that Calais, Carlisle, and Berwick must be victualled and prepared for defence. The English navy must be in readiness for immediate service. The commission of the peace must be purged of all but "men of worship and wisdom meet for the same"; and letters must be sent to all justices to keep special watch for seditious persons; as a further precaution certain of the nobles would be ordered to live in their own counties for a time.

The Pope was trying to reconcile the Emperor and Francis in order that all three might attack England; the King must contrive to have one friend at least, and as alliances were generally concluded by a marriage, the King's two daughters, though illegitimate, must have such provision made for them that their hands would be accepted by foreign princes. The Queen was pregnant, but still it was expedient that one of the King's daughters should be declared legitimate "to take away the remainder hanging upon the King of Scots," who might be tempted by the French to bring forward his claim[4].

Meanwhile the Border was alive with rumours of war. No one had yet been appointed deputy warden of the West Marches, but Sir John Lowther, the Earl of Cumberland's deputy captain at

[1] L. and P. xii (2), 80. [2] Ibid. 74. [3] Ibid. 80.
[4] L. and P. xii (1), 815–6; 816 printed in full, State Papers, i, 545.

Carlisle, was doing the work. Hearing a rumour on Easter Eve [31 March 1537] that the Scots were mustering, Lowther sent Edward Story the warden-serjeant with a letter to Lord Maxwell the Scots warden, in order that Story might pick up news by the way. Story talked for a long time with Maxwell, who told him that general musters had been proclaimed in every borough town in Scotland. Each man was expected to appear with "a jack of plate, a steel bonnet and splints, and a spear six ells long, and all who can, a horse." The King of Scots was expected at any time; he was waiting for a fair wind and he hoped "to escape the ships of the sea." Maxwell declared that if the King had been at home during the rebellion he would "have kept his house in Carlisle before this."

Lowther forwarded this news to the Earl of Cumberland on 6 April, and reminded him that Maxwell's boast might well be true, for neither the city nor the castle was strong, and he lacked ordnance, powder and gunners[1]. The Earl received the letter at Skipton, and sent on the warning to the King. He thought that a Scots general would attack either Berwick or Carlisle, and he dwelt upon the weakness of the latter[2].

In February Henry had sent a request to the Regents of Scotland by Ralph Sadler that rebels flying from the Duke of Norfolk's justice might be carefully returned to England. He received a flowery answer from the Scots Council, promising all that he asked[3]; but though the Scots wardens were charged not to harbour English fugitives[4], they were not expected to take their orders seriously, and such of the Pilgrims as escaped across the Border were safe.

On 7 April Norfolk at Newcastle-upon-Tyne wrote to inform the Regents that John Charleton, Rinian Charleton and John Dod, the slayers of Roger Fenwick, were being sheltered at Jedburgh Abbey. He demanded that they should be arrested and delivered to the English wardens[5]. Henry Ray, Berwick Pursuivant, a very important personage on the Borders, carried the letter. He was given no credence, but he was instructed to enlarge upon the peace, contentment, prosperity and riches of England to the Regents and all other Scots. On his way he was to find out all he could as to whether the people wished for war, how the new taxes were taken, and why some of the lords had gone with a large company into Fife.

On 9 April Berwick Pursuivant arrived at Edinburgh and dined

---

[1] L. and P. xii (1), 843. [2] Ibid. 882.
[3] L. and P. xii (2), Append. 12; printed in full, Hamilton Papers, i, p. 41, no. 38.
[4] L. and P. xii (2), p. xviii n. [5] L. and P. xii (1), 859.

with the Bishop of Aberdeen, who was Treasurer of Scotland. The Bishop made enquiries about the insurrection in England. Ray replied that the realm was never in better order than it was at present. The Treasurer said, "That is very well, but ye have put down many good Christian men." Ray admitted that they were Christian men, but if they had been good men they would not have been put down,—"I trow, my lord, we are as good Christian men as any in the world." The Treasurer replied, "Ye that are poor men are good, but the heads are worst; for if ye English men be so good, then is France, Italy and many other countries clearly deceived." Adam Otterburn, a member of the Scots Council who was dining with them, asked what ships were set on the sea. Ray answered that he knew of none. He gave them the English news according to his instructions. The Treasurer said that he was very glad to hear of so much peace and rejoicing, and that he would pray for the King of England and all the realm, "that ye may be good men." Ray retorted, "Ye can not, my lord, so soon begin your prayer, but it is had, for we are good already." He asked why the Scots Borderers were so sure that there would be war when their King came home. The Treasurer merely said that it would not be Scotland's fault if there were a war.

This humourous hostility, half hidden by a jest, was one sign of the national feeling which watched Henry's despotism with such jealousy. On his return Ray reported that the commons of Scotland were greatly roused against England, because they believed that English ships had been sent to take their King on his homeward voyage, and that Henry and the Emperor were in league to attack France. If that happened, they said, they would take the French King's part. They called the English heretics, and were more inclined to war than peace. The new money was paid already, without any rebellion. Lord Maxwell was the only lord who had gone beyond Fife, but for what purpose Ray could not find out. When Ray spoke of the King of England's power and riches "they say (and in my judgment verily think) they are able to withstand us or any other. And they marvel that my lord of Norfolk lieth in the north parts so long, fearing that his delay and the sailing of the King's ships means some mischief to them."[1]

Ray brought back a letter, dated at Glasgow 11 April, from the Chancellor of Scotland to Norfolk. The Chancellor acknowledged Norfolk's letter in the name of the Regents. He could scarcely

[1] L. and P. xii (2), Append. 19; printed in full, Hamilton Papers, i, p. 44, no. 41.

believe that their strict orders against the receipt of fugitives had been disobeyed, but if Norfolk would give them time to make inquiries, anyone found in fault should be sharply punished[1]. The pursuivant reached Sheriffhutton Castle, where Norfolk had taken up his residence, on 17 April. The Chancellor's letter and the report were forwarded to Cromwell. Norfolk sent Ray back to Scotland to pick up some more news[2]. It was generally believed that there would be war. For example, Sir Thomas Clifford, the captain of Berwick, was in London. One of his servants wrote from Berwick to tell him that the Mayor and townsmen begged him to show their needs to the King and the Privy Council, as war appeared to be imminent and they were not prepared for a siege[3].

The urgent reminders of the Border captains were not unheeded. The King was as anxious as they to secure his frontiers. On 13 April lists were drawn up of the northern fortresses, classified according to whether they required repair or were defensible. Sir George Lawson, the Treasurer of Berwick, received orders to victual the town. On 18 April he wrote to Cromwell to ask for more explicit instructions, and for more money, as he had not nearly so much as Cromwell expected[4]. Norfolk gave Cumberland similar orders for the victualling of Carlisle, and the Earl sent a similar plaint to head-quarters. The country was almost desolated by the recent risings, and food of all sorts was very difficult to procure. At Carlisle there was the old story of lack of guns and men, which he had repeated times out of number[5].

Norfolk had now taken up his quarters at Sheriffhutton Castle, which he left only to hold assizes or suppress a monastery. He had the chief pledges of Tynedale and Reedsdale in his hands, and hoped by their means to be able to extort restitution from their kinsfolk. He was troubled about the matter, for the honest subjects who had been harried demanded a great deal, and the raiders possessed very little[6]. The ravages of the Scots did not improve the honest men's chances of compensation. In April there were several Scots raids on both the East and the West Marches, and Lord Maxwell would not appoint a date for redress. In point of fact both the English and the Scots wardens were convinced that war would break out in a few weeks; and they thought it useless to make appointments that

---

[1] L. and P. xii (2), Append. 18; printed in full, Hamilton Papers, i, p. 43, no. 40.
[2] L. and P. xii (1), 967.   [3] Ibid. 952.
[4] Ibid. 968.   [5] Ibid. 993.
[6] Ibid. 967.

would not be kept and to administer law in a district which might any day be plunged into anarchy[1].

Lowther's spies brought him word that James V was expected daily. All the ships on the west coast had gone out to meet him[2]. In all Scotland the common bruit was that there would be war when the King came home[3]. Great preparations were made for his reception. He was expected on May Day, for at length the wind was in his favour. Lowther wrote to Cumberland that provision could hardly be made for Carlisle in time, "for either now war of Scotland when the King's purse is full of the French gold, or never." He cheerfully added that if corn were sent to Carlisle there was no mill in the castle to grind it, and if they obtained good ordnance, there was no one who could shoot guns. He had sent a spy to Edinburgh to bring news of James' arrival. This letter was sent on St Mark's Day, 25 April[4].

Amid the rising excitement Norfolk was calm. He understood the situation better than the gentlemen of the Marches, who were soldiers, but not statesmen. He knew that peace or war depended on Francis I, and that England was not on such terms with France as to cause immediate alarm. Still, he thought it well to be prepared. He had such good espial in Scotland that no move could be made without his knowledge. Berwick Pursuivant reached Edinburgh on his second mission on 23 April. He carried to the Chancellor another letter which demanded the delivery of English rebels. The Scots Council was heartily tired of these demands. When Ray appeared before them he was asked, "What is the cause ye send your friars to us?" He replied, "We send none, we had liever keep them ourself."

"If they tarried with you, ye had made martyrs of them." "Nay," interposed the Chancellor, "but patriarchs."

On 25 April Ray waited on the Bishop of Aberdeen to give him Norfolk's thanks for a present of hawks. In answer to the Bishop's promise that he would pray that the King and all England might be made good men, Norfolk sent the message that in no country was God better served, and that the Bishop of Rome had no authority out of his own diocese. The Treasurer replied that he felt no grudge towards England for that matter, "but for the cruelness of you that put down your own poor commons."[5] Ray brought back to Norfolk

[1] L. and P. xii (1), 982, 991, 994, 1030, 1050, 1060.
[2] Ibid. 1026.   [3] Ibid. 1058.   [4] Ibid. 1038.
[5] Ibid. 1094; printed in full, State Papers, v, 75-7.

a reply from the Chancellor which again promised that the cases which he mentioned should be investigated[1], and a secret message from the Queen Mother that no lord in Scotland would give the King her son counsel friendly to England[2].

On 2 May Henry sent a gracious letter of thanks to Norfolk for his services in the north. The King still intended to make a royal progress to York, where he would declare a general pardon, with only a few exceptions. He would see about paying Norfolk's expenses, though "to be plain with you we think that divers of the gentlemen ...might well have served us better cheap, for some part of a recompense of their former offences.... We do accept in good part the declaration of your opinion touching the Marches. Nevertheless we doubt not but you will both conform your own mind to find out the good of that order which we have therein determined, and cause other by your good mean to perceive the same." Finally money had been sent for the victualling of Berwick and Carlisle[3]. Berwick was now in process of being put into a thoroughly defensible condition[4]. The other Border fortresses were constantly in the King's mind, and suggestions on the subject were often laid before the Privy Council, but they seem to have had no immediate effect[5].

At this time Norfolk was vainly petitioning the King for leave to come to court. On 9 May he excused his repeated requests. He explained that his character was being attacked in his absence. He mentioned the rumours that he had encouraged the rebels[6]. It was said that he had sent for his son, the Earl of Surrey, to instruct him in northern affairs in order that he might presently take his father's place. Norfolk protested that all these tales were false. He had never encouraged the rebels. He had sent for his son partly because he had hoped the King would give him leave to come south for a short time, and he could not have kept his retinue in the north without Surrey; and partly because "in truth I love him better than all my children, and would have gladly had him here to hunt, shoot, play cards, and entertain my servants, so that they should be less desirous of leave to go home to their wives." Norfolk besought the King, if he thought him a true man, to allow him to come up and answer his enemies[7]. He protested that if he had not been on the King's service not all the Earl of Northumberland's lands would

---

[1] L. and P. xii (1), 1048.
[2] Ibid. 1094; printed in full, State Papers, v, 75-7.
[3] L. and P. xii (1), 1118; printed in full, State Papers, i, 547.
[4] L. and P. xii (1), 1024.   [5] Ibid. 1091-2.
[6] See above, chap. xi.   [7] L. and P. xii (1), 1162.

have kept him so long in the north[1]. If he stayed much after Michaelmas, he thought it would cost him his life. He had also many private reasons to justify his wish to return to London[2].

Henry replied on 13 May that he had heard none of the slanders to which Norfolk referred; if he had, he would have mentioned them to the Duke. "You know our nature is too frank to retain any such thing from him that we love and trust." Norfolk must not credit all the light tales that reached his ears. He could not be spared from the north until after the King's progress, which would shortly take place. Henry hoped that the Duke would settle all disputes, so that he might not be troubled with petitions. The tone of the King's letter was friendly, but, though he declared himself assured that Norfolk had not sent for Surrey for "any purpose not to our good contentment," yet he pointed out that as the Duke had summoned his son without consulting the King, it gave an occasion for people to think evil, which might have been avoided[3].

In fact Norfolk protested too much about Surrey. The cautious old nobleman believed that he had recovered after his first false step, and was beginning once more to feel his way towards the object of his ambition, the dictatorship of the north. It was the dream of many powerful men to hold the place there which the Percys alone had held. Norfolk had declared that a nobleman must rule there— that this man must have the joint powers of Warden of all the Marches and Lieutenant of the North. Then he held off and suggested that the Earl of Cumberland should have the West Marches and the Earl of Rutland the Middle and East. Norfolk did not suggest anyone to fill the great office his imagination had summoned up; he intimated that it would not become him to suggest the obvious man. In fact all his letters were full of his hatred of the north, and his fear that the climate would be the death of him. "For all the lands the Earl of Northumberland hath and had" he would not tarry there after Michaelmas[4]. "All the Earl of Northumberland's land,"—at that time they become a refrain in Norfolk's letters, the refrain of his ambition. He kept a careful eye on the dying Earl's extravagances. If the Earl wished to sell wood, Norfolk saved the Percy forests from the axe[5]. Northumberland was giving away his goods and houses, even the bricks of Wressell Castle, perhaps in a vindictive effort to save something from the King.

---

[1] L. and P. xii (1), 1157.
[2] Ibid. 1162.
[3] Ibid. 1192.
[4] Ibid. 1157, 1162.
[5] See above, chap. xviii.

Norfolk reported this to Cromwell and declared that it must be stopped[1].

At the same time the Duke suggested that the household stuff of Jervaux and Bridlington, and of Darcy, Sir Robert Constable, and Sir John Bulmer, should be stored in the King's wardrobe at Sheriffhutton Castle, for the use of the Council of the North, or of any nobleman whom the King might send to those parts. If the goods were sold he said that the King would not receive a third of their value[2]. This is another sign of the way his thoughts were tending. Later he wrote that Cromwell would marvel if he knew how often Norfolk had been urged by the northern gentlemen to ask for some of Northumberland's lands and to settle down among them. But he was determined never again to cross the Trent northwards, unless he were with the King, or marching against the King's enemies[3].

Clearer hints were never dropped. Norfolk loathed the north,— but if the King made it worth his while, very well worth his while, he was the nobleman who would be lieutenant and warden at once. Henry must have laughed with Cromwell over Norfolk's palpable ambition. The King had fairly rid himself of the Percys, and he would never put a Howard or any other nobleman in their place. Without a considerable grant of land, Norfolk could not turn to advantage the influence which he thought he possessed in the north; nor was his fear or favour there so great as to enable him to take the Percys' place, even though he held their lands. He had deceived the northern men, and they were not likely to forget all that they owed to "this false duke."

The Howards had no ancient connection with the north; their influence began at Flodden and might well have ended at Doncaster, if fate had not been contrary. The Percys had been surrounded by all the splendour of hereditary right and traditional leadership; they had made the north famous, and a hundred tales gave them a place in the hearts of the people. Now the great house was represented by the old Countess who outlived all her sons, and by Sir Thomas Percy's two little boys. Fallen though it seemed, the house of Howard could not take its place; nor did the White Lion ever put down the Blue. The Dacres might have filled the place of the greatest lords in the north, but after years of true service on the Borders the King and the Clifford feud had left Lord Dacre a ruined man. Henry had little to fear from the Earl of Cumberland, because of his many

---

[1] L. and P. xii (1), 1178. [2] Ibid. 1172.
[3] L. and P. xii (2), 291.

feuds and the hatred of his own tenants. As to the Earl of Westmorland, he was one of the few noblemen who cared less for place and power than for a quiet life and a safe head. Norfolk was allowed to imagine that he was winning the north for himself when he was really buying service for the King. No doubt Henry thought that the illusion did no harm and might make him work better.

James V of Scotland had at last embarked on his homeward voyage. It was a long and slow one. About six o'clock on the evening of Tuesday 15 May his ships lay at anchor off Scarborough. Norfolk wrote to Cromwell: "If God would have sent such good fortune, that he might have landed in these parts, I would so honestly have handled him that he should have drunk of my wine at Sheriff-hutton, and the Queen also, before his return to Scotland."[1] There is a sinister ring in the words. Kings of Scotland were not so often guests as prisoners in the King of England's castles.

If Norfolk had tried the experiment, he might have found unexpected difficulty in taking James. A party went ashore from the King's fleet to buy victuals in Scarborough, and several boats put out to James' ship. To one Englishman James said: "Ye Englishmen have let me of my return; an if ye had not been, I had been at home forty days past. But now I am here and will be shortly at home, whoso saith nay."

A party of twelve English fishermen came to speak with the King of Scots. On coming into his presence, they fell on their knees and "thanked God of his healthful and sound repair, showing how they had long looked for him, and how they were oppressed, slain and murdered, desiring him for God's sake to come in, and he should have all." To this pass had Norfolk's pacification brought the northern men, who had hitherto hated the Scots worse than the devil. James was a good deal troubled by this offer from his uncle's subjects. He refused to speak to a gentleman who came aboard, lest the man should say the same thing.

Presently the fleet sailed from Scarborough with so light a wind that Norfolk thought they might make Aberdeen, but not the Forth. At Whitburn, near Tynemouth, James cast anchor again, and ten Englishmen came to him with the same complaints, "promising plainly that if the said King of Scots would take upon him to come in all should be his."[2] One or two boats went ashore and a party of Frenchmen and Scots landed. With them was an Englishman,

[1] L. and P. xii (1), 1237; printed in full, State Papers, v, p. 78.
[2] L. and P. xii (1), 1286; printed in full, State Papers, v, 79.

James Crane, who was in the service of the French Vice-Admiral. He was really one of Cromwell's spies, but he probably passed as a refugee. With his companions he met the priest of the parish, and asked what news there was in England. The priest replied, "Ill news, for they kill and hang up men in this country." Crane seems to have abused the King of England, to lead the unsuspecting priest into further conversation. He asked where the Duke of Norfolk lay, and the priest said either at Sheriffhutton or at York; he added that the Duke dealt so cruelly with the north parts that he wished Norfolk were hanged on one side of a tree and Cromwell on the other. If the King of Scots had come home five months sooner and had entered England, the priest declared that he would have helped to carry him in triumph to London. As they talked by the seaside, he pointed out the lie of the coast: "Lo, here is as good and as ready landing for men as any place in England."[1]

On 18 May eleven of James' ships were sighted from Berwick. They lay becalmed in sight of the town from noon that day until the morning of the 19th. A party from one of the vessels landed at Alnmouth, and the Queen's gentleman usher rode on to Edinburgh to prepare for the royal reception. Sir Thomas Clifford kept good watch while the King of Scots lay so near, and sent out horsemen during the night to see if any man came ashore[2]. James must have been moved by the petition of the English fishermen. When his ship drew to the northwards of Berwick, he looked back upon the town and said to the gentlemen in attendance on him, "if he lived one year he should himself break a spear on one Englishman's breast."

Berwick Pursuivant was again on mission to Scotland. He saw the King and Queen land at Leith haven at ten o'clock on Whitsun Eve, 19 May 1537. The Vice-Admiral of France and the Bishop of Limoges were the only great men with him. His fleet consisted of ten great ships of France and four Scots ships. On Whit Monday the King and Queen made their entry into Edinburgh "and took their lodging in the Abbey of Holyrood House."

In Edinburgh Berwick Pursuivant met James Crane, the English spy in the French Vice-Admiral's service. Crane, seeing by the arms of England "in a box upon his breast" that Ray was an Englishman, took him aside to talk to him. He asked Ray to carry credence to Ralph Sadler "upon a token that when the said Ralph

[1] L. and P. xii (2), 422; printed in full, State Papers, v, 96.
[2] L. and P. xii (1), 1256.

Sadler was in France, he did inquire for the said James at his own house in Rouen." The credence was an account of the voyage, especially of the two embassies of English fishermen and peasants who had spoken with James. All the French ships were going home, except the *Salamander*, which was a present from Francis to his son-in-law. Crane was obliged to go with his master, though he would have "given £20 on the condition that he might himself come through your Highness' realm to show further his mind in the premisses."

Ray reported this to Sir Thomas Clifford at Berwick, and on 26 May the account was sent on to the King[1]. By this time all the French ships had passed Berwick on their homeward voyage[2]. Norfolk called Crane's story "some lies out of Scotland," and assured Cromwell that it was totally false, for he himself had been at Bridlington the day after James passed, and had examined the only Englishman on the coast who had spoken to the Scots King[3]. Norfolk was anxious to discredit the report, as he had been insisting for some time past that the north was reduced to perfect obedience and loyalty. Sir John Neville wrote that all the people rejoiced that the King and Cromwell were coming to the north. It was a pity that Richard Cromwell was not there to hear them talk; no men ever repented so sorely as they did[4].

With his usual prudence Cromwell paid more heed to the foul than the fair reports. In spite of Norfolk's scepticism Crane was summoned from France, and sent on 20 July to Norfolk at Sheriffhutton[5]. The Duke still made light of his story, as his geography had been much confused by the long voyage. He described a place which he said lay to the south of Scarborough, but no one could recognise it, and he could not give the names of the "false knaves" who had spoken to James[6]. To settle the matter Norfolk sent him with a sure, wise and secret gentleman to ride all along the north coast from Flamborough to Tynemouth in order to see if Crane could recognise the place. His description of it was that the church steeple was a sea-mark, that the church was dedicated to St Andrew, and that the vicar was one of the King's chaplains; it was with his parish priest that Crane had held the seditious conversation. When Crane and his companion came in sight of Whitburn, Crane declared that that was the steeple. On inquiry the wise gentleman learned

---

[1] L. and P. xii (1), 1286, printed in full, State Papers, v, 79.
[2] L. and P. xii (1), 1287.   [3] Ibid. 1307.   [4] Ibid. 1317.
[5] L. and P. xii (2), 122, 236, 269, 270.   [6] Ibid. 291.

that the church was dedicated to St Andrew and that the vicar was Dr Marshall, one of the King's chaplains. Norfolk was obliged to admit that there might be truth in Crane's story[1].

Crane could not say where the fishermen lived, and he did not know their names, but he described the leader of the party as a mariner with black hair and a weather-beaten countenance[2]. The priest of Whitburn, Robert Hodge, was examined by Norfolk and his council. He confessed his words, but declared that Dr Marshall had never spoken sedition and often preached against the Pope[3]. Norfolk sent Sir Thomas Hilton, the sheriff of Durham, to discover those who had been aboard the French Admiral's ship, and to arrest the leader of the party, if he had not gone to Shetland for the fishing[4]. James Crane was given a pardon and leave to return to France[5]. On 22 September Robert Hodge and two unnamed mariners, one of whom was the leader of the fishermen, were hanged in chains at Newcastle-upon-Tyne[6].

In order to prevent James' interviews with the discontented peasants from raising false hopes in Scotland, Henry sent Ralph Sadler as ambassador to James with professions of friendship and instructions to urge the King of Scots to follow his lead by throwing off the Pope and confiscating Church property[7].

All this while the Duke of Norfolk had been gradually going through an immense amount of law-work. A great many people had been plundered or had lost their goods during the rebellion. Most of them must have been poor men, for little or nothing can be learnt about their wrongs. If any full account of Norfolk's proceedings for redress remained, it would contain many local details of the Pilgrimage. On 18 May he wrote to Gardiner and Sir Francis Brian, who were on an embassy in France, with some natural self-satisfaction:—

"This country, thanked be God, is, I think, at this hour in as good obedience as any part of the realm and of such sort that of late at my coming hither I had not thought possible it should of long time have been brought to so good pass. There was marvellous spoils at the time of the insurrection through all these countries and divided in thousands of men's hands; and yet such restitution made that at this day there is very few that is not agreed withal, and the parties satisfied. It should be a very unreasonable thing that I would command to be done here that should not be shortly accomplished in all my Lieutenancy; save

---

[1] L. and P. xii (2), 340. [2] Ibid. 431.
[3] Ibid. 422; printed in full, State Papers, v, p. 96.
[4] L. and P. xii (2), 431. [5] Ibid. 796 (1). [6] Ibid. 479, 732.
[7] L. and P. xii (1), 1313; printed in full, State Papers, v, p. 81.

only in Tynedale and Reedsdale, of whom I have ten pledges at Sheriffhutton which lie upon their lives if their country men do not well. Finally I pray God send us three grace merrily to meet this winter at London."[1]

There are details of two cases of spoil and restitution, but as they both concern rich men, they are probably not characteristic of the rest. The first concerned the plundering of Blythman's house at York, and has already been described[2]. The second was the case of Robert Holdsworth, vicar of Halifax; his vicarage was appropriated by the rebels, his goods carried off by his enemies the Tempests, and his hidden pot of gold was found by Thomas Lacy[3].

During the first week of Lent 1536-7 Thomas Lacy went to confession. He told his ghostly father how he had found the money and asked what he should do with it. The confessor advised him to keep it until after Low Sunday [8 April]. Two or three days after the appointed date, Lacy brought the money to his ghostly father's room in a canvas pepper poke, and from there carried it to the vicarage, dropped it over the wall into the court, and left it. With an impulse as natural as dishonest, he kept £67 for himself; but presently he repented again and gave it up to Sir Alexander Emmet, Holdsworth's parish priest. Out of the whole sum Lacy had spent only 26s. 6d. "about his seeding."[4]

The Vicar returned to Halifax from London "after Mid-Lent Sunday" [11 March]. He had been urging his own cause with Cromwell, while Sir Henry Saville petitioned the Duke of Norfolk on his behalf. When he reached home and found the treasure gone, he did not complain to Norfolk and mentioned his loss only to the friends who knew of its hiding-place, Sir Henry Saville, Alexander Emmet, his sister and her son[5].

While Holdsworth was in London he had obtained writs of attachment against the Lacys and others who had plundered his vicarage. During Easter Week he went to York and begged Norfolk's favour in the matter. The Duke promised that he should have restitution or the writs should be executed. Holdsworth was still too prudent to mention the great sum that he had lost.

About a week later Alexander Emmet delivered £789. 8s. 9d. to Holdsworth in gold, simply saying that it came to him in confession.

[1] L. and P. xii (1), 1233; printed in full, State Papers, i, 549.
[2] See above, chap. viii.
[3] See above, chaps. iii and xii.
[4] L. and P. xii (2), 369 (4).
[5] L. and P. xii (1), 425; xii (2), 369 (8).

The priest must have been waiting in the vicarage court for the heavy bag that came over the wall[1].

The matter might have ended there to the satisfaction of everyone concerned, but too many people were in the secret. The Vicar had subpoenas against Lacy and his servants, but they did not appear. Lacy said contemptuously, "If they will have my head they shall fetch it." He had nicknamed one of his servants Audley and another Cromwell, and said he could not fail to do well having both the Lord Chancellor and the Lord Privy Seal with him. He admitted that he had robbed the Vicar, but he said that the money was treasure-trove; apparently he argued from this that he had as good a right to it as any man[2]. By this means the rumour of "treasure-trove" reached the ears of the Duke of Norfolk, and he determined that the government should be no loser.

On 12 July Norfolk sent for all the parties to appear before him[3]. On 20 July the Vicar was a close prisoner, allowed to speak only to those whom Norfolk appointed. The Duke had consulted Chaloner and Babthorpe about the law of treasure-trove, and they agreed that unless the Vicar could prove the money to be his, it was the King's. Before examining the witnesses Norfolk proposed to send the money to the King, and then, if Holdsworth had too strong a claim to be denied, the Duke would give him licence to sue for its restoration[4]. It was easy to guess the result of such an application.

The witnesses proved quite conclusively that the money was the Vicar's, and that he had hidden it himself. There was no evidence that any part of it had ever been treasure-trove. Norfolk's council believed that the money was really the Vicar's because there were many crowns of five shillings among the coins found in the pot, and this coin had come into use very recently[5]. Norfolk was vexed at this turn of the case, and asked Cromwell for instructions. He collected all the Vicar's money that he could lay hands on and accused Holdsworth of cheating the revenue, "living covetously like a man of £40 promotions," when he could well spend £200 a year[6].

On 25 July Sir Henry Saville wrote to Cromwell on the Vicar's behalf[7]. Holdsworth brought an action in the Court of Star Chamber against Lacy, but the result is unknown[8]. It is possible that the government obtained for Holdsworth restitution of his

---

[1] L. and P. xii (2), 369 (3).   [2] Ibid. 389.   [3] Ibid. 248.
[4] Ibid. 291.   [5] Ibid. 316, 369.
[6] Ibid. 369.   [7] Ibid. 389.
[8] Yorks. Star Chamber Proc. (Yorks. Arch. Soc. Rec. Ser.), ii, no. lxxi.

plundered goods, and at the same time robbed him of his fortune, but if this were so, the Vicar was not ruined. On the contrary, he retained too much money for his own safety, as in May 1556 he was murdered by thieves in the night-time in the vicarage house[1].

Norfolk was empowered to attend to the doctrine of the north as well as its peace. He encouraged the various anti-papal preachers who were sent there, such as Dr Layton and Dr Addison[2], and suggested that the Archbishop of York and the other principal ecclesiastics might not only promote "such well-learned and also well-willed priests," but also "find others at their own charges continually to go about and preach." If this had been done before he thought "no such follies had been attempted as hath been."[3]

About the beginning of June Norfolk sent round circulars to all justices of the peace and to the remaining monasteries, forbidding them to give any relief to sturdy vagabonds. He said that the alms of the religious houses had encouraged beggars, and that the justices were slack, but now he intended so to deal with them that Cromwell would probably hear of great numbers coming southward[4].

On 3 June the good news of the Queen's pregnancy was confirmed. Norfolk was in York and gave orders for general rejoicings. The Te Deum was sung in the afternoon and at night bonfires were lighted all through the city. To increase the merrymaking Norfolk gave four hogsheads of wine from his own cellar to be broached in different parts of the city for all passers-by.

York was in a ferment of preparation for the King's visit; the country-side had to prepare lodging and stabling for a large and magnificent company. Two or three hundred extra beds were being made. Fortunately the hay-harvest was good, or it would have been hard to provide for the horses in the royal train[5]. But all the preparations were in vain. The King changed his mind. It is clear from Norfolk's letters that he had never really believed that Henry would come, and had been only partly convinced by his repeated assurances. On 12 June the King sent the Duke his reasons for delaying his visit to the north until another year. The reasons were many and ingenious, such as his reluctance to leave the Queen at this critical period, and the delicate state of foreign affairs; but the real motive for delay, which Norfolk was to keep strictly to

[1] T. Wright, Hist. of Halifax (ed. 1834), p. 21.
[2] L. and P. XII (2), 9.
[3] L. and P. XII (1), 1158; printed in full, Wilson, op. cit., no. xxiii.
[4] L. and P. XII (2), 14.   [5] Ibid. 22.

himself, was the King's physical condition. His legs were worse, and his physicians advised him not to travel in the heat of the year. As he could not come to pardon the north in person, he would shortly send down "a personage of honour" with a general pardon; Norfolk might announce this. The King graciously said that he could not be better served than he was at present, but as the Duke desired his recall so earnestly, he should soon receive it. The King intended to establish a standing council and desired the Duke's advice as to its composition[1].

This was the first explicit statement of the King's intentions for the future government of the north, but it was so vaguely worded that it did not seriously clash with Norfolk's ambition. The north might be ruled by a council, but the council might be ruled by the King's lieutenant. Norfolk was still cautious. In his next letters, dated 16 June, he thanked the King for the promise of release. If his master knew how ill he had been he would not wonder at his desire "to be out of this cold country, where hath been two days this week great frosts in the morning, with the most cold weather that ever I saw in such a time of year." For the Council of the North he thought the King should either send down a lieutenant or make the Bishop of Durham president; he did not recommend either of the northern earls. For the councillors he recommended Sir Thomas Tempest, Sir Marmaduke Constable, Sir William Evers, Sir Ralph Ellerker, and Sir Brian Hastings. Dr Magnus was growing old and "less able every day." Norfolk spoke very highly of Babthorpe, Chaloner and Bowes, but they were badly paid. The Duke was heartily glad to hear that the King was sending a pardon to put despair out of "foolish, fearful heads." He asked that ten or twelve pardons might be sent him, with blank schedules attached, in which he could insert, with the advice of his council, the names of those to be excepted from the pardon[2].

At this time Border affairs loom large in Cromwell's memoranda and in the proceedings of the Privy Council, filling the place previously occupied by the northern insurgents. Lists of members proposed for the Council of the North, and of officers and pensioners on the Borders were drawn up, and amended, and drawn up again, until it is hard to say which is merely a "device" and which a final order[3].

[1] L. and P. xii (2), 77; printed in full, State Papers, i, p. 551.
[2] L. and P. xii (2), 100; printed in full, A Collection of Letters of Princes (ed. Howard), p. 272.   [3] L. and P. xii (2), 102, 249, 250.

The repairs of Berwick and Sheriffhutton were proceeding as fast as lack of money would allow[1]. Sir Thomas Clifford was at feud with Lionel Grey, the porter of Berwick[2]. Norfolk wished the King to have them reconciled, as Grey was a man whom Sir William Evers, the deputy warden of the East Marches, could not spare[3].

On the Middle Marches Sir Reynold Carnaby had succeeded the murdered Roger Fenwick in the dangerous office of Keeper of Tynedale. Norfolk disliked Carnaby, who was a creature of Cromwell's, and said sneeringly "that by hearing say he is more than half weary of his being in these parts." On 26 June Norfolk expected the Council of the Marches to wait on him at Sheriffhutton. He intended to "lay it sore to them" that their country was no stronger against the Scots raiders of Liddesdale, "which weekly doth run upon Carnaby's offices."[4]

The Duke was investigating the circumstances of Roger Fenwick's murder. The three murderers, John Charleton, Rinian Charleton and John Dod, fled to Scotland and were never captured. Lionel Grey accused Edward Charleton, Cuthbert Charleton, John Heron of Chipchase, George Heron his son and John Heron of the Hall Barns his kinsman, as instigators of the murder[5]. This accusation was very satisfactory to Norfolk, as the Charletons and Little John Heron of Chipchase were already wanted by the government for their share in the rebellion, but it would be safer and less awkward to punish them nominally for the murder. Little John Heron was captured and sent to London, where he was imprisoned in the Fleet. Heron of the Hall Barns fled to Scotland. George Heron appeared before Norfolk, but he established his innocence so clearly that the Duke wrote to Grey to require proof of the Herons' guilt[6]. On 7 July Lionel Grey brought to the Duke "one of the men that hath detected" the part played by the Herons in Fenwick's murder[7]. This sounds as if there were other witnesses, but later Jerry Charleton alias Topping is described as "the only accuser of the Herons,"[8] and his character was so bad that in the end his evidence was discredited[9]. At present, however, it was considered sufficient, but the Charletons could not be captured by force or stratagem[10].

---

[1] L. and P. xii (2), 10, 69.
[2] See above, chap. ix.
[3] L. and P. xii (2), 332.
[4] Ibid. 142.
[5] Ibid. 142, 203.
[6] Ibid. 142.
[7] Ibid. 229; printed in full, State Papers, v, p. 91.
[8] L. and P. xiii (2), 1010.
[9] State Papers, v, 203; L. and P. xvii, 219.
[10] L. and P. xii (2), 280; printed in full, Raine, op. cit. i, App. p. clix.

Cromwell suggested that John Heron of Chipchase might be sent north to stand his trial for Fenwick's murder. Norfolk replied on 20 July that he must not be sent north until the time was ripe. If he did not know that he was accused of the murder, he must be led to believe that he would soon be set free. If he had already been charged with it, he must be so closely imprisoned that he could send no word of warning to his son George or his son-in-law Cuthbert Charleton. It was important to lull the suspicions of the Charletons, for it was quite impossible to capture them while they were on the alert. Their own country was almost impenetrable, and if they were attacked with fire and sword they had only to cross the hills to Liddesdale[1].

On 27 August Norfolk was still hoping to apprehend Edward and Cuthbert Charleton and George Heron. As to Little John Heron, Norfolk directed Cromwell as follows:

"Which John I require your good lordship may be secretly conveyed hither and so delivered to the officers of my house, to be by them conveyed to me at Newcastle, to be ordered according to justice. I would he should be here on 20 September, and conveyed with a hood on his head, and so secretly kept by the way that no man should know him unto [until] his deliverance; which would also be in the night because I have many pledges of Tynedale and Reedsdale here. For an it were known he were here, I should neither take his son nor the others that I would have. And if it be not known in the Fleet whither he shall go, but conveyed in the night, the better."[2]

On 17 September Norfolk held an assize at Newcastle-upon-Tyne. He made George Heron foreman of the inquest, and the three murderers were condemned in their absence. George Heron did his part, not suspecting that Norfolk, who showed him such a fair countenance, was planning to convict himself and his father of the same crime. George offered to go home to Tynedale and arrest an arrant traitor. Norfolk sent him off with the comment, "If he do I shall have in my hands two false harlots." The Duke intended to arrest George Heron on his return, and to seize his father's house, goods and lands for the King's use. The news from Tynedale was that Cuthbert Charleton was dead[3].

At the next assizes, on 26 September, John Heron and Edward Charleton were indicted in their absence as accessories to the murder of Roger Fenwick. John Heron had not been sent north, and there was no evidence against George Heron, but nevertheless the latter

---

[1] L. and P. xii (2), 291.
[2] Ibid. 588; printed in full, State Papers, v, 101.
[3] L. and P. xii (2), 741.

was arrested and imprisoned[1]. The Charletons were outlawed, and the Keeper of Tynedale carried on a long guerilla war against them, in which the Charletons, having allies in Scotland, were on the whole successful[2].

Little John Heron of Chipchase was never sent north with a hood over his face to be hanged. He was called before the Privy Council and convinced the King of his loyalty and worth. In 1539 he rode home in triumph as Constable of Harbottle, with a pension in his pocket[3]. Edward Charleton was pardoned in 1539; even John Heron of the Hall Barns received mercy and was employed in carrying letters of importance to the north[4]. At length, in August 1540, Little John Heron was offered the post of Keeper of Tynedale. He refused, unless he were given Reedsdale as well, and he was given both[5]. Thus he completely superseded his old enemy Sir Reynold Carnaby. Sir Thomas Percy was avenged so far as vengeance lay in Little John Heron's power. The wily mosstrooper was one of the few men who discovered the length of Henry VIII's foot.

After this digression it is necessary to return to Norfolk at Sheriffhutton Castle. On 2 July 1537 Sir Cuthbert Radcliff, Thomas Carnaby, Cuthbert Shaftoe and George Heron waited on the Duke, and declared the true state of Northumberland. The raiding was chiefly the work of Liddesdale, reinforced by English outlaws. Norfolk daily expected an answer from the King of Scots to his repeated complaints of the protection which English outlaws received in Scotland. Sir John Widdrington was trying to capture certain Scots thieves in England who would be useful as exchanges. The Northumbrians convinced Norfolk that Tynedale had not done nearly as much harm as was reported, but no restitution had been made as yet[6].

The West Marches were reorganised about the beginning of July. Sir Thomas Wharton was made deputy warden, in spite of Norfolk's advice to the contrary. He was also made steward of the abbey of Holm Cultram and the priories of Carlisle and Wetherall. Under him there were four commissioners. Sir Thomas Wentworth became captain of Carlisle, and thirty-three gentlemen of those parts received patents as the King's pensioners. All these commissions and patents, with the oaths for the different officials, were dated

[1] L. and P. xii (2), 772.   [2] Ibid. 828, 878, 978, 979, 1076, 1242.
[3] L. and P. xiv (2), 481.   [4] Ibid. 781, f. 85 b.
[5] L. and P. xv, 570, 618, 987; Nicolas, Proc. and Ord. of the Privy Council (Rec. Com.), vii, pp. 6, 7.
[6] L. and P. xii (2), 229; printed in full, State Papers, v, p. 91.

28 June[1]. They were first sent to Norfolk, who forwarded them on 3 July to Wentworth, together with a summons to all the gentlemen to meet him at York, where he was going to witness Aske's execution on 12 July[2].

Norfolk thought that the arrangements for the West March were better than those for the other two. He wished to call Lord Dacre and Wharton before him and "knit them in amity." Dacre's friendship was far more important to the new Warden than that of the Earl of Cumberland, who had little influence with the marchmen. The prickers of Gilsland were always ready at Dacre's word. Unruly though they were, he kept them in awe, and he was respected even in Tynedale and Reedsdale[3]. When Dacre was Warden he had been both cruel and partial, sending word to his favourite ill-doers to fly when he intended to make a raid; yet he was very popular among the marchmen.

In spite of his general approbation, Norfolk as usual criticised the King's appointments[4]. The Duke constantly endeavoured to draw all the patronage of the north into his own hands. The dictatorship of the north would be within reach if every Border officer were the Duke's man, and owed his appointment to his master. Norfolk, being on the spot, could often choose better men than the King, who was guided only by report. Nevertheless, so long as the Duke remained in the north, the King would not reverse his decisions. After Norfolk's departure, the inefficient were replaced by more capable officers, but in the meanwhile he grumbled in vain. The King would not allow him to make any promotions on his own authority.

Norfolk was still urgently petitioning for leave to ride south. He was ailing and described all his symptoms to Cromwell at great length. Cromwell advised him to offer to stay longer in the north; the King had promised that he should come home at Michaelmas. Norfolk replied from Leckonfield on 8 July that if he stayed in the north until the cold weather began he would die. He was ready to serve the King to the death anywhere else; "but undoubtedly if I should know his pleasure to be to command me to remain here, I am sure I should never have one merry day in my life, and would incontinent determine myself for another world....I may well perceive I have some back friends that thinketh long to hear that I am out of this world." The north was now in such good order,

---

[1] L. and P. XII (2), 154–5, 254. [2] Ibid. 203.
[3] Ibid. [4] Ibid. 248.

that he considered there was no need for his presence; a lieutenant with a good council would be enough[1].

Sir Thomas Tempest, who had been attending on Norfolk, throughout his northern progress[2], wrote to Cromwell on 10 July. He said that Norfolk had shown him Cromwell's letter which advised him to remain in the north. To obey would certainly endanger Norfolk's life during the winter; nevertheless the Duke ought not to be recalled at once, because he was so much loved and feared throughout the north. "Although these parts be now well stayed, their late perversity should be noted, and, as many men of blood and well befriended have justly suffered, it is to be feared their friends are not well contented." Tempest suggested that Norfolk should stay until the end of October, and then leave a council with a good president to carry on the work until Easter, when the Duke could return for the summer[3]. Tempest wrote to Bishop Tunstall, who was then in London, to the same effect. Tunstall was the proposed president of the new council. Tempest urged that the Bishop knew well the need there was for Norfolk in the north[4].

These two letters were obviously inspired by Norfolk, and yet they were very different in effect from his own. Norfolk never wishes to see the north again; yet Tempest suggests that the Duke should return in the spring. Norfolk says that the country is quiet and can do without him; Tempest, that "the country is not so clearly reduced to all goodness that he should be taken from these parts." All this was the next move in Norfolk's game. He did not wish to bring the country into such order that the King could do without him. He hoped, on his return to the south, to be followed by a stream of petitions to the King that he might be sent back; even a minor disturbance would not be amiss. If Norfolk could prove to Henry that he was indispensable, he would be in a position to make terms. He had declared that he would not live in the north for all Northumberland's lands, but the King could test this by experiment. Henry, on the other hand, meant to keep the Duke in the north until it was reduced to order, but not a minute longer. When he did recall Norfolk, he had no intention of sending him back. Norfolk was told that he should be recalled before the cold weather set in. No word was said of a new mission in the spring, but he protested that he was immensely grateful.

[1] L. and P. xii (2), 229; printed in full, State Papers, v, p. 91.
[2] L. and P. xii (2), 152.   [3] Ibid. 238.   [4] Ibid. 239.

The Earl of Wiltshire's minstrel had composed a song about Norfolk, which he said had received the Duke's approval. The inference is that the song was in praise of true noble blood and predicted its triumph over upstarts. Norfolk promised Cromwell so to punish the minstrel that he would be afraid to sing such songs again[1].

Norfolk was impatient for the arrival of a general pardon. He advised that it should not extend beyond 20 February 1536–7. The murder of Fenwick and the welcome of the King of Scots both took place after that date, and consequently those who were involved in either would not be able to claim the benefit of the pardon thus limited. Norfolk sent about fifteen names to be excepted, and asked that room should be left for himself and his council to insert a few more. Those whom he mentioned were: Wilson and Woodmancy of Beverley, Marshall parish clerk of Beswick, Waflin and Leache of Lincolnshire, Bradford and Paris monks of Sawley, Roger Hartlepool monk of Jervaux, Helaigh canon of Coverham, Edward Middleton, Henry King and Simon Marshal of Masham, Esch friar of St Robert's of Knaresborough, Nicholas Musgrave, a friar of Appleby, John Priestman of Lillesdale Hall, John Priestman son of William Priestman of Helnesley [Helmsley?], Dr Marmaduke Walby, Towneley chancellor of the Bishop of Carlisle, and the Prior of the White Friars of Doncaster[2]. Most of these men had fled to Scotland, but the three last-named were prisoners in the Tower.

In Scotland James pursued an anti-English policy without actually provoking a breach of the peace. Norfolk wrote of him on 3 July "he doth keep so small an house that there is but only six messes of meat allowed in his house, and the Queen his wife not like to escape without death, and that not long unto as I am informed by divers ways."[3] The poor young Queen died before 24 July[4] of consumption, not, as might be supposed from Norfolk's letter, of starvation.

Sir Thomas Clifford's spies reported that James "doth not use nor give himself to any princely pleasure, like as he heretofore hath been accustomed, but continually yet doth go about framing his ordnance in most secret wise." He had paid several midnight visits to Dunbar, and Tantallon was prepared for war. Clifford contrasted with these preparations the destitute condition of

[1] L. and P. xii (2), 291. [2] Ibid. 291 (ii).
[3] Ibid. 203. [4] Ibid. 832.

Berwick[1], but as a matter of fact the town was being provisioned and the fortifications repaired.

It was thought possible that James might change his policy on the death of his French wife. It was reported that he was hesitating between a renewal of the matrimonial alliance with France and an application to England for the hand of Mary[2]. On 2 August James came as far as Dunbar with David Beaton, Abbot of Arbroath, whom he was about to despatch on a diplomatic mission first to Henry and then to Francis. Henry was making a short progress to Ampthill, and intended to receive the ambassador there[3].

Norfolk prepared to join the King at Ampthill to assist in the negotiations with Scotland, but on 7 August he received definite orders that he was not to leave Yorkshire. He replied with the bitterest complaints of his treatment, and indeed he had a right to expect better usage[4]. Henry must have felt that he might slight the Duke too much as he tardily consented, and Norfolk joined him at Grafton on 15 August, to give his advice upon the Scots negotiations and on the appointment of the Council of the North[5]. The Abbot of Arbroath promised that all the English fugitives in Scotland should be exchanged for Scots rebels in England, but his mission did not otherwise give satisfaction, as he was going to France to arrange a new French marriage for James, who was in perfect accord with Francis[6].

Norfolk and Henry together determined that the president of the Council of the North should be Bishop Tunstall of Durham[7]. Tunstall was very unwilling to undertake the arduous task. He protested that he was too old to be fit for anything but teaching and preaching. The people hated him, and whatever punishment he inflicted would be imputed to private malice, which would bring discredit on the King's justice. He was neither powerful enough to punish disobedience nor rich enough to keep up the hospitality which would be expected of him, and this would lead evil-doers to despise and mock the King's authority[8]. His objections went for nothing. Henry had decided that he was the most suitable man for the post, and Norfolk probably hoped that Tunstall would prove so

---

[1] L. and P. xii (2), 346; printed in full, State Papers, v, 94, and Scott's History of Berwick, p. 127.
[2] L. and P. xii (2), 332, 370.
[3] Ibid. 422, 430; 422 printed in full, State Papers, v, 96.
[4] L. and P. xii (2), 479; printed in full, State Papers, v, 99.
[5] L. and P. xii (2), 590. [6] Ibid. 566, 590.
[7] Ibid. 588; printed in full, State Papers, v, 101. [8] L. and P. xii (2), 651.

complete a failure that he himself would have to be reappointed. Tunstall was ordered to prepare himself and to forget his displeasure against Robert Bowes[1], who had plundered his palace at Bishop Auckland during the rebellion[2].

Norfolk's visit to the south was a short one[3]. He was back at Sheriffhutton on 27 August. Now that the Council of the North was an established fact he was impatient to be gone. It remained to be seen whether he could ever compass his return. On 27 August he wrote "I am...very desirous to bring Tynedale, before my departing hence, in better order than it is,"[4] but the task proved too long and he left it unaccomplished.

On the West Marches Sir Thomas Wharton was on the whole a successful warden, and under his rule there was at least a very fair appearance of regular justice, both on the Marches and in Cumberland, although this did not mean that there was any lack of such incidents as inspired the Border ballads[5].

The Middle Marches were a very different affair. Norfolk was longing to make his name terrible in the district which had treated his authority with such light-hearted contempt. He wished to arrange that James V should make a descent on Liddesdale at the same time as he attacked Tynedale. The Abbot of Arbroath held out some hope that his master would consent to this, but on 8 September James replied to Norfolk that he would give his wardens such charge that a simultaneous raid of this sort would be quite unnecessary[6]. Consequently the Duke was obliged to undertake the Borders without James' help.

While Norfolk awaited James' answer at Sheriffhutton he busied himself in reconciling the feuds of various Yorkshire gentlemen. Among others Sir Henry Saville came to an agreement with "all his neighbours and sisters" and might prove a good servant. On 5 September Norfolk was suffering from a cold in the head. He wrote to Cromwell, and after regaling him with his symptoms in great detail, proceeded to ease his temper by abuse of his subordinates. According to his account the whole of the north was in a state of Utopian peace except Tynedale and Reedsdale, for which the Keeper

---

[1] L. and P. xii (2), 589.   [2] See above, chap. ix.   [3] L. and P. xii (2), 547.
[4] Ibid. 588; printed in full, State Papers, v, 101.
[5] L. and P. xii (2), 422; printed in full, State Papers, v, 96; L. and P. xii (2), 537; 604, 642, 732; 828-9, printed in full, State Papers, v, 109-11; L. and P. xii (2), 836, 865, 990.
[6] L. and P. xii (2), 588; printed in full, State Papers, v, 102; L. and P. xii (2), 590, 666; printed in full, State Papers, v, 106.

and the warden were responsible. "Widdrington would fain do well, but surely it is not in him. Carnaby is so feared of his person that he doth nothing but keep the house. Men doth much doubt of his hardiness having yet shown no part of manhood since his coming hither. I would they were both in Paradise, so other good were in their rooms; for by their defaults I shall be enforced, as soon as I shall be able to travel, to ride to those cold parts which I fear shall not be without some danger. And yet had I rather to adventure the same, than to have the continual crying out of the poor people that I have to come thither."[1]

Norfolk rode to Newcastle-upon-Tyne on 14 September, and found that no restitution had been made for plunder taken during the rebellion, and that there were under a dozen offenders to be tried. In fact all the Border was very reluctant to deliver thieves to the law[2], not from mercy nor even from fellow-feeling, although the gentlemen of the country were not much more honest than the reivers, but because when a man was hanged his kinsmen would never forget the feud. The blood feud was the weapon which enabled the mosstrooper to keep up his war against the world; it was his last and best protection. The King's deputy warden might take a thief red-handed. If he brought him to the gallows many things would follow. The deputy warden's cattle would never be safe at the pride of the moon; his hay-stacks and barns would mysteriously take fire; wherever he went he would never ride safely, for on the open moors an arrow might fly from a whin-bush, and in the streets of a town a man might lurch against him with a knife in his hand. It generally happened that the warden let the thief go free.

Norfolk was very angry at this state of affairs. The blood feud made no difference to him, as he was leaving the north so soon. He made further complaints to the King of Carnaby and Widdrington, and proposed others to be promoted in their places. If Tynedale and Reedsdale refused to make restitution on the 20th and 21st September, "I will be busy with them." Reedsdale was not expected to give trouble, and if the men of Tynedale proved more obstinate Norfolk would make a descent upon their houses, burn them to the ground, set their standing corn ablaze, and when the people were driven into the hills, he would lay garrisons "to defend their malice," whenever they wickedly tried to get something to eat[3].

[1] L. and P. XII (2), 650; printed in full, State Papers, v, 104.
[2] L. and P. XII (2), 695, 732.   [3] Ibid. 696; printed in full, State Papers, v, 107.

The King answered on 18 September in one of those letters which must have been such a trial to his servants. He remained blandly determined that "whosoever kick against it" he would be served by the men of his own choice and no others. As to Tynedale, he sent orders very unlike his usual instructions. Clemency was to be shown. He expected Norfolk to reform, not to destroy[1]. It must be put to Henry's credit that if he had raised, for his own purposes, a breed of mosstroopers more savage than their fathers, he did not like them to be slaughtered wholesale, though it is doubtful whether this was due to some faint sense of his own responsibility or merely to an anticipation of the next war with Scotland.

Norfolk held two sessions at Newcastle-upon-Tyne, one on Monday 17 September, the other on Wednesday 26 September. Only nine thieves were executed altogether, but both Tynedale and Reedsdale were at last induced to make restitution or to put in sufficient pledges for it[2]. Norfolk said with natural pride that he had redressed above a hundred wrongs since he came to Newcastle-upon-Tyne, and that he would leave the country better contented[3]. He had "swept the houses so clean" that the Bishop of Durham and his Council would find little to do[4]. The King fully approved of all his proceedings and sent him a letter of thanks[5].

On 28 September 1537 Norfolk left Newcastle-upon-Tyne[6]. He was at Sheriffhutton on 4 October[7]. On 6 October he started on his journey southward[8]. His long mission was over. The government of the north passed into other hands.

Instead of the old expedient by which the supreme authority was conferred on a powerful nobleman, Henry had resolved that the north should be governed by a council. Although Cromwell was a warm advocate of this system, he cannot be given the credit for its invention. Government by council was a favourite Tudor device from the days of Henry VII onwards. It was said that in 1640 over a third of England was ruled by various councils, offshoots of the Privy Council[9].

Sufficient evidence has already been given to prove that the north required a better system of government than it had hitherto enjoyed. The Pilgrims at Pontefract had proposed that it should

---

[1] L. and P. XII (2), 712; printed in full, State Papers, I, 565.
[2] L. and P. XII (2), 782, 741.   [3] Ibid. 772.
[4] Ibid. 741.   [5] Ibid. 746.   [6] Ibid. 828.
[7] Ibid. 828; printed in full, State Papers, V, 109.   [8] L. and P. XII (2), 839.
[9] Dicey, The Privy Council, pt. III, sect. III, 2, c.

have adequate parliamentary representation, that parliaments should sometimes be held there, that law courts should be established at York competent to deal with all but the most important cases, and that in general the interests and welfare of the north should be treated as of equal importance with those of the south.

Instead of this, the King resolved to treat the north as a conquered province. It was placed under a form of government in which there was no representation and from which there was no appeal. If the Council of the North was to work at all, its decisions, however unjust, must be upheld by the central government. The north had already undergone an experimental foretaste of this method of rule, and had hated and protested against it[1], but the country was to groan under the Council of the North for another hundred years, until released by the Great Civil War. Yet the Council was not more autocratic than the Privy Council itself, and such partial success as it had in enforcing law and order was some compensation for the fact that it was entirely opposed to the independent spirit of the people.

Most of the new council's members had been leaders in the Pilgrimage; such were Sir Ralph Ellerker, Sir Thomas Tempest, Robert Bowes, William Babthorpe and Robert Chaloner. They were capable, ambitious men, bound to make their way upwards. They were not insincere Pilgrims, but the rising failed and they turned their energies to the King's service as the only course left open to them. Norfolk's business was to conciliate them and win them over, and he had succeeded: "all these men have their price." They had been willing to risk their lives for a cause, but having escaped, they would not sacrifice their careers. As members of the Council of the North, they helped to keep in subjection the country whose liberties they had so lately borne arms to defend.

Norfolk and his council in 1537 may be regarded as the forerunners of the new council, and the King's lieutenant, when there was one, was always the president of the Council of the North.

The advantages which the King derived from the establishment of the Council were obvious. It was small and could work easily and effectively, for although a large number of members were sometimes appointed, there were only five salaried members, who, with the president and vice-president, were obliged to attend and were competent to transact business[2]. Its members were chosen

[1] See above, chap. III.
[2] Prothero, Statutes and Constitutional Documents, 1559–1625, Introduction, v.

and dismissed by the King; there was no danger that the office would become hereditary or that individual members might be too powerful. It was therefore safe to trust them with very extensive powers.

The Council of the North had jurisdiction over the whole of the five northern counties, Northumberland, Durham, Westmorland, Cumberland and Yorkshire. Privileged districts such as the Palatinate of Durham were entirely abolished. The Council was authorised to hear and determine all offences connected with unlawful assemblies and breaches of the peace, and all actions concerning property and debts[1]. Its duties were to aid the ecclesiastical authorities in the repression of papists and heretics, to maintain uniformity and good morals, to protect agriculture, to defend the poor against the rich, to supervise the justices of the peace[2], and to provide for the defence of the Border. "It was empowered to inflict almost any penalty short of death," and although in cases of difficulty it might appeal for advice to the Privy Council, there was no appeal for suitors from its decisions[3]. It administered justice according to either the law of the land or the discretion of its members[4]. The Council also held sessions, oyer and gaol delivery, heard indictments for murder and felony, and executed felons. "In this respect their powers exceeded even those of the Star Chamber."[5] In short, the Council exercised all the powers previously held by Norfolk.

Before 15 October 1537 the Council of the North held its first meeting at York[6]. It was composed of Cuthbert Tunstall, Bishop of Durham, the president; Sir Thomas Tempest; Sir Ralph Ellerker; Sir Marmaduke Constable the elder; Robert Bowes; William Babthorpe; Richard Bellasis; Robert Chaloner; John Uvedale; Sir William Evers; and Thomas Fairfax, the King's serjeant-at-law[7]. Robert Holgate, Bishop of Llandaff and prior of Watton, also took part in its deliberations[8]. The officers of the court consisted of the Lord President, the Vice-President, four or more learned Councillors, the Secretary, the King's Attorney, two Examiners, one Registrar, fourteen Attornies, one Clerk of the

[1] Lapsley, op. cit. chap. VI, sect. 35.
[2] West Riding Sessions Rolls and Proc. in the Council of the North (Yorks. Arch. Ass. Rec. Ser.), III, pp. i–vi, 1–22.
[3] Prothero, op. cit., Intro. v, and Documents, Reign of James I, IV, no. 3.
[4] Lapsley, loc. cit. [5] Prothero, op. cit., Intro. v.
[6] L. and P. XII (2), 915; printed in full, State Papers, V, 116.
[7] L. and P. XII (2), 913, 914; 913 printed in full, State Papers, V, 112.
[8] L. and P. XII (2), 102 (3); see above, chaps. XII and XVII, and Baildon, Monastic Notes (Yorks. Arch. Soc. Rec. Ser.), I, p. 215.

Attachments, two Clerks of the Seal, one Clerk of the Tickets, one Serjeant-at-Arms, one Pursuivant, ten Collectors of Fines, two Tipstaves[1].

The first report of the Council of the North has not been preserved, but a letter from Tunstall to Cromwell, written at the same time (15 October), probably gives the information which was contained in it. Wide as the powers of the Council were, the members were not satisfied. They found that they had no power to levy men in order to enforce their precepts; the gentlemen had all sworn to levy none save at the King's command. The Council referred the matter to the King, "considering therewith that fire is more easily quenched in the spark than in the flame." They also referred two minor points to the King; they wished to know what seal they should use, and they requested that the decrees of the Duke of Richmond's late council might be sent to help them in their decisions[2].

Finally they wished for instructions concerning the little heirs of the house of Percy[3]. It was now represented by Sir Ingram Percy, who was dying by inches in the Tower, and Sir Thomas Percy's two sons. The Dowager Countess had been arrested by Sir Brian Hastings in February 1536–7. Her goods were seized and inventoried, but they were worth little, even the plate being valued at "an hundred pounds or very easy more." She had few jewels and robes for a lady of her position. Hastings good-naturedly wrote to Cromwell in her favour[4]. Before the beginning of October she had been released, her lands and goods were restored to her, and she was living at Catton in Yorkshire[5].

The Percy estates were viewed by the King's surveyor Robert Southwell in August[6]. The government kept a careful eye on the natural heirs of all this wealth, Sir Thomas Percy's sons Thomas and Henry. On 8 July Norfolk wrote: "As to Sir Thomas Percy's children, I have entreated good Sir Thomas Tempest to take them into his custody; they being at this time in the Bishopric within two miles of his house; and have promised him to have their costs paid for."[7] Sir Thomas soon grew weary of his charge. Tunstall

---

[1] Drake, Eboracum, bk I, chap. VIII.
[2] L. and P. XII (2), 915; printed in full, State Papers, v, 116. See Brown, Yorkshire Star Chamber Proc. (Yorks. Arch. Soc. Rec. Ser.), I, p. vii n. and no. xxxix.
[3] L. and P. XII (2), 915.
[4] L. and P. XII (1), 517.   [5] L. and P. XII (2), 955.   [6] Ibid. 548.
[7] Ibid. 229; printed in part, De Fonblanque, op. cit. II, chap. X, and State Papers, v, 91.

wrote on 15 October that Sir Thomas still kept the children at Norfolk's command; but "his house is not strong but very weak, and within sixteen mile of Tynedale, no town betwixt, nor other obstacle than the river of Tyne when the water is risen; for at low waters there be two fords that every man may pass, by which the thieves do much annoy our country. I know this to be true by experience, for I have ridden the same way. He desireth much to be rid of the custody of them, and demandeth of me licence to be absent for the keeping of them; which reasonably I cannot deny and yet his presence were very necessary. Some other place more within the country were more meet than his house, and the children be young and must be among women."[1] The Council must have feared that Sir Thomas Percy's old friends the reivers of Tynedale might carry off his children. Permission was given to place them wherever it was thought best[2].

With the fall of the house of Percy the old order of things ended. The new began with the Council of the North. There is this excuse for Bowes and the other Pilgrims who served on the Council; they probably believed that they were saving the country from the Duke of Norfolk's despotism. Norfolk never realised his dream of a northern dictatorship. It was improbable from the first that he would ever be able to force Henry to concede him such a position, and it is quite incredible that the King would have made such a grant willingly; but the northern gentlemen did not know that. Norfolk's pose was that of a faithful old servant who reluctantly performed a disagreeable duty laid upon him by his master. Partly because he needed Norfolk, and partly to gratify his love of playing with a man's hopes and fears, the King gave the Duke sufficient public countenance to make this pose appear plausible. Bad as the Council of the North might be, the gentlemen supported it, because they believed it to be the lesser of two evils. Its tyranny was not so unendurable as that of "this false Duke."

NOTES TO CHAPTER XXI

Note A. The Border pledges were hostages. When the reivers were in trouble they delivered up one of every surname or clan, in earnest of their better behaviour. The object of the government was to obtain a pledge who was sufficiently important to make his loss a matter of anxiety to his surname.

---

[1] L. and P. xii (2), 915; printed in full, State Papers, v, 116; De Fonblanque, loc. cit.

[2] L. and P. xii (2), 1016; printed in full, Merriman, op. cit. ii, no. 227.

The object of the reivers was to induce the government to accept as a pledge some man whom his friends did not mind losing. Theoretically the life of the pledge was forfeit if his people committed fresh offences, but the penalty seems very seldom to have been exacted in full. The pledges were not usually kept in strict confinement and were relieved by new comers every month or so. In the case of disorders, however, the pledges were more strictly imprisoned, and cases even occurred when they were half-starved until their kinsmen were reduced to obedience.

An example of the chaffering over pledges occurred on Tuesday, 17 July, 1537. Sir Cuthbert Radcliff and Sir Reynold Carnaby called the men of Tynedale to a meeting at Hexham for the restitution of spoil. Edward and Cuthbert Charleton came in "under assurance," and said that they were willing to follow any order taken by the meeting. Edward Charleton was anxious for the release of his pledge; he offered one of his tenants in exchange, but Carnaby did not consider a tenant sufficient. The other Charletons would neither pledge for nor with Edward; they proposed to lay a separate hostage for themselves when the first had returned. In this extremity Edward Charleton offered his son, a boy of thirteen, whom Carnaby was ready to accept, as he thought that his father would be loth to lose him[1].

When Norfolk left the north the eight Border pledges whom he had kept at Sheriffhutton Castle were removed to York, as no sufficient guard remained at Sheriffhutton. In York the marchmen boarded at a serjeant's house and showed themselves every day to the sheriffs[2]. The Council of the North dared not imprison them for fear "there would never more come in to be pledges." Bishop Tunstall, the president of the Council, objected to the presence of the pledges in York. He was also annoyed because "two of the most active men of all Tynedale" had come as pledges "to change and loose the others for a season as has always been accustomed." These two had promised Norfolk to resist the inroads of the outlawed Charletons, and Tunstall thought that they had come as pledges just before the full moon, when they were most needed at home, to be "honestly...quit of their premise." The Council of the North decided to move the pledges to Newcastle-upon-Tyne, because "it is within eighteen miles of their country, and coming thither they should learn no new ways, whereas now coming hither [to York] so far from home, by exchange, they learn all the byways of all countries adjoining unto them, which makes them more bold to steal, when they know which way to escape with their prey."[3]

The system of hostages is very characteristic of the age. Fundamentally unjust, it was a survival of primitive barbarism. It was clear that the pledges at Newcastle-upon-Tyne or York could not be guilty of outrages on the Border, but if the guilty could not be made to suffer, the innocent must be punished. This system was peculiarly congenial to Henry. He openly looked upon the mother and brothers of Reginald Pole, for instance, as hostages for his good behaviour. When he defied the King, it was only Henry's extreme benignity which prevented him from ordering the Cardinal's relations to instant execution.

---

[1] L. and P. XII (2), 280; printed in full, Raine, op. cit. I, Append. p. clix.
[2] L. and P. XII (2), 915, 1077; printed in full, State Papers, v, 116, 122.
[3] L. and P. XII (2), 1077; printed in full, State Papers, v, 123.

They were in the end put to death almost avowedly as a means of making the Cardinal suffer.

Note B. March treason was committed when an Englishman allied himself with a Scot to attack another Englishman. Such crimes were investigated and punished in the Wardens' Courts. The penalty was decapitation. Such a case was tried in October 1537 at Carlisle before Sir Thomas Wharton, the King's deputy warden[1].

Note C. This letter is not included among the Letters and Papers of Henry VIII. Raine's reference is MSS Cotton. Caligula B iii, 241.

---

[1] L. and P. xii (2), 829, 836, 865.

CHAPTER XXII

THE WHITE ROSE PARTY

With the leaders of the Pilgrimage died the spirit of active resistance to Henry. The gentlemen and commons had struck their blow and failed. There still remained the White Rose party at court. Its members had done nothing during the rebellion. They only whispered together and exchanged tokens and dreamed of better days. They were all under suspicion and constantly watched by royal spies, warned against consorting together, often in disgrace and banished from court. It was impossible that they could be dangerous to Henry. The proof of this has already been given. The Pilgrimage was the one good opportunity to carry out their long-cherished plans. If the Marquis of Exeter had raised the west and Lord Montague had raised Hampshire, the south would have been plunged into turmoil and the northern Pilgrims would have been able to march on London at leisure. Henry might have been forced to fly, and Mary proclaimed queen. But, as a matter of fact, Exeter marched to join Norfolk with all the force he could make; not one of the conservative nobles raised a man to second the Pilgrims; and Cardinal Pole, in spite of the Pope's encouragement, made not the slightest effort to improve the occasion. Their one chance slipped from the listless hands of the White Rose party. They did not even know that it was lost.

Why was Henry so bent upon the ruin of these very inefficient conspirators that he actually told the French ambassador that he meant to exterminate the house of Pole[1]? It is true that he was very angry with Reginald Pole; he regarded with jealousy all who could lay claim to the blood royal; and he may have believed them to be more dangerous than they were. He was already troubled by a disease so painful as partly to account for the savage hatred of opposition which became little less than madness towards the end of

[1] L. and P. XIII (2), 753.

his life. But all this is merely to say that he was a blood-thirsty tyrant, and that, however useful as abuse, is not a really satisfactory explanation of any human being's actions.

The answer to the problem is to be found in Henry's superb belief in his own divine right to rule. His admirers have tried to slur over the ferocity of his treason laws by vague talk of "compelled severity" and "temporary necessity." It may be modestly suggested that there is another explanation. There was no very pressing need for these laws, as the old treason law was quite sufficiently severe, but Henry honestly believed that they were just. To him treason was the blackest of all crimes, not a mere political offence which might be committed by a virtuous person with the highest motives, but a crime worse than murder or perjury against the innocent. The man who dared to criticise the title of Supreme Head of the Church was as guilty and as worthy of death as those who resisted him in arms; he made no distinctions between those who opposed him in thought, deed, or word. The catholic martyrs died for their opinions. The Pilgrims died for maintaining their opinions with their swords. The "Exeter Conspirators" died for a few careless words—for a wish —for a dream of majesty.

It is surprising that Pole's family remained in England. They might have fled to him at Rome, where their lives at least would have been safe. They considered flight,—they often talked of it, but apparently they could not bring themselves to face the results. The thought of becoming a landless exile was intolerable to most English gentlemen. Lord Montague might have chosen it rather than death, but he would not leave the country until the danger was imminent, and then it was too late for flight, for Henry struck swiftly. Sir Geoffrey Pole, with less to lose, often planned to join Reginald, but Montague and other friends dissuaded him, on the grounds that it would put the family in a worse position than ever. The Poles were always expecting a change of policy and a reconciliation with Rome. If this opinion was treasonable the King would have had to execute half the nobility to root it out. So the doomed family awaited the event, if not in security, at least with surprising calmness, as they were not by any means unwarned.

When Reginald Pole sent his book *De Unitate Ecclesiastica* to Henry in 1536[1], it was carried by an English servant who had followed his fortunes, a man named Michael Throgmorton[2]. He was of good family, and a suitable person to be intrusted with such a

---

[1] See above, chap. II. [2] Haile, op. cit. chap. IX.

delicate mission, as he was both faithful and quick-witted. He did not undertake his errand very willingly, for he had a natural fear that it would end in the Tower rather than in his return to Italy. His apprehension was well founded. Henry was furiously angry at Pole's opinions and Throgmorton was detained in London, in great danger, until January 1536-7. The country was in open rebellion throughout the autumn, and his brother, Sir George Throgmorton was in the Tower on a charge of spreading Aske's manifestos[1].

In January came the news that Pole had been created a Cardinal[2]. Before he set out on his journey Throgmorton had begged that if this promotion took place it might be kept secret until he had made his escape from England[3], but no attempt was made at secrecy, and Throgmorton might well feel his head unsteady on his shoulders. Nevertheless he lived to be one of the few men who could boast of outwitting Cromwell[4]. He played his cards well, declaring himself completely out of sympathy with Pole and the King's most loyal subject. He spoke of his influence over his master, and undertook to use every means to bring Pole back to England and his allegiance. He even consented to enlist in Cromwell's secret service, and became officially the King's chief spy on the traitor Pole. At the cost of such "crafty and subtle conveyance" he obtained leave to return to Rome, and by 26 January 1536-7 he was on his way thither with a light heart[5]. He had completely "bleared" Cromwell's eyes, for he never had the least intention of playing his master false.

Throgmorton arrived at Rome on 13 February. He carried letters for the Cardinal from the Privy Council, who professed themselves unspeakably shocked at Pole's ingratitude. But they offered to send certain wise men to meet him in Flanders in order to argue him into a better frame of mind, always provided that he came as a private person, without a commission from the Pope[6].

Throgmorton found his master dressed in his cardinal's robes, and delivered the letters together with credence to the same effect. He admitted in his first report to Cromwell that his persuasions had as yet been useless; "great men are not lightly persuaded and he especially." The writing of these reports must have been a great joy to Throgmorton[7].

Pole had been created a papal legate on 7 February, and he was about to set out for Flanders[8], in spite of the fact that the King had

[1] See above, chap. XIII.
[2] L. and P. XII (1). 105.
[3] Ibid. 88.
[4] L. and P. XIII (2), 507.
[5] L. and P. XII (1), 249.
[6] Ibid. 125, 429.
[7] Ibid. 429.
[8] Ibid. 367.

refused, in such a case, to send anyone to meet him[1]. Throgmorton represented him in this as the well-meaning tool of the scheming court of Rome; "let them mean as they will, he means all for the best, and to the honour of God and his Church, without dissimulation, covetousness or ambition."[2] Throgmorton hoped that Cromwell would not object to his going with his master, for although he was the King's man, he was loth to leave Pole on account of his rare virtues and good life. He referred the question to Cromwell, as no man could give better counsel in such a case, because no man had more proved the profit and comfort of true fidelity[3]. One of Cromwell's genuine spies recorded that Michael Throgmorton had an open and simple-minded manner[4]. It must have been a very simple manner to carry off remarks of that sort. But for some time Cromwell did not suspect that there was anything wrong.

Cardinal Pole was about to move at last. The avowed purpose of his legation was an attempt to help forward a general pacification, to inquire into the spread of heresy, and to announce a general council. Its real purpose was to arrange the affairs of England[5]. According to the news then current in Rome, Henry had given way to the Pilgrims, and intended to hold a northern parliament in the spring. It was taken for granted that this parliament would restore the Pope's authority in England, and it was essential that a papal legate should be present to see that everything was done in the right way. Also it was only proper that his Holiness should show his approval of "the manly and Christian demonstration those people are making." Pole never reproached himself for his delay at the time of the insurrection. His one anxiety was to be in time for the parliament. It was doubtful whether he would accomplish this, as he was a very bad traveller. It occurred to him that the King might be deceiving the Pilgrims, that he might intend no reform, but sought only to quiet them and then to dispose of their leaders; in fact that Henry might be doing the very thing that he was doing. Pole suggested that if this were the case, someone, not himself, should be sent to England to exhort the people, in the Pope's name, to stand firm, and that large sums of money should be ready in Flanders in case of need[6].

One of Pole's last acts before starting was to answer the letter of the Privy Council[7]. He stated his case well, but the matter had

---

[1] L. and P. xii (1), 429.   [2] Ibid. 430.
[3] Ibid. 429.   [4] L. and P. xiii (2), 507.
[5] L. and P. xii (1), 368.   [6] Ibid.   [7] Ibid. 444.

gone far beyond the reach of argument. Pole's only justification was that he was convinced he was right, and Henry's only reply was that Pole was hopelessly wrong. A meeting with Henry's agents in Flanders could have led to nothing more satisfactory, and perhaps Pole realised this when in reply to the Council's proposal he said that he would receive emissaries only if they were sent to him as to a cardinal and a legate.

At length Pole set out, but he was a long time on the journey. About 16 April 1537 he was at Cambrai[1], but he would not have reached even that point so soon if all had gone as he hoped on the way. There was a clause in the treaties between England and France that neither King should receive or assist the rebel subjects of the other; in marked contrast to the modern custom by which political offenders are especially exempted from extradition treaties, this clause was held to mean that a proscribed traitor who sought refuge in the other country must be seized and given up to his own government. Francis I sent word to Henry that Pole had entered his kingdom as legate[2]. The French King regarded the Pope as the Emperor's ally, and was ready to conciliate Henry at his expense, if he could do so without danger to himself. Henry commanded his ambassador in France, Gardiner Bishop of Winchester, to desire Francis to apprehend Pole and send him to England. Gardiner obeyed, and Francis replied that Pole had entered his dominions under safe-conduct, and that he could not arrest him, but he would send him word to depart within ten days[3].

Henry was not satisfied. He despatched Sir Francis Brian on 8 April to demand Pole again and to remind Francis I that the treaty did not recognise safe-conducts[4]. The French King did not dare to quarrel with Henry, but to apprehend Pole would have brought about an open breach with the Pope. The King was with the army, and when on 10 April Pole made his state entry as legate into Paris, he was met by a gentleman of the King's chamber, who informed him that he must press on to Cambrai without seeing Francis[5].

Henry was enraged at Pole's escape. He blamed Gardiner and Brian for lack of zeal and care. He bade them reproach Francis I with the legate's honourable reception[6], and at the same time he sent by the hands of John Hutton, his agent in the Netherlands,

---

[1] L. and P. xii (1). 949. [2] Ibid. 817.
[3] Ibid. 865. [4] Ibid.
[5] Ibid. 931. [6] Ibid. 939.

letters to the Regent of the Netherlands, which adjured her on pain of breaking solemn treaties to prevent Pole's entry into the Emperor's dominions. If he were already over the borders, she must send him injunctions to leave within the time specified by treaty[1].

Pole took refuge in the independent archbishopric of Cambrai. He was obliged to stay there all through May, though he was in considerable danger. Henry, who had not forgiven Gardiner and Brian for the first failure, wrote to them on 25 April: "And for as much as we would be very glad to have the said Pole trussed up and conveyed to Calais, we desire and pray you to consult and devise between you thereupon." Could not Brian secretly get together some men capable of such an enterprise? Francis I himself suggested that his Italians might "snap up" the legate some time when he was beyond the walls of the town[2]. Pole was careful to keep within the gates, for skirmishing parties were constantly about, and he soon discovered that, in obedience to their orders, Henry's agents had surrounded him with "spies and betrayers."[3]

The days at Cambrai must have been very bitter to Pole. The French King had ignominiously turned him out; the Regent of the Netherlands, though more truly his friend, dared not ignore Henry's protests[4]. All hope of a peaceful and honourable return to England had vanished. The Pilgrims were in the Tower awaiting death, and Pole was within measurable distance of joining them. He was told that 100,000 pieces of English gold would be given to any man who brought him to England alive or dead[5].

Sir Francis Brian had undertaken the mission, and that one-eyed "minion" declared that if the Cardinal returned to France he would kill him with his own hand[6]. All around Cambrai was the turmoil of a great European war. The Emperor's host was encamped round the city. The brave Queen of Hungary, Regent of the Netherlands, who wore over her kirtle "a jerkin of black leather with eyelet holes to wear harness upon," vowed that if Francis would await her forces but fifteen days she would show him "what God may strength a woman to do."[7] Pole, who had been sent to urge peace upon the combatants, was an embarrassment to all parties. The Regent peevishly exclaimed that her enemy had sent him simply to trouble her[8]. Evil days had fallen on the ambassador of the Holy See.

[1] L. and P. xii (1), 940.   [2] Ibid. 1032.   [3] Ibid. 1052.
[4] Ibid. 1061.   [5] Ibid. 1053, 1242, 1243.
[6] Ibid. 996.   [7] Ibid. 1220.
[8] Ibid. 1135.

It does Pole much honour that he was willing and even anxious to persevere against all these discouragements. His chief hope was that he might keep up the hearts of "these poor, good men" the commons of England. He imagined that his presence near at hand might encourage them to new endeavour. But he was too late, and the people of the north had other and nearer sorrows to mourn than the decay of the Pope's authority.

At last the Cardinal's friends in Flanders determined to help him to a place of safety, although they were hampered by the English King's constant threats that if Pole crossed the borders and were not arrested, he would consider that the treaties were broken[1]. They replied at length that a legate was outside such treaties, and that they had gone as far as possible to please Henry when the Regent refused to receive the Cardinal. The Pope had especially recommended Pole to the care of his fellow-cardinal Erarde de la Marck, the Prince Bishop of Liége, who was the head of the Regent's Council[2]. The Bishop secretly offered Pole a safe harbour in his own see, but he suggested that Pole should travel in disguise, to which the legate, feeling that in his person the dignity of the Apostolic See would be compromised, could not bring himself to consent[3]. During the last days of May an escort was sent, which conducted him honourably, but without all the state that was his due, through Flanders to Liége. Here he was received with pontifical honours, provided with money, and lodged in "the old palace."[4] "They take him there for a young god," wrote Hutton scornfully to Cromwell.

One day a starving Englishman came to John Hutton and begged for alms. His name was William Vaughan, and he had fled from England accused of manslaughter. He told Hutton that he had begged for help from Henry Phillips, an English student at Louvain who had betrayed Tyndale. Phillips had offered to introduce Vaughan into Cardinal Pole's service, or rather into the service of Michael Throgmorton. Phillips said that Throgmorton was about to sail secretly for England, carrying letters to Pole's friends hidden in a loaf of bread. Hutton seized this opportunity. He gave Vaughan money, and promised him a pardon and further reward if he would contrive to sail with Throgmorton; as soon as they reached England Vaughan must see that Throgmorton was arrested[5].

Vaughan set out for Liége with an uneasy conscience, but beggars

---

[1] L. and P. xii (1), 1220.   [2] Ibid. 1293.   [3] Ibid. 1242.
[4] L. and P. xii (2), 26.   [5] L. and P. xii (1), 1293.

cannot be choosers[1]. He went to Throgmorton, who regarded him with suspicion. It was so common, however, for one English exile to ask help of another that Pole consented to speak to him. When Vaughan came into his presence, the Cardinal said, "As I am informed, you be banished out of your native country as well as I"; he added that he liked to meet a Welshman, as his grandfather came out of Wales. Vaughan asked to be taken into the Cardinal's service, saying that he was destitute. Pole answered that he had all the servants that he needed while travelling, but if Vaughan would come to him again in Italy, he should have a place. He gave the man a crown, and bade him go back to gather news[2]. These newsbearers must often have been puzzled to know whose spies they were.

On 10 June Pole wrote to Italy, still in good hopes that his mission might prosper, although his life was in danger. He had discovered to whom he was indebted for Vaughan's visit[3]. Other spies were sent by Sir Thomas Palmer, the porter of Calais, and Pole heard that special assassins had been despatched from England[4]. Michael Throgmorton's expedition to England was abandoned, probably because the Cardinal received news from his family about this time. The messenger was Hugh Holland, who had formerly been in the service of Sir Geoffrey Pole, but was now a merchant in the trade with Flanders. Some years before Holland had secretly smuggled into France John Heliar, the vicar of East Meon and rector of Warblington, a dependent of the Poles, who fled partly because he wanted to study in Paris, but chiefly because he disliked the King's proceedings[5]. Holland was still in communication with Heliar and conveyed his correspondence[6].

"After Easter" 1537 Holland heard that wheat was selling well in Flanders, and arranged to carry a cargo across. Before he embarked Sir Geoffrey Pole sent for him and said, "I hear say you intend to go into Flanders. My brother, I hear say, is in those parts. Will you do me an errand unto him?"

Holland was quite willing, and Sir Geoffrey gave him the following message:

"I pray you commend me to my brother and show him I would I were with him, and will come to him if he will have me; for show him the world in England waxeth all crooked, God's law is turned upso-down, abbeys and churches overthrown, and he is taken for a

---

[1] L. and P. xii (2), 128. [2] Ibid. 107.
[3] Ibid. 71–3. [4] Ibid. 108.
[5] L. and P. xiii (2), 797. [6] See above, chap. xiii.

traitor; and I think they will cast down parish churches and all at the last. And because he shall trust you, show him this token, and show him also that Mr Wilson and Powell be in the Tower yet, and show him further that there be sent from England daily to destroy him, and that much money would be given for his head; and that the Lord Privy Seal said openly in the court that he, speaking of the said Cardinal, should destroy himself well enough; and that Mr Brian and Peter Mewtas was sent into France to kill him with a hand-gun or otherwise as they should see best."

The day before Holland sailed Sir Geoffrey sent for him again and said, "How sayest thou, Hugh, if I go over with thee myself and see that good fellow?"

Hugh replied, "Nay, sir, my ship is fully loaded, and the mariners be not meet for this purpose."

"Well then, I pray you remember what I have said unto you, and fare you well."

Holland sailed to Nieuport, sold his wheat, and went on to Cambrai, where he expected to find the Cardinal, but Pole had already set out for Liége. Holland overtook him at Alne Abbey. Throgmorton received the messenger and questioned him. Hearing that he came from Sir Geoffrey, Throgmorton went and told the Cardinal. After mass Holland was sent for and found the Cardinal in the church. He delivered his message. Pole said, "And would my Lord Privy Seal so fain kill me? Well, I trust it shall not lie in his power. The King is not contented to bear me malice himself, but provoketh other against me, and hath written to the French king that he should not receive me as Cardinal or legate; but yet I was received into Paris better than some men would."[1]

They talked for a little while about English matters, and then the Cardinal gave Holland the following messages:

"Commend me to my lady my mother by the same token that she and I looking upon a wall together read this, '*Spes mea in Deo est*,'[2] and desire her blessing for me. I trust she will be glad of mine also; and if I wist that she were of the opinion that other be there, mother as she is mine, I would tread upon her with my feet. Commend me to my lord my brother by this token, '*In domino Confido*,' and to my brother Sir Geoffrey, and bid him meddle little and let all things alone."[3] The Cardinal did not consider it expedient that

---

[1] L. and P. XIII (2), 797.
[2] See note A at end of chapter.
[3] L. and P. XIII (2), 797.

either of his brothers should join him. He bade them both tarry in England "and hold up yea and nay."[1]

It is impossible to avoid the thought that if the Cardinal had encouraged Geoffrey in his proposed flight, instead of snubbing him, the coming tragedy must have been, in part prevented. Lord Montague would probably have been put to death in any case, but England would have been spared the worst insult to humanity,—the degradation of the miserable Sir Geoffrey, the horror of a brother's betrayal by a brother, the agony of their mother. Unluckily Sir Geoffrey Pole was not a very desirable inmate for a Cardinal's household. He was stupid and extravagant, timid and untrustworthy. The Cardinal acted with his usual gentle selfishness. He refused to undertake the disagreeable responsibility, and left Lord Montague, in addition to all his other perils, to cope with this unsatisfactory younger brother.

Holland delivered all the messages to Sir Geoffrey Pole when he returned to England. Sir Geoffrey forbade him to repeat them to the Countess of Salisbury or to Lord Montague, because Montague "was out of his mind and would show all to the Lord Privy Seal."[2] He did not mean that Montague would betray the matter on purpose, but he was such a reckless speaker that his tongue was sure to endanger the secret. This was all the communication that Reginald Pole had with his brothers while he was in Flanders, and it cannot be said to have seriously threatened the throne of England.

The Cardinal stayed quietly at Liége until the Pope summoned him back to Rome[3]. His Holiness needed him and his present position was doing no good, nor was it very dignified. In August Pole prepared to set out for Rome[4]. In all his correspondence during his stay in Flanders there is strangely little reference to the Pilgrims. The months during which he was so near England were the very months of the King's vengeance. Pole must have known the English news, for Henry was eager to spread reports of the terrible justice that he was doing. Yet in all Pole's letters not one of the northern leaders is mentioned by name. Their effort for the Faith is spoken of only in the most general terms, and though there are vague allusions to the King's cruelty there is no word of their trial and death[5].

This silence effectually disposes of the idea that Pole had any

---

[1] L. and P. XIII (2), 804 (p. 315).   [2] Ibid. 797.
[3] L. and P. XII (2), 174.   [4] Ibid. 559.
[5] L. and P. XII (1), 1242, 1243; L. and P. XII (2), 71-3, 169, 310, 499, 559.

share in encouraging the rebellion, but when it is contrasted with the wide-spread horror at the martyrdom of More and Fisher, and with the admiration expressed for their constancy, the feeling arises that the Papal court and the catholic clergy generally were guilty of a snobbish callousness to the fate of less renowned but not less worthy upholders of their cause. The King's faithlessness to the insurgents was perfectly well known abroad. Laymen were not so absorbed in his attack on the Church as to overlook his treatment of his subjects[1], but the court of Rome would calmly have watched Henry grind Englishmen to powder so long as he did not interfere with the Pope's power and dignity. The Pope considered only his relations with the King and ignored the people, while his one chance of triumph lay in keeping his hold upon the nation, as was done in Ireland. There were two reasons for this indifference on the part of the Roman Church. In the first place, many of its supporters, Pole among them, shrank from the charge of encouraging rebellion. In the second, European statesmen in the spring of 1537 had little thought to spare on the internal state of England. The war absorbed the western states; in the south the Turks were threatening Rome itself.

Nevertheless Pole, an Englishman sent especially to watch English affairs, might have shown more interest in the fate of the Pilgrims. On 21 July, 1537, a week after Aske was hanged at York, the Cardinal wrote to the Pope to mention the suggestion of an English student at Louvain that all the Church should fast and pray for the return of England to the fold, and that certain days should be appointed for the fast. Pole was much pleased with the thought, and believed that it would do more good than any "censures or curses."[2] It would certainly be safer.

The Cardinal left Liége on 22 August, "riding solemnly through the city, giving his benediction to the people, with a cross borne before him and other ceremonies."[3] Two days before Michael Throgmorton had written his second and last report to Cromwell. Cromwell had commanded him to return to England, and much of the letter was filled with explanations as to why Throgmorton did not obey the summons. He protested that he could serve the King much better if he stayed at Rome with his master. He described the intended prayers for the unity of the Church, and added that if the King did not shortly repent Pole would publish his book as a defence against the charge of treason. Throgmorton insisted that

[1] See above, chap. xx.   [2] L. and P. xii (2), 310.   [3] Ibid. 598.

his master sought the King's honour and wealth, and that everyone about him marvelled that the King did nothing but try to procure his ruin[1].

Cromwell's first impulse on receiving this letter was to prevent Pole's return to Rome. A letter to Throgmorton was drafted which contained an offer that, though the King felt nothing but contempt for all that the Bishop of Rome could do against him, yet "to save him whom he hath from his cradle nourished and brought up in learning," he would send Dr Wilson and another of his own chaplains to confer with Pole in Flanders[2]. Instructions for the chaplains were drawn up[3], but they never started on their mission. There is nothing to show the reason which made Cromwell change his mind. Perhaps some fresh news came, or perhaps he merely decided on second thoughts that it was impossible to conciliate Pole, and the wider the breach with him became the better. Dropping his mask, he for once wrote his real mind and sent the letter after Throgmorton. It is too long to quote in full, and no mere extract can do it justice[4].

Cromwell began by denouncing the treasons of Pole and the treachery of Throgmorton, whom he had taken for a faithful subject. "I might better have judged that so dishonest a master could have but even such servants as you are.... You could not all this time have been a spy for the King, but at some time your countenance should have declared your heart to be loyal. No! you and your master have both well declared how little fear of God resteth in you, which, led by vain promise of promotion, thus against his laws works treason towards your natural prince and country, to serve an enemy of God, an enemy of all honesty, an enemy of right religion, a defender of iniquity, a merchant and occupier of all deceits." How foolish was Throgmorton to try to defend this "silly cardinal" from the name of traitor. All the world knew how well he deserved it. "Now if those that have made him thus mad can also persuade him to print his detestable book, where one lie leapeth in every line on another's neck, he shall be then as much bound to them for their good counsel as his family to him for his wise dealing. He will, I trow, have as little joy thereof as his friends and kinsfolk are like to take profit of it. Pity it is that the folly of one brainsick Pole, or, to say better, of one witless fool, should be the ruin of so great a family. Let him

---

[1] L. and P. xii (2), 552.
[2] Ibid. 619; printed in full, Merriman, op. cit. ii, 82.
[3] L. and P. xii (2), 620; printed in full, Merriman, op. cit. ii, 84.
[4] See note B at end of chapter.

follow ambition as fast as he can, these that little have offended (saving that he is of their kin) were it not for the great mercy and benignity of the prince, should and might feel what it is to have such a traitor to their kinsman." Let him bring forth his book. He is not out of reach of the King's "justice" even in Italy. "Amongst all your pretty news these are very pleasant, that the Bishop of Rome intendeth to make lamentation to the world and to desire every man to pray that his old gains may return home again....I have done what I may to save you. I must, I think, do what I can to see you condignly punished. God send you both to fare as ye deserve—either shortly to come to your allegiance, or else to a shameful death."[1] With this blessing hard on his heels Pole began his journey back to Rome. His first legation was ended.

The White Rose party in England had done nothing to help the Pilgrims. It would have been well for them if they had said as little; and yet the words that were afterwards objected against them were sometimes clearly innocent, sometimes just touched with disaffection to the government,—very seldom coming even under the most stringent treason law ever enforced in England. At the time of the rebellion a friend went to see Sir Geoffrey Pole at his house at Lordington, and found him mustering men who were to march with him against the insurgents.

"I must go northwards," said Sir Geoffrey, "but I will shift for one well enough, if they come to fighting—I will save one."

"Well, if you intend so," returned his friend, "you were best to have a good horse under you."[2]

It seems almost incredible that this old, old soldier's joke about running away at the first shot should have been interpreted by Froude as an avowed "intention of deserting in action, if an action was fought—real, bad, black treason."[3]

The Marquis of Exeter had gone northward to join Norfolk against the Pilgrims. One day when his wife was sitting alone, Sir Edward Neville came to her. He was an intimate friend of the family, and Lord Montague's brother-in-law. He greeted her with "Madam, how do you? Be you merry?"

She answered, "How can I be merry? My lord is gone to battle and he will be one of the foremost."

"Madam, be not afeared of this," said Sir Edward, "nor of the second, but beware of the third."

---

[1] L. and P. xii (2), 795. [2] L. and P. xiii (2), 822.
[3] Froude, op. cit. ii, chap. xv; see note C at end of chapter.

D. II.   19

"Ah, Mr Neville, you will never leave your Welsh prophecies," replied the Lady Marquis, "but one day this will turn you to displeasure."[1]

Sir Edward's mysterious words may have been treason, but they are even more unintelligible now than they were to the Lady Marquis. Sir Edward was much given to singing "merry songs"; in the Lady Marquis's garden at Horsley, where both Neville and Lord Montague were welcome guests, he would sometimes add political stanzas to his songs, such as that he "trusted knaves should be put down, and lords should reign one day."[2] Perhaps it was on the same occasions that he used to abuse the King "saying his Highness was a beast and worse than a beast."[3]

One day at court Sir Edward drew Sir Geoffrey Pole aside and said, "God's Blood! I am made a fool amongst them, but I laugh and make merry to drive forth the time. The King keepeth a sort of knaves here that we dare neither look nor speak; and if I were able to live, I would rather live any life in the world than tarry in the Privy Chamber." Another time he said, "Master Pole, let us not be seen to speak together; we be had in suspicion; but it forceth not, we shall do well enough one day."

The little group of friends were constantly being warned against each other. The King himself bade Sir Edward avoid the Marquis of Exeter. Sir Edward told his friend, "I may no longer keep you company"; and the Marquis quietly answered, "I pray Our Lord be with you," and no more[4]. Every act of friendship among the suspected nobles was used against them by Cromwell. A certain bearward of the Marquis was in trouble about the end of the year 1537[5]. He was "in prison for treason" in the west country. His offence does not appear, but it cannot have compromised the Marquis, as the affair was not mentioned at his trial. The bearward was executed at Gloucester in February 1537–8[6]. Sir Edward Neville heard of his arrest and very naturally told the Marquis "to look to it, as it was much against his honour."[7] Exeter sent to Cromwell to inquire about the matter. The result was unexpected. Cromwell told the King and a royal messenger was sent to Exeter to charge him on his allegiance to declare who had told him of the bearward's apprehension. Exeter was astonished and alarmed that so simple a matter should

---

[1] L. and P. xiii (2), 765.
[2] Ibid.
[3] Ibid. 804 (p. 318).
[4] Ibid. (p. 319).
[5] Ibid. 771 (iii).
[6] L. and P. xiii (1), 358, 371.
[7] L. and P. xiii (2), 804 (p. 319).

be taken so seriously. The messenger found him "the most appalled man that ever he saw." The Marquis answered at first that he would "liever die than to disclose his friend, for it did not touch the King." Afterwards he tried to smooth the matter over by producing a servant who said that he had heard about the bearward "in Paul's, but of whom he could not tell."[1]

Exeter was a loyal friend. On another occasion, when Montague was in trouble, he defended him in the Privy Council, and offered to be bound "body for body" for him[2]. The Marquis disliked the King's policy, but there is no proof that he ever engaged in treasonable practices. He contented himself with grumbling occasionally to his friends, and for the rest took things as they came. One day when Sir Geoffrey Pole was riding to London he met the Marquis and turned back a little way to talk to him. Exeter said that he had been compelled to give up his wardenship of Windsor and to take abbey lands instead.

"What!" cried Sir Geoffrey, "be you come to this point to take abbey lands now?"

"Yea," said the Marquis, "good enough for a time; they must have all again one day."

Exeter had on one occasion been obliged to receive Cromwell at Horsley; he gave his guest "a summer coat and a wood knife." At the first opportunity he winked at Sir Geoffrey Pole and said, "Peace! knaves rule about the King," and then holding up and shaking his fist, "I trust to give them a buffet one day."[3] It was very distasteful to a nobleman of the blood royal to play host to the lowborn favourite, who was also his personal enemy.

A fortnight before Christmas 1536 a story was told at Stoke in Somerset of a quarrel between the Lord Privy Seal and the Marquis of Exeter. It was said that the Marquis had drawn his dagger on Cromwell, whose life was saved only by his coat of fence. Cromwell ordered the Marquis to the Tower, "but if he had been put there... he would have been fetched out again though the best of the realm had said nay."[4] There is no reason to believe that this rumour had any foundation in fact; it bears a marked resemblance to the story that Lord William Howard had assassinated Richard Cromwell[5]. Nevertheless it illustrates the affection which the people of the west felt for Exeter.

---

[1] L. and P. xiii (2), 961 (2).
[2] Ibid. 772.
[3] Ibid. 804 (p. 317).
[4] L. and P. xii (2), 51.
[5] See above, chap. xvii.

The Marquis hated the new learning and his servants sometimes quoted their master's opinions indiscreetly. His "yeoman of the horse" used to go to a certain goldsmith in London for the garnishing of horse harness. Protestantism was now spreading rapidly in London, especially among the shop-keepers, and one day the yeoman of the horse found the goldsmith's wife reading the New Testament in English.

"What do you with these new books of heresy in English?" he said to her. "Well, well, there will a day come that will pay for all."

She asked what day that might be, and he answered, "The day will come there shall be no more wood spent upon you heretics, but you will be tied together, sacked, and thrown into Thames."

When she asked him who should do so, he said the Bishop of London [Stokesley].

"We care not for the Bishop of London," she cried, "thanked be God and our gracious King; but would to God my lord your master would read the Gospel in English, and suffer his servants to do the same."

On this the man affirmed with an oath, "If my Lord know any of his servants either to have any of these books in English or to read any of the same, they shall never do him any longer service."[1]

Lord Montague was as little inclined to conspire as his friends, but he was a careless talker. The cautious Lord Stafford, his brother-in-law, said, "I like him not, he dare speak so largely."[2] It is evident from his recorded sayings that he could not refrain from sallies against Henry and his favourites. He was a man of boldness and wit and took great pleasure in Sir Thomas More's books[3]. He thought that the Pilgrimage had been mismanaged: "Twishe, Geoffrey...the Lord Darcy played the fool; he went about to pluck away the council. He should first have begun with the head; but I beshrew them for leaving off so soon."[4] He was indignant that the commons had been quieted with false promises. "Time hath been when nothing was more surer to reckon upon than the promise of a prince but now they count it no promise, but a policy to blind the people, wherefore if the commons do rise again they will trust to no fair promise nor words."[5] In happier circumstances Montague thought his party might have helped the Pilgrims: "If my lord

---

[1] L. and P. xiii (2), 820.
[2] Ibid. 804 (p. 319).
[3] Ibid. 702 (p. 269).
[4] Ibid. 804 (p. 317).
[5] Ibid. 702, 876, 960; see note D at end of chapter.

Abergavenny (his father-in-law) were alive, he were able to make a great number of men in Kent and Sussex."[1]

Others of Montague's sayings were that "Wolsey had been an honest man had he had an honest master"[2]; "the King and Cromwell were both of one nature and what became of the nobility of the whole realm they cared not so they might live themselves at their own pleasure"; "the King gloried with the title to be Supreme Head next God, yet he had a sore leg that no poor man would be glad of, and that he should not live long for all his authority next God's"; and that "the King and his whole issue stand accursed."[3]

These words and many others of the same sort were treason under the new act. Montague "grudged" at this act, and thought that the Council should devise a "charitable punishment" for treason "so that men should not die therefore." He had "seen more gentleness and benignity in times past at the King's hands than he doth nowadays." Nor was it merely because the new laws pressed hardly on his own party that he disliked them. If he lived to see a better world, he hoped that Cromwell and the other "knaves" should "have punishment for their offences without cruelty."[4]

Montague lived on intimate terms with his brother Sir Geoffrey, but they had one estrangement when Sir Geoffrey entered the King's service against the advice of his brother and the Marquis. Montague tried to dissuade him by the argument that the King "would go so far that all the world would mislike him." He himself had never loved the King from childhood, and believed that Henry would some day go mad[5]. Moreover nothing was so dangerous as court favour; "the King never made man but he destroyed him again, either by displeasure or with the sword."[6] Nevertheless Sir Geoffrey made suit to the King and was received into his service. Lord Montague told him bluntly that "they were flatterers who followed the court and none served the King but knaves."[7] For a time Sir Geoffrey saw little of his friends, who no longer talked openly before him but treated him as if he had turned his back on his own party[8].

The news of Reginald Pole's arrival in Flanders and the attempts on his life put the whole court and especially the White Rose party in a flutter. A lady named Elizabeth Darrell, who was certainly a

---

[1] L. and P. xiii (2), 702.
[2] Ibid. 960.
[3] Ibid. 800.
[4] Ibid. 702, 875.
[5] Ibid. 804 (p. 818).
[6] Ibid. 960 (12).
[7] Ibid. 804 (p. 816).
[8] Ibid. (pp. 816–7).

great gossip, told Sir Geoffrey that Peter Mewtas had gone to Flanders to get rid of the Cardinal[1]. It was on this occasion that Sir Geoffrey sent the Cardinal the above-mentioned warning by Hugh Holland[2]. Later, forgetting their differences, he went to Lord Montague, whom he found in his garden.

"I hear our brother beyond the sea shall be slain," he said.

"No," replied Montague, "he is escaped. I have letters."[3] These letters must have contained news of the Cardinal's safe retreat to Liége. They were from someone who heard the court news, Mistress Darrell or the Lady Marquis of Exeter.

"By God's blood," swore Sir Geoffrey later to Mistress Darrell, "and if he [Mewtas] had slain him [the Cardinal] I would have thrust my dagger in him although he had been at the King's heels."[4] He was not as yet on his old terms with Montague, or he would surely have told him of the message from the Cardinal, however much he feared his brother's lack of discretion. Hugh Holland's errand was the only definite act of treason committed by any of the Poles, and Sir Geoffrey alone was responsible for it. The Cardinal's danger was discussed in Lord Montague's household, where the servants believed that the Cardinal "should do them all good one day," and that "it were a [meet] marriage betwixt my Lady Mary and the Cardinal Pole."[5] One of the servants, named Morgan Wells, said openly that he "would kill with a hand-gun Peter Mewtas or any other whom he should know to kill the Cardinal Pole, and that he was going overseas for that purpose." When he told this to Lord Montague's chaplain, John Collins, he was bidden to "be of good mind and make a cross in his forehead."[6]

In October 1537 Sir Geoffrey Pole went to court, "but the King would not suffer him to come in."[7] Thus banished he went down to Bockmore, his brother's place in Buckinghamshire, and was received again into Montague's confidence. "Geoffrey, God loveth us well," was Montague's greeting, "that will not suffer us to be amongst them; for none rule about the court but knaves."[8]

One night Montague told Sir Geoffrey "lying in bed" that he had just dreamt that the King was dead. "And now," quoth he, "we shall see some ruffling and bid Mr Cromwell good deane with all his devises."[9] Later he said, "The King is not dead, but he will

---

[1] L. and P. xiii (2), 804 (p. 315). [2] Ibid. 797.
[3] Ibid. 804 (p. 316). [4] Ibid. 766.
[5] Ibid. 702, 828 (2). [6] Ibid. 828.
[7] L. and P. xii (2), 921. [8] L. and P. xiii (2), 804 (p. 317).
[9] Ibid. 800.

one day die suddenly; his leg will kill him and then we shall have jolly stirring."[1] It must have been hope of this day that kept them in England, for they were well aware of their danger. Starkey, the King's chaplain, who had formerly been a great friend of Reginald's, warned the brothers that "if the King were not of a good nature," Cromwell "for one Pole's sake would destroy all Poles."[2] "The King, to be revenged of Reynold, I fear will kill us all," Montague told his brother, and added that he wished they were both with the Bishop of St Luke [Luik *i.e.* Liége], who was an honest man and a friend of the Cardinal. "Marry," said Sir Geoffrey, "an you fear such jeopardy, let us be walking hence quickly."[3] But Montague could by no means make up his mind to fly, though Geoffrey often urged it upon him. Reginald, when Geoffrey wished to join him, had advised them both to "tarry in England and hold up yea and nay there."[4] A non-committal attitude was impossible to Montague, but he determined to await the issue at home.

Sir Geoffrey was anxious to leave the realm for other besides political reasons. He often urged Hugh Holland to contrive his escape, with promises of ample reward when he reached Reginald's friends, but Holland was afraid to do more than he had already done and always refused[5]. Sir Geoffrey lacked ready money, and his debts were "a great occasion for him to flee." In this extremity he turned for help to George Croftes, the chancellor of Chichester Cathedral. Croftes was an ecclesiastic of the old school. When the Supremacy Act was passed he prepared to leave the country rather than take the oath, but Lord Delaware, his intimate friend, persuaded him to conform[6]. Sir Geoffrey told Croftes that he was determined to leave England with the next fair wind, for safe-guard of his life. Croftes lent him twenty nobles to help him on his journey.

Next morning Croftes wrote to Sir Geoffrey advising him to stay in England, for "he had the most marvellous dream that night that ever he had in his life, and that he thought Our Lady did appear unto him and she wed [*i.e. pledged*] him that it should be the destruction of the said Sir Geoffrey and of all his kin if he departed the realm."[7] The dream must have impressed Sir Geoffrey, for he gave up his plan and returned the twenty nobles[8]. Croftes went to John Collins, Montague's chaplain, and told him the whole matter,

---

[1] L. and P. xiii (2), 804 (p. 317).   [2] Ibid. (p. 316).
[3] Ibid. 800.   [4] Ibid. 804 (p. 315).
[5] Ibid. 797.   [6] Ibid. 829 (iii).
[7] Ibid. 829 (i).   [8] Ibid. 804 (p. 319).

begging him to ask his master to pay Sir Geoffrey's debts. "Whereupon there was a way taken by the said Lord Montague that all his said debts amounting to a great sum were paid."[1]

It is sad that this good-hearted old priest should have all unwittingly brought their fate on the heads of the house of Pole. Dreams were the curse of the White Rose party.

NOTES TO CHAPTER XXII

Note A. "Spes mea in Deo est" was a motto much used in the decoration of the Countess's house at Warblington[2].

Note B. The letter is printed in full by Froude, op. cit. II, chap. XIV, and by Merriman, op. cit. II, no. 218. It has so often been quoted and is so deservedly well known that it is necessary to include only a few quotations which are very much to the point.

Note C. Early in August 1914 a civilian was travelling in a carriage full of young miners just embodied in their Territorial unit and in the wildest spirits. "I suppose you're longing to meet a German?" he asked one of them. "By! If I meets a Garman, I'm off," said the lad. He was certainly avowing an intention to desert in action; but I wonder if he did? Froude was too hard upon the unfortunate Sir Geoffrey Pole in several respects. This was partly owing to the fact that he had not the full evidence, arranged and dated, before him.

Note D. This speech is pieced together from three different reports of the same words.

[1] L. and P. XIII (2), 829 (i).   [2] Ibid. 818.

CHAPTER XXIII

THE EXETER CONSPIRACY

On 12 October 1537, Queen Jane gave birth to a son. Froude enthusiastically describes the public rejoicings: "The crown had an undoubted heir. The succession was sure. The King, who was supposed to be under a curse which refused him male posterity, was relieved from the bane. Providence had borne witness for him and had rewarded his policy. No revolution need be looked for on his death. The Catholics could not hope for their 'jolly stirring.'—The insurrection was crushed. A prince was born. England was saved."[1] No doubt the birth of the prince greatly strengthened the King's position. But perhaps the rejoicings of the people were not quite so heart-felt nor so universal as appeared outwardly. At least the following story shows that the hidden hatred of the King extended itself to his innocent baby son.

Some months after the birth of the prince a group of idlers were watching the funeral of a child in a London church-yard. For some reason the priest became suspicious, and, opening the shroud, found no child but a waxen image with two pins stuck through it. One of the bystanders went to a friend, a scrivener, said to be skilled in conjuring, and asked what this might mean. "Marry," said the scrivener, "it was made to waste one. But," quoth he, "he that made it was not his craft's master, for he should have put it either in horse-dung or in a dunghill." "Why, may one kill a man after this sort?" cried the other. "Yea, that may be done well enough," said the man skilled in magic[2]. The story of the wax child was rumoured through the country[3], and it was said that the life so uncannily attacked was that of the baby Prince. On the death of Queen Jane rumours had been blown abroad that both the King and the Prince were dead as well[4].

---

[1] Froude, op. cit. II, chap. XIV.   [2] L. and P. XIII (1), 41.
[3] L. and P. XIII (2), 1200.   [4] L. and P. XII (2), 1185, 1205, 1208, 1256, 1282, 1298.

Any discussion of the general state of Europe would be out of place here, but a rough sketch of the situation is necessary. Henry was virtually at war with the Pope and though he was at peace with all the other powers he was on bad terms with his nephew James V of Scotland, his relations with the Emperor were strained, and his friendship with Francis far from cordial. His only real allies were the Protestant States of Germany. In these circumstances the Pope was naturally making every effort to obtain an ally who would fight for him against Henry. James would not invade England without French help; and Francis could not afford to have a second war on his hands. The Pope's scheme was therefore to reconcile Francis and Charles, and then publish his censures on the understanding that they would refuse to continue their treaties with Henry unless he returned to the pale of the Church. If this had not the desired effect they were to forbid all trade whatsoever between their dominions and England. This, as the court of Rome thought, could not fail to end in a complete and bloodless victory. It was a beautiful plan; wiser men in later ages have believed it possible to stop the trade of nations by a word. On account of her isolation both in place and policy, England has often been the intended victim of such interdicts. Once, long afterwards, one was really attempted; there is no reason to believe that the Pope would have been more successful than Napoleon.

The first step was to reconcile Francis and Charles; one bond between them was their common dislike of the King of England. On becoming a widower Henry proposed to use his hand as a prize in the game of international politics. To his intense annoyance he found it was a prize which no one very much coveted. It was in vain he tried to strengthen himself by proposing to the Emperor a marriage with the Dowager Duchess of Milan and hinting to Francis that he was anxious to bestow his hand on a French Princess. He even made overtures for Mary of Guise when she was already betrothed to the King of Scots. In December peace was concluded between Francis and the Emperor; Henry hoped that by a skilful use of all opportunities to inflame their jealousy it might be a short and disturbed one, but for once the Pope decidedly had the advantage. In May 1538, Charles and Francis met at Nice: the Pope joined them there, with Pole among his attendant Cardinals. The two princes agreed on a ten years' truce and parted the best of friends. They did not pledge themselves to anything with regard to England, though they listened politely to the Pope's schemes and made no definite refusal. They were firm in their temporary friendship and Henry in vain tried to make Francis distrust his new ally by sending reports that Mary was to be betrothed to Don Luis of Portugal and the Duchy of Milan settled upon them. Moreover he had deeply offended the whole French Court by suggesting that several of the princesses might meet him at Calais and he would choose a bride among them.

If Henry was no nearer his re-marriage in August 1538 than he had been nine months before, neither was the Pope nearer his dream of the submission of England. Charles was preoccupied with the Turks and his own Protestants in Germany, and had no time to look for infidels and heretics in other countries. As to Francis, all his ambitions were fixed on strengthening his position on the continent, nor did he care in the least about the unity of the Faith, for which Charles had some regard. Neither of them would take the risk and expense of invading England without the other's help; but a joint expedition was out of the question, for Charles would only have undertaken it on behalf of Mary, and Francis only in hopes of establishing James V on the thrones of both kingdoms. The appearance of a legitimate male heir to Henry was equally embarrassing to the rival schemers; and no doubt they determined to wait for a better time. The Prince might die in infancy, as all Katharine's sons had done, or in youth, like the Duke of Richmond. As to the Pope's plan of stopping England's trade, it would mean considerable loss and no particular profit for both, and that matter was tacitly dropped. In spite of the truce and the meeting at Nice, Henry was in little more danger than before, and in much less than he appeared to be. The fate of the Poles was hastened because Henry feared an invasion by the Emperor at the Pope's instigation—and feared it more than he need have done. But in them he was punishing if not exactly the innocent, at least the helpless. No European monarch had Exeter's claim to the crown at heart: quite the contrary. If Charles relied on the Pole faction to raise a popular commotion in his favour (as Froude suggests), he was leaning on a very feeble reed[1].

Meanwhile in England itself the King's policy was triumphant. The destruction of the shrines, the surrenders of the great monasteries went merrily forward. Our Lady's images and the bones of St Thomas were burnt in company with numerous "heretics," who

---

[1] Gairdner, Introductions to Vols. XII and XIII of Letters and Papers; Froude, Reign of Henry VIII, chaps. XIV, XV and XVI.

denied orthodox doctrines, and Friar Forest, who denied the King's Supremacy[1]. More commonplace executions for treason made a little variety. One of these was a sequel to the Pilgrimage, and the victim was no other than Thomas Miller, Lancaster Herald. He had been zealous for the King if ever man was: he had gone fearlessly to and fro between the rebels and the King's troops, respected by all; he had turned the course of the Archbishop's famous sermon at Pontefract; he had been "ungoodly handled" when he carried the King's pardon to Durham; and all to end in his sharing the Pilgrims' fate. In the summer of 1538 the following charges were brought against him:—

(1) He encouraged the rebels by kneeling before Robert Aske in Pontefract Castle.

(2) He promised the rebels that Cromwell should be delivered to them and their demands granted.

(3) He discouraged the King's troops by saying the rebels had ten thousand horsemen, each with twenty angels in his pocket.

(4) He showed the King's plans to the rebels.

(5) He defamed Cromwell and spread lying rumours against him, which chiefly made the northern men hate him.

(6) He answered, when asked how the northern men could be brought together seeing they had but two flags and no trumpets, drumslades, tabors or other instruments, that "it was marvel, but such was God," by which he traitorously implied that God could help rebels[2].

All these accusations, except the first and the last, were based on the unsupported evidence of two of the other heralds, who were his personal enemies, and could not possibly know what he had said while in the rebel host[3]. Lancaster had knelt to Robert Aske, but from anything rather than disloyal motives; the remark in the last articles might have been made without any treasonable intent; all the rest look much like pure inventions. It was very easy in Tudor times to swear an enemy's life away; if he had no near kinsfolk, there was nothing to trouble the perjurer afterwards but his own conscience.

Thomas Miller was hanged at York on 1 August, and the judge "devised that Lancaster's head should be set up by the body of Aske."[4] It was not two years since Aske had greeted the herald so

---

[1] Froude, op. cit., chaps. xiv and xv.
[2] L. and P. xiii (1), 1311.
[3] Ibid. 1312-13; see note A at end of chapter.
[4] L. and P. xiii (2), 20.

proudly in Pontefract Castle Hall. Two others, the vicar of Newark and a monk of Fountains, died for treason at the same time[1].

At most of the northern assizes at this time one or two priests were executed for preaching against the Supremacy, or kindred offences. John Dobson, who dealt so largely in prophecies[2], paid a heavy penalty for his string of rhymes, and another priest suffered with him. A third offender was a woman accused of witchcraft[3]. Her name was Mabel Brigg, and she was a widow and farm-servant in Holderness. She was condemned for keeping the "Black Fast" or "St Trynian's Fast" against the King and the Duke of Norfolk. It was said that she had once before fasted in the same way "for a man, and he brake his neck or it were all fasted, and so she trusted that they should do that had made all this business, and that was the King and this false Duke." The witnesses did not agree as to how the fast was kept. It seems to have lasted six weeks, one day in each week being kept a fast day, and each week a day later than the last. This method of fasting was also used when money had been lost, in hopes of bringing about its recovery. It seems possible that Mabel Brigg was really fasting for this end and not for the King's death, for the evidence is not very satisfactory, and the whole case is complicated by blackmail and private malice[4].

These stories are told for the sake of such light as they may throw on the state of England during 1538. The outstanding events of the year, especially the universal destruction of the abbeys, are too well known to need any description[5]. The Protestants, in spite of the burning of heretics, were rapidly increasing. The Papists, still vastly more powerful in numbers, were crushed in spirit. Everyone, from the greatest noble to the poorest commoner, could if he tried make something out of the fall of the monasteries; this fact influenced all classes, but especially the gentlemen, who sold, if not their souls, at least their honour, for a parcel of abbey lands. Only a few of the commons had enough intelligence to see that the King was killing the goose that laid his subjects golden eggs. Even if the worst accusations against the monks were true, if they all lived in idle luxury, careless of their old-time hospitality, spending on themselves the alms due to the poor; still as long as the abbeys remained in their hands they were not wholly lost to the people. The lands were still there; a religious revival might return them to their original

[1] L. and P. xiii (2), 142.
[2] See chap. iv.
[3] L. and P. xiii (1), 533, 705.
[4] Ibid. 487.
[5] See Froude, chaps. xiv and xv.

uses; wise legislation might convert the abbeys into schools and hospitals. But when all the dedicated wealth of the religious passed through the King's hands into those of extravagant favourites and grasping landlords, then, indeed, they were lost for ever to the poor of England. Whether the Reformation was good or bad it is useless to consider; that it was inevitable is quite clear; but that it was most grossly mismanaged and caused endless misery and injustice it is surely impossible to deny.

When Cardinal Pole returned to Rome from his first legation he found that the Pope had caused his book, *De Unitate*, to be printed. Characteristically he objected to this decided step, and had the entire edition bought up[1]. Concluding too much from the King's anger on reading it, he believed it was a good weapon to hold over Henry's head. It seems almost pitiful that any man should expect to frighten Henry into better behaviour with a book. After the meeting at Nice, Pole retired to Venice for the summer of 1538. Theobald, an English student in Italy, and also a member of Cromwell's secret service, sent amusing accounts of his way of life to the English Government[2]. He got his news from Michael Throgmorton, who may have been unsuspicious, or may have sent through him such reports as he thought would do good in England. Cromwell heard of the Cardinal's fear of assassination, and the precautions taken against it, which Theobald rather humorously imputed to his evil conscience[3]. Pole lived quietly in Venice, and it was there that he heard in September of Sir Geoffrey's arrest.

During 1538 the conduct of the White Rose party was neither better nor worse than before. They were still out of favour, and still grumbled among themselves, but they were becoming more indifferent to the King's proceedings[4]. They contented themselves with showing their dislike to the religious changes by dismissing any servants who favoured the new learning, and keeping conservative priests about them. Montague and Exeter assumed a fictitious "strangeness" towards each other on account of the suspicion in which they were held. By the court they were slighted and insulted. In the summer of 1538 Henry made a progress through the south, and stayed near Warblington where the Countess of Salisbury lived, but he passed by and did not come to visit her, although she was his kinswoman, and in the days of Queen Katharine's power he had loved and venerated

[1] Haile, op. cit. chap. XII.
[2] L. and P. XIII (2), 117, 337, 507-9, 813, 1034.
[3] Ibid. 507. [4] Ibid. 695 (2).

her. "Well, let it pass," said Montague, speaking of this slight, "we shall thank them one day. This world will turn upso-down, and I fear me we shall have no lack but of honest men." A little while before this Geoffrey had told Montague of the messages he had received from Reginald a year before.

About the same time Cromwell sent his nephew Richard to Exeter to beg him "to be frank in opening certain things." This seems to mean that the Marquis was offered safety and pardon if he would accuse his friends. He refused[1]. The King set about finding other witnesses.

The first that presented himself was Gervaise Tyndale, late a schoolmaster at Grantham[2], a "new-fangled fellow" of "heretic" opinions. Three or four years before, the friars had driven away his pupils. In the spring of 1538 he came to Warblington in bad health and took up his quarters with Richard Eyre, a surgeon, who administered a kind of hospital kept up by the Countess of Salisbury's bounty. Here he heard all the whispering and gossiping of her household and was filled with the true Protestant horror of her Papist bigotry. She dismissed any servants who favoured the new learning, or as Tyndale said "God's word"; she openly forbade her tenants to read the New Testament in English and other books which the King had licensed; nothing passed in all the country-side but the Lady presently knew it, for the priests learnt everything in confession and then told her. No wonder this was resented, though people admitted that the Countess used her power kindly; her servants blamed the chaplains rather than their mistress. "There were a company of priests in my lady's house which did her much harm and kept her from the true knowledge of God's word."

Tyndale was discovered to be a heretic and asked to depart. He refused stoutly; "I would not depart neither for lord nor lady till I were better amended." The Countess then ordered the surgeon to send away all his patients. Tyndale did not leave the neighbourhood until he had picked up a good deal of information. Eyre told him "very secretly" that "there is a knave which dwelleth by, whose name is Hugh Holland, and he beginneth now of late to act the merchant man and the broker, for he goeth over sea and conveys letters to Master Heliar...and he playeth the knave of the other hand and conveyeth letters to Master Pole the Cardinal, and all the secrets of the realm of England is known to the Bishop of Rome."

As far as can be made out (for the document we quote is mutilated

---

[1] L. and P. XIII (2), 804 (p. 316). [2] See chap. IV.

in parts) Tyndale wished to open a school in the neighbourhood and was opposed by all the priests. In a quarrel with one of them he called him a knave and accused him of "scarcely" being the King's friend. The constable, standing by "in a great fume," defended the priest saying, "It was merry in this country before such fellows came, which findeth such faults with our honest priests"; but he was rather frightened by the turn the conversation had taken, and told the whole matter to Sir Geoffrey Pole[1]. Sir Geoffrey was troubled on finding that Hugh Holland's voyages were so much talked about. He took Holland and Eyre, who was a gossip and a grumbler but not really ill-disposed to his mistress, and rode to the Lord Privy Seal. He had an explanation with Cromwell about his correspondence with Heliar[2] "and made such shift that the matter was cloaked." Heliar's goods had been seized on the report that he had fled after speaking traitorous words; they were now restored, and no doubt Sir Geoffrey thought the affair settled, probably by a bribe to Cromwell. But the little group of heretics at Warblington were very ill satisfied: they believed that if only they could get word with the Lord Privy Seal they could "so discover the matter that they should no longer blind him in it as they have done." At length they drew up a long and rambling statement of everything suspicious they had seen or heard in the Countess' household and despatched it to Cromwell. It is undated but probably belongs to May or June 1538[3].

The only serious accusation was that Hugh Holland had carried treasonable letters to the Cardinal, and the first result was his arrest. He was taken at Lord Montague's house at Bockmore and there was a "ruffle" with the King's officers[4]. As he was being carried prisoner "with his hands bound behind him and his legs bound under his horse's belly," along the London road, he met Sir Geoffrey who asked him where he was "bound to go." Hugh answered he could not tell, but he bade Sir Geoffrey "keep on his way, for he should not be long after."[5] This was the popular story, spread through the country by a certain harper of Havant, and there is something rather ballad-like about it, though that is no reason for supposing it untrue.

Sir Geoffrey kept on his way to Bockmore, where he was living at the time, and took counsel with his brother[6]. He suggested "that the keeping of letters might turn a man's friends to hurt." Montague

[1] L. and P. xiii (2), 817.
[2] Ibid. 817.
[5] Ibid. 392.
[3] Ibid. 875 (1).
[4] Ibid. 804 (p. 816).
[6] Ibid. 804 (p. 816).

answered, "Nay, they shall hurt no friend of mine, for I have burnt all my letters."[1] Sir Geoffrey had not been so prudent, and he at once despatched John Collins, the chaplain, to his house at Lordington[2]. He gave him a ring as a token to his wife, Dame Constance, and on receiving this she took the priest to her husband's closet, and there he burnt all the letters he could find[3].

This burning of letters was afterwards made much of by the Government prosecution, which said that they must have contained treasonable matter. The circumstances were certainly suspicious, but not a single treasonable paper was proved to have existed, though the papers of both brothers were remembered and described by servants and friends. Among Geoffrey's there was an old letter to Heliar, which may have contained treason, but seems to have been quite harmless[4]. There was also a bundle of letters from John Stokesley, the Bishop of London, who was a friend of Sir Geoffrey[5]. He was reported to be one of the few honest bishops[6], and though heretics might preach at Paul's cross it was with none of his goodwill[7]; he may have been the friend Sir Geoffrey feared bringing to harm. There was a copy of a letter from Sir Geoffrey to the Imperial Ambassador; Collins loyally declared that it merely begged favour for Heliar, but of all described this is the most likely to have contained treason. Finally he burnt a letter or letters concerning Latimer; when told of this last, Sir Geoffrey said, "What, you have burnt that also? Those letters were shown before the Council, and my lord of Norfolk told me I might keep those letters well enough." Collins rode back to Bockmore and told Montague his errand was done. His master asked him how Dame Constance did, and he replied "as a woman in her case might, meaning that she was in heaviness for such news as was of her husband...and opening of Hugh Holland's going overseas."[8]

Montague had been in the habit of burning all his letters shortly after receiving them; a habit perhaps not common in the days when letters were scarcer than they are now. Among them had been copies of three letters from Reginald Pole to the King, Cromwell, and the Bishop of Durham respectively. These were the letters brought by Michael Throgmorton in 1536[9]; Starkey must have given Montague the copies; and as both he and his mother had been required to write and reprove Reginald for sending them there seems

[1] L. and P. XIII (2), 772.
[2] Ibid. 829 (2).
[3] Ibid. 796.
[4] Ibid. 829 (2).
[5] Ibid. 803.
[6] Ibid. 797.
[7] Ibid. 695.
[8] Ibid. 829 (2).
[9] Ibid. 804 (p. 316).

nothing very strange in that. Montague had showed them to Collins with some triumph; the chaplain said his brother " wrote somewhat roughly to the Lord Privy Seal." "Marry, I warrant you," cried Montague, " he uttereth his mind plainly."[1] There were two other letters from Reginald to his mother and brother; but they had been written before the quarrel with the King and were about family affairs; in the one to his brother, Reginald advised that his nephew Henry, Montague's only son, should be brought up at home to live an active life[2]. Montague had also burnt letters from Exeter and his wife—at least he had received such letters several times during the last three years, and they were not found on his arrest: none of their contents was discovered except the most ordinary enquiries and answers about health[3]. They may very well have contained nothing else, for they seem to have passed only when one or other of the friends was ill.

After Collins's return from Lordington, Montague and Sir Geoffrey rode together to London[4], determined to face the matter out as well as they might. All these things, from Hugh Holland's arrest onward, happened "between Whitsuntide and Midsummer," or about "the feast of Corpus Christi" (10 June). They spent many weeks of uncertainty before Sir Geoffrey was committed to the Tower on 29 August[5].

Some time before Lord Montague had told his brother to disclose nothing if ever he were examined "for if he opened one all must needs come out."[6] This was very sound advice. A study of various confessions shows that a prisoner often began by intending to say very little, and ended by blurting out everything he knew, and sometimes even more. At first Sir Geoffrey tried to do his brother's bidding, but he lacked the strength of body and mind which can carry a man silent through two months in the Tower. His wife was allowed to visit him and she presently told Montague that her husband " was in a frenzy and might utter rash things." Montague replied, "It forceth not what a madman speaketh."[7] On 26 October Sir Geoffrey made his first answers to the interrogatories administered. They did not satisfy the examiners, for he accused hardly anyone but himself. Montague, Exeter, and Delaware, he said, had once disliked the King's proceedings but of late years their minds had changed. At the end he beseeches the King " that he may have good keeping and

---

[1] L. and P. XIII (2), 829 (p. 339).   [2] Ibid. 702 (2).
[3] Ibid. 779.   [4] Ibid. 796.   [5] Ibid. 232 (p. 91).
[6] Ibid. 804 (p. 817).   [7] Ibid. 796.

cherishing, and thereby somewhat comfort himself, and have better stay of himself," and he will then tell all he knows even though it touch his own mother or brother[1].

In the first days of November his friends heard that, knowing his steadfastness gone, he had made one last effort to save their lives and his own honour, and had "almost slain himself."[2] He must have made the attempt immediately after the first examination, for it was known in London on 28 October, when John Hussee wrote to Lord Lisle, "Sir Geoffrey Pole was examined in the Tower by my Lord Admiral. They say he was so in despair that he would have murdered himself, and has hurt himself sore. Please keep this secret as yet."[3] There is a contemporary account of the matter though it really throws less light on poor Geoffrey's character than on the religious ideas of the court party. It tells how for a long time the prisoner would reveal nothing though "conscience and God" worked in his mind against "blood and nature," urging him to tell all. "This motion ran oft in his head, but the devil, continual adversary to God's honour and man's wealth, put in his foot, and so tossed this wretched soul, that out of many evils he chose even the worst of all, which was a full purpose to slay himself. The commodities of his death were many, as the devil made them to show: his brother should live still, their family continue in honour, the Lord Marquis should have great cause to love all his blood, which had killed himself to save him; with many such fantasies as desperate men find to help them to their end.... His keeper being absent, a knife at hand upon the table, he riseth out of his bed, and taketh the knife, and with full intent to die, gave himself a stab with the knife upon the breast. The devil lacketh strength, when God has anything to do, and can better begin things than bring them to effect." The knife was blunt and the wound not mortal. But in great fear of death and hell he began to think it better his friends should lose their heads than he his soul. He sent for the Lieutenant of the Tower and certain of the Privy Council and disclosed everything then and there. Thus the devil's subtle provision of the knife was turned against himself[4].

The last part of this account is more or less untrue. Sir Geoffrey did not reveal everything in instant fear of death; he was examined seven times in all at intervals of a day or two[5]. But of course the

---

[1] L. and P. XIII (2), 695 (2).   [2] Ibid. 772.   [3] Ibid. 703.
[4] Moryson, An Invective against Treason.
[5] L. and P. XIII (2), 695 (2), 804.

examiners made the most of the state of moral collapse likely to follow a weak man's attempted suicide.

Chance played into their hands. Fitzwilliam, the Lord Admiral, who had lately been created Earl of Southampton, was at Cowdray, his seat in Sussex, during September. On the 17th he was out hawking with Lord Delaware when a poor man came to beg favour of him. His wife, he said, had been committed to Chichester prison by John Gunter, J.P., for saying that Sir Geoffrey Pole would have sent a band of men oversea to the Cardinal if he had not been sent to the Tower. Southampton seized upon the clue like a modern sleuth hound, and brought to light a great deal of country gossip about the Poles, who were the great family of the neighbourhood[1]. Going abroad to the Emperor's wars was a recognised career for adventurous young men, as the following story shows. In May 1538, a serving-man of Chichester said: "Master, I can have no living here. I will go beyond sea: for I know one John Stappill hath been there in the Emperor's wars, and is now come home like a jolly fellow apparelled in scarlet, and a hundred crowns in his purse"; this friend would get the King's licence for him to go abroad, and also "for half-a-score more of my Lady of Salisbury's servants." If they could not get service under the Emperor they would go to Cardinal Pole, "and there we shall be sure to be retained."[2] According to popular rumour Sir Geoffrey had intended to despatch this band to his brother in March. It was also whispered that the King and his Council would have burnt my Lady of Salisbury when they were in Sussex if she had been a young woman. The reports were traced to Lawrence Taylor, the harper of Havant, who confessed he had heard of the matter from the surgeon Richard Eyre, the tattler who was at the bottom of all the trouble. After examining him, John Gunter had released Taylor, who went off to a wedding. When Southampton heard this he turned on the unfortunate magistrate, accusing him of negligence and saying he had acted "like an untrue man. He waxed pale and with tears and sobbing besought me (Southampton) to be good to him; he had not seen the importance of the matter at the beginning, but would make amends by his diligent search for the said Lawrence."[3] He delivered the harper to Southampton next day[4], and was so worked upon by his fears that he himself reported to Southampton some private conversations he had had with Sir Geoffrey Pole. Two years afterwards Sir Geoffrey "did sore hurt and wound"

---

[1] L. and P. XIII (2), 392.　　　　　[2] Ibid. 592.
[3] Ibid. 892.　　　　　　　　　　　　[4] Ibid. 893.

John Gunter, because "he had dealt unkindly with him in his trouble by uttering things they had communed of in secret."[1]

Primed with so much information, Southampton rode to London to conduct Sir Geoffrey's examination. He knew quite enough to make it appear that he knew everything; he had only to perform the common lawyer's trick of making a desperate man believe it is useless to conceal what he knows, that he may save himself by confession but can save no one else by silence. It is easy for a man like Froude, who was a weak sentimentalist and so unable to sympathise with weakness in others, to condemn Sir Geoffrey as a traitor. But the prisoners of those days had to undergo something far worse than the most savage modern cross-examination. To begin with, a man charged with treason was in a hopeless case: no jury would acquit him. His one chance was the King's mercy, and that could only be gained by accusing others.

A man who does not fear death (Sir Geoffrey had tried to destroy himself) may fear torture. There is nothing to prove that Pole was threatened with the rack, and it seems to have been the custom to spare men of noble birth. Popular rumour said he was so threatened[2], and Richard Moryson denied it with much elaboration[3]: both assertions are quite untrustworthy. An openly spoken threat was not needed; a prisoner worn out with two months of close confinement and low living does not need any reminder; the fact that he is in the Tower, helpless before men who wield the powers of life and death and pain is threat enough. We can understand this only too clearly when we read this letter to the King, added in Sir Geoffrey's hand to his second examination, taken on 2 November[4]:—

"Sir, I beseech your noble Grace to pardon my wretchedness that I have not done my bounden duty unto your Grace heretofore as I ought to have done, but, Sir, grace coming to me to consider your nobleness always to me, and now especially in my extreme necessity, as I perceive by my Lord Admiral and Mr Comptroller (*the examiners*), your goodness shall not be lost on me, but surely as I found your Grace always faithful unto me, so I refuse all creature living to be faithful to you. Your humble slave, Geffrey Pole."

When this letter was written he had as yet accused no one but himself and Hugh Holland of serious offences[5]. But his confessions became rapidly more and more compromising to his friends[6]. He

---

[1] L. and P. xvi, 19.
[2] Spanish Chronicle, chap. lx.
[3] Moryson, op. cit.
[4] L. and P. xiii (2), 743.
[5] Ibid. 695 (2).
[6] Ibid. 804.

told the details of many political conversations with Exeter, with Sir Edward Neville, with Croftes the chancellor of Chichester Cathedral, but chiefly with his own brother. Jerome Ragland, a confidential servant of Montague "who was as it were his right hand,"[1] made a long confession against his master on 28 (?) October[2]. Perhaps Sir Geoffrey was confronted with this. The most pitiful record of all is a statement in Sir Geoffrey's own hand telling of Montague's words against the King[3]. It seems to have been written in a frenzy of hysterical rage against the man who had chosen to stay in England when they might have escaped safely across the seas. Everything came out, as Montague had foreseen; and not only through Sir Geoffrey, but, as more and more of the little faction were brought to the Tower, many others made equally long and unwilling confessions.

Montague and Exeter were committed on 4 November. The French Ambassador wrote to the Constable of France, in cypher, the following account of the King's intentions:—

"En escrivant ceste lettre ce matin, este adverty que le Roy d'Angleterre fit mettre hier au soir en la Tour de Londres Monsieur le Marquis d'Exestre..., qui est apres les enfans du Roy le plus proche de ceste couronne, et milort de Montagu.... Il y a bien longtemps que ce Roy m'avoit dict qu'il vooloit exterminer ceste maison de Montagu, qui est encore de la Rose Blanche, et de la maison de Polle dont est le Cardinal. Je ne scay encore qu'on veult faire dudit Marquis; par le premier je vous en advertiray. Il semble qu'il cherche toutes les occasions qu'on peult penser pour se ruyner et destruyre. Je croy que peu de seigneurs sont asseures en ce pays; je ne croy pas qu'il n'en advienne quelque miquemaque. Je vous advertiray eu diligence de ce que j'en entendray."[4]

Sir Edward Neville, George Croftes of Chichester, John Collins, and several servants were all arrested shortly after the two lords[5]. Gertrude, the Lady Marquis of Exeter, followed her husband to the Tower before 21 November[6], with her little son Edward Courtenay. It is not certain whether Henry Pole, Montague's heir, went at this time with his father, or later with his grandmother. Of the evidence given in their examinations little need be said; the most important consists of reports of conversations which came within the new treason act, and several of these have been mentioned already. The evidence is singularly full and we probably have more before us than was read at the trials, for there are two copies of many of the papers, and a great

[1] L. and P. XIII (2), 828 (2).
[2] Ibid. 702.
[3] Ibid. 800.
[4] Ibid. 758.
[5] Ibid. 822, 827, 828–9.
[6] Ibid. 884.

many repetitions in successive examinations. The only paper which may possibly be missing is the answer of the Marquis of Exeter to a set of interrogatories[1]; but as no statement of the Marquis is mentioned in Cromwell's notes and summaries or in the indictments, he may never have answered, and if he did his evidence must have been unimportant.

There is absolutely no proof of a conspiracy: the White Rose party were working on no sort of plan and had come to no definite agreement among themselves. We have once or twice spoken of their dreams of Cardinal Pole's marriage with Mary, after an invasion in her favour by the Emperor[2]. But a careful study of their statements shows that we have put these aims in a much more definite form than they ever did themselves. Even Froude, who finds no difficulty in believing in an organised plot just about to take effect, was puzzled by the fact that their schemes must have included two pretenders to the throne, Mary and Exeter[3]. The explanation is that they never thought the matter out. They were less a political party than a group of friends, who loved the old Faith, hated Cromwell, and longed for a change of policy. They met and talked treason and sang political songs in the Marquis's garden at Horsley, and in the woods at Bockmore. They did not trouble themselves about anything so strenuous and intellectual as a plot. The King's version of the matter, that Exeter meant to seize the Crown and slay the entire royal family, was simply ridiculous, considering that he had no one to help him but Mary's especial friends[4].

Montague and the rest were guilty of treason under the new laws but not under the old[5]. The case against them rested on nothing but words. They had not done anything treasonable with the exception of Sir Geoffrey Pole and Hugh Holland who had sent warning to a traitor beyond the seas. They had not compassed or purposed the King's death: they had only said they would be glad if he died. They had not levied war against him: they had only wished someone else would. There must have been some feeling against the new treason law, for Henry himself was troubled at putting it into execution and did his very best to make the world believe that the "conspirators" were guilty of more serious offences than those for which they were indicted.

Under the Act of 1534 there was no difficulty in convicting

[1] L. and P. xiii (2), 771 (iii).
[2] See chap. ii.
[3] Froude, op. cit. ii, chap. xv.
[4] L. and P. xiv (1), 233, 280.
[5] Stubbs, op. cit. iii, section 469.

Montague and Sir Edward Neville; quick and careless of tongue, they had both fallen under the law "that if any person...do maliciously wish, will or desire, by words or writing or by craft, imagine any bodily harm to be done or committed to the King's most royal person" he is guilty of high treason[1]. Against both of them Sir Geoffrey was the chief witness; both made short confessions in the Tower, in which there was nothing that could be used against their friends[2]. "I have lived in prison all these six years," Montague told his examiners; he thought it better to lie in the Tower than to go abroad in suspicion, and he had never felt free since Reginald had offended the King[3].

The two priests, Collins and Croftes, both confessed their secret attachment to the Pope[4]. Croftes had said, "The King is not Supreme Head of the Church of England but the Bishop of Rome is Supreme Head of the Church," and also "There was none act or thing that ever he did more grieved his conscience than the oath which he took to renounce the bishop of Rome's authority"; Lord Delaware had persuaded him to receive it after he had determined rather to fly abroad[5]. Collins said "the King will hang in hell one day for the plucking down of abbeys"; and when talking with Montague of the fall of monasteries: "I fear that within a while they will pull down the parish churches also."[6] He had instructed a friend to burn his sermons if he was sent to the Tower[7]; the burning of papers was in the King's eyes quite sufficient proof that they contained treason.

It was against Exeter that the Government had most difficulty in making out a case. Neither Montague nor Neville would accuse him, and in none of his conversations with Sir Geoffrey had he spoken against the King. In 1531 he had been banished the court and perhaps put under arrest for a short time, on account of the gossiping of his servants[8], who had gone about saying "My Lord Marquis would be King and they lords," and "our master shall wear the garland at the last."[9] But if this charge was not thought serious in 1531, there was no reason why it should be seven years later; nevertheless the King's lawyers thought it worth reviving.

Another charge, this time against the Lady Marquis, was equally out of date. As her gentlewoman confessed, she had gone in disguise

[1] Gee and Hardy, op. cit. no. lvii.
[2] L. and P. xiii (2), 772, 804 (p. 319).
[3] Ibid. 827 (8).
[4] Ibid. 829 (iii).
[5] Ibid.
[6] Ibid. 830 (p. 341).
[7] Ibid. 829 (p. 339).
[8] L. and P. v, 340, 416.
[9] L. and P. xiii (2), 961 (1); see above chap. xix, note D.

to speak with the Nun of Kent, and had afterwards received her at Horsley[1]. It was not about political hopes she had consulted the Holy Maid; all her babies had died at birth, and she desired the Nun's prayers for the child she was then expecting[2]; there was no proof that they had conversed treasonably. If the King knew of the Lady Marquis's correspondence with Chapuys a really grave charge might have been brought against her[3]. But the Marquis was not implicated in either of these mysterious expeditions. The straits to which Cromwell was put to make out a rational case against him is shown by this passage in one of the depositions:—

"About three years past when lord Montague began to recover from his sickness he sent examinate (*his servant Jerome Ragland*) to Horsley to show the lord Marquis of his recovery: the lord Marquis said he was glad thereof";

This is solemnly noted in the margin "Against the Lord Marquis."[4]

In the end the Crown lawyers were obliged to be contented with two scraps of conversation—"I trust once to have a fair day upon these knaves which rule about the King, and I trust to see a merry world one day"; and "Knaves rule about the King; I trust to give them a buffet one day." Also the general declaration "I like well the proceedings of Cardinal Pole, but I like not the proceedings of this realm,"[5] which is not to be found in the evidence, and was a kind of profession of faith attributed to all the prisoners. To one who is no lawyer these sayings do not appear to bring the Marquis under the Act of 1534. There is no wish or thought expressed against the King's person; at the worst they are against the King's ministers and policy, and these are not mentioned in the Act; no doubt by an oversight.

Exeter was to be tried by his peers on 3 December, Montague on 2 December[6]. On this last date Thomas West, Lord Delaware, was committed to the Tower[7]. It was whispered that he had dared to refuse to take a place in the jury of peers[8]. This rumour may have been true, for on 1 December the Council wrote to Henry humbly apologising for not having sent Delaware to the Tower; they had done their best, they assured the King, but as yet they had found nothing sufficient against him. They had commanded him to keep to his house, and to make a full confession[9]. It may

---

[1] L. and P. xiii (2), 802.
[2] Trans. of the Royal Historical Society, New Series, Vol. xviii (1904); D. A. Cheney, Holy Maid of Kent, pp. 117-8 (n.).
[3] See above, chap. ii.
[4] L. and P. xiii (2), 702.
[5] Ibid. 979 (15).
[6] Ibid. 979.
[7] Ibid. 982.
[8] Ibid. 1062.
[9] Ibid. 968.

have been merely through Henry's impatience that he was sent to the Tower next day; or perhaps he had determined after Darcy's trial to pass no more of the King's sentences. It would be good to think there was one nobleman in England who was capable of so acting.

Montague was brought to trial on 2 December[1], indicted of speaking against the King, approving Cardinal Pole's doings, and dreaming that the King was dead[2]. He pleaded not guilty and was condemned to death.

Exeter was brought to the bar on the 3rd, and the same judgment was pronounced against him[3]. There is an account of a strange scene which took place at his trial, given by a contemporary but not by an eye-witness. Exeter, Montague and Neville

"all the time of their arraignment stood stiff, with a casting up of eyes and hands, as though those things had been never heard of before that then were laid to their charge. The Marquis of all the rest stuck hardest, and made as though he had been very clear in many points, yet in some he staggered, and was very sorry so to do, now challenging the King's pardon, now taking benefit of the act, and when all would not serve he began to charge Geoffrey Pole with frenzy, with folly, and madness. It is much to be noted what answer Geoffrey made to the Marquis in this point. Some men, saith Geoffrey (as I hear), lay to my charge that I should be out of my wit and in a frenzy. Truth it is, I was out of my wit, and in a great frenzy when I fell with them in conference to be a traitor, disobedient to God, false to my prince, and enemy to my native country. I was also out of my wit and stricken with a sore kind of madness when I chose rather to kill myself than to charge them with such treasons, as I knew would cost them their lives, if I did utter them. But Our Lord be thanked, God wrought better with me than I thought to have done with myself. He hath saved my soul at the last, the knife went not so far as I would have had it gone: His goodness it is that I have not slain myself:...His work that I have declared myself, my brother, the Marquis, with the rest to be traitors. And where I thought, said Geoffrey, rather to have put my soul in hazard for the saving of these men, God, I thank Him, so wrought in me and so changed my mind, that if I had ten brethren, yea, ten sons, I would rather bring them all to this peril of death than leave my country, my sovereign lord, and mine own soul in such danger as they all stood in if I had kept these treasons secret. Let us, let us die, we be but a few, better we have according to our deserts than our whole country be brought to ruin....

"Geoffrey hath never been taken for any pleasant or sage talker, his wit was wont to serve his tongue but so so. I dare say, they that were the wisest of the King's most honourable council did much wonder that day, to hear him tell his tale, and looked for nothing less than that he should have so handled himself. God is a marvellous God, He can make both when Him list and whom He will eloquent, wise, pithy; He can make the tongues of the

---

[1] L. and P. xiii (2), 979 (3).   [2] Ibid. 979 (7).   [3] Ibid. 979 (19).

dumb serve His elect, when His will is. The Marquis was stiff at the bar, and stood fast in denial of most things laid to his charge, yet in some he failed and staggered in such sort that all men might see his countenance to avouch that, that his tongue could not without much faltering deny."[1]

Sir Geoffrey Pole with Sir Edward Neville, George Croftes, John Collins, and Hugh Holland, were brought to trial on 4 December. All pleaded guilty but Neville, who maintained his innocence to the last. All were found guilty[2].

Exeter, Montague and Sir Edward Neville were beheaded on Tower Hill on 9 December and buried within the Tower. The same day Croftes, Holland and Collins were executed at Tyburn, and "their heads set on London Bridge."[3] Sir Geoffrey Pole remained in the Tower[4]; the state of mind in which he had borne evidence against the others can hardly have outlasted their deaths. On 28 December he again attempted suicide by suffocating himself with a cushion[5].

Meanwhile the Countess of Salisbury had not been left to mourn her sorrows in quiet. She had been plunged into anxiety by Geoffrey's arrest in August. About the beginning of November the news of his first attempted suicide found its way to Warblington. "I pray God, madame, he do you no hurt one day," said her frightened steward. "I trow he is not so unhappy that he will hurt his mother," she answered, "and yet I care neither for him, nor for any other, for I am true to my Prince."[6] It must have been at this time that she wrote to her eldest son:—

"Son Montague I send you heretely goddes blessing and myne. This is the gretist gift that I can send you for to desire god of his helpe wich I perceave is great need to pray for. And as to the case as I ame informed that you stand in myne advise is to refer you to god principally and upon that ground so to ordre you both in word and deed to serve your prince not disobeyeng goddys commandment as far as your power and lief woll serve you for of to doo above all ordre for...hath brought you upe and maynteyned you...but his highnes who if you woll...with your lerning serve to the content...of his mynd as your bounden duetie is...that you may so serve his highness...daylie pray to god...orelles to take you to his mercy." It appears that he did not receive it until he was in the Tower[7].

[1] Moryson, An Invective against Treason.
[2] L. and P. xiii (2), 986, 987.
[3] Wriothesley, op. cit. i, p. 92; L. and P. xiii (2), 1056. [4] Ibid. 1163.
[5] L. and P. xiv (1), 87 (p. 19). [6] L. and P. xiii (2), 875 (1).
[7] Ibid. 855 (2); copied from original at the R. O.

On 12 November, Southampton and the Bishop of Ely were sent down to Warblington to interrogate the Countess. She had spoken truly of Sir Geoffrey; in all his confessions there is no word that could be twisted into an accusation against her. Nor had the other prisoners laid anything to her charge; she strongly disliked heretics, but no one accused her of speaking against the Royal Supremacy. Nevertheless Southampton had no doubt that he could soon make her commit herself. He was an experienced examiner and had just come from questioning her sons in the Tower. He was much disappointed with his first results. The Countess answered every question in the most straightforward way. She had had, she said, no secret confidences with, nor any letter from, her son Reginald and the Vicar of East Meon. She knew nothing of Holland's voyage. She had never heard Montague or Sir Geoffrey wish they were abroad or propose to go; she solemnly denied that they ever uttered treasonable words in her presence. She had never burnt letters concerning the King, nor was there any agreement between herself and her sons to conceal anything. This was the substance of Margaret Pole's confession[1].

The examiners wrote to Cromwell—"Yesterday, 13 Nov., as we wrote we would do, we travailed with the Lady of Salisbury all day, both before and after noon till almost night; but for all we could do she would confess nothing more than the first day." On the 14th they went to her again, as they were ordered; first they called all her men-servants before them and arrested one called Standish. "We then entreated her with both sorts, sometimes with douce and mild words, now roughly and asperly, by traitoring her and her sons to the ninth degree, yet will she nothing utter, but maketh herself clear." They thought such a woman had never been heard of, she was so earnest and precise and "manlike in continuance." Everything was so "sincere, pure, and upright on her part that we have conceived and needs must deem and think the one of two things in her: that either her sons have not made her privy nor participant of the bottom and pit of their stomachs, or else she is the most arrant traitress that ever lived."

They seized her goods and told her that it was the King's pleasure that she should leave her home at once. "She seemeth thereat to be somewhat appalled. And therefore we deem that if it may be so, she will then utter somewhat when she is removed, which we intend shall be tomorrow." They spoke with the neighbouring

[1] L. and P. xiii (2), 818.

gentlemen and bade them "to have vigilant eye to repress any stirring that may arise."[1] They examined Thomas Standish, the clerk of the kitchen, but he confessed nothing[2]; the Protestants who lodged the first information against the Countess had named him as a crafty fellow from whom it would be hard to get information[3]. Hugh Holland had told him of his visit to the Cardinal, and if the Countess knew of it, it would probably be through him[4].

On 15 November the Countess was taken from her home to Cowdray, Southampton's house. It was no wonder that the thought of being left in the keeping of such a man appalled even so brave a lady. Southampton and the Bishop of Ely wrote again to Cromwell on 16 November. They were rather better pleased with themselves. They had got something out of Standish, whose confession is lost, though apparently nothing against his mistress. They despaired of making the Countess accuse herself. "We assure your Lordship we have dealt with such a one as men have not dealt withal to fore us; we may call her rather a strong and constant man than a woman."

Their hopes revived when some papers were found at Warblington: two or three old bulls in Standish's room, and a copy of the Countess's letter to Montague in a gentlewoman's chest. "Travailing sundry times and after sundry sorts with her," the examiners thought she had at last admitted something of importance[5]. She did not deny the letter was hers; she had caused it to be written before Montague was in the Tower but after Sir Geoffrey was taken[6]. She described a conversation with the comptroller of her household who said he was afraid Sir Geoffrey would "slip away."[7] The servant himself gave a different account of the matter, and if he used these words he must have meant Sir Geoffrey was likely to die, for he had just injured himself in the Tower[8]. Finally the Countess was asked whether Sir Geoffrey had not told her that the King went about to cause Reginald to be slain; she answered that he had "and she prayed God heartily to change the King's mind." Both her other sons told her that he had escaped "and for motherly pity she could not but rejoice."[9] These were "the principal points" of her confession. Southampton, "putting her in such order [and] surety here as the King's pleasure is she should be left in," hastened

[1] L. and P. xiii (2), 835.   [2] Ibid. 835, 838 (iii).
[3] Ibid. 817 (p. 326).   [4] Ibid. 797 (ii).
[5] Ibid. 855.   [6] Ibid. 818 (21).
[7] Ibid. 818 (19).   [8] Ibid. 875.
[9] Ibid. 818 (5).

back to court[1], and two weeks later took his part in the condemnation of her eldest son[2].

The fate of the White Rose party caused more stir in court circles than in the country. Except for the disturbance that Southampton feared at Warblington, there is no sign that the sympathy of the lower orders was roused on their behalf. On the other hand the only people really pleased were the favourers of the New Learning; Exeter and Montague had been too long out of favour to be much disliked by the nobility. Latimer's congratulations to Cromwell on their fate and the Cardinal's terrible position have been too often quoted to need inclusion here[3]. The Londoners, who every year inclined more towards Protestant opinions, were distinctly against Exeter and the Poles. A goldsmith was chatting with two men in a boat at Paul's Wharf on 13 November. One of these was "a servant of the King's within the Tower"; said he, "We have great pain in watching of these naughty men lately brought into the Tower. Would to God every man would know their duties to God and their Prince." The goldsmith asked if Sir Geoffrey Pole were dead or alive, and what was the news "of that naughty fellow Pole, his brother beyond sea." The King's servant said he was made Bishop of Rome.

"How know you that?" asked the goldsmith.

"I have heard it of great men."

"Of whom?"

"Of some of my Lord Privy Seal's house."

The third man broke in, "I have heard as much as this comes to, for the council doth know this thing well enough."

"I pray you," said the goldsmith, "how do you know they know it?"

"By the ambassadors and others."

"There was one in our house (i.e. the Tower) prisoner," said the King's servant, "who being delivered by the King's favour and sent to the said Pole beyond sea, to show unto him the King's pleasure, doth yet there remain, and now is one of the greatest in favour with him." The goldsmith asked his name, and was told "Throgmorton."[4]

A Protestant community sending the London news to friends abroad referred to the executions, not without triumph:—"The principal supporters of Popery among us have been cut off."[5]

---

[1] L. and P. xiii (2), 855.
[2] Ibid. 979 (5).
[3] Ibid. 1036; see note B at end of chapter.
[4] L. and P. xiii (2), 820 (iii).
[5] L. and P. xiv (1), 466.

Strangely enough most indignation was aroused abroad, especially in France, where the nobility had long regarded Henry with aversion. In a letter to Montmorency, the French ambassador urged that such an opportunity for a successful invasion of England had never before been offered to a Constable of France. What glory he might gain by avenging at length all the wrongs that England had done their country in times past[1]! In another letter he related how Henry complained to him of the way he was spoken of in France, and wished to know if Francis could not prevent his subjects from using such unseemly railing against his (Henry's) heresy and inhumanity. For the first, they should rather praise him; for the second, the Exeter party had been most justly punished. The ambassador replied that in France people had so much greater liberty of speech than in England that it was very difficult to prevent talking; Francis allowed his people "to say many things" of himself[2].

Lord Delaware was set free on 21 December[3]. Nothing had been deposed against him as far as is known except that he disliked the New Learning and certain new laws, such as the Act of Uses; also that he was intimate with Exeter and Croftes and had heard the latter deny the royal supremacy without informing against him[4]. This was little enough, but it might have cost him his head. He was, however, released on heavy securities and went back to his quiet life as an undistinguished baron[5].

On the last day of December the last man to suffer for this visionary conspiracy was sent to the Tower. This was Sir Nicholas Carew, the Master of the Horse[6], and a certain mystery surrounds his fate. For years he had been high in the King's favour[7]. The only explanation of his sudden fall is given by Chapuys, who, writing on 9 January, tells all the court gossip about this arrest and the late executions. Cromwell himself explained to the ambassador that Exeter had been plotting to destroy the King and the Prince, seize the throne himself and marry his little son to Mary. He added that "their treasons had been fully proved since their deaths." It was true they had burnt the incriminating letters, but fortunately a number of copies of them had been found in a coffer belonging to the Lady Marquis[6]. There is no evidence beyond this bare statement

---

[1] L. and P. xiii (2), 1162.
[2] Ibid. 1112.
[3] Ibid. 1168.
[4] Ibid. 821, 822, 829.
[5] Ibid. 1117.
[6] L. and P. xiv (1), 37 (p. 18).
[7] Ibid. Introduction, pp. i–iv.
[8] Ibid. 37.

that these letters ever existed except in Cromwell's brain. One of them, however, was supposed to implicate Carew[1]. "The testimony of young Pole is not sufficient," wrote Chapuys, "these men...want to form the process after the execution."

At court it was said that Carew was especially urged to accuse Exeter, and that he had confessed that when he told the Marquis of the Prince's birth he seemed sad; "which," wrote Chapuys, "I believe was only on account of the love he bears to the Princess, in whose service he would willingly, as he had often sent to tell me, shed his blood."[2] Exeter had never made any secret of his attachment to Queen Katharine and her daughter[3]. Chapuys thought that if Carew had written to the Lady Marquis it must have been about Mary, for he too had always shown himself her devoted servant. "It would seem they wish to leave her as few such as possible." Carew had looked for help rather from France than from the Emperor, "for which he has been frequently reproached by good Edward Neville."

Cromwell hinted that some compromising letter from Chapuys himself might be found in the Lady Marquis's collection; but the ambassador felt safe, for he had written no private letters except to Mary and Katharine, and he was sure that these had been destroyed. But as burning letters was now as dangerous as keeping them, he wrote the Princess half a dozen which she could show to anyone if commanded; he lived in hopes that Henry would discover them[4].

Sir Nicholas Carew was brought to trial on 14 February, 1539. The charge against him contained the following clauses:—That he knew Exeter to be a traitor and falsely encouraged him; that he talked to him of the state of the world; that they exchanged letters which they afterwards burnt. Carew was on the Surrey jury which sat on Exeter's indictment, and had indiscreetly said, "I marvel greatly that the indictment against the Lord Marquis was so secretly handled and for what purpose, for the like was never seen."[5]

Very little of the evidence against him has been preserved. He was Mary's friend. He was one of the guests who frequented the Marquis's garden at Horsley. He seems to have tried to intercede for the Lady Marquis when she was sent to the Tower[6]. But the slightness of the indictment points to the flimsiest of evidence. He pleaded not guilty and was sentenced as usual[7].

---

[1] L. and P. xiv (1), 280. [2] Ibid. 37. [3] L. and P. v, 238, 340.
[4] L. and P. xiv (1), 87. [5] Ibid. 290.
[6] L. and P. xiii (2), 830; see note C at end of chapter.
[7] L. and P. xiv (1), 290.

He was beheaded on Tower Hill, 3 March, 1539[1], "where he made a goodly confession, both of his folly and superstitious faith, giving God most hearty thanks that ever he came in the prison of the Tower, where he first savoured the life and sweetness of God's most holy word, meaning the Bible in English, which there he read by the means of one Thomas Philips then Keeper."[2]

Chapuys remarked that when confiscating Sir Nicholas' goods the King would do well to remember "the most beautiful diamonds and pearls and innumerable jewels" which he formerly gave to Lady Carew, and which once had been Queen Katherine's[3]. No doubt Henry did remember, for Lady Carew was soon begging for some provision for herself and her daughters[4]. As to the offices held by the late Master of the Horse, they had been promised to others even before his arrest[5].

Though there was little popular feeling about the death of the Exeter conspirators, it must have alarmed all but the most secure of the nobility. Some men must have been revolted by the severity of the new treason laws; the story of the Lady Marquis's letters, found after the trial, was meant to reconcile these malcontents. Henry made another attempt to persuade public opinion to take his view of the case. Richard Moryson, one of those quick-witted, talented, heartless, faithless "knaves" of Cromwell's, was commissioned to write a book setting forth the heinousness of treason with special reference to the White Rose party. This was the tract called "An invective against the great and detestable vice, treason, wherein the secret practices, and traitorous workings of them that suffered of late are disclosed," which was published in London during 1539.

In defiance of the title the book contains no coherent account of Exeter's alleged plot. We have twice quoted from it at some length, but it is really more remarkable for its blood-curdling theology and spirited abuse than for serious historical worth. The letters of the Lady Marquis are never even mentioned and no proofs of treason are produced at all. Montague and the rest were detestable traitors; their guilt is assumed and they are abused for it with abundance of classical and scriptural illustrations. There is only one belated allusion to their possible motives for being so gratuitously wicked. It was because they were Papists; anyone who believes the Pope to be Supreme Head of the Church "may well lack power or stomach

---

[1] Wriothesley, op. cit. I (p. 93).
[2] Hall's Chronicle, Ann. 1539.
[3] L. and P. xiv (1), 87.
[4] Ibid. 408.
[5] Ibid. 87.

to utter treason, but he can not lack a traitorous heart."[1] Henry was pleased with the book. He wrote to Hutton, for circulation in the Netherlands, his own account of the conspiracy, "whereupon of late there is a pretty book printed in this our realm which ye shall receive herewith."[2]

As an example of Moryson's style we may quote a part of his invective relating to Cardinal Pole: "To come at the last, to the archtraitor, and to speak somewhat of him whom God hateth, nature refuseth, all men detest, yea and all beasts too would abhore, if they could perceive how much viler he is than is even the worst of them: what man would ever have thought that Reynold Pole could have been by any gifts, by any promotion, by any means in this world brought from the love which for so many the King's high benefits of all men he ought (owed) his grace the most?" His true friends are those who wish him dead, for only by death can he escape "the gripes, the wounds, the tossing and turmoiling, the heaving and shoving that traitors feel in their stomachs." Probably God leaves him alive "only because thy life hath many more torments, much more shame in it, than any cruel death can have....What greater shame can come to thee than to be the dishonour of all thy kin, a comfort to all thine enemies, a death to all thy friends?" "O Pole, O whirl pole, full of poison, that wouldest have drowned thy country in blood....God be thanked thou art now a Pole of little water, and that at a wonderful low ebb." Moryson in fact is quite unable to keep off the subject of the Cardinal, and always strays back to him. In another place he says: "Pole came somewhat too late into France, at the last commotion. If he had come in season, he would have played an hardier part than Aske did, he would surely have jeopardied both his eyes, where Aske ventured but one. He would have had not only a foot in their boat but in spite of Aske and his company would have ruled the stern."

As an example of Moryson's theology his remarks on the end of the Pilgrimage are instructive. He is never tired of bidding England praise God's goodness in sending so wise and beneficent a Prince to reign over her. She must also give praise for the ending of the rebellion without bloodshed; God's goodness was still further shown by His causing the "rank captains" and deceivers of the people to commit further treason and "testify upon the gallows that traitors must come to shameful death." And though the King in his mercy pardoned the common people, "God hath this last summer by a

[1] Moryson, "An Invective against treason." [2] L. and P. xiv (1), 280.

strange kind of sickness well declared unto the commons of the north that he was not contented so few were punished where so many offended." Also the plague had been in other parts of the country, which, as God knew "had hearts evil enough, though their deeds were unknown."[1] This is a particularly revolting form of the ancient superstition that any great calamity is a punishment from God, especially if it befalls an enemy. Men who sincerely love God have striven against this relic of devil-worship ever since Euripides wrote:—

"This land of murderers to its god hath given
Its own lust; evil dwelleth not in heaven";

but the superstition is not yet dead.

Of the surviving members of the White Rose party, Sir Geoffrey was pardoned early in the New Year[2]. The Lady Marquis of Exeter remained in the Tower, with the two boys, her son Edward Courtenay, who was twelve years old, and Henry Pole "a child, the remaining hope of our race," as the Cardinal called him with a touch of human feeling[3]. Courtenay must have been a spirited boy even in his childhood. Some months before, his schoolmaster had fled the Marquis' household because certain of the young gentlemen had threatened him for administering correction to the young lord[4]. The Countess of Salisbury was still at Cowdray[5].

Parliament met in April 1539 and sat until 28 June. During May it passed an Act of Attainder including all who had suffered after the Pilgrimage, Exeter and his friends, Cardinal Pole and other Englishmen who had fled abroad; Gertrude Courtenay, Marchioness of Exeter, and Margaret Pole, Countess of Salisbury[6]. It has commonly been said that the two boys were also attainted; but it can have been only by implication as an examination of the Parliament Roll shows that they were not named[7]. An account of the passing of the Act was sent by a correspondent in London to Lord Lisle:—

"Pleaseth your lordship, so it is that there was a coat armour found in the Duchess of Salisbury's coffer, and by the one side of the coat there was the King's Grace his arms of England, that is the lions without the flower de lys, and about the whole arms was made pansies for Pole, and marygolds for my lady Mary. This was about the coat armour. And betwixt the marygold and the pansy was made a tree to rise in the midst, and on the tree a coat of purple hanging on a bough, in token of the coat of Christ, and on

---

[1] Moryson, op. cit.
[2] L. and P. xv (1), 191 (3).
[3] L. and P. xiv (2), 212.
[4] L. and P. xiii (2), 217.
[5] L. and P. xiv (1), 520.
[6] L. and P. xiv (1), 867 (15).
[7] Parl. Roll 1539, R. O.; see note D at end of chapter.

the other side of the coat all the Passion of Christ. Pole intended to have married my lady Mary and betwixt them both should again arise the old doctrine of Christ. This was the intent that the coat was made, as it is openly known in the Parliament house, as Master Sir George Speke showed me. And thus my lady Marquis, my lady Salisbury, Sir Adrian Fortescue, Sir Thomas Dingley, with divers other are attainted to die by act of Parliament. Other news here is none....At London the xviiith day of May" (1539)[1].

Froude gives the following account:

"A remarkable scene took place in the house of Lords on the last reading of the act. As soon as it was passed Cromwell rose in his place, and displayed in profound silence, a tunic of white silk which had been discovered by Lord Southampton concealed amidst the Countess' linen....It was shown, and it was doubtless understood, as conclusive evidence of the disposition of the daughter of the Duke of Clarence and the mother of Reginald Pole."[2]

Of course such a piece of evidence cannot be conclusive. The work might have been done years before, when a match between Mary and Reginald Pole was proposed by Queen Katherine. The symbol of the Five Wounds was far too common to fix the date as the time of the Pilgrimage. The Countess may have been innocent; but we may prefer to believe she was guilty. It is pleasant to think of her setting her maids to work when the first news came from the north, and of all the prayers for the faith and the hopes for her banished son that must have gone to the embroidering. The bill was passed on 12 May and shortly after she was removed from Cowdray to the Tower. This change must have been very welcome, for Southampton and his lady had treated her with all discourtesy, and in the Tower she would be near her grandson[3].

She spent two years in the Tower. Her experience there and that of the Lady Marquis may be gathered from a petition presented on their behalf to a Privy Councillor by the kind-hearted warder, Thomas Philips, who had given Sir Nicholas Carew the English Testament[4]. "By reason that I am daily conversant with them that are pensive," he wrote, "(*I*) can no less do but utter the same to your honourable lordship." The Lady Marquis begs favour and "saith she wanteth raiment, and hath no change but only that that your lordship commanded to be provided." Her gentlewoman, Mistress Constance Bontane, "hath no manner of change and that that she hath is sore worn. Another gentlewoman she hath, that is Master Comptroller's maid, and hath been with her one whole year

---

[1] L. and P. xiv (1), 980.
[3] L. and P. xiv (2), 287, 554.
[2] Froude, op. cit. chap. xvi.
[4] See above.

and more, and very sorry is she that she hath not to recompense them, at the least their wages." Finally, " the Lady Salisbury maketh great moan for that she wanteth necessary apparel both for to change and also to keep her warm."[1]

This petition must have been presented before April 1540, when the Lady Marquis was released[2]; it was expected at the time that the old Countess would be pardoned shortly. But she remained alone, except for her waiting woman and the two boys, who were not kept very close and would probably be allowed to see her.

On 1 March, 1541, the Council sent an order to the Queen's tailor for certain apparel and necessaries for the Countess[3]. All thanks be to Thomas Philips who has left one kindly story to adorn the Tower; he had been himself a prisoner there some years before[4]. In April the clothes were delivered:—"a night-gown furred, a kirtle of worsted and petticoat furred, another gown of the fashion of night-gown of saye, lined with satin of Cyprus and faced with satin, a bonnet with a frontlet, four pairs of hose, four pairs of shoes and a pair of slippers." But the Countess did not long enjoy this ample provision[5].

In May 1541 Henry was about to set out on his gorgeous progress through the north[6]. Before he left London the Tower was cleared of traitors[7]. The Countess was the first to suffer, at seven o'clock on the morning of May 27. Chapuys briefly records the event:—

"About the same time took place the lamentable execution of the Countess of Salisbury at the Tower, in the presence of the Lord Mayor and about one hundred and fifty persons. When informed of her sentence, she found it very strange, not knowing her crime; but she walked to the space in front of the Tower, where there was no scaffold, but only a small block. There she commended her soul to God, and desired those present to pray for the King, Queen, Prince and Princess."[8]

The Lady Marquis of Exeter had been pardoned a year before[9], and her son, who was still a prisoner, lived to be set free by Queen Mary[10]. The Countess suffered under the Act of Attainder without any trial; the two boys were not even included in the Act[11];

[1] Everett Wood, op. cit. III, no. xlii.
[2] L. and P. xv, 487.
[3] Everett Wood, op. cit. III, no. xlii.
[4] Hall's Chronicle.
[5] Everett Wood, op. cit. III, no. xlii.
[6] L. and P. xvi, 941; printed in part, Correspondance de Castillon (ed. Kaulek), no. 350.
[7] L. and P. xvi, 868.
[8] Ibid. 897.
[9] L. and P. xv, 487.
[10] Haile, op. cit. chap. xiv.
[11] See note D at end of chapter.

and were simply held by a sovereign power that no one dared to question. Henry Pole had been allowed to go about inside the Tower before his grandmother's death; after it he was more strictly guarded. "It is to be supposed that he will follow his father and grandmother," wrote Chapuys[1]. Edward Courtenay had a tutor, but Henry Pole was "poorly and strictly kept, and not allowed to know anything."[2] He is last mentioned in 1542[3]. Nothing more is known of him. The Tower must have been an unhealthy place for any child, and this one was an orphan without friends. He had, indeed, two uncles living. The Cardinal was helpless, for if he had attempted interference through the Emperor it would certainly have had an unhappy effect. Perhaps Sir Geoffrey did all he dared and lost touch with the boy on his closer confinement. He was, besides, hardly responsible for his actions.

Southampton, of all people least inclined to mercy, advised that Pole's assault on John Gunter should be overlooked "considering the ill and frantic furious nature of the unhappy man."[4] An account of his subsequent life is given in the Spanish Chronicle. Although the greater part of this work is entirely untrustworthy, particular passages may be accepted when the writer describes facts which he had himself witnessed, and his account of Sir Geoffrey Pole is fairly reliable because there is reason to believe that the Chronicle was written at Liége while Geoffrey was living there[5]. The Chronicler gives the following story of how Sir Geoffrey crossed the seas at last[6]. After he was pardoned "he went about for two years like one terror-stricken, and, as he lived four miles from Chichester, he saw one day in Chichester a Flemish ship into which he resolved to get and with her he passed over to Flanders, leaving his wife and children. Thence he found his way to Rome, and throwing himself at the feet of his brother the Cardinal, he said, "My lord, I do not deserve to call myself your brother for I have been the cause of our brother's death." The Cardinal, seeing he had sinned through ignorance, pardoned him, and brought him to the feet of the Pope, and procured forgiveness and absolution for his sin. Then the Cardinal sent him back to Flanders, with letters to the Bishop of Liége, who has him with him

---

[1] L. and P. xvi, 897.
[2] Ibid. 1011; printed in part, Correspondance de Castillon (ed. Kaulek), no. 351.
[3] L. and P. xvii, 880, f. 23 b, f. 29, f. 43 b.
[4] L. and P. xvi, 19.
[5] Spanish Chron. (ed. Hume), preface.
[6] See note E at end of chapter.

to this day, treating him with all honour, and allowing him a ducat a day, and food for himself, two attendants and a horse."¹

It was quite right of the Cardinal to forgive Sir Geoffrey; but should all the forgiveness have been on one side? Geoffrey, yielding to circumstances, had endured all that Reginald had escaped by taking his own path. Reginald had been in safety while Geoffrey had seen imprisonment and despair. Did the man whose uprightness had brought ruin on all he loved never for a moment accuse himself? When the Cardinal first heard the news of his mother's death, he spoke of it in these words: "Until now I had thought God had given me the grace of being the son of one of the best and most honoured ladies in England, and I gloried in it, returning thanks to His Divine Majesty; but now He has vouchsafed to honour me still more by making me the son of a martyr....Let us rejoice for we have another advocate in Heaven."² Perhaps it is because this speech has an appearance of having been thought out beforehand that it sounds cold and even heartless. The Cardinal seems more human in a letter written to one of Montague's daughters, who, after Mary's accession, sent him good news of herself and her children, the first he had received from his kinsfolk for many years:—"Albeit as I say all this did comfort me greatly, yet I ensure you I could not read your whole letter through, though it were not long, at all one time, for the sorrowful remembrance it brought me of the loss of those which I left in good state at my departing, to whom you were most dearest. But when I consider even what servants of God they were and so died, this ever doth comfort me with that certain hope of their good estate in all felicity to the which all we trust to come when it shall be God's pleasure to call us."³

NOTES TO CHAPTER XXIII

Note A. The internal dissensions of the College of Heralds are described at length in Lancaster Herald's statement, L. and P. XIII (1), 1313. The details are intimate and rather sordid.

Note B. L. and P. XIII (2), preface; Haile's Life of Cardinal Pole, chap. XII. The Romanist writers do not generally add that the same letter contains a kindly appeal for a well-famed priory, the head of which "is old and feedeth many.... Alas! my good lord, shall we not see two or three in each shire changed to such remedy?"⁴

---

¹ Spanish Chron. (ed. Hume), chap. LX.
² Haile, op. cit. chap. XIV.
³ English Hist. Rev. XXVIII, 528.
⁴ L. and P. XIII (2), 1036.

CHAPTER XXIV

CONCLUSION

The Pilgrimage of Grace failed completely. Its only result was to hasten the very events which the Pilgrims dreaded. The greater monasteries were suppressed, the north was bridled by the Council of the North, the Poles were all but exterminated. It is not a sufficient explanation of this failure to say that the Pilgrims were contending against the spirit of the age. Although certain revolutions in thought are broadly speaking inevitable, a reaction may have a temporary success, and may delay or modify the operation of the changes. The immediate causes of the Pilgrims' failure have appeared in the course of this history and may be summarised here:—

(1) The most striking was the Pilgrims' fundamental misconception of Henry's character. They believed him to be a weak, good-tempered sensualist, always the tool of some favourite. Consequently they thought that if only the King could be given ministers who shared their own views of public matters, they would be able to guide his policy without difficulty. Henry himself took some pains to hide his despotic temper and his iron will under a mask of careless good humour, and with his northern subjects the deception was completely successful. The Pilgrims never realised that to change the King's policy they must change the King; on the contrary they professed loyalty to the King's person and would not countenance pretenders. They saw that it would be more convenient to be able to change the policy of the government by changing the chief ministers, than by the old method of deposing or killing the King, as in the case of Richard II, Henry VI, and Richard III, but the theory of ministerial responsibility had not yet developed, and it did not accord with the facts of the case.

(2) Closely connected with this first blunder is a marked weakness in the opposition to Henry. It had no leader of genius.

The leaders of the Pilgrimage were honest men and men of ability, but they were nothing more. They had not the unconquerable energy needed to withstand Henry's determination and the sinister power of Thomas Cromwell. They were brave, they were unselfish, they were lovable, but all that counts for nothing. Henry possessed none of these qualities, but he had that force of character which alone is able to carry through great designs. He stamped himself upon the memory of the nation, while the names of the Pilgrims are forgotten.

(3) These reasons for failure may seem too personal to suit scientific history, but there were other weaknesses in the Pilgrims' movement of a more general nature. The chief of these was the conflict between the interests of the gentlemen and of the commons

The gentlemen wanted certain parliamentary reforms. If they could obtain them, they would be able to redress their own grievances. The commons wanted certain social reforms, which they were much more likely to obtain from the King than from Parliament. Briefly the gentlemen wanted higher rents and lower wages, while the commons wanted lower rents and higher wages. It seemed impossible that anything could reconcile these discordant aims.

(4) There was one power strong enough to bring the gentlemen and the commons together, a power which might have so united and inspired them as to carry them through to victory. This was the power of the Church. Yet though the force of religion accomplished much, the clergy of England, as a body, gave little countenance to the Pilgrims. The lower clergy, both regular and secular, devoted themselves to the cause, but the higher ecclesiastics were supine. The bishops who really opposed the King's innovations, such as Tunstall, fled from the rebels. The Archbishop of York and most of the abbots who were forced to join them were reluctant to share their danger, and gave them no encouragement. The Papacy was inert. Cardinal Pole refused to stir. The Pope was anxious to help the movement, but he was baffled by the passive indifference of the men through whom he might have acted. This inaction to a great extent caused the failure of the most promising attempt to preserve the Church of Rome which was ever made in England.

The reluctance of the higher clergy to take part in the Pilgrimage was due to the principles in which they had been brought up. The Church had always taught that obedience to the King was a duty second only in importance to obedience to the Church. In return the King had protected the Church against heresy. Henry VIII had suddenly broken the old alliance in the most startling manner, but ecclesiastics could not all at once throw over their old political theories. The Church of Rome was the church of tradition and authority; her priests preached law and order and submission to the appointed governors temporal and spiritual. They could not suddenly take up the opposite watch-words, and ally themselves with the partisans of freedom and reform. They were dazed and terrified by the overthrow of the old order, and in their bewilderment they stood aside while the Pilgrims marched to death, without attempting to add the weight of the Church to her champions' cause.

The Papacy ignored the Pilgrims while they lived and forgot them after their death; they were not sufficiently well-born to do her credit. To this day those who are curious in such matters may find recorded in Roman Catholic calendars the death of Bishop Tunstall and of the Blessed Thomas Percy, Sir Thomas' son, the seventh Earl of Northumberland, but there is not a word concerning Robert Aske, who was more steadfast in his faith than the first, more nearly successful than the second, and morally a better man than either.

The points enumerated were the sources of the Pilgrims' two great errors, over-confidence in themselves and over-trust in the King. They were over-confident because they had been taught that the Church was irresistible. Hence they had no doubt that their cause must triumph, and they imagined that the victory was theirs when the struggle had scarcely begun. They trusted the King too much because they misconceived his character. They believed him to be weak but well-meaning, whereas he was strong but unscrupulous.

Among the causes of their failure need not be reckoned the lack of foreign assistance. It was an advantage to the Pilgrims that interference from abroad did not arouse national feeling in Henry's favour. This abstinence on the part of the continental powers was due to accident, not policy. Francis I and Charles V fully intended some time to settle English affairs each in his own way, but the time never arrived. At every crisis in England it happened to be inconvenient for either of the great rivals to stir in the matter, but on every occasion, particularly after the Pilgrimage, they excused their inaction to the Pope by saying that the movement had been premature, but that there would be no difficulty in rousing a fresh revolt at a more suitable opportunity.

Henry knew better than that. He was thoroughly aware that a king is never so powerful as when he has crushed a rebellion. The leaders of the opposition are dead, the rank and file are frightened into silence, the waverers are confirmed in their allegiance. Henry took advantage of this interval to put in force all the measures against the Church upon which he had resolved, but when the attempt at revolt was almost forgotten on the continent, Henry began to remember it.

Many influences united to bring about Cromwell's fall and the religious reaction at the end of the reign. Among these influences should probably be reckoned the numerical strength of the religious conservatives revealed by the Pilgrimage. After the blow which they had received had spent its first effect, they might once more be dangerous. Henry had escaped the first time, but he might not be so successful the second. The memory of his treachery would be against him. Therefore he forestalled opposition by bringing about a small reaction of his own, which he could control. By this means he satisfied all but a few extremists, whom he did not fear. This is not put forward as the sole cause of Henry's change of policy, but it was probably one of the causes.

After Henry's death the moderate reaction was swept away by violent religious changes, which oscillated from extreme to extreme. The only effect of the Pilgrimage disappeared, and from that day to this the movement has been regarded as a picturesque episode having no real bearing on national history. Yet if not noteworthy in its effects, it had a political significance, which Henry VIII was the first to perceive. The important feature of the rising was the union between the gentlemen and the commons.

For the previous two hundred years revolts in England had been in character either feudal, that is, led by some great lord for his personal aggrandisement and supported by his relations and dependents, or social, blind outbreaks of the common people, due to general discontent, leaderless and without any definite purpose. Against risings of these types the King's best ally had been the middle class, the country gentlemen, the burgesses, the professional men, priests and lawyers. The middle class hated equally the tyranny of the nobles and the anarchy of the commons. In return for their constant support the King shared with them the greater part of the executive government. The gentlemen passed laws in parliament and administered them in the country as magistrates; they voted the taxes and assessed them; they called out the musters and commanded them. They were the chief support of the throne, and if they were alienated from the King the royal power would totter.

The interests of the middle class were so closely bound up with those of a strong central government, and so much opposed to those of the labouring classes, that it seemed impossible for the alliance between King and gentlemen to be weakened. The Pilgrimage of Grace was the first indication of the manner in which this alliance was to be broken. A difference in creed was powerful enough to divide the gentlemen from the King; a similarity in creed was powerful enough to unite a very large proportion of the gentlemen and commons in spite of their previous antagonism. So long as practically everyone in England belonged to the same Church, the common creed was not felt as a bond of union, but now that religious dissensions had inevitably arisen, the aspect of the political world was altered.

Henry quickly grasped the significance of the alliance between the gentlemen and commons, and used all his arts to destroy it. At the time he was successful. The wrongs which the commons had suffered were too recent and bitter for the new-found allies to be able to resist so skilful an opponent as the King. Dissension and suspicion awoke, and the power which might have held them together, the power of the Church, was not employed to help them. The Pilgrimage fell to pieces and ended in disunion. The revolts in Edward VI's reign, though led by minor country gentlemen, were chiefly social, those in the reigns of his sisters were feudal, and it was more than a century before the gentlemen and commons again united to oppose the King.

In Charles I's reign the whole face of the nation had changed, but the same forces were at work as those which had produced the Pilgrimage of Grace. Religion was no longer hampered by timidity and tradition. The new creed in which the puritans opposed the throne gave its whole strength to the union and support of its champions. Many of the men who opposed Charles I were lineal descendants of the Pilgrims. Philip and Brian Stapleton, the great-great-grandsons of Christopher Stapleton, both distinguished themselves in the cause of the Parliament. Richard Aske, the great-great-grandson of young Robert Aske, the nephew and namesake of the grand captain, was one of the lawyers who drew up the indictment of Charles I. The great Lord Fairfax was descended on his father's side from Sir Nicholas Fairfax, an enthusiastic Pilgrim, and on his mother's from young Robert Aske. Sir William Constable, who signed the death-warrant of Charles I, was the great-great-grandson of Sir Robert Constable. These are not mere genealogical freaks. The spirit which had defied Henry VIII overwhelmed Charles I.

Finally, in estimating the value of the Pilgrimage of Grace, its moral importance must be taken into account. The following judgment has been passed upon England in the reign of Henry VIII:—

"The nation purchased political salvation at the price of moral debasement; the individual was sacrificed on the altar of the State; and popular subservience proved the impossibility of saving a people from itself. Constitutional guarantees are worthless without the national will to maintain them; men lightly abandon what they lightly hold; and, in Henry's reign, the English spirit of independence burned low in its socket, and love of freedom grew cold. The indifference of his subjects to political issues tempted Henry along the path to tyranny."[1]

The Pilgrimage of Grace removes a part of this responsibility from the shoulders of the nation. It was a matter of the utmost moment to her future regeneration that, in an age of selfish cruelty and materialism, there were men who willingly died for justice and freedom, who still cherished the ideal of "England's ancient liberties," which were not less inspiring because they had never existed. If the flame of independence burned low, at least their hands were ready to pass on the torch, still unextinguished, and England is not yet last in the race.

[1] Pollard, op. cit. chap. xvi.

LIST OF WORKS CITED

[Those marked with an asterisk contain copies of original documents relating to the Pilgrimage of Grace or the Exeter Conspiracy]

*Acts of the Northern Convocation, ed. G. W. Kitchin (Surtees Society) (1907).
*Acts of the Privy Council, vol. II, ed. J. R. Dasent (1890).
*ANSTIS, J. The Order of the Garter (1724).
*The Antiquary (1880).
*Archaeologia, vol. XVI (1812).
Archaeologia Aeliana (new series), vols. III (1859), XVI (1894).
**Archaeological Journal*, vols. XIV (1856), XXV (1868).

BAILDON, W. P. Monastic Notes, vol. I (Yorkshire Archaeological Society Record Series) (1895).
*Ballads from MSS. vol. I, ed. F. J. Furnivall (Ballad Society) (1868).
*BAPST, E. Deux Gentilshommes Poètes de la Cour de Henry VIII (1891).
*BATES, C. Border Holds (1891).
BAX, E. B. The Peasants' War in Germany 1524-5 (1899).
*BECK, T. A. Annales Furnesienses (1844).
Beverley Town Documents, ed. A. F. Leach (Selden Society) (1900).
BERENS, L. H. The Digger Movement (1906).
Boldon Buke, ed. W. Greenwell (Surtees Society) (1852).
BOOTHROYD, S. History of Pontefract (1807).
BRAND, J. History of Newcastle-upon-Tyne (1789).
BRENAN, G. and STATHAM, E. P. The House of Howard (1907).
BREWER, J. S. The Reign of Henry VIII to the Death of Wolsey (1884).
*BURNET, G. History of the Reformation in England (1865).

Calendar of Inner Temple Records, ed. F. A. Inderwick (1896).
Calendar of Spanish State Papers, vol. V (2), ed. P. de Gayangos (1888).
Calendar of Venetian State Papers, vol. V, ed. R. Brown (1873).
Cambridge Modern History, vol. II, The Reformation (1903).
CAVENDISH, G. Life of Wolsey, ed. S. W. Singer (1827).
Chronicle of the Grey Friars of London (Camden Society) (1852).
*Collection of Letters of Princes, ed. L. Howard (1753).
*COOPER, C. H. Annals of Cambridge (1842-1908).
Correspondance Politique de MM. de Castillon et de Marillac, ed. J. Kaulek (1885).
*Correspondence of Edward 3rd Earl of Derby, ed. J. N. Toller (Chetham Society) (1890).

Cox, J. C. Churchwardens' Accounts (The Antiquary's Books) (1913).
*Cox, J. C. William Stapleton and the Pilgrimage of Grace, reprinted from the Transactions of the East Riding Antiquarian Society, vol. x (1902).
*CRANMER, T. Works, ed. J. E. Cox (Parker Society) (1844-6).
CUNNINGHAM, W. The Growth of English Industry and Commerce (1905).

*Depositions and Ecclesiastical Proceedings at York Castle (Surtees Society) (1861).
*Deputy Keeper's Reports on the Public Records, vols. III (1842), XLIV (1883).
Dicey, A. V. The Privy Council (1887).
Dictionary of National Biography.
Dixon, R. W. History of the Church of England (1878).
*Documents relating to the History of the Church of England, ed. H. Gee and W. J. Hardy (1896).
*DODD, C. (H. Tootell). Church History of England, ed. M. A. Tierney (1839-43).
*Domesday of Inclosures, ed. I. S. Leadam (Royal Historical Society) (1904).
DOWELL, S. History of Taxation in England (1888).
DRAKE, F. Eboracum (1736).
DUFF, E. GORDON. English Provincial Printers to 1557 (1912).
*Durham Account Rolls, ed. J. T. Fowler (Surtees Society) (1898-1901).

Early English Dramatists, Anonymous Plays, vol. II, ed. J. S. Farmer (Early English Drama Society) (1906).
*English Historical Review, vols. V (1890), XXVIII (1913).

FERGUSON, R. S. Westmorland (1894).
*FLOWER, W. Visitation of Yorkshire, ed. C. B. Norcliffe (Harleian Society) (1881).
*FONBLANQUE, E. B. DE. Annals of the House of Percy (1887).
*FOSTER, J. Durham Visitation Pedigrees (1887).
*FOSTER, J. Yorkshire Visitation Pedigrees (1874).
FOSTER, J. *Collectanea Genealogica*, vol. x (1881-5).
FOXE, J. Book of Martyrs, ed. J. Milner (1863).
*FROST, C. History of Hull (1827).
FROUDE, J. A. Essays on Literature and History (1906).
*FROUDE, J. A. History of England from the Fall of Wolsey to the Defeat of the Armada (1856-70).

GAIRDNER, J. Richard III (1878).
GAIRDNER, J. The English Church in the 16th Century from the Accession of Henry VIII to the Death of Mary (History of the English Church Series) (1902).
GAIRDNER, J. Lollardy and the Reformation (1908).
GASQUET, F. A. Henry VIII and the English Monasteries (1888).
GASQUET, F. A. The Eve of the Reformation (1900).
The Gentleman's Magazine (1754) (1835).
*GLOVER, R. Visitation of Yorkshire, ed. J. Foster (1875).
GOWER, LORD RONALD SUTHERLAND LEVESON. The Tower of London (1901-2).

HAILE, MARTIN. Life of Cardinal Pole (1910).
HALL, E. The Union of the Families of Lancaster and York (1809).
HALLAM, H. Constitutional History of England (1827).
Halmota Prioratus Dunelmensis, ed. J. Booth (Surtees Society) (1889).
*Hamilton Papers, ed. J. Bain (1890–2).
*HARDWICK, C. History of the Articles (1884).
HARLAND, J. The Monastery of Salley (1853).
HERBERT, LORD, OF CHERBURY. The Reign of Henry VIII (ed. 1672).
*Historical MSS. Commission Report VI (1878).
History (1913), (1914).
HOLDSWORTH, W. S. History of English Law (1903–9).
HOLINSHED, R. Chronicles (1807).
HOLME, WILFRED. The Fall and Evil Success of Rebellion (1572).
HOWARD, H., Earl of Northampton. A Defensative against the Poison of Supposed Prophecies (1583).
HUNTER, J. History of South Yorkshire (1828).

LANG, A. James VI and the Gowrie Mystery (1902).
LANG, A. History of Scotland (1900).
LAPSLEY, G. T. The County Palatine of Durham (Harvard Historical Series) (1900).
*LATIMER, H. Sermons and Remains, ed. G. E. Corrie (Parker Society) (1844–5).
*Letters and Papers of Henry VIII, vols. XI, XII (1) and (2), XIII (1) and (2), and others, ed. J. Gairdner (1888) (1890–1).
*Letters of the Kings of England, ed. J. O. Halliwell-Phillipps (1846).
*Letters of Royal and Illustrious Ladies, ed. M. A. Everett Wood (Green) (1846).
The Library (1913).
LODGE, S. Scrivelsby.
*LONGSTAFF, W. H. D. A Leaf from the Pilgrimage of Grace (1846).
*LONGSTAFF, W. H. D. History of Darlington (1854).

MAITLAND, F. W. English Law and the Renaissance (1901).
*MERRIMAN, R. B. Life and Letters of Thomas Cromwell (1902).
*MILNER, E. and BENHAM, E. Records of the House of Lumley (1904).
*Miscellaneous State Papers, ed. the Earl of Hardwicke (1778).
MORE, Sir T. Richard III (1883).
MORE, Sir T. Selections from his writings, ed. T. E. Bridget (1892).
MORRIS, J. The Troubles of our Catholic Forefathers (1872–7).
MORYSON, R. An Invective against Treason (1539).
MURRAY, J. A. H. Thomas of Ereildoun (Early English Text Society) (1875).

*NICOLSON, J. and BURN, R. History of Westmorland and Cumberland (1777).
North Country Wills, ed. J. W. Clay (Surtees Society) (1908).
**Notes and Queries*, 11th series, vols. IV (1911), VIII (1913).
*NOTT, G. F. Lives of the Earl of Surrey and Sir Thomas Wyatt with their works (1815–16).

ORD, J. W. History of Cleveland (1846).
*Original Letters illustrative of English History, ed. Sir H. Ellis (1825–46).

PARK, G. R.   Parliamentary Representation of Yorkshire (1886).
PLANTAGENET-HARRISON, G. H.   History of Yorkshire (1879).
*Plumpton Correspondence (Camden Society) (1839).
*POLLARD, A. F.   The Reign of Henry VII from Contemporary Sources (1914).
POLLARD, A. F.   Henry VIII (1905).
POLLOCK, Sir F.   The Land Laws (English Citizen Series) (1883).
PORRITT, E. P. and A. G.   The Unreformed House of Commons (1903).
POWELL, E.   The Rising in East Anglia in 1381 (1896).
*Proceedings and Ordinances of the Privy Council, ed. Sir N. H. Nicolas (Record Commission) (1834–7).

*RAINE, J.   Memorials of Hexham Priory (Surtees Society) (1864–5).
Return of the Names of all Members of Parliament 1213–1874 (Blue Book).
*Richmondshire Wills, ed. J. Raine (Surtees Society) (1853).
Rites and Monuments of Durham, ed. J. T. Fowler (Surtees Society) (1903).
ROSE-TROUP, F.   The Western Rebellion of 1549 (1913).
ROUND, J. H.   Peerage Studies (1901).
Royal Historical Society's Transactions, vol. XVIII (1904).
*RUSSELL, F. W.   Ket's Rebellion (1859).

SANDERS, N.   De Origine ac Progressu Schismatis Anglicani (1585).
SCOTT, J.   Berwick-upon-Tweed (1888).
SEEBOHM, F.   The Oxford Reformers (1867).
Select Cases in the Court of Chancery, ed. W. P. Baildon (Selden Society) (1896).
*Select Cases in the Court of Star Chamber, ed. I. S. Leadam (Selden Society) (1903).
SHARP, Sir C.   Memorials of the Rebellion of 1569 (1841).
Spanish Chronicle of King Henry VIII, ed. M. A. S. Hume (1889).
SPEED, J.   Theatre of the Empire of Great Britaine (1611).
*SPEED, J.   History of Great Britaine (1632).
Star Chamber Cases, Index (Index Society) (1901).
*State Papers during the Reign of Henry VIII, vol. I, Domestic (Record Commission) (1830).
*Statutes and Constitutional Documents 1559–1625, ed. G. W. Prothero (1898).
Statutes of the Realm (1810–28).
*STEVENS, J.   History of antient abbeys, monasteries, hospitals, cathedrals, and collegiate churches, being two additional volumes to Dugdale's Monasticon (1722–3).
STOW, J.   Chronicle (1615).
*STRYPE, J.   Ecclesiastical Memorials (1822).
STUBBS, W.   Constitutional History of England (1883).
*SURTEES, R.   History of Durham (1816).
SWALLOW, H. J.   De Nova Villa (1885).

TAWNEY, R. H.   The Agrarian Problem in the Sixteenth Century (1912).
*Testamenta Eboracensia, ed. J. Raine (Surtees Society) (1836).
THOMAS, W.   The Pilgrim, ed. J. A. Froude (1861).
*TONGE, T.   Visitation of Yorkshire in 1530, ed. J. Raine (Surtees Society) (1863).

*_Transactions of the East Riding Antiquarian Society_, vols. VI (1898), X (1902).
TREVELYAN, G. M.   England in the Age of Wycliffe (1904).
*TURNER, J. H.   Yorkshire Anthology (1901).

USHER, R. G.   The Rise and Fall of the High Commission (1913).

Valor Ecclesiasticus (Record Commission) (1810–34).
Victoria County History of Cumberland, vols. I and II (1901–5).
Victoria County History of Durham, vols. I and II (1905–7).
*Visitation Articles and Injunctions, ed. W. H. Frere and W. M. Kennedy (Alcuin Society) (1910).
*Visitation of Lincolnshire, ed. A. R. Maddison (Harleian Society) (1902–6).

WEIR, G.   Historical Sketches of Horncastle (1820).
West Riding Sessions Rolls and Proceedings of the Council of the North, ed. J. Lister (Yorkshire Archaeological Society's Record Series) (1888).
WHITAKER, T. D.   History of Richmondshire (1823).
WHITAKER, T. D.   Whalley and the Honour of Clitheroe (1818).
*WILKINS, D.   Concilia Magnae Britanniae et Hiberniae (1737).
*WILSON, J.   The Monasteries of Cumberland and Westmorland (1899).
WRIGHT, T.   History of Halifax (1834).
*WRIGHT, T.   Three Chapters of Letters on the Suppression of the Monasteries (Camden Society) (1834).
WRIOTHESLEY, C.   Chronicle (Camden Society) (1875–7).

*York City Records in MSS.
*_Yorkshire Archaeological and Topographical Journal_, vols. II (1873), VIII (1884), XI (1891), XIII (1895), XXI (1911).
*Yorkshire Star Chamber Proceedings, ed. W. Brown (Yorkshire Archaeological Society's Record Series) (1909–11).

INDEX

Aberdeen II, 253
Aberdeen, the Bishop of. *See* Stewart, William
Abergavenny, George Neville, Lord I, 14, 15; II, 298
Acclom, John I, 186
Acclom (Aclom), William I, 186, 278–9, 312, 345; II, 38, 218–9
Acklam II, 66, 131
Acomb I, 231
Adderstone I, 199
Addison, Dr II, 259
Admiral, the Lord. *See* Fitzwilliam, Sir William
Aglabe, Dr II, 193
Aglionby, Edward II, 9, 42, 122
Ainstey of York I, 168, 174–5, 181, 262
Aire, the river I, 234, 282, 300
Aldham, the parson of II, 185
Alford I, 100
Allerton, — I, 345
Alne Abbey, Flanders II, 285
Alnmouth II, 254
Alnwick I, 198, 199, 200, 201; II, 28, 41, 42
  Castle I, 198, 199
  the Abbot of I, 198
Amarton (Hamerton?), Harry II, 43
Ambrogio (Ambrosius de Recalcatis), papal secretary I, 336
America I, 2
Amersham I, 244
Ampthill I, 117, 118, 119, 123, 241–7, 324, 330; II, 267
Anabaptists, the I, 346
Ancaster I, 109, 111, 114, 119, 129; II, 155
Ancrum Moor I, 211–2
Angoulême, the Duke of. *See* Orleans, the Duke of
Annan, the Earl of I, 211
Annates. *See* First Fruits
Anne, St I, 43
Anthony, a canon of Watton II, 59
Antwerp I, 336
Appleby II, 28, 120
  a friar of II, 266
Appleby, Alexander I, 299
Applegarth, Thomas I, 58
Appointment at Doncaster, the First. *See* Truce of Doncaster

Appointment at Doncaster, the Second. *See* Pilgrimage of Grace, the Second Appointment at Doncaster
Arbroath, the Abbot of. *See* Beaton, David
Army, the Royal
  character of the forces I, 123; II, 55, 170
  disaffection in I, 184, 219, 233, 264, 265, 269, 302–3, 326, 327, 329, 330; II, 36
  disbands I, 270, 327
  discipline I, 305
  its condition at Doncaster I, 257, 260, 268
  finances I, 184, 206, 244, 245, 246–7, 248, 251, 279, 294, 296, 320, 330, 331; II, 8
  at Flodden I, 272
  in Lincs. I, 122–3, 128–30, 168, 281–2, 299, 319; II, 8, 11, 24
  musters I, 108, 113, 119, 132–3, 134, 140, 148, 241–2, 243, 244–5, 247, 273, 326; II, 7–8, 52–3, 170, 289
  numbers I, 257
  ordnance I, 119, 122, 128, 129, 130, 134, 135, 136, 241, 247, 250, 259, 324, 327; II, 11, 24, 26, 48
  in touch with the Pilgrims I, 251, 255–6
  spies from I, 119, 287, 289, 324; II, 8
  uniform. *See* Badge, St George's Cross
  its weakness I, 122, 249, 250, 253, 254, 257, 278, 279
  its position during the rebels' advance on York I, 174
  advance to Yorkshire I, 244–50
  reference I, 153, 166
Arras, Yorks. II, 48
Array, Statute of I, 65; II, 243
Arthur, Prince, son of Henry VII I, 14
Articles of the rebels. *See* Demands of the rebels
Articles of Religion, the Ten I, 9, 10, 266, 324, 343, 352, 353, 374, 379, 380, 388; II, 9, 164, 166
Arundel, Sir John II, 141
Asheton, Thomas I, 344
Ashton (Esch), Robert I, 151, 153, 163; II, 266
Aske, Yorks. I, 36, 39, 49; II, 180

Index 341

Aske, family of I, 49, 80; II, 92
Aske, Christopher I, 49, 51–54, 61, 72, 141, 144, 145, 150, 208, 209, 210, 295, 312, 313, 316; II, 131
Aske, Eleanor, wife of John I, 51
Aske, Elizabeth, wife of Sir John I, 40, 49
Aske, Elizabeth, wife of Sir Robert I, 49
Aske, Sir John I, 40, 49
Aske, John I, 49, 50, 51, 54, 72, 105, 141, 144, 145, 149, 150, 151; II, 136, 137, 210, 224
Aske, Richard, of Aughton I, 49
Aske, Richard, brother of Robert I, 61
Aske, Richard II, 333
Aske, Sir Robert II, 49–51, 54, 61
Aske, Robert
  his account of the Pilgrimage of Grace I, 191; II, 18, 19, 37, 50
  his appearance I, 55; II, 3, 322
  announces the second appointment at Doncaster to the Pilgrims II, 16–17, 19, 20, 54
  his arrest II, 38, 133, 207
  his articles. *See* Demands of the rebels
  his authority I, 149, 185–6, 227, 262; II, 53, 322
  and Sir Francis Bigod II, 57, 72–4, 89, 98, 102, 119, 131, 205
  his character I, 54; II, 331
  and his brother Christopher I, 210–1, 312–3
  his questions for the clergy I, 342–3, 348, 352–3, 359–60, 362, 377–8, 382, 386–7
  his council I, 158, 181
  his criticism of the Government I, 351, 364–6. *See also* Cromwell, Thos, and Robt Aske
  and Lord Darcy I, 168, 170, 186–7, 189, 291, 301, 312, 327; II, 32–3, 48, 50, 53–4, 128, 188–9, 209, 223, 360
  and the Earl of Derby I, 214–5, 227–8
  and the first conference at Doncaster I, 252–4, 258–9, 265
  at the second conference at Doncaster II, 13, 16–9
  his part in the East Riding insurrection I, 141–2, 145–6, 148–9, 155–7
  his examinations I, 387; II, 134, 207–8, 223
  excepted from the first Yorkshire pardon I, 273; II, 126
  his execution I, 267; II, 194, 208, 220, 222–5, 264, 287
  evidence against II, 92–3, 208–10, 225
  his family and relatives I, 40, 49–55, 80, 141, 218, 289, 305–6; II, 222, 333

Aske, Robert
  and the Pilgrims' finances I, 286; II, 209
  hostages demanded for him I, 317; II, 3–4, 11–2, 23
  and the siege of Hull I, 159–60, 164
  garrisons Hull I, 285, 286
  his imprisonment II, 207–8, 216
  attempts to kidnap him I, 142, 168, 170, 204, 267, 289, 291, 292, 294–8, 301, 304, 309, 311
  interview with Lancaster Herald I, 228–30, 240; II, 300–1
  lays down his office II, 17, 86, 98
  and Archbishop Lee. *See* Lee, Archbishop, and Robert Aske
  letters attributed to him I, 145–6, 289; II, 34, 208
  and the Lincs. Articles I, 156, 174
  in the Lincs. Rebellion I, 105–7, 139, 141, 142, 143, 289; II, 209
  and the messengers to the King I, 291, 308–9
  his moderation I, 257, 258, 315
  and the monasteries I, 51, 233, 251, 285, 286, 287, 317, 348–9; II, 20, 38, 39, 58, 83, 84, 209
  and the Duke of Norfolk I, 267, 289–91, 312; II, 102, 104, 130, 131, 138, 147, 208, 209, 211, 220, 224–5
  and the Earl of Northumberland I, 288–5; II, 188
  pacifies the north II, 48, 49, 50, 51, 104
  his papers II, 38, 210, 211
  his pardon II, 32, 209, 224
  his petitions II, 207, 208, 222–3
  calls the rebellion the Pilgrimage of Grace I, 157
  composes the Pilgrims' oath. *See* Oath of the Pilgrimage of Grace
  his company of pilgrims I, 262
  at the musters at Pontefract I, 233, 237, 238–9
  and the surrender of Pontefract I, 181, 185–91, 302; II, 127
  at the council at Pontefract I, 344–6, 353, 361, 384, 385, 387; II, 10, 12
  his proclamations. *See* Proclamations, Rebel
  promises of help from Lincs. II, 151, 223
  promises of help from the West Marches I, 304
  his property and early career I, 54–5; II, 222
  his protection of Bigod's followers II, 78, 81, 89–92, 98, 131, 209
  his protection to loyalists I, 282, 284, 278, 283, 306
  his reception at court II, 32–3, 36–8, 45, 50, 217, 241
  reports of his agents I, 256, 257; II, 151

Aske, Robert
  and the rumours of new laws I, 78
  correspondence with southern sympathisers I, 327-8, 332, 333; II, 228
  his reported secession to the King II, 3, 4, 45, 79, 89, 95
  his servants I, 50; II, 32, 78, 210, 222
  and William Stapleton I, 58, 157-9, 167, 235
  his trial II, 135, 136, 140, 198, 206, 211
  announces the truce I, 211, 220, 269, 279, 288
  and the alleged breaches of the truce I, 292, 293, 314
  and the muster at Wighton Hill I, 154, 157
  his headquarters at Wressell Castle I, 285, 288, 293; II, 210
  and the council at York I, 293, 312, 318
  the taking of York I, 158, 160, 163, 174-5, 176, 178, 180
  reference I, 36, 48, 61, 72, 79, 110, 168, 190, 216, 226, 230, 236, 255, 264, 271, 310, 311, 347, 357; II, 105
Aske, Robert, the younger I, 51, 105, 148-9, 235; II, 333
Aske, Roger I, 36, 89; II, 180
Askew, Anne II, 180
Askew, Christopher I, 111, 116, 234, 244
Askew, Sir Christopher I, 112-3, 116, 124
Askew Robert I, 106
Askew, Sir William I, 97-100, 110, 126; II, 180
Aslaby, James I, 163, 203
Atkinson, James I, 140
Atkinson, John I, 71, 213, 216, 217, 218; II, 113, 144
Attainder, Acts of I, 318; II, 153, 323-5
Auckland. See Bishop Auckland
Audley, Sir Thomas, Lord Chancellor I, 26, 352, 353, 357, 358, 366-7; II, 14, 186, 225, 258
Aughton I, 40, 49, 51, 141, 142, 144, 150; II, 32, 39, 50, 84, 91, 210
—— Church I, 49, 54, 61
—— manor-house I, 49, 55
Augustine, St II, 57
Axholme, the Isle of I, 100, 148-9, 282
Aylesbury II, 165
Aylesham II, 177
Ayrey, John I, 345
Ayton I, 84

Babthorpe, William I, 144, 145, 148, 150, 186, 238, 308, 309, 312, 314, 316, 342, 345, 346, 357; II, 92, 104, 201, 229, 258, 260, 271-2
Bachelor, Mr I, 388
Badge
  of Sir Robert Constable I, 240

Badge
  of the Five Wounds of Christ I, 19, 238-9, 240, 255, 261, 274; II, 17, 190, 324
  St George's Cross I, 175, 245, 256; II, 77
  of the Howards I, 245; II, 252
  of I.H.S. I, 255
  of the Princess Mary II, 323
  of the northern families I, 83
  of the Percys I, 84, 232; II, 252
  of the Poles I, 23; II, 323
  Tudor I, 84-5
Bainton II, 72-4
Baker, John, attorney-general II, 200, 211
Bale, John I, 43, 324; II, 166
Balliol, family of I, 86
Balderstone, William I, 101
Bamborough I, 199; II, 41
Banister, Simon I, 47
Bankes, Robert I, 306
Banner
  the church cross used as I, 156, 175, 221, 236, 330; II, 114, 147
  of Sir Robert Constable I, 336
  of the Cornish rebels II, 171, 181
  of St Cuthbert I, 205, 238, 261
  of the Five Wounds of Christ I, 139, 238, 261, 344; II, 300
  the King's I, 119, 122; II, 119, 121, 122
  of the Lincs. rebels I, 106, 114, 124, 129, 130, 139; II, 154
Bapst, M. 'Deux Gentilshommes Poètes de la Cour de Henry VIII' I, 272
Bardney Abbey I, 104, 114; II, 152, 153, 154
Bardon I, 211
Barker, William I, 155, 160; II, 62
Barlings Abbey I, 104, 107, 128; II, 138, 152, 153-5
Barlings, Abbot of. See Mackerell, Matthew
Barlings Grange I, 107
Barlow, William, Bishop of St David's I, 67, 353. See also Demands of the rebels
Barnard Castle I, 36, 190, 202, 207, 237, 239; II, 28, 34, 44, 110, 117, 128
Barnes, Robert I, 68, 324, 346, 353
Barnesdale I, 208, 252
Barnfield, John II, 116
Barnsley I, 208
Barton-on-Humber I, 78, 104, 105, 282, 289, 301, 319
Barton, the bailiff of I, 130
Barton, —— I, 345
Bashall in Bolland I, 210; II, 211
Bateman, Harry I, 345
Bath I, 326
Bawne, George I, 157
Baynton, Mary I, 87

Baynton, Thomas I, 87
Bax, E. B. 'The Peasants' War' I, 78, 139–40, 225
Beacons I, 104, 128, 143, 145, 148, 151, 153, 300, 318; II, 66, 96, 106, 175
Beaconsfield I, 247
Beamish I, 33
Beaton, David, Privy Seal of Scotland, Abbot of Arbroath II, 242, 267, 268
Beauchamp, Viscount II, 198, 206
Beck, John I, 221
Becket, Thomas a I, 64; II, 169
Beckwith, Leonard I, 154, 234, 243, 278; II, 38, 80, 133, 138, 139, 218, 219
Beckwith, Mrs I, 234-5, 279
Bedall I, 202
Bede, St I, 83, 84, 86
Beetham II, 106, 113
Belchford I, 101, 124
Belchford, the vicar of. *See* Leache, Nicholas
Bell, John II, 47
Bellasis, Richard II, 272
Bellay, John du, Cardinal I, 333, 334
Bellingham, II, 234
Bellingham, Sir Robert I, 50, 218
Bellingham, Margaret, wife of Sir Robert I, 50, 218
Bellowe, John I, 95, 112, 126, 135, 165
Benefit of Clergy, Act limiting I, 8, 355
Benham II, 175
Bentham Moor I, 218
Berlichingen, Gotz von I, 140
Berwick upon Tweed I, 35, 174, 187, 190, 192, 200, 201, 223, 225, 239, 286; II, 9, 28, 34, 94, 104, 106, 228, 230, 231-3, 245, 246, 248, 250, 254, 255, 261, 267
—— the mayor of II, 248
Berwick pursuivant. *See* Ray, Henry
Berwick, Thomas I, 221
Beswick, the parish clerk of. *See* Marshall, Dr
Beverley
and the Archbishop of York I, 48, 143, 150
Bigod's appointed meeting-place II, 61-3, 67, 80, 97
Bigod at II, 74-6, 78, 90
the Grey Friars I, 57, 146, 147
rivalry with Hull I, 159, 161, 282
communications with the Lincs. rebels I, 104, 115, 130, 145; II, 156
its liberties I, 61, 355; II, 61
meeting at, after the Pilgrimage II, 48-51, 54, 59
the Minster I, 45
outbreak of the rebellion at I, 58, 115, 144-8, 151-60, 168, 201, 208
pardon proclaimed at II, 27
parliamentary representation of I, 359, 388

Beverley
printing press at I, 252
sedition at I, 78, 88, 144; II, 49, 51, 52, 56, 62
the Tabard inn I, 145
the town hall I, 145
the town seal I, 115, 146, 152
West Wood Green I, 145, 146, 147, 151, 152, 160; II, 90
reference I, 57, 79, 150, 164, 192, 235, 270, 273, 288, 298, 314; II, 60, 72, 82, 87, 98, 102, 126, 194, 198, 266
Bewley, Richard I, 222
Biggis, James II, 178
Bigod, family of I, 40
Bigod, Agnes, wife of Sir Ralph I, 40
Bigod, Dorothy I, 41
Bigod, Elizabeth, wife of Sir John I, 40
Bigod, Sir Francis
his arrest II, 106, 110, 133, 136
his book on the King's supremacy I, 347; II, 57, 58, 60, 75, 211
his chaplain. *See* Pickering, John, priest
his character and opinions I, 22, 43-44; II, 56, 71-2, 199
his confession II, 196-9
early life and family I, 40-41; II, 136, 185, 199
his execution II, 216
his flight II, 75-7, 80, 87, 88, 90
and John Hallam II, 57, 60-3, 65, 67, 72, 75, 213
his insurrection II, chap. xvii, pp. 55-98, 101, 104, 114, 126, 131, 132, 158, 187, 188, 198, 199, 201-3, 205, 211-3
and the monasteries I, 42-3; II, 56, 58, 59, 60, 211
his papers II, 75, 205
his share in the Pilgrimage of Grace I, 205-6; II, 56-7
a prisoner II, 114, 118-9, 121, 198
his speech to the rebels II, 67-9
his trial II, 135, 136, 197-9
reference I, 214; II, 97, 111
Bigod, Joan, wife of Sir John I, 40
Bigod, Sir John, the elder I, 40
Bigod, Sir John, the younger I, 40
Bigod, Katherine, wife of Sir Francis I, 41-2; II, 87, 199
Bigod, Margaret, wife of Sir Ralph I, 40
Bigod, Sir Ralph I, 38, 40, 40
Bigod, Ralph I, 40; II, 57, 59, 199
Bigod, Ralph, son of Sir Francis II, 185
Bilborough I, 180, 231
Bilsby, Sir Andrew I, 100
Bilsdale II, 97
Bird, John I, 86
Bishop Auckland I, 203, 204, 205, 206; II, 44, 66, 268
Bishop Burton I, 159
Bishopdale I, 210
Blackborne, Thomas I, 53

Blackborne, William, vicar of Skipton I, 53, 210
Blackburn, the proctor of II, 169
Blackburn, the vicar of. *See* Lynney, Randolph
Black Death, the I, 369; II, 173
Black Fast II, 301
Black Lands, the I, 196, 223; II, 120
Blackheath, the battle of I, 45
Blackley I, 56
Blackmoor I, 41; II, 96
Blades, John of II, 110
Blaunde, Christopher I, 288
Blenkhow, Richard I, 223
Blenkinsop, — II, 159, 180
Blenkinsop, Christopher I, 221
Bletsoe I, 34
Blyth Priory II, 89
Blythe I, 234
Blythe Law I, 233
Blytheman, William I, 183, 184, 206, 207; II, 134–5, 138, 139, 257
Bockmore II, 294, 304, 311
Boleyn, Anne I, 1, 5, 7, 10, 16, 25, 26, 31, 56, 67, 69, 72, 76, 81, 82, 108, 149, 271; II, 15, 181
Bolingbroke I, 89, 91, 92, 96, 101
Bolton I, 40, 201
Bolton Castle II, 79, 102, 108, 214
Bolton Priory I, 210
Bonaventure. *See* Johnson, Thomas
Bonner, Edmund I, 367
Bontane, Constance II, 324
Booth, Mr I, 97
Borders, the, between England and Scotland
 their characteristics I, 29, 35, 89, 198; II, 269
 jurisdiction of the Council of the North on II, 272
 exempted from the Statute of Handguns I, 364
 fortresses I, 190; II, 228, 235, 238, 248, 250
 the King's plan for their government II, 227–9, 234 236, 237, 240, 250, 270–1
 Council of the Marches II, 228, 232–3, 237, 238, 261
 the East Marches II, 227–9, 236, 238, 239, 248, 251, 261
 law of the Marches II, 235
 the Middle Marches II, 41, 228–9, 232, 234, 236, 238, 239, 251, 261, 268
 March treason II, 234, 276
 the West Marches II, 224, 228, 229, 236, 239, 245, 248, 251, 263, 268
 officers and pensioners I, 18–9, 80–2, 198–9, 284, 285; II, 79, 103, 227–8, 229, 230–1, 232, 233–4, 235–6, 238–9, 240, 248, 260–1, 263–4, 268–9
 influence of the Percys on I, 32; II, 227

Borders
 the Pilgrims ready to defend I, 199, 221, 253, 304–5
 raids I, 29, 31, 33, 190, 192–3; II, 228, 248, 261, 263
 expected war with Scotland. *See* Scotland, expected war with England
 reference I, 19, 45, 190, 272; II, 246, 252. *See also* Norfolk, the Duke of, and the Borders
Borough II, 66, 67, 72
Borough, Thomas, Lord I, 93, 97, 98, 99, 100, 101, 103, 106, 108, 110, 112, 182, 319; II, 193, 196
Borough-under-Stainmore I, 220
 the vicar of. *See* Thompson, Robert
Borrodale, Gawen II, 138
Boston I, 87, 111, 121
Bowes, family of I, 36
Bowes, Alice, wife of Robert I, 36
Bowes, Elizabeth, wife of Richard I, 36; II, 180
Bowes, George I, 202
Bowes, Margaret, wife of Sir Ralph I, 36
Bowes, Sir Ralph I, 36
Bowes, Richard I, 36, 39, 202, 345; II, 180
Bowes, Robert
 King's attorney II, 119
 his character I, 37; II, 289, 260
 the commons attack him II, 61
 his company of Pilgrims I, 202–5, 237, 239, 252, 255, 261, 262
 at the first conference at Doncaster I, 259, 262, 263, 265
 and the second conference at Doncaster II, 12, 21
 at the council at Pontefract I, 345, 346
 at the council at York I, 312, 313, 316, 318
 his influence in Durham II, 239
 his mission to the King I, 267, 270, 274, 278–80, 289, 290, 292, 293, 296, 297, 298, 308, 311–3, 320, 326, 330, 331, 333, 339; II, 1, 31, 119, 194
 on the Council of the North I, 37; II, 271, 272, 274
 on the Duke of Norfolk's council II, 229
 pacifies the North Riding II, 94
 his servant I, 377
 and the spiritual articles I, 342, 378
 and the suppression of the monasteries II, 21
 his feud with Tunstall II, 268
 reference I, 36, 55, 231, 238; II, 95, 130, 135, 139
Bowgham, George I, 90
Bowyer (Bowier), Richard I, 174, 175, 176, 344, 346, 353, 378, 382; II, 130, 219

Boynton, Matthew II, 75, 76, 88, 98, 212
Brabson, — I, 368
Brackenbury, Anthony I, 253
Bradford II, 28
Bradford, Brian I, 310
Bradford, Edward I, 200
Bradforde, —, monk of Sawley II, 83, 266
Brancepeth I, 204, 207; II, 66, 78
Brandling, Robert, mayor of Newcastle-upon-Tyne I, 206, 207
Brandon Bridge II, 175
—— Ferry II, 175
Brandsburton, the bailiff of II, 62
Brandsby, Dr John I, 377, 378, 382, 383
Brantingham I 154
Brasse, Henry II, 134
Bray, Lord II, 193
Brayton, the vicar of. *See* Maunsell, Thomas
Breamore Priory I, 380
Brenan and Statham, 'The History of the House of Howard' I, 61
Breyar, William I, 78, 145, 150, 207
Brian, Sir Francis I, 55, 122, 123, 135, 136, 246, 289, 293, 305, 319, 320, 358; II, 3, 6, 7, 8, 53, 256, 281, 282, 285
Bricket, — II, 30
Bridewell I, 303
Bridgewater I, 87
Bridlington I, 87, 281; II, 211, 255
Bridlington Priory I, 233, 280; II, 69, 121, 138, 139, 212, 252
—— the shrine of St John II, 139
Bridlington, the Prior of. *See* Wood, William
Brigg, Mabel II, 301
Brigham, — II, 133
Brighton II, 167
Bristol I, 65, 80
 Christchurch II, 167
 the Grey Friars II, 167
 the Friars Preachers II, 167
Broadfield Moor II, 116
Brocke, Edmund I, 70
Broderton, Richard II, 84
Brodly, Nicholas I, 61
Bromley II, 208
Bromsgrove, I, 328
Brougham Castle II, 113
Broughton I, 67; II, 44
Brown, — I, 156, 345
Browne, Sir Anthony I, 136, 247, 248, 289, 319, 327, 344, 377; II, 3, 8, 10, 103, 229-34, 237
Browne, George, Bishop of Dublin I, 98, 353
Browne, Humphry II, 200
Browne, John I, 95
Browne, Robert I, 95, 126
Browne, Walter, curate of Kendal II, 41
Bruchsal I, 370

Brussels I, 385; II, 224
Bucer (Bucerus), Martin I, 346
Buckenham Priory II, 173
Buckingham town I, 246
Buckingham county I, 69, 264; II, 165, 294
Buckingham, Henry Stafford, second Duke of I, 15
Buckingham, Edward Stafford, third Duke of I, 14, 15, 18, 37-8, 39, 332; II, 79, 186
Bug, — I, 109
Bulmer, family of I, 37-8, 40, 287
Bulmer, Anne, wife of Sir John I, 38-40
Bulmer, Anne, wife of Ralph I, 38
Bulmer, Anne, wife of Sir Ralph I, 39; II, 180
Bulmer, Elizabeth, wife of Sir William the younger I, 39-40; II, 200, 202
Bulmer, John of Pinchinthorpe I, 39, 61
Bulmer, Sir John
 his arrest II, 133, 163
 at the first conference at Doncaster I, 265
 his connection with Bigod's rising II, 76
 his confession II, 201-2
 his correspondence II, 52, 96, 160, 180, 183, 200-1
 his early life I, 37, 38, 39, 40
 evidence against II, 200-1, 213
 his execution II, 214-5
 his household goods II, 252
 and Guisborough Priory I, 317; II, 40, 57
 his imprisonment II, 182-3, 200
 his suspicion of the King II, 95-6, 158-9
 summoned to London II, 158-9, 161-3, 164, 185
 his preparations for a new rising II, 96-7, 159-62, 184-5, 201
 his trial II, 135-6, 197-8, 200-2, 204
 reference I, 237; II, 75, 88, 95
Bulmer, Margaret, wife of Sir John I, 39, 61; II, 76, 97, 135, 158-9, 161-3, 182, 198, 200-2, 204, 206, 215-6
Bulmer, Margery I, 37
Bulmer, Ralph I, 38, 345; II, 76, 95, 135, 158-60, 198, 200-2
Bulmer, Sir Ralph I, 37, 38, 39, 205, 345, 346; II, 110, 180
Bulmer, Robert II, 47
Bulmer, Sir William, the elder I, 37-8
Bulmer, Sir William, the younger I, 37-40, 237, 345; II, 95, 96, 97, 163, 200, 202
Bungay II, 176
Buntingford II, 207
Burbeck, Thomas I, 221
Burford (Brunfelde) Oak I, 223, 224
Burgh, Leonard I, 203

Burn I, 248
Burnley I, 219
Burnsall in Craven II, 43
Burscough Priory I, 316
Burton-upon-Stather I, 142, 145
Burton-on-Trent I, 282, 294, 299
Burwell, Richard I, 131
Bushell, James I, 217
Bushop, Richard II, 176, 177
Butley, the Prior of II, 166
Butts, Dr II, 89
Byland Abbey I, 233; II, 60, 97

Cadiz I, 19
Caistor I, 96-9, 113, 116, 124, 135, 347; II, 149, 154
Caistor Hill I, 96, 97
Calais I, 72, 335; II, 19, 245, 282, 284, 299
Caldbeck I, 222
Calkhill, I, 152; II, 61
Cambrai II, 281, 282, 285
Cambridge I, 63, 241, 242, 244-5, 246, 247, 249, 260, 266
　All Hallows II, 168
　university II, 168
Cambridge county II, 164
Canell, Robert II, 165
Cante, Andrew II, 63, 110
Canterbury I, 64, 65, 326; II, 219
Canterbury, the Archbishop of
　general reference I, 348; II, 57
　See Cranmer, Thomas, Archbishop of Canterbury
Captain Cobbler (Nicholas Melton) I, 92-96, 116, 133, 138, 140; II, 149, 150, 155
Captain Poverty I, 199, 220, 221, 226; II, 113
Carleton I, 211
Carew, Elizabeth, wife of Sir Nicholas II, 321
Carew, Sir Nicholas II, 319-21, 324
Carlisle I, 27, 35, 190, 208, 211, 223, 224, 225, 239, 305, 312, 382; II, 6, 8, 9, 28, 42, 44, 111, 113-20, 122, 123, 126, 138, 142, 219, 226, 245, 246, 248, 250, 263, 276
　the Captain of. See Cumberland, the Earl of, and Wentworth, Sir Thomas
　the Bishop of. See Kite, John
　Castle I, 223; II, 42, 110, 114, 116, 117, 138, 246, 249
　the mayor of I, 224; II, 42
　Priory I, 222; II, 263
Carlisle Herald I, 270
Carlton I, 124
Carnaby, family of I, 195, 199, 285, 299; II, 41, 231-2, 238
Carnaby, Sir Reynold I, 31-3, 193-4, 195, 199, 200; II, 9, 124, 203, 231-2, 239, 261, 263, 269, 275
Carnaby, Thomas I, 197; II, 263
Carnaby, William I, 194-7

Carpyssacke, — II, 171
Carr, family of II, 228, 231
Carr, Ralph I, 59
Carr, Mrs, wife of Ralph I, 59-60
Carre, Robert I, 113, 127, 181-2; II 153
Carter, Thomas, abbot of Holm Cultram I, 222-5, 312; II, 116, 122-3, 138
Carthusians
　of London I, 23, 62, 63, 75, 80, 189, 271; II, 137, 193
　of Hull I, 62, 163, 164; II, 137
Cartlogan Thorns I, 222
Cartmell Priory II, 20, 39, 142, 144
—— the Prior of I, 218; II, 21, 148
Castelforth, Robert II, 89
Castillon, Louis de Perreau, Sieur de, French ambassador II, 241, 277, 310, 319
Catherell, — II, 61
Catherick, — I, 211
Catton II, 273
Cavendish, John I, 299
Cawood I, 143, 150, 151, 170, 380
Cawood, Gervase I, 48, 148, 181
Caxton II, 168
Cervington, — II, 199
Chalcedon, the Bishop of. See Mackerell, Matthew, abbot of Barlings
Chaloner (Challoner), Robert I, 238, 262, 312, 345, 346, 353, 357, 383; II, 189, 258, 260, 271, 272
Chamber, Dr I, 244
Chamley. See Cholmley
Chancellor of the Augmentations. See Riche, Richard
Chancery I, 45, 273, 360, 366-7; II, 29-30, 68, 192
Chapuys, Eustace, Imperial ambassador in England I, 8, 22-3, 24-8, 55, 117, 144, 310, 325, 330-3, 335-6, 338; II, 25, 191, 205, 223-4, 305, 313, 319-21, 325-6
Chapuys, Eustace, nephew of the Imperial ambassador I, 138, 336
Charles I of England II, 55, 333, 334
Charles V, the Emperor I, 2, 11, 16, 17, 18, 24, 83, 87, 117, 134, 287, 310, 325, 333-4, 336, 340, 356-7; II, 25, 176, 243, 245, 247, 281, 282, 298-9, 308, 320, 326, 331
Charleton, family of II, 228, 275
Charleton, Cuthbert I, 195; II 41, 230-3, 261-3, 275
Charleton, Edward I, 195; II, 41, 230-3, 261, 262, 263, 275
Charleton, Gerrard, of Wark II, 238
Charleton, Gerry, of the Bourne II, 238, 261
Charleton, Gilbert II, 238
Charleton, John II, 234, 246, 261
Charleton, Rinian II, 234, 238, 246, 261
Charleton, Thomas II, 238
Cheshire I, 213, 215, 219, 282, 294, 314, 382; II, 7, 52, 141
Chester Castle I, 214

Index 347

Chester Herald I, 270
Chester-le-Street II, 244
Cheyne, Margaret. *See* Bulmer, Margaret
Cheyne, William I, 39
Chichester I, 70; II, 308, 326
Chichester, the Bishop of. *See* Sampson, Richard
Chichester Cathedral, the Chancellor of. *See* Croftes, George
Chideock I, 80
Chillingham Castle I, 199–201, 225, 239
Chipchase I, 195–7; II, 41, 230, 233, 261–3
Cholmley, — I, 281
Cholmley (Chamley), Sir Roger II, 136, 184
Chorley I, 319
Church of Rome I, 6, 9, 15, 16, 25, 28, 44, 48, 55, 60, 64, 70, 81, 82, 114, 178, 218, 225–6, 229, 263, 294, 337, 341–3, 347–8, 352–3, 355, 360, 370, 383–7; II, 57, 179, 287, 330–3
Cifuentes, Fernando de Silva, Count of, Imperial ambassador at Rome I, 335, 338
Civil Code of Justinian. *See* Common Law v. Civil Law
Civil War in England, the Great I, 388; II, 271, 333–4
Clapham, the vicar of I, 217
Clare, Stephen II, 68
Clarence, the Duke of I, 14; II, 324
Clarke, Sir John I, 328–9
Cleeve Abbey II, 172
Clement VII, Pope I, 20–1
Clementhorpe nunnery I, 244
Cleobury Mortimer (Cleeland) II, 166
Clergy of England
   Act regulating the I, 5
   commission to inquire into their condition I, 91, 96
   the council of divines II, 166
   and the Cumberland rebels I, 225, 370, 372
   and the Act of First Fruits I, 351
   and Henry VIII I, 5–10, 67–9, 244, 326, 383, 385; II, 164–5
   their influence I, 56–8
   and the New Learning I, 66
   and the Statute of Praemunire I, 6, 385
   their allegiance to the Pope I, 342–3
   punishment of, without degradation I, 9, 355, 384
   their part in the rebellion I, 58, 79, 96, 134, 203, 217, 221, 261, 342, 343, 386; II, 28, 40–41, 74, 159, 330–31
   submission of the I, 6
   taxation of the I, 351–2, 371–2, 384
   reference II, 68
Cleveland I, 202, 262; II, 67, 76, 80, 94–7, 105–6
Cliff, Dr William I, 382–4, 386

Clifford, family of I, 34–5, 224; II, 42, 115, 252
Clifford, Anne, wife of Henry, Lord I, 34
Clifford, Lady Eleanor I, 35, 210
Clifford, Henry, Lord, the 'Shepherd Lord' I, 34, 49
Clifford, Henry, Lord, son and heir of the first Earl of Cumberland I, 35, 208, 223–4; II, 6, 9, 9, 42, 43
Clifford, John, Lord I, 49
Clifford, Sir Thomas I, 35, 200–1, 223; II, 9, 104, 228, 230, 232, 248, 254, 255, 261, 266
Clifford, Thomas I, 35; II, 111–3, 116, 117, 120, 138
Clifton, — I, 155
Clifton, Walter I, 155
Clinton, Lord I, 96, 118, 128, 132; II, 193
Clitheroe, Hugh I, 154
Clyfton, Gervis I, 306
Cobham, Lord II, 193
Cockerell, James, quondam prior of Guisborough II, 40, 56–9, 135, 183, 211, 214
Cockermouth I, 223; II, 23, 44, 105, 112, 119, 120
Coinage, the I, 2
Coke, Henry I, 273
Cokke, John II, 175
Colchester I, 241
—— St John's Abbey II, 24
Colins, Lancelot, treasurer of York Minster I, 178, 133–4, 232
Collingwood, Robert I, 194, 198, 199; II, 232
Collins, John II, 294–5, 305–6, 310, 312, 315
Collins, William I, 213, 216, 345; II, 20, 21, 30, 31, 106, 113, 114, 144, 148, 219, 220
Colne I, 219
Colsell, John I, 65
Colwick I, 109, 113
Commission of the Peace II, 245
Commission, the King's. *See* Letters Royal
Common Law v. Civil Law I, 366–8; II, 182
Comperta, the I, 350
Compiègne II, 242
Confessa Germaniae (the Angsburg Confession) :, 346
Conishead Priory I, 218; II, 39
—— the prior of II, 21
Conisholm, the parson of I, 91
Constable, family of I, 44, 47, 48; II, 58, 206
Constable, Christopher I, 47
Constable, Eleanor I, 45
Constable, Elizabeth, wife of Marmaduke I, 46
Constable, James, of the Cliff I, 157
Constable, Jane, wife of Sir Robert I, 45

Constable, John, brother of Sir Robert
I, 45
Constable, Sir John of Holderness I,
46–7, 155, 158, 164, 345; II, 81
Constable, Joyse, wife of Sir Marmaduke
the little I, 45
Constable, Leonard I, 58
Constable, Sir Marmaduke the little I,
45, 46
Constable, Sir Marmaduke, brother of Sir
Robert I, 45–6, 109, 110, 116, 278,
283, 292; II 48, 50, 53, 102, 104,
133, 216, 229, 260, 272
—— his wife II, 216
Constable, Marmaduke, son of Sir William
I, 163
Constable, Marmaduke, eldest son of Sir
Robert I, 46; II 72, 103, 206
Constable, Ralph I, 155
Constable, Sir Robert
with the royal army at Nottingham
I, 170; II, 205
his arrest II, 125, 133, 204
his conduct during Bigod's rising II,
72–3, 75, 90–2, 98, 102, 119, 131,
205–6
warned by Bulmer II, 160
his classical allusion II, 46
his early life and character I, 45–6,
48, 61
evidence against II, 130–1, 140, 205–6,
209
his examination II, 134, 204, 207
his execution II, 194, 220–1, 223
his family I, 40, 45; II, 333
his feuds I, 46–8; II, 91
his friendship with Darcy I, 19, 21,
45–6; II, 189, 205, 220
and the first conference at Doncaster
I, 259, 264–5, 269
his household goods II, 252
his name used by Hallam II, 48
governor of Hull I, 286, 288, 293,
336
his imprisonment II, 207, 216, 220
and Archbishop Lee I, 342, 380
in command of the middle ward I,
252, 256, 261–2
his motto I, 48; II, 221
his papers II, 205
his petitions II, 206–7
becomes a leader of the Pilgrimage of
Grace I, 227
at Pontefract I, 171, 186, 228, 233,
238; II, 205
at the council at Pontefract I, 345,
347, 353
steward of Howden II, 40
summoned to London II, 50, 52,
158
and the suppression of the monasteries
II, 20
at Templehurst I, 308
his trial II, 135, 136, 140, 198, 205,
206, 211

Constable, Sir Robert
at the council at York I, 312–4, 316;
II, 9
reference I, 27, 116, 280, 310–1, 323,
325, 351; II, 96, 101, 103, 126
Constable, Sir Robert (grandfather of
above) I, 40
Constable, Thomas I, 47
Constable, Thomas, of Settrington I, 40
Constable, Sir William, brother of Sir
Robert I, 45, 46, 155, 163, 239,
286, 345, 346; II, 47, 81
Constable, Sir William, the regicide II,
333
Constable, William I, 325
Constable, William, of Settrington I, 40
Convocation
general reference I, 9, 360, 371, 383,
385; II, 37, 49, 72, 187, 198, 209
the Northern I, 6, 7, 9, 351, 384, 388
the Southern I, 6–7, 9, 10, 353
Conyers of Hornby, family of I, 36, 42
Conyers, Sir George I, 60, 157; II, 87
Conyers, Gregory I, 42–3; II, 77, 87–8,
133, 136, 158, 159, 163, 164, 199
Conyers, James I, 43
Conyers, Sir John I, 37
Conyers, John I, 42
Conyers, Sir Richard I, 36
Conyers, William, Lord I, 33, 41, 345;
II, 13, 34, 109, 184
Conyers, Sir William I, 37
Conyers, William I, 211
Cook, Lawrence, Prior of the White Friars
of Doncaster I, 251; II, 266
Cooper, William II, 68
Copindale, Edmund I, 157, 286
Copledike, Sir John I, 101, 102
Corbridge I, 33; II, 235
Coren, Richard II, 223–4
Cornage. See Neat geld
Corney, George I, 221
Cornwall I, 88; II, 170, 171, 180, 181
Corthrop, Thomas I, 68
Cottam, Bartholomew II, 159, 160, 161
Cottingham I, 151, 153, 159, 160, 161;
II, 75
Cotton, Richard I, 248
Council, the King's
its composition I, 136, 229, 263, 276,
290, 331, 357; II, 1, 36
examinations before I, 26, 118, 244
Exeter and Fitzwilliam excluded from
I, 25–6
and Lord Delaware II, 313
its deliberations II, 245, 248, 263,
291, 305, 325
and the King's reply to the Pilgrims
I, 278; II, 24, 35
and Mary's marriage I, 325; II, 245
correspondence with Norfolk I, 121,
244–5, 247, 268, 295; II, 6, 9, 11,
103, 105, 118, 125, 132, 150, 229,
230, 235–6, 241
negotiations with Pole II, 279–80

Council, the King's
 its offshoots II, 229, 270–5
 proposals for the settlement of the North II, 26–7, 33, 52–3
 reference I, 5, 13, 20, 86, 99, 131, 143, 180, 181, 186, 274, 285, 290, 313, 329; II, 79, 104, 126, 234, 260, 293, 307, 308, 318
Council of the North
 established II, chap. xxi, pp. 226 et seq., 260, 267–8, 270–3, 329
 its first meeting II, 272–3
 its members and officers II, 260, 272–3
 its origin I, 30–1
 and the Border pledges II, 275
 its powers II, 272–3
 president of. See Tunstall, Bishop
 and seditious prophecies I, 82–4
 reference II, 185, 200, 228, 234, 252
Court of Arches I, 383
Courtenay, Edward II, 310, 319, 323, 325, 326, 328
Coventry I, 70
Coventry, the Bishop of. See Lee, Roland
Coverham Abbey I, 201; II, 266
Cow Cross, London II, 59
Cowdray II, 308, 317, 323, 324
Cowper, James I, 217
Cox, J. C., 'William Stapleton and the Pilgrimage of Grace' I, 52
Crake, Robert I, 143, 150; II, 49
Crane, James II, 254–6
Cranmer, Thomas, Archbishop of Canterbury I, 8, 14, 98, 111, 114, 133, 236, 353–4, 356; II, 165, 167
Craven I, 73, 150, 207–8, 237, 316; II, 48
Crawford, the Earl of I, 272
Cresswell, Katherine II, 195
Cresswell, Percival I, 289–94, 326; II, 195
Cressy, Simon II, 177
Crockey, William II, 63–4, 82
Croftes, George, Chancellor of Chichester Cathedral II, 295, 310, 312, 315, 319
Croftormount I, 371
Cromwell, Richard I, 108, 117, 119, 120, 122–3, 128, 185, 164–5, 293, 319, 377; II, 8, 11, 12, 14, 46, 150, 255, 291, 303
Cromwell, Thomas, Lord Privy Seal, afterwards Earl of Essex
 his arrest II, 222, 332
 and Robert Aske I, 60, 291; II, 207, 224–5
 and Sir Francis Bigod I, 41, 43–4
 his character I, 4; II, 330
 and Darcy I, 20, 266, 304, 305; II, 186–9, 192–3
 the rebels demand his head. See Demands of the rebels
 and Lady Margaret Douglas I, 317–8; II, 58

Cromwell, Thomas
 his letter to young Sir Ralph Evers I, 313–4, 317
 examinations before I, 78; II, 199
 and the Marquis of Exeter II, 290–1, 303, 318, 319, 320
 his extortions I, 352, 357; II, 185
 Knight of the Garter II, 195, 222
 and the King I, 244, 326–7, 374; II, 4, 83
 supposed to be the King's heir I, 317–8, 361, 363; II, 58
 scapegoat for the King I, 21, 189, 358; II, 15, 36, 60
 and the Lincs. Rebellion I, 117
 and Mary I, 26, 317
 his commission for the Visitation of the Monasteries. See Visitation of the Monasteries
 and the monasteries I, 4, 43, 75, 208–9, 213–4, 285; II, 39, 40, 56, 58, 82, 124, 189, 201
 his correspondence with the Duke of Norfolk I, 5, 241–2, 244–5, 272; II, 99, 102, 105, 109, 110–2, 118, 121, 123, 124, 126, 130–1, 133, 185, 187, 139, 185–6, 210, 218, 221, 224, 239–40, 252–3, 258–9, 262, 264–5, 266, 268–9
 and the Earl of Northumberland I, 31–2
 and Parliament I, 3, 4; II, 55
 petitions to
  from Robert Aske II, 222
  from Richard Bowyer II, 219
  from Sir Robert Constable II, 206–7
  from Sir Arthur Darcy I, 74
  from young Sir Ralph Evers II, 88
  from Archbishop Lee I, 193
  from John Madowell II, 167
  from Sir Thomas Percy I, 33
  from Edward Stanley I, 53
  from Sir Richard Tempest I, 56; II, 218
  from Robert Thompson II, 219
 his account of the Pilgrimage II, 25, 217
 and Sir Geoffrey Pole II, 304
 and Reginald Pole II, 285, 288, 295, 305–6, 318
 his policy I, 4, 10, 57, 63–4, 378
 and prisoners II, 153, 220, 245, 311
 see also above, petitions to
 prophecies about. See Prophecies
 and the rebels I, 303, 314, 358; II, 37, 118, 127, 224
 and the reformers I, 63, 370
 reports of his agents I, 64–7, 71, 87, 109, 111–2, 118, 123, 128, 165, 190, 214, 220, 248, 329, 335; II, 25, 40–1, 50, 92–5, 122, 129, 145–6, 148, 150, 165, 168, 170–2, 177, 181, 190–1, 208, 215, 224, 248, 254–5, 263, 273, 279, 280, 283, 287, 302, 316, 317

Cromwell, Thomas
  rhymes against. *See* Sedition, rhymes
  his servants I, 248, 352, 368
  his correspondence with Shrewsbury
    I, 109, 116, 294
  his correspondence with the Earl of
    Sussex II, 142, 144, 147
  his unpopularity I, 1, 59–60, 69, 79,
    103, 111, 120, 139, 183, 207, 214,
    235, 236, 263, 266, 271, 281, 285,
    290, 292, 307, 315, 323, 326–7, 357,
    368, 377; II, 4, 14, 37, 51, 57, 79,
    80, 110, 160, 164, 183, 254, 293–4,
    300
  reference I, 13, 24, 54, 66, 72, 86,
    95, 108, 122, 126, 131, 140, 173,
    194, 206, 215, 234, 267, 278, 284,
    336, 343, 353, 381; II, 79, 137,
    257, 270, 286, 321, 324
Crossthwaite I, 307
Crow, John I, 153
Crowle, the vicar of I, 70, 79
Crowley, Richard I, 67
Crummock Water I, 307
Cumberland county
  arrest of Sir Francis Bigod in II,
    110
  character of the rising in I, 192, 225,
    226, 370
  commons and the clergy I, 222, 224,
    354; II, 120
  the commons' rising II, 114–8, 122,
    208. *See also* Westmorland county,
    the commons' rising
  disturbances there after the rebellion
    II, 105, 112
  the rebels' grievances I, 217, 220,
    226, 369; II, 112, 119–20
  parliamentary representation of I,
    388
  the Pilgrimage in I, 221–6
  the second appointment at Doncaster
    proclaimed in II, 43
  the pardon proclaimed in II, 28
  riots there I, 78, 220; II, 42, 56
  the sheriff of. *See* Curwen, Sir
    Thomas
  escapes taxation I, 192, 372
  the truce I, 224, 279, 283, 292, 298,
    299, 304, 381
  reference I, 29, 50, 70, 196, 305, 318,
    364; II, 6, 134, 234, 268, 272
Cumberland, Henry Clifford, first Earl
    of
  captain of Carlisle I, 35; II, 245–6,
    248–9
  his character I, 34
  and the commons' rising II, 122,
    123
  his feud with the Dacres I, 35; II,
    42, 115, 229, 230, 236, 252–3
  at Darcy's trial II, 193
  his family I, 49, 51, 150, 200, 210,
    223
  Knight of the Garter II, 229

Cumberland, the Earl of
  and the King I, 35; II, 43–4, 183,
    246
  ordered to dissolve Hexham Priory
    I, 194–5, 208
  his influence I, 29
  and the Duke of Norfolk II, 102, 240
  his feud with John Norton I, 52,
    209; II, 43
  and the outbreak of the Pilgrimage
    I, 201, 207–10
  his proceedings after the second
    appointment at Doncaster II, 43–4
  his defence of Skipton Castle I, 208–
    11, 312, 316; II, 6
  his correspondence with Suffolk I,
    301, 312
  his unpopularity I, 35, 52–3, 73, 192,
    305; II, 103, 252–3, 264
  Warden of the West Marches I, 35;
    II, 123, 228–9, 251
  sheriff of Westmorland II, 123
  reference I, 50, 53–4, 185, 238, 313;
    II, 111, 160, 165
Cumberland, Margaret, Countess of I,
  34, 51, 54
Curtis, Anthony I, 79–80, 152–3, 155,
  156, 162, 288–9; II, 152
Curtis, Leonard I, 105
Curwen, Sir Thomas I, 74; II, 110, 112,
  114, 120, 122
Cuthbert, St I, 36, 238
  his banner. *See* Banner, of St Cuthbert
Cuthbert, a priest II, 243–4
Cutler, George I, 110, 112–3, 131; II,
  148, 149, 196

Dachant, Roger I, 207
Dacre, family of I, 35, 84; II, 42–3,
  115, 252
Dacre, Sir Christopher I, 224; II, 115–8,
  120–1, 138
Dacre, Richard I, 299; II, 42
Dacre, William, Lord (Lord Dacre of the
  North) I, 22, 30, 35, 224, 250,
  299; II, 42, 115, 186, 229–30,
  235–6, 240, 252, 264
Dacre, Thomas Fiennes, Lord (Dacre of
  the South) II, 193
Dakyn, John, vicar-general of the diocese
  of York I, 201–3, 206, 211, 283,
  377–8, 382–4, 386, 388; II, 20–1,
  40, 44, 130, 148
Dakyns (Cromwell's servant) I, 368
Dalison, Mr I, 97
Dalston I, 224
Dalston, Thomas I, 223
Dalton, the vicar of II, 146
—— the bailiff of II, 145
Dalyvell, Robert II, 244–5
Danby, Sir Christopher I, 201–3, 205,
  211, 212, 228, 231, 262, 269, 345;
  II, 92, 108, 136
Dantzig I, 42

Index 351

Darcy, Sir Arthur I, 18, 74, 118–9, 121, 143, 171–2, 184, 259, 269, 293, 297; II, 83, 86, 88, 127–9, 139, 142–3, 145, 195
Darcy, Dorothy, wife of Sir George II, 51
Darcy, Dousabella, first wife of Lord Darcy I, 18, 27
Darcy, Edith, second wife of Lord Darcy I, 18, 27
Darcy, Euphemia, mother of Lord Darcy I, 18
Darcy, Sir George I, 18, 142, 168, 170, 186, 188–9, 269, 294, 297–8, 345; II, 33, 51, 92–3, 95, 109, 189, 195, 218
Darcy, Richard I, 18
Darcy, Thomas, Lord
 and the divorce of Katherine of Arragon I, 20
 his arrest II, 133, 186, 195, 204
 and Robert Aske. See Aske, Robert, and Lord Darcy
 and the plan to kidnap Aske I, 267, 290–6, 304
 his attempts to keep order after the rebellion II, 38, 41, 44, 50, 51–2, 72–3, 109, 187–8
 and the Badge of the Five Wounds I, 239; II, 190
 his services on the Borders I, 18–19, 30
 and the mission of Bowes and Ellerker I, 292, 308
 warned by Bulmer II, 160, 188–9
 his correspondence with Chapuys I, 22–3, 27, 310; II, 191, 233
 his character and opinions I, 20, 24, 304, 353; II, 14, 187, 191, 194, 197
 a member of the King's Council I, 276; II, 1
 and Thomas Cromwell. See Cromwell, Thomas, and Lord Darcy
 and the first appointment at Doncaster I, 253–4, 258–9, 264–6, 269, 283, 302
 and the second appointment at Doncaster I, 309, 314; II, 2, 13, 18
 his message to the Emperor. See Waldby, Marmaduke
 evidence against I, 190; II, 92–3, 95, 119, 130, 147–8, 187–92, 196, 206, 208, 209, 225
 his examination I, 267; II, 134, 186–7, 207
 his execution I, 380; II, 193–5, 217
 his expedition to Spain I, 19, 45, 239
 his family I, 18, 46
 in France I, 19
 correspondence with Sir Brian Hastings I, 169, 308, 321, 344
 his household goods II, 252
 and the House of Lords I, 20, 360–1
 and Lord Hussey I, 21–2, 290–2
 his imprisonment II, 194–5, 216

Darcy, Thomas, Lord
 and the King I, 20, 118, 121–2, 143–4, 169, 171, 173–4, 184–5, 189–90, 207, 208, 212, 243–4, 276, 292, 301–5; II, 50–2, 89, 92–3, 101, 109, 129, 190, 194–5
 and Levening's case II, 92, 131, 188
 his alleged letter to Lincs. II, 84
 and the Lincs. prisoners II, 17, 189
 and the Lincs. rebellion I, 99, 172; II, 191
 and the Duke of Norfolk I, 267, 269, 290–2, 296, 297, 302, 306, 309, 311, 321; II, 41, 102, 127, 128, 186, 188–9, 194
 his return to the North in 1536 I, 24
 his papers II, 186–90, 192, 194, 201, 205
 his pardon I, 305; II, 89, 190, 195, 217
 becomes a leader of the Pilgrimage of Grace I, 227–8, 230, 233, 238–9
 his company of Pilgrims I, 239, 261–2
 and the council at Pontefract I, 315, 344–6
 his responsibility for Pontefract Castle I, 190; II, 92–3, 109, 127–9, 189
 his surrender of Pontefract Castle I, 188–90; II, 92, 94, 190, 205
 his position at the beginning of the rebellion I, 144, 168–71, 180–1, 185, 188
 reports of his agents I, 169–70, 173, 213–4, 216, 233, 269
 his servants I, 156, 180
 and the Earl of Shrewsbury I, 130, 169, 172–4, 185, 188, 245, 252–3, 256–7, 266, 270, 297–8, 302, 310, 316, 344, 345; II, 6, 34, 80, 92, 188–9, 193
 his interview with Somerset Herald I, 299–305, 331–2
 his stewards. See Strangeways, Thomas, and Grice, Thomas
 summoned to London II, 50–2, 127, 129, 158
 accuses the Earl of Surrey I, 267
 suspected I, 20, 22–3, 144, 190, 244, 250
 and Sir Richard Tempest I, 172; II, 218
 his trial II, 135–6, 140, 185–7, 193, 195–6, 314
 his anxiety during the truce I, 296–8
 letter to, from the commons of Westmorland I, 299
 and Cardinal Wolsey I, 19–20; II, 192
 absent from the council at York I, 311, 314–6
 reference I, 32, 40, 50, 74, 203, 215, 226, 254, 256, 280, 288, 293, 330, 351; II, 23, 52, 105, 126, 292
Darcy, Sir William I, 18
Darcy, William I, 18
Darlington I, 202; II, 94–5
Darrell, Elizabeth II, 293–4

Dartnell, Jacques I, 313
Davy, — II, 167-8
Dawnye, Sir John I, 186, 238, 345
Delariver, — I, 345
Delariver, Robert I, 253
Delariver (Delaryver), Thomas I, 74; II, 132-3, 136
Delaware, Thomas West, Lord II, 186, 193, 217, 295, 306, 308, 312-3, 319
Demands of the rebels
  the articles of St Thomas I, 64
  of Cornwall II, 171
  of Durham I, 197
  of Lancashire I, 216
  of Lincolnshire
    general I, 109, 156
    at Boston I, 111
    at Caistor I, 98
    the Horncastle articles I, 102-4, 111, 124
    the first petition to the King I, 98-9, 107, 109, 118
    the second petition to the King I, 114-5, 123, 136-7, 142
    as reported in London I, 134
    sent to Yorkshire I, 78, 115, 152
    their influence in Yorkshire I, 153, 156, 174, 176, 352-3, 364
  in Northumberland I, 199
  of Yorkshire
    Aske's speech upon, at Pontefract I, 186-7
    distributed during the truce I, 298
    the terms of the second appointment at Doncaster II, 15-24, 27
    the first Yorkshire articles I, 176-8, 180-1, 191
    the five articles I, 229, 263-5, 267, 271, 275, 291, 315, 328, 331-3; II, 1, 29, 35, 45, 51, 170, 174, 279
    the articles drawn up at Hunsley I, 166-7
    a free pardon and a free parliament I, 293; II, 6-7, 8, 13-18. *See also* Pardon *and* Parliament
    proposal to print the five articles I, 252
    the twenty-four articles of Pontefract I, 191, 264, 315, 332, 344, 346-374, 384, 387; II, 1, 2, 12, 13-15, 35, 59, 130, 270-1
    the Richmondshire articles II, 80, 97
    the restoration of the monasteries II, 14-6, 18-26, 38, 45, 86, 100, 111, 141
    the spiritual articles I, 315, 318, 342-3, 353, 377, 383-8; II, 13, 14, 57, 129-31, 166. *See also* Aske, Robert, his questions for the clergy
    reference I, 253, 258, 295; II, 100, 105. *See also* Proclamations, Rebel
Denmark I, 334

Dent I, 143, 207, 216-8, 298, 316, 369
  the bailiff of II, 144
Derby county I, 113, 282, 314
Derby, Edward Stanley, third Earl of I, 169-70, 210, 214-20, 227-8, 269-70, 282, 287, 294-6, 298, 306, 316, 376; II, 6, 7, 43, 52, 119, 141-4, 146, 176, 204
Derby town I, 294, 296, 311, 319
  the bridge I, 282
Derwent, the river, Cumb. II, 112
Derwent, the river, Yorks. I, 49, 144, 174
Devon county I, 78, 88; II, 171
Dewsbury I, 288
Diamond, — I, 344
Dickering wapentake II, 68-9
Dickson, Isaac I, 307
Dighton Mr I, 101, 124
Dilston I, 193
Dingley, Sir Thomas II, 324
Disney, — I, 114
Dispensations from the Pope, Act declaring them void I, 8, 385
Dissolution of the monasteries. *See* Suppression of the monasteries
Dix, John II, 177
Dobsone, John I, 82-4; II, 301
Dockwray, Thomas I, 216
Dod, family of II, 228
Dod, Archie II, 238
Dod, John II, 234, 246, 261
Dod, Henry II, 238
Don, the river I, 91, 149, 227, 238, 239, 249, 255-7, 260, 282, 300, 344; II, 4, 5, 7, 8, 23, 217
Doncaster I, 169, 180, 184-5, 205, 227, 234-5, 238-9, 245-6, 249-52, 255-7, 259-60, 262, 266-7, 270, 283, 290, 293-5, 297, 305-6, 308-9, 313, 319-21, 323, 327, 346, 377, 388; II, 2, 4, 10-13, 15-17, 19, 20, 22, 34, 52, 93-5, 97, 99, 101-6, 108-9, 166, 194, 198, 223, 229, 252
  bridge I, 235, 265, 268, 327, 344
  the first appointment at I, chap. xi, pp. 241-272. *See also* Truce of Doncaster
  the second appointment at. *See* Pilgrimage of Grace, the second appointment at Doncaster
  the Grey Friars' house II, 13, 16
  the White Friars' house II, 13, 266
  the Prior of the White Friars of. *See* Cook, Lawrence
Donne, Thomas I, 115, 152-3, 155-7
Donnyngton, John II, 132
Doomright, John II, 243
Dorset county I, 80, 326
Dorset, Henry Grey, Marquis of II, 193
Douglas, Lady Margaret I, 317-8, 363; II, 58
Dover I, 134
Downes, Dr Geoffrey, chancellor of York I, 382
Drewy, John II, 167-8

Index

Driffield 1, 47, 157
Duckett, — 1, 345
Dudley, — 1, 221
Dudley, Edmund 1, 21
Duke, Thomas 1, 74, 86
Dunbar 11, 86
    Castle 11, 266–7
Dunholm Heath (Lings) 1, 106, 110
Duns Scotus 1, 65
Durham, the Bishop's Chancery 1, 205
Durham Cathedral 1, 205
Durham city 1, 205, 207, 239, 273; 11, 28, 30, 44, 61, 66, 78–9, 83–5, 95, 122, 125–6, 133–4, 170
    the mint 1, 288
Durham county
    arrests there 11, 119
    its liberties 1, 8, 30, 85–6, 144, 355; 11, 125, 272
    pardon proclaimed in 11, 28, 30
    not represented in parliament 1, 355, 388
    Pilgrims from 1, 237–8, 251–2, 256, 262
    the rebellion in 1, 178, 192, 197, 199, 201, 205, 207
    sheriff of. See Hilton, Sir Thomas
    escapes taxation 1, 192
    tenure in 1, 369
    unrest there during the truce 1, 304
    unrest there after the rebellion 11, 30, 44, 61–2, 66–7, 78–80, 94–6, 213, 300
    reference 1, 29, 182, 210, 227, 289, 349, 364; 11, 234, 272–3
Durham Priory 1, 205, 238; 11, 126
Dymmoke, family of 1, 130; 11, 148
Dymmoke, Arthur 1, 124
Dymmoke, Sir Edward, sheriff of Lincolnshire 1, 101–2, 106, 111, 124, 127; 11, 149
Dymmoke, Sir Robert 1, 101
Dymmoke, Thomas 1, 124

Eamont Bridge 1, 221
Easington, Yorks. 11, 158
    the parson of. See Watts, John
East Anglia 11, 173, 177
Eastbourne, the vicar of 1, 69
Easterford 1, 120
East Meon, the vicar of. See Heliar, John
Ebberstone 11, 87
Eden, the river 1, 221–2
Edenhall, the vicar of 1, 222
Edinburgh 11, 244, 246, 249, 254
Edmund, a priest 1, 107
Edward I 1, 359; 11, 182
Edward III 1, 18, 359
Edward IV 1, 15, 21, 30, 362
Edward, son of Henry VIII, afterwards Edward VI 1, 77, 240, 349, 374; 11, 297, 299, 319–20, 325, 338
Egremont 11, 112
Eland, John 1, 164, 166; 11, 65–6, 76, 88, 90

Eleyn, William 1, 95
Elicampadus (Oecolampadius), John 1, 346
Elizabeth, afterwards Queen 1, 1, 7, 10, 81, 108, 374; 11, 25, 245, 333
Ellerker, Yorks. 1, 105; 11, 91–2
Ellerker, family of 1, 48, 49, 287; 11, 72, 91–2
Ellerker, — 1, 244
Ellerker, Agnes 1, 50, 105
Ellerker, Sir Ralph, the elder 1, 48, 50, 151–2; 11, 74–5, 88
Ellerker, Sir Ralph, the younger
    his warning to Aske 11, 91–2
    and the Beverley rebels 1, 147, 159, 163–4, 167
    suppresses Bigod's rising 11, 74–5, 81, 88, 90–1, 98, 126–7, 132
    his feud with Sir Robert Constable 1, 46; 11, 91
    at the first conference at Doncaster 1, 262
    captain of Hull 1, 48, 165, 318; 11, 52, 74, 78, 125
    King's marshal 11, 119
    his mission to the King. See Bowes, Robert, his mission to the King
    and Archbishop Lee 1, 342
    his company of Pilgrims 1, 239, 261
    at the council at Pontefract 1, 345–6
    a commissioner of the Subsidy 1, 105, 141
    at the council at York 1, 312
    reference 1, 143, 155, 235, 238; 11, 20, 33, 97, 198, 260, 271–2
Ellerker, Ralph 1, 159
Ellerker, Sir Robert 1, 199–201
Ellerker, Thomas 1, 159, 161
Ellerker, William 1, 50, 105, 141
Ellerton Priory 1, 51
Ellerton, the Prior of. See Lawrence, James
Elmedon 1, 39
Elmedon, William 1, 39
Embleton, Cumb., the bailiff of. See Jackson, John
Emett, Alexander 1, 57; 11, 257–8
Empress, the. See Isabella
Empshot 1, 54
Empson, Richard 1, 21
Enclosures
    acts regulating 1, 12–3, 89, 372
    of the common land 1, 373
    in Cumberland and Westmorland 1, 220, 371–2; 11, 112, 121
    the King's instructions about 11, 100, 141
    in Lincolnshire 1, 89
    their progress and effect 1, 73, 349, 369
    rising directed against 1, 225–6, 318, 372
England
    Clergy of. See Clergy
    communications with the Continent closed 1, 333–4, 336, 340, 356

England
    dangers of a renewed civil war I, 123, 253; II, 55–6
    espionage in II, 179
    the Established Church of I, 374, 376
    feudal dues in I, 371–2
    relations with France I, 11, 333–4, 340; II, 240, 243, 249, 281, 319
    government by council II, 270
    the law of inheritance in I, 362–3
    proposed invasion of I, 16–7, 23, 134; II, 298–9, 311, 319, 331
    its isolation I, 17, 72; II, 298
    land tenure in I, 369–70
    and the Netherlands I, 335–6; II, 282–3
    its political condition I, chap. i, pp. 1–13, 361; II, 334
    and the Pope I, 7, 8, 271, 339, 341; II, 280, 287, 298–9, 301, 330
    prophecies about I, 82–3
    the rebellion in, compared to the German Peasant Revolt I, 139–40, 226, 364
    character of rebellions in II, 332–3
    the Reformation in I, 51, 59, 75, 340, 347–8; II, 287, 299–302
    state of religion in I, 9
    expected war with Scotland I, 334–5; II, 238, 243–5, 247
    Scots outlaws in II, 263, 267
    Supreme Head of the Church of. *See* Henry VIII, Supreme Head of the Church of England
    forms of trial in II, 182
    weapons used in I, 364
    reference I, 15, 19, 26, 36, 63, 81, 85, 270, 310, 333, 336–7; II, 19, 22, 55, 136, 144, 162, 170, 173, 217–8, 228, 241–2, 246, 250, 254, 278–9, 284, 286, 289, 295, 303, 322, 327–8
Ennesmore I, 217
Erasmus, Desiderius I, 379
Errington, Anthony II, 41
Errington, Arthur I, 197
Esch, Robert. *See* Ashton, Robert
Escheators I, 368
Esk, the river I, 35, 196, 223; II, 113, 117, 233
Essex county I, 68, 70, 74, 248; II, 185
Essex, Henry Bourchier, Earl of II, 193
Essex, Sir William I, 328–9
Estgate, John II, 142–3
Estgate, Richard II, 83, 142–5
Estoft, Thomas II, 53
Eton, George I, 100
Everingham I, 240
Everingham, Sir Henry I, 186
Evers, family of I, 37, 44
Evers, John II, 184
Evers, Sir Ralph, the elder II, 70
Evers, Sir Ralph, the younger I, 40, 44, 157, 211, 313, 323; II, 33, 52, 70, 77, 88, 96–8, 125, 160, 183–4, 211

Evers, Ralph I, 157
Evers, —, wife of Sir Ralph the younger II, 184, 216
Evers, Sir William II, 103, 229, 232, 238–9, 260–1, 272
Exeter city II, 171
Exeter, Henry Courtenay, Marquis of
    accusations against II, 190
    his arrest II, 310
    attainted II, 323
    his royal blood I, 15; II, 299, 311
    in command against the rebels I, 243, 245–7, 249, 257, 259–60, 269, 329–30; II, 277, 289
    unconnected with the Cornish plot II, 180–1
    and Cromwell. *See* Cromwell, Thomas, and Exeter
    a member of the King's Council I, 276; II, 36
    expelled from the Council I, 25–6
    banished from court II, 181, 312
    evidence against II, 310–3, 319–21
    his execution II, 315, 318–9, 321
    his friends II, 290–1, 303, 306, 319
    receives a grant of monastic lands I, 330; II, 291
    his opinions II, 292
    a plot in his favour II, 180–1
    his popularity II, 291
    Lord High Steward at Darcy's trial II, 193
    his trial II, 314–5
    reference I, 18, 247; II, 23, 186, 293, 307
Exeter, Gertrude Courtenay, Marchioness of (the Lady Marquis) I, 15, 24–5, 330; II, 289–90, 294, 306, 310, 312–3, 319–21, 323–5
Eynesham, the Abbot of II, 168
Eyre, Richard II, 303–4, 308

Faenza, Ridolfo Pio, Bishop of, papal nuncio at Paris I, 333–4, 336, 339; II, 240–2
Fairfax, Sir Nicholas I, 231–2, 312, 345; II, 83, 333
Fairfax, Thomas, King's serjeant at law II, 272
Fairfax, Sir William I, 162, 237–8, 345; II, 40, 101
Fairfax, Thomas, Lord II, 333
Farforth I, 91
Farrore, Harry I, 236
Fawcett, —, I, 209
Featherstonhaugh, the laird of II, 42
Felton I, 31
Fendale I, 262
Fenton, Ralph II, 61, 69, 77, 110
Fenwick I, 49
Fenwick, family of II, 228
Fenwick, George II, 229, 232
Fenwick, Roger II, 229, 234, 236, 246, 261–2
Ferdinand, King of Spain I, 19

Index

Fermor, —, I, 327
Fermor, Sir Henry I, 327
Fermour, Adam I, 69
Ferriby I, 105, 162
Ferriby Priory I, 154. 162, 217; II, 20
   the Prior of I, 162
Ferrybridge (Ferrybridges) I, 184, 234, 270, 327
Feversham I, 79
Fewaryn (Fitzwarren), Lord I, 87
Field, John I, 324
Fife II, 246–7
Fifteenth, the I, 11, 137, 372–3
Fincham II, 174
Fincham, John II, 174
First Fruits (Annates), Act of I, 6, 56, 91, 98, 187, 187, 347, 349, 851–2, 384–5; II, 14, 34
Fishe, Guy II, 70
Fisher, John, Cardinal, Bishop of Rochester I, 11, 23, 63, 68–9, 271, 354, 384; II, 192, 287
Fisher, Matthew II, 208
Fittleworth I, 326
Fitzgerald, Thomas, Earl of Desmond I, 302
Fitzherbert, Sir Anthony II, 141, 148
Fitzwilliam, Sir William, Lord Admiral I, 26, 117, 119, 123, 128, 131, 133, 135, 169, 245–6, 274, 276, 278, 290, 295–6, 306, 309, 311, 316, 319, 321–2, 331; II, 2, 6, 7, 10, 22, 52, 308–9, 316–8, 324, 326
Five Wounds of Christ. *See* Badge and Banner
Flamborough I, 40, 44, 46, 116, 186; II, 125, 198, 255
Flanders I, 88, 286, 357; II, 190, 223, 242–3, 279–84, 286, 288, 293–4, 326
Fletcher, Bernard II, 153
Fletcher, Richard I, 327
Flodden, the battle of I, 19, 37, 40, 46, 58, 250, 265, 272; II, 45, 252
Follansby, John II, 184
Ford Castle II, 230, 235
Forest, Friar II, 300
Forsett, Edward I, 100
Forster, family of II, 228, 231
Forster, Thomas I, 199
Fortescue, Sir Adrian II, 324
Forth, the frith of II, 253
Foster, Thomas I, 92; II, 150
Fountains Abbey II, 50, 107, 114, 301
   the Abbot of I, 211
   the quondam Abbot of. *See* Thirsk, William
Fowbery, John I, 312; II, 64, 65, 81
Fox, Edward, Bishop of Hereford I, 276, 290
France I. 15–6, 19, 21, 45, 60, 83, 132, 247, 325, 332–4, 338, 340, 357, 375; II, 10, 25, 95, 217, 238, 240–3, 247, 249, 255–6, 267, 281–2, 284–5, 319–20, 322

France
   ambassador in England. *See* Castillon, Louis de Perreau, Sieur de
   Constable of. *See* Montmorency, Anne de
   the court of parliament of II, 240
   Vice-Admiral of. *See* Moy, Charles de
Francis I, King of France I, 2, 11, 17, 325, 331, 333–5, 338, 340; II, 240, 242–3, 245, 247, 249, 255, 267, 281–2, 285, 298–9, 319, 331
   his daughter. *See* Madeleine
Francis, John II, 61–2, 82
Franke, Thomas, rector of Lofthouse I, 148–9; II, 159, 161–4
Frankishe, John I, 93–4
Franklin, William, Archdeacon of Durham I, 203–4; II, 61
Fredewell, James II, 243–4
Freeman, John II, 155
Friars
   Austin I, 105, 118
   Black (Preachers) I, 65–6, 82, 280, 382; II, 167
   Grey I, 65, 88; II, 167
   Observant I, 57, 63, 352, 388; II, 21, 89, 127
   White I, 64–5, 83; II, 166
Froude, J. A. 'History of England from the Fall of Wolsey to the Defeat of the Armada' I, 44–5, 75, 240, 387; II, 53, 154, 180–1, 215, 289, 296–7, 299, 300, 311, 324
Frythe (Frith), John I, 93
Fulstow I, 98
Fulthorp, — I, 345; II, 92, 184
Fulthorp, Thomas II, 95
Furness I, 369
Furness Abbey I, 81, 218, 225, 283; II, 144–8
   the Abbot of I, 217; II, 145–6, 156

Gainsborough I, 108, 293, 319
Galant, John II, 175
Galowbaughen I, 202
Galtres Forest I, 73, 74
Ganth, Hans I, 42
Ganton II, 61
Gardiner, Stephen, Bishop of Winchester I, 132, 276, 325, 333, 367, 374, 375; II, 256–7, 281–2
Gargrave II, 48
Gascoigne, Master I, 148
Gascoigne, Sir Henry I, 202, 345; II, 21, 182
Gasquet, F. A. 'Henry VIII and the English Monasteries' I, 140; II, 138
Gateforth II, 51
Gateshead II, 244
Gaunt, William I, 216
Gawan, Archbishop of Glasgow, Chancellor of Scotland II, 247–9
Genoa I, 335
Gentlemen of the North
   and the Church I, 55–6

23—2

Gentlemen of the North
  their lack of education I, 50; II, 18
  a typical example I, 54
  their family history I, 29
  their feuds I, 46; II, 268
  their grievances I, 3, 28, 59; II, 330
  their share in local government I, 29; II, 332
  their good and bad qualities I, 60
  their part in the rebellion II, 92–4, 100, 157–8
  their conduct after the rebellion II, 90, 137, 157
  and their tenants I, 89, 369–70, 372–3; II, 96, 100, 105, 108–9, 112, 115, 121, 156–7, 175, 177
  sympathy with rioters I, 73
Germany I, 17, 367; II, 298–9
  the Peasant Revolt of 1525 in I, 28, 78, 80, 126, 139–40, 225–6, 364, 370–2; II, 226
Gibson, — I, 101
Gifford, — I, 264
Giggleswick I, 209; II, 43
Gill, Harry, sub-prior of Watton I, 231–2, 286; II, 58–60, 62, 64, 81–2, 110
Gilsland II, 42, 115–6, 235, 264
Girlington, Nicholas I, 106
Gisburn, the vicar of I, 213
Glamis, Lady II, 216
Glaskerion, William II, 167
Gloucester city I, 287; II, 290
Gloucester county I, 245–6
Godalming I, 117
Goldsmith, William I, 98
Gonson, William I, 122, 299, 319
Goodall, — I, 324
Goodrich, Thomas, Bishop of Ely I, 98, 111; II, 168, 316–7. *See also* Demands of the rebels
Goole I, 298
Goole Dyke I, 250
Gostwick, John I, 246, 251; II, 34, 44
Gower, Sir Edward I, 345; II, 136
Gower, Ralph II, 44, 85
Grafton I, 45; II, 267
Graham, the family of II, 117
Grame, Robin II, 117
Grantham I, 65, 274; II, 303
Gray, Lionel I, 194, 200; II, 228, 232, 261
Gray's Inn I, 54, 58, 80, 155; II, 223
Graystoke, — II, 110
Green, Dorothy I, 51; II, 38
Green, Richard I, 51–2; II, 38
Greenwich I, 23, 46, 63; II, 25, 99
  the Friary II, 194
Gressoms. *See* Ingressum
'Grey Friars' Chronicle' II, 198
Grey (Gray), family of II, 41, 231
Grey (Gray), Sir Roger I, 200, 285
Grey, Roger II, 63–4
Grey, Sir Thomas I, 200; II, 41
Greystoke I, 222
Grice (Gryce), Thomas I, 169, 235, 237–8, 269, 295, 310, 311, 343, 347; II, 189, 215
Griffith, Sir Rhys ap I, 287–8
Grimsby I, 79–80, 95, 105, 110–1, 118, 162, 282, 286, 299, 301, 314, 318–9, 322; II 104
Grinston, — I, 155
Grinton II, 110
Grysanis, Anne I, 45, 61
Guaras, Antonio I, 240
Guildford I, 117
Guisborough II, 97, 110, 127, 160
  the Bishop's palace II, 40
  the priest of I, 71
  Priory I, 233; II, 40, 56, 201
  Prior of. *See* Silvester, Robert
  quondam Prior of. *See* Cockerell, James
Guisborough, George II, 175–6, 178–9
Guisborough, William II, 176, 178–9
Guise, Mary of. *See* Mary of Guise
Gunter, Geoffrey I, 328–9
Gunter, John II, 308–9, 326, 328

Haggar, Stephen I, 102
Hagnaby I, 101
Hailes, the Abbot of II, 169
Hales, Sir Christopher, Master of the Rolls I, 103, 111; II, 199. *See also* Demands of the rebels
Halifax I, 115, 235; II, 28, 257
  the vicar of. *See* Holdsworth, Robert
Hall, family of II, 228, 231
Hall, Anthony II, 230
Hall, Edward, 'The Union of the Families of Lancaster and York' I, 55
Hall, John II, 230
Hall, Sandy II, 230–1
Hallam, John
  his arrest II, 65–6, 73, 76, 90, 221
  restrained by Aske II, 48–50
  in the Beverley rising I, 153, 157
  and Sir Francis Bigod. *See* Bigod, Sir Francis, and John Hallam
  his character and opinions I, 152; II, 46–7
  captures Cromwell's letter to young Sir Ralph Evers I, 314
  his execution II, 82, 89, 91, 98
  his attempt on Hull. *See* Hull, Hallam's attempt to seize
  his insurrection II, chap. xviii, pp. 55 *et seq.*, 99, 102, 199
  dissatisfied with the general pardon II, 31, 69
  at the council at Pontefract I, 343, 347
  a prisoner II, 73, 78, 81–2, 88, 91, 98, 206, 209
  attempts to cause a new rising II, 46–8, 59
  and seditious songs I, 280
  his quarrel with the Prior of Watton II, 58–60
  at the council at York I, 318; II, 57

Index

Hallam, John
  reference II, 16
Haltemprice Abbey I, 154; II, 20
Halton, Northumberland I, 194–7, 201
Halton Castle, Cheshire I, 214
Hambleton Hill, Lincs. I, 106–7, 141
Hambleton Hills, Yorks. II, 97
Hamell II, 171
Hamerton, the family of I, 51
Hamerton, — I, 345
Hamerton, Elizabeth, mother of Sir Stephen I, 53
Hamerton, Elizabeth, wife of Sir Stephen I, 40
Hamerton, Henry I, 53; II, 204
Hamerton, John I, 53
Hamerton, Roger I, 53
Hamerton, Sir Stephen I, 40, 51, 53, 209–10, 219, 312, 345; II, 39, 43, 83, 85–6, 133, 135, 148, 198, 201, 204, 211, 214
Hampole nunnery I, 251–2, 254–6, 259–60, 264
Hampshire I, 54, 326, 332; II, 222
Handguns and Crossbows, the Statute of I, 363–4; II, 243
Harbottle, — I, 33
Harbottle Castle II, 42, 235, 289
  constable of. *See* Heron, John
Hardwick in Sherwood I, 118–9
Hardy, William Keing. *See* Captain Cobbler
Harland, J. 'Salley Abbey' II, 143
Harlaw Woods II, 233
Harrington, Mr I, 112
Harrington, William, lord mayor of York I, 143, 168, 174–6, 243, 344; II, 76
Harrison, — I, 156
Harrison, Richard, Abbot of Kirkstead I, 104, 106; II, 152
Harrison, William II, 31
Hartlepool I, 205
Hartlepool, Roger II, 107–8, 266
Harwich I, 68
Hastings, Sir Brian, sheriff of Yorkshire 1536–7 I, 49, 121, 148, 168–9, 185, 208, 250, 261, 282, 288, 293, 296–8, 300, 306, 308, 311, 319, 321, 344; II, 132, 134, 260, 273
Hastings, Sir George I, 49
Hastings, Sir John I, 49
Hastings, Dame Katherine I, 49
Hatcliff, Thomas I, 314
Hatfield, Yorks. I, 169, 185, 250, 282; II, 10–11
Havant I, 332; II, 308
  a harper of. *See* Taylor, Lawrence
Haverfordwest, the Prior of I, 67
Hawley, Thomas, Clarencieux King-of-Arms II, 21, 23, 28, 53
Haynton I, 90
Headcorn, the curate of II, 168
Hebyllthwayte, John I, 217
Hedge, John I, 155
Hedon I, 388

Helaigh, — II, 266
Heliar, John, vicar of East Meon and rector of Warblington I, 332; II, 284, 303–5, 316
Hellifield Peel I, 53
Helmsley II, 266
Hemingborough I, 141, 144
Henneage, John I, 93–5, 99, 107, 109–10, 320
Henry II I, 64
Henry III I, 84
Henry IV I, 84–5, 362, 383
Henry VI I, 30, 359; II, 329
Henry VII I, 15, 18, 34, 45, 63, 85, 218, 303, 332, 337, 362, 366, 373
Henry VIII
  his accession to the throne I, 19, 21, 30
  and Robert Aske I, 191, 289–91, 294, 298, 304, 313, 321, 323; II, 6, 18–19, 32–3, 36–8, 45, 48–51, 54, 72–3, 76, 89–91, 99, 104–5, 180, 207–10, 222–5
  receives news of Bigod's insurrection II, 75–6
  and the Borders I, 30, 35, 190. *See also* Borders, the King's plan for their government
  compared to
    David I, 358
    Henry II I, 64
    Herod I, 72
    Nero II, 167
    Rehoboam, Edward II and Richard II I, 357
  and Thomas Cromwell. *See* Cromwell, Thomas, and the King
  and Darcy. *See* Darcy, Thomas, Lord, and the King
  and the Earl of Derby I, 214–7, 316
  his disease II, 260, 277, 293, 295
  his domestic relations I, 1, 20–21, 24–6, 31, 37, 108, 133, 325, 354, 356
  and the first appointment at Doncaster. *See below* and the truce
  and the second appointment at Doncaster II, chap. xv. pp. 1–23, 56, 88, 102, 111, 126, 188, 206, 287, 292, 332
  his ecclesiastical policy I, 2–4, 5–11, 44, 56, 63–7, 72, 74–5, 77, 80, 104, 193–4, 208, 214–5, 324, 339, 341, 343, 350–2, 374–6; II, 14, 21–2, 25–6, 38–9, 85, 111, 121–2, 127, 138–9, 143–8, 292, 298, 330–2
  his finances I, 2, 11–2, 154, 168, 244, 246–7, 330–1, 349, 357, 372–3; II, 9, 17, 26, 33–5, 44–5, 49, 100, 184
  foreign affairs I, 2–3, 16–7, 132, 324–5, 333–6, 338, 340, 356–7; II, 241–3, 245–7, 255–6, 267, 298–9, 319
  fears a general rising throughout England I, 166, 214, 330

358   Index

Henry VIII
  land held in chief from 1, 12, 365, 368
  and Archbishop Lee 1, 150, 195, 380, 382
  his reply to the Lincs. rebels. *See* Proclamations, Royal
  and the Lincs. rebellion 1, 89, 91, 98–9, 107–8, 117, 119–20, 123, 134–6, 140, 165–6, 242, 335; II, 151
  misapprehension of his character 1, 60, 87, 190, 207, 209, 236, 253, 257–8, 271, 281, 358; II, 15, 87, 45, 172, 292, 329, 331
  and the nobles 1, 14–5, 21, 35, 87; II, 185–6, 227, 252–3
  and the Duke of Norfolk. *See* Norfolk, the Duke of, and the King
  his proposed visit to the north II, 89, 100, 134, 242, 250–1, 255, 259–60, 325
  reorganisation of the northern counties II, 103, chap. xxi, pp. 226 *et seq.*
  heir of the Earl of Northumberland. *See* Northumberland, the Earl of, act assuring his lands to the King
  Oath of allegiance to. *See* Oath of allegiance
  and the pacification of the north II, 99–101, 121–2, 127, 141, 144, 226–7, 286
  reluctant to grant a general pardon 1, 273–4; II, 7, 27, 52–3, 68, 100
  his pardons. *See* Pardon
  his private promises of pardon 1, 323; II, 6, 37
  his influence on parliament 1, 3, 21, 359–61, 388; II, 26, 55
  the rebels' petitions to. *See* Demands of the rebels
  proposes to lead an army against the Pilgrims 1, 112, 242–3, 278, 331, 338; II, 8
  his replies to the Pilgrims' Demands 1, 211, 263–4, 267, 274–8, 280, 289, 291–3, 295, 309, 315, 321–3, 331, 357; II, 1–2, 4, 11–4, 31, 35, 45, 51, 53, 72, 194
  receives the Pilgrims' messengers 1, 274, 308–9, 313, 334
  his policy with the Pilgrims 1, 278–81, 295–6, 308, 311, 314, 321–2, 324, 376; II, 3–4, 6, 12–4, 18, 23, chap. xvi, pp. 24 *et seq.*, 55, 59, 68, 82, 88, 105, 112, 280, 333
  his preparations against the Pilgrims 1, 178, 240, 241–9, 279, 282, 294–5, 319–20, 331; II, 6–7
  his first proclamation to the Pilgrims. *See* Proclamations, Royal
  and Reginald Pole 1, 16–7, 336–8; II, 277, 279, 281–3, 285–9, 295, 302, 305–6, 310, 317, 322

Henry VIII
  prophecies about. *See* Prophecies
  Rhymes and rumours about. *See* Rumour, *and* Sedition, rhymes
  the question of safe-conducts 1, 309, 317, 322, 345–6, 379; II, 2, 8, 10–12, 23
  correspondence with the Earl of Shrewsbury. *See* Shrewsbury, the Earl of, and the King
  the problem of his successor 1, 1, 317–8, 356, 362–3, 374; II, 297
  correspondence with the Duke of Suffolk. *See* Suffolk, the Duke of, correspondence with the King
  Supreme Head of the Church of England
    acceptance of the title 1, 73, 76, 98, 189, 263, 347, 385; II, 316
    the King asserts the title 1, 2, 6, 7, 10–11, 71–3, 275; II, 80, 85, 101
    the clergy's opinion of the title 1, 6; II, 59
    the nation's opinion of the title II, 36
    opposition to the title 1, 6, 11, 16, 69, 71, 72, 76, 212–3, 263, 326, 344, 347–8, 383–5; II, 57, 59, 60, 68, 79, 82, 137, 145–6, 198, 278, 293, 295, 300–1, 312, 319
    proposed limitations of his powers 1, 348, 374, 383, 385
    treason to discuss the title 1, 366
    reference 1, 9, 339, 353; II 166
  and the Treason Act 1, 11; II, 191, 192–3, 278
  his influence on trials II, 131–3, 185–7, 192–3, 204
  and the truce of Doncaster 1, 270–4, 279, 282
  his unpopularity 1, 69–70, 79, 207, 218, 258; II, 179, 247, 254, 293, 297–8, 301, 319
  and the White Rose Party 1, 17–18; II, 275–6, chap. xxii, pp. 277 *et seq.*, chap. xxiii, pp. 297 *et seq.*
  reference 1, 13, 19, 22, 28–9, 35, 46, 54–6, 61, 88, 115, 130–1, 142, 167, 186, 187, 198, 204, 226, 233, 235, 239, 240, 248, 254, 265, 286, 300, 319, 335, 355, 364, 371–2, 379; II, 24, 47, 58, 66, 69, 70, 71, 74, 76, 81, 84, 87, 90, 96–7, 173, 175, 181–2, 197, 199, 201, 207, 215–6, 300, 303
Henryson, — 1, 344
Herbert, Lord, of Cherbury, 'Life of Henry VIII' 1, 267
Hereford, the Bishop of. *See* Fox, Edward
Heresy. *See* New Learning
Herington, — 1, 264
Heron, Anthony 1, 44

Heron, George I, 197; II, 261-3
Heron, John, of Chipchase I, 195-7, 199, 299; II, 41-2, 230, 232-3, 261-3
Heron of Ford II, 235
Heron, John, of the Hall Barns II, 261, 263
Hert, Robert I, 93
Hert, William I, 93
Hertford I, 326; II, 244
Hessle I, 152-3
Hexham *alias* Topcliffe, John, Abbot of Whitby I, 41-3, 350
Hexham Priory I, 41, 75, 193-6, 198, 200, 208, 225; II, 121-2, 124, 232-3
  the sub-prior of I, 193-4
Hexham town I, 194; II, 41, 122, 124, 275
Hexhamshire II, 41, 235
Heydock, William II, 142
Heydon, Sir John II, 175
Heyton Wansdale. *See* Marston
Hilliard (Hillyard), Sir Christopher I, 155, 159, 161, 345; II, 81
Hilsey, John, Bishop of Rochester I, 98, 111, 353; II, 208
Hilton Castle I, 204
Hilton, family of I, 36-7
Hilton, Hugh I, 312
Hilton, Robert I, 221
Hilton, Sir Thomas, sheriff of Durham I, 204-6, 252, 262, 264-5, 284, 345-6, 376; II, 11, 21, 38, 104, 256
Hinde, John, the King's solicitor I, 87; II, 151, 204
Hinderwell II, 88, 159
Hodge, Robert, curate of Whitburn II, 254-6
Hogon, John I 266; II, 174
Holderness I, 145, 153, 155, 157, 159-61, 163, 167, 232, 242, 318; II, 9, 27, 47, 49, 62-4, 74-5, 82, 90, 301
Holdsworth, Richard I, 61
Holdsworth, Robert, vicar of Halifax I, 56-7, 61, 236, 286; II, 257-9
Holgate, Robert, Prior of Watton I, 285-7; II, 40, 58, 60, 82, 272
Holidays
  Christmas customs I, 41, 68; II, 61
  May games II, 176
  Michaelmas 1536 I, 78, 84, 86, 91
  Midsummer customs I, 41
  order for I, 9, 10, 383
  Plough Monday II, 47
  their prohibition causes discontent I, 152-3, 202, 220; II, 170-1, 174
  the rebels demand their restoration I, 383; II, 171
  shooting at the flyte and standard II, 175
Holinshed, Raphael, 'Chronicles of England' I, 116, 272
Holland, Lincs. I, 103, 111-2, 113, 121, 131

Holland, Hugh II, 284-6, 294-5, 303-6, 309, 311, 315-7
Holm Cultram Abbey I, 222, 225; II, 116, 123, 138, 263
  the Abbot of. *See* Carter, Thomas *and* Ireby, Thomas
Holme-in-Spalding Moor II, 50, 72-3, 75, 91
Holme, Wilfred, 'The Fall and Evil Success of Rebellion' I, 84, 179, 191, 287, 306; II, 118, 138, 160, 217
Holy Island, Northumberland I, 226
Holyrood II, 244, 254
Hooke Moor I, 156
Hopton, Sir Arthur I, 122
Horncastle I, 89, 101, 103-6, 111, 114, 124-5, 128, 129, 130, 135, 139, 153; II, 106, 149, 153
Hornchurch I, 74
Horncliff, Robert I, 162, 288-9; II, 152
Horner, Thomas I, 87; II, 172
Horskey, William I, 343; II, 47, 49, 61, 63-4, 81-2, 90
Horsley II, 290-1, 311, 313, 320
Horsley, John II, 232
Horwood, William II, 151
Hotham, Robert I, 157-8
Houghton juxta Harpley II, 179
House of Commons. *See* Parliament
House of Lords. *See* Parliament
Howard, family of II, 252
Howard, Queen Katherine II, 325
Howard, Katherine, widow of Rhys ap Griffith I, 287-8
Howard, Lord Thomas I, 242, 318; II 23
Howard, Lord William I, 259; II, 10, 23, 46, 291
Howden I, 142, 144, 156, 293, 298, 318; II, 27, 40
Howdenshire I, 141-2, 148-9, 154-8, 160, 169-70, 192, 230, 262; II, 163
Hudson, Clement II, 62
Hudswell, George I, 96, 105, 113, 125, 130, 289; II, 148-9, 153
Hugill, Robert II, 159
Hull
  Beverley gate I, 161; II, 65, 220-1
  the Busse ditch II, 65
  captain of. *See* Ellerker, Sir Ralph, the younger
  the Charterhouse. *See* Carthusians of Hull
  the parish church I, 158
  proposed fortification of II, 45-8, 51-2, 67, 71, 78-9, 88
  Hallam's attempt to seize II, 47-8, 60-8, 71-3, 76, 81, 97
  the Hermitage I, 161, 164
  its loyalty to the King I, 155, 159, 282; II, 47, 74, 77
  market II, 63-4, 220
  the mayor of. *See* Rogers, William
  Bigod's messengers to II, 73-4. *See also below*, prisoners
  vessels of I, 161, 286, 299, 336; II, 51

Hull
  pardon proclaimed in II, 27
  parliamentary representatives I, 359, 388
  in the Pilgrim's hands I, 167, 235, 286, 288, 297, 299, 301, 309, 318, 324; II, 8–9
  the plague in II, 222
  prisoners in II, 73–8, 81, 88–91, 98, 102, 126, 206, 209
  the siege of I, 146, 155–61, 163–6, 183, 228, 231, 235
  surrender of I, 163–4; 166–8, 239, 244; II, 65, 77, 90
  reference I, 79, 153, 174, 285, 310; II, 52, 80
Hullshire I, 160–1
Humber, the river I, 42, 78, 91, 105–6, 130, 141, 143, 145, 153, 157, 160–1, 164, 172, 245, 282, 319
Hume, Lord I, 37
Hundred Years War, the II, 55
Hungate, Thomas II, 82
Hunsley Beacon I, 148, 153, 166–7
Huntingdon town I, 120–2, 128, 133, 241–2; II, 82, 220
Huntingdon, George Hastings, Earl of I, 118, 122, 129, 131, 265, 312, 361
Huntington, Yorks. I, 84
Husee, John II, 19, 141, 193, 307
Huss, John I, 346
Hussey, Master I, 148
Hussey, Anne, wife of John, Lord I, 21, 25–6, 113, 130–1; II, 195, 215
Hussey, John, Lord I, 21–5, 96, 99, 100–1, 103–4, 108–10, 112–3, 116, 118–9, 130–2, 246, 289–92, 331; II, 149, 185–6, 195–7, 205
Hussey, Sir William, father of Lord Hussey I, 21
Hussey, Sir William, son of Lord Hussey I, 118, 131
Hutchinson, William I, 101
Hutton, Cumberland I, 222
Hutton Cranswick I, 157; II, 62
Hutton, Anthony I, 221; II, 106
Hutton, John, governor of the Merchant Adventurers of Antwerp I, 335–6; II, 224, 281, 283, 322
Hutton, Thomas, of Snaith I, 273; II, 126, 134

Indictments II, 135, 153–4, 198, 211, 314, 320
Ingleby, Sir William I, 45
Ingressum, the I, 369–72; II, 96, 121, 141
Injunctions of the Court of Chancery I, 366–7
Injunctions, the First Royal I, 10; II, 170
Inner Temple I, 90
Inns of Court I, 55, 367
Interdict, the Bull of I, 11, 72
Ipswich II, 166
—— the White Friars II, 166

Ireby, Anthony I, 112, 131
Ireby, Thomas, Abbot of Holm Cultram II, 188
Ireland I, 38, 287, 302; II, 159, 162, 287
Isabella, Empress of Charles V I, 335–6
Isle, the, Durham I, 204, 205, 226
Isle of Wight I, 326
Italy I, 4, 16, 47, 364; II, 247, 279, 284, 289, 302

Jackson, John II, 118, 120
Jackson, Richard II, 164
Jakes, — I, 209
James IV, King of Scotland I, 272
James V, King of Scotland I, 1, 28, 287, 333–5, 340, 355–6, 363; II, 10, 86, 95, 134, 216, 240–50, 253–6, 263, 266–8, 298–9
Jay, Edward, Prior of Hexham I, 193–5
Jedburgh Abbey II, 246
Jedworth Forest II, 233
Jeffreys, Judge II, 120
Jenney, Christopher I, 59, 62
Jepson, Isabel I, 61
Jerusalem I, 82, 214
Jervaux Abbey I, 43, 202–3, 206, 211, 288; II, 106–8, 188–9, 145, 214, 252, 266
  Abbot of. See Sedbarr, Adam
Jervyse, Harry II, 174
Jewel House, the I, 244
Jherom, — II, 199
Jobson, Brian I, 216
John the Baptist, St I, 72
John, St, of Beverley I, 45, 144
John, St, of Jerusalem II, 40
John the Piper I, 319
Johnson's house II, 46
Johnson, Mr II, 64
Johnson, Thomas (Brother Bonaventure) I, 57–8, 62, 147–8
Johnson, Dom Thomas I, 62
Johnson, Sir Thomas I, 345
Jons, Robert II, 215, 217
Jonson, William I, 248
Julian Bower I, 100

Katherine, youngest daughter of Edward IV I, 15
Katherine of Arragon I, 1, 7, 14–18, 20, 21, 22–25, 69, 80–1, 133, 178, 339, 354, 356; II, 299, 302, 320–1, 324
Kedington I, 92, 126
Kelet Moor I, 217
Kelsey II, 180
Kendal, barony I, 307, 345, 349, 369; II, 96
Kendal, borough I, 213, 216–8, 226, 316, 319, 345, 359; II, 20–1, 28, 30, 41
  the bailiff of. See Collins, Wm
Kendall, — II, 181
Kendall, Thos., vicar of Louth I, 92; II, 153–4
Kene, John II, 167

Index

Kenilworth Castle II, 170
Kenninghall I, 107, 121, 242; II, 99, 101
Kensey, — I, 156
Kent, county I, 134, 326; II, 167, 243, 293
Kent, George Grey, Earl of I, 21
Kermounde I, 98
Kesteven I, 131
Kettlewell II, 43, 85, 129
Kevin, St II, 170
Kexby I, 174
Kilton II, 160
Kilwatling How I, 222
Kimbolton I, 23, 122
King, Henry II, 266
King's Lynn II, 170, 174, 179
Kingston, Sir Wm I, 247, 290
Kingswood I, 65
Kirkby in Cleveland II, 159
Kirkby Lonsdale I, 207
Kirkby Malzyerd I, 52
Kirkby Ravensworth I, 201; II, 21
  the rector of. *See* Dakyn, John
Kirkbyshire I, 202, 262, 369; II, 51
Kirkby Stephen I, 221; II, 44, 106, 112–3, 117, 120
  the curate of I, 220
Kirk Deighton I, 382
  the rector of. *See* Waldby, Marmaduke
Kirkham Priory I, 233
Kirkstall, the Abbot of. *See* Ripley, John
Kirkstead Abbey I, 104, 106, 114, 126; II, 152–3
  the Abbot of. *See* Harrison, Ric.
Kirton, Thos I, 107
Kirton Soke I, 106–7, 110
Kitchen, Roger I, 145, 148, 150, 273; II, 61–4, 78, 82
Kitchin, 'Acts of the Northern Convocation' I, 388
Kite, John, Bishop of Carlisle I, 78, 117, 220
Knaresborough I, 388
  the forest of I, 163
  St Robert's Friary I, 151, 153, 175; II, 61–2, 68–9, 106, 121, 266
Knevet, Mr I, 234
Knight, — II, 3
Knolles, John I, 164, 166; II, 65, 90
Knutsford II, 169
Kyme, Guy I, 78–80, 94–6, 98, 111, 115, 130, 152–7, 174; II, 152–3, 180
Kyme, Thos II, 180

Lacy, family of I, 236; II, 257
Lacy, John I, 57, 61, 235–6
Lacy, Lancelot II, 70–1
Lacy, Thomas I, 236–7; II, 257
Lambart, John I, 286
Lambeth, John I, 233
Lamerside Hall I, 221
Lamplough, Sir John II, 110, 120
Lamprecht, K., 'Deutsche Geschichte' I, 225
Lancashire
  boundaries I, 226

Lancashire
  the Earl of Derby's musters I, 215–6, 219, 282; II, 7, 52
  disaffection in I, 169, 171, 212–5, 227; II, 188
  pardon proclaimed in II, 28
  the Pilgrimage of Grace in I, 212–3, 215, 216–9, 236, 314; II, 144
  trials II, 141–8
  the truce in I, 219–20, 269–70, 279, 292, 294, 316, 317, 319; II, 147
  reference I, 294, 304–6, 349; II, 119, 170
Lancaster, the House of I, 362
Lancaster Herald. *See* Miller, Thomas
Lancaster town I, 216–9, 239; II, 28, 142–3
  Castle II, 146–7
  the mayor of I, 218
Lanercost Priory II, 121–2
Langdale, Hugh II, 47, 49, 58, 63–4, 81–2, 90
Langgrische, Richard I, 332
Langley, barony of II, 235
Langley Castle I, 197, 201
Langrege, Dr, Archdeacon of Cleveland I, 382
Langthorn, Anthony I, 345
Langton, Sir John I, 18
Langwith Lane End I, 111
Lartington, the chantry priest of. *See* Tristram, William
Lasingham, — II, 158
Lassells, George II, 53
Lassells, Richard I, 345
Lassells, Roger I, 238, 261, 345–6
Lastingham II, 95, 97, 159
Lateran, the Council of the I, 384
Lather, Thomas, cellarer of Watton Priory II, 63, 82
Lathom I, 217, 220; II, 43
Latimer, John Neville, Lord I, 163, 182, 185, 201–3, 205–6, 231, 235, 237–8, 252, 262, 265, 312, 345, 377–8; II, 4, 13, 33, 61, 80, 87, 108–9, 160, 184–6
Latimer, Hugh, Bishop of Worcester I, 1, 43, 65, 98, 111, 114, 274, 326, 353; II, 25, 166, 199, 305, 318
Lawrence, James, Prior of Ellerton I, 287; II, 58, 60, 62
Lawson, Sir George I, 143, 174, 180–1, 232, 235, 243, 316, 344, 382; II, 34, 44, 138–9, 248
Layborne, Parson II, 31
Layton, Dr Richard, clerk of the Chancery I, 71, 114, 183, 318, 354, 367; II, 199, 204
Layton, Dr, preacher II, 259
Leache, Nicholas I, 101, 124; II, 151, 153–4
Leache, Robert I, 129; II, 151, 153–4
Leache, William I, 101–2; II, 83–6, 106, 113, 121, 129, 151, 202, 266
Leckonfield II, 80–1, 264

Ledam, John I, 42
Lee, Christopher I, 299
Lee, Edward, Archbishop of York
    and Robert Aske I, 191, 240, 254, 342–3, 377, 380–2, 385, 387
    his disputes with Beverley I, 147
    his brother I, 161
    and Lord Darcy I, 150, 252, 377, 379–81; II, 14, 34
    and the King's policy I, 9, 71, 193–5
    and the Pilgrims' demands I, 254, 263, 315, 342–3, 347, 352, 377–8, 383
    at Pontefract Castle I, 150–1, 170, 185–8, 190–1, 227, 228, 240, 252, 292, 302
    his sermon at Pontefract I, 377–82; II, 10, 12, 154, 300
    and the rebellion I, 143, 150, 175, 201, 256, 330, 340, 343, 376–81, 385–6; II, 130, 330
    his servants I, 212
    his steward I, 151
    and the taxation of the clergy II, 34, 49
    reference I, 264; II, 14, 33, 40, 259
Lee, Sir Robert I, 311
Lee, Roland, Bishop of Coventry II, 166
Leeds II, 28, 51, 111, 127
Legate, Robert II, 145–6
Legbourne Nunnery I, 95, 112; II, 154
Legh, Thomas I, 114, 133, 183, 318, 354, 367; II, 112, 184, 199, 204, 208
Leicestershire I, 113
Leicester town I, 321; II, 3, 244
Leith Haven II, 254
Lenton Priory II, 39, 179
Letters, Royal, Letters Missive, Royal Commissions
    circular letter to the Bishops I, 324; II, 9, 14
    commission on the condition of the clergy I, 91, 94
    commission to the Earl of Derby I, 215
    concerning Hexham Priory I, 194
    to the Lincs. rebels I, 123, 126–7
    to muster troops I, 108–10, 112, 116–8, 121, 173–4
    for attendance on the Duke of Norfolk II, 101
    citation to London II, 104–5, 125, 133, 157–62, 165, 185, 211, 215, 218
    concerning the title of Supreme Head of the Church I, 7
    joint commission of lieutenancy to Shrewsbury and Norfolk. See Norfolk, 3rd Duke of, his joint commission of lieutenancy with Shrewsbury
Levening, William II, 47, 66, 92, 131–3, 136–7, 188, 206, 209, 216
Lewes, Adam II, 248
Ley, Thomas II, 34

Leyborne, Sir James I, 216–7
Leyborne, Nicholas I, 216
Liddesdale II, 233, 238, 261–3, 268
Liége II, 283, 285–7, 294–5, 326
Lillesdale Hall (Bilsdale?) II, 266
Limehouse II, 195
Limoges, Bishop of II, 254
Lincoln city
    the Angel Inn I, 142
    assizes II, 153
    the Bishop's palace I, 111
    the cathedral I, 127, 135, 319
    the castle II, 150
    the Castle Garth I, 129
    the chapter house I, 115, 123, 127, 140
    the close I, 111, 115, 127, 135
    the dean's house I, 319
    executions there. See Lincs. rebellion, executions
    monastery of St Katherine II, 58, 60
    the mayor of. See Sutton, Robert
    Mile Cross towards Nettleham I, 114
    New Port I, 113
    prisoners in I, 281, 288–9, 319; II, 24, 148, 150–1, 153
    the rebels in I, 109–15, 126, 128–30, 140
    Suffolk's advance to I, 128, 135, 208, 245
    See also Suffolk, the Duke of, at Lincoln
    reference I, 79, 101, 103–4, 106, 109, 113, 119, 122, 164, 166, 274, 298, 301, 314, 320; II, 82, 102, 154
Lincoln, John I, 101
Lincolnshire
    its character I, 89
    condition of, after the rising I, 135, 164–5, 298; II, 84, 149, 151, 153, 197, 220, 223
    the King's lieutenant there. See Suffolk, the Duke of
    opposition to the New Learning in I, 67, 93–4, 96
    monastic debts in I, 320
    the royal army in. See Army, the Royal, in Lincs.
    a centre of sedition I, 78, 80
    the false Princess Mary in I, 87
    the subsidy men I, 192
    reference I, 18, 21, 50, 98, 131, 149, 151, 155, 228, 234, 247, 283, 287, 326; II, 26, 75, 80, 107, 214–5, 266
Lincolnshire rebellion
    accounts of, on the continent I, 132–3, 325, 335, 336, 338
    its characteristics I, 90–1, 123
    the commons and the gentlemen I, 91, 97–8, 100, 104, 114–5, 123–7, 138–40, 142; II, 148–51
    Lord Darcy's opinion of. See Darcy, Lord, and the Lincs. rebellion
    Demands of the rebels. See Demands of the rebels of Lincs.

Lincolnshire rebellion
  executions I, 79; II, 45, 94, 108, 148-9, 150-4, 158, 168, 197, 213, 220
  execution of the rebels delayed I, 269, 281, 319; II, 17, 148-51, 189
  causes of its failure I, 85, 126, 129, 138-9, 166, 265, 334, 358, 381
  finances I, 106-7, 113, 118, 153
  examination of the gentlemen I, 135, 140; II, 148-51
  the rebels at Lincoln. See Lincoln city, the rebels in
  monks in I, 104-5, 107, 118, 126; II, 152, 155-7
  murders and plundering I, 98, 101-2, 104, 111, 113, 115, 157; II, 196
  numbers of the rebels I, 97, 109, 111-2, 119, 125, 128, 133
  oath of the rebels. See Oath of the Lincs. rebels
  outbreak at Caistor I, 96-7
  outbreak at Horncastle I, 101
  outbreak at Louth I, 92
  the pardon I, 135, 273, 320; II, 84-5, 108, 150-1
  the parish priests in I, 91-2, 94, 96, 102
  prisoners sent to London I, 135; II, 148-9, 151
  prisoners pardoned II, 152-3
  refugees I, 306; II, 83, 93, 96, 129, 202
  royal letters to the rebels. See Letters, Royal, and Proclamations, Royal
  spreading of the rebellion I, 100-1, 104, 106, 111; II, 174
  and the commissioners of the Suppression I, 95
  surrender and dispersal of the rebels I, 129-30, 138, 162, 166, 173, 228, 244, 288
  trials II, 148, 151-4, 204
  connection with the Yorkshire rebellion I, 24, 79-80, 95, 105-6, 115, 129, 130, 139, 141, 142-3, 145, 146, 151-3, 156-7, 162-3, 166, 172, 174, 177, 201, 207, 229-30, 244, 288, 353; II, 150-2
  reference I, 154, 214-5, 279, 295, 377; II, 1, 40, 74, 166, 169, 180, 205
Lindsey I, 89
Line (Leven), the river I, 35, 196, 223; II, 113
Lisle, Arthur Plantagenet, Lord I, 335; II, 307, 323
Lisle, Lady II, 19
Lisle, Sir Humphry I, 31, 199, 201
Lisle, Sir William I, 31
Littlebury, Thomas I, 101, 107
Littleton, — I, 264
Llandaff, the Bishop of. See Holgate, Robert
Lobley, — II, 106, 203
Lockwood, — II, 70
Loder, John I, 42
Loder, William I, 42
Lofthouse, the rector of. See Franke, Thomas
Lofthouse, the bailiff of II, 161-2
Lollardy II, 172-3
Londesborough I, 62, 72, 82
London
  Bethlehem without Bishopgate I, 68
  Bishop of. See Stokesley, John
  the Black Friars nigh Ludgate II, 193
  London Bridge II, 195, 214, 216, 315
  Chancery Lane II, 46
  the Charterhouse. See Carthusians
  Cheapside I, 145, 328; II, 198
  Crossed Friars' Churchyard II, 195, 216
  Darcy detained in I, 20-4, 189-90
  districts in. See under their names, as Smithfield, Limehouse, etc.
  the Fleet prison II, 200, 218, 261-2
  the gates II, 214
  the Guild Hall II, 153-4, 206
  the King's Bench prison II, 219
  Our Lady Friars in Fleet Street II, 193
  news of the Lincs. rebellion reaches I, 107, 133
  the Lord Mayor of II, 325
  the Marshalsea II, 163-5, 213
  Newgate I, 62; II, 198
  Pardon Churchyard by the Charterhouse II, 154, 185
  St Paul's I, 328. See also Paul's Cross
  the plague in II, 27, 218
  preparations to suppress the rebellion I, 108, 117, 134
  rebel proclamations in. See Proclamations, Rebel, in London
  Protestant feeling in II, 292, 318
  its unprotected position I, 125
  the Queen's Head in Fleet Street I, 328
  the Rolls II, 46
  royal progress through II, 25
  rumours in I, 80, 122, 298; II, 19, 23, 25, 118, 165, 307
  news of the Yorkshire rebellion reaches I, 173, 244
  reference I, 25, 39, 50, 55-8, 69, 73, 99, 105, 118, 121, 123, 131, 141, 145-6, 157, 190, 191, 193, 205, 224, 229, 234, 236, 274, 278, 284, 293, 308, 310-1, 313, 326, 329, 340, 360, 366, 368, 377; II, 4, 24, 30, 32-3, 39-40, 42, 45, 50-2, 54, 58, 76, 79-80, 84, 95-6, 129-31, 135, 137-9, 142, 145, 163, 166, 171, 175-6, 184, 187-8, 194, 197, 200, 202, 204, 206-7, 209, 213, 222, 230, 233, 235, 242-5, 248, 251, 254, 257, 261, 265, 277, 279, 291, 304, 309, 321, 324-5
Longbottom, William II, 154

Longland, John, Bishop of Lincoln I, 67, 92, 98, 101, 111, 113, 114, 188; II, 40. *See also* Demands of the rebels
Lonsdale I, 317; II, 129
Lordington II, 289, 305-6
Louth
 Church I, 79, 92
 commissary's court at I, 91-2
 the Corn Hill I, 93
 the High Cross I, 94, 96
 the Tolbooth I, 126, 135
 the vicar of. *See* Kendale, Thomas
 reference I, 79, 91, 95-107, 111, 124, 128, 135, 136, 158, 326; II, 40, 126, 149-50, 152-4
Louthesk I, 79, 98
Louth Park II, 106
 Abbey I, 92-3, 112; II, 153
Louvain II, 283, 287
Lovell, Sir Francis I, 122
Lovell's rebellion I, 21
Low Countries. *See* Netherlands, the
Lownde, Thomas II, 47, 59, 63
Lowrey, John II, 63
Lowther I, 221
Lowther, Sir John I, 221-3; II, 116, 245-6, 249
Loyalists I, 155, 157, 159, 169-70, 180, 183, 196, 198-201, 206, 211, 223, 225, 280, 282, 287, 293-4, 297, 299; II, 92, 183
Luis of Portugal I, 325; II, 299
Luke, Sir Walter II, 151
Lumley Castle I, 204
Lumley, family of I, 86, 83
Lumley, George I, 204-5, 282-3; II, 66-72, 77, 80, 87, 135, 159, 185, 197-200, 208, 212, 216
Lumley, Jane, wife of George I, 205; II, 66, 200
Lumley, John I, 197, 199
Lumley, John, Lord I, 182, 204-6, 232, 237, 238, 252, 262, 265, 344-5; II, 13, 16, 96, 159-62, 185, 199-200
Lupton, Dr I, 244
Luther, Martin I, 346, 358
Lutherans I, 72
Lutton, — II, 181-2
Lygerd, — I, 157
Lynn I, 327
Lynney, Randolph, vicar of Blackburn II, 147-8, 189
Lynton II, 43
Lythe I, 151; II, 69, 71, 96, 184, 211, 213

Mackerell, Matthew, Abbot of Barlings I, 107, 111, 114, 116; II, 149-51, 153-6
Madeleine (Magdalen), daughter of Francis I I, 333-4, 340; II, 240, 242-3, 253-4, 266-7
Madeson, Sir Edward I, 96-9, 107, 118
Madowell, John II, 167

Magna Carta I, 360, 387
Magnus, Thomas, Archdeacon of the East Riding I, 72, 143, 150, 170, 185-6, 227, 292, 302; II, 33, 188, 260
Maidstone II, 168
Maitland, F. W. 'English Law and the Renaissance' I, 367-8; II, 182
'Year Books of Edward II' I, 36-7
Mallory, — I, 345
Mallory, Sir William I, 59, 212, 262, 345; II, 78
Maltby, Simon I, 91
Malton I, 40, 163, 281, 388
 Priory I, 283; II, 58-9
 the Prior of. *See* Todde, William
Maltravers, Lord II, 193
Manby, Thomas I, 95, 165
Manchester II, 142
 College I, 213
Manne, John I, 327
Manser, Edward I, 345
Manser, Henry II, 174
Mansfield I, 108, 116
Mansfield, — II, 133
Marches, Council of the. *See* Borders, Council of the Marches
Marck, Erard de la, Bishop of Liége II, 283, 295, 326
Margaret, Queen-Dowager of Scotland II, 250
Markby Priory I, 95
Markenfield, family of I, 212, 262
Market Rasen I, 107, 110
Marney, Henry, Lord I, 276; II, 1
Marshall, William I, 324, 346
Marshall, —, clerk of Beswick II, 65, 266
Marshall, Dr Cuthbert, Archdeacon of Nottingham I, 382-3, 385-6
Marshall, Dr II, 256
Marshall, Simon II, 266
Marshland I, 141-2, 148-50, 155-6, 168-9, 282, 293, 299, 318, 323; II, 9, 27
Marston *alias* Heyton Wansdale I, 58
Marton Priory I, 286
Mary, afterwards Queen
 and Charles V I, 325, 331, 333; II, 299
 danger of her position I, 22-5
 her friends I, 21, 25-6; II, 311, 320, 325
 her governess I, 14
 her proposed flight from Greenwich I, 23
 impersonated I, 87
 question of her legitimacy I, 1, 10, 21, 325, 331, 356, 363; II, 245
 proposals for her marriage I, 15, 17, 317, 324-5, 331, 337, 340; II, 267, 294, 299, 319, 323-4
 the Pilgrims support her claims I, 264, 318, 331, 339, 355-6, 383; II, 14, 277
 her popularity I, 1, 356-7

Mary
　reconciled to her father　I, 1, 26, 108
　her reign　I, 81; II, 325, 327
　reference　I, 27, 335; II, 25
Mary of Guise　II, 298
Mary of Hungary, Regent of the Netherlands　I, 133-4, 310, 335-6, 339; II, 282-3
Masham　II, 266
Mashamshire　I, 201-3, 208, 239, 252, 262, 369
Master of the Rolls. *See* Hales, Christopher
Maston　I, 82; II, 132
Maunsell, Thomas, vicar of Brayton　I, 170, 180, 184-6, 188-90, 261, 278, 297; II, 92
Maunsell, William　I, 180, 297; II, 84
Maxwell, Lord　II, 246-7
Maydland, Dr　I, 82
Meat, act regulating the price of　I, 13
Melanchthon, Philip　I, 346
Melling, the constable of　II, 113
Melmerby, the parson of　I, 227
Melton, Nicholas. *See* Captain Cobbler
Merlay, Thomas　I, 205
Merlin　I, 81, 83-6, 209; II, 244
Merriman, R. B. 'Life and Letters of Thomas Cromwell'　II, 296
Metcalf, Sir James　I, 86, 208
Metham, Sir Thomas　I, 149, 151
Metham, young　I, 148-9, 157-9, 181, 185, 345
Meux　I, 388
Mewtas, Peter　II, 32, 285, 294
Middleham　I, 201, 208; II, 28, 34, 105, 184
Middleham Moor　II, 108
Middleton, Lancs.　I, 217
Middleton, —　I, 345
Middleton, —, yeoman, and his wife　I, 236
Middleton, Edward　I, 203; II, 38, 107-8, 110, 208, 214, 266
Middleton, John　I, 217
Middlewood, Roger　II, 87-8, 117
Middlewood, William　II, 87
Miffin, Philip　I, 155
Milan, Christina, Dowager-Duchess of　II, 298
Milan, the Duchy of　II, 299
Milburn　I, 371
Milburn, the family of　II, 238
Milburn, Christopher　II, 230-1
Milburn, David　II, 230-1
Milburn, Humphrey　II, 238
Mileham, Nicholas, sub-prior of Walsingham　II, 175, 179
Miller, Thomas, Lancaster Herald　I, 128-30, 134, 166, 172, 228-30, 238, 240, 249, 252, 256, 259, 346, 379-80; II, 10, 17, 28, 30, 40, 44, 61, 83, 134, 300-1, 327
Millthrop Hall　I, 237
Milner, Sir John　I, 152
Milnthorpe, the bailiff of　II, 144
Milsent, John　I, 95, 126, 135, 165
'Mirror for Magistrates'　I, 85
Missenden, Sir Thomas　I, 97
Moigne, Thomas　I, 36, 55, 90, 98-100, 106, 110, 126-7, 140-1; II, 150-2
Moke, William　II, 215, 217-8
Monasteries
　capacities for monks　I, 92, 116, 218; II, 125, 145
　proposed crown rent charge from their lands　I, 352, 374-5
　and the Statute of First Fruits　I, 351
　grants of monastic lands　I, 28, 51, 95, 162, 190, 193, 280, 332, 349; II, 138-9, 219, 301-2
　and Henry VIII. *See* Henry VIII, his ecclesiastical policy
　Queen Jane pleads for them　I, 108
　not restored by the Lincs. rebels　I, 112, 153
　restored by the Pilgrims　I, 112, 162, 178-9, 213, 218, 244, 274, 317; II, 17, 20-1, 24, 39, 35-6, 109, 111, 129, 212
　and the Pilgrimage of Grace　I, 208, 218-9, 222, 225, 232-3, 283, 287; II, 38-40, 121, 128, 145-6, 152, 154-7, 212-4
　their popularity　I, 348-51
　prophecies in. *See* Prophecies
　the rebels demand their restoration. *See* Demands of the rebels
　draft act for their reorganisation　I, 375
　suppressed, receivers of their goods　I, 278; II, 20
　refounding of, after suppression　I, 193; II, 25-6
　opinions of the suppression in　I, 74-6; II, 107, 157, 166, 175
　suppression or surrender of the greater　II, 121-2, 138-9, 142, 144-7, 153, 155, 166
　general suppression of　II, 299, 301-2, 329
　and their tenants　II, 156, 173, 213
Monketon, Anne　I, 50
Monketon, William　I, 50, 148-9, 181; II, 32-3, 78
Monmouth's Rebellion　II, 120
Montague, Henry Pole, Lord
　his arrest　II, 310, 315
　his character and opinions　I, 361; II, 217, 236, 292-4, 303
　his danger　I, 15; II, 275-7, 295
　evidence against　II, 310-2, 321
　his execution　II, 286, 315, 326-7
　his correspondence with Exeter. *See* Exeter, the Marquis of, his friends
　his family and connections　I, 14-5, 22
　his proposed flight from England　II, 278, 286, 295, 310, 316

Montague, Henry Pole, Lord
  his friends II, 290–2, 313
  his papers II, 305–6, 315, 317, 319
  message from Cardinal Pole II, 285–6, 294, 303
  and Sir Geoffrey Pole's arrest II, 306
  his trial II, 314, 318
  reference I, 17, 330; II, 289, 296, 304, 307
Montague, Jane, Lady I, 14
Monteagle, Thomas Stanley, Lord I, 53, 216, 218, 319; II, 119
Montmorency, Anne de, Constable of France II, 310, 319
Monubent I, 210, 219
Monyhouse II, 69
Moors, the I, 19
Mordaunt, Lord II, 193
More, Sir Thomas I, 11, 23, 63, 65, 68–9, 271, 354, 358; II, 136, 182, 192, 287, 292
Moreton, John I, 285
Morland, William, *alias* Burobe I, 92–4, 96–8, 100–4, 124, 126, 128, 138, 288, 336; II, 106, 153
Morley, Lord II, 193
Morpeth II, 28, 81, 233
Morris, John, 'The Troubles of our Catholic Forefathers' I, 59
Mortlake I, 303
Moryson, Richard, 'An Invective against Treason' II, 307, 309, 314–5, 321–2
Mountgrace Priory I, 43, 233
Mountjoy, William Blount, Lord II, 193
Mousehold Heath II, 176
Moy, Charles de, vice-admiral of France II, 254, 256
Mulgrave I, 41, 205–6; II, 59, 87
Muncaster II, 112
Musgrave, family of II, 115
Musgrave, Cuthbert II, 116
Musgrave, Sir Edward I, 222
Musgrave, Nicholas I, 221, 345; II, 106, 111–3, 266
Musgrave, Sir William II, 6, 9, 42
Muskham I, 319
Mustone. *See* Maston
Mustone, the vicar of. *See* Dobsone, John

Napoleon I, 17; II, 298
Nassau, the Count of I, 108
Navy, the English II, 95, 242–3, 245, 247
Naworth Castle I, 224, 250
Neales Ynge I, 209
Neat geld I, 370–2; II, 44
Nesfield, John I, 72
Nethe Abbey II, 143
Netherdale I, 52, 262, 369
Netherlands, the I, 27, 335–6; II, 281, 322
  the Regent of. *See* Mary of Hungary
Nettleham (Netlam) II, 154
Neville (Nevill), Edith, Lady I, 18; II, 194

Neville, Sir Edward II, 289–90, 310, 312, 314–5, 320
Neville, Henry, Lord I, 204–5, 231, 235, 237, 238, 252, 262, 345; II, 13, 16, 96
Neville, Sir John II, 255
Neville (Nevill), Margaret II, 185
Neville (Nevill), Marmaduke I, 262, 312, 345; II, 20, 24, 53
Neville (Nevill), Mary II, 185
Neville (Nevill), Sir Robert I, 186, 238, 345
Neville (Nevill), Thomas II, 185, 217
Neville, William II, 87–8
New, Roger II, 153
Newark I, 63, 245, 249, 251, 293–4, 296, 311, 319–20; II, 5, 8, 107
  Castle I, 250, 282
  the vicar of II, 301
Newbald I, 151; II, 64
Newborough I, 146; II, 60, 133
Newburgh Priory I, 233
Newbury I, 51
Newcastle-upon-Tyne I, 31, 36, 59, 63, 65, 72, 183, 185, 192, 196, 204–7, 225, 239, 288, 336; II, 21, 28, 30, 38–9, 94–5, 102, 104, 122, 124, 126, 133, 233–4, 237–8, 246, 256, 262, 269–70, 275
Newdyke, Richard I, 145
New Learning, the
  and the ten articles of religion I, 10
  bishops inclined to I, 178, 280, 324, 348, 353–4
  in East Anglia II, 173, 177
  in Germany II, 299
  the King's persecution of I, 324, 374, 379; II, 13, 166, 180, 299–300
  literature I, 24, 67, 98, 353
  in the monasteries I, 65, 75; II, 166
  its progress I, 24, 93; II, 168, 177, 197, 199, 292, 301, 318
  the rebels demand its suppression. *See* Demands of the rebels
  its unpopularity I, 59, 66, 68, 71, 82, 271, 348, 354; II, 164–9, 196, 199, 292, 302–3, 305, 316, 319
  reference I, 64, 84, 86; II, 259
Newminster Abbey II, 121–2
Newstead I, 200
Newton, William I, 43
Nice II, 299, 302
Nicholas, — I, 93, 98
Nicholson, William II, 49, 62, 64, 66, 82
Nidd, the river I, 231
Nidderdale I, 201, 208
Nieuport II, 285
Noble, Thomas I, 96
Norfolk county I, 78, 107, 120, 241, 327–8; II, 26, 99, 173–4, 178
Norfolk rebellion of 1549 I, 364
Norfolk, Thomas Howard, second Duke of, formerly Earl of Surrey I, 272, 276; II, 154

Index

Norfolk, Thomas Howard, third Duke of, formerly Lord Admiral
  and Robert Aske. *See* Aske, Robert, and the Duke of Norfolk
  and the Borders II, 103, 124, 126, 133–4, 230–9, 248, 257, 261–4, 268–70, 275–6
  his plan of campaign I, 249
  plot to capture II, 60–1, 97, 107, 111, 176
  his character I, 4–5, 14
  and the commons' rising II, 114–24, 128
  his council II, 8, 16, 52, 99, 126, 229, 256, 271
  his correspondence with the Privy Council. *See* Council, the King's, correspondence with Norfolk
  his correspondence with Cromwell. *See* Cromwell, Thomas, his correspondence with Norfolk
  his rivalry with Cromwell I, 5, 107, 109, 120, 265–6, 358; II, 4, 14, 37, 46, 221–2, 224, 261
  and Darcy. *See* Darcy, Thomas, Lord, and the Duke of Norfolk
  suppresses disturbances in Norfolk I, 78, 120–1; II, 174
  at the second conference at Doncaster. *See* Pilgrimage of Grace, the second appointment at Doncaster
  and Sir Ralph Evers II, 183–4
  his family I, 260; II, 28, 250
  his finances I, 244, 246–7; II, 9, 250
  at the Battle of Flodden I, 19, 265, 272
  hated in the north II, 254, 301
  and the King I, 20, 107, 120, 130, 241–3, 245–7, 249, 251, 259–60, 266–8, 270, 274, 276, 273, 279, 290, 329–30; II, 4–11, 15–6, 19, 22–4, 26, 31, 36, 50, 95, 99, 101–3, 109, 111, 114, 117–8, 120–4, 126–7, 131, 133–5, 138–9, 186, 194, 211, 229, 239, 250–1, 253, 259–60, 264–5, 267, 269–70, 273
  his mission to the north II, 9, 11, 18, 21, 27–32, 44–46, 48–53, 55, 60, 67, 71, 73, 76, 80–2, 92–7, chap. xviii, pp. 99 *et seq.*, 141, 158, 160, 187–8, 202, 206, 209, 215, 244, 245, 253, 254–6, 259, 270, 272
  his first journey north I, 244–5, 247, 249–51
  his opinion of northern gentlemen I, 18, 37, 46; II, 236, 239, 269
  his designs on the Percy inheritance II, 125, 234–7, 239–40, 251–3, 260, 264–5, 274
  his opinion of the Pilgrims' army I, 257, 269
  collects evidence against the Pilgrims II, 85, 124–5, 130–1, 194, 199–201, 210–1, 218–9

Norfolk, Thomas Howard, third Duke of
  his sympathy with the Pilgrims I, 266–7, 279, 287, 327, 329–31, 338–9; II, 15, 111
  sent to treat with the Pilgrims I, 253–4, 256–9, 264–5, 309, 311, 315, 317, 321–3, 330–1, 342, 344–5, 377, 381, 385; II, 2, 3, 7, 10, 12
  his policy I, 4–5, 260, 266–8
  his popularity I, 19, 250–1, 258, 265, 271, 315; II, 45–6, 217–8
  his promise to keep no terms with the rebels I, 259–60; II, 5, 15
  reports of his agents I, 318; II, 3, 123
  rumour of his arrest. *See* Rumour, of the Duke of Norfolk's arrest
  his troops I, 118–9, 183, 241–2, 244–5, 248, 257, 268–9
  superseded in the command of the royal army I, 120–1, 241
  reappointed to command the royal army I, 173, 241
  and Scottish affairs II, 238, 241, 247–50, 266, 268
  and the Earl of Shrewsbury. *See* Shrewsbury, the Earl of, and the Duke of Norfolk
  his joint commission with Shrewsbury I, 173, 215, 243, 245; II, 8, 9, 29
  and the Duke of Suffolk I, 241–2, 247, 268, 321; II, 8, 9, 11, 17, 22
  his trial II, 186
  holds trials II, 109–111, 118–122, 125–6, 129, 131–7, 140, 143, 151, 164, 257–8, 262
  at York. *See* York city, the Duke of Norfolk at
  reference I, 38, 204, 218, 238, 262, 264, 294, 300, 302, 320, 326; II, 77–9, 84, 98, 108, 113, 144, 151, 163, 182, 193, 197, 277, 289, 305

Norham Castle I, 203–4, 240; II, 33, 78
Norman, Robert I, 92
Northallerton I, 388; II, 78, 180
Northamptonshire I, 113
North Cave I, 152
North Charlton I, 200
North Tynedale. *See* Tynedale, North
Northumberland county
  escapes taxation I, 192
  gentlemen of II, 228, 230–1, 235, 239
  pardon proclaimed in II, 28
  the rising in I, 115, 118, 122, 143, 192–201; II, 41
  the truce proclaimed in I, 299
  unrest there after the rebellion II, 61, 81, 105, 120, 122, 203, 230–3, 263
  reference I, 29, 150, 205, 345, 364; II, 80, 103, 234, 238, 244, 272
Northumberland, the Earls of. *See* Percy, family of
Northumberland, the first Earl of I, 15

Northumberland, the fifth Earl of I, 31, 33, 34, 46–7, 232
Northumberland, the seventh Earl of II, 331. *See also* Percy, Sir Thomas, his children
Northumberland, Henry Percy, sixth Earl of I, 23, 29–34, 41, 45, 54–5, 57, 73, 149–50, 184, 194, 197–9, 230, 232, 235, 246, 283–6; II, 9, 33, 103, 125, 131, 228, 235, 237, 239, 250–2, 265
  Act assuring his lands to the King I, 33, 199, 264; II, 125, 183, 235
Northumberland, Katherine, dowager countess of I, 81, 34, 150, 230–1; II, 67, 81, 85, 203, 215, 252, 273
Northumberland, Mary, Countess of I, 32, 285
Norton, family of I, 212, 238, 262
Norton, John I, 52, 209, 211, 345–6; II, 43
Norton, Richard I, 209, 345
Norton, Thomas I, 209
Norton, Cheshire, the Abbot of I, 213–4, 226
Norton Conyers I, 52, 209
Norway I, 83, 86
Norwich I, 65, 78, 327; II, 99, 175, 177–9
  Castle II, 176
Nottingham county I, 234; II, 89
Nottingham town I, 109, 113, 118–9, 121–2, 128, 130–1, 148, 168, 170, 172–4, 185, 249, 259, 266, 294–6, 311, 320, 322, 360; II, 3, 8, 59, 205
  Castle I, 282
  the Archdeacon of. *See* Marshall, Dr Cuthbert
Nunney (Nonye) I, 87–8; II, 172
Nun of Kent, Elizabeth Barton, the II, 313
Nuttles I, 155

Oath
  of allegiance to the King I, 68, 147, 342; II, 2, 9, 99–101, 109, 122, 127, 141–2, 149, 231–3
  devised by Sir Francis Bigod II, 60, 66, 70, 73, 78
  of the Cornish rebels II, 171
  of the rebels at Kendal I, 216
  of the Lincs. rebels I, 93–5, 97, 99, 105, 107, 109, 111, 124, 141, 181, 182, 198, 289; II, 87
  the obligation of contradictory oaths I, 304, 342, 387
  of the Pilgrimage of Grace I, 139, 181–4, 190, 200, 202, 209–10, 216–9, 222, 227–9, 231, 234, 252, 263, 298, 310, 319, 321, 328, 342; II, 41, 47, 92, 101, 112–3, 164, 170, 174, 183, 190, 202
  of canonical obedience to the Pope I, 342
  of the Richmondshire rebels II, 80

Oath
  acknowledging the King's supremacy I, 343; II, 295, 312
  a treasonable, taken in the Yorkshire dales I, 79, 207
  of the Yorkshire rebels I, 145, 147, 150, 152, 154, 163–4, 180, 197, 199, 204–5
Observant Friars. *See* Friars, Observant
Ogle, family of II, 228, 231
Ogle, Lewis I, 197
Ogle, Robert, Lord I, 32, 197, 285; II, 81
Oldfelden, John II, 169
Oldfelden, Philip II, 169
Oldfelden, Richard II, 169–70
Ombler, William I, 155, 160–1, 163, 273
Order of the Garter II, 195, 229
Orders. *See* Proclamations, Royal
Orleans, the Duke of I, 325, 331, 340
Ormsby I, 95
Ortiz, Dr Pedro I, 336
Osborne, Harry I, 287–8
Oseney, the Abbot of II, 168
Osgodby II, 72
Otterburn II, 230
Otterburn, — II, 110
Otterburn, Adam II, 247
Otterburn, James, priest of Rosedale II, 160
Oughtred, Sir Robert I, 186, 379
Ouse, the river I, 130, 134, 141–2, 148–9, 156, 170, 172, 174, 231, 282
Ovingham, the master of I, 193–4
Oxford city II, 170
  the vicar of St Peter's in the East. *See* Serls, —
Oxford county I, 67; II, 170
Oxford, John de Vere, 15th Earl of I, 120–1, 276, 290; II, 25, 193
Oxford University I, 43; II, 168–70
  Oriel College II, 169
Oxneyfield I, 202–3

Page, Sir Richard I, 259
Palmer, Sir Thomas II, 284
Palmes, — I, 345
Palmes, Dr George, rector of Sutton-upon-Derwent I, 382, 384
Papal Dispensations declared void by Act of Parliament I, 8
Pardon
  persons excepted from I, 273; II, 9, 12, 22, 27, 126, 260, 266
  the general I, 79; II, 7, 11, 15–21, 23, 27–31, 35, 37, 42, 48, 52–4, 73, 77–8, 82, 100, 106, 120, 127–8, 131, 141, 147, 152, 158, 187–8, 190, 191, 198, 200–2, 204, 206, 209, 211–2, 217–8, 224, 250, 260, 266, 300
  dissatisfaction caused by the general II, 30–1, 45, 51, 59–60, 68, 76, 82, 106, 114, 211
  the final II, 328

Index

Pardon
  the Lincs. rebels petition for I, 98–9, 127. *See also* Demands of the rebels, of Lincs.
  proposed, to the Lincs. rebels I, 129, 135
  to Marshland and Holderness II, 9
  by act of parliament I, 318, 361. *See also* Demands of the rebels, of Yorks.
  a limited, offered to the Pilgrims I, 273, 295; II, 2, 6–7, 12, 126
  sale of I, 366, 373; II, 146
Paris I, 339, 357; II, 240, 242, 284–5
Parishe, — II, 83, 266
Parker, Edmund II, 188
Parker, George I, 95, 126
Parkyns, John II, 168
Parliament
  complaints of abuses in I, 3, 28, 331, 339, 358–61; II, 330
  of December 1529 to March 1536 I, 3, 11, 20, 24–5, 264
  of June to July 1536 I, 1, 3, 8, 25
  of 1539 II, 323–4
  acts of. *See under separate heads as* Treason, Act of
  its composition I, 3, 358; II, 31, 45
  freedom of access to I, 318
  freedom of speech in I, 361; II, 26
  the King relies on its authority I, 331, 358; II, 14
  confirms the Lancastrian title to the crown I, 362
  the ancient customs of the House of Lords I, 360
  petition of the Commons 1532 I, 6
  the Pilgrims appeal to its authority I, 355, 360, 374; II, 14
  places not represented in I, 355, 359, 388; II, 15
  proposed, after the rebellion I, 360–1, 375; II, 16, 18–24, 26, 27, 31, 37, 45, 48–9, 51, 55, 60, 68, 71–3, 79, 86, 100, 102–3, 130, 168, 187–8, 198, 206, 209–10, 280
  social legislation I, 12
  the Speaker I, 358
  modification of the Treason Act I, 11
  reference I, 2, 19, 98, 372, 385
Parr, Sir William I, 122–3, 126, 320; II, 53, 151, 153–4, 220–2
Parry, Thomas I, 203
Paslew, John, Abbot of Whalley II, 142–5, 147, 169, 189
Pater, William I, 299
Paul III, Pope (the Bishop of Rome)
  his authority in England denied I, 2, 7, 10, 65, 67–8, 71, 304, 343, 385; II, 35, 41, 165
  letters of censure on Henry VIII I, 337; II, 241–2, 287–8, 298
  and his English supporters I, 8, 64–9, 72, 75, 82, 258, 287, 310, 331, 336, 338–40, 383–4; II, 30, 120, 127, 219, 277, 280, 287, 312, 321, 330–1

Paul III, Pope (Bishop of Rome)
  his relations with France I, 334; II, 281
  tries to reconcile Francis I and Charles V I, 2, 3, 335, 338; II, 242, 245, 298
  possible reconciliation with Henry VIII I, 1; II, 278
  his Bull of Interdict against Henry VIII I, 11, 334, 339, 341; II, 298–9
  and James V of Scotland II, 240–2, 256
  at the meeting at Nice II, 298–9
  and Cardinal Pole II, 279, 283, 286, 302
  sermons against his usurped power. *See* Sermons, loyal
  reference II, 244, 249, 303, 326
Paul's Cross I, 274, 324, 374; II, 25, 291, 305
Paul's Wharf II, 318
Paulet, — II, 172
Paulet, Sir William I, 247, 276, 290; II, 118, 309, 324
Pavia, the battle of I, 364
Pawston (Fawston?) II, 238
Payne, Hugh II, 165
Peacock, Anthony II, 110–1, 180
Pecock, John I, 42
Pennell, Harry I, 96
Penrith I, 70, 79, 221–4, 226, 312, 345, 370; II, 28, 120–3
  the Captains' Mass I, 223
  chapel I, 222
  Fell I, 221
Percebay, William I, 230–1
Percy, family of I, 31, 84, 115, 192; II, 43, 114, 183, 227, 232, 252, 273–4
Percy, Agnes, wife of Sir William I, 45
Percy, Eleanor, wife of Sir Thomas I, 33; II, 124–5
Percy, Henry. *See* Percy, Sir Thomas, his children
Percy, Sir Ingram I, 32–3, 150, 196, 198–201, 220, 224, 284–5, 299, 306; II, 10, 41–2, 104–5, 158, 202, 219, 228, 230, 273
Percy, Thomas. *See* Percy, Sir Thomas, his children
Percy, Sir Thomas
  his arrest II, 104–5, 130, 158, 202, 230
  and Robert Aske I, 231, 284–5
  his character I, 34
  and Bigod's insurrection II, 61, 67, 71, 80–1, 36–7, 203
  captured by the Pilgrims I, 163, 280–1; II, 163
  his feud with the Carnabys I, 33, 199–200; II, 41, 124, 281–2
  his children I, 33; II, 252, 273–4
  his petition to Cromwell I, 33
  disinherited I, 33–4, 122, 232, 284
  evidence against II, 86, 124, 202–3
  his execution II, 216, 228
  and little John Heron I, 195; II, 41–2, 232, 263

Percy, Sir Thomas
  his imprisonment II, 125, 219
  his alleged letter to Lincs. II, 84
  and the monasteries I, 233
  his quarrels with the Earl of Northumberland I, 32–3, 283–4
  his conduct in Northumberland I, 115, 299; II, 41–2
  his company of Pilgrims I, 280–1, 239, 251, 262
  his popularity I, 34, 232; II, 71, 203
  his connection with the Richmondshire rising II, 203, 214
  and the Abbot of Sawley's supplication II, 83–6, 98, 124, 127, 142, 201, 203, 212
  his trial II, 185, 198, 204
  his entry into York I, 281–2, 285
  reference I, 122, 149, 198, 238, 285, 345; II, 10
Percy, Sir William I, 45–8
Percy, William, Lord II, 83
Perith, Edward I, 221
Peter, — I, 91
Peter, St I, 383
Peterborough I, 112
Petitions of the rebels. *See* Demands of the rebels
Philips, — I, 170; II, 205
Philips, Thomas II, 321, 324–5
Phillips, Henry II, 283
Picardy I, 339
Pickburn I, 256, 260
Pickering I, 388
Pickering Lythe. *See* Lythe
Pickering, Friar John I, 280–1, 307, 373, 382–3, 385–6, 388; II, 61–2, 121, 125, 130, 188, 211–4
Pickering, John, priest II, 163–4, 211, 213
Piercebridge I, 208
Pilgrimage of Grace
  its political antecedents I, chap. i, pp. 1–13, 73–4, 341–2
  badge of the Five Wounds. *See* Badge, the Five Wounds of Christ
  the mission of Bowes and Ellerker. *See* Bowes, Robert, his mission to the King
  its captain. *See* Aske, Robert
  reports of, on the continent I, 330, 333–6, 338–40; II, 217, 241, 280
  discipline I, 148, 160–2, 176, 178, 183, 221, 229–30, 312–3
  its dual character I, 208, 225–6, 283, 370; II, 96, 100, 213, chap. xxiv, pp. 329 *et seq.*
  the advance to the Don I, 238–9, 251–62
  the first appointment at Doncaster. *See* Truce of Doncaster
  the second appointment at Doncaster I, 287, 313, 315, 317–8, 321, 332, 342, 346, 359, 373, 376–7; II, chap. xv, pp. 1–23, 24–5, 27, 31–4, 38–9, 42–3, 46, 52, 54–5, 73,

Pilgrimage of Grace
  79, 84, 95, 97–8, 111, 129, 141, 147, 158, 164, 166, 189, 223, 252
  its early stages. *See under* Yorkshire rebellion
  executions II, 195, 214–7, 220–1, 225, 226, 278, 282, 286, 322
  prospects of success or failure I, 253–4, 258, 279, 381; II, 55
  causes of its failure II, 55–6, 292, 322, 329–333
  finances I, 162, 183, 188, 206, 232–3, 267, 286, 288, 331; II, 44, 209
  suspicion between gentlemen and commons I, 252, 254, 265, 280, 308, 341, 381–2; II, 16, 20, 31–3, 45–7, 51, 330, 333
  lists of grievances I, 315, 332, 342, 345–7, 354, 357, 370–2
  siege and surrender of Hull. *See* Hull
  the Pilgrims' attitude to the King I, 253, 281, 305–6; II, 292, 329
  and the King's intrigues. *See* Henry VIII, his policy with the Pilgrims
  the King's replies to the Pilgrims' Demands. *See* Henry VIII, his replies to the Pilgrims
  its leaders I, 29, 36–7, 55, 254, 261–2, 271, 367–8, 373, 376; II, 18, 55, 72, 90, 164, 271, 277, 322, 330, 333
  restoration of monasteries during. *See* Monasteries restored by the Pilgrims
  proposed appeal to the Netherlands for help I, 310; II, 190, 223
  means of communication between the hosts I, 211, 288
  negotiations with Norfolk. *See* Norfolk, the Duke of, sent to treat with the Pilgrims
  settlement of the north after II, chap. xxi, pp. 226–276
  numbers I, 70, 154, 157, 160, 173, 175, 180, 185, 191, 205, 212, 217, 234, 237, 252, 261–2, 330–1, 336; II, 300, 332
  oath of the Pilgrims. *See* Oath, of the Pilgrimage of Grace
  opinion in the ranks I, 264–5, 268, 290; II, 12, 19–20, 22, 24
  siege and surrender of Pontefract Castle I, 184–90, 192; II, 92, 129
  the musters at Pontefract I, chap. x, pp. 227–40
  Council at Pontefract I, 191, 312, 315, 317, 332, chap. xiv, pp. 341–88; II, 7, 10, 20, 24, 57, 129–30, 185, 189, 213, 270
  plundering by the Pilgrims I, 183–4, 204–5, 211, 261, 279, 283, 287, 297, 300; II, 218, 256–8
  rhymes in praise of I, 85, 213, 261, 280–1, 307, 349–50; II, 169–70, 212–3
  the Pilgrims in touch with the royal army I, 251, 255–6

Index

Pilgrimage of Grace
  the Pilgrims demand safe-conducts.
    See Henry VIII, the question of safe-conducts
  Scarborough Castle besieged I, 212, 314
  the siege of Skipton Castle. *See* Cumberland, the Earl of, his defence of Skipton Castle
  the alarm at Snaith I, 296-8, 300-1
  spread of I, 171, 230-1, chap. ix, pp. 192-226
  sympathy with, in the south I, 266-7, 305-6, 327, 329-30, 375; II, 24, 26, 36, 59, 164-5, 167-9, 171, 174, 190, 223, 243-4, 292
  council of captains at Templehurst I, 308-11
  trials II, chap. xx, pp. 182-225
  the Pilgrims' determination during the truce I, 295-6, 344; II, 4, 6
  preparations during the truce I, 281-3, 286, 309-10, 313, 316-7, 344
  the capture of Edward Waters' ship I, 314, 317, 322-3; II, 9, 17, 57
  the advance to York I, 154, 158, 164, 168-9, 171, 174-5, 178, 181-2
  the council at York I, 233, 306, chap. xiii, pp. 308-40, 342, 354; II, 57, 201
Pinchinthorp I, 39
Pittington I, 369
Place, — I, 345
Pledges, the Border II, 281, 283, 237-9, 248, 257, 262, 270, 274-5
Plumland II, 112
Plummer, John I, 66
Plumpton, — I, 181, 345
Plymouth I, 19
Poland I, 15
Pole, family of I, 14, 332-3, 338; II, 277-8, 299, 308, 329
Pole, Constance, wife of Sir Geoffrey II, 305-6, 326
Pole, Sir Geoffrey I, 22, 330, 332; II, 275-6, 278, 284-6, 289-96, 302-12, 314-18, 323, 326-8
Pole, Henry II, 306, 310, 323-5, 328
Pole, Reginald, Cardinal
  approves of the ten articles of religion I, 352
  attainted II, 323
  his book 'De Unitate Ecclesiastica' I, 16-7, 337-9; II, 278-9, 287-9, 302
  his cardinalate I, 338, 340; II, 279
  and Charles V I, 16-17
  delay in his ordination I, 27, 337
  leaves England I, 15
  communications with England II, 283-6, 303-6, 311, 316-8
  his proposed mission to England I, 331, 337-9; II, 241, 280, 282-3, 287
  his family endangered by his conduct I, 338; II, 275-8, 288-9, 295, 312, 314, 318, 322, 326-7

Pole, Reginald
  plot to kidnap II, 282, 284-5, 293-4, 317
  papal legate II, 279-83, 286-7, 289, 293, 302, 322
  his proposed marriage with Mary I, 15, 17, 337; II, 294, 311, 324
  and Montague's children II, 306, 323, 326-7
  at the meeting at Nice II, 298-9, 302
  and the rebellion in England I, 337; II, 286-7, 330
  at Rome I, 336, 338; II, 277, 286-9
  spies in his household II, 284
  at Venice II, 302
  reference I, 22, 330, 367; II, 278, 295, 308, 313
Pollard, A. F. 'Henry VIII' II, 334
Pollard, Richard II, 189, 208
Pommeraye, Gilles de la (Pomeroy) I, 325
Pontefract Castle I, 121, 143, 150-1, 167-8, 170, 173-4, 180-1, 184-90, 208, 227-8, 235, 237, 244, 246, 250, 289, 291-2, 302, 309, 344, 377-8; II, 52, 61, 89, 92-3, 109, 127-9, 131, 189-90, 200, 205, 300-1
Pontefract, the council at I, chap. xiv, pp. 341-388. *See also* Pilgrimage of Grace, the council at Pontefract
Pontefract town I, 144, 184, 211, 212, 227-40, 243-4, 250-4, 256, 262, 269-70, 280, 283, 298, 300, 310, 327, 372; II, 7, 10, 12-3, 16-7, 19-21, 54, 99, 101, 108-9, 129, 198, 300
  the parish church, All Hallows I, 340, 379, 388; II, 12, 300
  the market cross I, 229; II, 16, 19
  representation in parliament I, 359, 388
Pontefract Priory I, 184-5, 344, 346, 378, 382; II, 127
  the Prior of. *See* Thwaites, James
Pontefract, St Thomas' Hill I, 233, 237; II, 17
Pontefract, the honour of I, 296; II, 92
Pope, the
  general reference I, 16, 45, 61, 82, 342-3, 347-8, 351, 356, 374, 384; II, 36, 57, 177. *See also* Clement VII *and* Paul III
Porman, John I, 98
Porter, Thomas II, 43
Portington, Julian I, 50
Portington, Thomas I, 50, 97-9, 105, 151
Portugal II, 299
  Don Luis of. *See* Luis
Potter Hanworth I, 131
Powell, — II, 285
Powes (Powys), Lord II, 193
Praemunire, Statute of I, 6, 385
Pratt, James I, 70, 79
Preston in Lancs. I, 217-9; II, 113, 142, 144, 146
Preston in Holderness I, 155; II, 49, 64

24—2

Priestman, — ii, 96
Priestman, John ii, 266
Priestman, William ii, 266
Privileged Districts, act abolishing i, 8, 144, 355
Proctor, John i, 52
Proctor, Robert i, 93
Proclamations
  Rebel
    Aske's first i, 148; ii, 163
    Aske's second i, 175, 182, 209, 227, 327
    summons to Beverley in Aske's name i, 145
    issued by Bigod ii, 78, 97-8
    against Bigod's rising ii, 72-4, 102
    summons to Cleveland i, 202
    in Cornwall i, 327
    the terms of the second appointment at Doncaster ii, 48-9
    summons to Lancashire i, 216, 217
    in Lincs. i, 96, 125
    in London i, 327-9
    in Norfolk i, 327-8
    in Northumberland i, 199
    prohibited ii, 106
    rhyming i, 305, 307; ii, 96
    for a rising in Richmondshire ii, 97, 106, 108
    for a new rising ii, 51, 79-80, 93-4, 96-7, 102, 105, 198
    against spoiling i, 160-1, 176, 178, 183, 204, 318; ii, 69
    against unlawful assemblies i, 318; ii, 51
    in Westmorland i, 220, 221, 370; ii, 113-4
    in Worcester i, 328
  royal, mandates, orders
    after the commons' rising ii, 119
    order concerning Holy Days i, 9. *See also* Holidays
    carried by Lancaster Herald to Pontefract i, 229, 240, 249
    for the observance of Lent ii, 167-8
    sent to Lincoln i, 122, 128, 129, 135, 172
    the King's reply to the Lincs. rebels i, 136-8, 142, 324, 328; ii, 1, 2, 149, 151
    the pardon to the Lincs. rebels. *See* Lincs. rebellion, the pardon
    concerning the price of meat i, 13
    a limited pardon proclaimed to the Pilgrims i, 295
    affirming the general pardon ii, 106
    prepared for the Pilgrims i, 273-4
    for preaching and bidding of beads i, 7, 67
    against the Bishop of Rome i, 7; ii, 165
    Shrewsbury's, sent into Yorkshire i, 172, 173, 228

Proclamations
  order for declaring the Royal Supremacy i, 71-2
  torn down i, 70; ii, 167
  against sturdy vagabonds ii, 259
  to suspend the Statute of Woollen Cloths i, 108
Prophecies i, 57, 78, 80-6, 326; ii, 58, 146, 169, 171, 176, 243-5, 289-90, 294-5
Prowde, John ii, 63, 66
Prudhoe Castle i, 33, 230; ii, 41, 85, 124
Pullen (Pulleyn), Robert i, 221, 312, 345; ii, 16, 44
Purgatory i, 8, 9, 66, 71, 72, 266, 326, 383
Purveyance ii, 172
Py, John i, 87

Quarrendon i, 311
Quinzine. *See* Fifteenth
Quondam Prior of Guisborough. *See* Cockerell, James
Quyntrell, — ii, 181

Radwell i, 326
Raffells, Robert i, 145, 147
Ragland, Jerome ii, 310, 313
Raine, J. 'Memorials of Hexham Priory' ii, 276
Rasen i, 98, 100
Rasen Moor i, 100
Rasen Wood i, 106
Rasshall, Henry ii, 132-3
Rastell, John i, 324, 346
Ratcliff, Sir Cuthbert ii, 232, 263, 275
Ratcliff, Roger i, 269, 295, 306
Ratford, Thomas, parson of Snelland i, 127; ii, 153
Ravenspur i, 388
Ravenstonedale i, 81
Rawcliff i, 208
Ray, Henry, Berwick pursuivant-at-arms i, 219, 306; ii, 217, 246-50, 254-5
Raynes, Dr John, chancellor of the Bishop of Lincoln i, 91, 101-2, 104, 133, 202
Reading i, 328-9
Rede, William ii, 169-70
Redman, — i, 345
Reedsdale i, 196, 198; ii, 6, 41, 81, 120, 122, 228-33, 235, 238-9, 248, 257, 262-4, 268-70
  keepers of. *See* Fenwick, George, *and* Heron, John, of Chipchase
Reformation, the. *See* England, the Reformation in
Retford i, 78
Reynton, Thomas ii, 170
Ribble, the river i, 219
Ribblesdale ii, 43
Rice, John ap ii, 208
Richard III i, 14, 84, 337
Richardin, Robert ii, 169

Richardson, Alexander II, 145
Richardson, Cuthbert II, 78
Riche, Sir Richard, Chancellor of the Court of Augmentations I, 103, 111, 114, 268, 280, 357-8; II, 14
Richmond, Surrey I, 63, 327; II, 7, 30
Richmond, Yorks. I, 210, 221, 283, 359, 377; II, 28, 44, 79, 83, 85, 105-6, 108, 110, 112, 114
   the monastery of St Agatha II, 21, 85, 121-2
   the Grey Friars II, 106
   Moor II, 110
Richmond, Henry Fitzroy, Duke of I, 1, 30, 302; II, 273, 299
Richmondshire I, 163, 182, 201-4, 206, 216, 220, 226, 237, 251, 262; II, 62, 66, 74, 78, 80, 97, 106, 108, 110, 128, 180, 203, 208, 214
Rievaux Abbey I, 233
Ringstanhirst I, 149, 155
Ripley, John, Abbot of Kirkstall I, 382; II, 92
Ripon I, 143, 201, 238, 262, 355, 359, 388; II, 28, 50-1, 111
Risby I, 48
Rising of the North I, 209; II, 58, 120
Rither, — I, 345
Robin Hood's Cross I, 252
Robin, William I, 224
Robson, family of II, 228
Robson, Archie I, 196; II, 238
Robson, Geoffrey II, 41, 230, 238
Robson, Henry II, 230-1
Robson, John I, 196
Robson, John, of Fawston II, 238
Roche Abbey I, 349
Rochester II, 165
Rochester, the Bishop of. *See* Fisher, John
Rochester, John II, 187
Roddam, John I, 199
Rogers, William, mayor of Hull I, 155-6, 158-9, 161, 288-9; II, 68-4, 72, 76, 81, 206
Rogerson, Ralph II, 175, 178
Rokeby, Dr John I, 377-8, 382-3, 388
Rokeby, Lady I, 48
Rokeby, Thomas I, 202
Rokeby, William I, 388
Romaldkirk, the priest of I, 203
Rome, Church of. *See* Church of Rome
Rome I, 6, 82, 333, 335-9, 341, 351, 354, 356, 383; II, 279-80, 286-9, 302, 326
Rooper, Thomas II, 177
Roos, Edward I, 155
Rose, Mr II, 44
Rosedale nunnery II, 76, 160, 162
Ross I, 325
Rossington Bridge I, 250-1
Rothbury I, 299; II, 41, 202
Rotherham I, 310, 319, 323, 344
Rothwell I, 74, 98
Rouen II, 242, 255

Rous, Anthony II, 188
Royston, Herts. II, 244-5
Rudston, — I, 157
Rudston, Nicholas I, 157-60, 164, 181, 184, 235, 288-9, 345-6; II, 74-5, 90-1, 136, 140, 163-4, 206
Rumour
   of Aske's execution II, 45, 50
   of the King's death II, 297
   of the King's intentions after the rebellion II, 45-6, 67, 77, 94-6, 105-6, 108, 112
   of the King's strength I, 167, 250, 324, 327, 331
   of new laws and taxes I, 13, 76-80, 91-2, 96-9, 102, 112, 121-2, 129, 153, 228, 243, 321; II, 30, 85, 93, 114, 142, 165, 169, 177
   of murders committed by the Lincs. rebels I, 95, 112, 133
   of Norfolk's arrest II, 46, 291
   of the Pilgrims' strength I, 122, 287-8, 293, 321, 329, 331, 389
   that Pole had become Pope II, 318
   of new risings II, 171, 174, 176
   of the defeat of the royal army I, 122-3, 334
Ruskington, the bailiff of I, 181
Russell, Sir John I, 122-3, 128, 245, 293, 305, 319; II, 4, 6, 7, 8, 22
Rutland, Thomas Manners, Earl of I, 118-9, 122, 129, 265, 294-6, 319-20; II, 23, 52, 206, 237, 239, 251
Rycard, Thomas I, 24
Rydale I, 81, 151, 153; II, 58
Ryder, Henry I, 186
Rye, the curate of I, 68
Rylston I, 52; II, 43, 56
Rysse, Lady. *See* Howard, Katherine
Ryther, Sir Ralph I, 51
Ryton I, 230-1

Sadler, Ralph I, 86, 207; II, 93-4, 104, 246, 254-6
St Asaph, the Bishop of. *See* Warton, Robert
St Clare's Bradfield (Senkler's Bradfield) I, 69
St David, diocese of II, 166
St German, Christopher I, 346
St John Ley I, 196
St John, Sir John I, 84
St Kerverne II, 170-1, 181
St Lo, Sir John I, 87; II, 172
St Oswald's I, 184
St Vincent I, 19
Sais, Harry I, 234, 244
Salisbury II, 167
Salisbury, the diocese of II, 167
Salisbury, Margaret, Countess of I, 14, 15, 17; II, 275-6, 285-6, 296, 302-3, 310, 315-7, 323-7
Saltmarsh, Thomas I, 148-9, 181, 185, 345; II, 58
Sampoul, Mr I, 107

Sampson, Richard, Bishop of Chichester I, 276
Sanctuary, act restricting the right of I, 8, 355, 384
Sandall Castle II, 52
Sanderdale Hill I, 223
Sanders, N. 'De Origine ac Progressu Schismatis Anglicani' II, 142
Sanderson, Mr I, 101, 124
Sanderson, Christopher I, 147, 151; II, 49
Sandes (Sandys), William, Lord I, 18, 23, 276; II, 36, 79
Sandforth Moor I, 221
Sandon, Sir William I, 101
Sandsend II, 87
Sandwich I, 134
Saville, Sir Henry I, 56–7, 61, 172, 190, 235–6, 250, 282, 286, 288, 297–8, 310–1, 316, 321; II, 52, 92, 136, 140, 212, 257–8, 268
Saville, Thomas I, 61
Sawcliff I, 50, 105–7
Sawl, — I, 156, 158
Sawley Abbey I, 210, 213, 215, 217–9, 225, 261, 270; II, 39, 56, 83–6, 111, 121–2, 127–9, 142–3, 145, 212, 266
Sawley, the Abbot of I, 213; II, 39, 83–6, 98, 122, 124–5, 127–9, 142–3, 180, 203–4, 212
Sawley, the Prior of I, 317
Sawley, Henry II, 145–6
Scarborough I, 88, 281, 318, 359, 388; II, 9, 45–7, 57, 60–2, 66–9, 71–2, 77–8, 80, 88, 98, 110, 125, 159, 198, 212, 253, 255
  the bailiffs of II, 67, 70, 97–8
  Castle I, 44, 150, 157, 183, 211, 212, 225, 239, 286, 298, 313–4, 317, 322–3; II, 33, 52, 67–70, 77, 98, 183
  the Grey Friars' House II, 70
Scarlet, — II, 188
Scawby Hill I, 255
Scawsby Lease I, 260
Scotherne I, 107
Scotland
  Border officers I, 299; II, 227, 238, 246, 248–9, 268
  the Chancellor of. See Gawan
  Council of II, 246–7, 249
  English spies in II, 117, 228, 249, 266
  alliance with France I, 340; II, 267
  dislike of Henry VIII in II, 242, 250
  James V's return to II, 238, 241–3, 246–7, 249, 253–5
  the King of. See James V
  days of march I, 222; II, 41–2, 238–9, 248–9
  murder of an English herald I, 306; II, 86
  sympathy with the Pilgrimage of Grace II, 217, 247, 249

Scotland
  a refuge for rebels I, 31, 65; II, 65, 77, 86, 93, 108, 159, 244, 246, 249–50, 261, 263, 266–7
  the Regents' correspondence with Norfolk II, 246–7, 249–50
  expected war with England I, 198, 201, 258, 335; II, 230, 238, 240, 243–9, 270
  previous wars with England I, 19, 40, 238, 272, 359; II, 144
  reference I, 187, 193, 304; II, 10, 28, 59, 95, 103, 134, 216, 219, 230, 256
Scott, Sir Walter, quoted I, 212, 272; II, 69, 77
Scriptures in English, the I, 10, 51, 66–7, 93; II, 243, 292, 303, 321, 324
Scrivelsby I, 89, 101, 106, 124
Scrooby I, 228, 234, 249, 257
Scrope, Henry, Lord I, 40, 185, 201, 208, 212, 238, 250, 262, 269, 312, 316, 345; II, 13, 79, 102, 108, 214
Sculcotes I, 160–1
Seamer I, 150, 230–1, 285
Sedbarr, Adam, Abbot of Jervaux I, 202–3, 206, 208; II, 38, 107–8, 127, 135, 156, 203, 211, 213–4, 216
Sedbergh I, 143, 207, 217, 298, 316, 369
Sedgefield I, 226
Sedition
  bills I, 70; II, 43–4, 86, 96–7, 105, 110, 112, 159, 164, 167
  books I, 72, 175
  plays II, 176
  rhymes I, 83–6, 213, 286, 266, 280–1, 305, 307, 350; II, 105, 169–70, 174, 178, 212, 290
  offers to the King of Scotland II, 253–6
  sermons. See Sermons, seditious
  speeches I, 24, 57, 64, 66, 69–72, 79, 91, 112, 118, 120, 131, 133, 145, 207, 218, 319, 326; II, 39, 111, 146, 169, 175–9, 185, 215–7, 243, 290–8, 308, 312–3
  watch for, in the southern counties I, 325; II, 245
Selby I, 151, 170, 180, 285, 291
Serls, —, vicar of St Peter's in the East, Oxford II, 168
Sermons
  heretical I, 22, 66, 68, 71, 324, 353; II, 14; 166–7
  loyal I, 7, 8, 10, 43–4, 64, 71, 274, 280, 324, 353; II, 25, 35, 44, 52, 100, 146, 167, 168, 256
  on Purgatory. See Purgatory
  seditious I, 7, 64–8, 72, 92, 213, 326; II, 154, 164–5, 167
Servant, — II, 106, 203
Seton I, 40
Settle Spring II, 88
Settrington I, 40; II, 59, 61, 66, 87, 98, 160, 198

Seyman, Robert II, 176-7
Seymour, Jane I, 1, 2, 108, 117, 145, 207, 244, 330; II, 25, 27, 37, 48-9, 139, 171, 181, 206, 245, 259, 297
Shaftoe, Cuthbert II, 263
Shakespeare, W. 'Henry IV' I, 85
Shaxton, Nicholas, Bishop of Salisbury II, 167
Sheffield Park I, 99; II, 24
Shepcotes Heath II, 175
Sherburn II, 198
Sheriff of Lincolnshire. *See* Dymmoke, Sir Edward
Sheriff of Yorkshire. *See* Hastings, Sir Brian
Sheriffhutton Castle I, 46, 208; II, 34, 105, 110, 112, 134, 139, 248, 252-5, 257, 261, 263, 268, 270, 273
Sherwood, Dr, Chancellor of Beverley minster I, 382-3
Shetland II, 256
Shewlton I, 222
Shipton I, 158
Shirburn I, 235
Shrewsbury II, 165
Shrewsbury, George Talbot, Earl of
correspondence with Cromwell. *See* Cromwell, Thomas, correspondence with the Earl of Shrewsbury
and Lord Darcy. *See* Darcy, Thomas, Lord, and the Earl of Shrewsbury
and Sir George Darcy I, 294, 297-8
his daughters I, 32, 84, 285
his advance to the Don I, 215, 238, 245-6, 249-51, 257, 260, 268-9; II, 5
and the first appointment at Doncaster I, 219, 259-60, 265-6, 270, 300, 302
at the second conference at Doncaster II, 6, 10
finances I, 119, 244, 246, 293
and Lord Hussey I, 113, 130-1
and the King I, 108, 116, 119, 135, 173, 242-3, 249, 294, 298; II, 6, 34, 89
and the Lincs. rebels I, 99, 112, 119, 121, 128-30, 228
his musters I, 108, 113, 116, 118, 121, 122, 233-4
his joint commission with Norfolk. *See* Norfolk, the Duke of, his joint commission with Shrewsbury
in command against the Pilgrims I, 135, 143, 173, 185, 188, 230, 243, 249
correspondence with the other commanders I, 129-30, 134, 208, 245-6, 249-50, 298
his preparations during the truce I, 282, 319-20
reference I, 168, 187, 223, 224, 235-6, 258, 262, 276, 285, 311, 329; II, 24, 27, 33, 43, 52-3, 148
Shropshire I, 67, 113

Shuttleworth, George II, 39, 83-5, 98, 142, 202
Siena I, 336
Siggiswick, — I, 211
Silvester (Sylvester), Robert, Prior of Guisborough I, 317; II, 40, 56-7, 201
Simondburn Castle II, 235
Simpson, Percy I, 224
Simpson, Richard II, 66
Skerne, the river I, 226
Skipton I, 295, 359; II, 28
the vicar of. *See* Blackborne, William
Castle I, 51-2, 54, 150, 183, 206-12, 225, 238-9, 250, 312, 316; II, 6, 43, 246
Skipwith Moor I, 148-9, 170
Skipwith, Mr I, 154
Skipwith, Sir William I, 95, 125-6; II, 148
Sleaford I, 21, 24, 26, 104, 109-10, 112-3, 118, 126-7, 130-2; II, 153
Smithfield, London II, 59, 198, 215
Smythely, — I, 154
Smythely, Richard II, 81
Snaith I, 284, 296; II, 126, 134
Snaith, the bailiff of II, 49, 64
Snape I, 74, 273; II, 80, 108
Snelland I, 124; II, 153
the vicar of. *See* Ratford, Thomas
Snow, Richard I, 328
Somerset county I, 87-8; II, 26, 172, 215
Somerset Herald. *See* Treheyron, Thomas
Sotby II, 152
Soulay, Henry II, 87
Southampton I, 63; II, 171
Southampton, the Earl of. *See* Fitzwilliam, Sir William
Southbye, Robert II, 153
South Cave I, 154
Southwell I, 246
Southwell, Richard II, 164
Southwell, Robert II, 164, 273
Sowerby, the vicar of I, 222
Sowle, Thomas I, 70, 79
Spain I, 19, 22, 45
Spalding I, 111-2
the Prior of I, 112
'Spanish Chronicle' I, 240; II, 23, 86-7, 54, 217, 326-7
Speed, John, 'History of Great Britain' I, 191, 287, 387; II, 97-8
Speke, Sir George II, 324
Spencer, Bishop II, 173
Spencer, Sir Robert I, 31
Spennymore I, 204-6
Spittel, the Wold beyond I, 231
Spittels II, 69, 71
Stafford II, 165
Stafford, Henry I, 39
Stafford, Henry, Lord I, 14, 287; II, 292
Stafford, Sir Humphry I, 45
Stafford, Ursula, wife of Lord Stafford I, 14

Stafford county I, 113, 215
Staindrop II, 66
Staines, George I, 103, 114-5, 128
Stainton, John II, 107-8
Stamford I, 109, 112, 122-3, 128, 246, 305; II, 59, 149
Standish, Thomas II, 316-7
Stanger, Leonard I, 327
Stanley, family of II, 204
Stanley, Edward I, 53; II, 204
Stanley, Thomas I, 169, 214-6
Stanley, Sir William I, 215
Stanton Lacy I, 67
Stapleton, family of I, 57
Stapleton, Sir Brian I, 58, 146-7, 151, 158, 160, 235, 239
Stapleton, Brian II, 333
Stapleton, Christopher I, 57-8, 146-7; II, 333
   his wife I, 58, 146-8; II, 216
Stapleton, Philip II, 333
Stapleton, William I, 36, 55, 58, 62, 78-9, 146-7, 151-4, 157-63, 167, 174, 176, 235, 239, 255, 270, 284-5, 312
Stappill, John II, 308
Star Chamber, Court of
  Order for the government of Beverley I, 48
  Sir William Bulmer before I, 87
  Cases
    Beckwith v. Aclom II, 218
    Leonard Constable v. Sir Oswald Wolsthrope I, 58-9
    concerning the Earl of Cumberland's servants I, 34, 53
    relating to enclosures I, 369
    Hans Ganth v. the Abbot of Whitby I, 42
    Holdsworth v. Lacy I, 61; II, 258
    Thomas Moigne v. George Bowgham I, 90
    the burgesses of Newcastle-upon-Tyne I, 206
    John Norton v. the Earl of Cumberland I, 52
    Sir William Percy v. Sir Robert Constable I, 47
    John Proctor v. Thomas Blackborne and others I, 53
    between Tempest and Saville I, 56, 61
    the Abbot of Whitby v. the town I, 41-2
  fines recalcitrant juries I, 60
  reference I, 89; II, 272
Starkey, Thomas I, 16, 338; II, 295, 305
Staunton, Gloucestershire I, 66
Staveley, Ninian I, 203; II, 107, 108, 110, 113, 188, 208, 214, 219
Staynhus, William II, 76, 159-64, 200-1, 219
Steward, the Lord. *See* Shrewsbury, George Talbot, Earl of

Stewart, William II, 10, 22
Stewart, William, Bishop of Aberdeen II, 217, 247, 249
Stillingfleet II, 80
Stilton I, 109
Stockwith I, 293
Stoke-on-Trent I, 120
Stoke, Somerset II, 291
Stoke Nayland II, 165
Stokesley, John, Bishop of London II, 292, 305
Stokton, — II, 110
Stonar, Francis I, 106
Stone Fair II, 173
Stonor, Sir Walter II, 190
Stony Stratford I, 246
Stonys (Staines), Brian I, 101-2; II, 153
Story, Edward II, 246
Stow, John, 'Chronicle' II, 148
Stowe I, 325
Stowping Sise I, 260, 262
Strangways, Sir James I, 40, 205, 235, 312, 345; II, 96, 136, 160
Strangways, Thomas I, 180-1, 185, 188-9; II, 127-9, 193-4, 216, 219
Streatlam I, 86
Strebilhill, John II, 215
Strebilhill, Thomas II, 169
Strickland, — I, 345
Strickland, Walter I, 219
Strype, J., 'Ecclesiastical Memorials' I, 388
Stuard, —, bailiff of Beverley I, 145, 151
Sturley I, 78
Sturley, Sir Nicholas I, 319
Sturton I, 101, 124
Subsidy, the I, 11, 72, 74, 76-7, 91, 96-8, 141, 192, 372-3; II, 99, 125, 172, 174-5, 177
Succession, the three Acts of I, 10, 76, 355-6
  the second Act of I, 11, 26, 72
  the third Act of I, 1, 264, 317-8, 361-3
Suffolk county I, 12, 69, 121-2, 241, 326; II, 164-5, 173-4, 176
Suffolk, Charles Brandon, Duke of
  his council I, 319; II, 150
  and the second conference at Doncaster II, 2, 6-8, 11, 17, 189
  correspondence with the King I, 129, 133-6, 289, 296, 311, 320, 323; II, 6-8, 28, 148-9, 197
  at Lincoln I, 135-6, 165-6, 245, 282, 293, 319; II, 148-50, 220
  commander against the Lincs. rebels I, 120, 122-3, 132, 134, 142-3, 241, 247-8, 305
  his correspondence with the other commanders I, 211, 246, 274, 293, 297, 301, 313
  and the Lincs. gentlemen I, 127-30, 136, 172; II, 148-9

Suffolk, Charles Brandon, Duke of
  his second mission to Lincs. II, 52
  returns to London II, 24
  and the Duke of Norfolk. *See* Norfolk, the Duke of, and Suffolk
  communications with the Pilgrims I, 288–9, 297, 300–6
  his position during the truce I, 278–9, 281–2, 286, 293, 297–8, 301, 318
  reference I, 95, 121, 210, 218, 244, 249–50, 266, 269, 276, 306; II, 9, 27, 45–6, 220
Suffolk, Duchess of. *See* Tudor, Mary
Sulyard, Mr II, 19
Suppression of the Smaller Monasteries
  act for I, 3, 8, 14, 25, 186–7, 178–9, 222, 264, 351, 353, 374; II, 19, 25–6, 141
  begun I, 74, 87
  commissioners for I, 91, 95, 133, 204, 206, 377, 387; II, 16, 26, 56, 99, 101, 155
  the commissioners resisted I, 169, 193–5, 218–4, 316
  expenditure of the spoils. *See* Monasteries, grants of
  a motive for rebellion I, 28, 73, 98, 133, 186–7, 189, 212–3, 222, 271, 316, 333, 348–51, 379, 384; II, 35, 40, 79, 85, 156, 173, 175, 177, 312. *See also* Demands of the rebels
  continued after the rebellion II, 99–100, 111, 121–2, 124–5, 127–9, 141, 172, 174–5
  by Wolsey I, 75, 213, 271, 307
  reference I, 76, 153, 265, 326, 339; II, 15, 68, 155, 227. *See also* Monasteries
Supremacy, Act of I, 7, 23, 26, 43, 64–5, 68–9, 73, 76, 98, 139, 213, 347; II, 14–5, 295. *See also* Henry VIII, Supreme Head of the Church of England
Surrey county II, 320
Surrey, Henry Howard, Earl of I, 120, 242, 244–5, 259, 265–6; II, 23, 64, 186, 250–1
Sussex county I, 51, 69, 82, 326; II, 164, 293, 308
Sussex, Robert Ratcliff, Earl of I, 276, 290; II, 52, 111, 141–8, 158, 193, 218, 225
Sussex, the Countess of II, 141
Sutton, Sir John I, 114
Sutton, Robert, mayor of Lincoln I, 99–101, 114, 132; II, 196
Sutton-upon-Derwent I, 174, 382
  the rector of. *See* Palmes, Dr George
Swaledale I, 182, 209; II, 61, 78, 110–1
Swalowfield, — II, 128
Swan, John II, 177
Swanland I, 162
Swayne, Michael II, 134
Swensune, Ralph II, 89
Sweton II, 155

Swinburne, Dr I, 344; II, 62
Swinburne, John II, 112
Swinhoe, Robert I, 199
Swinnerton, — I, 67

Tadcaster I, 57, 150, 235, 270; II, 94
Tailboys, Elizabeth Blount, Lady I, 107
Tailboys, Gilbert, Lord II, 235
Talbot, Francis, Lord I, 250–1, 253, 274, 294
Talbot, William I, 296; II, 147, 189
Talentire II, 44
Tantallon Castle II, 266
Taunton I, 87; II, 172
Tavistock, the Abbot of I, 75
Taxation I, 2, 3, 11, 29, 98, 114, 182, 192, 332, 352, 371–3
Taylor, John I, 93
Taylor, Lawrence, a harper II, 304, 308
Tees, the river I, 36–7
Tempest, family of I, 87, 285; II, 148, 257
Tempest, John I, 210
Tempest, Nicholas I, 210, 215, 219, 226, 312, 317; II, 89, 86, 133, 135, 144–5, 201, 211–2, 214
Tempest, Sir Richard, of the Dale I, 18
Tempest, Sir Richard I, 36–7, 61, 172, 190, 210, 235–6, 239, 250, 269, 312, 316, 345; II, 48, 52, 128, 144, 215, 218
Tempest, Sir Thomas I, 38, 61, 172, 345–6, 357–8, 366, 368, 373; II, 133, 135, 260, 265, 271–4
Templehurst I, 18, 24, 118, 143, 170, 188, 207, 288, 290, 300, 308–12, 327–8, 344; II, 34, 48–50, 52, 93, 109, 147, 189, 198
Tenande, — II, 43
Tenant, Mr II, 207
Tenant, Richard, of Holderness I, 155, 160
Tenant right I, 369
Tenth, the lay I, 11, 372
Tenths, ecclesiastical I, 6, 98, 187, 349, 351–2, 384–5; II, 14, 34, 45, 49, 51, 53, 139
Terouanne I, 19
Teshe, Tristram I, 157; II, 139
Tewkesbury I, 70
Thame II, 169, 215
Thames, the river I, 23; II, 25, 292
Theobald, — II, 302
Thetford I, 266
Thicket Priory I, 51
Thimbleby, Sir John I, 128, 136
Thimbleby, young I, 128
Thingden I, 369
Thirleby, Thomas II, 201
Thirsk I, 388
Thirsk, William, quondam Abbot of Fountains II, 107, 127, 135, 208, 211, 214
Thomas a Becket, St I, 64; II, 299

Thomas the Rhymer I, 82–4, 86
Thomas, William, 'The Pilgrim' I, 263; II, 86, 217
Thomlynson, — I, 202
Thompson, Robert, vicar of Borough-under-Stainmoor I, 220–5, 370; II, 219
Thomson, John II, 62
Thoresway I, 98
Thorley I, 326
Thornbury II, 189
Thorndon II, 166
Thorne I, 296
Thorneton, John I, 166
Throgmorton, Sir George I, 328–9; II, 279
Throgmorton, Michael I, 16; II, 278–80, 283–5, 287–8, 302, 305, 318
Thwaites, — II, 182–3
Thwaites, James, Prior of Pontefract I, 382
Thwaites, William, vicar of Londesborough I, 62, 72–3
Thwing (Thweng) I, 205, 232; II, 66, 72
Tibbey, Thomas II, 106, 111–3, 117
Tickhill I, 251
 Castle I, 319, 388
Tithes I, 225, 370; II, 21, 44, 56, 106, 112
Todde, William, Prior of Malton I, 81, 163; II, 58, 59, 66
Tonge, T. 'Visitation of Yorkshire' I, 61
Toone, Thomas I, 70
Topcliff I, 184; II, 125
Topcliffe, John. See Hexham, John, Abbot of Whitby
Tortington I, 82
Tournelles II, 240
Towcester I, 321
Tower of London
 as an arsenal I, 108, 117, 119, 120, 134, 327
 the Beauchamp Tower II, 202
 the lieutenant of the. See Walsingham, Sir Edmund
 as a prison I, 26, 31, 38, 191, 208, 324, 329, 348, 353, 360, 366; II, 25, 33, 46, 53, 105, 125, 143, 151, 153–4, 159, 168, 182–3, 185–7, 193, 195, 197–200, 202, 206–8, 213, 215–6, 219–20, 223, 266, 273, 279, 282, 285, 291, 306–10, 312–21, 323–6
Tower Hill II, 216, 315, 321
Towghtwodde, Thomas I, 87
Towneley, Bernard, Chancellor of the diocese of Carlisle I, 222–4; II, 121–2, 266
Townley, — I, 216
Townley, John I, 216
Townley, Sir John I, 216
Towse Athyenges Heath I, 106; II, 154
Towton, battle of I, 40
Tranby I, 153
Treason. See Sedition
Treason, Act of I, 10–11, 76, 263, 332,
365–6; II, 14, 176, 192–3, 201, 211, 215, 289, 293, 310–13, 321
Treasury, the II, 59, 195
Treglosacke, — II, 171
Tregonwell, Dr John II, 170, 199, 204
Treheyron, Thomas, Somerset Herald I, 299–306; II, 86, 190
Trent, the river I, 29, 180, 141–2, 148–9, 172, 245, 249, 260, 268, 282, 294, 310, 314, 319, 368, 375; II, 4, 5, 23, 106, 252
Tristram, William, chantry priest of Lartington I, 203, 377–8; II, 40
Trotter, Philip I, 125; II, 153
Trowen, Sir Charles I, 287
Truce of Doncaster I, 201, 211, 219–20, chap. xi, pp. 241–72, chap. xii, pp. 273–306, 317, 327, 330, 340, 342; II, 1, 9, 21, 84, 102, 115, 151
Tudor, Mary, sister of Henry VIII, Duchess of Suffolk I, 35, 87, 210
Tunstall, Cuthbert, Bishop of Durham I, 6, 9, 35–6, 72, 203–4, 207, 354; II, 38, 40, 78, 102, 200, 231, 260, 265, 267–8, 270, 272–5, 305, 330–1
Tunstall, Sir Marmaduke I, 218
Turkey I, 17, 269, 304, 330; II, 287, 299
Turner, Richard I, 329
Tuxford I, 259, 269
Tweed, the river II, 217
Tyburn II, 154, 214, 216, 315
Tyndale, Gervase I, 65–6; II, 169, 303–4
Tyndale, William I, 346, 353; II, 243–4, 283
Tyndale Wood, Suffolk II, 176
Tyne, the river I, 38, 86; II, 41, 274
Tynedale I, 230
 North I, 35, 115, 195–8, 299; II, 6, 41, 81, 120, 122, 228–35, 237–8, 248, 257, 262–4, 268–70, 274–5
 North, keepers of. See Fenwick, Roger, Carnaby, Sir Reynold, and Heron, John of Chipchase
 South II, 235
Tynemouth Priory II, 38, 40, 253, 255
Tyrwhit, Sir Robert I, 97–100, 106, 116, 126, 165; II, 148, 154
Tyrwhit, Robert I, 109–10, 116
Tyrwhit, Sir William, sheriff of Lincs. 1537 II, 151, 153

Unlawful Games, act forbidding II, 243
Uses, Statute of I, 12, 28, 69, 102–3, 114, 124, 187, 189, 264, 266, 362, 364–5, 368, 387; II, 24, 319
Usselby I, 99
Uty, Philip II, 47, 63–4
Uvedale, John II, 138, 201, 272

Vachell, Richard I, 222
Valor Ecclesiasticus I, 388
Vaughan, William II, 283–4
Vavasour, Sir Peter I, 345; II, 3, 4
Venice II, 302

Vernon, Roger II, 169
Vienna, the Council of I, 384
Villiers, — I, 264
Visitation of the Monasteries I, 63, 183, 318, 354; II, 56, 135, 146, 173

Wade, — I, 343; II, 60, 62
Waflin, William II, 266
Waid, Robert I, 58
Wakefield I, 56, 169, 172, 180, 184-5, 235, 237, 250, 282, 295, 306, 310, 321, 843-4, 359; II, 28, 34
Walbourne Hope II, 176
Waldby (Walby) Marmaduke, prebendary of Carlisle and vicar of Kirk Deighton I, 23-4, 27, 310, 382-3; II, 90-1, 266
Waldeby, Philip I, 157-8
Waldron I, 69
Wales I, 215; II, 165, 284, 290
Walker, — I, 312, 318
Walkington, — I, 156
Wall, Robert II, 222
Wallace, William I, 313
Wallop, Sir John, ambassador in France I, 132, 325, 333; II, 240
Walsingham I, 328; II, 174, 176-9
Walsingham Priory II, 175, 177
 the sub-Prior of. *See* Mileham, Nicholas
 the shrine of Our Lady II, 174
Walsingham, Sir Edmund, lieutenant of the Tower II, 46, 198, 207, 307
Warblington I, 332; II, 296, 302-4, 315-8
 the rector of. *See* Heliar, John
Wardens of the Marches
 English. *See* Borders, officers
 Scottish. *See* Scotland, Border officers
Ware I, 119; II, 32
Wark II, 288
Warrington II, 141-2
Wars of the Roses I, 14, 359; II, 55
Warter Priory I, 72; II, 110
Warton, Robert, Bishop of St Asaph II, 165
Warwick, Richard Neville, Earl of, the Kingmaker I, 14, 15, 36
Water, Thomas II, 66
Waters, Edward I, 314, 317; II, 9, 17, 57
Watton Priory I, 152, 285-6, 344; II, 40, 58-63, 66, 82, 98, 102
 the confessor of the nuns II, 59
 the Prior of. *See* Holgate, Robert
 the sub-Prior of. *See* Gill, Harry
 the cellerar of. *See* Lather, Thomas
Watton village I, 153, 157, 280, 343; II, 47, 58-61, 63, 110
 parish church I, 152; II, 47-8
 the curate of I, 343
 the vicar of II, 47, 59
Watton Carre II, 59
Watts, John II, 158-64, 200
Waverton I, 382

Wednesborough, the parson of I, 82
Weeley I, 70
Welbeck I, 259-60; II, 6, 10, 23
Wells, Morgan II, 294
Wensleydale I, 143, 182, 207, 209-10, 237, 262; II, 61
Went, the river I, 234, 239
Wentbridge (Ferrybridge) I, 233-4, 238-9, 251, 256
Wentworth, — II, 132
Wentworth, Sir John I, 186
Wentworth, Sir Thomas II, 197, 220, 263-4
Wentworth, Thomas I, 297; II, 199
West Malling II, 243
Westminster I, 30, 36, 303, 359-60
Westminster Abbey II, 27
Westminster Hall II, 193, 198, 206
Westmorland, the barony of I, 371
Westmorland county
 boundaries I, 226
 attitude of the clergy to the rebels I, 354; II, 120
 the commons' rising II, 105-6, 111, 113-24, 128, 138, 142
 the first rising there I, 192, 220-5, 331, 370
 disturbances there after the first rising II, 44, 111-2
 the rebels' grievances I, 217, 220, 226, 299, 318, 369-72; II, 112-3, 119-21
 loyalists in II, 6
 pardon proclaimed in II, 28
 the sheriff of. *See* Cumberland, the Earl of
 the truce proclaimed in I, 279
 escapes taxation I, 192, 372
 reference I, 29, 81, 218, 226, 292, 304, 305, 307, 318, 349, 364; II, 234, 272
Westmorland, Charles Neville, sixth Earl of II, 58
Westmorland, Katherine Neville, Countess of I, 18, 88; II, 79, 239
Westmorland, Ralph Neville, fourth Earl of I, 18, 29, 38, 157, 182, 185, 204, 237, 312; II, 44, 56, 78-80, 96, 103, 111, 119, 134, 227, 229, 236, 239, 253
Westwood, Thomas II, 179
Wetherall Priory II, 263
Wetherby I, 285
Whalley Abbey I, 219-20; II, 138, 142, 144-8
 the Abbot of. *See* Paslew, John
 the Prior of II, 145, 189
Whalley village II, 142-3
Whalworth, James II, 137
Wharfe, the river I, 231
Wharton, George I, 327
Wharton, Richard I, 151, 155; II, 62
Wharton, Sir Thomas I, 74, 220-1, 292; II, 33, 80, 114, 120, 128, 239-40, 263-4, 268, 276
Whelpdale *alias* Whelton, Gilbert I, 221

Whenby I, 345
Whitaker, T. D. 'History of Craven' II, 143
Whitburn II, 253, 255–6
Whitburn, the priest of. *See* Hodge, Robert
Whitby I, 40–2; II, 184
Whitby Abbey I, 41–3, 233, 350; II, 127
the Abbot of. *See* Hexham, John
White Rose Party, the I, 14, 17–8, 22–4, 28; II, chap. xxii, pp. 277–96, 302, 311, 318, 321, 323
Whitgift I, 156
Whorwood, William, solicitor-general II, 212–3
Wickham I, 326
Wicliff (Wycliff), William I, 59–60; II, 131, 136
Widdrington, Sir John I, 285; II, 81, 103, 229, 232, 238–9, 263, 269
Wighill I, 57–8, 146, 160, 235, 270
Wighton I, 154–9
Wigmore, the Abbot of II, 165
Wilfred, St I, 153
Wilkins, D. 'Concilia' I, 388
Wilkinson, Hugh II, 173
Wilkinson, John II, 238
Wilkinson, Lancelot II, 62
Wilkinson, Richard II, 82
Willen, George I, 216
William, servant to Anthony Curtis I, 288
Williams, John I, 123, 140
Williamson, Anthony I, 96
Willoughby, family of I, 89
Willoughby, — I, 327
Willoughby, Lady I, 106
Willoughby, Sir Thomas II, 206
Wilson, Mr II, 285
Wilson, Dr II, 288
Wilson, John (Jockey Unsained) I, 92
Wilson Richard I, 145, 150, 155; II, 61–2, 266
Wilton I, 37–8, 40; II, 95, 97
Wiltshire I, 65
Wiltshire, Thomas Boleyn, Earl of II, 193, 266
Wimbourne I, 326
Winchester, Bishop of. *See* Gardiner, Stephen
Windermere I, 307; II, 106
Windsor I, 86, 118, 133, 185, 173, 241, 243–4, 274, 278, 289, 291–2, 326; II, 165, 184, 291
Windsor, Lord II, 193
Winestead, the priest of I, 72
Wingfield I, 282, 294, 311
Wingfield, Sir Anthony I, 122
Wistow I, 151
Witchcraft I, 66, 82; II, 297, 301
Witnesham, the parson of. *See* Jackson, Richard
Witton II, 108
Witton Fell I, 202
Woburn, the Abbot of I, 75

Wold, the I, 314
Wolsey, Thomas, Cardinal I, 6, 19–20, 31–2, 40, 46, 75, 102, 134, 213, 271, 307; II, 192, 293
Wolsey, Thomas, a servant I, 102, 104
Wolsthrope, Sir Oswald I, 58–60, 174, 181, 231–3, 288, 345; II, 33, 48, 74, 80, 83, 101, 127, 200
Wood, Elizabeth II, 177
Wood, William, Prior of Bridlington I, 282; II, 69, 130, 133, 135, 211–3, 216
Woodhouse, the Prior of II, 166
Woodmansey (Woodmancy), William I, 115, 146, 152–3, 163, 288; II, 74, 266
Woodward, John II, 165
Woollen Clothes, Act of I, 12, 108, 120
Woolpit I, 121, 241
Worcester, city I, 70, 326
Worcester, county I, 12, 56, 70, 113
Worcester, the diocese of II, 166–7
Worcester, the Bishop of. *See* Latimer, Hugh
Wothersome I, 345
Wotton, Shropshire II, 170
Wotton-under-Edge I, 66
Wressell Castle I, 149, 184, 198–9, 230, 283–5, 288, 293, 308, 312; II, 183, 210, 251
Wright, *alias* West, Anthony II, 62
Wright, John I, 155, 163
Wright, Thomas II, 179
Wriothesley, Charles, 'Chronicle' I, 87–8; II, 215
Wriothesley, Thomas I, 140, 173; II, 22, 150
Wyatt, Sir Thomas II, 217
Wyclif, John I, 346
Wycliff, Henry II, 110, 180
Wycliffe, the rector of I, 377–8. *See also* Rokeby, Dr John
Wyfflingham I, 90, 99
the bailiff of I, 100
Wynd Oak I, 159–60
Wyndessor, George II, 150
Wyre, William I, 328
Wyvell, John II, 71, 77, 110

Yarborough Hundred I, 106
Yarm I, 388
Yarmouth II, 179
Yarrow, Henry II, 288
Yeddingham Bridge II, 87
Yersley Moor II, 110
Yoell, Thomas, parish priest of Sotby II, 152
York, the Archbishop of. *See* Lee, Edward
general reference I, 45, 48, 348
York, the Ainstey of. *See* Ainstey of York
York city
monastery of St Andrew II, 58
the Archbishop's prison I, 72

York city
  assizes I, 43, 46–7, 56–7, 59, 73; II, 109–11, 120, 122, 131–3, 135–7, 151, 193, 198
  Botham Bar I, 175
  Castle II, 133
  the Clifford Tower II, 224
  proposed coronation and convocation in II, 27, 37, 48–9, 72–3
  the Council at I, chap. xiii, pp. 308–340. *See also* Pilgrimage of Grace, the Council at York
  the Council of the North at II, 272–3
  the dean and chapter of II, 41, 74
  disaffection there I, 144, 169, 171, 175; II, 40
  executions at I, 267; II, 110–1, 114, 220, 222, 264, 287, 300–1
  the Priory of the Holy Trinity II, 38
  market II, 222–3
  St Mary's Abbey I, 179
  —— the Abbot of I, 231–2; II, 39
  the Lord Mayor of I, 47. *See also* Harrington, William
  minster I, 178, 180, 183, 237, 355, 382; II, 27
  Minstergate II, 46
  the mint I, 288
  restoration of the monasteries there I, 179
  the Duke of Norfolk in II, 80, 99, 101, 104, 109–10, 113, 122, 126–7, 129, 131–2, 136–7, 254, 257, 259
  Observant Friars of I, 57
  pardon proclaimed in II, 28
  proposed parliament in. *See* Parliament, proposed, after the rebellion
  its parliamentary members I, 359
  the Pilgrims advance upon I, 154, 156, 168–9, 173–5
  the Pilgrims in I, 141, 163, 178, 180–1, 183–5, 205–6, 209, 231–2, 235, 239
  represented at the Council of Pontefract I, 344
  printing-press I, 252
  prison I, 44, 47
  prisoners I, 81, 87, 102
  the sheriff of II, 275. *See also* Lawson, Sir George
  White Friars I, 47
  reference I, 146, 150, 160, 182, 190–1, 193, 195, 206, 212, 234, 243, 283–5, 299, 306, 310, 328, 336, 345, 368, 379; II, 3, 8, 34, 45, 59, 60, 74, 76, 93, 97, 112, 130, 134, 185, 244, 250, 271, 275
York, the vicar-general of the diocese of. *See* Dakyn, John
Yorkshire
  the Dales of I, 79, 192, 207, 239, 252; II, 61, 107
  news of the Lincs. rebellion in I, 99, 104

Yorkshire
  proposal to refound monasteries in II, 26
  the King's oath in II, 109
  representation of, in parliament I, 359–60, 388; II, 15
  unrest in, after the rebellion II, 44–5
  sedition in I, 24, 44, 72, 78–9, 121, 207
  the sheriff of, in 1536. *See* Hastings, Sir Brian
  reference I, 18, 40, 47, 50–1, 55, 59, 71, 87, 91, 105, 110, 153, 192, 227, 262, 281, 294, 300, 325, 349–50, 364; II, 6, 16–7, 52, 54, 61, 84–5, 89, 102–3, 106, 109, 112, 125–6, 151, 184, 208, 223–4, 234, 267, 272–3
  East Riding
    outbreak of the rebellion there I, chap. vii, pp. 141–167
    the pardon proclaimed in II, 27, 31
    unrest there after the pardon II, 46–50, 61
    rebel forces from I, 157, 168, 235, 239, 252, 262
    watch kept during the truce I, 283
    reference I, 48, 298; II, 71, 75, 78, 205
  North Riding
    character of the rising in I, 192, 208–9
    outbreak of the rebellion in I, 157, 171, 201, 208, 230–1
    pardon proclaimed in II, 28
    unrest there after the pardon II, 50–1, 61, 76, 79–80, 94, 96, 106–8, 158
    rebel forces from I, 252, 283
    reference I, 37, 150
  West Riding
    outbreak of the rebellion I, 170–1
    pardon proclaimed in II, 28
    unrest there after the pardon II, 76, 78
    rebel forces from I, 239, 252, 262
    reference I, 18, 149; II, 99
Yorkshire Rebellion
  the signal of the bells I, 142, 148
  communications with Lincs. *See* Lincs. Rebellion, connection with Yorks.
  musters I, 149, 151, 153, 155, 157
  outbreak I, 115, 129, 132, 141, 145, 195
  called the Pilgrimage of Grace I, 157
  for subsequent references see under Pilgrimage of Grace
  the rising at Wakefield and Halifax I, 115, 285–7; II, 218
Yorkswold I, 105, 141, 152, 157–8, 160

Zealand I, 134, 336
Zion, the fathers of I, 68

ImTheStory.com

Personalized Classic Books in many genre's

Unique gift for kids, partners, friends, colleagues

Customize:
- Character Names
- Upload your own front/back cover images (optional)
- Inscribe a personal message/dedication on the inside page (optional)

Customize many titles Including
- Alice in Wonderland
- Romeo and Juliet
- The Wizard of Oz
- A Christmas Carol
- Dracula
- Dr. Jekyll & Mr. Hyde
- And more...

For Product Safety Concerns and Information please contact our EU representative GPSR@taylorandfrancis.com
Taylor & Francis Verlag GmbH, Kaufingerstraße 24, 80331 München, Germany

www.ingramcontent.com/pod-product-compliance
Lightning Source LLC
Chambersburg PA
CBHW071239300426
44116CB00008B/1098